EFFECTIVE
and
RESPONSIBLE
TEACHING

EFFECTIVE
and
RESPONSIBLE
TEACHING

The New
Synthesis

Fritz K. Oser, Andreas Dick,
Jean-Luc Patry, Editors

Jossey-Bass Publishers · San Francisco

For sales outside the United States, contact Maxwell Macmillan
International Publishing Group, 866 Third Avenue, New York,
New York 10022.

Manufactured in the United States of America

Library of Congress Cataloging-in-Publication Data

Effective and responsible teaching : the new synthesis / Fritz K.
   Oser, Andreas Dick, Jean-Luc Patry, editors.
       p.   cm. — (The Jossey-Bass education series)
   Includes bibliographical references (p.   ) and index.
   ISBN 1-55542-449-X
   1. Teaching.   2. Teaching—Research.   3. Learning.   4. Teachers—
Training of.   I. Oser, Fritz K.   II. Dick, Andreas, [date].
III. Patry, Jean-Luc.   IV. Series.
LB1025.3.E35   1992
371.1'02—dc20   92-11511
                                                            CIP

FIRST EDITION
HB Printing   10 9 8 7 6 5 4 3 2 1   *Code 9251*

The Jossey-Bass
Education Series

To our children
Carole, Ellen, Eric, Ingeborg, Juliano,
Philippe, Sigrid, and Wilfried,
who effectively teach us to be permanent
responsible learners

Contents

Preface

When we first asked ourselves, What is good teaching? we tried to identify techniques and approaches in method or subject matter that are particularly effective. What we discovered was essentially all techniques, methods, and approaches are effective only insofar as they are humanely applied in the service of the learner. Even "good" approaches to content or efficient techniques may destroy children's desire to learn and pride in learning. Our deep conviction is, therefore, that didactic knowledge must be coupled with responsibility, professional intentions with ethical care. Neither effectiveness nor responsibility is more important than the other; rather, it is the combination of the two that gives strength and makes for excellence. When we tried to separate the two parts of this synthesis, we found that responsibility was clearly the weaker of the two. For most people effectiveness is what counts, not whether something is based on ethical, responsible action. This bias can be seen in research and in teacher training. Three questions thus arise: Why this imbalance? What does responsibility in relation to effectiveness mean? How should it be intertwined with knowledge?

The synthesis postulated here can be illustrated by a few of the outstanding educators in the history of education. In the European tradition, examples of the particular kind of responsibility we attempt to model can be found in the life of the famous Swiss educator Johann Heinrich Pestalozzi (1746–1827). Pestalozzi was very creative in developing new instructional methods that adhered to the belief that all teaching should be directed by and oriented to ethical norms. Another example is Janusz Korczak (1878–1942), who was a Jewish medical doctor, novelist, and educator in Poland. Korczak was the founder of orphanages in Warsaw that insisted on democracy and mutual respect as fundamental criteria for everyone. A sense of caring and community was embedded in all teaching. He also formulated a number of fundamental rights for children (rights that are still not viewed as self-evident today), and he himself lived up to these standards. Korczak clung so tenaciously to his ideals that he paid with his own life for the responsibility he felt toward "his" children of the orphanages. Given the choice to be freed or to accompany the 200 Jewish orphans that were being sent to the Nazi death camp at Treblinka, he did not hesitate in insisting that he would prefer death with the children rather than leaving them to their horrible fate alone. Korczak was not only an extraordinary teacher but also a living example of the highest form of responsibility.

In the American educational tradition, John Dewey (1859–1952) is an example of an outstanding educator. Known for his "progressive" approach, Dewey espoused developmentally oriented teaching methods that focus on learning by doing and on education by experience. However, he is also known for his vision of a society that, through cooperation, mutual responsibility, and participation, reaches social and moral maturity — a maturity that Dewey viewed as essential for democracy. It may not be apparent what such extraordinary professionals, who lived and worked at a particular moment and place in time, can offer to our general understanding of teaching. Nonetheless, we feel that their experiences, commitment, and work can help us discover just what responsibility is and inspire us.

From the work of Pestalozzi, Korczak, and Dewey we learn that while efforts to develop more effective ways of teaching are done with present gains in mind, responsibility requires us to assess the impact of our effectiveness for the long term. Professional responsibility in teaching encompasses an adaptive teaching approach, both guiding and assessing the structuring and managing of teaching content. While our efforts at effectiveness look forward to the future, as we strive to succeed and be our best, responsibility requires us to look at the present from the vantage point of the future, judging whether our actions were ones that enabled even our weakest students to benefit. How can we learn to look both forward and back at the same time? This is not an easy task, but we feel that it is necessary if we are to get to the root of what makes for good teaching. A first step in this direction is to ask, What makes good learning? How can we synthesize responsibility and effectiveness in both teaching and learning? The chapters in this book, written by education researchers of many different schools of thought, offer partial but hopeful answers to these questions.

The work presented here is the result of a week of intensive talks and discussions among internationally renowned education researchers at a conference on the study of teaching held to celebrate the centennial of the University of Fribourg, Switzerland. The university is located in a city with a distinguished tradition of education for all children, both the poor and the rich. The chapters in this book were inspired by the theme that eventually crystallized from the conference: the urgent need to synthesize effectiveness with professional morality and ethics in the teaching professions.

This edited collection is addressed particularly to researchers in education, who need to include both dimensions, effectiveness and responsibility, in their research paradigms if they are to find practical relevance and impact in our research, but it will also be of value to anyone working in the field of education — teacher educators, school administrators, students of education, and teachers in the field.

This book is not a new bundle of do's and don'ts. Research on teaching and teacher education has been a normative enterprise for too long. What teachers need is not a knowledge base that distinguishes either more effective methods from less effective ones, or more responsible ones from less responsible ones, but rather one that distinguishes more effective *and* responsible ones from less effective *and* responsible ones. Thus, we maintain a concept of teaching that is broad and inclusive and view teaching as essentially both a moral activity and a pedagogy of substance.

The authors' contributions to this work do not express a consensus. They are meant primarily to stimulate and provoke discussion and only secondly to report research findings. As research, thinking, and debate continue, other possibilities for achieving a synthesis between effectiveness and responsibility will surely turn up. Thus, this book should be regarded as a first step toward building a foundation for the new synthesis that will encourage readers from differing methodological and analytical approaches to reflect on their concept of education and on the need for meaning and worthwhile improvement in the practice and profession of education.

Readers may perceive limitations, omissions, or contradictions, depending on their own particular field of expertise. This is to be expected in any new endeavor. For instance, while some authors presupposed that there is agreement regarding the definition of *responsibility,* others felt obligated to develop a new and differentiated meaning of the term. In addition, a number of topics and specific projects in teacher education and school reform could not be included. In spite of whatever shortcomings the reader finds, we hope that we have attained our primary goal in publishing this edited collection: to inspire reflection, to trigger debate, and to stimulate research that will lead to a more humane approach toward schooling.

Overview of the Contents

The book is divided into eight sections dealing with specific aspects of effective and responsible teaching. As volume editors, we compiled the introductory and concluding comments of the book in the first and last sections. For most sections, a contributor served as the special editor of the chapters discussing the issues in which he and the coauthors hold specific expertise. Each editor of Sections Two through Seven provides an introductory overview of the succeeding chapters.

Section One opens with an introductory chapter (Chapter One) in which Fritz K. Oser, Andreas Dick, and Jean-Luc Patry discuss research in teaching from the perspective of combining effectiveness and morality and propose that this complementarity be reconstructed according to four possible synthesis models. In Chapter Two, Lee S. Shulman offers a historical perspective on research on teaching with an overview of the five foundational themes of cognition, content, context, culture, and character, themes that are treated more thoroughly in the following sections.

The chapters in Section Two discuss a number of different approaches to integrating responsibility and effectiveness. In Chapter Three, Gavriel Salomon discusses evidence that the role of the teacher is already changing from that of "information transmitter" to that of "orchestrator of learning," whereby the teacher designs, implements, coordinates, and monitors the open learning environment. In Chapter Four, Richard T. White presents nine principles deduced from long-term action research that suggest ways to raise the quality of students' learning by encouraging them to be purposeful and responsible in the classroom. In Chapter Five, Walter Doyle examines the question of how teachers and students together shape and manage "the experienced curriculum" by choosing and interpreting knowledge, rather than having only one individual "teach" it. Richard J. Shavelson and Gail P. Baxter, in Chapter Six, add to the holistic discussion of how teachers and students must collaboratively confront the curriculum by reflecting on the symmetry of teaching and testing. They propose reforming testing programs by offering more hands-on performance tests and fewer multiple-choice tests and discuss the implications for teachers' instructional decisions.

Section Three addresses the moral dimension of responsible teaching. In Chapter Seven, Gary D Fenstermacher frames the discussion in terms of a new concept of method and manner in education and shows how this concept can form the basis for a "profound engagement" of teachers and students that fosters intellectual and moral development in all students. Fritz K. Oser, in Chapter Eight, emphasizes the ethical dimensions of teachers' professional decision making and advocates a discourse approach through roundtable discussion. In Chapter Nine, Mordecai Nisan proposes the cultivation of a sense of "ought"—the motivation to maintain and affirm self-identity, as an essential school aim. Exemplifying the broad notion of teaching as a moral craft or enterprise, William Damon proposes in Chapter Ten teaching strategies that advance the developmental goals of a spirit of tolerance and critical thinking through respectful engagement.

Section Four focuses on the developmental perspectives in education. In Chapter Eleven, Wolfgang Edelstein revisits the slogan "Development as the Aim of Education," stressing that the interplay between development and education is more complex and less linear than usually thought and that it encompasses multiple goals and bi-directional relationships between content, structure, and process in the two interlocking domains. In Chapter Twelve, Lothar Krappmann discusses the "joint venture" between students and teachers, emphasizing the social embedding of the teaching and learning process and comparing teacher-centered instruction with open, self-organized learning. Rolf Oerter (Chapter Thirteen), focusing on students, and Ronald Gallimore and Claude N. Goldenberg (Chapter Fourteen), focusing on teachers, present Vygotsky's theory about the careful mapping of the zone of proximal development between teacher and students and then go on to show the result of the teaching-learning path of teachers and learners with mutual responsibility: teaching transforms itself into an "instructional conversation."

Section Five looks at experts and expertise in teaching. In Chapter

Fifteen, David C. Berliner offers a "master teacher approach." He lists characteristics of experts in the pedagogical domain, comparing them with experts in other professional domains and showing that expert teachers clearly demonstrate effectiveness and responsibility. In Chapter Sixteen, Franz E. Weinert, Andreas Helmke, and Friedrich-W. Schrader present a more general "teaching model approach," which tries to model the complex pattern of classroom interactions through a system in which a small number of variables define some general features of teacher-student relationships. In contrast, Elliot W. Eisner argues in Chapter Seventeen that theoretical models provide mostly comfortable security to "professorial life." The complex setting of a classroom often enough belies conceptually neat notions because of the highly nuanced and qualitative features of the extremely wide range of human and social interactions found there. In Chapter Eighteen, Brigitte A. Rollett takes one set of such variables, examines expert teachers' interpretations of critical incidents in the classroom in cross-cultural contexts, and finds expert teachers to be especially caring and loving toward their students.

The authors in Section Six address the content of teaching. In Chapter Nineteen, Magdalene Lampert examines practices and problems in teaching and learning with a focus on student negotiation in mathematics. In particular, she examines the relationship between teacher and students that allows (or prevents) a negotiation of content knowledge. In Chapter Twenty, Frank Achtenhagen treats two specific content areas (English as a foreign language and business education) as special forms of a pedagogy of substance that require network thinking. And in Chapter Twenty-One, Anne-Nelly Perret-Clermont stresses an "outsider" view of the sociopsychological factors that affect the teaching process, examining teachers' and students' differing views of "knowledge."

Section Seven includes chapters that examine a number of research projects dealing with effectiveness and responsibility in schools and teacher education. In Chapter Twenty-Two, Trygve Bergem analyzes teacher education programs in Norway and suggests developing responsibility and identity in teacher education through the development of critical reflectiveness, viewing teachers as moral agents with moral obligations. In Chapter Twenty-Three, Andreas Dick proposes an approach based on ethnographic methods to get student teachers to reflect and deliberate on the observed personal and practical knowledge of experienced teachers and on schools as cultural settings. On the macro level of schooling, Daniel Solomon, Marilyn Watson, Victor Battistich, Eric Schaps, and Kevin Delucchi (Chapter Twenty-Four) describe efforts to promote children's sociomoral development through a school-based program with components such as developmental discipline, cooperative learning, and literature-based approaches to reading. Sigrún Adalbjarnardóttir (Chapter Twenty-Five) views development on the micro level of schools, the classroom, and shows how fostering children's ability to resolve social conflicts in the classroom represents such an approach. In Chapter Twenty-Six, Heinz Schirp describes a holistic school-based program aimed at improving education's ability to foster moral-cognitive development by "opening the schools."

In Section Eight, Christopher M. Clark and Karen I. Jensen (Chapter Twenty-Seven) shift the discussion into a framework of relational responsibility, urging a research agenda focused on a more caring dimension in teaching. The book concludes with an afterword by Fritz K. Oser, Andreas Dick, and Jean-Luc Patry, which reemphasizes the points made in the previous chapters and highlights the three central elements of the book's approach: the direction of responsibility, the act of taking responsibility, and the engendering of mutual understanding.

Acknowledgments

We are glad to take this opportunity to thank a number of people for their "hidden" work and friendly advice. We would like to thank Susan Rose for her huge amount of editorial and translation work, which tremendously increased the coherency and clarity of our manuscript, and Susanne Gutknecht, not only for collecting and coordinating the manuscripts from the beginning to the end but also for being an extraordinary all-rounder. The authors and especially the section editors deserve special thanks for accepting the strict though friendly deadline reminders repeatedly sent them from Fribourg. We also owe special thanks to everyone in the Department of Education and Marie-Tony Walpen for their important roles in the conference in honor of the centennial of the University of Fribourg (made possible through grants from the University of Fribourg, the canton of Fribourg, the Swiss National Science Foundation, and the Swiss Educational Research Association), which eventually led to this book.

We are very indebted to Christie Hakim, Frank Welsch, and especially Lesley Iura of Jossey-Bass Publishers for their unconditional confidence in the topic and, without the faintest idea of how efficient or responsible we were, in our team from tiny Switzerland. In all sincerity, it was a great pleasure working with them.

Fribourg, Switzerland   Fritz K. Oser
August 1992   Andreas Dick
                                                              Jean-Luc Patry

The Editors

Fritz K. Oser is professor of education and educational psychology and director of the Department of Education at the University of Fribourg, Switzerland. He received his M.A. degree (1973) in education, theology, and philosophy and his Ph.D. degree (1975) in education, both from the University of Zurich. He was a postdoctoral fellow at the University of California, Los Angeles, and at Harvard University, working with Richard Shavelson and Lawrence Kohlberg. He earned his postdoctoral degree in education in 1979. In 1987, he received a doctorate honoris causa in theology from the University of Mainz, Germany. His research focuses on moral development, reconstruction of religious judgment in ontogenetic development, and professional morality (ethos) of teachers. He has assisted in the creation of three "just community" schools in North Rhine–Westphalia (Germany) and a new seminar for negotiation on the topic of ethical culture and effectiveness. His courses include educational psychology, the choreography of teaching, and moral development. His publications on developmental, intervention, and evaluation studies include the chapter "Moral Education and Values Education: The Discourse Perspective" in the *Handbook of Research on Teaching* (edited by M. C. Wittrock, 1986); *Religious Development During Childhood and Adolescence* (with G. Scarlett, 1990); *Moral Problem Solving in Small Groups* (1981); *How Much Religion Does Man Need?* (1988); and *Moral Autonomy* (with W. Althof, 1992).

Andreas Dick is a senior lecturer and faculty member in the Department of Education at the University of Fribourg, Switzerland, where he teaches graduate courses in teacher education, cultural awareness, and reflective ethnography. He taught at the elementary and high school levels before traveling extensively and living abroad. He received his B.A. degree (1971) from the Teacher's College of Fribourg and his secondary school teaching certificate (1978), his M.A. degree (1982) in education, social psychology, and philosophy, and his Ph.D. degree (1992) in education from the University of Fribourg. From 1986 to 1988, he was a visiting scholar at Stanford

University, where he worked with Lee S. Shulman in the Knowledge Growth in Teaching and Teacher Assessment projects. His major professional interests and publications are in the area of teacher education, and he has published works on teacher thinking and the practical knowledge of teaching, inquiry-oriented teacher education, and collaborative frameworks for teacher education. He is currently involved in the development of a preservice teacher education curriculum that encourages reflective inquiry through the collaboration of experienced teachers. His teaching and research interests also include multicultural education and he is a founding member of the Association for Intercultural Research based in Switzerland and France.

Jean-Luc Patry is a privatdocent in the Department of Education at the University of Fribourg, Switzerland. He received his M.A. degree (1972) in natural science and his Ph.D. degree (1976) from the Swiss Federal Institute of Technology in Zurich. His dissertation was on visual perception of geometric forms, and he received the *habilitation* (1987) for his work on empirical research in education. His main research activities have focused on situation specificity of human actions; on methodological questions such as evaluation theory, field research, and critical multiplism; on the relationship between theory and practice; and on metatheoretical questions of educational research.

His publications, in German, French, and English, include a number of articles as well as books on field research (1982), situation specificity (1991), counseling (with M. Perrez and others, 1985), and theory and practice (with G.-A. Eckerle, 1987). He was a visiting scholar at Stanford and Lehigh universities and the University of Salzburg from 1982 through 1984. He has been vice president of the Swiss Educational Research Association and is currently editor of the journal *Bildungsforschung und Bildungspraxis* [Educational Research and Practice].

The Contributors

Frank Achtenhagen has been a full professor of economics and business education and management training at the Georg August University of Göttingen, Germany, since 1971. He received his M.A. degree (1963) from the Free University of Berlin in economics and business education, his assessor degree (1965), the highest state examination for teachers, from the Senate of Berlin, and his Ph.D. degree (1969) from the Free University of Berlin in economics and business education. He received an honorary doctorate in economics (1991) from the University of St. Gallen, Switzerland.

Sigrún Adalbjarnardóttir is associate professor of education in the Faculty of Social Sciences of the University of Iceland. She received her teacher's diploma (1969) from the Teacher Training College in Iceland, her B.A. degree (1983) from the University of Iceland in education, and her M.A. (1984) and Ed.D. (1988) degrees from the Harvard University Graduate School of Education in human development and psychology. For the last twenty years, she has worked as an elementary school teacher and teacher trainer, a curriculum developer in social studies, and a researcher in educational psychology.

Victor Battistich is deputy director of research at the Developmental Studies Center, San Ramon, California. He received his B.A. degree (1974) from California State University, Sacramento, in psychology and his M.A. (1976) and Ph.D. (1979) degrees from Michigan State University in personality–social psychology. He was previously an assistant professor of psychology at Cleveland State University.

Gail P. Baxter is a researcher in the Department of Education, University of California, Santa Barbara. She received her Ph.D. degree (1991) from the University of California, Santa Barbara, in psychometrics in educational psychology. She has done extensive developmental and evaluative work on performance assessments in both science and mathematics. Most recently, her work has examined the psychometric qualities of hands-on performance assessments in science and the exchangeability of less costly and less time-consuming surrogates of hands-on investigation, including laboratory notebooks, computer simulations, and paper-and-pencil exercises. She is currently involved in training teachers in the use of performance assessments in the classroom.

Trygve Bergem is associate professor of education at the Norwegian Laererakademi (teachers college), Bergen, Norway. After earning his Ed.D. degree (1967) at the University of Oslo, he became an assistant professor at the Institute for Educational Research. He joined the faculty of the Education Department of the academy in 1976, and he has also served as its president. His most recent research has investigated how students, teachers, and parents perceive what is presently taught in Norwegian primary schools; the relationship between teacher thinking, social sensitivity, moral reasoning, and teachers' effectiveness; and how teachers are trained as moral educators.

David C. Berliner is professor of curriculum and instruction and professor of psychology in education in the College of Education at Arizona State University. He received his Ph.D. degree (1968) from Stanford University in educational psychology. He has taught at the University of Massachusetts and the University of Arizona and served as director of research at the Far West Laboratory for Educational Research and Development. He is a former president of the American Educational Research Association. His interests are in the study of teaching, teacher education, and educational policy.

Christopher M. Clark is professor of education in the Department of Counseling, Educational Psychology, and Special Education at Michigan State University. He received his B.S. (1963) and Ph.D. (1976) degrees from Stanford University in educational psychology. His professional interests and publications include research on teacher thinking, teacher professional development, and the relationship between research and practice. He is the recipient of the Palmer O. Johnson Award for empirical research (1979) and the Interpretive Scholarship Award (1987), both from the American Educational Research Association, and of a Spencer Fellowship from the National Academy of Education (1979–1984).

William Damon is professor and chair of education at Brown University. He received his B.A. degree (1967) from Harvard University in social relations and his Ph.D. degree (1973) from the University of California, Berkeley, in developmental psychology. He has also been distinguished visiting professor at the University of Puerto Rico. His research has focused on several areas of social and cognitive development. His books include *The Social World of the Child* (1977), *Social and Personality Development* (1983), *Self-*

Understanding in Childhood and Adolescence (1988), and *The Moral Child* (1988). He was the founding editor of the Jossey-Bass quarterly sourcebook serial New Directions for Child Development and has served as its editor-in-chief since 1978.

Kevin Delucchi is senior statistician at the San Francisco Treatment Research Unit, University of California, San Francisco. He received his B.A. degree (1976) from the University of San Francisco in psychology and his M.A. (1979) and Ph.D. (1986) degrees from the University of California, Berkeley, in educational psychology. He was previously a senior research associate at the Developmental Studies Center, San Ramon, California.

Walter Doyle is professor of teaching and teacher education at the University of Arizona, where he specializes in curriculum theory and research on academic tasks. He received his B.A. degree (1962) in English, his M.A.T. degree (1963) in education and English, and his Ph.D. degree (1967) in curriculum and instruction from Notre Dame University. He taught at North Texas State University and served as research scientist in the Research and Development Center for Teacher Education at the University of Texas. He is a former editor of the *Elementary School Journal* and associate editor of the *American Educational Research Journal* and has served as vice president of Division K of the American Educational Research Association.

Wolfgang Edelstein is codirector of the Max Planck Institute for Human Development and Education in Berlin, Germany, and heads the institute's Center for Development and Education. He received his M.A. degree from the Sorbonne University in Paris in general linguistics, Latin, English, and Scandinavian philology and his Ph.D. degree from the University of Heidelberg in medieval Latin philology. He is adjunct professor of education at the Free University of Berlin. From 1966 to 1984, he was chief scientific adviser for the Icelandic Ministry of Education where he was responsible, among other things, for curriculum development and qualitative planning of change in the country's educational system and headed the major curriculum project, Integrated Social Studies, for grades 1 through 9.

Elliot W. Eisner is professor of education and art at Stanford University. His major research interest is the use of critical methods from the arts for studying and improving educational practice. He has received numerous awards for his work, including the Palmer O. Johnson Memorial Award, a John Simon Guggenheim Fellowship, a Fulbright Fellowship, and an award for Distinguished Contributions to the Field of Curriculum from Division B of the American Educational Research Association. He has served as president of the National Art Education Association and the International Society for Education Through Art. He is currently president of the American Educational Research Association.

Gary D Fenstermacher is professor of education at the University of Arizona, Tucson. He received his B.A. degree (1961) in political science and his Ph.D. degree (1969) in philosophy and education from Cornell University. Following faculty appointments at New York University, the University of California, Los Angeles, and the Virginia Polytechnic Institute, he became dean of the College of Education at the University of Arizona. After serving six years in this position, he resumed full-time teaching and research. His primary research specialties are the philosophy of teaching and the study of educational policy.

Ronald Gallimore is professor of psychology in the Department of Psychiatry and Biobehavioral Science and the Department of Education at the University of California, Los Angeles. He received his B.A. degree (1960) from the University of Arizona and his M.A. (1963) and Ph.D. (1964) degrees from Northwestern University in clinical psychology. He is the author of *Rousing Minds to Life* (with R. G. Tharp, 1988).

Claude N. Goldenberg is assistant research psychologist in the Department of Psychiatry and Biobehavioral Sciences at the University of California, Los Angeles. He received his A.B. degree (1977) from Princeton University in history and his M.A. (1982) and Ph.D. (1984) degrees from the University of California, Los Angeles, in developmental studies.

Andreas Helmke is a research associate at the Max Planck Institute for Psychological Research in Munich, Germany. He received his M.A. degree from the Technical University of Braunschweig in psychology and his Ph.D. degree from the University of Constance in psychology. His main research interests are teaching, student achievement, and motivational development.

Karen I. Jensen is a research fellow in the Department of Education at the University of Oslo. She holds degrees in nursing and education and from 1981 to 1985 served as chair of the National Council for Education of Habilitation Workers in Norway. She is the editor of *Images of Caring* (1990). Her current research project is a study of modes of practice among care personnel serving the developmentally disabled.

Lothar Krappmann is senior researcher in the Center for Development and Socialization at the Max Planck Institute for Human Development and Education in Berlin, Germany, and adjunct professor in the School of Education at the Free University of Berlin. He received his Ph.D. degree (1969) from the Free University in sociology. His main theoretical and research activities have been in the fields of social interaction and identity development, socialization in the family and peer group, school and instruction as a field of social interaction, and qualitative research methods. His publications include *Sociological Dimensions of Identity* (7th ed., 1988).

Magdalene Lampert is associate professor of teacher education at Michigan State University, where she is codirector of the Mathematics and Teaching Through Hypermedia project and senior researcher at the Institute for Research on Teaching. She is also a fifth-grade mathematics teacher at Spartan Village School in East Lansing, Michigan. She received her Ph.D. degree (1981) from Harvard University in teaching, curriculum, and learning environments. She was recipient of the Raymond B. Cattell Early Career Award for Programmatic Research from the American Educational Research Association in 1991 for her research on teaching practice.

Mordecai Nisan is professor of educational psychology and head of the School of Education at the Hebrew University of Jerusalem. He received his B.A. degree (1963) in psychology and literature and his M.A. degree (1965) in psychology from the Hebrew University of Jerusalem and his Ph.D. degree (1969) in psychology from the Committee on Human Development at the University of Chicago.

Rolf Oerter is professor of developmental and educational psychology and current dean of the Department of Psychology and Pedagogy at the University of Munich, Germany. He received his M.A. degree (1960) and his Ph.D. degree (1963) from the University of Würzburg, Germany, in psychology, and in 1969 he completed the *habilitation* in psychology. His research focuses on cognitive development in adolescence and early adulthood from a cross-cultural perspective and on the role of play in human development. He was director of preschool education in Bavaria from 1969 to 1971 and participated in several research projects investigating learning with media during the 1970s. Among his many publications is the book *Psychologie des Spiels* [The Psychology of Play].

Anne-Nelly Perret-Clermont is professor of psychology at the University of Neuchâtel, Switzerland. She received her M.A. degree (1971) and her Ph.D. degree (1976) from the University of Geneva in psychology and her M.Sc. degree (1973) from the University of London in child development. She is coeditor of the *European Journal of Psychology of Education* and of the Swiss Society for Research on Education's book series *Exploration*. Her current research deals with the social psychology of cognitive processes.

Brigitte A. Rollett is head of the Department of Development and Educational Psychology and of the Center for Child, Youth, and Family Therapy at the University of Vienna, Austria. She received her Ph.D. degree (1957) from the University of Graz, Austria, in psychology and education. She has held several chairs in psychology at German educational institutions, including the Universities of Ruhr and Kassel and the Teachers' Training College of Osnabrück. She is an accredited educational expert for the European Common Market, president of the Society of Learning Therapy, and the national correspondent of Austria for the European Association for Research on Learning and Instruction. Her book *Educational Psychology* is now in its third edition.

Gavriel Salomon is a professor in the College of Education at the University of Arizona. He received his Ph.D. degree (1968) from Stanford University in educational psychology and communication and has taught at the Hebrew University, Tel Aviv University, Harvard University, Stanford University, and the Universities of Michigan and Southern California. His areas of interest include the cultivation of thinking skills and the use of technology and media in educational settings. He has published three books and numerous articles. He is a fellow of the American Psychological Association, president of the Educational and Instructional Division of the International Association of Applied Psychology, and editor of *Educational Psychologist*.

Eric Schaps is president of the Developmental Studies Center, San Ramon, California, and project director of the Child Development Project. He received his B.A. degree (1964) from Northwestern University in history, his M.A. degree (1966) from Pennsylvania State University in psychology, and his Ph.D. degree (1970) from Northwestern University in social psychology. His previous institutional affiliations were with the Pacific Institute for Research and Evaluation and the University of Chicago.

Heinz Schirp is head of the Curriculum, Education, and School Research Department in the State Institute for School and Adult Education in North Rhine–Westphalia, Germany. He received his M.A. degree (1966) in German history and social science and his Ph.D. degree (1979) in education from the University of Dortmund. He is also head of school- and research-based innovation projects concerning the development of school quality.

Friedrich-W. Schrader is a research associate at the Max Planck Institute for Psychological Research in Munich, Germany. He received his M.A. degree (1977) from the Technical University of Braunschweig in psychology and his Ph.D. degree (1988) from the University of Heidelberg in psychology.

Richard J. Shavelson is dean of the Graduate School of Education and professor of research methods in the Department of Education at the University of California, Santa Barbara, and past president of the American Educational Research Association. He received his Ph.D. degree (1971) from Stanford University in psychometrics in educational psychology. He conducts research in the areas of social science measurement methods, psychometrics, and related policy issues. His most recent measurement research involves the development and evaluation of performance assessments in mathematics and science education. His policy research includes two recent monographs on alternative designs for educational indicator systems and the research basis underlying the system.

Lee S. Shulman is Charles E. Ducommun Professor of education at Stanford University. He received his B.A. degree (1959) in philosophy as well as his M.A. degree (1960) and his Ph.D. degree (1963) in educational psychology from the University of Chicago. From 1963 to 1982, he was a professor of educational psychology and medical education and the founding codirector of the Institute for Research on Teaching at Michigan State University. His research and writing have dealt with the study of teaching and teacher education and the growth of knowledge among those learning to teach. He has conducted a five-year research program to design and field test new strategies for the assessment of teaching. He is the current president of the National Academy of Education and past president of the American Educational Research Association.

Daniel Solomon is director of research at the Developmental Studies Center, San Ramon, California. He received his B.A. degree (1956) from Antioch College in sociology, his M.A. degree (1956) from the University of Michigan in psychology, and his Ph.D. degree (1960) from the University of Michigan in social psychology. Before coming to the Developmental Studies Center, he conducted developmental and educational research at the Institute for Juvenile Research in Chicago and at the Montgomery County public schools in Maryland.

Marilyn Watson is program director at the Developmental Studies Center, San Ramon, California. She received her B.A. degree (1959) from Connecticut College in philosophy and her M.A. (1972) and Ph.D. (1975) degrees from the University of California, Berkeley, in education. Prior to her position at the center, she was assistant professor of education and director of the Children's School at Mills College, Oakland, California.

Franz E. Weinert is codirector of the Max Planck Institute for Psychological Research and research professor at the Universities of Heidelberg and Munich. He received his Ph.D. degree (1958) from the University of Erlangen in psychology and his postdoctoral degree (1966) from the University of Bonn in psychology. From 1968 to 1981, he worked as a professor and director of the Psychological Institute at the University of Heidelberg. He has also served as president of the German Psychological Association.

Richard T. White is professor of education at Monash University, Melbourne, Australia. He received his B.Sc. (1956) and B.Ed. (1958) degrees from the University of Melbourne and his Ph.D. degree (1972) from Monash University in education. His scholarly interest, which follows from his ten years as a secondary school teacher, concerns learning. His books include *Learning Science* (1988) and *Probing Understanding* (1992, with R. F. Gunstone). He was president of the Australian Association for Research in Education in 1982.

Section Editors

Frank Achtenhagen
David C. Berliner
Ronald Gallimore
Mordecai Nisan
Jean-Luc Patry
Richard J. Shavelson

EFFECTIVE
and
RESPONSIBLE
TEACHING

Section One

WHAT IS GOOD TEACHING?

1

Responsibility, Effectiveness, and the Domains of Educational Research

Fritz K. Oser, Andreas Dick, Jean-Luc Patry

Successful teachers are both effective and responsible. They want both teaching success and a respectful way to interact: in other words, good learning and human satisfaction. The challenge of the new synthesis is to discover the relationship between effectiveness and responsibility and to integrate the two concepts as a base for teaching practice and research on teaching. Aristotle first touched on this issue when he distinguished technical discourse (*techne*) from practical discourse (*praxis*). *Techne* is a disposition that guides and directs action in a reasoned way in order to bring about some determinate end according to the rules of the craft, thus enhancing skill in and understanding of the craft. *Praxis* is a moral disposition aimed at acting appropriately, truly, and justly in order to realize ethical values and goals, thus reviewing actions and the knowledge that informs them (see Carr and Kemmis, 1986, for an in-depth discussion). The two dispositions, he argues, must be regarded not as separate and distinct but as complementary elements that are in a dynamic interrelationship, mutually constitutive and reciprocally enriching.

In the course of the history and development of psychological and educational research, it was deemed necessary to separate the two concepts. The results of the separation have been useful at times but in the long run unsatisfactory. This becomes clear when we glance back at the past several decades of research on teaching. We therefore carefully summarize each side separately before we expand on the combination of the two.

Teaching Effectiveness Research

When people talk about effectiveness in teaching, they are usually referring to research on effectiveness in teaching. This research, most of it begun during the 1950s, has tended to focus on effectiveness as a process-product relationship: what teachers do has been defined as the "process" of teaching, what students do as the "product" of the teaching (in other words, learning), and the relationship between the two as a measurement of effectiveness. For researchers to reach quantitative results, the complex situation of teaching and learning had to be simplified. This approach led to research on such topics as teacher effectiveness programs, direct instructional models, active teaching, and time on task. For example, the Academic Learning Time research program (Fisher and others, 1980; influenced by Carroll's model of school learning [1963; 1989] and Bloom's concept of mastery learning [1974]) chose time as the central construct for the teaching-learning process. The program was concerned with relationships among variables differentiating the attributes of instruction (opportunity to learn and quality of instruction) and the attributes of the learner (ability, aptitude, and perseverance). Unfortunately, the research on academic learning time led to prescriptions of longer time spent in schooling, including more time spent on the microtask level as well as a longer school year, without dealing adequately with the substantive instructional quality of teaching (Clark, 1987). A positive outcome, however, was that it brought attention to the neglected domain of students' thought processes and the crucial question of how they make sense of the teaching-learning processes going on in the classroom. This led to "student mediation" programs designed to fill the "empty time vessel" (Doyle, 1990; Shulman, 1986).

Another outcome of the process-product approach to research was the studies of direct instructional models conducted in the late 1960s and the 1970s. This work suggested that the components of direct instruction — pacing, sequencing, and structuring — were effective because they made most lessons clearer and easier for students to follow. (The researchers did not consider the possibility that learners' prior knowledge might influence their findings.) This behavior-oriented (or technical) research was then transferred to the practical domain of teaching, eventually leading to the competency-based teacher education movement and performance-based teacher education programs: researchers identified the skills and behaviors of effective teaching processes, or "competencies," and then developed lengthy checklists of prescribed behavior and teacher testing systems. (For a summary of the major research findings from the teaching effectiveness literature, see Brophy and Good, 1986.)

Since competency-based teacher education was thus based on the process-product research, both were subject to criticism based on the same conceptual and methodological issues: they are empirical but nontheoretical; they are based on exclusive and/or molecular units of analysis; they tend to concentrate only on skills and classroom management; and they consider the standardized achievement test as the ultimate criterion of effectiveness. Shulman (1986) has described this quantitative (or, as it is known in Europe, "positivistic") research as employing pragmatic or "correlative conceptions of effectiveness" — in other words, assuming that effectiveness correlates strongly with a desired outcome. Schön (1983) has referred to it as the "technical rationality" approach, which offers the concept of usable knowledge (that is, practical knowledge) without answering the crucial question of when and how to use it.

In response to this criticism, new areas of research have been developing. Two of them, the "discovery" and the integrative perspectives on educational research, are less likely to assume that data establish "facts" than that they suggest theory (Biddle and Anderson, 1986). Findings are viewed as being bound by context and method, thus allowing research to also focus on the search for contextual variation. A third area, termed the "epistemology of practice," is concerned with looking at the practical knowledge of teaching and teachers. Propositional knowledge (leading to predictability and control of teaching processes) is replaced by situational knowledge created by teachers and educators. This important knowledge concerns the relationship between the teacher and the taught in the classroom and provides insights into how decisions and actions with serious moral implications look and feel in context. Thus, this is the first type of research that begins to recognize the need to include responsibility when examining what *teaching practice* really means. In Shulman's words, "A distinctive alternative is the *normative* conception of effectiveness, in which a given exemplar of instruction is compared to a model or conception of good teaching derived from theory or ideology. This criterion of effectiveness uses *correspondence* rather than *correlation* as its test" (Shulman, 1986, p. 28). Thus, correspondence to normative models rather than correlation with empirical outcomes is the criterion of effectiveness.

Responsibility in Teaching

In the pedagogical literature, the concept of responsible teaching can be found in three different forms. The first form, found in the earlier literature, is as a normative base. European teacher education traditions seem especially prone to very general statements of how teachers should behave. These statements shared something in common with the competency-based teacher program: they did very little to convey to teachers how to behave responsibly in the idiosyncratic situations that a particular teacher may be confronted with. But while the competency-based program could at least show results in terms of test scores, the normative literature could only assert that teachers following these responsibility norms would be better teachers (which would imply a clear-cut criterion for what *better* means).

More recent literature has presented responsibility in terms of a developmental theory such as the Kohlbergian framework. For example, an article by Strom (1989) entitled "The Ethical Dimension of Teaching" promotes ethical sensitivity as a means for fostering moral reasoning in order to reach a developmentally higher moral stage. While reaching a higher moral stage is a societal value, it is not specific enough to be a professional one. This apparent shortcoming has led to newer literature that tends to embody responsibility in a more procedural concept of professional morality. Strike

(1990), for example, sees professional morality as an intensive process learned step by step, as follows:

1. A serious dealing with the ethics of teaching requires a detailed discussion of the ethical standards that are to govern the characteristic activities of teachers.
2. A serious dealing with the ethics of teaching requires that teachers act in ways that respect the values and mores internal to subject matter.
3. A serious dealing with the ethics of teaching requires that we connect the characteristics and behavior of teachers with the moral purposes (and the overall purposes) of education [p. 206].

However, even though we agree that education is a moral endeavor, wherein the teaching act is a deliberate effort to develop values and sensibilities as well as skills, the question remains whether moral imperatives pervade the whole process of teaching. Responsibility and morality in teaching suffer in general from a lack of empirical analysis. Questions such as "Do we have responsible teachers in our schools?" "In what way are they responsible?" "Are these teachers effective as well?" and "How many are there?" remain to be asked. In contrast to effectiveness, which is seen as analyzable and observable, responsibility is assumed to be an innate part of one's character. Or it is assumed, implicitly, that it is learned through contact or by osmosis: the simple act of reading classical authors who emphasize responsibility automatically enhances responsible action. Both assumptions are obviously problematic.

After reviewing the literature in research on teacher effectiveness and on teacher responsibility, we are left with two mutually exclusive traditions and many questions: How can we conceive responsibility in the realm of research? How can we assess the interdependency between responsibility and effectiveness? What can we say about the necessity to supply them? What could be prototypes of professional action that demonstrate the interaction of the two concepts?

Effectiveness and Responsibility in the New Synthesis

In the "new synthesis," we are arguing for a new understanding of effectiveness, an understanding that will affect what teachers expect of themselves as effective teachers and what researchers will attempt to define and examine when studying teacher effectiveness. We see effectiveness as a much broader concept than heretofore—one that encompasses and integrates not only high marks for correct answers on a certain test but overall, self-motivated achievements; one that includes the teachers' and the students' sense of well-being; one that views effectiveness as a result of teachers' and students' mutual desire to master a certain subject matter.

The effectiveness research has been generally shortsighted on both theoretical and methodological grounds. By our own concept, teachers are successful, or effective, if they reach their goals with students *and* take the needs of their students into consideration. In other words, we are looking for a sense of effective responsibility that must emerge over time and that eventually yields higher involvement and commitment and, finally, success. Thus, the criterion for success needs to include curricular goals, as well as goals oriented to the social and self-concept (in other words, curricular or cognitive domain, social domain, and general domain).

In the new synthesis, we would like to see responsibility as a mutual undertaking, with teachers trying to coordinate human needs with means-ends thinking. Rather than educators taking responsibility for children's education by actually taking responsibility away from the children in order to uphold some prescribed normative curriculum, mutual responsibility is concerned with the giving and sharing of responsibility among all concerned in the learning process. Such a construct of the term *responsibility* entails three basic sets of criteria:

1. Preconditions for responsibility in any setting
    a.   A positive communication base (discourse)
    b.   Moral dimensions (often balanced against each other)
    c.   A sense of obligation of the responsible person
2. Functional criteria for the individual teacher's responsibility
    a.   Setting optimal conditions for learning
    b.   Optimal accompanying of the learner
    c.   Presupposition of the students' positive ability and morality
3. Reversibility criteria of responsible acts of any education professional
    a.   Universalization
    b.   Meaning making

The first set of criteria consists of three universal preconditions necessary for achieving responsibility in any social situation: a positive communication base, a moral dimension, and a felt sense of obligation. The communication base is the means for making responsibility apparent and attainable. The moral dimension highlights the issues of justice or fairness, care, truthfulness, and honesty and the justification of each of them. And the sense of obligation provides the feeling of commitment and guides the mode (or manner) of teaching (see Chapter Seven).

The second set of criteria is particular to the context of teaching. These functional criteria are the process of setting optimal conditions for learning; the readiness to help the learner by consistently accompanying the learner along the learning path; and a fundamental belief in the child's ability to learn, to participate, to decide, to choose, and so on. Although all three must be achieved before we can say that responsibility is present, we think that the third criterion, presupposition of students' ability and morality, is the most valuable. This presupposition means that the teacher assumes that learners are really able to act by themselves. The teacher communicates the message "I believe you can do it! And I believe you want to do it!" by offering students the role of cothinkers, coworkers, codeciders, and cocontrollers. By accompanying students and by actively participating, teachers promote autonomy rather than dependency. By presupposing the ability to learn through mistakes, the teacher is able to accept wrong steps, wrong logics, and wrong results, thus helping sharpen students' ability to think and reason.

The last set of criteria embraces *reversibility,* which is the most important construct of moral philosophy and is based on the Kantian idea of categorical imperative. It means that the core concept of qualitative higher morality is such that what applies to oneself, applies to everyone else. It includes the criteria of universalization and of meaning making. *Universalization* means that the functional criteria must be applied to any child independent of race, gender, socioeconomic status, or intelligence. This does not mean that every child should be treated exactly in the same way; rather, it means that each child should be treated according to his or her actual needs. It also means that students learn to mutually presuppose the qualities of thinking and social action among themselves. Learning of this sort is a great aid to social integration. Similarly, *meaning making* means that every child should feel that his or her work is important and that he or she is a unique person in the world.

It should be apparent by now that, in our view, both responsibility and effectiveness need to be constructed and produced in teaching research and teaching practice. Each must be viewed in terms of its counterpart. The concept of effectiveness in teaching needs to include human goals, not just curricular ones. And the concept of responsibility means that there is a communication base between teacher and students that presupposes mutual respect, ability, and obligation and that leads to the mutual taking of responsibility for the learning process, where students function as coparticipants and cocreators of the classroom environment. The aim of this volume is to provoke thought and debate on how best to achieve this conception of effectiveness and responsibility.

Structural Models for Research Using the New Synthesis

The four models of synthesis between effectiveness and responsibility that we propose here are aimed clearly at research on teaching. This is because we feel that, with the system of teacher training that exists throughout most of the Western world, it is necessary to start with research in order (1) to affirm and recognize the responsible and effective teaching practice that has thus far escaped empirical quantification and (2) to provide a research base for future teacher training that will promote responsible and effective teachers. We do not mean to imply that these are the only four models possible—in fact, quite the reverse. We think that there are other models, and it is our hope that this book will encourage the discovery of those models and the eventual selection and refinement of the best ones to form a research base. None of these four models is presented in the other chapters in this book as clearly as they are presented here. Rather, each author in the volume has his or her own conceptualization of a synthesis that has evolved from one of the four models. We support the diverse methods of inquiry used by the various chapter authors by quoting Fenstermacher's (1986, p. 43) thoughtful distinction between knowledge production and knowledge use, a distinction derived from Aristotle's differentiation between theoretical wisdom and practical wisdom: "The logic of knowledge production consists of statements or propositions about the world. This logic terminates in assertions, in claims about events, states, or phenomena. These assertions are testable using such disciplined methods as are available to the researcher. The logic of knowledge use also consists of statements, but arguments in this logic terminate in actions rather than propositions." This view allows the researcher a methodological pluralism and thus methodological freedom.

The Interpretive Synthesis Model

In this model, whenever one of the two approaches is addressed, the other is implicitly addressed as well. Morality is implicit wherever aims of education are at stake. Implicit morality is also involved when certain "humane" forms of effectiveness are employed; for example, when as much consideration is given to a weak learner as to a strong one, when a teacher takes responsibility for a child's learning, or when a teacher acts as an orchestrator rather than just a transmitter of information. The same principle applies to effectiveness as well: it is implicit wherever responsibility is the key factor within a learning process. It is implicit when, for example, activities are chosen for a child that lead to a strong sense of self or when a child is encouraged to complete a task that gives him or her a sense of obligation. It is also implicit when teachers who have ethical misgivings about the use of punishment as a method for handling disciplinary problems nonetheless use it because they know of no other effective methods for reaching their goals.

The Additive Synthesis Model

This model contrasts effectiveness and responsibility in such a way that the reader must make the synthesis. This may occur through some kind of inner conflict. A good example of this model is achievement evaluation: the more strictly an evaluation concerns only the results of an achievement, the less consideration can be given to the elements of "care" in respect to effort, originality, or the process of solving the task and the systematic mistakes that occur.

The Complementary Synthesis Model

This model concerns the idea of "the lived value system." It assumes that responsibility and effectiveness are mutually dependent on one another. To become an effective teacher, one must act responsibly, and one cannot act responsibly without considering issues of effectiveness. The more effectiveness is required, the more it becomes necessary to consider the intentions, ideas, and needs (sense of obligation) of the partners; the more one takes morality (obligation toward the learners) into consideration, the more effective a procedure becomes. This model views one dimension as the condition for the success of the other.

The Regulative Synthesis Model

This model addresses the limits placed on effectiveness by responsibility. Effectiveness is acceptable only to the extent that it is not achieved at the expense of individual students. Where efforts at effectiveness are undermining individual children's feelings of security, value, and self-acceptance, they must be stopped by some outside interference. Thus, the pedagogical ethos of teachers consists of being sensitive to such conflicts either in their own teaching or in their environment, making the participants aware of such conflicts, and contributing appropriately to the search for a responsible solution without necessarily denying that effectiveness might be justified.

The New Synthesis in Practice

Over the past decades, reponsibility and effectiveness have been separate and unrelated traditions in research on teaching, with effectiveness the primary focus of such research. Much the same has been true in the practice of teaching: teachers have been concerned primarily with questions of effectiveness, often feeling that responsibility is simply innate or intuitive. The reasons for this, although not clear-cut, are nonetheless understandable when we look at, for example, an experience of a teacher in the Australian Project for Enhancing Effective Learning (PEEL), directed by Richard T. White (see also Chapter Four). After specifically encouraging students to think about what they were doing and to ask questions, the teacher wrote a nonsense text on the board, pretending to copy it from a book. The students copied the text without hesitation; only one student per class had a question (Hynes, 1986, p. 30f.). As the teacher reported,

> It is from this point on that I realized three things:
> Firstly, I thought I had been teaching in a fashion that encouraged student involvement and initiative. I now realized that I had not been challenging the students enough. My reaction to these two classes was one of concern about my teaching methods.
> Secondly, I was surprised to see to what extent students expect teachers to dictate and dominate class situations. Students either believe that teachers should not be questioned or

believe that it is much easier not to get involved in class discussion.

Thirdly, that as a teacher I had an obligation to alter my teaching strategies. Even though I believed that I was using strategies that the PEEL program professed, I had to have a much closer look at the program and adapt it to my classroom methods [Hynes, 1986, p. 31].

This example shows the complexity of issues involved when both effectiveness and responsibility are taken into account. The teacher quoted above chose to judge his teaching according to the criterion of helping students to become more active, critical, and reflective rather than simply according to curricular aims. Thus, he felt a sense of obligation, and he acted on the presupposition of the students' ability and willingness to engage in a fair discussion (see Chapter Eight for further discussion). Furthermore, the teacher set up an evaluation situation to assess whether the criterion was satisfied. Assessment of some kind is a necessary condition for any effectiveness study, whether scientific or not. The question is whether the assessment method is appropriate with respect to the criterion. In this case, the teacher had to conclude that his teaching was a failure. In the words of Hynes (1986, p. 28), "There is a subtle difference between telling students to ask questions, telling them to think about what they did last lesson, telling them to find problems in the topics being studied and teaching them to perform those activities, or creating an atmosphere in which they can take more initiative for their own learning."

As more teachers make conscious efforts to combine effectiveness and responsibility in their teaching, and as more researchers attempt to analyze concrete teaching situations to find how effectiveness and responsibility are intertwined, the less such ambiguous experiences as the one described above should occur. The important thing is to start the dialogue so that the process of laying a foundation for the new synthesis can begin.

Summary

Research on teaching has tended to measure teaching effectiveness through constructs such as teacher variables, student variables, context variables, and process and product variables (see Dunkin and Biddle, 1974). In addition, by identifying important causal effects and their magnitude through comparative studies or meta-analyses, we presumed to know what effectiveness was. However, we are finally realizing that, purposely or not, we have left out a very important intervening factor: responsibility. Instead of making responsibility an integral part of effectiveness, we have allowed it to exist as a normative demand. Recent efforts—such as the psychology of content learning, the analysis of expert teachers' inspired actions, and proximal developmental stimulation—demonstrate the plausibility of the relationship of effectiveness and responsibility and yet our operational helplessness with respect to it.

In the literature on teaching, there exists as yet either an unclear synthesis between the two concepts or no synthesis at all. However, the process of research in the field of responsibility is beginning. We believe that the three sets of criteria mentioned above—preconditions, functional criteria, and universalization and meaning making—are useful to create a process model of professional responsibility and to assess through possible operationalization of the criteria how responsibility affects the choice of a method, handling of knowledge, evaluation, selection procedures, and so on. Responsibility is a "control" that ensures that fairness, accountability, honesty, and care will be introduced into any decision-making process in a professional field. Using the "new synthesis" as a guideline, we can say that a method is both effective and responsible if the criteria of performance are combined with the criteria of morality and commitment: reinforcement of good student behavior is effective *and* responsible if the reinforcement technique is combined with truthfulness; an individual learning sequence can be considered effective *and* responsible if the strategy used is appropriate (or fair) with respect to the learning capacity of the child.

We would also hope that not only will intertwining of responsibility with effectiveness become a standard for researchers in teaching and teachers but the teachers and researchers themselves will become links in a long chain of effective responsibility, along with students, parents, administrators, teachers' pressure groups, school boards, community, business and industry representatives, and policy makers. All of these people should be informed and involved in the decision processes that shape the education of our children, aiming to act not only appropriately but also truly and justly in a sociopolitical context.

References

Biddle, B. J., and Anderson, D. S. "Theory, Methods, Knowledge, and Research on Teaching." In M. C. Wittrock (ed.), *Handbook of Research on Teaching.* (3rd ed.) New York: Macmillan, 1986.

Bloom, B. S. "An Introduction to Mastery Learning Theory." In J. H. Block (ed.), *Schools, Society, and Mastery Learning.* Troy, Mo.: Holt, Rinehart & Winston, 1974.

Brophy, J. E., and Good, T. L. "Teacher Behavior and Student Achievement." In M. C. Wittrock (ed.), *Handbook of Research on Teaching.* (3rd ed.) New York: Macmillan, 1986.

Carr, W., and Kemmis, S. *Becoming Critical: Education, Knowledge and Action Research.* London: Falmer Press, 1986.

Carroll, J. B. "A Model of School Learning." *Teachers College Record,* 1963, *64*(8), 723–733.

Carroll, J. B. "The Carroll Model." *Educational Researcher,* 1989, *18*(1), 26–31.

Clark, C. M. "The Carroll Model." In M. J. Dunkin (ed.), *The International Encyclopedia of Teaching and Teacher Education*. New York: Pergamon Press, 1987.

Doyle, W. "Themes in Teacher Education Research." In W. R. Houston (ed.), *Handbook of Research on Teacher Education*. New York: Macmillan, 1990.

Dunkin, M. J. and Biddle, B. *The Study of Teaching*. New York: Holt, Rinehart & Winston, 1974.

Fenstermacher, G. D. "Philosophy of Research on Teaching: Three Aspects." In M. C. Wittrock (ed.), *Handbook of Research on Teaching*. (3rd ed.) New York: Macmillan, 1986.

Fisher, C., Berliner, D., Filby, N., Marliave, R., Cahen, L., and Dishaw, M. "Teacher Behaviors, Academic Learning Time, and Student Achievement: An Overview." In C. Denham and A. Lieberman (eds.), *Time to Learn*. Washington, D.C.: National Institute of Education, 1980.

Hynes, D. "Theory into Practice." In J. R. Baird and I. J. Mitchell (eds.), *Improving the Quality of Teaching and Learning: An Australian Case Study — the PEEL Project*. Melbourne, Australia: Monash University, 1986.

Shulman, L. S. "Paradigms and Research Programs in the Study of Teaching: A Contemporary Perspective." In M. C. Wittrock (ed.), *Handbook of Research on Teaching*. (3rd ed.) New York: Macmillan, 1986.

Schön, D. A. *The Reflective Practitioner: How Professionals Think in Action*. New York: Basic Books, 1983.

Strike, K. A. "The Legal and Moral Responsibility of Teachers." In J. I. Goodlad, R. Soder, and K. A. Sirotnik (eds.), *The Moral Dimensions of Teaching*. San Francisco: Jossey-Bass, 1990.

Strom, S. M. "The Ethical Dimension of Teaching." In M. C. Reynolds (ed.), *Knowledge Base for the Beginning Teacher*. Oxford, England: Pergamon Press, 1989.

2

Research on Teaching: A Historical and Personal Perspective

Lee S. Shulman

I expected something much greater — an instructor of the young, training the mind in order to train the heart.

Père Girard
(quoted in Compayre, 1894)

This book was inspired by a conference to celebrate the centennial of the University of Fribourg. It is appropriate that we celebrate the birthday of a university with a conference on the study of teaching, for deliberations on teaching and learning lie at the heart of the educational enterprise. In this chapter, I develop five central assertions about this enterprise:

- Teaching is and has always been at the center of all education and educational reform.
- Theory underlies research on teaching, even when that research is assertively practical and self-consciously atheoretical; much of current policy and practice in education reform rests on research and theory.
- A major failing of both practice and policy is that they typically rest on incomplete, partial views of teaching. The most widespread view emphasizes observable performance of teachers — a perfectly legitimate feature to address — but ignores other critical aspects of teaching, such as cognition, content, context, culture, character, and collaboration.
- All approaches to the study of teaching entail both epistemic and moral commitments. These two facets of thought are intertwined in fundamental ways.
- The contemporary movement in the study of teaching to reclaim a more complete view of pedagogy and pedagogical inquiry is consistent with concurrent developments in the social sciences and with dramatic changes in the condition and organization of the teaching profession itself.

Beginnings

The concept of teaching as a profession, which implies a field of knowledge that can be systematized and thus imparted to others, began long ago.

14

However, I shall begin my story at the turn of the nineteenth century in Switzerland.

The Ideas of Père Girard

I devote special attention to the work of the eminent Swiss educator Père Girard for several reasons. First, he was the great educational pioneer of Fribourg, site of the university whose centennial the conference leading to this volume celebrated. Second, although far less famous than his contemporary Johann Heinrich Pestalozzi, his ideas carry a wisdom and value that deserve the attention of the modern reader. Finally, his conjoining of skill and understanding, especially of the intellective and the moral, foreshadowed the work of his compatriot Fritz Oser and the subject of the present book, effective and responsible teaching.

Père Grégoire Girard was born in Fribourg in 1765. He was a marvelously patient man, waiting until he had reached the age of seventy-nine to publish his masterwork (Girard, 1844). Girard believed strongly in the primacy of ideas over skills and in the necessary fusion of intellectual with moral work in the schools. For example, Girard argued that the purposes of elementary instruction, even in a subject such as grammar, should include development of the mind and of the judgment—grammar should not be taught for cultivation of the memory alone. He is quoted as asserting that "This [grammar] instruction becomes a pure affair of memory, and the child becomes accustomed to pronounce sounds to which he attaches no meaning. The child needs a *grammar of ideas*. . . . Our *grammars of words* are the plague of education" (Compayre, 1894, pp. 470–471). Perhaps anticipating somewhat the contributions of his future compatriot Jean Piaget, Girard argued that grammar should be an exercise in thinking, a movement toward "the logic of childhood."

As for the links between mind and morality, Girard argued that all subject matters could be learned in ways that improve the moral fiber of the students as well. He wrote of both moral arithmetic and moral geography. The following is an example of Girard's arithmetic: "A father had the habit of going every evening to the dramshop, and often left his family at home without bread. During the five years that he led this life, he spent, the first year, 197 francs, the second, 204 francs, the third, 212 francs, and the fourth, 129 francs. How many francs would this unfortunate father have saved if he had not had a taste for drink?" (Compayre, 1894, pp. 471–472).

I am not eager to claim that contemporary theorists, even his successors in Fribourg, would find Girard's particular strategies of intellectual and moral education compelling. However, when we read the work of educational thinkers of the nineteenth century such as Girard, we encounter images of teaching that are broad and inclusive. They see no problems in joining the intellectual and the moral elements of education. For further evidence of this comprehensiveness of view, let us cross the Atlantic to a contemporary of Girard, the American educator David Page.

David Page

One of the most widely used textbooks of pedagogy in nineteenth-century
United States was that of David Page, founder of the first normal school
in the state of New York, a disciple of Horace Mann, and particularly inspired by Pestalozzi's work. One grasps a sense of his broad, inclusive view
of teaching from the chapter titles of his textbook, *Theory and Practice of Teaching
or The Motives and Methods of Good School Keeping* (Page, 1885):

1. "The Spirit of the Teacher"
2. "Responsibility of the Teacher"
3. "Habits of the Teacher"
4. "Literary Qualifications"
5. "Right Views of Education"
6. "Right Modes of Teaching"
7. "Conducting Recitations"
8. "Exciting Interest"
9. "School Government"
10. "School Arrangements"
11. "Relating to Parents"
12. "Teacher's Care of His Health"
13. "Teacher's Relations to His Profession"
14. "Rewards of Teaching"

Unfortunately, the rewards of teaching for Page included an early demise
at the age of thirty-seven, brought on, we are told by his biographer, by
his overwork to establish the state normal school. The biographer describes
Page the pedagogue thus: "As a teacher, he exhibited two valuable qualifications: the ability to turn the attention of his pupils to the *principles which
explain facts,* and in such a way that they could clearly see the connection;
and the talent for reading the character of his scholars so accurately that
he could at once discern what were their governing passions and tendencies, what in them needed encouragement and what repression" [from the
biographical essay in Page, 1885].

   A concern for both principles and character permeated David Page's
thought and writing as an educator. He equally values both effective and
responsible teaching.

John Dewey

Another thirty-seven-year-old educationist, John Dewey, was invited to the
University of Chicago in 1896 (when the university itself was barely five
years old) by its president, William Rainey Harper, to become professor
of philosophy, psychology, and pedagogy. Dewey addressed the questions
of why a research university (in itself a new conception in American higher

education) should include a school of pedagogy and how such a school should differ from the already existing normal schools. Dewey too employed a broad and comprehensive vision of pedagogy. He argued for the conjunction of interest and intelligence, of the needs of the child as well as the progressive organization of the subject matter. He did not hold a narrow view of education.

Dewey argued that a school of pedagogy within a research university was to have a special role. It would not only prepare practitioners, both teachers and administrators; it would also be expected to contribute to the development of a "science of education," the systematic investigation of the processes and institutions of educating that would place education on a par with physics and the other sciences. The disciplinary key to a science of education was likely to be the emerging science of psychology, thought Dewey, and the laboratory for its investigations would be the schools themselves. In that spirit, Dewey established the Laboratory School of the University of Chicago. It was not a demonstration school, like those found in the many existing normal schools, whose purpose was solely the training of teachers. It was intended to serve as a site for the scientific study of learning, teaching, and child development, as well as the systematic investigation of school curriculum and organization.

Although Dewey was caught up in the creation of the Laboratory School, his spirit of educational experimentation and investigation captured the imagination of several presidents of the university as well. Both President Ernest D. Burton and President Robert M. Hutchins asserted that the University of Chicago's undergraduate college was itself an educational experiment. Just as the Laboratory School was to be a site for experimentation from kindergarten through secondary school, the college would be a site for research on and evaluation of higher education. It was no accident that many of the leading educationists of the University of Chicago emerged from the University Examiner's Office, where the evaluation functions for the college were placed. Among its leading figures were university examiners Ralph Tyler and Benjamin Bloom.

In spite of the genius of his vision, Dewey made two fundamental errors. The first was his undue optimism regarding the adequacy of psychology for providing a comprehensive scientific base for education and even the likelihood that psychology could ever achieve the status of a science such as physics. The second was his failure to recognize the costs of treating education — a complex field of practice — as a science, the most profound consequence of which was a tragic narrowing of its investigations as we entered the modern era.

The Modern Era: The Implicit Roles of Theory and Moral Stance

When we come to the modern era, we encounter a paradoxical narrowing of the conception of teaching found in the writing of scholars. Ironically, this narrowing came about in the interest of developing the very *science* of education that Dewey envisioned, and the effects of this quest were particularly visible in the study of teaching. To achieve such a science, scholars were required to do what any science quite properly requires of its savants: to narrow the field of study sufficiently to permit systematic and controlled observation of and experimentation with the phenomena of interest. To do science, we seek objectivization, abstraction, and generalization. These all demand a simplification and narrowing of the field of view so that lawlike statements can be made. The goals of scientific inquiry also demanded a degree of decontextualization, with "all other things being equal" standing as the implicit credo for generalizations emerging from the research. Thus, though Dewey held a highly complex and contextualized conception of education, his call for a science of education undermined precisely the view of the enterprise that he most valued.

For scholars (or policy makers), a theory, however implicit and unacknowledged, determines the questions that they ask; their data will be answers to their questions, and they really cannot ask about everything at once. The theories that underlie such research both sharpen and narrow their efforts. I shall show how each successive paradigm for research on teaching typically begins with a criticism of the blindness of its predecessor, only to blinker its own eyes in a somewhat different manner. These problems of theoretical myopia (or, more precisely, tunnel vision) become particularly acute when research findings and methods are translated into educational policies by bureaucrats and political leaders. As the economist John Maynard Keynes once observed, "Practical men, who believe themselves to be quite exempt from any intellectual influences, are usually the slaves of some defunct economist. . . . [I]t is ideas, not vested interests, which are dangerous for good or evil" (Keynes, 1936, pp. 383–384).

Policies act comprehensively even when they employ narrowly formulated theories. Policy makers are almost never conscious of the pervasively theoretical cast of their educational mandates. I have been involved in such activity over the past four years as I have worked with colleagues to develop new approaches to the evaluation of teachers. Approaches to teacher assessment and evaluation constitute the ultimate policy statement; they enshrine in standards and instrumentation the tastes and theoretical preferences of political leaders. That does not make them evil; on the contrary, political leaders are often more sensitive to the interests of disenfranchised or underrepresented groups than are the cloistered scholars of the academy.

What of morality? Is there any connection between the epistemic and methodological conceptions carried by alternate theories and any moral visions that they embody? If competing paradigms for the study of teaching have been myopic with regard to their implicit theories, they have been positively blind in failing to grasp the moral philosophy underlying their work. I can attest to that blindness from personal experience. In my own work over the past twenty-five years, much influenced by my teacher Joseph

Schwab, I have constantly sought to identify those critical aspects of the process of education that have been ignored by other scholars and then to design a program of research to repair the gap. I have typically failed to recognize that my critiques of other paradigms, as well as those criticisms skillfully leveled at my own work, reflect both epistemic and moral values.

A Succession of Paradigms

In the balance of this chapter, I shall have two interwoven stories to tell. First, I shall recount the succession of approaches to the study of teaching with which I have been personally associated since the 1960s. These will be limited primarily to work in the United States, and for this I apologize. As I summarize each approach, I shall emphasize its critique of prior work, its own theoretical approach, and the often implicit moral theme that permeates its concepts and methods.

Process-Product Research

In the modern era, research on teaching began as an attempt to answer a straightforward question: How are the behaviors and actions of teachers related to variations in student achievement? This research was dubbed "process-product" research because its goal was to discern the links between teaching *processes* and the kinds of student achievement that constituted the sought-after *products* of formal education. The research usually proceeded by having observers use categorical observation scales to record classroom teacher behavior and student responses. Observations might be made as few as three or as many as fifteen times during the school year. At the end of the year, children in each observed class were tested through the use of standardized achievement examinations. The teachers' behavior was correlated with student performance, and those forms of teacher behavior found to be positively correlated with student achievement were hypothesized to be part of "teaching effectiveness." Whenever possible, those correlations were replicated in further studies or tested more rigorously in experimental studies.

Much was gained from this research. Careful, systematic observation of practice occupied the center of the research program. The arena of inquiry shifted from the laboratory or the questionnaire to the classroom itself, with the actions of the teachers and students at its heart. (For an analysis of the different paradigms and programs in the study of teaching, see the *Third Handbook of Research on Teaching* [Shulman, 1986], which reviews these programs more formally and with numerous references. In this chapter, I wish to examine the progression of alternate research programs in a more personal and even autobiographical mode.)

Although the proponents of this research program claimed it to be atheoretical (perhaps motivated by the bloody and unproductive wars between learning theorists that characterized the 1930s and 1940s in the United

States), it was far from that. While its goal was not to create and test formal theory, it rested undeniably on a host of implicit theoretical and ideological claims. Thus, research in the process-product tradition rests on the assumption that teaching can be divided into molecular acts, which in turn can be counted, combined, and analyzed. It assumes that teaching is, by and large, a singular phenomenon, about which much can be learned without worrying too much about context. It also assumes that teaching is an activity in which the representatives of the society, in this case teachers, learn to act on their students to bring them the educational benefits that the greater society has deemed best for them. We therefore learn which teacher behaviors are most effective so that we can encourage all teachers to engage in them for the benefit of their pupils.

Process-product research dominated the study of teaching for about fifteen years (1960–1975), reaching its peak in the late 1960s and early 1970s. It was especially effective in providing a response to critics who claimed that teaching was incapable of making a difference in the learning of children, because school achievement was overwhelmingly determined by social class and other characteristics of students' home background. Whether one agreed with the conceptual framework of process-product research or not, the enterprise certainly demonstrated that teacher behavior could be related to student achievement.

Another important feature of process-product research was its moral component. While it did not particularly emphasize moral behavior on the part of teachers or moral outcomes as its student products, it unambiguously rested on a moral claim: teaching ought to be understood and valued primarily through its effects on student learning. The purpose of teaching is the amelioration of ignorance, and studies of teaching that make claims of excellence for some kinds of pedagogy must buttress those claims with evidence of the impact of the teaching on the lives and capacities of students. Thus, although some critics (including this writer) have been rather harsh judges of process-product research on epistemic and methodological grounds, we must acknowledge the importance of its clear moral stance.

Nevertheless, the image of teaching found in the process-product literature was quite narrow. The teacher *behaved.* Those behaviors were observed, counted, and combined without reference to teachers' intentions or cognitions, oblivious to their contexts and constraints. Of all those omissions, that most striking to me in 1975 was the ignoring of thought as a central element of teaching. By the mid 1970s, the cognitive revolution was well under way. Every human being was acknowledged to engage in thinking, reasoning, judgment, decision making, and problem solving; everyone, that is, except teachers, who were still described exclusively in terms of their behavior. It was time to introduce a new research paradigm. (Nathaniel Gage humorously criticized my cognitive approach during a debate between us at an annual meeting of the American Educational Research Association. Paraphrasing the learning theorist Edwin R. Guthrie's critique of his contemporary Edward

Tolman, Gage opined that "Shulman leaves teachers lost in thought." A number of years later, in a paper prepared for Gage's own *festschrift*, I finally found the proper response. "Better to be lost in thought than missing in action." Neither fate is desirable.)

Teacher Thinking

When my colleagues and I established the Institute for Research on Teaching (IRT) at Michigan State University in 1975, we formulated its mission in reaction to the dominant process-product paradigm and its emphasis on behavior rather than cognition. As consistent with the growing cognitive revolution in psychology, we designed a research program built around the "mental life" of the teacher. Research on teacher planning, decision making, diagnosis, reflection, and problem solving dominated our research agenda. We pursued one of the earliest studies examining the ways in which teachers' decisions mediated the effects of administrative policies and mandated textbooks. Our critiques of process-product research were successful in pointing out the overly narrow focus of its efforts, especially its blindness to the centrality of thinking in the work of teachers.

The orientation of our work on teacher thinking, however, remained as dominated by psychology as the process-product tradition had been; it simply took a cognitive rather than a behaviorist slant. Like Dewey, we continued to "psychologize" teaching. Nevertheless, once again a moral perspective could be discerned in this work. Teachers were not merely automatons, machines that emitted behavior that could be measured. They were intelligent, thoughtful, sentient beings characterized by intentions, strategies, decisions, and reflections. Thus, their work could not be studied in the old-fashioned ways, as if they were mere "subjects" to be examined like rats in mazes or first-year psychology students in required laboratory courses. We could not merely do research *on* teachers; we were obligated to work collaboratively with teachers in our research.

Collaboration in Research on Teaching

A parallel movement, which began during our IRT days and has continued to grow in strength in the past few years, has been the emergence of *collaboration,* the design and pursuit of research on teaching with teachers themselves playing an increasingly collaborative role in the enterprise. In the IRT, we had "teacher collaborators," active classroom practitioners who spent half the day teaching and the other half at the university participating as researchers. We were not alone. Classroom ethnographers had begun to work with classroom teachers as coethnographers, full partners in the endeavor. The action research movement in the United Kingdom was taking shape, and this group too emphasized the importance of their partnership with teachers.

The emphasis on the need for more active collaboration between teachers and researchers carried both a moral and an epistemic quality. The moral perspective reflected a recognition that if research were to be used to influence the ways in which teachers worked, then they were entitled to be full partners in any efforts destined to affect their lives. The epistemic perspective was somewhat more subtle. If teachers' thoughts and judgments were indeed so central to understanding teaching, then how could any reasonable insights into teaching be accomplished without their active participation? Ironically, in this argument, the perspectives of morality and validity joined together. Not only were teachers entitled to be treated as full collaborators in research; the validity of the investigations might well be suspect without evidence of their collaboration.

In conjunction with these research developments, the occupation of teaching began to take a new turn toward greater professionalization. Teachers began to speak of autonomy and empowerment, of moving control of school policies to the building and classroom levels, and of the need for more research that documented teaching from the perspective of the classroom teacher. They began to call for research that would carry the "teacher's voice," rather than the "outsider" perspective of the ostensibly objective observer. Slowly but surely, collaboration has evolved from a courtesy practiced by a few scholars to an emerging norm for the relationship between researchers and teachers.

And Then We Discovered Context and Culture

During the second year of the IRT, we began to bring anthropologists into the picture. They addressed a totally new set of issues, methodologically, conceptually, and ideologically. Far more was changed than merely a shift from quantitative to qualitative methods. They formulated different questions, conceptualized utterly distinctive programs, and conducted research in the interests of other parties. With the coming of the ethnographers, we added context and culture to a picture that had previously included only cognition and behavior.

The contexts were both cultural and political. While some of our researchers—predominantly the anthropologists—were especially taken with the cultural mismatches between the school and the home, others, taking a perspective from political science, looked at the school and the teacher's cognitions in the classroom within a policy context of federal, state, local, and building-level organizations. Here again, a methodological paradigm carried both epistemic and moral weight. The anthropologists argued that prior research had emphasized an "*etic*" perspective, seeing the world— however acutely—from the point of view of the research observer, an outsider. The ethnographer's interest was in an "*emic*" view, reconstructing how the participants in a situation made their own sense of their worlds.

How did this methodological stance carry moral views as well? Ethnographers have in recent years been particularly interested in capturing the perspectives of those individuals and classes in a society least likely to be able to speak for themselves. These politically weakest members of a society often include teachers but more frequently include pupils, their parents, and especially the poor and disenfranchised elements of the society. Moreover, ethnographers tend to believe that the most critical aspects of classrooms are their social arrangements, the ways in which power relationships are distributed, the affinities between students afforded by systems of grouping or tracking, and the ways in which groups function interactively. The anthropologists therefore focus our attention on aspects of classroom life, those involving culture and context, that other methods tend to ignore. On the other hand, this emphasis is not accomplished without paying some price.

Teacher behavior had been augmented by teacher cognition, though at some expense, because the more attention we paid to thought, the less we were likely to attend to action. Then we added collaboration, culture, and context, putting more ingredients on the plate but undoubtedly leaving room for smaller amounts of each. Nevertheless, I was soon to discover that there were quite important ingredients still missing from our diet, an insight I failed to achieve until I had physically moved from one university to another.

The Missing Paradigm: Teacher Knowledge

In 1983, after moving from Michigan State University to Stanford, I observed that there still remained a significant "missing paradigm" in the study of teaching: the *content*, or substance, of the curriculum being taught and learned. The subject matter was missing. Whether conducted in traditions of behavioral study, cognitive research, or ethnography, most investigations treated teaching as a generic activity rather than as one that changed significantly as a function of what was being taught, to whom, and at what level. I initiated a research program in the interests of recovering the missing paradigm.

We began to ask a new question: How do people who already know something learn to teach what they know to others? That is, how does someone who had learned Shakespeare's *Hamlet* learn to teach that play to others? How does one learn to teach the principles of human evolution, or the concept of democracy, or the equivalence of fractions, or the past perfect conjugation in French? We conducted longitudinal studies of men and women becoming secondary school teachers and negotiating the transition from "expert learners" to "novice teachers" with special reference to the subjects they taught. We also studied experienced teachers in a variety of content areas.

As we conducted that research, we realized that our question was not quite right. Teachers did not either know something or not know it. They knew their subjects in different ways and with different areas of specialization or familiarity. The teacher of social studies or science, for example, was sometimes teaching topics that he or she knew very well and at other times teaching topics with which he or she had only superficial acquaintance. In addition, teachers had different explicit or implicit theories of their disciplines and how they are learned. So we began to ask: How do teachers who know their subjects in different ways and at different levels teach their subjects to others? And as we proceeded further into our studies, these questions became further differentiated and deepened to accommodate variations in contexts and in the backgrounds of students.

As I have come to examine the ways in which these perspectives on the processes of teaching have emerged in response to one another, I have become especially conscious of the ways in which the syntax of the research questions determined the shape of the investigation that followed. "What do good teachers do that distinguishes them from ordinary teachers?" yields very different studies than the question "What do good teachers of history do that distinguishes them from ordinary ones?" or "that distinguishes them from good teachers of mathematics?" Similarly, what effective teachers *do* is a different question from what effective teachers *know*. And "What do good teachers of biology for urban minority children do and think?" yields yet another challenge for scholars.

With the defining of the "missing paradigm," I began to feel that we had finally arrived at a comprehensive view of teaching. Content had now joined the mix, and the picture was complete—or so I had deluded myself into thinking. No sooner had our work on the "pedagogy of substance" begun to flourish than a cogent critique appeared in response to a paper I had published in the *Harvard Educational Review*, "Knowledge and Teaching" (Shulman, 1987). Hugh Sockett (1987) asserted that I had missed the point completely. The essence of teaching was no more content than it had been behavior, cognition, or culture. Teaching was essentially a moral activity; I had missed the centrality of *character*, or what my friend Fenstermacher (Chapter Seven of this volume) would call *manner*.

I will not presume to characterize the research program proposed by those who would place character or manner at the center of their problem definition. To some extent, much of this volume examines this idea as it explores notions of responsible teaching. In other ways, Sockett, Fenstermacher, and other members of the moral wing of teacher education are more comfortable playing the role of astute critic than they are at conducting their own empirical research. But I am confident that the research will come, and I am equally optimistic that this research will also add significant new facets to our understanding of teaching.

Quest for the Grand Strategy

The question remains whether it is possible to ask research questions that simultaneously include all the important perspectives—behavior, cognition, culture, context, collaboration, character—and still preserve the precision and reproducibility associated with classical social scientific models, or whether we need quite different research models that approach the study of teaching in quite new ways.

I have expressed in several other publications my admiration for the research in mathematics teaching pioneered by one of the other contributors to this volume, Magdalene Lampert of Michigan State University. Other colleagues at Michigan State—Lampert's collaborator Deborah Ball in math, Suzanne Wilson in history and social studies, Katherine J. Roth in science— have pursued similar investigatory styles. I present this approach to you as a case in point of research that manages to blend in an uncanny way the full gamut of perspectives that I have identified.

Lampert's approach to research on the teaching of mathematics exemplifies a new conception of the teacher as investigator, a new way of thinking about the university professor as a classroom-based researcher, and a broad, comprehensive perspective on the teaching of school subjects. Her approach to the study of math teaching is best exemplified in a recent paper (Lampert, 1990) as well as in her contribution to the present volume (Chapter Nineteen). She conducts her research by assuming full responsibility for all the mathematics teaching in a fifth-grade classroom during an entire school year. She documents her teaching and her students' learning meticulously, through a combination of classroom videotapes, daily journal keeping, clinical interviews with students, observations by research assistants, and active commentaries solicited from outside experts.

In her 1990 paper, Lampert begins her exposition with several pages on the nature of mathematics, drawing heavily from the writings of the eminent mathematicians Georg Polya and Imre Lakatos. She emphasizes the intellectual aspects of mathematical learning as explicated by such mathematicians. She also gives surprising and enlightening attention to the moral and social aspects of the mathematical discourse community, as discussed by those same mathematicians. After laying out the intellectual, moral, and social parameters of mathematics as a knowledge-finding and knowledge-testing collegium, she proceeds to provide a detailed analytical account of her own teaching of a unit on exponentiation. In this elaborated case study, we can vividly see the ways in which she incorporates and instantiates her understanding of mathematics as a way of knowing and of socially engaging in the everyday workings of her classroom.

At the end of her paper, Lampert deftly relates her case to broad national concerns for the learning of mathematics with understanding and to the practical issues of how to accomplish such an extraordinarily difficult agenda in the setting of real classrooms. Lampert's work is both teacher's work and mathematics educator's work; it is both practice and theory. It informs and inspires practitioners while enlightening and stimulating researchers.

But is this social science? When the focus of the research is a single teacher, and that teacher is also the investigator, what forms of generalization and theoretical knowledge are possible? And even if Lampert's work does succeed in addressing behavior, cognition, context, character, and collaboration, is it not inevitable that there yet remain one, two, and more theoretical or practical perspectives that even she has not included?

I conclude that our quest for the full picture, the complete pedagogue, is a fruitless one if we insist on maintaining a traditional conception of social science. We are, as human thinkers, actors, and believers, unable to achieve completeness, destined to be partial from a disciplinary, an ideological, and a policy perspective. To be properly comprehensive, we will need to forgo our traditional dream of a social *science* of education. We will instead move toward a more local, case-based, narrative field of study, as exemplified in Lampert's research.

Meanwhile, unfortunately and dangerously, educational policy makers remain most heavily influenced by the older work on teacher behavior. In part, the influence of process-product research is stronger because its findings are older and more easily translated into prescriptions for policy. Unlike most other research on teaching, it ties the acts of teaching directly to socially valued student outcomes. Perhaps most significantly, this work is also most readily compatible with a top-down view of educational reform and policy making, in which the best approaches are determined at the top and teachers are then trained, advised, and mandated to behave accordingly.

I have already argued that all approaches to teaching rest on both an epistemic and a moral foundation. I have attempted to describe those approaches, their foundations, and their implications for practice and policy. Before concluding the chapter, I should like to comment directly on the overall topic of this book, effective and responsible teaching.

Effective and Responsible Teaching

This volume addresses the interacting topics of effective and responsible teaching. They are most typically addressed independently, as if educators trade off intellectual against moral ends, in a zero-sum game in which an emphasis on effectiveness must entail a sacrifice of responsibility or vice versa. Alternately, they are viewed hierarchically, as in Sockett's (1987) assertion that all aspects of teaching must be subordinated to the moral, for all teaching is fundamentally, to use Allan Tom's (1984) lovely phrase, a moral craft.

I too assert that all teaching represents a confluence of the intellectual and the moral, but in ways that are not normally addressed in these discussions. I treat as my text the most famous sentence ever written about education by the eminent American psychologist Jerome Bruner (1960). In paraphrase, he claimed that any child could learn any subject at any stage of development in an intellectually honest way. Most of the discussions of his claim have focused on its developmentally ambitious manifesto that any learning is attainable by any child. But for a pedagogy of substance, the most significant phrase is contained in the words "in an intellectually honest way."

(I was most recently reminded of this connection in a paper by Deborah Ball [forthcoming].) In those four words, we recognize the essential conjunction of the moral and the intellectual, of the responsible and the substantive, in all pedagogy.

All teaching entails a fundamental tension between ideas as they are understood by mature scholars of a discipline and as they might be grasped by schoolchildren. Teachers explain complex ideas to children by offering examples, analogies, or metaphors, by telling stories or providing demonstrations, by building bridges between the mind of the child and the more developed understanding in the mind of the teacher. These bridges carry two-way traffic, as children offer their own representations to the teacher and to one another as well. Teachers not only represent the content of their disciplines; they model the processes of inquiry and analysis, the attitudes and dispositions of scholarship and criticism, and they purposively create communities of interaction and discourse within which ideas are created, exchanged, and evaluated.

How can these experiences of the mind be accomplished "in an intellectually honest way"? What are the teacher's responsibilities to both the student and the subject matter, to the child and the curriculum? This tension captures an inherently moral aspect of all teaching, a tension central to any definition of effective *and* responsible pedagogy. The implicit social contract between teacher and students implies that the mathematics that the teacher offers will be real mathematics and the history, honest history. To the extent that teachers themselves can grasp the complexities and uncertainties of a field, these subtleties will be shared with the student, not obscured or camouflaged. But the pedagogical contract presumes that the teacher is capable of gauging the likely compatibility between mind and idea in much the way that a physician is responsible for discerning the physical compatibility of body and medication. In these situations, the moral and the substantively pedagogical fuse.

Dewey's conception of education, to which I enthusiastically subscribe, rests on the unity of his epistemology and his political philosophy. Dewey's theory of knowledge rests on a never-consummated neo-Hegelian spiral of alternating, competing, and inherently incomplete knowledge claims. Anticipating, perhaps, the modern information processing psychologist's view that human cognition is severely limited in its capacities to grasp the richness of the world in its full complexity, Dewey argued that no knowledge claim, however well grounded and soundly argued, can ever be immune to critical attack. In principle, any thesis will have left some part of the argument inadequately covered. There is always room for another opinion. Indeed, another opinion is mandatory. Knowledge is socially constructed because it is always emerging anew from the dialogues and disagreements of its inventors.

Similarly, the ideal classroom must be a setting where opposing views collide, where every thesis is subjected to critical scrutiny and communally sanctioned doubt. Recognize that this is not only a conception of knowing and teaching. It is a moral argument as well. To permit knowledge claims to be offered that appear immune to critical examination, that appear to be warranted *in principle* without the negotiated warrant of a learning community, is to violate both the intellectual and the moral code of Dewey's conception of education. Moreover, it is nearly impossible to discern where the intellectual ends and the moral begins in this formulation.

Conclusions

What, then, is the future for research on teaching? First, because we are both educators and scholars, women and men of action as well as students of human behavior, we are fated to be frustratedly schizophrenic. We must be both impassioned and dispassionate, deeply committed and objectively accurate.

Second, our work will grow increasingly cognitive, substantive, contextual, and — in several senses — local. We will tell stories more often than we conduct true experiments, we will modify situations more than we manipulate variables, we will construct allusions to history as often as we rely on psychology, and disciplinary boundaries will fade and blur.

Third, we will take ever more seriously the wisdom of practice, both in the definition of what we study and in our design of collaborative, interactive studies. Teachers will become research agents as well as research subjects. We will watch as the profession of teaching and the community of scholarship intersect and interpenetrate.

Fourth, in this sense, the activity of research and the practice of teaching will become purposefully and mutually *reactive*. In spite of decades of preaching in manuals of research design that warn against reactivity as a threat to validity, we will come to see educator reactivity as one of the signs of its vitality and validity. Research on teaching will contribute to the increased professionalization of teaching by rendering teachers full partners in the making of research. We will resist the deskilling of teachers through the uses of research as a source of elite expertise. We will begin to judge the validity of research by its consequences for the improvement of teaching and learning.

We will not forgo entirely our search for generalizations about human learning, teaching, and classrooms, for generalization and simplification are essential to the understanding of our work. But the teachers and scholars who are at the center of our field, I am confident, will be prepared to exchange the quest for a science of education for a much higher goal — a search for meaning and worthwhile improvement in the practice and profession of education.

References

Ball, D. L. "With an Eye on the Mathematical Horizon: Dilemmas of Teaching Elementary School Mathematics." *Elementary School Journal,* forthcoming.

Bruner, J. *The Process of Education*. Cambridge, Mass.: Harvard University Press, 1960.

Compayre, G. *The History of Pedagogy*. (2nd ed.) (W. H. Payne, trans.) Lexington, Mass.: Heath, 1894.

Girard, G. *De l'enseigment réguli de la langue maternelle dans les écoles et les familles* (On the systematic teaching of the mother tongue in schools and families). Paris: Dezobry, 1844.

Keynes, J. M. *The General Theory of Employment, Interest and Money*. New York: Harcourt Brace Jovanovich, 1936.

Lampert, M. "When the Problem Is Not the Question and the Solution Is Not the Answer." *American Educational Research Journal,* 1990, *27,* 29–63.

Page, D. P. *Theory and Practice of Teaching or the Motives and Methods of Good School Keeping*. New York: Barnes & Noble, 1885.

Schwab, J. J. "The Practical: A Language for Curriculum." *School Review,* 1969, *78*(5), 1–23.

Shulman, L. S. "Paradigms and Research Programs in the Study of Teaching: A Contemporary Perspective." In M. C. Wittrock (ed.), *Handbook of Research on Teaching*. (3rd ed.) New York: Macmillan, 1986.

Shulman, L. S. "Knowledge and Teaching: Foundations of the New Reform." *Harvard Educational Review,* 1987, *57*(1), 1–22.

Sockett, H. "Has Shulman Got the Strategy Right?" *Harvard Educational Review,* 1987, *57*(2), 208–219.

Tom, A. *Teaching as a Moral Craft*. White Plains, N.Y.: Longman, 1984.

Section Two

NEW ROLES
FOR TEACHERS AND STUDENTS

Richard J. Shavelson,
Section Editor

Teaching effectiveness and responsibility arise, ultimately, in the transaction between students and teachers. Teachers and students enact the curriculum in their classrooms, mutually constructing knowledge, attitudes, and values about learning and about one another. The contributions presented in this section address the interdependence of teaching effectiveness and responsibility from different perspectives. The authors agree that knowledge is constructed through the enactment of the curriculum in a constructive process that places teachers and students in new roles. Students must be given responsibility for mindfully constructing knowledge, individually and together, while teachers have to take responsibility for creating and orchestrating classroom tasks that stimulate knowledge construction. The authors agree that the manner in which this orchestration takes place sends a message to students about what is valued about knowledge and interpersonal interaction.

Walter Doyle (Chapter Five) addresses effectiveness and responsibility in teaching from a curricular perspective. He argues that curricular issues have an impact on effective and responsible teaching at multiple levels of education. Although the institutional level is not the focus of the chapter, he points out that curriculum provides at this level a set of expectations regarding what schooling and teaching should be. These content and value expectations are translated into concrete experiences in the classroom. At the classroom level, he argues, teaching is an interpretive process that is based in how teachers understand what they are teaching and the value of that content for students and citizens. Teachers and students together construct knowledge and negotiate the terms of that knowledge construction. This process is enacted through the tasks that frame both the curriculum and the pedagogy, since it is the tasks that organize students' cognitions. Moreover, curriculum is locally constructed, creating an interpretive context for learning, unique to the classroom.

Doyle's conception of teaching can be illustrated by an example that characterizes both the constructive nature of teaching and the way in which the teacher's manner in carrying out a lesson communicates values. An elementary school teacher, using an excerpt from an autobiography that detailed the experiences of a Mexican-American upon entering school, elicited students' personal reactions to the narrator's feelings and constructed an interpretation of the text. This interpretation was largely shaped by the teacher's interpretation — one that emphasized patriotic behavior. Indeed, the teacher kept tight control over the lesson and, when students' reactions did not reflect this emphasis, drew on personal experiences to model the appropriate interpretation. The manner in which this lesson was conducted communicated to the students a set of values, perhaps unintended by the teacher. In jointly constructing knowledge with students, the teacher became the final arbiter of interpretations. Moreover, students learned that there is one interpretation of text — the teacher's — and that personal contributions that deviated from that interpretation were not valued.

Gavriel Salomon (Chapter Three), Richard T. White (Chapter Four), and Richard J. Shavelson and Gail P. Baxter (Chapter Six) all argue that the transformation of our knowledge about learning has profound consequences for what is considered effective teaching, the manner in which teaching is carried out, and the values conveyed. Learning is a constructive process, one that students must be mindfully engaged in. No longer are lectures to fill the intellectual vessel adequate to the task. Rather, incremental learning that develops knowledge in an activity context is needed to enable students individually and together to construct knowledge. In this effort, teaching effectiveness — knowledge construction — cannot be divorced from responsibility.

Such a change in the prevailing conception of learning requires a change in both the teacher's and the student's roles in education. The teacher's role shifts from that of "the deliverer of information, the solo player of a flute in front of a less than appreciating audience, to that of a designer, tour guide, and orchestra conductor," as Salomon writes in Chapter Three. By creating an environment in which students construct knowledge, by orchestrating the knowledge-construction performance, and by ensuring that all students continue to be mindfully engaged and to make the mental effort needed, the teacher engages in responsible effectiveness. Such a role shift clearly requires that students, too, take on a surprisingly new role. They are given the responsibility for constructing, individually and with their peers, their own knowledge. They become valued members of a community in the learning process. Their contributions come to be respected, and they come to respect the diversity of perspectives and contributions made by their peers.

However, the authors recognize that the transformation from traditional views of teaching to this reformed view will not be easy. Salomon believes that the prod to reform is the rapidly emerging information technology. With the widespread availability of technology in the schools and with the public's insistence on its use, computers will help us make the shift from knowledge as something to be owned to knowledge as something to be constructed. Salomon also hopes that attention will be shifted from instruction as transmission of knowledge to instruction as an act of guiding socially based exploration in intellectually rich settings.

Shavelson and Baxter (Chapter Six) argue, as does Doyle, that teaching is the enactment of a subject-matter curriculum that creates a particular learning culture. As do Salomon (Chapter Three) and White (Chapter Four), they argue that learning is constructive in nature, shifting the responsibility for knowledge construction from teacher to student. They see changing views about both the curriculum and learning stimulating a reform in teaching that will lead to more effective and responsible teaching. Teaching will become more effective because knowledge will be constructed by students in meaningful contexts, and it will become more responsible because of the set of values communicated in the process.

Shavelson and Baxter view testing as the needed prod to reform teaching effectiveness and responsibility. If teachers teach to the test (and they do), and if students learn (some of) what is taught (and they do), then by creating performance assessments wherein hands-on classroom activities are translated into tests, teachers will reform their pedagogy in teaching to the test. Indeed, Shavelson and Baxter argue that the typical scripts that teachers use in carrying out teaching will, of necessity, change. For example, the recitation script, with teacher questioning and students responding, will give way to an orchestration script, with students working with hands-on activities constructing knowledge. Typical classroom scenes will change from "frontal" teaching to the extensive use of materials and equipment, with students working together, socially constructing knowledge. These changes in teaching and classroom processes, they argue, may lead to a restructuring of schooling.

White (Chapter Four), however, is not sanguine about the effectiveness of any prod in reforming teaching. His extensive experience in moving schools and teachers toward a constructivist curriculum in the Project to Enhance Effective Learning (PEEL) leads him to recognize that extensive support is required to implement a new conception of effective and responsible teaching. He agrees with the other authors in this part that students must be made aware of their responsibility for their own learning. This touches at the core of the problem, as he describes it: learning is often ineffective because it is so often irresponsible. To reform this, he formulates nine principles that guide innovation and implementation. For example, the Principle of Innovation states that "things get worse before they get better."

All four chapters send a strong, consistent message. Assumptions and knowledge about teaching have changed radically over the past decade. These changes have led to a new understanding and view of what constitutes effective teaching — teaching that enables students to construct knowledge individually and socially — and to a change in the conception of the teacher's role from that of information dispenser to that of orchestrator of tasks that enable mindful knowledge construction. The student's role is also changing, from that of one who memorizes facts conveyed by teacher and text to that of one who is responsible for his or her own learning. Inherent in these changes is a set of values; for example, students are valued as capable of constructing knowledge, and students value one another's diverse contributions. These chapters also envision a change in the very nature of research on teaching: research on teaching should take a reformist position, one that no longer describes the model teacher but prescribes a teaching model (see Chapter Sixteen). However, if any of these reforms are to be realized, systematic, concerted efforts will be needed to begin training preservice and in-service teachers.

3

The Changing Role of the Teacher: From Information Transmitter to Orchestrator of Learning

Gavriel Salomon

The conception of teachers' roles emanates directly from conceptions of teaching, while these are affected, as they have always been, by conceptions of learning and the ways in which learning is studied. This relationship is justified, since teaching is an activity designed to facilitate the process of learning by providing the desired information, by arranging circumstances, activities, and opportunities that are likely to promote skill and knowledge acquisition, and by providing the necessary guides to keep the processes of learning on the desired track. But as the conceptions of and opportunities for learning change, so should the conceptions of effective and responsible teaching.

Both teaching and research on teaching as we have come to know them face at least three challenges today. One challenge arises from our changing conceptions and understandings of what learning, particularly *good* learning, in school is all about. A second challenge is posed by the new learning opportunities that technology affords. A third challenge, following from the other two, pertains to the thorny question of responsible teaching. Once learning is seen in a new light, and once the conceptions and practices of teaching change accordingly, one needs to answer such questions as who is responsible for learning and what constitutes responsible teaching. The bad news about all this is that such challenges create much uncertainty and confusion and a growing discrepancy between the newly evolving conceptions of teaching and the unchanged practical reality of teaching in the schools (see, for example, Cuban, 1990). The good news is that the three factors that challenge conceptions of teaching—new understandings of learning, new opportunities, and new responsibilities—are congruent with each other, thus increasing the changes that when they operate in concert, they might also affect the practice of teaching.

New Conceptions of Learning

With the rediscovery of cognitive processes as legitimate mental activities and legitimate objects for study, the conception of learning has changed.

Of particular interest and importance is the idea of learning as a *constructive process,* whereby, rather than knowledge being simply associated with responses or copied or "assimilated" from external sources, information is turned into knowledge by means of interpretation, by active relating of information to existing bodies of knowledge, by the generative creation of representations, and by processes of purposeful elaboration and transformation. Such a conception, as pointed out by Resnick (1987), integrates functionalist and structuralist theories of development, information processing, and cognition. But this conception also suggests additional elements of importance. One such element is the crucial role played by *specific* knowledge (Anderson, 1984), not only in terms of the acquisition of new knowledge but also in terms of the acquisition and employment of skill. Thus follow the conceptions of knowledge and skill as situated in particular contexts and knowledge schemata (Brown, Collins, and Duguid, 1989).

Another important element is the degree to which construction takes place. Indeed, there is more to the conception of learning than its constructive, knowledge-dependent, and situational nature: there are different *degrees* of construction (Langer, 1989) and different *qualities* of construction (Bereiter and Scardamalia, 1989) and these have an important influence on the depth, width, durability, and transferability of the learning that results (Salomon and Perkins, 1989). Listening to a talk while letting one's understanding be handled by automatic processes is not the same as listening to the talk while guiding one's own nonautomatic processes, selecting comprehension strategies, and effortfully and deliberately elaborating on selected ideas conveyed by the speaker. Similarly, it is one thing to elaborate the presented material for purposes of satisfying the demands of a multiple-choice test; it is another to elaborate the material with the purpose of fully understanding it and its implications (Bereiter and Scardamalia, 1989).

Following the work of Langer (1989) on mindlessness and mindfulness, the late Tami Globerson and I began to study mindfulness as it pertains to school learning. We defined mindfulness in learning as the deliberate, goal-directed and metacognitively guided expenditure of mental effort in the employment of nonautomatic processes (Salomon and Globerson, 1987). This is very similar to (but less well specified than) what Bereiter and Scardamalia (1989) call "intentional learning." Intentional learning is the expenditure of effort "in pursuit of cognitive goals, over and above the requirements of tasks" (p. 385), when these tasks could be accomplished by far less expenditure of effort. And it is not just the effort expended that is important. What is crucial is *the goal of learning as learning,* not as satisfying an immediate and concrete task requirement. Similarly, it is intentional in the sense that the effort is expended not just for the sake of solving a problem but for the sake of acquiring new knowledge and deeper understanding. Good learning, then, is not just constructive; it is intentional, motivated, self-guided, effortful, and learning-goal-oriented. It is thus the opposite of incidental learning that takes place when students try to "satisfice" some task requirements by going through the motions of an instructional activity.

Few students engage in intentional or mindful learning on their own, given that the typical school environment strongly emphasizes good form, going through the motions, and learning for the sake of concrete goals such as grades. Learning, as Bereiter and Scardamalia (1989) point out, degenerates into schoolwork. And work, whether in school or on the assembly line, is something that one tries to get over with quickly, efficiently, and with the least possible effort.

Teaching must take into serious consideration the conception of good learning as intentional or mindful by providing the necessary opportunities for it to take place. For, as Bereiter and Scardamalia (1989) hypothesize, "In order to learn what is ostensibly being taught in school, students need to direct mental effort to goals over and above those implicit in the school activity" (p. 385). But even a mindfully inclined learner needs the occasion and reason to engage in effortful intentional learning. What, then, would constitute such opportunities, and, knowing that not all opportunities are necessarily taken (Perkins, 1985), what would increase the likelihood that they *are* taken?

Obviously, there are a few instructional and situational ingredients, such as arousing and maintaining intrinsic motivation (Malone and Lepper, 1985) and providing "procedural facilitation" (Bereiter and Scardamalia, 1987), that we are already familiar with and have good reason to believe are likely to promote intentional learning. Here I wish to discuss an issue that goes beyond the ones mentioned above. Specifically, I want to ask what kind of learning *activity* would make even the less mindful students engage in such intentional mental activity? To answer this question, I need to revive a theory initially proposed by David Olson (1970), a theory that was published far ahead of its time and therefore did not receive the attention it deserves.

According to Olson, every kind of activity—listening, drawing, discovering, writing—entails a series of unique points for making choices or encountering alternatives (for example, how do I represent depth while drawing a ball? How do I determine the speed of a ball coming at me so that I can catch it? What should I emphasize first when teaching a child to catch a ball?). Clearly, we could say today that the alternatives encountered are very much a function not only of the activity itself but also of what the learner already knows about it and perceives to be entailed in its execution (hence the important role played by specific and well-organized previous knowledge). Each such choice requires for its resolution its own kind of information to be collected, generated, or retrieved, lest the activity come to a halt. The choice points that a student encounters in writing a paper are certainly different from the ones that her readers encounter. Accordingly, the student and the readers must consider different information. It is the elaboration of this performance-specific information needed when one is faced with activity-determined choice points that leads to its reconstruction and acquisition as knowledge. Hence, the information acquired while trying, for example, to draw an object may be very different from that acquired by looking at it. (Notice how close this comes to the notion of situated cognitions, developed nearly twenty years after Olson's publication of his theory; see Brown, Collins, and Duguid, 1989).

This is where learning by doing — *experiential* learning, or the employment of knowledge in an activity context (Lave, 1988) — may play a crucial and distinctive role. For the choice points that students face when designing a new galaxy, actively participating in a simulation of World War I, or solving a real-life science problem are dramatically different from those that they face when reading about these issues or listening to a lecture about them. It is not that experiential learning is necessarily "better" than other modes of learning (although numerous scholars would argue that under some conditions it actually is better for many students) but that it is qualitatively different by virtue of the choice points that one encounters through it and the information that one has thus to elaborate and consider.

But there is more to it than this. Experiential, activity-in-practice learning is accompanied by more mindful engagement in the processing of information, as it requires self-guidance, sustained motivation (Kuhl and Kraska, 1989), and the construction of self-explanation (Chi and Bassok, 1989) for the resolution of the choice points encountered. Moreover, as pointed out by Lave (1988), "knowledge in practice, constituted in the settings of practice, is the locus of the most powerful knowledgeability of people in the lived-in-world" (p. 14). And it is so powerful because, first, one encounters choice points that one would have neither encountered nor considered without that in-context practice and, second, it is knowledge genuinely *owned* by the learner.

But in and of itself, experiential, in-context practice has its limitations when seen from the perspective of intentional learning, particularly when seen from the point of view of transfer of knowledge and skill to novel situations. As pointed out by Bereiter and Scardamalia (1989), even under conditions of self-guided, practice-based activities, one would still need to consider whether students entertain the necessary *learning* goals (as contrasted with immediate performance goals), whether the teacher has such goals in mind, and whether the situational constraints favor or disfavor the pursuit of learning goals. Indeed, in our own research, we have found, as others found long before us, that the more open the learning situation, the more the quality of learning depends on students' perceptions, motivations, goals, intentions, and proclivities. Hence, we face a dilemma: on the one hand, experiential, practice-based learning activities provide an opportunity for the promotion of intentional learning; on the other hand, the extent to which this opportunity is taken greatly depends on the student's volition.

There are no fast and simple solutions to this dilemma. Perhaps one way to resolve it is through yet another element that current research on learning has rediscovered and formulated: the critical role played by the social context in which learning takes place. Not only is learning a socially distributed activity, whereby meanings are socially negotiated and "appropriated" (Newman, Griffin, and Cole, 1989), but its goals, as entertained by the individual, are greatly dependent on those entertained and shared by the other partners in the learning situation. Thus, whether students play the role of Italy during World War II only for the sake of finding a strategy to strengthen their position or for the sake of learning what makes a nation enter and win or lose a war may greatly depend on the shared, consensually held perception of the task and activity.

A second problem with experiential learning is that, while the ownership attained through it may indeed allow the *acquisition* of the new knowledge and skill, it may not suffice for their *sustained utilization in new situations*. This is a typical problem of far transfer. According to our theory (Salomon and Perkins, 1989), far transfer can be attained only when the ideas, behaviors, or attitudes to be flexibly transferred to novel situations have been mindfully abstracted (that is, decontextualized) and are mindfully searched for when new situations are encountered. For example, one does not transfer anything from chess to political campaigning except for an abstracted principle such as "get hold of the center." But such a principle needs to be actively, deliberately, and effortfully abstracted by the learner. Practice alone may not suffice; it may teach how to play chess, but the developing cognitions are likely to be highly situated (Brown, Collins, and Duguid, 1989), not easily transferred to novel situations (Salomon and Perkins, 1989). However, we can expect the desired far transfer to be attained when practice is accompanied and followed by mindful reflection.

It is the well-orchestrated interplay of socially and practice-based experiential learning and the demand for active, mindful abstraction, the reflection on and verbalization of what one is doing and why one is doing it, that may promote the desired intentional learning. But this, it appears, is a very pretentious expectation, one that would be unfair to impose on a teacher facing thirty students. Moreover, there is large discrepancy between the standard operating procedures of common teaching, procedures that often work relatively well, and the demands implied by this expectation. As Ann Brown (1990) has recently pointed out, novel teaching approaches that do not fit well into standard operating procedures are not very likely to be adopted or, if they are adopted, to be sustained. Indeed, some novelties, such as instructional television, computer programming, and drill and practice computer usages, have been smoothly incorporated into school practices precisely because they fit so well the existing procedures, while others, such as collaborative learning, have not because they require major and effortful changes. One needs a lever, a new tool, the introduction of which affords the latter kinds of changes in ways that change the whole instructional system, not just isolated elements of it.

New Learning Opportunities Afforded by Technology

Enter the second challenge to teaching: the computer. Two assumptions can be made about computers and related technologies in education. One assumption is that their availability, accessibility, and versatility are constantly increasing and are likely to continue to increase. Computers are gradually becoming a ubiquitous component of the school learning environment. The second assumption is based on Herbert Simon's (1987) assertion that computers are a "one in many centuries invention," implying that this technology is not just one more set of instructional means, serving more efficiently old educational ends, but carries with it a whole new conception of knowledge and of ways of attaining it in educational settings. The effective use of computers in education helps us shift our focus from knowledge as possession to knowledge as construction and from learning as externally guided to learning as self-guided. It also carries with it a renewed conception of instruction that shifts attention from the imparting of knowledge to the guidance of socially based exploration in intellectually rich settings. It is no coincidence that these shifts happen to be highly congruent with the new conceptions of learning.

Computers can accomplish many functions in education, ranging from electronic workbooks to music making, from communication to media exploratory devices, and from a rich source of information to a rich soil for construction. What makes computers unique is their capacity to serve as multiple symbolic tools for making, doing, and creating and as tools that afford access to large and remote sources of knowledge with which one can interact (Brown, 1985; Sheingold, 1987). Never before have we had a technology that not only *exposed* students to knowledge but afforded them the opportunity to *construct* it in interaction with peers, knowledge repositories, and experts. Six interrelated elements are likely to characterize education once the challenge of computers is seriously taken: exploration, commuication, collaboration, disciplinary integration, curricular variation, and teachers' and students' autonomy.

With traditional instructional practices, students are passively exposed to the sciences, thus following their well-established two dimensions — theory building and theory testing. With the introduction of computers and computer networks, students can now also engage in the activity of *(re)creating* phenomena in imaginary and intellectually daring settings: creating new chemical compounds and testing their properties, designing and testing galactic processes, simulating revolutions and economic forces, testing physical laws and simulating their derivations. From passively learning about the sciences, students can become explorers and doers of science through intellectual partnership with intelligent technologies (Brown, 1990; Pea, 1987).

Exploration is never carried out in a social and intellectual vacuum. One explores with peers and consults sources of knowledge. As shown by Newman (1990), computers can serve as invaluable sources of knowledge through networks that provide access to large sources of knowledge and remotely located peers and experts. The single student thus turns into a team member engaged in guided learning through exploration, communication, and collaboration that become integrated into a well-orchestrated learning environment (Salomon, 1991). Indeed, never before could teams of students thousands of miles apart engage in a dialogue through which they jointly construct a model of their respective economies, cultural surroundings, or ecologies and then collaboratively test its far-reaching implications. Never before could students engage in a team-based project of writing, guided by the intelligent advice of an expert writing partner, while being able to consult encyclopedias, high-resolution disks, and live experts, all through their computers.

Let me briefly illustrate the above discussion with a real-classroom example. On the basis of previous experimental findings, I planned to introduce the use of a data base into the study of the U.S. Constitution, a rather unexciting and difficult subject for eighth-graders. However, it became clear to me that students' construction of a data base would not in and of itself be effective — it had to be integrated into a whole new conception of classroom learning activities. Indeed, it came to serve as a trigger for major changes in almost everything else in these social science classes. Students started working in teams, assuming the roles of adversarial parties (Loyalists, New Yorkers, Federalists) whose task it was to rewrite the Constitution in light of their particular interests. They also prepared for a reenactment of the Constitutional Convention, where a new constitution was to be debated and written. The construction of the data base served to assist the intellectual process; in fact, it afforded the students the opportunity to engage in intentional learning. Observations and interviews provided evidence that this was indeed the case. Each article of the constitution had to be entered into the data base, disputable elements had to be paraphrased, and other teams' proposed changes had to be seriously considered. There was much excitement in the air as students prepared to debate and discuss their adversarial positions at the forthcoming constitutional convention. They hurried to class and were late to leave when the period was over; they exchanged hints about history and ways to get the most out of their data bases. The teacher moved around, directing, guiding, suggesting, and advising, more like an orchestra conductor than a composer. All this reached its peak at the constitutional convention; the school principal, dressed as George Washington, led the debate among the teams in a congresslike fashion, guiding the attempts to reach compromises and formulate the students' new constitution.

This example shows where the teacher's new role comes in. No wondrous technology, in and of itself, can meet the challenges of the new opportunities. While computer technology affords a number of important possibilities, none of them can be assumed to become automatically realized simply because of the technology's presence. Unfortunately, it is all too often erroneously assumed that the very existence of computers is itself the opportunity, with everything else falling into place more or less on its own. Taking advantage of the opportunities afforded by computer technology requires a whole new conception of education and instruction to be developed and adopted in interaction with the emergence of new technological capabilities. For education to realize any of technology's potentials, classroom practices, curricula, teachers' roles and behaviors, social structure, and the nature of classroom activities all need to be orchestrated into a well-integrated learning environment. The computer is no more than the yeast, and no yeast suffices to make an edible cake.

Implications of the Challenges to Teaching

It is only the teacher who can design, implement, coordinate, and monitor the changes occurring in the learning environment. These changes are shifting the teacher's role from the deliverer of information, the solo player of a flute in front of a less than appreciative audience, to a designer, tour guide, and orchestra conductor. Such a shift has three kinds of implications, pertaining to the teacher's perceptions of the classroom as a learning environment, the way teacher training is carried out, and the question of responsibility in teaching.

Teachers' Perceptions of the Classroom

To design their classrooms so that the cognitively based conceptions of learning become manifest and the new opportunities afforded by computer technology are seriously taken advantage of, teachers will be required to engage in *systemic thinking*. Such thinking is based on a number of principles, such as the multiplicity of causes, the interdependence of variables, the reciprocal relationship between cause and effect, and the self-feeding, often self-sustaining nature of the system as a whole (Salomon, 1981; Weick, 1979). This is not the way most people think of events in the world or the systems within which they operate. But such modes of thinking can be acquired and deliberately applied when complex systems such as the classroom are considered or designed. Given the changing conceptions of learning and the newly afforded opportunities, school administrators and particularly teachers will have to acquire such systemic modes of thinking. They will have to learn to think of the classroom as a multivariate environment, akin perhaps to Barker's (1963) "behavior settings," in which they play the role of conductor of a whole system of ever changing, mutually affecting factors. What implications does this have for teacher training programs?

Teacher Training

It is all very nice to think of how to facilitate intentional learning, mindful transfer, and other cognitively based conceptions of learning when it comes to the young learner in school, while more or less ignoring the possibility that the same applies to the teacher and to the student teacher. If experientially based, activity-in-practice learning, coupled with mindful abstraction, is expected to be essential for students in school settings, would not the same apply to teaching students in institutions of higher education? For teachers to become well versed in systemic thinking and to be daring designers of whole new learning environments, they need to experience the actual process of designing and orchestrating such learning environments and to accompany these experiences with mindful reflection. This implies major changes in the way teachers are trained and supervised, not an unfair expectation from those institutions of higher education that pioneer changes in public schools.

Responsibility in Teaching

Underlying the above discussion of the teacher's new role, with its shift from knowledge transmission to activity orchestration, is the implicit assumption that the newly designed classroom is a more effective one. However, two things need to be said about this expected effectiveness. First, there is more than one kind of "effect"; second, what is "effective" for one student may not be for another. This is where the question of responsible teaching comes in.

Efficiency and Two Kinds of Effect. Two distinctions need to be made here. The first distinction, a rather old yet useful one (see, for example, Argyris, 1973), is between "effective" and "efficient" teaching. Many teaching activities and classroom environments may be highly efficient in the sense that things are accomplished properly, smoothly, promptly, and with little fuss or disruption. But efficiency is *not* the ultimate goal of classroom learning, and it may not even be a useful means to reaching the goals of socially based experiential learning by construction. The U.S. Constitution project described above was very inefficient in terms of the time devoted to the topic, as the teams learned how to study jointly and slowly experienced what could have been easily and speedily transmitted ready-made. But it was an effective way of teaching, inasmuch as it provided the opportunity for construction, for the social appropriation of shared meanings, and for the entertaining of alternative points of view.

The second distinction, a distinction not often made, is that between two kinds of "effects" (see Salomon, Perkins, and Globerson, 1991). A new approach to teaching—or, for that matter, any teaching procedure, strategy, or method—can be effective in the sense that it promotes desired activities and performances while it is in place. For example, while constructing different data bases in teams, students engage in intellectual and social activities that meet the goals of such an experiential project. These are effects *within* the learning environment, akin, perhaps, to the improvement in performance that occurs when one is equipped with a powerful tool or supported by a strong decision-making team. Contrast this kind of effect with another: the effect that engagement in a project such as the one described above has in the form of some desirable residues to be manifested later on, long after the project is completed. These are effects *of* the project, effects that endure after the students are no longer within it.

This distinction raises important normative and ethical questions pertaining to the goals of education. On the one hand, one could argue (as does, for example, Pea, 1987) that in this age of computers, when the tools for socially based learning by construction are available, one needs to aim at the improved *distributed* performance of students-plus-peers-plus-technology (Pea, forthcoming). It is the activity that counts, supported as it is by peers and technology. This conception is akin, for example, to one's desire to see an improvement in students' ability to construct complex economic models when they are equipped with a powerful computer model builder. The question of the residue that such an activity leaves behind becomes moot, so goes the argument, as students will hardly ever construct complex models without the support of peers or technology. On the other hand, one could argue that effects *within* a project are but means to the attainment of desirable residues *of* it, whether in the form of better generalizable skill mastery, a better sense of others' points of view, or improved ability to solve problems in teams. Taking the latter viewpoint, Perkins (forthcoming) argues that not all knowledge can be distributed and that therefore there is no way one can avoid aiming at the attainment of students' "solo" residues beyond the effects within classroom activities. Similarly, Salomon, Perkins, and Globerson (1991) argue that it is education's moral obligation to prepare students to solve novel and challenging problems that no technology and no well-designed environment will be able to support. Classroom environments and the new role of the teacher in them are in this sense means for the attainment of this residue, and their joint effectiveness is to be judged in this light.

The kind of learning environment described here, with the newly formulated role of the teacher in it, is not and cannot be of equal effectiveness for all students. Neither effects *within* that environment nor effects *of* it are attained by all students. Recent research clearly shows that slower, less mindfully inclined students, or those with a poorer perceived self-efficacy as autonomous learners, do not seem to benefit from such environments, at least in terms of their performance while within them, as opposed to the residues that are left behind. Such students seem to feel quite comfortable in experiential learning environments but to benefit more in terms of learning residues from a better-structured less self-guided environment. Hence, while the new conceptions of learning appear to be well grounded and to lead to new conceptions of teaching and new definitions of teachers' roles, some students may not benefit from them. For such students, more didactic styles of teaching appear to be more beneficial. This is where the question of responsible teaching enters.

Responsibility for Learning and Responsible Teaching. Another important distinction is that between *responsibility for learning* and *responsible teaching.* Quite clearly, the new role of the teacher described here entails the shifting of much responsibility for learning to the students. It is they who volitionally expend mental effort in poorly defined, exploratory, and interdisciplinary activities, who define tasks and objectives, and who control the pace of learning and depth of construction. The teacher, having become the orchestrator of the activities, does not dictate but coordinates and guides. In this sense, we may see a true change in schools inasmuch as the power structure, one of the impediments to change (Sarason, 1990), is itself undergoing change. One residue that such a learning environment is likely to foster is students' increased sense of responsibility for their own activities and learning outcomes. Another expected outcome—an effect of that kind of learning environment—is students' improved ability to respect the points of view of others and the relative validity of even the most deplorable of perspectives, as was the case in the constitution project, wherein students came to accept the relative validity of slavery defenders.

The shifting of responsibility for learning, while it is not the same as responsible teaching, is fully complementary to it. I can see at least three elements for responsible teaching. The first element is the proper carrying out of the role of teacher as orchestrator. This is not an easy task. As the result of personal experience as students, of traditional teacher training programs, and of the examples set by others, many teachers tend to "take charge," particularly when things do not go the way they envisioned they ought to. Moreover, experiential learning environments do not have standard operating procedures or a clear scenario to follow. Teachers design such environments and monitor them by constant improvisation, but they cannot easily control them as they can control more authoritative learning settings. Hence, properly carrying out the new roles of teaching as envisioned here, particularly catering to different students, becomes a tricky and rather fluid task.

The second element, even more demanding than the first, is the teacher's perception of his or her responsibility for the learning process and outcomes. Now, this may appear to contradict the idea of shifting the responsibility for learning to the students, but it does not. While the students become responsible for their own activities and learning outcomes, it is still the teacher who sets the stage and conducts and guides life in the classroom. Shifting learning responsibility to students is an unfortunate invitation to also see them as responsible for their failures and to blame them for those failures. Such blaming of students, seeing them as either "mad, bad or stupid" (Watzlawick, Wickland, and Fisch, 1974), is common even in more authoritarian learning environments and can certainly be expected in environments characterized by experiential learning. Experiential learning environments and the new role that teachers are to play in them still leave to the teachers the ultimate responsibility of creating the proper and differentiated settings for students.

The third element of responsible teaching is perhaps the most difficult of all. It is the serious consideration, selection, and design (as contrasted with the mindless adoption) of instructional means, activities, materials, tasks, and the like in light of normative and moral criteria. This element of responsible teaching concerns the question of what is a more and what a less valuable skill, piece of knowledge, or activity for the students to encounter and experience. Having students operate in teams, deal with real-life problems, use computers extensively, and be evaluated in other than simple tests of recitation comes at the expense of other things, such as testable mastery of disciplinary information. The new learning environment, by necessity, may promote the development of certain skills, abilities, and points of view at the expense of others. This is what March (1987) has described as the inevitable process of "deskilling" that accompanies the introduction of any new technology. Can good spelling be laid aside when spell checkers are easily available? Can the skills associated with receptive learning be neglected to make room for those associated with the self-construction of knowledge? Can students be taught science without also adopting the authority of experts and time-honored scientific methods and knowledge?

Obviously, there are no clear-cut answers to such questions, and it is the teacher who, in his or her new role, needs to seriously ponder such questions and take responsibility for answering them. Moreover, such considerations need to take into account not only of effects *within* the new learning environment but also, and perhaps primarily, of the more lasting effects *of* it. As correctly pointed out by Sarason (1984, p. 480), "Because something can be studied or developed is in itself an insufficient base for doing it however wondrous it appears to be." Indeed, students' activities may appear to be exciting, engaging, and worthwhile while they carry them out, but what are the residues that they are likely to leave behind? What about the students who do not flourish in such environments? To illustrate, could it be the case that some of the students in the U.S. Constitution project learned that fighting with adversaries is better than compromising? That secret deals are more effective than straightforward negotiations? That working in a team allows one to become a free rider (Kerr and Brunn, 1983)?

Responsible teaching, then, is related to shifting responsibility for learning over to students but the two are not the same. Responsible teaching means being fully committed to the role of effective activity orchestrator; taking responsibility for the processes and outcomes of learning, despite the power shift that experiential learning entails; and giving serious consideration to the desirable and less desirable long-term effects of the constantly improvised learning environment.

Conclusion

In this chapter, I have argued that the conception of teaching, justifiably related to conceptions of learning, has to change as it is being challenged by new conceptions of learning and by new technologically afforded opportunities for learning. The changed conceptions of learning lead us to believe that learning is a constructive socially and knowledge-based process whose quality greatly depends on the extent to which it is mindfully and intentionally carried out. To promote intentional learning, one needs to create opportunities for experiential, in-context active learning accompanied by mindful abstraction of basic ideas and principles. This is a tall order needing a lever, something potentially provided by the computer if it is used as a tool for socially shared design, construction, and communication. The introduction of the computer for such purposes, serving in fact as a Trojan Horse, or as a subversive element, brings about major changes in the whole classroom culture. But it is only the teacher who can introduce and orchestrate these changes. Shifting such responsibility to the teachers has numerous implications concerning their autonomy, self-image, ability to deal with whole systems, and, of course, teacher training programs.

In relating the changes in the teacher's role to questions of effective and reponsible teaching, I have argued that effectiveness needs to be distinguished from efficiency and that there are at least two classes of effects: those *within* a given classroom environment and those *of* it. The latter represent longer-lasting cognitive, emotional, developmental, and social residues. I have further distinguished between two related kinds of responsibility: responsibility for learning, now shifted to students, and responsibility for teaching, which, as I have tried to show, is particularly demanding for the teacher as activity orchestrator in the new kind of learning environment.

I believe that teachers' roles are about to undergo radical changes. These changes can take two paths. One is the incidental path, whereby the very presence of computers and the growing availability of them as tools, not tutors, force teachers' roles to change. The second is a more deliberate, planned, thoughtful, and thus *responsible* path, whereby the changes in our conceptions of learning and the opportunities opened up by technology are seriously considered and studied, affecting policy, teacher education, and gradual implementation. Most of technology's more profound effects are usually unforeseen (March, 1987) and thus tend to surprise us. However, we are sufficiently experienced today to be able to plan for many of the unintended effects, select out those that we consider desirable, and transform them into intended changes.

References

Anderson, R. C. "Some Reflections on the Acquisition of Knowledge." *Educational Researcher,* 1984, *13* (9), 5–10.

Argyris, C. *Intervention Theory and Method.* Reading, Mass.: Addison-Wesley, 1973.

Barker, R. G. *The Stream of Behavior.* New York: Appleton-Century-Crofts, 1963.

Bereiter, C., and Scardamalia, M. *The Psychology of Written Composition.* Hillsdale, N.J.: Erlbaum, 1987.

Bereiter, C., and Scardamalia, M. "Intentional Learning as a Goal of Instruction." In L. Resnick (ed.), *Knowing, Learning and Instruction: Essays in Honor of Robert Glaser.* Hillsdale, N.J.: Erlbaum, 1989.

Brown, A. L. *"Technology and Restructuring: Creating a Context for Learning and Evaluation."* Paper presented at the annual meeting of the American Educational Research Association, Boston, Apr. 1990.

Brown, J. S. "Process Versus Product: A Perspective on Tools for Communal and Informal Electronic Learning." In M. Chen and W. Paisley (eds.), *Children and Microcomputers*. London: Sage, 1985.

Brown, J. S., Collins, A., and Duguid, P. "Situated Cognition and the Culture of Learning." *Educational Researcher*, 1989, *18* (1), 32–42.

Chi, M., and Bassok, M. "Learning from Examples via Self-Explanations." In B. L. Resnick (ed.), *Knowing, Learning and Instruction: Essays in Honor of Robert Glaser*. Hillsdale, N.J.: Erlbaum, 1989.

Cuban, L. "Reforming Again, Again, and Again." *Educational Researcher*, 1990, *19* (1), 3–13.

Kerr, N. L., and Brunn, S. E. "Dispensability of Member Effort and Group Motivation Losses: Free Rider Effects." *Journal of Personality and Social Psychology*, 1983, *44*, 78–94.

Kuhl, J., and Kraska, K. "Self-Regulation and Metamotivation: Computational Mechanisms, Development, and Assessment." In R. Kanfer and P. L. Ackerman (eds.), *Abilities, Motivations, and Methodology*. Hillsdale, N.J.: Erlbaum, 1989.

Langer, E. J. *Mindfulness*. Reading, Mass.: Addison-Wesley, 1989.

Lave, J. *Cognition in Practice*. New York: Cambridge University Press, 1988.

Malone, T. W., and Lepper, M. "Making Learning Fun: A Taxonomy of Intrinsic Motivations for Learning." In R. E. Snow and M. J. Farr (eds.), *Aptitude, Learning and Instruction: III. Conative and Affective Process Analyses*. Hillsdale, N.J.: Erlbaum, 1985.

March, J. G. "Old Colleges, New Technology." In S. B. Kiesler and L. S. Sproull (eds.), *Computing and Change on Campus*. New York: Cambridge University Press, 1987.

Newman, D. "Opportunities for Research on the Organizational Impact of School Computers." *Educational Researcher*, 1990, *19* (3), 8–13.

Newman, D., Griffin, P., and Cole, M. *The Construction Zone*. New York: Cambridge University Press, 1989.

Olson, D. R. *Cognitive Development*. San Diego, Calif.: Academic Press, 1970.

Pea, R. D. "Integrating Human and Computer Intelligence." In R. D. Pea and K. Sheingold (eds.), *Mirrors of Minds*. Norwood, N.J.: Ablex, 1987.

Pea, R. D. "Distributed Intelligence and Education." In G. Salomon (ed.), *Distributed Cognitions*. New York: Cambridge University Press, forthcoming.

Perkins, D. N. "The Fingertip Effect: How Information Processing Technology Shapes Thinking." *Educational Researcher*, 1985, *14* (7), 11–17.

Perkins, D. N. "Person Plus: A Distributed View of Thinking and Learning." In G. Salomon (ed.), *Distributed Cognitions*. New York: Cambridge University Press, forthcoming.

Resnick, L. B. "Constructing Knowledge in School." In L. Liben (ed.), *Development and Learning: Conflict or Congruence?* Hillsdale, N.J.: Erlbaum, 1987.

Salomon, G. *Communication and Education*. London: Sage, 1981.

Salomon, G. "Transcending the Qualitative-Quantitative Debate: The Analytic and Systemic Approaches to Educational Research." *Educational Researcher*, 1991, *20* (6), 10–18.

Salomon, G., and Globerson, T. "Skill May Not Be Enough: The Role of Mindfulness in Learning and Transfer." *International Journal of Educational Research,* 1987, *11,* 621–638.

Salomon, G., and Perkins, D. N. "Rocky Roads to Transfer: Rethinking Mechanisms of a Neglected Phenomenon." *Educational Psychologist,* 1989, *24* (2), 113–142.

Salomon, G., Perkins, D. N., and Globerson, T. "Partners in Cognition: Extending Human Intelligence with Intelligent Technologies." *Educational Researcher,* 1991, *20* (3), 2–9.

Sarason, S. B. "If It Can Be Studied or Developed, Should It Be?" *American Psychologist,* 1984, *39,* 477–485.

Sarason, S. B. *The Predictable Failure of Educational Reform: Can We Change Course Before It's Too late?* San Francisco: Jossey-Bass, 1990.

Sheingold, K. "The Microcomputer as a Symbolic Medium." In R. D. Pea and K. Sheingold (eds.), *Mirrors of Minds.* Norwood, N.J.: Ablex, 1987.

Simon, H. A. "Computers and Society." In S. B. Kiesler and L. S. Sproull (eds.), *Computing and Change on Campus.* New York: Cambridge University Press, 1987.

Watzlawick, P., Weakland, J., and Fisch, R. *Change: Principles of Problem Formulation and Problem Resolution.* New York: Norton, 1974.

Weick, K. E. *The Social Psychology of Organizing.* Reading, Mass.: Addison-Wesley, 1979.

4

Raising the Quality of Learning: Principles from Long-Term Action Research

Richard T. White

Teaching is a means to an end: it is responsible and effective only when it leads to a valued and morally defensible change in students. In much education, students have no share in determining the value and the morality of the goal, but when they do, their learning as well as the teaching can be effective and responsible.

The relationship between effectiveness and responsibility is subtle. They do not necessarily go together — it is possible to think of teaching and learning that are only too effective while being irresponsible (brainwashing in totalitarian states or in some religious cults is an example) — but neither are they independent of each other. The reason why learning is often ineffective may be because it is so irresponsible. In present school systems, learners see that the teacher has the responsibility to control their attention in lessons as well as to present information in a form that they can digest without effort. They see that they are responsible to an authority, the teacher, and not to themselves.

Making students aware of their responsibility for their own learning and giving them the opportunity to exercise it constitute the theme of a substantial body of case studies and action research on learning by teachers and academics associated with Monash University in Melbourne, Australia. Rather than being tightly designed tests of hypotheses in which the conclusions are supported by comparisons of scores of competing groups, case studies and action research are reflective experiences that yield insights. The Monash research has led me to formulate nine such insights, or principles.

Any insight may be obvious, mistaken, or trivial. My colleagues and I think that the nine principles are not obvious; they emerged only through our research. They should not be mistaken, since they are based on long classroom experience by many teacher-researchers. Nor do they appear trivial: we see them as useful guides to better conduct of teaching and learning.

Origin of the Principles

The research on which the principles are based arose from concerns about the quality of learning in schools and universities, especially in regard to the acquisition of scientific knowledge. In the late 1970s, reports began to appear that revealed that many students took what they were taught about scientists' portrayal of the world only as a veneer of knowledge, beneath which they maintained the contradictory beliefs that they had formed earlier from unguided interpretations of experience. Physics students versed in Newtonian mechanics clung to pre-Galilean views of force and motion (Champagne, Klopfer, and Anderson, 1980), and biology students who could recite Darwinian principles thought as Lamarckians (Brumby, 1979). Other studies probed understandings of the shape of the earth (Nussbaum and Novak, 1976), heat and temperature (Erickson, 1979), electricity (Tiberghien and Delacôte, 1976), gravity (Gunstone and White, 1981), and light (Stead and Osborne, 1980). Although these studies are well known now, their results at the time caused surprise. They demonstrated that there is much more to learning than the simple acquisition of knowledge: it involves revision of beliefs, which will occur only if people process deeply what they are being told. Thus, the studies directed attention to styles of learning.

Baird and I carried out three case studies of learning styles (Baird and White, 1982a, 1982b; Baird, 1986), first identifying and then trying to remedy defects such as failing to determine the task and to evaluate progress in understanding. In the third study, Baird (1986) worked for six months with one teacher and three of his classes to encourage the students to become more purposeful and reflective learners. He was trying to put into practice with science classes the notions of metacognition that Brown (1980) had applied in reading. The students did improve their strategies of learning, but success was limited, because the teacher had no support from colleagues, so that the students regressed to poor learning behavior in lessons in other subjects. It was clear that we needed a more consistent attempt, so in the next study, the Project to Enhance Effective Learning, we started with ten high school teachers who shared the same students.

The Project to Enhance Effective Learning (PEEL) is action research. When it began in 1985, the purpose was clear: to raise the quality of students' learning by encouraging them to be purposeful and responsible in lessons. At the beginning of the project, no teaching procedures had been worked out; they evolved from experimentation from lesson to lesson and frequent discussion among the teachers and Monash researchers. Baird and Mitchell (1986) describe experiences of the first year. The project has now expanded to a score of schools. The teachers have invented or adapted many procedures that promote purposeful learning. Within each school, they meet weekly to share ideas and results from trials of techniques, there are frequent interschool meetings, and a newsletter circulates to broadcast experiences. The success of this project inspired a parallel effort in preservice teacher education (Gunstone, Slattery, and Baird, 1989) and action research projects by teachers working for master's degrees (Bakopanos, 1988; Macdonald, 1990; Swan, 1988).

PEEL and the related projects attended to cognition and metacognition. My colleagues and I were slow to study the relationship between cognition and affect. More recent action research (Baird and others, 1990; Baird, Fensham, Gunstone, and White, 1991; White and others, 1989) has been concerned with why students often lose their liking for science and how that depressing result may be reversed. Table 4.1 summarizes the research. While each study has specific findings, reflection on the whole body of our action research has led to another level of conclusion, the nine general principles that follow.

The Nine Principles

Principle of Vocabulary

This principle holds that knowledge of terms for processes of learning improves a student's rate of acquisition of learning strategies. When Baird (1986) asked students in grades 9 and 11 whether they wanted to become better learners, nearly all said yes; but when he asked them what they might do to become better learners, most could not cite anything other than concentrating or working harder. "Just concentrate harder on my work . . . that's probably it." "Spend more time going over it . . . getting the things in my mind" (Baird, 1984, p. 213). Later, Macdonald (1990) found that he had to teach twelfth-year students the meanings of linking, concepts, processing, learning strategies, metacognition, and short-term and long-term memory before they could understand what he meant by becoming purposeful learners. Given the terms, they were able to discuss their learning behavior in and out of lessons with insight and could tell what they had to do to improve. After they had developed extensive meanings for words such as *fix, link,* and *reflect,* two of his students commented, "If you asked people to name negative strategies they were using or positive strategies they should use they probably would not have been able to say 'this, this, and this' until the language was there. When you see the words you think of learning now." "Having words like that, and understanding the meaning behind them, . . . triggers your learning. So when you have words that you associate with it, you have something to think about within class" (Macdonald, 1990, p. 45).

Principle of Innovation

Concern that their students were not learning as well as they should prompted teachers at one high school to join PEEL. Although they had been comfortable in their teaching, they were prepared to employ new procedures because they thought that their students would benefit from them. They un-

Table 4.1. Summary of Studies.

Outline	Length	Number of Students	Age of Students	Number of Teachers	References
Case study of adults' learning styles	2 hours + retention tests	3	20, 34, 34	0	Baird and White, 1982a
Observation of learning styles and attempt to remedy defects	6 weeks	3	18	1	Baird and White, 1982b
Action research in high school science classes to promote better learning strategies	6 months	74	14–16	1	Baird, 1986
Action research in high school classes for various subjects to promote better learning strategies	5 years+	Initially 200, now 2,000+	11–17	Initially 10, now 100+	Baird and Mitchell, 1986
Promotion of question asking by students	3 months	19	16	1	Bakopanos, 1988; White, Bakopanos, and Swan, 1988
Use of "thinking" books to promote greater awareness of learning	6 months+	24	8	1	Swan, 1988; White, Bakopanos, and Swan, 1988
Training pre-service student teachers in reflection on teaching and being a teacher	8 months	13	20+	2	Baird, Fensham, Gunstone, and White, 1989; Gunstone, Slattery, and Baird, 1989
Action research with teachers and students of science on how their actions promote or inhibit learning	3 years	2,000+	11–17	Initially 9, total now 33	Baird, Fensham, Gunstone, and White, 1989; Baird and others, 1990; White and others, 1989
In classes outside normal lessons, training students to apply learning strategies in all contexts	1 year	9	16	1	Macdonald, 1990

derestimated the changes that they had to make. The introduction of PEEL produced strain between new teaching and old learning, as the students took time to learn how to benefit from lessons in which they were encouraged to ask questions as well as answer them or to take part in discussions in which the teachers withheld their own opinions. Thus, the early months of PEEL were more difficult for teachers and students than the preceding time, when they had been working comfortably. One teacher wrote:

> Over the years it's easy to develop defences which are protection against failure, but which limit the amount of interaction between students and teacher. I'd worked out how I could achieve a "quiet, busy" classroom. From the outside I looked like a good teacher. But the dynamics were mostly me giving and them taking; I didn't allow much rope. PEEL changed all that! The techniques we came to develop meant a much more open, honest approach, and deliberately handed over much of the business of learning to the students. This was risky, as it was easy to fail. Classes were rowdy and disorganized. Kids became demanding and argumentative. There wasn't any time to sit up the front and correct essays! Every lesson was a 3-mile hurdle race, and I usually came last. There were many days when I threw up my hands in horror and said "To hell with all this PEEL stuff, today they can copy notes off the board" [J. Mitchell, 1986, p. 99].

The principle was clear: *In innovations, things get worse before they get better.* Teachers need time to develop and become skilled at new practices, and students need time to learn how to benefit from them.

Principle of Matching

Reflection on the early months of PEEL illuminates two parts of a principle of matching. The first is fairly trite: *Teaching method and learning style must match for effective learning of content.* When the PEEL teachers first introduced new procedures into their lessons, the students were puzzled. They did not know how to frame questions; they were unable to sustain discussions or to wait until they had considered several points of view before forming opinions; they were poor at devising means of testing alternative views. Consequently, they did not benefit immediately from the lessons and learned little.

The second part of the principle is more subtle: if methods and styles match exactly, there is no strain; there is then stagnation in development of strategies of learning. The students may continue to acquire subject matter, but they will not become better learners. Therefore, *in order for new strategies of learning to develop, teaching method and learning style must not always match.*

The two parts of the principle of matching appear to conflict, but the clash is merely an instance of another principle, that of balance. Of course, if there is a continual discord between teaching method and learning style, communication will break down. There must be the right proportion of new and established procedures for there to be the best balance between acquisition of subject matter and development of better strategies.

Teaching methods and learning styles must match the values and purposes of the teachers and students. In my book *Learning Science,* I reported a conversation between a tenth-grade student and a teacher in the PEEL program:

> "We see what all this is about now," one said. "You are trying to get us to think and learn for ourselves."
>
> "Yes, yes," replied the teacher, heartened by this long-delayed breakthrough, "that's it exactly."
>
> "Well," said the student, "we don't want to do that" [White, 1988, p. 1].

Methods and learning styles must also match values and purposes of the broader community, of parents, and of school administrators. Radical schools such as Summerhill (Neill, 1937) could not become common because few parents believed that the procedures accorded with their values of discipline and work. We had no trouble convincing parents and administrators that PEEL was useful, since they were in accord with its purpose of increasing the quality of learning.

Principle of Minimum Expenditure of Energy

PEEL introduced a beneficial amount of strain between teaching method and learning style. Strain is unnatural, however, and needs energy to be maintained. We saw an instance of that in PEEL. One of the first techniques that we tried was encouraging students to ask questions that began with "What if . . . " We thought that framing questions this way would require students to reflect on knowledge and lead them to ask other thoughtful questions, thus promoting purposeful learning. Indeed, it did for a while; for example, with tenth-grade students asking questions on the law such as these: "How would a person go about learning of the laws and their rights if not at school? Is there a place which records these matters and puts them on display for the public? What if a person broke both the civil and criminal laws—would he be charged for both? What would happen if my dog wandered onto next-door's lawn . . . and next-door's dog badly injured my dog. Would I be able to sue for payments for my dog, even though it was on the other dog's lawn?" (Brooks, 1986, p. 215). Another example comes from tenth-grade science students, who after lessons on cells asked, "What happens when [cells] die? Do they shrivel, decompose, etc.? Are they all the same colour? How many times can one cell break (multiply)? If blood renews it-self every 3 weeks, do cells do as well? If bacteria invade both plant and animal cells, which can fight [them] off more easily?" (I. Mitchell, 1986, p. 67).

After a few months, however, Hanna Arzi, who had joined the aca-demics in the project, observed that some students had developed an al-gorithm for framing "What if . . . " questions without thinking (Arzi and White, 1986). It is amazing how widely the question "What if the tempera-ture had dropped sharply?" may be applied in science, geography, history, social studies, and even literature. Overuse led to a similar decline in value for concept mapping, a useful procedure that Novak and Gowin (1984) describe in detail.

For increasing numbers of students, procedures that at first required thought, such as framing questions and concept mapping, became automatic. We should not have been surprised by this. There is evolutionary advan-tage in making repetitive actions automatic: it enables more attention to be given to coping with new events. People do it all the time — in driving, playing sports — and so, of course, they do it in learning.

We have, then, a principle that *frequently repeated actions become automatic.* This is an aspect of the broader principle that *people expend as little energy as they need.* These principles apply to teachers as well as to students. Teaching can become automatic, too. Two challenges then follow: how to maintain continuous input of energy into learning and teaching and how to establish more effective forms of automatic learning and teaching. These are not al-ternatives; it might be possible, and indeed necessary, to meet both.

The first challenge, fueling a continuous input of energy, is easy to meet in innovations. Missionary zeal and encouragement from others pro-vide the energy. Invitations to speak at other schools, even from as far away as Canada, made the PEEL teachers aware that they had something to give to their profession, an impression that was supported by regular visits from Monash academics and occasional ones by foreign professors. However, the excitement of the innovatory phase cannot last. A more permanent fuel is needed. What that fuel might be remains uncertain. For teachers, perhaps it is the reward they receive from having students who are eager and pur-poseful, more ready to carry some of the weight of a lesson; for students, it might be realization of their greater control over their learning and the activities promoting it and appreciation of their greater understanding. (See Chapter Nine for a discussion of motivation.)

Even if permanent rewards are found for high inputs of energy into learning and teaching, a lot of human action must go on at a lower level of consciousness. We cannot be metacognitive all day. Yet it would be good if even the automatic actions of learners and teachers were ones that led to deep understanding. One of the main goals of our research is, in fact, to find out how to make application of good learning strategies a matter of rou-tine. A difficulty is that symptoms of good learning, such as students' asking of questions, may become automatic, without the strategies themselves being applied. It is as if there were a hump to get over. Once over it, the learner finds it easy to apply strategies, automatically *and* effectively, without excessive use of energy. A few learners manage to get over that hump in any school system. What we are trying to do is to increase that few to many.

Training in automatic application of learning strategies can be an integral part of normal lessons or given in special sessions. The PEEL researchers and Bakopanos (1988) and Swan (1988) took the former approach; Macdonald (1990) took the latter. Each approach has its advantages and weaknesses. Training in normal lessons can be frequent and permits the teacher to shape learning behavior directly. Bakopanos (1988) observed, however, that where the person coaching change in learning behavior is also the giver of the lesson, students may exhibit good symptoms, such as asking lots of questions, merely to please the teacher and not because they value the behavior for themselves. In such cases, they are not applying the strategies automatically. Training in special sessions can be intense, but there is the problem of transferring the promoted skills to the context of the normal classroom. It is too early to tell whether one approach is superior.

Principle of Variation

The Principle of Minimum Expenditure of Energy implies that if you keep doing the same thing long enough, the strain will approach zero, and stagnation will set in. The positive principle from this is that *variation in activity is essential for the maintenance of good learning.* This is, of course, a long-established dictum that most teachers will say they subscribe to and apply. There may, however, be less variation in most classrooms than people claim. Transcripts of non-Peel lessons recorded by Clarke (1987), Theobald (1977), and Muralidhar (1989) contain almost no variation in teaching procedure from lesson to lesson. The PEEL teachers, driven by their perception that overuse blunted the effect of concept mapping and student questions, increased their total repertoire to more than eighty techniques, with each teacher using frequently as many as ten. Though a fine achievement, this highlights the fact that before PEEL, they used far fewer—perhaps only one or two.

Even when the teacher thinks that there is variation, the students may not perceive it. One of the PEEL teachers ran a series of four lessons in one week in which the students used microscopes. Although the students had to use the microscope for different purposes, because it was used in all four lessons, they saw the lessons as being of the same sort. It is important to note that as few as four lessons were enough for them to become bored with the activity. Perhaps students in PEEL have had their expectations raised too high and have lowered their tolerance for routine, but more probably, they know from experience that useful variation is possible and have gained the confidence to speak out in protest against humdrum teaching.

Students who have not had an experience such as PEEL may also perceive that routine lessons are boring but be fearful to tell the teacher so. They might reveal their feelings when an independent person asks for them. Here are formerly unpublished comments about science lessons that my colleagues and I collected from seventh-grade students in a non-PEEL school:

> On a scale from 1 to 10 it rates about minus 999,999,999,999,990! It's nothing what I expected it to be. The teacher does all the pracs and we're not allowed to touch anything except our books and pens. All we ever do is sit there copying notes off the board or from sheets. We've had about two practical lessons all year.

> Nothing like what I expected: we hardly do any experiments and we copy from the board and books and his mouth and the dictation drives me crazy.

> It is *much* worse than I thought it would be. It's worse because we always do heaps of writing and never any prac. work. I used to want to do science in grd 6 but now I don't even look forward to science lessons because it's so boring.

> It is much worse than I expected. All we do is write notes off the blackboard and write down dictation and the science teacher does all the experiments and we have only done about 3 experiments. Most people I know got a C in report cards and it's no wonder with all the uninteresting things we do!

> We hardly do anything except copy notes that the teacher has written (not our own words) and do experiments that the teacher does for us. In other words we aren't given any real work.

One cannot imagine that students who feel like that about their lessons are ready to expend energy in thinking about their learning.

Principle of Balance

The Principle of Variation holds that teaching methods must change frequently enough to keep alive conscious, purposeful learning. The PEEL teachers, however, found that students need time to learn how to work with each new procedure. Thus, too frequent introduction of new procedures will lead to poor learning. The relationship between rate of introduction of procedures and quality of learning is an inverted U. This relationship is an instance of the Principle of Balance: *the optimum resolution of issues in education is some balance point between extremes* — or extreme positions in education are unworkable.

In nearly all their actions, teachers have to find the right balance between competing demands. Examples are discovery learning versus recitation and process versus product. There are instances in PEEL and in the study that preceded it (Baird, 1986) of tension between the need to cover content and the need to encourage students to think deeply about it. Evaluating one of his lessons, the teacher in the six-month-long pre-PEEL study recognized that "direction by me [was] prompted by the lack of time left to teach the course . . . little opportunity for pupils to grasp the [ideas]" (Baird, 1984, p. 362).

If we want students to better understand what they learn, we may have to teach fewer topics — but we must teach something, so we cannot concentrate wholly on strategies of learning. Given the usual practice in schools today, we should want to shift the balance toward less content and more attention to learning strategies. The paradox that teachers and curriculum developers have to appreciate is that fewer topics may produce more real learning. If the movement has gone too far, we should shift the balance back to more content. Similarly, we should shift some control over the lesson from teacher to students, but not so far that anarchy develops.

Principle of Maximum Opportunity

A special case of the Principle of Balance refers to the conduct of lessons: *the pace and style of each lesson must be chosen to give students the maximum opportunity to learn.* Carroll (1963) recognized this in his equation that the amount of learning is a function of the ratio between time needed to learn and time available to learn.

If the teacher presents too much information, the students have little opportunity to process it, and if he or she presents too little, there is nothing to process. Either way, not much is learned. Thus, there is an optimum rate for the introduction of new matter, but what the rate is depends on so many factors — the complexity of the content, its interest for the students, the state of the students both as individuals and as a group — that no precise, quantified rule is possible. Further, individuals vary so much that a graph of learning curves for a class will show lines peaking at different rates, as in Figure 4.1. What makes teaching an art is the judgment of the best overall pace. (See also Chapter Seventeen.)

Principle of Divergence

The goal in attempts such as PEEL to encourage good learning strategies can be pictured as a lift in the heights of the individual curves of Figure 4.1 without any regression of the maximums to the left. That is, we can teach the same amount while having it learned better. That, too, was Bloom's goal when he applied Carrol's equation in the mastery learning movement (Bloom, 1968, 1971). There is, however, little about changing learning styles in the mastery learning literature. Rather, styles are accepted as they are, and teaching methods are to be selected to fit learning styles. The end result is portrayed as lifting the weaker, or at least slower, students up to the achieve-

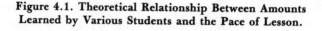

Figure 4.1. Theoretical Relationship Between Amounts Learned by Various Students and the Pace of Lesson.

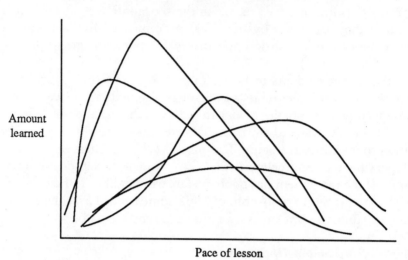

Amount learned

Pace of lesson

ment now attained by the best or fastest. The mastery literature is silent about the performance of the best students. Apparently, they are expected to continue doing about as well as they always did, while the other students will draw level with them. Our research on strategies of learning leads me to a different view, that *all effective interventions increase the range of differences in quality of learning.*

The Principle of Divergence is a conclusion that, though education may counter inequalities of birth and fortune, it will produce inequalities of its own. The only way to keep people level in learning is to leave them equally ignorant. As soon as you start to teach them, some will learn more than others, and when they develop learning strategies, they will do so at different rates, and so some will learn even more.

Rank order of learning may alter when teachers promote learning strategies. This happened in PEEL, where some students who were doing relatively well under the former teaching saw no reason to change and were surpassed by others who entered wholeheartedly into the project. Some were unable or unwilling to acquire new skills of learning, while others gained much, so that orders of performance changed while the range stretched.

Divergence may seem to cause problems for teachers, but in practice, it does not, because it results from students taking on more responsibility for their own learning. As they acquire good strategies of learning, they become less dependent on the teacher.

Principle of Support

Learning is an individual act, but in schools, individuals work within a social group. Attitudes of the group determine the public behavior of its members, including expressing opinions, volunteering information, asking questions, and other overt acts that demonstrate engagement in learning.

The teacher is a part of the social group in the classroom, and, of course, the teacher can promote or inhibit learning. So can the students influence each other. One of the PEEL teachers recorded for two months every instance in a class when a student asked a question about the subject matter or volunteered information without being stimulated by a direct question. There were wide differences among the students. One student, Teresa, made well over a hundred contributions, while another, Colin, made only five. The teacher rates Teresa and Colin as equally able, but when I asked him why Colin volunteered so rarely, he said that the other students inhibit him. Colin used to be more active, but when he asked a question, other students would groan and say, "Colin again" or "smart aleck." They did not say that to Teresa because, the teacher said, "She is bigger than the rest of them."

A strong personality such as Teresa can ride over the group and enforce favorable reactions for herself. Another form of strength was shown by a student named Joe in Bakopano's (1988) study, who said, "No one has ever told me to question. I do it because I want to—it's my personality I guess. If I don't understand I ask questions and I don't care what anyone else thinks" (pp. 34–35). For most students, however, negative comments from peers inhibit overt good learning behavior, so that they either carry on being good learners but do it covertly, which is fine for themselves but does not help others or contribute to the general quality of the lesson, or give up and become shallow learners.

When the PEEL teachers came to appreciate the importance of the group in learning, they introduced appropriate rules of behavior, such as "No one in this room will 'put down' anyone else." In another action research project (Baird, Fensham, Gunstone, and White, 1991), students in grades 8 through 11 (ages thirteen to sixteen) negotiated with their teachers three changes in behavior that each would try to make so that lessons would be more enjoyable and productive. In several classes, the changes to be made by teachers included using simpler words and making tasks clearer, not surprising aims; among those to be made by students was being supportive of and never negative toward each other.

It would be simpler if the principle that summarizes our observations of the influence of class groups were the strong one that *support is essential for overt good learning behavior, while criticisms destroys it.* Exceptional students such as Joe, however, weaken it to *unvarying support from the teacher and all classmates promotes display of good learning behavior, while criticism inhibits it.*

Value of the Principles

The nine principles are insights derived by reflection on studies of teaching and learning. They apply broadly. The Principle of Innovation, for instance, may well hold for almost any change in social practice and should rank high in the consciousness of all reformers who wish to act effectively and responsibly—effectively because they must determine how long it will take true gains to overtake initial losses and responsibly, because they must judge whether the initial loss and any associated suffering are justified by later gain. A historical example is the abolition of slavery in the United States: newly freed slaves without necessary skills or resources were cast into a new system where means of earning a living were not well developed, so that many were worse off for a while. With the detachment of time, we see the gain and do not feel the pain. A responsible teacher or administrator, however, does not have the luxury of a historical view and must consider the immediate negative effects of a change in practice.

The Principle of Vocabulary refers to learning but applies to any responsible teaching or attempt to promote social change. Responsible reformers will not use technical language to obscure their purposes and their reasons for their actions but will take pains to share their vocabulary with the people who are the targets of the change—in schools, ordinarily the students. Responsibility is a moral issue, but in the Principle of Vocabulary, we see that the moral course is also the effective course.

Similarly, the Principles of Matching, Minimum Expenditure of Energy, Variation, and Maximum Opportunity, which are closely related, apply to more human experiences than just teaching and learning. These four principles are almost corollaries of each other. When teachers apply them, they are acting responsibly because they are likely to be effective. The *and* between effective and responsible is not a conjunction between distinct terms, as in *animals and plants* or *cats and dogs,* but joins two aspects of the same behavior. When teachers act responsibly through following these principles, they make it easier for their students to act responsibly in turn and to learn more effectively. Thus, variations in procedure stimulate input of energy, and when new procedures are introduced at an appropriate rate, students can develop good strategies of learning that enable them to become more independent and thus responsible and effective.

The Principles of Matching, Minimum Energy, Variation, and Maximum Opportunity are all ruled by the Principle of Balance, which may be the most fundamental and widely applicable of the nine principles. In its light, we might see that many controversies in education are arguments about where to place a balance between extremes rather than choosing one extreme or the other. A classic instance is the 1960s debate about the relative merits of discovery learning and didactic teaching, which spurred many short-term experiments. With hindsight, one can see that elements of both approaches are useful and that the question is really whether the present mix is the most effective. Other instances are the debates about process and product and whether examinations should be set by teachers in each school or by an external authority. In each case, there is something to be said for each point of view—otherwise, there would be no debate—but instead of it being all or nothing, the end of the argument is often settling on a balance. That settlement may be continually reviewed.

The Principle of Support provides a controversial example of application of the Principle of Balance. Although the Principle of Support is morally acceptable, it is contrary to much common practice, teacher folklore, and notions of competition. It is easy to find instances of politicians, administrators, businesspeople, and others, including teachers, arguing that society is competitive and that therefore children need to be taught in competitive classrooms. Such a simple argument overlooks the fact that society, by its very nature, involves cooperation as well as competition and that the proportion of cooperation has to outweigh that of competition if the society is to cohere. It seems more sensible for classrooms to reflect that mix. Our judgment from our research is that the balance in the school systems with which we are familiar needs to be shifted a long way toward greater support and away from individualistic competition. Note that support is not apathy or laissez-faire indifference but active cooperation and encouragement by all members of the class with respect to all other members. The Principle of Support should allow a healthier form of competition, in which students strive to do better against a standard, not against each other — for the latter can lead to irresponsible acts such as trying to get in front by holding others back.

The final principle, Divergence, is also controversial. It runs counter to many current ideals of equality, to hopes that education will be a means of eliminating discrimination of all types and that all can be lifted, as the mastery learning movement intended, to a common high plane. The flaw in those hopes is that quality of learning is not linear with a finite upper bound. Understanding is multifaceted and can increase without limit. So although an effective intervention will raise the quality of learning for all or most participants, it may enable some to make much greater leaps than others. That appears to be the outcome in our studies.

Differences in quality of learning do not necessarily mean that the teaching or the learning was ineffective or irresponsible. Teachers are behaving responsibly and as effectively as they can when they implement the Principle of Maximum Opportunity, and students are doing so when they make as much use of their opportunities as each individually can. Differences in abilities and resources of both teachers and students are the cause of differences in quality of learning. Responsibility lies in teachers and students being as effective as they can within the limits that apply to them.

I have tried to show how, in their broad applications, the principles can explain difficulties in teaching and learning caused by lack of vocabulary or opportunity, mismatching or overmatching, or need for time to get used to an innovation. The principles, especially that of balance, also can help resolve contentious debates and guide decisions both on the large scale, such as determining the organization of school systems or the nature of curricula, and on the small, such as momentary actions in classrooms. Through these uses, the principles guide the way to effective and responsible education and thus a marked rise in the quality of learning.

References

Arzi, H. J., and White, R. T. "Questions on Students' Questions." *Research in Science Education*, 1986, *16*, 82–91.

Baird, J. R. *"Improving Learning Through Enhanced Metacognition."* Unpublished doctoral thesis, Monash University, 1984.

Baird, J. R. "Improving Learning Through Enhanced Metacognition: A Classroom Study." *European Journal of Science Education*, 1986, *8*, 263–282.

Baird, J. R., Fensham, P. J., Gunstone, R. F., and White, R. T. *Teaching and Learning Science in Schools*. Melbourne, Australia: Faculty of Education, Monash University, 1989.

Baird, J. R., Fensham, P. J., Gunstone, R. F., and White, R. T. "The Importance of Reflection in Improving Science Teaching and Learning." *Journal of Research in Science Teaching*, 1991, *28*, 163–182.

Baird, J. R., and Mitchell, I. J. (eds.). *Improving the Quality of Teaching and Learning: An Australian Case Study — The PEEL Project*. Melbourne, Australia: Monash University, 1986.

Baird, J. R., and White, R. T. "A Case Study of Learning Styles in Biology." *European Journal of Science Education*, 1982a, *4*, 325–337.

Baird, J. R., and White, R. T. "Promoting Self-Control of Learning." *Instructional Science*, 1982b, *11*, 227–247.

Baird, J. R., and others. "Researching Balance Between Cognition and Affect in Science Teaching and Learning." *Research in Science Education*, 1990, *20*, 11–20.

Bakopanos, V. "Encouraging Reflective Thinking in an Upper-Secondary School Classroom." Master of educational studies project, Monash University, 1988.

Bloom, B. S. "Learning for Mastery." *Evaluation Comment*. Los Angeles: Center for the Study of Evaluation of Instructional Programs, University of California, 1968.

Bloom, B. S. "Mastery Learning." In J. H. Block (ed.), *Mastery Learning: Theory and Practice*. New York: Holt, Rinehart & Winston, 1971.

Brooks, A. Untitled chapter. In J. R. Baird and I. J. Mitchell (eds.), *Improving the Quality of Teaching and Learning: An Australian Case Study — The PEEL Project*. Melbourne, Australia: Monash University, 1986.

Brown, A. L. "Metacognitive Development and Reading." In R. J. Spiro, B. C. Bruce, and W. F. Brewer (eds.), *Theoretical Issues in Reading Comprehension: Perspectives from Cognitive Psychology, Linguistics, Artificial Intelligence, and Education*. Hillsdale, N.J.: Erlbaum, 1980.

Brumby, M. "Problems in Learning the Concept of Natural Selection." *Journal of Biological Education*, 1979, *13* (2), 119–122.

Carroll, J. B. "A Model of School Learning." *Teachers College Record*, 1963, *64*, 723–733.

Champagne, A. B., Klopfer, L. E., and Anderson, J. H. "Factors Influencing the Learning of Classical Mechanics." *American Journal of Physics*, 1980, *48*, 1074–1079.

Clarke, J. A. "The Influence of the Content and Structure of Curriculum Materials and Dialogue on Achievement in Science." Unpublished doctoral thesis, University of Queensland, Brisbane, 1987.

Erickson, G. L. "Children's Conceptions of Heat and Temperature." *Science Education,* 1979, *63,* 221–230.

Gunstone, R. F., Slattery, M., and Baird, J. R. "Learning About Learning to Teach: A Case Study of Pre-Service Teacher Education." Paper presented at the meeting of the American Educational Research Association, San Francisco, Mar. 1989.

Gunstone, R. F., and White, R. T. "Understanding of Gravity." *Science Education,* 1981, *65,* 291–299.

Macdonald, I. "Student Awareness of Learning." Master of educational studies project, Monash University, 1990.

Mitchell, I. Untitled chapter. In J. R. Baird and I. J. Mitchell (eds.), *Improving the Quality of Teaching and Learning: An Australian Case Study — The PEEL Project.* Melbourne, Australia: Monash University, 1986.

Mitchell, J. Untitled chapter. In J. R. Baird and I. J. Mitchell (eds.), *Improving the Quality of Teaching and Learning: An Australian Case Study — The PEEL Project.* Melbourne, Australia: Monash University, 1986.

Muralidhar, S. "An Exploratory Study of a Science Curriculum in Action: Basic Science in Fiji." Unpublished doctoral thesis, Monash University, 1989.

Neill, A. S. *That Dreadful School.* London: Jenkins, 1937.

Novak, J. D., and Gowin, D. B. *Learning How to Learn.* Cambridge, England: Cambridge University Press, 1984.

Nussbaum, J., and Novak, J. D. "An Assessment of Children's Concepts of the Earth Utilizing Structured Interviews." *Science Education,* 1976, *60,* 535–550.

Stead, B. F., and Osborne, R. J. "Exploring Science Students' Concepts of Light." *Australian Science Teachers Journal,* 1980, *26* (3), 84–90.

Swan, S. M. "Helping Children Reflect on Their Learning." Master of educational studies project, Monash University, 1988.

Theobald, J. H. "Attitudes and Achievement in Biology." Unpublished doctoral dissertation, Monash University, 1977.

Tiberghien, A., and Delacôte, G. "Manipulation et représentations des circuits électriques simples par des enfants de 7 à 12 ans" [Manipulation and representation of simple electric circuits by seven- to twelve-year olds]. *Revue Française de Pédagogie* [French review of education], 1976, *34,* 32–44.

White, R. T. *Learning Science.* Oxford, England: Blackwell, 1988.

White, R. T., Bakopanos, V., and Swan, S. "Increasing Metalearning: Two Classroom Interventions." Paper presented at the meeting of the Australian Association for Research in Education, Armidale, Nov. 1988.

White, R. T., and others. "Teaching and Learning Science in Schools: An Exploration of Process." Paper presented at the meeting of the American Educational Research Association, San Francisco, Mar. 1989.

5

Constructing Curriculum
in the Classroom

Walter Doyle

Until quite recently, the dominant theme in most discussions of teaching and teacher education has been the remote control of teaching quality; that is, defining what teachers should do and how to ensure that their behavior will reliably conform to these specifications (see Doyle, 1990). As a result, issues of effectiveness and responsibility in teaching have been treated largely as problems to be resolved outside the classroom. Specifying how best to teach has been seen primarily as the responsibility of policy makers, school administrators, and researchers. Teachers, in turn, have been viewed as instruments to be managed to ensure that they carry out these system-level requirements for teaching effectively.

This traditional view has had a substantial impact on conceptions of what teaching is, how it can be studied, and what the issues of effectiveness and responsibility in teaching, especially at the classroom level, might mean. The purpose of this chapter is to critically examine the foundation and consequences of this traditional view and to explore the implications for both research and practice of the emerging emphases on subject matter in teaching and on the experienced curriculum that evolves within the interaction between a teacher and students. Throughout the discussion, attention is directed to how issues of effectiveness and responsibility can be understood and fruitfully analyzed in this emerging intellectual context.

The distinctive character of this chapter derives from its focus on curriculum processes in teaching (see Doyle, 1992). For most of this century, curriculum has been virtually invisible in studies of teaching and its effects. Rather, attention has focused largely on generic interpersonal processes or the "how" of schooling. If invoked at all, the term *curriculum* has generally been used to refer simply to the content of schooling or to the materials used in the classroom, items that are treated as if they were fixed and inert rather than dynamic aspects of classroom events. Pedagogy, on the other hand, is seen as beginning where curriculum leaves off; that is, with the human interactions that occur during teaching episodes.

It is becoming increasingly apparent, however, that this stripping of content from the study of teaching has severely restricted our capacity to understand how teaching effects occur and, thus, how effective teaching is jointly constructed or achieved by teachers and students in classroom situations. Moreover, the separation of curriculum from teaching has made it quite difficult to keep issues of values and responsibility in focus during the analysis of pedagogy.

In this chapter, a deliberate attempt is made to identify curriculum processes in teaching. The inherent assumption in this emphasis on processes is, of course, that the curriculum is a dynamic rather than a static element in teaching. The focus, therefore, is on the curriculum in motion. The chapter begins with a brief analysis of the themes and issues that have shaped research on effective teaching. Attention then turns to curriculum studies in an attempt to clarify the meaning of the term *curriculum* at both institutional and classroom levels. Particular attention is given to recent work that reveals how the curriculum actually unfolds in classroom environments. The chapter ends with a summary designed to integrate the study of curriculum processes with deliberation about issues of effective and responsible teaching.

Underlying Themes in the Study of Teaching

The search for knowledge about teachers, teaching, and teacher education has been driven largely by the themes of effectiveness and quality control (see Doyle, 1990). These themes emanated from a basic assumption in North American society that excellence in education can be achieved only if teachers are governed remotely by administrators and policy makers. From this quality-control perspective, teachers are viewed as instruments or tools in the production of school achievement rather than agents who interpret situations and make decisions. As tools, teachers are to be directed from a distance by the imposition of uniform practices on all teachers and/or by the employment of a common set of indicators to evaluate performance. Research came to serve schooling by generating effectiveness indicators or classroom practices that reliably predict achievement-test scores.

The Emergence of Educational Science

How did this view of research on teaching evolve, and what were its consequences? The following brief exploration of the history of research on teaching provides a background for understanding these issues.

Over the course of this century, educational psychology, as expounded in its early decades by such leading figures as Edward L. Thorndike at Teachers College, Columbia University, and Charles Judd at the University of Chicago, became the foundational discipline for educational research (see Lagemann, 1989). This psychology, designed to mirror the forms of the physical sciences, was behavioral, experimental, and atomistic. The focus was on precise measurement of specific behaviors and the use of controlled experiments to verify scientific laws. These laws, in turn, were intended to be prescriptive; that is, they would define precisely what teachers must do in order to cause student learning (see Joncich, 1968; Lagemann, 1989).

Toward a Generic Understanding of Teaching

The impact of the new psychology on knowledge about teaching was specially strong since pedagogy was historically viewed as a branch of psychology. The result was research on pedagogy driven by the theme of effectiveness; that is, a search for the best way to teach or the criteria for identifying the best teachers (see especially Barr, 1929).

One of the distinctive features of this educational science was a lack of attention to content or subject matter in the study of teaching. The language of behavioral psychology focused on overt actions; behaviors rather than content were measured during classroom observations. Moreover, the effectiveness question focused on teachers or teaching methods as the direct causes of outcomes. Taken together, these frameworks excluded students and curriculum from the analysis of teaching. Questions of what was being taught to whom slipped into the background.

From a practical perspective, a generic educational science modeled on the emerging physical sciences had distinct advantages. In particular, it provided the necessary scientific authority for the social efficiency movement, which, through the efforts of Joseph Mayer Rice and Frederick Taylor, had already begun to influence schooling and business (see Kliebard, 1986; Lagemann, 1989). In addition, a generic view of teaching was quite compatible with the administrative uses of effectiveness research for the remote control of teaching through evaluation and training. If one were making decisions about a large number of teachers for an entire school system, indicators of effectiveness needed to be few in number, easily applied, and highly generalizable across teaching situations. If indicators had to be specific to each teaching area, it would soon become impossible to find a common metric with which to judge teachers.

On the other hand, the new educational science swept aside the rich intellectual heritage of teaching methods, a tradition characterized by philosophical and curricular arguments about the nature of knowledge, the character of learners and the learning process, and the impact of teaching activities (see Bayles and Hood, 1966; Kliebard, 1986). With the loss of these complex frameworks and a move toward the seeming simplicity and precision of science, pedagogical thought also lost its capacity to deal with reciprocity, negotiation, meaning, and constructive processes in teaching events. Effectiveness became a matter of prediction rather than understanding. Effective teaching became a mechanical process of behaving in conformity with scientifically derived standards of performance rather than a deliberative process of interpretation, judgment, and responsibility. Students, in turn, had little visible role in either comprehending instruction or contributing to the meaning that emerged from their experiences in the classroom.

Emerging Directions

At present, however, there are clear signs that conceptions in the field of teaching are changing fundamentally. Interest in curriculum is spreading rapidly among researchers who have traditionally studied teaching (see Shulman, 1986). At the same time, the emergence of cognitive science and qualitative-interpretive research perspectives has given rise to a fundamental reformulation of the disciplinary foundations of educational inquiry. This reformulation is opening exciting new theoretical and empirical corridors for research framed around issues of learning, teaching, and curriculum (see, for example, Brown, Collins, and Duguid, 1989; Connelly and Clandinin, 1986; Golden, 1989). Moreover, this ferment appears to be leading to fundamentally different conceptions of the character of educational science and of the relationship between research findings and classroom practice.

The remainder of this chapter represents an attempt to make curriculum an analytical concept in the study of teaching. As will be seen, this effort to frame teaching as a curriculum process has significant implications for understanding issues of effectiveness and responsibility in teaching.

What Is Curriculum?

The first task in identifying curriculum processes in teaching is to establish a foundation for understanding what the term *curriculum* means. As several observers (for example, Glatthorn, 1987) have noted, this term has multiple definitions, no one of which completely captures the various meanings commonly associated with it. This multiplicity of meaning exists in large part because curriculum processes operate at several levels of schooling. There are the official curriculum, the curriculum represented in textbooks and materials, the curriculum actually taught in the classroom, the curriculum that students learn, and the curriculum embodied in the tests that students take.

For the purpose of this analysis, attention will focus on curriculum processes at two levels: the institution and the classroom. As will be seen, these levels represent distinct but interrelated domains of curriculum discourse and, thus, different types of curriculum processes. Similarly, issues of effectiveness and responsibility differ between these levels.

Curriculum as Social Paradigm

At an institutional level, there are two major curriculum domains or centers: the abstract or ideal curriculum, which defines the connection between schooling and society, and the analytical or formal curriculum, which translates curriculum policy into instruments that are used in actual curriculum events.

The abstract curriculum serves primarily to define or typify schooling. If one asks what goes on in a school or school system, the answer is likely to be framed in terms of broad goals and general experiences (for example, a process approach to science or a whole-language emphasis in reading) or symbols (for example, standards, discipline, or free expression) rather than the multiplicity of particular incidents that occur daily. Schooling is often typified, in other words, through a relatively abstract model or description of what a school or school system is and does.

This abstract model serves as a means of capturing aspects of the educational ideals and expectations that exist within a society and representing the forms and procedures of schooling as responses to these ideals and expectations (see Lazerson, McLaughlin, McPherson, and Bailey, 1985). As a result, this model serves the important function of establishing the terms of the connection between schooling and society.

It is important to underscore that the abstract curriculum is not equivalent to the official statements or written documents that are often issued by school authorities. At its core, the abstract curriculum is a tacitly understood and shared conception or paradigm of schooling. Official statements and documents are certainly shaped by this shared conception and often capture important aspects of it. Nevertheless, the operating form of the abstract curriculum is the shared social understanding that is used to judge the adequacy of proposals about what should constitute the experience of schooling.

Curriculum at the intersection of schooling and society consists largely of images or metaphors that are relatively nonspecific with respect to classroom practice. These images are fundamentally important because they embody conceptions of what is desirable in a society, what is to be valued and sought after by members of a community or nation (see Chapter Nine). At this level, curriculum becomes an instrument for both clarifying social norms and responsibilities and bringing them to bear on the special role that schooling is to play in contributing to the achievement of these ideals. Curriculum, in other words, is the means by which moral significance is carried forward into the activities of teaching.

A moment's reflection suggests that the institutional curriculum in all probability reflects the fundamental character of a society. In societies that are deeply heterogeneous with respect to basic values, curriculum agreements are likely to be tenuous at best. At the same time, this heterogeneity is likely to influence teaching effectiveness. As Nisan argues in Chapter Nine, social norms play a key role in influencing students' motivation in classrooms. To the extent that consensus regarding basic social values is lacking, it is hardly reasonable to expect that the social group, including parents and children, will cooperate with and support the activities of schooling.

From the perspective of this volume, the abstract curriculum can be viewed as an important arena for examining issues of effectiveness and responsibility in teaching. The basic educational issue is not simply "What works?" The more fundamental question is "What should the members of a society desire?" Whether intended or not, the abstract curriculum, as a social paradigm with respect to education, is a statement about what is desirable within a social group. And the responsibility for formulating this statement is not simply the province of educational experts. It extends to all citizens. Thus, deliberating about curriculum can be an occasion for citizens to understand what they believe in. Unfortunately, such public discourse is rare.

Similarly, effectiveness is not something that schools achieve in spite of society and, therefore, is not a responsibility that can be delegated solely to teachers. It is rather a product of educators, students, and citizens working toward comparable ends. Thus, curriculum processes, even at the somewhat remote level of the intersection between society and the institution of schooling, have substantial and immediate consequences for teaching effectiveness.

Curriculum as a Theory of Content

The institutional curriculum, as a paradigm of schooling with respect to society, is also important as the starting place for a complex transformational process through which curriculum policy is translated into instruments for use in classrooms. Herein lies a second basic meaning of the term *curriculum* — an elaboration or theory of content with respect to both the aims of schooling and the activities of teaching. The formal process of constructing curriculum, in other words, consists of framing a set of arguments that rationalize the selection and arrangement of content (knowledge, skills, and dispositions) and the transformation of that content into school subjects; that is, a form suitable for use in classrooms (see Fenstermacher, 1984). In this way, the formal curriculum, as a theory or set of theories of content, bridges the gap between the abstract curriculum and the classroom.

From this perspective, it is imprecise to say that the curriculum is the content. It is more accurate to say that a curriculum is a theory of the content, an elaboration of the fundamental nature of the content and how it is to be represented to children at various grade levels (see Kirsch, 1977). Unfortunately, little attention has been given to theories of content in the United States. For many of the reasons discussed earlier in this chapter, the traditional focus has been on the managerial or regulatory uses of curriculum to organize levels of schooling and synchronize the work of teachers within and across these levels.

With content deliberation made invisible or relegated to the relatively obscure domain of experts in philosophy or the academic disciplines, basic issues of effectiveness and responsibility in teaching are ignored in the formation of school subjects. Moreover, within a managerial emphasis, there is little room to consider teachers' and students' responsibilities; what teachers and students think is relevant only insofar as it might constitute a deviation from the faithful enactment of the formal curriculum. As will be seen, when content theories are neglected, it is easy to overlook the important impact of teachers' and students' conceptions of content on the curriculum as it is actually experienced in the classroom.

Curriculum Processes in Classrooms

Recently, attention among curriculum specialists has shifted from the curriculum as a regulatory mechanism to the curriculum as an event experienced in the classroom (see Cornbleth, 1988; Posner, 1988) and as "an evolving construction" resulting from the interaction of teacher and students (Zumwalt, 1989, p. 175). Similarly, pedagogy is being seen not simply as a neutral pipeline for delivering content but as a social context that has fundamental curricular effects (see Doyle, 1986).

This modern surge of interest in the experienced curriculum signals fundamental changes in educational discourse. The emphasis on the remote control of teaching is increasingly being replaced by a concern for teachers' personal practical knowledge and their role as responsible curriculum makers (Connelly and Clandinin, 1986; Zumwalt, 1989) and for students' paradigms and how they operate in the construction of shared meanings in the classroom (Confrey, 1990). Attention is being directed to teachers' and students' curriculum knowledge, how it is constructed, and how it affects what the curriculum actually comes to be in the events of teaching.

One of the fundamental effects of this emerging emphasis is an awareness of how the curriculum is shaped in powerful ways by local factors in classrooms. What follows is a brief survey of two research programs, one on knowledge construction processes and one on academic tasks, that are helpful in identifying curriculum processes in classrooms, especially the processes of interpretation and construction, and how these processes shape and are shaped by teaching. For a more complete discussion of research that sheds light on the experienced curriculum, see Doyle (1992).

Knowledge Construction in Classroom Lessons

Using reader-response criticism from literary theory and text analytical procedures, Golden (1988, 1989) has demonstrated ways in which the meaning of a text is constructed by students in lessons. Her basic argument is that a text is "a highly organized arrangement of cues which evoke a range of cognitive operations resulting in the formulation [by the reader] of the aesthetic work" (Golden 1988, p. 71). In one study, Golden (1988) used this perspective to analyze story-reading lessons taught by two teachers. Golden described the episodic structure of the text itself and then the structures of the instructional texts (instructional moves and themes) produced by the two teachers in reading the story and asking questions. She noted that both teachers appeared to be sensitive to the episodic structures of the story text but that they differed in their emphasis on themes. The first teacher focused on episodic information from the text itself as a central point of reference, whereas the second teacher emphasized text-related themes (that is, information relevant to but not included in the text). What students recalled from the lessons was consistent with the teachers' instructional texts.

In a second study, Golden (1989) analyzed a five-day lesson in a sixth-grade class in which the principal text was an excerpt from an autobiography focusing on a Mexican-American's acculturation experience upon entering school. During lessons, the teacher elicited personal reactions to the narrator's feelings, but she maintained tight control over which interpretations were acceptable—namely, those that reinforced her emphasis on patriotic behavior. When students' responses did not reflect this emphasis, the teacher drew on her own experiences to model the appropriate interpretation. The teacher, in other words, was the primary interpreter of the text, who controlled which interpretations were allowed on the floor.

These studies by Golden, as well as similar ones by Heap (1985) and Lemke (1990), are important for at least two reasons. First, they demonstrate ways of examining content itself rather than simply the processes surrounding the use of that content. This is a significant breakthrough for understanding curriculum processes in teaching. Second, these studies show that texts read and written in classrooms are embedded in interpretive structures created and governed by teachers as they struggle to transform and represent the curriculum to students in a complex social setting. More needs to be known about these structures and how they function over time to affect the range of realizations of curriculum in classrooms.

Classroom Task Structures

Recently, attempts have been made to analyze academic tasks as central organizing frameworks in classroom settings (see Doyle, 1983). In these studies, the concept of "task" is used to refer to the way in which students' work is organized or structured in a classroom.

In describing classroom tasks analytically, investigators focus on three essential components: a goal or end state to be accomplished; a problem space or set of conditions and resources (such as information or tools) available to accomplish the task; and the operations (that is, thoughts and actions) involved in assembling and using resources to reach the goal state (Doyle, 1983).

In classrooms, goal states for curriculum tasks are usually embedded in a product—such as answers to a set of work-sheet or test questions or an original essay—that must be generated to complete an assignment. Resources in classrooms vary widely. For some tasks students can consult peers, while for others they must work strictly alone. The operations that students are to use to accomplish work are not always clearly specified by teachers and sometimes are difficult to communicate. Moreover, students often circumvent task demands or invent their own strategies for getting work done.

A fundamental premise of task investigators is that tasks organize students' cognitions and, therefore, have powerful treatment effects in classrooms (see Doyle, 1983). In other words, they provide situational instructions for thinking and acting with respect to curriculum, and students learn the information and processes that they use to accomplish the tasks that they encounter. If someone were asked, for example, to count the number of times the letter *s* appears in a paragraph, it is unlikely that this person would acquire much of an understanding of the substance of the text.

From this perspective, tasks frame both curriculum and pedagogy. Regardless of the announced or presented curriculum, students experience the curriculum as it is encountered through the tasks that they are asked to accomplish. Moreover, the significance of a teacher's actions in explaining, questioning, and praising students depends on their relationships to the task system in a classroom. If, for instance, a teacher asks higher-order questions during class discussions but holds students accountable in written work only for knowing definitions of key terms, it is unlikely that students will, over time, pay much attention to classroom questions. To capture the curriculum in use, then, one must describe not only the information represented to the students but also the tasks enacted with respect to that information (see Doyle, 1986).

Finally, because tasks are enacted in the complex social setting of a classroom, they have an inherently dynamic quality that requires participants to do a considerable amount of interpretive work to ascertain what a particular task is and how it can be accomplished.

A major portion of task research has focused on the types of tasks that occur in classrooms (see, for example, Doyle and Carter, 1984; Sanford, 1987). Typologies of tasks are usually constructed around the presumed cognitive processes or operations that are required to accomplish tasks. Doyle (1983), for instance, distinguished among tasks involving (1) memory or the reproduction or recognition of information previously encountered (for example, spelling tests); (2) routines or algorithms that reliably generate answers (for example, arithmetic or grammar exercises); (3) opinion or the expression of a disposition toward content (for example, reactions to a poem); and (4) understanding, including recognizing transformed versions of text, selecting appropriate procedures to solve complex problems, and drawing inferences or making predictions from information given (for example, solving word problems in math, performing science experiments, or reading a new passage with comprehension).

Doyle (1986) argues that tasks are deeply entwined with the structure and flow of action in classroom environments and that these circumstances shape the curriculum. When academic work is routinized and familiar to students (for example, spelling tests or recurring work-sheet exercises), the flow of classroom activity is typically smooth and well ordered. When work is problem-centered — that is, students are required to interpret situations and make decisions to accomplish tasks — activity flow is frequently slow and bumpy.

From the students' perspective, problem-centered work involves high levels of ambiguity concerning the precise character of the product and the risk that they will not be successful. Students often respond to the ambiguity and risk involved in such work by negotiating directly with teachers to increase the explicitness of product specifications or reduce the strictness of grading standards. Otherwise, error rates may go up and engagement and completion rates go down, creating pressures on work flow and order in classrooms.

Teachers sometimes respond to these pressures by excluding higher-level tasks from the classroom altogether. More often, however, they revise or simplify task demands by clearly defining specifications, emphasizing procedures for completing assignments, providing prompts and resources, and adjusting accountability for work. When this happens, students' attention shifts from meaning and the underlying operations with content to obtaining correct answers and completing the work.

In summary, the research on tasks and task structures is beginning to provide useful insights into the fate of curriculum within classrooms. At a classroom level, tasks are pushed around by intrinsic factors related to management, activity flow, and direct student negotiation. Novel or problem-centered work, in particular, appears to stretch the limits of classroom management and to intensify the complexity of the teacher's task of orchestrating classroom events.

Curriculum Process in Effective and Responsible Teaching

In this final part of the chapter, I attempt to distill and integrate the various lines of thought surveyed above to construct a framework for inquiry into curriculum processes in teaching and to examine how issues of effectiveness and responsibility can be understood within this framework. While several important issues of effectiveness and responsibility in teaching emerge at the institutional level, the discussion in this part centers on issues of effectiveness and responsibility at the local level.

Interpretation and Construction in Teaching

The premise of this chapter is that understanding issues of effectiveness and responsibility at the local level requires a model of teaching as a curriculum process. Such a conception of teaching means that classrooms are contexts in which students encounter curriculum events — that is, must act with respect to some content. These events can be thought to consist of written, oral, and behavioral "texts" that must be interpreted and acted on (see Green, Weade, and Graham, 1988). Teachers "author" curriculum events to achieve effects on students. In this sense, teachers are curriculum makers who guide students through the texts, shape the interpretations that are allowed on the floor (see Golden, 1989), and, importantly, define the tasks that students are to accomplish with respect to these texts (see Doyle, 1986).

At the same time, students contribute to the authoring of curriculum events as they participate in these enactments. By providing information, asking questions, and participating in classroom events, students shape what the curriculum comes to mean. Moreover, the meaning that they take away from their experiences within these events is dependent on the frames that they bring to the situation (see Confrey, 1990). This perspective also suggests that moving through the curriculum successfully involves a large amount of basic theoretical work as categories are reformulated, propositions understood, and interpretation revised.

There are, of course, limits on this constructive process in classrooms. Students, who often share the broader social norms embodied in the institutional curriculum, witness classroom curriculum events and judge them as "proper" or not (see Burgess, 1984). These definitions and judgments would seem to play an important role in sustaining curriculum events within classrooms. At the same time, as curriculum events become visible in various ways to administrators, parents, and other citizens, forces can be brought to bear at the classroom level. Through these mechanisms, the classroom curriculum is indirectly connected back to the abstract curriculum and the formal curriculum.

This analysis highlights at least two important aspects of teaching. First, interpretation and knowledge are placed at the center of curriculum processes. These constructs are likely to be much more powerful than "learning" and "behavior" for understanding teaching, because they direct attention to the frameworks of meaning that students and teachers bring to a situation and how these interact with the curriculum contexts in which they find themselves.

Second, the analysis underscores a theme that emerges in several lines of inquiry: students' curricular knowledge is deeply embedded in the fabric and culture of a classroom (see Doyle, 1986; Golden, 1989; Green, Weade, and Graham, 1988). Indeed, there is evidence to suggest that curriculum is locally produced and jointly constructed as teachers and students go about enacting and accomplishing tasks. Remote control of this process, especially through a small set of generic indicators of teaching effectiveness or students' achievement, is likely to distort the process itself (see Madaus, 1988).

Effectiveness and Responsibility

This conceptualization of teaching as a curriculum process suggests that teachers and students have powerful theories of the content that shape classroom plans, choices, and outcomes in fundamental ways. To understand effective teaching, then, it is necessary to understand these curriculum theories and how they operate. Clearly, effectiveness in teaching is not a mechanical process of using the correct behaviors but rather a matter of interpretation and choice.

Because teaching effectively is a matter of choice, issues of value and responsibility are at the heart of the enterprise at the local level. As teachers and students interpret and select within the classroom, they are jointly shaping the consequences of schooling. Thus, teachers and students must give attention to fundamental education questions as they participate in defining what that education will be. These issues cannot, in principle, be settled or controlled remotely.

The view of teaching advanced in this chapter implies, then, that teaching and teacher education can never be treated solely as a matter of technical proficiency. Teaching is, at its core, an interpretive process grounded in conceptions of what one is teaching and what value that content has for students and society. And the choices that teachers make with respect to their content have enormous consequences for the lives of students and the health of the society. To teach effectively, teachers must be responsible curriculum theorists.

References

Barr, A. S. *Characteristic Differences in the Teaching Peformance of Good and Poor Teachers of Social Studies.* Bloomington, Ill: Public School Publishing, 1929.

Bayles, E. E., and Hood, B. L. *Growth of American Educational Thought and Practice.* New York: HarperCollins, 1966.

Brown, J. S., Collins, A., and Duguid, P. "Situated Cognition and the Culture of Learning." *Educational Researcher,* 1989, *18* (1), 32–42.

Burgess, R. G. "'It's Not a Proper Subject: It's Just Newsom.'" In I. F. Goodson and S. J. Ball (eds.), *Defining the Curriculum: Histories and Ethnographies.* London: Falmer Press, 1984.

Carter, K., and Doyle, W. "Classroom Research as a Resource for the Graduate Preparation of Teachers." In A. E. Woolfolk (ed.), *Research Perspectives on the Graduate Preparation of Teachers.* Englewood Cliffs, N.J.: Prentice-Hall, 1989.

Confrey, J. "A Review of the Research on Student Conceptions in Mathematics, Science, and Programming." In C. B. Cazden (ed.), *Review of Research in Education.* Vol. 16. Washington, D.C.: American Educational Research Association, 1990.

Connelly, F. M., and Clandinin, D. J. "On Narrative Method, Personal Philosophy, and the Story of Teaching." *Journal of Research in Science Teaching,* 1986, *23,* 293–310.

Cornbleth, C. "Curriculum In and Out of Context." *Journal of Curriculum and Supervision,* 1988, *3,* 85–96.

Doyle, W. "Academic Work." *Review of Educational Research,* 1983, *53,* 159–199.

Doyle, W. "Content Representation in Teachers' Definitions of Academic Work." *Journal of Curriculum Studies*, 1986, *18*, 365–379.

Doyle, W. "Themes in Teacher Education Research." In W. R. Houston (ed.), *Handbook of Research on Teacher Education*. New York: Macmillan, 1990.

Doyle, W. "Curriculum and Pedagogy." In P. W. Jackson (ed.), *Handbook of Research on Curriculum*. New York: Macmillan, 1992.

Doyle, W., and Carter, K. "Academic Tasks in Classrooms." *Curriculum Inquiry*, 1984, *14*, 129–149.

Fenstermacher, G. D. "Some Superficial Thoughts on a Profound Problem." Paper prepared for the Conference on the Study of Curriculum in Graduate Education, College of Education, Michigan State University, 1984.

Glatthorn, A. A. *Curriculum Leadership*. Glenview, Ill.: Scott, Foresman, 1987.

Golden, J. M. "The Construction of a Literary Text in a Story-Reading Lesson." In J. L. Green and J. O. Harker (eds.), *Multiple Perspective Analyses of Classroom Discourse*. Norwood, N.J.: Ablex, 1988.

Golden, J. M. "Reading in the Classroom Context: A Semiotic Event." *Semiotica*, 1989, *73*, 67–84.

Green, J. L., Weade, R., and Graham, K. "Lesson Construction and Student Participation: A Sociolinguistic Analysis." In J. L. Green and J. O. Harker (eds.), *Multiple Perspective Analyses of Classroom Discourse*. Norwood, N.J.: Ablex, 1988.

Heap, J. L. "Discourse in the Production of Classroom Knowledge: Reading Lessons." *Curriculum Inquiry*, 1985, *15*, 245–279.

Joncich, G. M. *The Sane Positivist: A Biography of Edward L. Thorndike*. Middletown, Conn.: Wesleyan University Press, 1968.

Kirsch, A. "Aspects of Simplification in Mathematics Teaching." In H. Athen and H. Kunle (eds.), *Proceedings of the Third International Congress on Mathematics Education*. Karlsruhe, Germany: University of Karlsruhe, 1977.

Kliebard, H. M. *The Struggle for the American Curriculum: 1893–1958*. New York: Routledge & Kegan Paul, 1986.

Lagemann, E. C. "The Plural Worlds of Educational Research." *History of Education Quarterly*, 1989, *29*, 185–214.

Lazerson, M., McLaughlin, J. B., McPherson, B., and Bailey, S. *An Education of Value: The Purposes and Practices of Schools*. Cambridge, England: Cambridge University Press, 1985.

Lemke, J. L. *Talking Science: Language, Learning, and Values*. Norwood, N.J.: Ablex, 1990.

Madaus, G. F. "The Influence of Testing on the Curriculum." In L. N. Tanner (ed.), *Critical Issues in Curriculum*. The eighty-seventh yearbook of the National Society for the Study of Education, Part 1. Chicago: University of Chicago Press, 1988.

Posner, G. J. "Models of Curriculum Planning." In L. E. Beyer and M. W. Apple (eds.), *The Curriculum: Problems, Politics, and Possibilities*. Albany: State University of New York Press, 1988.

Sanford, J. P. "Management of Science Classroom Tasks and Effects on Students' Learning Opportunities." *Journal of Research in Science Teaching,* 1987, *24,* 249–265.

Shulman, L. S. "Paradigms and Research Programs in the Study of Teaching: A Contemporary Perspective." In M. C. Wittrock (ed.), *Handbook of Research on Teaching.* (3rd ed.) New York: Macmillan, 1986.

Zumwalt, K. K. "Beginning Professional Teachers: The Need for a Curricular Vision of Teaching." In M. C. Reynolds (ed.), *Knowledge Base for the Beginning Teacher.* Oxford, England: Pergamon Press, 1989.

6

Linking Assessment
with Instruction

Richard J. Shavelson, Gail P. Baxter

In the United States, educational reforms of the 1980s sought to improve curricula, increase high school graduation standards, raise teachers' pay, improve administrative leadership, and hold schools accountable for student achievement (see, for example, National Commission on Excellence in Education, 1983). These reforms have, for the most part, failed (Shanker, 1990): students improved basic skills at the expense of understanding and problem solving (Mullis and Jenkins, 1988). This finding reaffirms what was learned in the 1960s mathematics and science reform: students learn, to a greater or lesser degree, what they are taught (Walker and Schaffarzick, 1974). Moreover, teachers, not surprisingly, teach what they are held accountable for — student achievement on fact-driven multiple-choice tests (Shavelson, Carey, and Webb, 1990; Smith, 1991). The inevitable conclusion is that by directly influencing *what* teachers teach, achievement testing has had a profound effect on the *content* and the *manner* of instruction.

Alternatives to traditional multiple-choice achievement testing are currently being proposed (Wiggins, 1989; Gough, 1989; Nickerson, 1989). They rest on a set of assumptions about effective and responsible teaching that differ significantly from assumptions of the past. Perhaps the most fundamental assumption is that learning is an active, mindful process (Glaser, 1984; Resnick, 1987). In this process, students construct meaning and knowledge: they do not have meaning and knowledge handed to them in a book or lecture. Learning, then, is a process of students "making sense" of how things fit together; factual and procedural knowledge is built along the way.

Note: Research reported in this chapter was supported by grants from the National Science Foundation (No. SPA-8751511) and a University of California President's Grant for School Improvement. The views expressed in this chapter, however, are those of the authors and are not necessarily endorsed by either granting agency.

A second, related assumption deals with the important role played by the context in which knowledge is constructed. For knowledge to be meaningful to students and for students to develop the attitude and manner of inquiry in a discipline, a culture of inquiry into the subject matter must be created (Lave, Smith, and Butler, 1988). The context is a culture of "doing" science or mathematics, not receiving scientific or mathematical truths. Students learn not only a set of cognitive tools (for example, facts and procedures) but, more importantly, a set of beliefs about the subject and about valuing and caring for other students' contributions to knowledge construction. These cognitive and social tools, perpetuated in everyday practices and rituals of the culture, define the context in which knowledge is constructed.

One implication of these two assumptions for the development of alternative assessment technologies is that not just individually but also socially constructed solutions (for example, cooperative groups of students solving problems) should be encouraged (compare Resnick, 1988; Shavelson, Webb, Stasz, and McArthur, 1988). A second implication is that assessments should contain concrete, meaningful tasks. These tasks should respond to students' actions, providing feedback as they test ideas about problem solutions. A third implication is that tests should contain tasks for which there are alternative solutions. Hence, the tasks confronting students should be holistic in nature; the amount of time to solve them will exceed the usual thirty seconds allocated to an exercise provided by the teacher or a multiple-choice question on a test. Evaluation of performance on such tasks should capture the diversity of problem-solving strategies, compare them on a common metric, and provide credit for partial knowledge and well-reasoned, even if somewhat erroneous, solution strategies.

Changing the way we test, then, may well have a direct impact on what and how science and mathematics are taught. Teaching to tests that reward diverse problem solving in concrete, well-contextualized situations may directly influence teachers' instructional decisions to be consistent with the assumptions underlying effective and responsible teaching. In this chapter, we illustrate the nature of changes in teachers' decisions, goals, and plans through concrete examples and draw implications for educational reform.

Alternative Technologies for Assessing Achievement

For the past several years, a team of researchers at the University of California, Santa Barbara, and the California University of Technology has been developing and evaluating alternative assessment technologies in science — assessments that are consistent with assumptions about effective and responsible teaching (Shavelson and others, 1991; Shavelson, Baxter, and Pine, forthcoming). These alternatives are based on students' performance of concrete, meaningful tasks (for example, a laboratory experiment to determine which of three paper towels soaks up the most water). Moreover, they are scored in a way designed to capture not just the "right answer" but also the reasonableness of the procedure used to carry out the task or solve the problem. Finally, these alternatives recognize the symmetry between testing and teaching; that is, a good assessment makes a good teaching activity, and a good teaching activity makes a good assessment. The project focused on upper elementary and middle school children (ages eleven through fourteen years) and provides a concrete example of the new vision of assessment and, indirectly, of effective and responsible teaching.

The researchers developed a number of alternative assessments, including observation of hands-on experimentation, notebooks based on the experiment, computer simulations of the experiment, and paper-and-pencil tests related to aspects of the experiment. We focus here on two examples. The first, the paper towels investigation, shows how assessments may reinforce science process understanding and encourage diversity of student performance. The second, an "electrical mysteries" simulation, reinforces application of knowledge in a problem-solving setting and demonstrates the symmetry of teaching and testing. Teaching to these assessments will change teachers' decisions about how to organize and present instruction.

For the paper towels investigation, students conducted an experiment to determine which of three kinds of paper towels soaked up the most water. A laboratory setup including towels, water, trays, graduated beakers, scissors, a scale, a timer, and so on was provided. Students were told that they could use all or some of the equipment available, as they felt necessary. After completing the investigation, students recorded procedures, findings, and conclusions in a lab notebook.

The diversity of student performances was striking. More than sixteen different procedural sequences were recorded—some legitimate, some flawed. The challenge to the researchers was to preserve this diversity and yet score the student performance on a common metric (see Baxter, Shavelson, Goldman, and Pine, 1992). To this end, a procedure-based scoring scheme was developed. It ordered the variety of performances as to their "scientific soundness" while preserving the actual procedures used. The scoring system recognized that several different procedures could result in the same quality of performance. For example, a student who poured equal amounts of water into three beakers, saturated a towel in each, removed the towels, and measured the amount of water remaining in each beaker would get the same score as a student who dipped each towel into a pitcher of water until saturated and then weighed each.

For the "electrical mysteries" simulation, students had to determine the contents of each of six mystery boxes (for example, battery and bulb) by connecting a circuit to the box. Students used a Macintosh computer and a mouse to connect the circuits, with the software emulating the behavior of an actual circuit. Students could connect a multitude of circuits on the screen at once if they so desired, or they could leave one completed circuit on the screen as an explicit model of what they thought was in the box and compare this circuit to the one hooked up to the box. Most germane to the present discussion was the finding that some students completed no fewer than 150 circuits in about thirty minutes. They had gone beyond the intended assessment to explore the nature of electrical circuits and to construct new knowledge through experimentation. The assessment had been viewed by the students as a teaching activity, not a test; hence the symmetry of teaching and testing.

This research on science assessments has several implications for learning how to teach science *effectively* if investigations such as the paper towels and electrical mysteries experiments are used to measure achievement. First, the materials typically found in elementary classrooms are going to have to change — from book learning to laboratory experiments, from pencil and paper to computers. Second, the typical arrangement of the classroom will have to change to accommodate the availability and use of lab equipment and computers. Third, teams of students are likely to be working together on a problem, partly because of limited access to equipment but more importantly because such an arrangement is consistent with the culture of doing science. Fourth, some concepts and norms of classroom discipline will need to change as students walk around and talk to one another. Fifth, writing up experiments, part of the science culture, will become routine. Indeed, science offers a concrete, meaningful occasion for practice in writing. And, sixth, teachers will have to deal with the diversity of solutions that students invent.

This research also has implications for what is considered *responsible* teaching. To prepare to take the test, students need to take responsibility for their own learning. The teacher becomes an orchestrator, responsible for developing learning activities and helping students construct knowledge. The goal is to create a culture in which students learn to work together cooperatively, to construct knowledge, and in the process to learn to value one another's unique contributions.

If teachers teach to the test, will they teach effectively and responsibly? To do so, we suspect that many teachers will have to change the way they plan and carry out instruction.

Changes in Instructional Decision Making

To describe some of the changes in teaching that alternative assessment technologies may bring about, we have first to characterize instructional planning and action and the kinds of decisions that teachers make. Then we can characterize the impact of changes in the nature of assessments on these plans and actions.

A Framework for Teachers' Instructional Decision Making

Research has shown that teachers' planning is opportunistic. That is, their focus is on creating a flow of activities that enact the curriculum while balancing multiple goals. The nature of those activities, the manner in which they are carried out, and students' acquisition of knowledge and values reflect the extent to which the teaching is effective and responsible.

Teachers' instructional planning and action focus on the instructional task (Doyle, 1986; Shavelson, 1983). As Figure 6.1 illustrates, this task contains two fundamental components: a goal state and a problem space. The

Figure 6.1. Components of the Instructional Task.

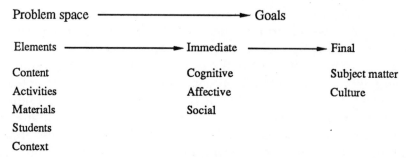

goals are not just cognitive but intrapersonal (affective) and interpersonal (involving social skills and values) as well. The problem space is defined by "a set of instructions, conditions, and resources available to reach the goal state" (Doyle, 1986, p. 394). It contains at least five elements (Shavelson, 1983; Shavelson and Stern, 1981):

1. Content: the subject matter of instruction.
2. Activities: what the teacher and students will be doing during the lesson. This element encompasses the other elements of the problem space and sequences, paces, and times the instructional content and materials.
3. Materials: those things that students can observe and/or manipulate in order to explore content and construct understandings.
4. Students: especially their abilities, needs, and interests.
5. Context: the class as a whole and its sense of "groupness," a specially created community around a subject matter. It also includes the teacher's grouping of students for instruction (for example, cooperative learning, tutoring), which establishes the sociocultural context of valuing the subject matter and individuals' unique contributions to knowledge construction.

Teachers create instructional tasks when they plan instruction. The central concern is the construction of activities that connect goals with the other elements of the problem space to create the flow of classroom instruction. Teachers' plans for instruction, which exert a strong influence on classroom teaching, are guided by a conceptual framework or schema (Shavelson, 1986). A schema is an abstract information structure. It can be viewed as a structured set of expectations. "Information that neatly satisfies expectations can be encoded into memory so as to 'instantiate' the slots [expectations] in the schema" (Anderson, 1984, p. 5). These expectations are linked to the elements of the problem space and the instructional goals. When teachers plan instruction, they instantiate the slots in their instructional schema. These slots correspond to the elements of the problem space and their instructional goals.

Three types of instructional schemata appear to be particularly important: knowledge structures, scripts, and scenes. Each type addresses a subset of the elements in the problem space. Scripts are action-oriented and guide classroom instruction. Knowledge structures and scenes provide the subject matter and pedagogical basis for scripts.

Knowledge structures are centrally concerned with subject matter, students, and pedagogical assumptions and arguments for action. That is, knowledge structures represent teachers' understanding of subject matter and knowledge of students' abilities, interests, and classroom behaviors. They also include teachers' beliefs about effective and responsible teaching and the assumptions that link these beliefs to teaching actions.

Scripts are schematic representations of familiar, everyday experiences, such as getting dressed or teaching reading to a high-ability group of elementary school children. Scripts are temporally and hierarchically ordered, concrete, stereotypical knowledge structures about common routines. They embody the sequence, pacing, timing, and groupings of instruction. They are instantiated with the particular content and materials of an activity (lesson). They have been used to characterize interactive teaching, guiding classroom instruction until something unexpected occurs (Shavelson and Stern, 1981).

Scenes are cognitive structures that organize knowledge about places. For example, we have scene schemata for a kitchen, a supermarket, and a classroom. The scene represents recurring, well-established inventories of people and objects and their spatial relations. They are topological in Piaget's sense, not Euclid's, in that they represent left, right, up, down, in, out, next to, and so on. Scene schemata may be particularly apt for describing teacher's knowledge about classrooms and common activity structures found in them, such as reading groups and seat work (Berliner, 1983). These schemata guide the spatial location of materials and students within the classroom.

Taken together, scripts and scene schemata create the sociocultural context of the classroom. They are greater than the sum of their parts, creating a whole culture—a manner of approaching subject matter and the individual and social construction of knowledge.

Impact of Alternative Technologies on Instructional Decisions

As we have seen, the alternative assessment technologies are based on two important assumptions about the nature of learning: that knowledge is constructed and that this construction takes place within a cultural context of a discipline. If teachers want to teach to the new tests, they will have to align their professional knowledge—schemata—with these assumptions.

The teacher's primary role—conveyor of knowledge—must change. The teacher must provide opportunities for students to make meaning and construct new knowledge. To do so, the teacher needs to value the capabilities and contributions of all students and establish a culture of doing mathematics or science. This culture is one in which its members—teacher and students together—find problems, debate and establish criteria for solving them, and construct alternative solutions.

To create ths culture, the teacher must possess "a strong mastery of the practice of mathematics" and science and have "the autonomy to engage with learners in the practice of problem solving in inventive ways" (Lave, Smith, and Butler, 1988, p. 77). Moreover, the teacher has the responsibility of modeling care and respect for student contributions, creating a strong sense of self and capability in the learners. In short, the usual goals of instruction (often acquisition of facts and basic skills) and the usual scripts and scenes will have to be replaced by new ones. They may shift from primarily cognitive—teaching basic operations in mathematics or definitions in science—to cultural—constructing a supportive culture in a subject matter. Within this culture, teachers will seek to intertwine intellect, values, attitudes, and social interaction.

To teach to the alternative assessments, teachers will need a firm grounding in subject matter knowledge. They may need a much greater understanding of mathematics, for example, than they now possess if they are to facilitate students' recognition of a mathematical problem and its representation in alternative symbolic forms, identification of criteria against which to evaluate solutions, and so on (Lave, Smith, and Butler, 1988; Leinhardt and Smith, 1985). The usual pedagogical assumptions and rationales that underlie teachers' instructional decisions, such as those that lead to whole-class instruction with the teacher as primary information conveyor ("direct instruction"), may also be called into question; assumptions and values embodied in the constructivist reform will affect teaching scripts and scenes and lead to different instructional decisions and practices.

The most common teaching *script* in the United States is recitation: teachers ask questions and students give quick, short answers; teachers talk about 80 percent of the time and students 20 percent. A second common script is seatwork: after a brief explanation of a concept in mathematics or science, students work individually on exercises or definitions in a workbook (Romberg and Carpenter, 1986). Neither script gives rise to an intellectual community respecting individual and joint contributions to knowledge or to a culture within a subject matter.

Teachers will need to acquire new scripts, scripts that are just emerging. Their task will be to facilitate the development of an intellectual community. A new set of responsibilities and values regarding knowledge and its construction may be needed. No longer will teachers make decisions within the constraints of a fifty-minute hour. Knowledge construction does not recognize these time barriers. Hands-on activities and apparatus will find their way into the script. Sequencing will be guided by student exploration, unpredictable in the specifics but predictable at the macro level. The pace will be set by the students, as will the timing of activities. The content will be built from the concrete activities. In short, teachers' decisions about the content, materials, sequencing, pacing, and timing of classroom activities will change.

The physical and social organization and operation of classrooms may very well change substantially as well. Typical scenes associated with seatwork and recitation, with no social contact, will decrease in frequency as task-oriented social interaction and knowledge construction emerge. Students will no longer be seated at individual desks; larger work spaces will be needed. Decisions about allocation of classroom space, equipment, and materials will have to serve the need for students to interact and to use equipment in the discovery of knowledge.

For most teachers, this view of instruction and the decisions that give rise to it are not routine today. The nature of the scripts and scenes that teachers instantiate to motivate and support knowledge construction are not well established (but see, for example, Lampert, Chapter Nineteen in this volume). They will emerge and become recognizable if the alternative assessments have the impact expected. They will become a necessary precursor of teaching to the test. These new teaching routines are going to challenge the boundaries of schooling as we know them today. They may very well lead to the restructuring of schooling. However, a caveat is in order. Without substantial commitment to training and supervision of teachers, without public support, without the necessary materials and facilities, there are no guarantees that the picture of effective and responsible teaching painted here will emerge in the curriculum reform. Indeed, even with this support, the reform goals may get warped.

An anecdote may serve to illustrate the importance of our concern. One of the teachers whose classes participated in our research knew of the paper towels experiment. Teaching to the test, she instructed her students to saturate the towels completely, using the timer to ensure that at least ten minutes were given to saturating each towel separately (a total of thirty minutes for saturation!), when, in reality, the towels could be saturated in a matter of seconds. The result was that the students performed in a clearly stylized manner. The teacher had informed them, perhaps unintentionally, that science is a set of precise steps that must be carried out invariably, regardless of whether they make sense. This was not particularly conducive to scientific exploration; although the teacher could teach the students how to "do" the experiment, what was missing was the cultural context of doing science.

Implications: A Basis for Restructuring Education

One of the most often cited solutions to educational problems in the United States is "restructuring." Shake up the schools organizationally, the assumption goes, and when the pieces are reassembled, things will be better. For example, place greater decision-making responsibility with teachers and less with administrators: shifting decision making to those more closely linked to the function of schooling—teaching and learning—will (somehow) improve education. Or place decision making at the local school site, not at a central office. The incentives for quality schools, politicians argue, reside in the community. Somehow, nonprofessionals will discover a way to improve education.

None of these "solutions" paints a picture of what effective and responsible teaching would look like and why student learning and performance would improve. These suggestions place form—organization of schools—before function. Suppose that the function of schools were to create an intellectual community in which students and teachers value one another and together construct knowledge and use it in meaningful ways to solve problems, resolve dilemmas, or make meaning out of the unexpected. Suppose further that our accountability systems held teachers accountable with assessments congruent with school functions—not just in individual academic achievement but also in the ability to work together constructing knowledge and solving problems. Teachers would design instruction to this end. The design decisions would lead to changes in scripts and classroom scenes. The physical organization of the classroom, the temporal organization of the school day, and the relations among teachers and students would reflect the functions of education. If teachers, educational systems, policy makers, and the public respond to and support changes in assessment technologies as we envision, changes in teaching may very well lead to restructuring schools in an effective and responsible way.

References

Anderson, R. "Some Reflections on the Acquisition of Knowledge." *Educational Researcher,* 1984, *13* (9), 5–10.

Baxter, G. P., Shavelson, R. J., Goldman, S. R., and Pine, J. "Evaluation of Procedure-Based Scoring for Hands-On Science Assessment." *Journal of Educational Measurement,* 1992, *29*(1), 1–17.

Berliner, D. C. "Developing Conceptions of Classroom Environments: Some Light on the T in Classroom Studies of ATI." *Educational Psychologist,* 1983, *18*(1), 1–13.

Doyle, W. "Classroom Organization and Management." In M. C. Wittrock (ed.), *Handbook of Research on Teaching.* (3rd ed.) New York: Macmillan, 1986.

Glaser, R. "Education and Thinking: The Role of Knowledge." *American Psychologist,* 1984, *39*(2), 93–104.

Gough, P. B. (ed.). Special section on testing. *Phi Delta Kappan,* 1989, *70*(9), 683–725.

Lave, J., Smith, S., and Butler, M. "Problem Solving as Everyday Practice."

In R. I. Charles and E. A. Silver (eds.), *The Teaching and Assessing of Mathematical Problem Solving*. Hillsdale, N.J.: Erlbaum, 1988.

Leinhardt, G., and Smith, D. A. "Expertise in Mathematics Instruction: Subject Matter Knowledge." *Journal of Educational Psychology*, 1985, *77*, (3), 247–271.

Mullis, I. V., and Jenkins, L. B. *The Science Report Card: Elements of Risk and Recovery*. National Assessment of Educational Progress report no. 17-S-01. Princeton, N.J.: Educational Testing Service, 1988.

National Commission on Excellence in Education. *A Nation at Risk: The Imperative for Educational Reform*. Washington, D.C.: U.S. Government Printing Office, 1983.

Nickerson, R. S. (ed.). "New Directions in Educational Assessment." *Educational Researcher*, 1989, *18* (9), 3–32.

Resnick, L. B. *Education and Learning to Think*. Washington, D.C.: National Academy Press, 1987.

Resnick, L. B. "Treating Mathematics as an Ill-Structured Discipline." In R. I. Charles and E. A. Silver (eds.), *The Teaching and Assessing of Mathematical Problem Solving*. Hillsdale, N.J.: Erlbaum, 1988.

Romberg, T. A., and Carpenter, T. P. "Research on Teaching and Learning Mathematics: Two Disciplines of Scientific Inquiry." In M. C. Wittrock (ed.), *Handbook of Research on Teaching*. (3rd ed.) New York: Macmillan, 1986.

Shanker, A. "The End of the Traditional Model of Schooling—and a Proposal for Using Incentives to Restructure Our Public Schools." *Phi Delta Kappan*, 1990, *71* (5), 345–357.

Shavelson, R. J. "Review of Research on Teachers' Pedagogical Judgments, Plans, and Decisions." *Elementary School Journal*, 1983, *83* (4) 392–413.

Shavelson, R. J. *Pensamientos de los Profesor y Toma de Decisiones* [Teacher cognition and decision making]. Seville, Spain: University of Seville, 1986.

Shavelson, R. J., Baxter, G. P., and Pine, J. "Performance Assessments in Science." *Applied Measurement in Education*, forthcoming.

Shavelson, R. J., Carey, N. B., and Webb, N. M. "Achievement Indicators: Options for a Powerful Policy Instrument." *Phi Delta Kappan*, 1990, *71* (9), 692–697.

Shavelson, R. J., and Stern, P. "Research on Teachers' Pedagogical Thoughts, Judgments, Decisions, and Behavior." *Review of Educational Research*, 1981, *51* (4), 455–498.

Shavelson, R. J., Webb, N. M., Stasz, C., and McArthur, D. "Teaching Mathematical Problem Solving: Insights from Teachers and Tutors." In R. I. Charles and E. A. Silver (eds.), *The Teaching and Assessing of Mathematical Problem Solving*. Hillsdale, N.J.: Erlbaum, 1988.

Shavelson, R. J., and others. "Alternative Technologies for Large-Scale Assessment: Instrument of Education Reform." *School Effectiveness and School Improvement*, 1991, *2*, 1–18.

Smith, M. L. "Put to the Test: The Effects of External Testing on Teachers." *Educational Researcher,* 1991, *20* (5), 8–11.

Walker, D. F., and Schaffarzick, J. "Comparing Curricula." *Review of Educational Research,* 1974, *44* (1), 83–111.

Wiggins, G. "A Trust Test: Toward More Authentic and Equitable Assessment." *Phi Delta Kappan,* 1989, *70* (9), 703–713.

Section Three

THE MORAL DIMENSION

Mordecai Nisan,
Section Editor

Responsible teaching encompasses several dimensions, the most prominent being the responsibility to pass on knowledge in a valid and appropriate way. This aspect of responsibility, discussed in other sections of this book, complements effectiveness as it is commonly defined as the successful acquisition of knowledge. Yet responsible teaching entails more than the diffusion of knowledge per se; it also involves the nurturing of values that permeate the overall school context. Such values are implicit in the content of the material taught, the manner of its transmission, the teacher's behavior, how moral and value dilemmas are handled, and the school's perceived ideals and aims (school ethos). The chapters in this section deal with responsibility in this latter sense.

Expectations of responsible teaching regarding values are not as explicit and clear-cut as expectations regarding efficiency and the responsibility to impart appropriate knowledge. Many value messages — quite likely the more influential ones — are transmitted unintentionally and unconsciously through what has been termed "the hidden curriculum." This curriculum is hidden from child and teacher alike. An important task of the researcher interested in responsibility is to reveal these latent value messages, as well as the ways in which they are transmitted to the child.

There is also less general consensus regarding the responsibility to impart values than regarding the responsibility to impart knowledge. First, we may expect disagreement as to which values ought to be transmitted in school. Second, being "hidden," these values are not subject to reflection or public discussion, which could lead to a certain measure of agreement. This is true also of many moral and value dilemmas that the teacher is likely to encounter in his or her work. Thus, an educational researcher who wishes to enhance responsible teaching will have to venture beyond the accepted descriptive role and suggest solutions to the problematic issue of values in education. Such solutions may be formal in nature—for instance, procedures to deal with value dilemmas—or they may be substantial, pointing to a set of values about which there is or should be consensus.

The chapters in this section address these very issues. They demonstrate that teaching cannot be free of value judgments and implications, not only because it is based on interpersonal relations, which inevitably raise moral considerations, but also because of factors inherent in it. They present some major values and value dilemmas that the teacher is bound to consider and encounter in teaching, and they suggest directions for the responsible educator to take in this regard.

Teaching is not merely a matter of method (skills for transmitting knowledge). It also involves manner (exhibition of personal traits), which transmits value messages, as described by Gary D Fenstermacher in Chapter Seven. Even an ostensibly noncontroversial act such as the teaching of critical thinking may arouse value controversy, as William Damon suggests in Chapter Ten. And even the type of motivation mobilized for instruction carries a value message, as Mordecai Nisan argues in Chapter Nine. Values involved in the teacher's work, which are often latent, may conflict with one another, with other considerations of classroom teachings, and with the teacher's personal interests. No wonder, therefore, that at times teachers avoid the values inherent in their work or only partially take them into account, as Fritz K. Oser observes in Chapter Eight.

Conflicts such as those just mentioned often give rise to value dilemmas, several of which are raised in the chapters in this section. Without presuming to comprehensively cover the place and range of values in school instruction, the chapters offer a broad outline of types of values and value dilemmas involved in teaching. These include the tension between effectiveness (success in imparting knowledge) and responsibility (adherence to moral values; dilemmas related to basic dimensions of morality in teaching, such as justice, truthfulness, and caring; and issues concerning the limits and constraints of the teacher's authority).

Mere awareness of the existence of value dilemmas, as well as identification of their components, is certainly not enough. Once the teacher has recognized and identified the dilemma, he or she has to make a decision and act on it. Can we prepare teachers for responsible decisions and actions? Can we suggest ways to help them teach responsibly? There is surprisingly limited treatment of these issues in the educational literature, and it is encouraging to find that the chapters in this section offer some suggestions. In Chapter Seven, Fenstermacher suggests the development of practical reasoning related to teaching, "of the capacity to deliberate and reflect on one's action and to react on the basis of this deliberation and reflection." He offers steps for such development and suggests that it requires critical discourse with another person. In Chapter Eight, Oser proposes the stimulation of discourse morality and roundtable discussions of value dilemmas in which all participants, including children, are considered equals. In Chapter Nine,

Nisan proposes constructing the entire school enterprise in terms of desirable rather than instrumental behavior, where such an orientation is reflected at all levels of school activity, from the teacher-student interaction to the school ethos. Finally, in Chapter Ten, Damon discusses teacher-student interactions based on the principle of respectful engagement, where the child is encouraged to actively participate in a dialogue in which the adult clearly expresses his or her own perspective.

These suggestions offer a mix of what we have called formal and substantial solutions to the value dilemmas in teaching, implying agreement about a set of values that should instruct educators. Common to the suggestions is that they have both cognitive and dialogical elements — that is, that responsibility can be fostered both through reflection and understanding and through interactions based on mutual respect. The suggestions differ, though, in certain respects, such as the teacher's status in the discourse (higher than the student's in Chapters Seven and Ten, equal to the student's in Chapter Eight), the weight given to the cognitive as opposed to the dialogical element (greater in Chapter Seven than in the other chapters), and the relative importance of the roles of the school as a whole and the individual teacher (a greater role for the school in Chapter Nine than in the other chapters).

These differences notwithstanding, the cognitive and logical elements common to the above suggestions seem highly suited to classroom instruction, affording the above propositions strong plausibility and making them largely noncontroversial. It is clear, however, that many empirical data are needed to examine the prospect of applying these ideas to a real school context. A salient obstacle in this regard may be the developmental level of the teacher and tendencies to avoid a true dialogue that Oser discusses in Chapter Eight.

What we identify as responsibility from the viewpoint of the teacher can be seen from the student's perspective as moral or value education. The decisions and behavior of the responsible teacher in a value dilemma carry a clear educational message, precisely because they are personal decisions rather than intentional efforts to influence students. Such decisions and behavior express to students the teachers' convictions, the values that they accept as universally (or at least culturally) valid, and their commitment to act accordingly. At the same time, the joint reasoning and decision making imply acknowledgment not only of the students' competence but also of their responsibility for their decisions and their consequences. This seems to encourage a sense of obligation in the student. A child who discovers that responsibility is a characteristic of the environment — from the teacher's behavior, the school ethos, and the way in which the child is perceived and treated — will come to view responsibility as a constitutive part of the self; that is, will internalize it.

7

The Concepts of Method and Manner in Teaching

Gary D Fenstermacher

The concept of pedagogy consists of two critical attributes: method and manner. The notion of method has been and continues to be extensively discussed and analyzed by educators and researchers. The notion of manner, whether called by this name or another name with similar meaning, has received scant attention in recent scholarship and is not well understood. Until both attributes of pedagogy are thoroughly understood and developed in practice, we are unlikely to have teaching that is both effective and responsible. This chapter is an attempt to effect a synthesis between effectiveness and responsibility in teaching by demonstrating the complementarity of method and manner in pedagogy.

What follows may be thought of as a variation on an old but honorable theme: Can virtue be taught? Debated since the early dialogues of Plato, this question continues to vex educational practitioners and researchers. Much of the formal scholarship in English, save for that of a small group of educational philosophers, has for decades avoided any serious consideration of the moral and ethical aspects of teaching. Instead, the primary purpose of the study of teaching has, for the last thirty years, been to increase our general understanding of instruction in classrooms and to enhance the effectiveness of that instruction. Little attention has been given to the moral and ethical dimensions of teaching, to those features that make teaching responsible as well as effective.

As a result, our inquiries have been devoted to method, to that attribute of pedagogy pertaining to the skills and techniques of teaching. This preoccupation with method provides little opportunity to consider another important aspect of pedagogy, the development of valued dispositions and traits of character. Dispositions and traits of character are fostered not by method but by manner. Manner, in turn, is shaped by two forces: (1) habituation and training and (2) reasoning about intentions and actions.

The purpose of this analysis is to establish the case for both method and manner as critical attributes of a fully specified concept of pedagogy and to show how manner may be fostered through the development of teachers' capacities to reason about their practice: teachers who are capable of practical reasoning are better able to nurture the moral and intellectual development of their students.

Distinguishing Method from Manner

Method is the general descriptive term that we give to a broad range of teaching behaviors whose purpose is to convey content. It includes many of the practices that characterize the activities of teaching, such as planning, instruction, evaluation, and grading. Our very strong interest, at least in the United States, in the students' acquisition of content has led us to think of content area learning as the sine qua non of teaching. In a recent report on the Provisional Teaching Program in the state of New Jersey, the Council on Basic Education states that "Of the assumptions that undergird the Provisional Program, first and most striking are the notions that substantial knowledge of an academic subject is the most crucial qualification for an effective teacher, and that professional skills essential to success in teaching students and managing classrooms can be imparted in fairly short order" (Gray and Lynn, 1988, p. 6).

This focus on the acquisition of knowledge and understanding within subject areas or disciplines leads us to think of pedagogy almost exclusively in terms of method, of skill and technique. Yet more often than we recognize, we are stymied by this preoccupation with method. Because it is a useful — indeed, powerful — way to think about how knowledge and understanding are conveyed, we assume that it is also a useful, perhaps powerful way to think about how valued traits and human dispositions are developed. Thus, when it is contended that children lack problem-solving or critical thinking skills, the tendency is to isolate and describe the "knowledge base" of critical thinking and then to identify the skills required to use this knowledge base. In so doing, we presuppose that critical thinking is a cluster of facts, ideas, and skills, just like the clusters of facts, ideas, and skills in mathematics, history, or woodshop.

We appear to believe that if we find the right methods to teach critical thinking, we can produce students of great ability in problem solving and critical thinking. This view of critical thinking can lead to quite ludicrous situations, as when a teacher says that her intention is to teach critical thinking, then assigns students to read about logicians and memorize the square of opposition, the truth tables, and thirty-one common fallacies of reasoning, all followed by multiple-choice tests to determine whether the students now know about critical thinking. It is in just such a cockeyed example that we see that critical thinking is something more than a cluster of facts and skills.

The British philosopher John Passmore (1975, p. 28) argues that "being critical' is, indeed, more like the sort of thing we call a 'character trait' than it is like a skill. To call a person 'critical' is to characterize him, to describe his nature." In his seminal analysis of teaching children to be critical, Passmore sets forth three "levels" of critical thinking. The first level is that of critical ability, which is in fact a kind of skill — the skill of being able to criticize performance, one's own and others, as when the teacher criticizes the student for shoddy work. The second level of critical ability is the critical spirit, wherein one "is alert to the possibility that the established norms themselves ought to be rejected, that the rules ought to be changed, the criteria used in judging performance modified" (p. 30). Teaching a child to embrace a critical spirit is more than teaching skills or facts. It involves encouraging the child "to look critically at the value of the performances in which he is taught to engage, as distinct from the level of achievement arrived at within such a performance" (p. 30). To achieve this second level of critical ability, the teacher is called on to develop an enthusiasm for the give-and-take of critical discussion. The third level of critical ability is called critico-creative thought. Here the critical spirit combines with imagination to produce what we think of as the great achievements in literature, philosophy, science, and other fields of higher learning.

One does not, Passmore contends, acquire the second and third levels of critical ability in the same way one acquires the first level. The first level consists of facts and skills, conveyed through the use of proper and appropriate methods. The second and third levels consist of certain dispositions and traits and must be conveyed differently from the first level. They are attained by engaging in manner of a certain kind.

The Concept of Manner

Manner is the term that I apply to human action that exhibits the particular traits or dispositions of a person. It refers to such characteristics as compassion, selfishness, caring, meanspiritedness, industriousness, narrow-mindedness, tolerance, and so forth. When we say that a person is thoughtful or snobbish, we are referring to the manner of that person. The term may also refer to a cluster of dispositions and traits that are the result of a certain form of upbringing. Shakespeare used the term just so when, in act 1, scene 4, Hamlet says,

> Ay, marry, is't;
> But to my mind, though I am native here
> And to the manner born, it is a custom
> More honored in the breach than the observance.

The notion of manner is clearly revealed when we ponder human virtue and how it is engendered in people. Few scholars speak as eloquently to this topic as Gilbert Ryle, who considers the case of a surgeon who is offered a bribe to murder a patient on the operating table:

If Jones is a conscientious surgeon, then his conscientiousness is no part of his dexterity, and vice versa; and the training that made him dexterous is not what made him care more for the welfare of his patient than for any other competing consideration that might be suggested to him. So how did he learn to care more for his patient's recovery than for any rival bonus? Unless we surrender and say that Jones was just born to be both asthmatic and conscientious, we seem now to be postulating a kind of learning by which he acquired not information and not proficiencies, but the caring for some sorts of things more than for others; a kind of schooling as a result of which, to put it in metaphor, Jones's heart came to be set on some things and against other things [Ryle, 1975, p. 50].

Jones's conscientiousness is part of his manner, and this characteristic of his personhood is different from his proficiency or dexterity as a surgeon. One could say that in the performance of his surgery, he exhibits the method of his craft, and in his demeanor and disposition, he exhibits the manner of his personhood. Viewed in this way, it is apparent that method and manner occur together, such that Jones is at the same time being both dexterous and conscientious, though it is also possible for him to be dexterous and not conscientious, or the other way around.

Manner and method are thus concurrent and, when one serves the other, complementary. Method pertains to skill or to skilled performance; manner, to traits of character or general human dispositions or their exercise in behavior. Manner is acquired less directly than skill and over a longer period of time. To foster manner of a certain kind in others, it is necessary to engage in the formation of habits and to assist the individual so that he or she responds to situations in specific ways. It is also necessary to engage the person in thinking about his or her actions so that he or she understands and reflects on them (this kind of thinking will later be identified as practical reasoning).

Habituation and training are what take place when we are encouraged or admonished to act in certain ways. To pick up on Ryle's (1975, p. 47) felicitous phrasing one more time: "What will help make us self-controlled, fair-minded or hard-working are good examples set by others, and then ourselves practising and failing, and practising again, and failing again, but not quite so soon, and so on. In matters of morals, . . . we learn first by being shown by others, then by being trained by others, naturally with some worded homily, praise and rebuke, and lastly by being trained by ourselves."

In his analyses of child rearing in the United States and the Soviet Union, Bronfenbrenner (1972) reached much the same conclusion. He argued that such qualities as mutual trust, kindness, cooperation, and social responsibility "are learned from other human beings who in some measure exhibit these qualities, value them, and strive to develop them in their children" (p. 117). Bronfenbrenner tells that one of his teachers, Walter Fenno Dearborn, used to say, "He's a chip off the old block—not because he was knocked off it, but because he knocked around with it" (p. 117).

In this chapter, the consideration of manner is generally restricted to a consideration of those traits and dispositions that we regard as human virtues. Thus, this analysis is, for the most part, limited to "good manner," to the manner that we value and praise in fellow human beings. This good manner is usually known as virtue and is of two kinds, intellectual and moral. Though these two categories overlap, it is helpful to distinguish them in the context of pedagogy. Manner that is productive of the intellectual virtues is manner that promotes a respect for evidence, a sense of tentativeness and willingness to suspend one's pet notions as the exploration proceeds, an appreciation of and regard for the canons of inquiry and the demands of truth telling, and an openness to alternative and competing ideas. Manner that is productive of the moral virtues is manner that encompasses such traits as compassion, fairness, tolerance, caring, and honesty.

Having distinguished between method and manner in this way, we are now in a position to ask whether a teacher might be prepared to foster virtue in students through manner as the teacher is prepared to foster knowledge through method. Raising the question in this way calls for assuming a somewhat different perspective on the notion of manner.

Manner as an Attribute of Pedagogy

Like *method,* a general term in our language until it is formalized by being located in the context of pedagogy, *manner* means something more specific and precise when placed in the context of pedagogy. Here it refers to dispositions and traits of the teacher as he or she undertakes the tasks of teaching. Thus, we speak of a teacher being fair or unfair, considerate or harsh, high-minded or base, while also engaging in explaining, leading a discussion, organizing a study group, or illustrating a difficult concept. It is in this way that manner and method occur together, as two dimensions of pedagogical activity.

The question for consideration at this point in the argument is whether teachers can employ manner to impart virtue in somewhat the same way they employ method to impart knowledge. That is, is it possible to train or perfect the manner of the teacher in somewhat the same way in which we train teachers in the methods of teaching? Framing the question in this way points out a problem in the parallelism between method and manner. When we speak of method in the context of pedagogy, we are speaking specifically of the methods of teaching. But when we speak of manner in the context of pedagogy, are we referring specifically to the manner of teaching?

In other words, is there a general manner of some sort, as well as a manner specific to teaching? Perhaps one could build a case for there being a manner specific to teaching, though that seems to me to be taking a wrong turn. The charge to educators is to impart those virtues that are generally regarded by humankind as noble and proper virtues, not to impart virtues specific to the school or to classroom teaching. Thus, the manner of teaching is generally not something that is specific to teaching in the way that the methods of the teacher usually are. Rather, the manner of the teacher should be exemplary of good manner writ large.

Thus, our task is not to find a manner particular to being a teacher but rather to find out how to exemplify good manner while instructing in the subject areas and disciplines of study. Understanding this point calls for us to return to an earlier part of this chapter. Recall that Passmore, Ryle, and Bronfenbrenner argue that one acquires virtue by being around virtuous people and that these virtuous people engage the young in certain ways when they seek to impart a capacity for virtuous conduct to the young. Given these views, the first step is to ask whether the teacher him- or herself is virtuous and thus able to demonstrate virtuous conduct and call for it from his or her students. This last point raises the issue of whether those who teach are themselves sufficiently imbued with the intellectual and moral traits of character that we regard as essential to engage in the education of fellow human beings. Though this is an important question, it raises an issue that is not central to this argument. Our concern here is whether, even if we were amply supplied with teachers who were otherwise virtuous persons, these teachers would know *how* to exercise their virtue in the context of modern schooling and would have full and sufficient opportunity to exercise their virtue as teachers.

The remainder of this chapter takes up the matter of how teachers may be helped in the exercise of virtue as teachers. But before we turn directly to this matter, it is worth another moment to consider whether teachers have full and sufficient opportunity to deploy manner as robustly as they are called on to deploy method. There are two impediments that come immediately to mind. The first is the restrictions that custom, policy, and law place on what can occur in schools. If classroom settings are restricted to dealing only with what is not controversial or offensive to certain special-interest groups, the teacher's capacity to evidence manner, especially manner indicative of intellectual virtues, is greatly diminished.

A similar point may be made about the subject matter of instruction. If the texts, the visual aids, and the other materials of instruction are diluted in substance and sophistication, then the opportunity of the teacher to "rise" to topics of great import or significance is also thereby diminished. Consider the difference between teaching reading through structured reading materials, such as primers, basals, and workbooks, and teaching through stories and works of literary value. The teacher's opportunity to employ manner for the purpose of nurturing virtue is far greater in the latter case. It is not at all difficult to establish a connection between the nature of the texts and materials used in instruction and the opportunity of a virtuous teacher to engage in manner of the kind that advances desirable traits and dispositions in students.

These brief considerations of opportunity for employing manner are somewhat afield of the main line of the argument here. In returning to the central thesis of this chapter, it may be helpful to summarize the key contentions of that argument as developed thus far. First, manner is different from method in that method encompasses the skills and techniques used to impart knowledge, while manner encompasses the traits and dispositions that characterize a person as rational or moral, irrational or evil, or something in between. Second, traits and dispositions are acquired differently from knowledge and ideas. The former are the result of training, habituation and practical reasoning, while the latter are the result of direct instruction as well as more formal processes of reasoning. Third, manner and method occur together, as when a skill is demonstrated to some end that is worthy or demeaning. Fourth, in the context of pedagogy, manner may be thought of as somewhat, although not precisely, parallel to method; that is, manner is not specific to teaching, while method typically is. The fifth point is a contention that we are now examining: that manner, like method, can be purposefully developed in teachers.

One way to ensure that teachers have the requisite manner is to screen those entering the profession for the proper dispositions and traits of character. However, it is not always possible to do screening of this kind, and even if it were, the means of doing so are without proven validity, as well as being subject to legal challenge. And even if such screening were possible and acceptable, there is no assurance that people so screened would have a conception of what it means to engage manner in the classroom for the purpose of nurturing the intellectual and moral virtues of the young. Some development or perfecting of the concept of manner as an attribute of pedagogy is called for, else people whose traits and dispositions outside of school seem quite proper and appropriate may never pay attention, as a matter of pedagogy, to these traits and dispositions within the classroom.

There are thus two phases, if you will, to perfecting or developing manner. One is enhancing manner itself; that is, working on perfecting the traits and dispositions that evidence an agile and curious mind and high character. The second is assisting the teacher in understanding what it means to treat or employ manner as an attribute of pedagogy; that is, what is involved in purposefully setting out to foster intellectual and moral virtue in the young. Our understanding of these two facets of manner is illuminated and advanced by a careful consideration of the concept of practical reasoning.

Practical Rationality as a Constituent Part of Manner

As already noted, manner is in part formed and shaped by habituation and training. Yet for purposes of my argument here, I shall assume that habituation and training have already occurred for most people by the age of sixteen or so. Whatever we do about habituation and training after late adolescence is primarily a matter of changing what is already there. Eliminating punishment and grosser forms of behavioral conditioning as means for altering the habits and training of those entering teaching or now engaged in it, we are left with processes of reasoning as a way of changing many of the habits and dispositions acquired during one's childhood and youth. The processes of reasoning pertinent to this type of change fall within the category of practical rationality.

Practical rationality is reasoning about actions. It is distinguished from theoretical or formal reasoning in that it is not entirely propositional in form, it is not intended to advance our knowledge or understanding through deductive or inductive inference, and it is not strictly subject to logical canons for appraisal of its adequacy. I emphasize the fact that practical reasoning is not strictly subject to logical canons of appraisal because it will later be argued that practical reasoning is subject to certain conditions of form and coherence.

Much of our thinking about practical reasoning stems from the work of Aristotle, particularly *De Anima* and the *Nicomachean Ethics*. Aristotle's notion of *phronesis,* or practical wisdom, states Dahl (1984, p. 4), "seems to be the first recognition of a uniquely practical form of knowledge." As described by Aristotle, practical reasoning follows the form of a syllogism, wherein the major premise describes a desired end, the minor premise specifies the means to that end, and a third premise marks the situation as one in which the major and minor premises apply, leading to a conclusion in the form of an action. An example follows:

> Major: Health is a desirable end for all persons.
> Minor 1: Blood circulation is a means to health.
> Minor 2: Morning runs circulate the blood.
> Situation: This is the morning.
> Action: Running.

A fully elaborated practical syllogism would specify a desired end state, the means to obtain that end, a decision or choice to pursue the end through these means, a recognition of what circumstances call for one to act accordingly, and acting accordingly when these circumstances obtain (Ross, [1923] 1959).

Aristotle's notion of practical reasoning (within this general term, I include both *proairesis,* deliberative choice, and *phronesis,* prudence or practical wisdom) has been the source of discussion and commentary for much of the history of philosophy. Of interest have been whether Aristotle regarded practical reasoning, particularly the practical syllogism, as anything more than an almost automatic process and whether practical reasoning is related in any important way to ethical conduct. There is a growing body of scholarship (Audi, 1989; Dahl, 1984; Sherman, 1989; Sorabji, 1980; Wiggins, 1980) that places the Aristotelian concept of practical reasoning at the center of moral reasoning and the formation of character. This body of scholarship sustains much of what is argued in the remainder of this chapter.

In some of my prior work (Fenstermacher, 1986, 1987), I attempted to cast the education of teachers as, in part, a transformation of the practical arguments that they use to explain and justify their practice. This work began with Green's (1976) contention that "we may identify the competencies required of a teacher successful in instruction by identifying what is required to change the truth value of the premise of the practical argument in the mind of the child, or to complete or modify those premises or to introduce an altogether new premise into the practical argument in the mind of a child" (p. 252). While Green referred to the practical arguments in the mind of the child, my interest is in the practical arguments in the mind of the teacher. Early attempts to frame this thesis were subject to a fair amount of criticism (see Buchmann, 1987, 1989; Confrey, 1987; Morine-Dershimer, 1987; Munby, 1987; Kilbourne, 1987; Russell, 1987). With the subsequent help of Virginia Richardson (Richardson, 1990; Richardson and Anders, 1990; Richardson-Koehler and Fenstermacher, 1988), my conception of practical rationality has been broadened, as I hope will become evident in the next few pages.

Practical rationality may be defined as the capacity of a person to reason in a relatively coherent and logical fashion from action to the grounds for that action and back again. Using this notion as a working definition of practical rationality, I want to argue that the development of manner is, in part, the development of the capacity to reason practically, to deliberate and reflect on one's action, and to re-act on the basis of this deliberation and reflection. The philosophical foundation for these claims is quite extensive and will not be pursued here. Those who wish to explore the relevant arguments are referred to the work of Dahl (1984) and Sherman (1989).

At this point in the argument, we could branch out to an analysis of how practical rationality is related to manner, maintaining a tight scholarly style, with a concomitant high level of abstraction. While there would be a benefit to this approach insofar as it would offer a better opportunity to appraise the logic and reasonableness of the argument, I prefer to turn to what Scheffler (1985) calls "practical theory" as a way of illustrating and defending the claims made thus far about the connections among pedagogy, manner, and practical rationality.

Developing Manner Through Practical Rationality

Scheffler (1985, p. 5) states that a practical theory "organizes its propositions so as to provide guidance to some practical enterprise, for example, the healing of the sick, the construction of shelters, the rearing of the young." It is in this spirit that I advance a conception of how practical rationality serves as a means to enhance the manner of the teacher and to assist the teacher to employ manner as an aspect of pedagogical practice.

Both teachers and their students arrive at their schools as givens. They come to their respective roles already shaped and formed by their experiences, understandings, and reflections. If we accept that what is "given" is merely the base on which enlightenment and empowerment are constructed, we are thereby challenged to seek a means of further educating our fellow human beings. Method and manner are two of the primary means for undertaking such an education. This section is an exploration of how we might engage in the development of manner.

In the course of this exploration, I want to set aside an important aspect of the development of manner, and that is the formation of particular and specific traits of character. This formation happens frequently in the rearing of children, as we point out to them that they must share their toys, use fairness in competition, show respect for their parents, and treat their siblings with forbearance. This didactic pedagogy is quite essential to the development of character, but there is another part as well, and that is the formation and use of practical reasoning.

The consideration of practical reasoning opens a broad avenue for venturing into the development of manner on the part of the teacher. By "practical reasoning," I mean how the teacher reasons about his or her action as a teacher. Every teacher exhibits some practical rationality with respect to his or her actions in the classroom. That is, every teacher is able to put together some statements—premises, if you will—in explanation or defense of a course of action that the teacher pursued in the classroom. This line of reasoning may be nearly inchoate, but it is usually enough to begin a discussion of the action and its undergirding rationale.

A discussion of the teacher's practical reasoning is intended to "unearth" or elicit the basis for the action taken by the teacher. The initiating purpose of the inquiry is to gain a sense of why the teacher did what he or she did. In the course of eliciting the teacher's sense or rationale, certain avenues of exploration are important. The first is the teacher's description of the situation: What is the nature of this specific situation? What is taking place here? Who are the participants, and what are they doing? These questions are intended to aid the teacher in becoming more discerning in appraising the situations encountered in the course of teaching (see Pendlebury, 1990).

The next segment of the discussion involves the teacher's reasons for responding to the situation as he or she did. This inquiry typically has three parts—stipulative, empirical, and moral. In the stipulative part, the teacher sets forth his or her understanding of the central ideas undergirding an action or series of actions in the classroom. For example, if the action pertains to teaching seven-year-olds to read, the teacher may have a set of ideas about what reading is and how it is learned (see Richardson and Anders, 1990). These ideas will influence what the teacher does by way of teaching children to read. They are thus framed as stipulations underlying the action of the teacher.

The empirical statements pertain to contentions that the teacher makes that can be assessed or appraised with empirical evidence. If the teacher explains his or her action with the statement that children learn better when grouped with peers of similar intellectual ability, this explanation is subject to evaluation on the basis of the empirical evidence available to the professional community of educators. These statements are not unlike the minor premises shown in the Aristotelian practical syllogism illustrated earlier.

The moral statements provide the moral or ethical grounds for the action of the teacher. The teacher may say something like "The child will be at a disadvantage if she doesn't know how to share things" or "Jean cannot be allowed to disrupt the class every time he feels bad about something." These statements often indicate the root principles that undergird the action of the teacher.

Given that practical reasoning consists of statements that, when complete, include a description of the situation, the stipulative meaning of the act, the empirical basis of the action, and the moral or ethical grounds for the action, what can we say of the teacher's general capacity to offer a set of practical reasons for explaining or justifying his or her conduct? Some recent research (Hamilton, 1989; Richardson and Anders, 1990) indicates that when teachers are asked for the basis of their classroom actions, they most frequently provide stipulative statements, with few statements pertaining to situation, empirical evidence, or moral grounds. These stipulative statements are often descriptions of perceived requirements external to the classroom; for example, "This is required by the principal or the school board" or "I have to do this to satisfy the students' parents."

One gains little sense from these early responses that the teachers have a definitive idea about why they do what they do. One begins to wonder just how much consideration they have given to alternative ways to think about the situation (situational premise), to the empirical evidence available to support or repudiate certain practices, and to the moral principles that may or may not supply justification for this activity. It is, perhaps, not so much that teachers lack alternative premises as that they are not able to express them readily, that they feel somewhat uncomfortable discussing them openly, or both.

It is the discussion and elaboration of the different types of premises in a practical argument that enhance the practical reasoning of the teacher and thereby promote the capacity of the teacher to engage manner as an attribute of pedagogy. Given this, the problem becomes one of how to move from the relatively truncated and perhaps highly compressed statements offered by the teacher to a far more elaborate and thought-through understanding of the basis for the teacher's actions. To effect this change requires a shift from the elicitation of the practical rationality of the teacher to the construction of a practical argument that explains and offers clear justification for the teacher's practice.

Note the change here. The move is from eliciting, in as unintrusive a way as possible, the rationale that a teacher offers for his or her practice to constructing an elaborated practical argument for the teacher's actions.

The act of constructing a practical argument usually requires the participation of another person, one whom I shall call simply the "other." The other engages the teacher in a critical discourse about his or her practice, in a way that has parallels with Habermas's notions of the ideal speech situation (Habermas, 1971, 1979) or Bernstein's (1983) notion of dialogical communication and practical discourse.

There are, however, constraints that must be imposed on the discourse between the teacher and the other. The task of the other is to work with the teacher to construct a practical argument that includes robust accounts of situation, stipulation, empirical claims, and moral and ethical grounds. After a short period of time, the rationale initially elicited no longer belongs only to the teacher but is a construction of both the teacher and the other. As an aside, it is in this act of construction that one finds a place for what might be called a "master teacher educator."

The construction of the practical argument is a process of calling the teacher's attention to the different aspects of pedagogical actions and enlarging the teacher's awareness of choices available, choices made, and the grounds for these choices. Thus, the teacher's habits and dispositions are opened to scrutiny, primarily by the teacher himself or herself. The teacher's capacity for self-study, reflection, and revision of thought and action is thereby increased.

How might these considerations of manner and practical rationality be understood as an attribute of pedagogy in relation to manner? The answer to this question constitutes the conclusion of this chapter.

Method and Manner as Attributes of Pedagogy

Moral action, as should by now be clear, is grounded in both habituation and practical reasoning. By intruding, if you will permit so bold a term, into the practical reasoning of a person, we may alter the actions that are the consequence of habit and conditioning. Thus, it is in working with the teacher on the practical reasoning that accounts for the teacher's practice that it becomes possible to influence the moral conduct of the teacher qua teacher.

But there is more here than influencing the conduct of the teacher. Of equal interest is the other's treatment of the teacher in a way that exemplifies a moral engagement between them. The other calls on the teacher to take explanation and justification of action seriously and assists the teacher in constructing grounded descriptions of practice. As the teacher gains in understanding of and facility with this process, he or she gains in the capacity to treat students in the same way. He or she is thereby able to serve as the other for the students and in this way engage in a manner appropriate to tasks and functions of teaching while also displaying a manner that he or she calls on the students to imitate and test.

It is in this sense and in this way that method and manner are critical attributes of pedagogy. Neither offers much of educational significance without the other. Both working together provide the basis for the profound engagement of teachers and students in their own and their mutual educations. Method and manner provide the basis for teaching that is both effective and responsible. Through an understanding of their complementarity, it is possible to achieve a new sythesis in the way we think about and study teaching.

References

Audi, R. *Practical Reasoning.* London: Routledge & Kegan Paul, 1989.

Bernstein, R. J. *Beyond Objectivism and Relativism: Science, Hermeneutics, and Praxis.* Philadelphia: University of Pennsylvania Press, 1983.

Bronfenbrenner, U. *Two Worlds of Childhood: U.S. and U.S.S.R.* New York: Simon & Schuster, 1972.

Buchmann, M. "Impractical Philosophizing About Teachers' Practical Arguments." *Educational Theory,* 1987, *37,* 409–412.

Buchmann, M. "Practical Arguments Are No Account of Teacher Thinking: But Then, What Is?" In J. M. Giarelli (ed.), *Philosophy of Education, 1988.* Normal, Ill.: Philosophy of Education Society, 1989.

Confrey, J. "Bridging Research and Practice." *Educational Theory,* 1987, *37,* 383–394.

Dahl, N. O. *Practical Reason, Aristotle, and Weakness of the Will.* Minneapolis: University of Minnesota Press, 1984.

Fenstermacher, G. D. "Philosophy of Research on Teaching: Three Aspects." In M. C. Wittrock (ed.), *Handbook of Research on Teaching.* (3rd ed.) New York: Macmillan, 1986.

Fenstermacher, G. D. "Prologue and Reply to My Critics." *Educational Theory,* 1987, *37* (4), 357–360, 413–422.

Gray, D., and Lynn, D. H. *New Teachers, Better Teachers: A Report on Two Initiatives in New Jersey.* Washington, D.C.: Council for Basic Education, 1988.

Green, T. F. "Teacher Competence as Practical Rationality." *Educational Theory,* 1976, *26* (Summer), 249–258.

Habermas, J. *Knowledge and Human Interests.* (J. Shapiro, trans.) Boston: Beacon Press, 1971.

Habermas, J. *Communication and Evolution of Society.* (T. McCarthy, trans.) Boston: Beacon Press, 1979.

Hamilton, M. L. "The Effects of a Practical Argument Staff Development Process." Unpublished dissertation, University of Arizona, 1989.

Kilbourne, B. "The Nature of Data for Reflecting on Teaching Situations." *Educational Theory,* 1987, *37,* 377–382.

Morine-Dershimer, G. "Practical Examples of the Practical Argument." *Educational Theory,* 1987, *37,* 395–408.

Munby, H. "The Dubious Place of Practical Arguments and Scientific

Knowlege in the Thinking of Teachers." *Educational Theory,* 1987, *37,* 361–368.

Passmore, J. "On Teaching to Be Critical." In R. F. Dearden, P. H. Hirst, and R. S. Peters (eds.), *Education and the Development of Reason,* Part 3: *Education and Reason.* London: Routledge & Kegan Paul, 1975.

Pendlebury, S. "Practical Arguments and Situation Appreciation in Teaching." *Educational Theory,* 1990, *40* (2), 171–179.

Richardson, V. "Significant and Worthwhile Change in Teaching Practice." *Educational Researcher,* 1990, *19* (7), 10–18.

Richardson, V., and Anders, P. *Final Report on the Reading Instruction Study.* Tucson: College of Education, University of Arizona, 1990. (ED 324 655)

Richardson-Koehler, V., and Fenstermacher, G. D. "The Use of Practical Arguments in Staff Development." Paper presented at the annual meeting of the American Association of Colleges for Teacher Education, New Orleans, 1988. (ED 030 047)

Ross, W. D. *Aristotle.* Cleveland, Ohio: World, 1959. (Originally published 1923.)

Russell, T. "Research, Practical Knowledge, and the Conduct of Teacher Education." *Educational Theory,* 1987, *37,* 369–376.

Ryle, G. "Can Virtue be Taught?" In R. F. Dearden, P. H. Hirst, and R. S. Peters (eds.), *Of Education and the Development of Reason,* Part 3: *Education and Reason.* London: Routledge & Kegan Paul, 1975.

Scheffler, I. *Of Human Potential.* New York: Routledge & Kegan Paul, 1985.

Sherman, N. *The Fabric of Character: Aristotle's Theory of Virtue.* Oxford, England: Oxford University Press, 1989.

Sorabji, R. "Aristotle on the Role of Intellect in Virtue." In A. O. Rorty (ed.), *Essays on Aristotle's Ethics.* Berkeley: University of California Press, 1980.

Wiggins, D. "Deliberations and Practical Reason." In A. O. Rorty (ed.), *Essays on Aristotle's Ethics.* Berkeley: University of California Press, 1980.

8

Morality in Professional Action: A Discourse Approach for Teaching

Fritz K. Oser

Morality in professional action, or professional ethos, has become an important issue not only for its own sake but also because of its implications for the success of functional expertise. How can we understand the "ethos of the teacher"? How can we distinguish professional morality from the general claim that people should be "good"? The following example is illustrative.

As a part of the final selection phase for filling a new position in training student teachers in high school–level biology, the two final candidates had to present an hour-long biology lesson. The first candidate talked about segmentation of cells. He performed excellently, using clear structuring of the subject matter and showing high expertise in changing and combining instructional methods. The evaluators saw effective group work, a fine-tuned self-control system, and highly active students who were seeking information by performing an experiment, using textbook information, and generating their own results. As students displayed any insecurity, difficulty, or interactional incorrectness, the teacher immediately intervened and suppressed it. In fact, his whole attention was focused on suppressing students' personal reactions, making the didactic technique seem more important than the interactional free zone of school life.

The second candidate organized his lesson around an experiment using fish in an aquarium-type basin. The students' task was to stabilize the environmental conditions so that the animals would survive. They had to look for technical instructions and to develop explanations and justifications for their actions. Suddenly, one of the groups started teasing the fish,

Note: The research reported here was conducted with the help of a grant from the Swiss National Science Foundation. The author wishes to express his gratitude to Michael Zutavern, Jean-Luc Patry, Roland Reichenbach, Richard Klaghofer, Wolfgang Althof, and Heinz Rothbucher, members of the project team.

including taking them out of the water. Although the teacher tried to draw their attention back to the task, they continued to misbehave. The teacher reacted by interrupting the whole enterprise, thereby putting his lesson plan at risk. All the fish were put back into the aquarium, and the teacher created a roundtable situation in which he articulated his standpoint that such behavior threatens animals' life and well-being and is counter to the interest of the other groups in the classroom. He talked about the need to protect the fish and nature in general and asked the students to justify their actions. A heated discussion ensued. Some students said that they wanted to continue their work. Others reproached the malefactors for their disrespect for life. The group in question apologized and said that they had not meant to be insensitive; they had just wanted to have a little fun. The discussion lasted about fifteen minutes; finally, the teacher asked the class to accept the group's apology, but he also stressed the necessity of learning that in certain situations a joke can be misplaced because the dignity of a living being is at stake. Thereafter, the lesson continued very effectively, but the teacher failed to reach the goal that had been set by the election committee because he ran out of time.

After the lesson, the election committee began a heavy debate about which of the two lessons was better. Only a minority interpreted the instructional brilliance of the first candidate as decisive; the majority voted for hiring the second teacher because, in addition to his didactic know-how, he showed a commitment to helping students to be responsible for their actions. Thus, we can say that the second teacher's actions were interpreted as showing more "professional morality" or "ethos" than the first one's. In the long run, it was thought, the second teacher would do better in training student teachers because he would teach them how to integrate important insights and attitudes toward nature, life, and social issues into the process of daily teaching.

This example offers a prototype of a characteristic of professional morality: that responsibility either inhibits or nurtures efficiency. In the Kohlbergian framework (Kohlberg, 1971, 1984), moral issues arise when one moral value, such as life, stands against another value, such as property. In the professions, a moral value often stands against the direct success of the professional craft. Many teachers feel that if they care about social and pedagogical aims and about morality standards, they risk not fulfilling the expected curriculum content plan. Their model is one of separating responsibility from efficiency with the silent assumption that morality hinders success. We could say that they find themselves in a situation similar to that of salespeople whose success is measured in turnover numbers and is endangered if too much thought is given to whether they would buy their product themselves.

It is my hypothesis that the teacher who does not care about moral issues but concentrates only on didactic or content matters (sticks to the content as asked for by the formal curriculum, to methods only, or to other one-sided teaching skills) will be more successful in the short run and in curricular matters only than the teacher who also engages in a moral discourse, who will be more successful over a longer time and when curricular or didactic as well as sociomoral aims are used as criteria to evaluate success.

On an even broader level, I would like to advocate a normative demand: every professional, including teachers, has to consider and actively address within his or her technical, economical, or productivity-oriented activity aspects of dignity, care, and justice toward the human beings who are affected by his or her function and action as a moral duty. In this sense, the teacher in my example who was only — as we assume — didactically engaged will not be successful in the long run, whereas the morally engaged teacher will enhance the students' academic motivation as well as the societal relevance of his or her teaching, because the students will have learned to take responsibility for their actions.

The Moral Discourse Position in Professional Ethics

A recently developed approach, based primarily in Europe, attempts to resolve moral problems using the method of discourse ethics. This approach can be distinguished from Kantian ethics in the following ways: while Kantian ethics focuses on the individual's use of rationality to create a more complex and internally consistent form of moral reasoning, discourse ethics focuses on a group of individuals' use of a more inclusive procedure that allows each person to present and absorb moral points of view. In discourse ethics, moral decisions are made by use of a moral group-centered procedure (Apel, 1988). Habermas (1981) speaks about the process of legitimation of norm through an imagined "ideal speech community" (see also Oser, 1986). Further, while the focus of Kantian ethics is on whether the proposed maxim of a solution is in accordance with a generalizable law, discourse ethics is a procedural approach to morality in which *process* is at stake; the most appropriate procedure is one in which the "ideal speech community" is realized.

Such an ethical discourse can be implemented in the classroom. But the *real* discourse in the classroom does not satisfy the conditions of an ideal communication community; it is never idealistic, never with equal rights for all participants, never without fears, limits of capacity, and constraints of other kinds. One cannot assume that the participants are fully rational, unselfish, and so on. However, in contrast to Apel's (1988) discourse ethics, the task in discourse morality is not to justify universal norms but to resolve specific conflicts, which is possible under certain conditions. In discourse morality, people discover moral norms by using and legitimizing them instead of justifying them (Döbert, 1986).

How can this discourse method be fostered? There are four fundamental conditions that should be met. First, the professional (the teacher) must create a "roundtable" situation in which all concerned people are invited to participate. The roundtable can be, for example, a group meeting, a classroom setting, or a school assembly. Sometimes there are many difficulties in engaging people in this interactional setting: the demands of the curriculum,

the tendency to avoid extra efforts, organizational impediments, a preference not to intervene in conflicts. It is the ethical duty of the teacher to overcome such difficulties and to work to create the roundtable. (We assume
here that no students misuse the roundtable just to detract the teacher from
his or her work and that the teacher knows when the roundtable is really
important.)

Second, the presentation of statements regarding needs, justifications,
blame, proposed solutions, and so on must be coordinated so that all participants listen to each other and commonly search for the best solutions. The
teacher has two roles: to function as chair of the discussion and to be an
engaged participant with an important message to share and interests to defend. Evidently, children and adolescents have to learn to be a serious-minded
part of this procedure. Every argument should be allowed to be presented;
the criterion for the final decision making should be the rationality of the
best argument. The main goal here is for all the participants to listen to
each other and to fully consider the arguments for and against a proposed
solution.

Third, the teacher must strongly believe and expect that every person involved in the roundtable is able to take responsibility, to search for
truth, to decide freely, and to consider (and balance) aspects of truthfulness, care, and justice. These are the three main moral principles encountered in professional ethical dilemmas. Especially children and adolescents
who have been stigmatized as lazy, slow to learn, impudent, or disadvantaged must have the feeling that they are taken seriously and that they are
expected to play an important role. The belief in the students' abilities and
demonstrated confidence in them are important pedagogical elements of this
method.

Fourth, the teacher must strongly believe that if the first three conditions are met, the outcome will always be moral and in the best interest of all.

But what if the solution arrived at is not the "best"? Procedural morality
assumes that the moral judgment of individuals cannot be imposed by external forces but has to be constructed by individuals themselves, in a process
of mutual help with a balance between autonomy and control. We have to
accept that this must be learned and that it takes time. But there is no reason to wait until some imaginary point of self-generated maturity arrives
before children are included in the process of problem solving. Instead, by
creating the conditions proposed here, the reasoning behind them will gradually become self-evident. At the same time, caring and responsible behavior
will become more deeply rooted and genuine. It is through the communicative process, the real-life decision-making experience, that we learn not only
good solutions but the process for arriving at them.

In an educational setting, discourse morality requires a framework
within which every child is protected, taken seriously, and given appropriate responsibility for what is going on — and that means the opportunity to
care about others, to participate, to justify a viewpoint, to consider other

viewpoints, and to be responsible for following through on decisions. (This combination of protection and inclusion is like letting a young child freely explore but putting a barrier in front of the stairway so that the child cannot fall.) It is only by practicing a strong commitment to mutual respect that children are able to learn it.

There is another advantage of this method, even if it does not result in the "best" solution. When the discussion has addressed all the possible consequences of a proposed course of action and when the common intentions have taken into account criteria of responsibility, care, and justice, a fundamental moral consensus can emerge. Even when there is some dissent, the agreed-upon course of action is better than a solution that has been achieved simply by way of persuasion or indoctrination. While the solution may represent only minimal consensus, the moral quality of the solution must be maximal.

Pedagogical discourse requires a great deal of energy from teachers, because they must constantly be investing trust in advance and must make no distinctions among children, even when (or perhaps especially when) a student is in some sort of crisis, is having learning difficulties, or seriously argues against the teacher's position. Children and adolescents are able to take responsibility, to participate in thinking, deciding, and acting—we just have to expect them to do so without communicating the message that they are left alone with all this responsibility. We know from the whole body of research on the Pygmalion effect (Brophy and Good, 1974) that expectation is a power that can be used positively or negatively. If the four elements mentioned above (creating a roundtable situation, giving all participants the opportunity to validate their claims, presupposing that every participant is rational, and having faith that this procedure will result in the morally best solution) are taught to teachers and student teachers as a primary and very important goal of their action as teachers, we can actualize and enhance the social and cognitive potential of each child. And in the long run, this will lead to greater didactic effectiveness.

Triple Disequilibrium: The Balance Between Success and Morality

In the example given at the beginning of this chapter, a concrete method was used to solve a professional ethical problem. Let us look at another area where ethos can play an important role: pedagogical grading, a particularly sensitive domain. In our research on teachers' ethos, we have used the following dilemma to stimulate reflection and discussion on this topic:

> Mrs. G. is teaching mathematics in a fourth-grade class. Twice a year, rather than giving grades on the basis of a score or the average performance of the class, as is usual, she assesses individual increases in achievement as compared to the students'

previous tests. She has explained and justified this form of grading to students and parents. The parents were not enthusiastic about the idea, but they did not object. Now she is making use of this procedure for the third time. Peter, who ordinarily is poor in math, attains quite a good grade because he made fewer mistakes in this test than he has in the previous weeks. Of course, Peter is very pleased, and he tells his classmate Jim about it. However, Jim cannot share Peter's happiness. He is one of the best in math. As always, his performance on the test has been much better than Peter's, but this time, they both got the same grade. Jim perceives this as an injustice, and he complains angrily to his parents and his teacher, Mrs. G. Other students join in these complaints. The next day, a father calls the teacher and insists that Mrs. G. renounce her unconventional style of grading.

In this situation, as in the example presented earlier, there are three types of disequilibrium to overcome (see Figure 8.1). The first type is between conflicting aims: in the case of Mrs. G., between continuing the grading system for the sake of the students and abandoning it to satisfy the demands of some students and their parents; in the earlier example, between attempting to make a good impression on the selection committee by giving a "perfect lesson" and interrupting the lesson to create a roundtable to discuss the issue of protecting life, which might fail to meet the evaluation criteria of the committee.

When a teacher recognizes his or her responsibility and acknowledges it as a necessary dimension of the situation, a second type of disequilibrium will follow that requires finding a balance among the three moral dimensions of justice, care, and truthfulness. It is a major characteristic of situations of moral conflict that we cannot be just, caring, and truthful at the same time toward all the people involved. In the case of Mrs. G., justice toward other students (and toward their claim to be treated equally) would inhibit care for weak learners, and vice versa. To openly accept conflicts with certain parents (truthfulness) may not be in the interest of a good and caring classroom atmosphere (see Chapter Twenty-Four for a discussion of the caring classroom). In the candidate selection case, being just toward the students who worked well by continuing the lesson may have meant being insufficiently caring toward the fish and untruthful toward the students who misbehaved.

The third disequilibrium concerns commitment: it is the disequilibrium between the teacher's preference as to whether to implement a solution and his or her other interests. For example, when the teaching candidate interrupted the lesson for the unplanned roundtable discussion, he jeopardized his chances to be hired. Similarly, in the pedagogical grading situation, it might be quite costly for Mrs. G. to openly accept conflicts with certain parents.

In our empirical research with dilemmas such as these, my colleagues

Figure 8.1. Elements of Moral Discourse.

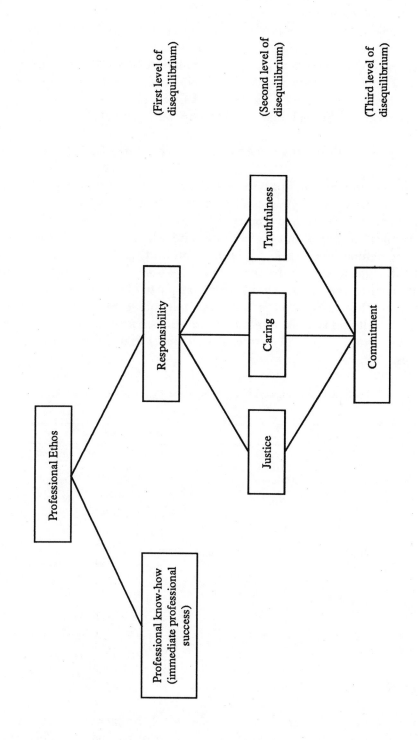

(First level of disequilibrium)

(Second level of disequilibrium)

(Third level of disequilibrium)

and I have found that at least two of these three moral dimensions are always involved in professional decision-making situations where there are ethical issues that cannot be solved to everyone's satisfaction. Adopting discursive problem-solving procedures necessarily requires facing this specific type of conflict, and facing it with a deliberately developed balance among these dimensions. However, as I will show later, the core notion of discourse morality is that not only the teacher but everyone involved in a problem must produce this balance in a coordinated way.

Types of Equilibrium Among Justice, Care, and Truthfulness

Central to the theory of professional discourse morality that I am attempting to outline here is the hypothesis of qualitatively different forms of coordination for claims of care, justice, and truthfulness in interpersonal decision-making or conflict-solving situations (see Oser and others, 1991). My colleagues and I have defined five types of coordination and ranked them hierarchically. At the highest level is the "complete discourse." The roundtable situation described above, in which all members participate, is an example of this level. At the lowest level is "avoiding"; at this level, responsibility is only vaguely felt and not taken into consideration as something that urgently requires action. Table 8.1 defines the elements that distinguish the different types.

Table 8.1. Discourse Elements in Five Types of Decision Making.

Levels of Discourse	Characteristics				
	Participation in Decision Making	Presupposition of Reasoning Competence	Implementation of a Solution	Commitment to a Solution	Awareness of Necessary Responsibility
1. Avoiding	No	No	No	No	Yes
2. Security seeking	No	No	No	Yes	Yes
3. Single-handed decision making	No	No	Yes	Yes	Yes
4. Incomplete discourse (discourse 1)	No	Yes	Yes	Yes	Yes
5. Complete discourse (discourse 2)	Yes	Yes	Yes	Yes	Yes

Avoiding

In this type of discourse, at the lowest level, a teacher tries to avoid considering action necessary for the resolution of a problem. The reason for this may be a feeling of incompetence or helplessness or fear of being blamed or wasting time. Conflicting responsibilities are often offered as an argument: "Subject matters are so important, I can't always interrupt the lesson when there's trouble with some students." In terms of professional criteria, I assume that the main reason for consistent avoiding is that the avoider does not believe that children are able to take responsibility or that they are moral personalities.

Delegating or Security Seeking

At the second level, the teacher sees and accepts responsibility to act in a given situation and implicitly believes that an equilibrium among care, justice, and truthfulness must be found but tends to shift responsibility for making the final decision to some authority (the principal, the school psychologist, the school board). People who delegate often have a fear of failing and a feeling that they lack experience and competence. But I believe that in most such cases, the fear of losing control plays a dominant role: there are so many problems with discipline and organizing good interactions that have to be taken into account. In other cases, teachers seem to play a power game, attempting to strengthen their own position and indirectly to pursue their own interests by reference to an authority person or to the hierarchical structure. We also find a kind of mixture between the belief that a teacher has to teach but not solve interpersonal problems and the conviction that specialists and authorities outside the classroom exist for the purpose of dealing with tricky decisions.

Single-Handed or Unilateral Decision Making

This type of problem-solving strategy includes not only a commitment to finding a solution but also an attempt to justify the chosen solution. Single-handed decision making means taking the matter firmly in one's own hands, proceeding without ceremony, putting into practice all the strategies that one is equipped with and that one intuitively feels are justified. This type of decision maker, whether more contemptuous or more respectful of others, regulates things as quickly, efficiently, and unobtrusively as possible in order to return to the "real thing" — the subject matter. Such decision makers believe that intuitive decisions do not require justification. Reasons for preferring this type of strategy are the wish to minimize disturbances in the classroom; the assumption that rules exist to be followed; the fear of professional failure; and, finally, a sort of "king syndrome": the belief in the necessity of leadership and the conviction that a teacher is supposed to lead.

Incomplete Discourse (Discourse 1)

Those who engage in this level of discourse are characterized by a willingness to consider the viewpoints of the various people concerned in a particular problem situation and an acceptance of these people as rational beings. Discourse 1 problem solving or decision making includes listening to others and taking their knowledge, interests, and viewpoints into consideration. It is presupposed that others are essentially truthful and that they try to be just and cooperative. But the actual decision remains the teacher's responsibility (which is why people who often use this strategy sometimes become martyrs). Reasons for discourse 1 decision makers acting as they do are that they believe in their professional expertise and in the fundamental responsibility connected with their function; they believe that, while you can expect a lot from children, children still are children, and it is necessary to take responsibility for them; and they believe that being a teacher means being a part of the helping professions, whose obligation to the welfare of the society is primarily expressed in being responsible for other people.

Complete Discourse (Discourse 2)

This highest level of discourse is a form of equilibrium among care, justice, and truthfulness in which the teacher not only presupposes goodwill, rationality, and autonomy of all people concerned but additionally focuses on real participation. Teachers who engage in this level of discourse know that the procedure of seeking the morally best solution is more important than the immediate result and consistently employ the four conditions necessary: creation of a roundtable situation; initiation of a common search for the best solution; the presupposition that every participant is able and willing to collaborate; and the belief that this is the most morally adequate approach. They view problem solving as a common endeavor, in which different points of view have to be accepted and one should be open to any decision as long as every participant — including the teacher — can feel fully accepted as a person and as the proponent of a point of view. These teachers are more than observers and more than instructors or trainers. With highly inner- and outward-directed activity and sensitivity, they watch over the right *process*, rather than concentrating on achieving the right result. They believe fundamentally that not only themselves but all concerned are able to create an equilibrium among justice, care, and truthfulness as everyone participating in the roundtable cooperates and works toward a common decision. (One of the institutionalized forms of the discourse 2 model is the "just community" of Kohlberg [Power, Higgins, and Kohlberg, 1989; Oser and Althof, 1992], in which all students and teachers solve relevant problems by participating in community meetings and by creating new rules for dealing with old conflicts.)

These five decision types are forms of qualitatively different reconstructions of the moral dimensions of real-life professional situations. We have found that statistically there is a strong interaction between persons and situations such that some teachers decide discursively in some situations and single-handedly in others; other teachers may consistently prefer one particular type of decision making. It is also clear that, for example, not all problems in school life require the same type of discourse solutions. If, for instance, students are teasing the teacher, it may be perfectly all right to ignore this; that is, to "avoid" (level 1) further occupation with the incident. In other cases, it might be a grave failure not to call in a specialist (level 2) to settle a conflict or to help with a severe problem. However, whenever someone's human dignity is at stake (when a student insults another, when a teacher behaves autocratically and disrespectfully, when a teacher uses methods and instructional steps that students cannot follow, or simply when a person feels that he or she is being treated in an uncaring or unjust way), the complete moral discourse (level 5) is the best way to solve the conflict and to practice and teach professional morality. In a roundtable situation, such as in the sample teaching example, more will be learned than can be taught otherwise about procedural justice.

Alternative Models and Consequences for Teacher Education

With the moral decision-making frame outlined above, we are able to see new perspectives for training future expert teachers. The ethos (professional morality) of this profession is no longer seen as a collection of personality traits, a directly measurable variable, a set of virtues, or a knowledge base of ethics that can be directly taught or transmitted. Rather, it is a capacity to stimulate moral discourse about professional actions. Discursive professional morality is a process-oriented interactive practice with clear procedural rules and clearly defined situational conditions. It is a strategy that can be learned, but it is not unconditional: it presupposes that teachers change their conceptions of authority in order to create the conditions of a moral discourse (participation, presupposition of rationality, and search for a morally informed decision) when necessary.

In most books on teacher education, we find lists of virtues that teachers should learn or adopt. Fritz Schneider (1966, p. 50), for example, describes the perfect teacher in a page-long list of attributes, including that a teacher should "have an ethical character; be religious, just, lenient, loving, and cheerful; be gifted with a high intelligence, a reliable, extensive, and quick memory, a rich imagination, a deep sentiment, and the ability to suppress any involuntary expression of unpedagogical emotions; be of high activity and initiative; have a quick psychic tempo combined with inner tranquillity." Such lists of duties or virtues tend to mix up intellectual, professional, social, and moral virtues. What is important for the discussion here, however, is that they imply that it is possible to transmit duties, competencies, and characteristics and thus to teach professional norms and virtues. This approach, which suggests indoctrination, has been called the "value transmission model" and has been strongly criticized for being antidemocratic (see Kohlberg, 1981, pp. 6–28). Putting such an approach into practice would probably result in some superficial changes but would not succeed in changing a teacher's basic attitudes or the deep structure of his or her personality. In fact, young teachers today would feel suffocated and blackmailed by such a demand. Examples of more modern forms of the same approach (calling for new kinds of virtues) are character education in the United States (see, for example, Holmes, 1980) and value socialization in Europe (see, for example, Brezinka, 1978). Such norms as presented in the virtue approach have only a general guiding character and can never be operationalized.

Two approaches in values education that have attempted to provide an alternative to the value transmission model are the moral judgment stimulation method of Kohlberg (1981, 1984), which aims at helping teachers to reach a higher developmental stage, and the personality approach, which is designed to stimulate a strong moral character (see, for example, Levis, 1987). These methods, however, do not deal specifically with professional ethics; rather, they postulate a general sense of human responsibility.

The discourse approach contrasts with all of the three approaches mentioned above. It holds that professional morality is learned only if the professional (in our case, the teacher) learns to face and reconstruct the moral issues in specific professional action and decision-making situations. It is noteworthy that in the United States, there is no such concept as procedural morality or discourse approach in the field of teacher training. For example, the book entitled *The Moral Dimensions of Teaching* (Goodlad, Soder, and Sirotnik, 1990) discusses the moral sensitivity that teachers should have toward many structural factors in schools and toward critical situations that each teacher has to face ("If I give Michael a D in biology, he will not have the grades he needs for a driver's license — and his family badly needs the part-time job that a car will enable him to take"; p. 24). It addresses the moral consequences of teaching decisions and the moral model of the teacher (see also Chapter Seven in this book), and it offers a useful examination of how an active engagement with the materials and symbols of a society leads to an identification of the conditions that inhibit children from developing the skills that they need to participate fully in societal life (Feinberg, 1990, pp. 155–187). It shows how issues such as indoctrination, grading and evaluation, teachers' autonomy, and hidden values in the curriculum are all moral issues. We also find excellent examples in which the process of finding ethical solutions to teaching problems is developed and illuminated (Clark, 1990). But in the end, none of the major concepts in this book deals with something tangible or concretely comprehensible; it offers merely analyses of possibilities or normative suggestions. What is missing is a *procedural* concept that can be taught and learned.

The moral discourse concept is not only realizable; it is also operationalizable in the sense of the constructivist tradition. It can show how children and teachers deal together with ethical issues, how these issues become a complementary part of the didactic side of teaching, and how the procedural conditions can be learned through role taking, comprehension, and practice.

Here is the place to question again whether the discourse model has an influence on effectiveness. The more the four conditions of discourse 2 are introduced into settings in which effectiveness and responsibility are at stake, the more the participants will feel involved in the result (causal attribution). However, the time or efficiency sacrificed in the beginning of such a process is easily offset in the long run because any result achieved through balancing mutual care, justice, and truthfulness, even if difficult, is better. "Better" is when nonstrategic thinking, which takes the broader context into account, is allowed to guide strategic thinking, which is limited by focusing only on goals or success; when discourse is more important than gains; and when creating a roundtable is more valued than winning. In the "just community" schools, for example, the students eventually came to speak of "our" school and "our" decisions and of their responsibility for each other. These are precisely the variables most neglected in most effectiveness studies (see, for example, Coleman and others, 1966; Rutter, Maughan, Mortimer, and Ouston, 1979; Creemers and Scheerens, 1989), variables that go beyond organizational reforms and suggest member satisfaction and member cohesion.

A Research Program and Its Results

In our empirical research (Oser and others, 1991), we have tried to analyze critical aspects of the ethos construct. We wanted to find out in depth what really characterizes teachers' ethos and to be able to stimulate a long-term change in teachers' professional ethics toward a more discursive attitude. In addition, we wanted to show how much the discourse approach can really be practiced and how much influence it has on children's learning, on the school climate, and on the responsibility and moral commitment of the teacher.

In our first studies of how teachers felt that "ethos" came into play in their daily work, we assessed teachers' subjective theories with respect to the concept of professional ethos by a sentence completion test ("A teacher has a high ethos if he or she . . . ") with 192 teachers from all school types. Content analysis of the 210 answers (several answers had to be coded twice) showed that about 45 percent of the teachers chose care as the most important issue, about 17 percent truthfulness, and 15 percent general engagement or commitment; 7 percent relied on ethical codes, and 5 percent believed that every ethical problem can be solved with didactic knowledge. In only 6 answers was justice mentioned as an important value. Obviously, many teachers feel that care is the most important issue in their profession; in real situations, however, justice is much more often cited in defending selection processes and grading.

We also asked the teachers to elaborate solutions for certain situations that demand a discourse position and to judge a series of "should" statements, such as: "A teacher should integrate all students into the class community" or "A teacher should teach the students all necessary knowledge and skills."

Norms such as integration of students, discipline and order, participation, ability to admit mistakes, and caring for students outside the school were included. Each item was rated twice: on the degree to which the teachers thought that the norm was justified and on the degree to which they thought that they actually lived up to it in their classroom behavior. In most cases, differences beween normative conviction and everyday behavior became apparent. Obviously, teachers sense the tension between ideals and reality themselves. An interesting exception is participation, a variable that defines a crucial element of the discourse 2 perspective. Most teachers opposed the idea that students should participate in classroom decision making and, consequently, said that they did not practice participation. Learning to participate—that is, to take individual responsibility—seems not to be seen by teachers as a requirement for human autonomy (at least not in the classroom context). We saw the same tendency when we used a questionnaire on ethos orientations (based on the five types of morality described above). In this case, the teachers often preferred items representing discourse 1 or 2 orientations but in their normal practice chose nondiscursive ways of problem solving.

A second series of studies dealt with measurement problems. Here, we used a semiclinical interview format, posing various dilemmas from the professional life of a teacher. Elements such as the subject's dominant action tendency, normative orientation, strategy of justification, and proposed solutions to the conflict were considered. Most importantly, we tried to grasp subjects' conceptions of an adequate decision-making process (whether other people are involved, whether they participate in the decision making, who is to take responsibility for the final decision, and so on). Furthermore, we considered subjects' statements in terms of the probability of actual conflict occurrence and the likelihood of the proposed conflict solution in real school life. In these studies, the development of a fine-tuned scoring format was a major task. The overall format of the scoring sheet was based on the ethos elements summarized in Table 8.1. This instrument yielded a high interrater reliability (.85). On the basis of the first phase of qualitative analyses and experiences with the types of professional morality that we had constructed, we formulated an ethos questionnaire for the purpose of broader assessments.

A third topic of our research was changing teachers' conception of ethos. In an intervention study with eighty-four teachers from different school levels, we tried to develop a discourse position during a ten-week course (three hours per week) through confronting the participants with dilemma situations, role playing, case analyses and analyses of personal experiences, and application of the discourse model in real situations. In a quasi-experimental design (see Oser and others, 1991, for details), one group dealt exclusively with ethos issues, one with only didactic matters, and a third with combined ethos and didactics (mixed group). A fourth group was a delayed-treatment control group.

Results showed that over the course of time, the cognitive conception of the teachers in the ethos group changed remarkably, while the mixed group showed a general decrease in nondiscursive behaviors but no increase in discursive behaviors. In a follow-up assessment about one year later, the effects had diminished. We believe that this is due to the fact that the intervention took place not in the classroom with students but in a training setting. Thus, there was less transfer from the training situation to the classroom as we had expected.

In a further group of studies, we investigated the relationship between students' perception of the teacher's personality and the teacher's discourse attitude. Discourse-oriented teachers were rated more highly than other teachers on variables such as truthfulness, commitment, interpersonal respect, justice, and didactic competence, and students felt better in their classrooms. The higher rating on didactic competence is particularly interesting because it is consistent with our hypothesis that a good, discourse-oriented ethos is positively related to a teacher's technical and organizational competence. Further, we found that students prefer either teachers with a discursive orientation or those who tend to avoid decisions. We can only interpret this as the tendency to be consistent: a teacher either is committed, has a discursive ethos, or is not engaged at all. In both cases, students feel autonomous: in the first case with the explicit support of the teacher, in the latter case because the teacher does not take charge of the situation at all.

Finally, the discourse approach was compared to the moral development approach of Kohlberg (1981, 1984). It seems that the horizontal discourse approach (in the sense of viewing development within a certain stage) is a different measure from the vertical moral development measure (in the hierarchical sense of the Kohlbergian stages). Correlations between discourse orientation (by questionnaire) and stage of moral judgment were $R = .15$ ($n = 38$). It must be mentioned, however, that the eight teachers who showed a high discursive orientation in the questionnaire and a low stage of moral judgment had a low discursive orientation in the interviews. It might well be that these teachers responded to the questionnaire according to social desirability — discursively — without really being convinced of the desirability of the approach. Further research is necessary in this regard.

Conclusion: The Relationship
Between Effectiveness and Responsibility

As noted above, our research found that students rate discourse-oriented teachers significantly more highly than other teachers in didactic competence. This leads us back to the question of effectiveness and responsibility. Students feel that discourse 2 teachers are not only committed, truthful, respectful, and just but also well prepared, technically serious, and scientifically solid. It is this interaction between the two variables, didactic and discourse techniques, that makes our question so important. It seems that only the interaction of the two makes learning fruitful in the long run. Cool didactics leads to demotivation; discourse alone has no significance in respect to academic standards. But both together influence each other toward high performance, high motivation, and a high self-attributed learning outcome. While we agree that our research findings only partly validate this hypothesis, it shows that it is possible to learn the roundtable model and to influence students' judgment about teachers' didactic capacity through discourse and that the general classroom climate of discourse 2 teachers is better than that of nondiscursive teachers.

Thus, to be a discursive teacher means to take serious procedural responsibility for the learning path of children. It is an expertise that should be acquired during student teaching. Instead of basing actions only on perceived instructional strengths, on teaching and problem-solving competence, teachers should rely on the "practical" (ethical) reasoning of the students and of all people involved in a particular problem.

The tensions and dilemmas in the interactive school class are the best "material," the best situations in which to practice discourse 2. A teacher needs to know and appreciate what embarrasses children, what makes them feel neglected or unimportant, and so on. Procedural morality differs from the normative or structural approach in that it is not the result that is important but the process, which is repeated over and over again. Discourse 2 means fostering the voice of the child in order to produce a morally and socially better condition for learning. I believe that school life has an influence on life in general. And life means to create, step by step and in cooperation with other humans, a worthy existence. Effectiveness from this point of view is always moral.

References

Apel, K.-O. *Diskurs und Verantwortung: Das Problem des Übergangs zur postkonventionellen Moral* [Discourse and responsibility: the problem of transition to postconventional morality]. Frankfurt, Germany: Suhrkamp, 1988.

Brezinka, W. *Metatheorie der Erziehung: Eine Einführung in die Grundlagen der Erziehungswissenschaft, der Philosophie der Erziehung und der Praktischen Pädagogik* [Metatheory of education: an introduction to the science of education, the philosophy of education, and practical pedagogy]. Munich, Germany: Reinhardt, 1978.

Brophy, J. E., and Good, T. L. *Teacher-Student Relationships: Causes and Consequences.* New York: Holt, Rinehart & Winston, 1974.

Clark, C. M. "The Teacher and the Taught: Moral Transactions in the Classroom." In J. I. Goodlad, R. Soder, and K. A. Sirotnik (eds.), *The Moral Dimensions of Teaching.* San Francisco: Jossey-Bass, 1990.

Coleman, J. S., and others. *Equality of Educational Opportunity.* Washington, D.C.: U.S. Government Printing Office, 1966.

Creemers, B.P.M., and Scheerens, J. "Conceptualizing School Effectiveness." *International Journal of Educational Research,* 1989, *13* (7), 691–706.

Döbert, R. "Wider die Vernachlässigung des Inhalts in den Moraltheorien von Kohlberg und Habermas, Implikationen für die Relativismus/Universalismus-Kontroverse" [Against the neglect of content in the moral theories of Kohlberg and Habermas: implications for the relativity and universality controversy]. In W. Edelstein and G. Nunner-Winkler (eds.), *Zur Bestimmung der Moral* [Determining morality]. Frankfurt, Germany: Suhrkamp, 1986.

Feinberg, W. "The Moral Responsibility of Public Schools." In J. I. Goodlad, R. Soder, and K. A. Sirotnik (eds.), *The Moral Dimensions of Teaching.* San Francisco: Jossey-Bass, 1990.

Goodlad, J. I., Soder, R., and Sirotnik, K. A. (eds.). *The Moral Dimensions of Teaching.* San Francisco: Jossey-Bass, 1990.

Habermas, J. *Theorie des kommunikativen Handelns.* Bd. 1: *Handlungsrationalität und gesellschaftliche Rationalisierung.* Bd. 2: *Zur Kritik der funktionalistischen Vernunft* [The theory of communicative action. Vol. 1: Reason and the rationalization of society; Vol. 2: Lifeworld and system: a critique of functionalist reason]. Frankfurt, Germany: Suhrkamp, 1981.

Holmes, M. "Forward to the Basics: A Radical Conservative Reconstruction." *Curriculum Inquiry,* 1980, *10* (4), 383–418.

Kohlberg, L. "From Is to Ought: How to Commit the Naturalistic Fallacy and Get Away with It in the Study of Moral Development." In T. Mischel (ed.), *Cognitive Development and Epistemology.* San Diego, Calif.: Academic Press, 1971.

Kohlberg, L. *Essays on Moral Development.* Vol. 1: *The Philosophy of Moral Development. Moral Stages and the Idea of Justice.* New York: HarperCollins, 1981.

Kohlberg, L. *Essays on Moral Development.* Vol. 2: *The Psychology of Moral Development. The Nature and Validity of Moral Stages.* New York: HarperCollins, 1984.

Levis, D. S. "Teacher's Personality." In M. J. Dunkin (ed.), *The International Encyclopedia of Teaching and Teacher Education.* New York: Pergamon Press, 1987.

Oser, F. K. "Moral Education and Values Education: The Discourse Perspective." In M. C. Wittrock (ed.), *Handbook of Research on Teaching.* (3rd ed.) New York: Macmillan, 1986.

Oser, F., and others. *Der Prozess der Verantwortung: Berufsethische Entscheidungen von Lehrerinnen und Lehrern* [The process of responsibility: Ethical decisions of professional teachers]. Research project reports 1.188–0.85 and 11.25470.88/2 of the Swiss National Foundation. Fribourg, Switzerland: Pedagogical Institute of the University, 1991.

Oser, F., and Althof, W. *Moralische Selbstbestimmung: Modelle der Entwicklung und Erziehung im Wertebereich* [Moral self-determination: Models of development and education in the domain of values]. Stuttgart, Germany: Klett-Cotta, 1992.

Power, F. C., Higgins, A., and Kohlberg, L. *Lawrence Kohlberg's Approach to Moral Education.* New York: Columbia University Press, 1989.

Rutter, M., Maughan, B., Mortimer, P., and Ouston, J. *Fifteen Thousand Hours: Secondary Schools and Their Effects on Children.* London: Open Books, 1979.

Schneider, F. "Quotation." In *Methodik des Volksschulunterrichts* [Teaching methodology for elementary school]. Hochdorf, Switzerland: Martinusverlag, 1966.

9

Beyond Intrinsic Motivation: Cultivating a "Sense of the Desirable"

Mordecai Nisan

Imagine three students working hard on a history project. One finds the material intriguing and aspires to master it. Another has no particular interest in the material yet is motivated by the short- and long-term utility of receiving a high grade. The third student works on the project with the understanding that history is a valuable subject and that knowledge of history plays a significant role in one's personal development. This student is not intrigued by the subject matter, nor is he worried about grades; he feels that he should do a good job in order to better himself.

Of the three students, who is preferable: the first student, whose actions are intrinsically motivated; the second, who is extrinsically motivated; or the third, who is guided by motivation based on what is desirable, or what ought to be done? In other words, which type of motivation should be fostered in the school? Research in academic motivation over the past twenty years has focused on the first two types of students. Such research, much like prevailing educational thought, would suggest that the first student is preferable to the second. One reason for this, emphasized by several researchers (for example, Maehr, 1976), is the stability and consistency of the motivation—when learning is not evaluated and rewarded, the intrinsically motivated student will continue studying, while the one driven by extrinsic motivation will not. Intrinsic motivation is also likely to be considered preferable to motivation based on "what ought to be done." This is in accord with a central message underlying the psychology of academic motivation (and espoused by many educators years ago): study is best when based

Note: Research described in this chapter was supported by a grant from the United States–Israel Binational Science Foundation, Jerusalem. The author would like to thank Elliot Eisner and Ruth Butler for their helpful comments on an earlier version of this chapter and Helene Hogri and Mimi Schneiderman for their editorial assistance.

126

on genuinely free choice, when motivated by immediate interest in what one is doing, whether this is stimulated by features, such as incongruities, that arouse intrigue or by the challenge invoked by the task and an orientation toward mastering it.

It is my contention that the attempt to base scholastic motivation on intrinsic motivation in this sense is doomed to failure from the outset, as the curriculum of the educational system is based on other motivational elements. Rather, it is motivation based on a "sense of the desirable" that is consistent with the considerations guiding the school curriculum.

Value-Oriented Curricula

The primary objective of schooling is instilling knowledge, skills, and values that can ensure the child's development as a complete human being in his or her society and culture. Ostensibly, these goals are consistent with an instrumental theory of motivation, such as that proposed in the value-expectancy model (Weiner, 1980). They may be interpreted as directed toward enhancing students' ability to maximize their satisfaction (or utility). However, closer examination reveals a qualification that renders this claim inadequate.

Schooling does not aim toward satisfaction of what is desired but rather toward what is *desirable,* as constructed by the culture. The school curriculum is not directed, as one might mistakenly believe, at preparing the individual to obtain maximal satisfaction of his or her wishes. Rather, it is directed at designing a system of values — that is, at cultivating certain values rather than others and preparing the individual to behave accordingly.

Frankfurt's (1971) distinction between first- and second-order motivation suggests a conception of motivation that would seem to fit the above-mentioned goals of schooling. First-order motivation refers to the needs that the individual feels an urge or desire to satisfy. These can be primary, stemming from a physiological drive, or secondary, substantially conditioned by personal and cultural experience. Second-order motivation, on the other hand, is related to the individual's cognition and evaluation of desirable behavior. According to this conception, individuals judge their personal needs and desires in terms of "objective" criteria and, where these needs appear undesirable, attempt to suppress or change them. Similarly, individuals perceive certain goals as desirable and proper and therefore worth pursuing regardless (or in spite) of existing needs and preferences. First-order motivations thus provide a basis for what are commonly called considerations of utility, while second-order motivations are related to consideration of what is worthy and proper. Frankfurt points out how essential the latter type of motivation is for human beings. It is second-order motivation that distinguishes a human being from what he calls a "wanton." One cannot speak of autonomy without second-order motivation, without a "sense of the desirable," which is the product of reflection.

Frankfurt's analysis sheds light on a concept whose definition in motivational psychology is vague—the concept of "value" in a restricted sense (as distinguished from its broader usages, as in the value-expectancy model). Among the diverse definitions of the concept in the psychological literature (see, for example, Rokeach, 1973; Schwartz and Bilsky, 1987), a common thread is evident: value denotes a belief that an end state or behavior is desirable, as distinct from being desired. It is based on the image of a state of human perfection that is worth aspiring toward. Whether emerging directly from experience with reality or from cultural perceptions, value (in its restricted sense), like the "sense of the desirable," is perceived as having intrinsic validity—that is, as not being contingent on personal inclination or social convention. In this sense, values stand in opposition to needs. Values rely on reflection and consideration, while needs rely on existing desires. While reflection and consideration can lead the individual to attribute a positive value to an existing need, they can also lead him or her to ascribe to it a negative value and to make an attempt to repress it.

Hence, from a motivational perspective, the school curriculum is directed by values. The reasons for including subject matter in the curriculum are value-related. Indeed, the educator or curriculum designer is likely to explain the inclusion of a given subject in terms of its desirability. Accordingly, the school curriculum can be said to be directed toward the formation and development of values and teaching ways of realizing them. Moreover, above and beyond specific curricular goals, the educator aims to develop individuals who act on the basis of values—that is, of the desirable—rather than of desires.

The Limitations of Intrinsic Motivation in the School

The discussion above brings to light the problems inherent in motivational reliance on reward and punishment, as well as on intrinsic motivation. Both relate to first-order motivations, and neither is inherent in curricular objectives. Rather, they are used as means to increase the chances that students will engage in studies based on "values." One cannot expect these sources of motivation always to accord with the material taught in school.

Studies on the effect of external rewards have pointed to such an inconsistency on both cognitive and motivational levels. Extrinsic rewards have been found to confine learning and performance, emphasizing structured and measurable aspects of a task and hindering divergent thinking and creativity (Butler and Nisan, 1986; Kruglanski, Friedman, and Zeevi, 1971; Nisan, 1981). Moreover, they have been shown to suppress intrinsic motivation and a willingness to study spontaneously and to generate defensiveness and anxiety (Deci, 1975; Lepper and Greene, 1979).

Analogously, intrinsic motivation has limitations on the same two levels. A preliminary problem is that not all subject matters can arouse intrinsic motivation. Part—in fact, a large part—of the curriculum, though considered desirable by its designers, may not have the features appropriate for generating intrinsic motivation in most students. Whether educators continue to work on the present curriculum and try to "inject" it with intrinsic motivation, or whether subject matter that is problematic (from a motivational point of view) is simply omitted, the result is equally undesirable: a biased selection of curricular material, teaching methods, and possibly ways of learning and thinking. Moreover, the aim to achieve maximal coordination between the student's inclinations and the curricular material will create a tendency to give students inordinate freedom of choice in what they learn. The criterion of including curricular material of intrinsic interest will thus conflict with the basic educational criterion of teaching that which is "desirable." This is an important limitation that must be taken into account.

Another limitation of intrinsic motivation is that heavy reliance on it can develop and encourage an orientation toward first-order motivation—toward that which is of immediate interest, conforming with the individual's wishes and desires at a given time. To put this in extreme terms, individuals whose studying is intentionally confined to material of intrinsic interest may be handicapped when it comes to mobilizing the motivational resources required to study material that does not interest them.

This prediction is based on research on the effect of rewards on intrinsic motivation (Deci, 1975; Lepper and Greene, 1979). These studies found that a person who attributes his or her behavior to a certain source of motivation tends to lose interest in that behavior when the motivational source is absent (for example, when an external reward is no longer expected), even if another motivational basis exists. This suggests a hierarchy of motivational types, such that extrinsic motivation tends to overshadow intrinsic motivation. Taking this argument one step further, I contend that intrinsic motivation tends to prevail over "value" (in the sense of what is desirable); that is, heavy reliance on intrinsic motivation with regard to a given task will overshadow and consequently weaken the perception of value and desirability with regard to that task.

The vulnerability of values and motivation based on the "sense of the desirable" was demonstrated in a recent study by Kunda and Schwartz (1983), which found that the rewarding of a prosocial act led to a decline in altruistic motivation, as expressed in behavior at a later date. Though there is no empirical evidence indicating that intrinsic motivation has a similar effect, it can be reasonably assumed that heavy emphasis on interest in what one is doing, on the immediate satisfaction that the student derives from the material, can overshadow the sense of the desirable regarding that material. This argument echoes claims regarding the development of a narcissistic personality.

In short, intrinsic motivation cannot constitute a sufficient and stable motivational basis for schooling in general or a predesigned curriculum in particular. It will bias the content of the studies, lead students to think along confined lines, and encourage an orientation toward activity based on immediate satisfaction rather than on values. Contrary to claims made by some psychologists, intrinsically motivated students will not be consistently motivated. Certain aspects of the curriculum will interest them, while others will not; at times they will study, and at times they will not. Thus, students who rely exclusively on intrinsic motivation are likely to neglect a large part of their schoolwork.

Most students, however, do not do this. The average student in a good school tends to do the work expected of him or her or at least takes care to devote a minimum level of attention to studies, even when a subject does not arouse high intrinsic motivation and even when rewards and punishments are not salient. What, then, is the source of such students' hard work? An answer to this question has been alluded to above; that the students share the belief of the curriculum designers that the program is desirable and valuable. This perception, which I call the "sense of the desirable," has motivational force; it affects behavior.

The Sense of the Desirable

Observations of two special educational frameworks—the Israeli yeshivas (secondary schools and colleges for Orthodox Jews) and one-year college preparatory programs—as well as studies in regular classrooms (Nisan, 1987; Bauminger, 1988), have revealed a sort of motivational, or action-directing, consideration that is distinct from and may even contradict common motivational considerations of utility. Apparently students perceive the school as an integral part of their world order, where non-instrumental considerations serve not only as behavioral constraints but also as major reasons for action. The child perceives school attendance and related demands made by the educational system as part of a complex set of cultural expectations that are legitimate and desirable. Fulfillment of such expectations is not always a function of fear of punishment, nor can it be reduced to terms of immediate or delayed utility (or satisfaction). It is perceived as desirable in itself, as inherently worthwhile. It is my thesis that perception of "the desirable" creates a motivational force that can be of considerable importance in school.

The sense of the desirable, or "value" in the restricted sense described above, is assumed to be a basic component of human experience. The question of what determines whether behaviors are perceived as desirable is analogous to a major question in the sphere of morality—what determines whether behaviors are perceived as moral or immoral? From a cognitive-developmental perspective (Kohlberg, 1976), one might seek the intrinsic logic underlying the perception of certain types of behavior (for example, close friendship) as desirable. At the other end of the theoretical spectrum, the relativistic approach attributes perceptions of desirability to arbitrary conditioning or cultural conventions. A third perspective—the cultural-constructivist approach, the approach taken here—claims that culture provides a network of beliefs and conceptions that lend validity and logic to the perception of certain behaviors as desirable. Accordingly, perceptions of "the desirable" are largely based on the cultural image (whatever its sources—natural, traditional, the interests of power groups) of the ideal human being. Anything perceived as bringing the individual closer to this image (as well as everything perceived as contributing to his or her unique personal development, as will be suggested later) is judged as desirable and therefore as what "ought to be done."

The motivational force of the sense of the desirable thus derives from cognition. However, this need not be a well-developed cognitive structure, and the individual need not be continuously aware of what ought to be done. Research on the distinction between moral and conventional norms (Shweder, Turiel, and Much, 1981) suggests that, although young children are unable to provide fully developed reasons for their judgments, they do possess "intuitions" that are sufficiently developed to create a sense of the desirable.

One should not expect, of course, full coordination between the sense of the desirable and behavior. The gap between the two is well known. However, it should be noted that studies on the relationship between judgment and behavior, conducted by philosophers and psychologists alike, have sought to explain this gap rather than considering it to be natural. The prevailing expectation is that judgment of "ought" will affect behavior. Indeed, common sense suggests that the mere belief that something ought to be done creates pressure to do it (although this may be overcome by other, opposing forces). The motivational force of the sense of the desirable is particularly salient in the domains of morality and altruistic behavior, and it may be assumed that it also operates—and can be further developed—in the school.

An instructive example of the motivational force of the sense of the desirable concerns Holocaust studies offered in Israeli schools. The material taught in the framework of these studies does not arouse intrinsic motivation in the sense that it is intriguing or that it evokes a challenge to master a difficult task; nor is it related to extrinsic or instrumental motivation—that is, to short-term reward and punishment or long-term utility. Nevertheless, especially in recent years, students have taken these studies very seriously out of a sense of commitment. The efforts that they devote to their studies are directly related to the value that they attribute to the subject matter as an important component of their identity.

The Sense of the Desirable and Personal Identity

The example of Holocaust studies illustrates a special type of the sense of the desirable—one that is perceived not as having universal validity but rather as being valid for a specific group for whom the material has unique significance. The children who perceive Holocaust studies as desirable and behave accordingly do not necessarily believe that everyone ought to study the subject. In other words, we are dealing with a matter of particularistic desirability. Along these lines, there is also a perception of the desirable that is personal, holding only for a particular individual. This type of the desirable, illustrated in the following empirical study, demonstrates the creative and dynamic aspect of this motivational set.

Almost all subjects in a study on "ought motivation" (Nisan, 1989b) stated that it is unnecessary to encourage children to participate in an extracurricular astronomy course. Interest in astronomy is perceived as a "personal preference" (Nucci, 1981), so that it is up to the individual to choose whether to pursue it. Yet when astronomy was presented as a high priority in a student's life, responses were somewhat different. Two groups of Israeli subjects were presented with the same scenario: a seventeen-year-old boy who had to choose between attending a lecture on astronomy and going to a soccer match that he really wanted to see. To one group of respondents, the boy was described as "extremely interested in astronomy. The subject of astronomy plays an important role in his life—so important that Danny cannot envision himself without pursuing his interest in the subject." To the other group, he was described as "somewhat interested in astronomy." Both groups were then asked a number of questions. For example, they were asked to respond to the question "To what degree do you think Danny ought to go to the lecture?" by ranking their answers on a nine-point scale, from 1 = "not at all" to 9 = "very much." A total of 120 respondents answered this question; results showed that subjects were more likely to feel that Danny ought to attend the lecture when he was described as "extremely interested in astronomy" (average rating of 6.5) than when he was described as "somewhat interested" (average rating of 5.7). Similar results were obtained for other scenarios with a similar structure. It seems, thus, that the personal project of an individual creates a sense of the desirable regarding that project. People are expected to dedicate themselves to such personal projects even if the activities related to them are not perceived as having universal value—that is, as being desirable for everyone.

Examination of this research may also provide a clue to the motivational basis for behaving according to what is desirable. Respondents had difficulty explaining why one "has" to act according to commitments and projects. However, the reasons they gave included variations of the following: "If it is so important for the person, then he ought to do it" and "If he does not do what is so crucial to him, he is spineless." These reasons do not apply to the expectation that a person should always behave according to his preferences; if Danny likes to play bridge, we do not think that he ought to do that instead of attending a soccer match. Rather, he is expected to pursue projects that are very important to him and to fulfill deeply rooted commitments that constitute part of his self. Failure to behave in accordance with such projects and commitments—so long as they have not been abandoned—cannot be perceived as neutral behavior, as it would signify disregard for and even denial of that part of the self. Such denial is viewed as hindering and restraining the self. This same consideration holds for what is perceived as universally desirable. A child who believes that studying mathematics is desirable and important for the development of any person will also believe that he or she owes it to himself or herself to pursue those studies. To do otherwise would be to deny part of oneself, which is considered undesirable.

The study on the effect of commitment to astronomy and the previous example of learning about the Holocaust suggest that perceptions of the desirable are not limited to behaviors perceived as universally desirable ("Everyone should study poetry") but also include behaviors perceived as desirable for people belonging to a particular group or even for a specific individual ("I should persist in my efforts to excel in piano playing"). All of these perceptions can be encompassed by the following formulation: "It is desirable to develop oneself and actualize and act in accordance with one's personal identity." Such a perception regarding a personal project not only renders it desirable and motivating but also gives it a sense of value and legitimacy (for example, when it conflicts with other considerations).

The Sense of the Desirable in the School

In considering the possibility of fostering a sense of the desirable in the school, two questions come to the fore: Do schoolchildren possess a concept of desirability or value in the distinct sense described here? Is studying indeed perceived as desirable and intrinsically worthy behavior? These questions were examined in two recent studies (Nisan, 1988, 1989a) investigating the development of a distinct perception of values in children in the first, fourth, and seventh grades (ages six to seven, ten to eleven, and thirteen to fourteen, respectively). Subjects were presented with scenarios, each describing a child who behaves contrary to expectations of four different types (each study investigated three of the four types), labeled *morality* (for example, he steals), *value* (for example, she does not read books), *convention* (for example, he calls his teacher by her first name), and *personal preference* (for example, she does not go to the movies). Subjects were asked whether the behavior was bad, whether children should be brought up to behave in accordance with the expectation in question, and whether the described behavior should be punished.

A major finding emerging from the studies was that many first-graders and almost all of the fourth- and seventh-graders distinguished among the four types of expectations. This distinction was sharpest in respect to the questions on upbringing and punishment. Subjects said that children everywhere should be brought up in accordance with both moral and value expectations (but not personal preference) yet should be punished only for behavioral infractions involving issues of morality; expectations of convention were perceived similarly to moral expectations (regarding upbringing and punishment) only if there was a social convention regarding that behavior. This distinction among types of expectations was also evident in the reasons that the children gave for their responses. Moral expectations were reasoned mainly in terms of the welfare of others and of society, values mainly in terms of long-term utility and self-development, conventions in terms of social rules, and personal preferences in terms of the individual's right to free choice. (The results also revealed a clear developmental trend, which is not directly relevant to the present subject.)

One of the studies included a scenario specifically intended to examine children's expectations regarding school attendance. A large majority of subjects at all grade levels considered failure to attend school as bad behavior even when the protagonist lived in a country in which school attendance is not required and not common. Moreover, they even believed that there should be a law requiring school attendance (a response predicted for moral expectations but not for expectations of values). These responses were reasoned mainly in terms of the child's development and his or her long-term well-being—reasons typical of values in the sense used here. What is relevant to the present argument is that young children perceive school attendance as desirable and as necessary for proper development.

The preceding discussion provides firm ground for the claim that the sense of the desirable *can* and *should* serve as a basic motivation in school. It *can* do so because it is the only motivation that conforms to the main objective underlying curriculum design—to develop the whole person; it *should* do so because cultivation of a sense of the desirable and encouragement to behave accordingly are presumably central educational goals. These cannot be achieved through extrinsic or intrinsic motivation, which are based—as suggested above—on expected gratification. It does not seem plausible that one can cultivate, develop, and encourage values that, by definition, go beyond the principle of pleasure and utility on the basis of that very principle. The sense of the desirable thus serves both as an educational aim and as a source of motivation for studying.

As a source of motivation, the sense of the desirable has several advantages. Two of them seem to overcome the limitations of intrinsic motivation. First, perception of the desirable is largely consistent with the entire curriculum, as all the curriculum is presumably based on what is desirable. Second, it is a relatively stable and consistent motivation, since it does not rely on interest in the material or on the chances for external reward.

One should not conclude, however, that the sense of the desirable offers a complete and exclusive solution to the problem of motivation in school. The sense of the desirable only guides one toward a certain action; it does not obligate one to take that action. It can thus be expected that numerous deviations from the desirable will occur. Elsewhere (Nisan, 1987), I have suggested an additional element—the perception of a contract—that provides the sense of the desirable with motivational force. However, like morality, the sense of the desirable seems more effective in keeping the individual from slipping below a certain level of functioning than in motivating him or her to excel. Thus, from both practical and theoretical points of view, the sense of the desirable does not and should not rule out other motivations.

While it should be emphasized and developed as a basic reason for studying, it should be complemented by additional motivations that are subordinate to it. In such a context, there is room not only for intrinsic or achievement motivation, which some may consider worthwhile in themselves and desirable goals of education, but also for external rewards. Though empirical evidence is yet lacking, I would venture that external rewards that are clearly perceived as intended to further a "desirable" cause will not hinder motivations based on what "ought" to be done.

How can we develop the sense of the desirable as a basic motivation in schools? Two suggestions, based on observations and research conducted at a number of schools, will suffice here. The first suggestion refers to the school culture and the second to teacher behavior.

As mentioned, the primary basis for the sense of the desirable is recognition of the contribution of schooling to the development of the individual. While the individual may construct certain perceptions of the desirable by himself or herself, on the basis of what he or she considers "objective" features of the behavior or outcome at hand, in most cases perceptions of the desirable stem from cultural assumptions and beliefs — not only because the individual alone cannot know or predict all possible outcomes, but primarily because the value is often culturally dependent. A certain skill or behavior may be desirable in one culture and of no value in another culture, where it has a different set of meanings. Consequently, the clarity, force, and degree of cultural consensus regarding the desirability of a given behavior or outcome are likely to be major factors affecting the perception of that behavior or outcome. Although these cultural assumptions are transmitted to the child through a variety of channels (for example, parents, the media), the culture of the school — what has been recently referred to as the school's "ethos" — is undoubtedly a central factor shaping the student's evaluations and beliefs, particularly with regard to the value of studying in school.

Thus, a major factor affecting the development of the sense of the desirable in schoolchildren is the degree to which the school is value-oriented. The value orientation, in contrast to instrumental, achievement, and hedonistic orientations, is directed at developing the individual's personality and potential, at cultivating "good" people, whose lives are guided by values. The yeshiva is an extreme example of this conception, but secular institutions can be value-oriented as well. Indeed, we have observed that students in value-oriented institutions tend to have a stronger sense of the desirable than their counterparts studying in schools in which the prevailing orientation is instrumental or based on achievement.

As mentioned above, teacher behavior also plays an important role. The value orientation of a school is expressed in all aspects of schooling, including the criteria employed in teacher evaluations of students and the nature of the student-teacher interaction. Of particular significance in this regard is the respect exhibited by the teacher toward the students (Schwartz, Cohen, Kinreich, and Grad, 1987). Respect for the student seems to be an essential component of an orientation toward values, as it reflects consideration of the whole human being, rather than just a part of the person's self (for example, his or her achievements). Our preliminary study of eighth-graders has shown that teachers perceived as respecting their students were also perceived as guided more by the value orientation, emphasizing their students' personal development rather than high scholastic achievement. Furthermore, they were perceived as tending to prefer value considerations over personal ones when faced with a dilemma.

A Concluding Note

The argument favoring the sense of the desirable as a source of motivation in the school is likely to arouse certain reservations. I believe that our discussion disaffirms two central ones.

One such reservation stems from associating the sense of the desirable with the superego. This conjures up an image of the child as restrained and suffering, in contrast to the child who is positively motivated, free, and happy. Freud's discussion of the superego has led to a perception of the moral and value system as being directed at the restraint of the individual's natural inclinations. This is the source of the sharp distinction between motivation and morality: motivation is related to behaviors that derive from desire and free choice, while morality and value are perceived as being forced on the individual.

Obviously, the division between the two systems is not justified from a practical point of view. The direction and intensity of learning cannot be fully examined without taking into account the influence of values and morality. Even from a theoretical perspective, however, the distinction between moral and motivational factors is not sharp. In fact, scholars in the field of psychoanalysis (for example, Pattison, 1968) have widely recognized that the restraining aspect of the superego must be considered together with the constructive aspect of the ego ideal. Indeed, a sense of the desirable related to studying is closer to tendencies toward self-realization than to restraint of desires. True, the sense of the desirable will sometimes lead the individual to engage in behavior that contradicts his or her "natural" needs, but the same may be said of achievement-oriented motivation, for example. The conflict with other value systems is not limited to the sense of the desirable.

A second reservation stems from associating the sense of the desirable with obedience and conformity and with the imposition of values on the innocent child. These features are contradictory to the approach that seeks to view the school as a framework that fosters personal freedom and independent thinking. While values undeniably dictate behavior and therefore limit it, they always involve a degree of self-construction. Without denying the dominant effect of culture in forming beliefs and values, I submit that culture-transmitted values come to be justified within a coordinated system of beliefs and values. The value of schooling is based on an understanding of what is desirable, not on blind obedience. Indeed, that is how the child distinguishes between morality and values, on the one hand, and conventions, on the other.

The type of motivation emphasized in school may have broad implications for the student and his or her culture. The motivation that operates in schools not only reflects a cultural orientation but also contributes to the shaping of that orientation. For this very reason, we ought to consider what each motivational practice represents. While the sense of the desirable represents an orientation toward values or ideals, extrinsic motivation—and to some extent intrinsic motivation—represent an orientation toward self-interest. Cultivation of the sense of the desirable is therefore important not only for strengthening one's motivational set but also for enabling one to strike a balance between an orientation toward self-interest and one toward values.

References

Bauminger, L. "Sense of Obligation in the School." Unpublished master's thesis, School of Education, Hebrew University of Jerusalem, 1988.

Butler, R., and Nisan, M. "Effects of Evaluation on Intrinsic Motivation." *Journal of Educational Psychology,* 1986, *78,* 210–216.

Deci, E. L. *Intrinsic Motivation.* New York: Plenum Press, 1975.

Frankfurt, H. G. "Freedom of the Will and the Concept of a Person." *Journal of Philosophy,* 1971, *63,* 5–20.

Kohlberg, L. "Moral Stages and Moralization: The Cognitive-Developmental Approach." In T. Lickona (ed.), *Moral Development and Behavior.* New York: Holt, Rinehart & Winston, 1976.

Kruglanski, A. W., Friedman, I., and Zeevi, G. "The Effects of Extrinsic Incentives on Some Qualitative Aspects of Task Performance." *Journal of Personality,* 1971, *39,* 606–617.

Kunda, Z., and Schwartz, S. "Undermining Intrinsic Moral Motivation: Extrinsic Reward and Self-Presentation." *Journal of Personality and Social Psychology,* 1983, *45,* 763–781.

Lepper, M. R., and Greene, D. (eds.). *The Hidden Costs of Reward.* Hillsdale, N.J.: Erlbaum, 1979.

Maehr, M. L. "Continuing Motivation: An Analysis of a Seldom Considered Educational Outcome." *Review of Educational Research,* 1976, *46,* 443–462.

Nisan, M. "Motivational Aspects of Evaluation in School." In A. Levy (ed.), *Evaluation Roles.* London: Gordon & Breach, 1981.

Nisan, M. "Sense of Obligation as a Motivational Factor in School." In V. Last (ed.), *Psychological Work in the School.* Jerusalem: Magnes Press, 1987.

Nisan, M. "The Child as a Philosopher of Values: Development of a Distinct Perception of Values in Childhood." *Journal of Moral Education,* 1988, *17,* 172–182.

Nisan, M. "The Child's Distinction Between Value, Morality and Personal Preference." Unpublished manuscript. Hebrew University of Jerusalem, 1989a.

Nisan, M. "Identity and Ought Motivation." Unpublished study, Hebrew University of Jerusalem, 1989b.

Nucci, L. "Conceptions of Personal Issues: A Domain Distinct from Moral or Social Concepts." *Child Development*, 1981, *52*, 114–121.

Pattison, E. M. "Ego Morality: An Emerging Psycho-Therapeutic Concept." *Psychoanalytic Review*, 1968, *55*, 187–222.

Rokeach, M. *The Nature of Human Values*. New York: Free Press, 1973.

Schwartz, S., Cohen, O., Kinreich, L., and Grad, M. "Teacher's Respect for Pupils." *Psychology and Counseling in Education*, 1987, 66–109.

Schwartz, S. H., and Bilsky, W. "Toward a Psychological Structure of Human Values." *Journal of Personality and Social Psychology*, 1987, *53*, 550–562.

Shweder, R. A., Turiel, E., and Much, N. C. "The Moral Intuitions of the Child." In J. H. Flavell and L. Ross (eds.), *On the Development of Social Cognition in Children*. New York: Cambridge University Press, 1981.

Weiner, B. *Human Motivation*. New York: Holt, Rinehart & Winston, 1980.

10

Teaching as a Moral Craft and Developmental Expedition

William Damon

About a decade ago, Alan Tom made a compelling argument for the idea of teaching as a moral craft in a book of the same title (Tom, 1984). Tom urged us to think carefully about our implicit metaphors for the act of teaching and to find one that does full justice to this complex enterprise. He believed that many of the field's standard operating metaphors — such as teaching as a fine art, teaching as an expert profession, teaching as an applied science — were leading educators astray. He proposed the "moral craft" metaphor as an antidote to the misconceived standards by which a teacher's work was being guided and judged.

The distinctive message of a moral craft formulation is that teaching is fundamentally a practical activity directed by explicit or implicit values. As a practical activity, it must remain oriented to the particular situation that the teacher faces and be flexible enough to deal with the vagaries of situations that may change in unpredictable ways. As a values-driven activity, it must remain subjective as well as ever cognizant of its purposes and effects. In these regards, the moral craft formulation differs from approaches that imply that there could be objective standards of teaching independent of the communicational relationship between teacher and student, as well as from approaches that imply that there ever could be a definitive and generally applicable body of knowledge about teaching and learning.

Tom reserved his harshest criticism for the teacher effectiveness approach, which he considered mired in obsolete empiricist fallacies. Tom, in fact, was quite clear in his skepticism about educational research in general. While reviewing several decades of the research literature, he rarely located a finding that he found valid or useful, and he doubted that insight about a complex interpersonal endeavor such as teaching could be generated by normative studies.

Like many who argue for a new position, Tom took some rhetorical liberties in drawing his contrasts with opposing points of view. His denunciation of educational research was made easier—and ultimately less credible—by his refusal to review any studies other than those arising from a logical positivist framework. He chose to omit from his treatise Piaget, Dewey, Bruner, Vygotsky—in fact, the entire developmental tradition. Yet the developmental perspective has answered many of Tom's reservations about the misguided objectivism of positivist approaches while at the same time providing a solid conceptual framework for instructional practice.

Despite Tom's scholarly omissions and his rhetorical excess, the moral craft metaphor is an insightful and useful contribution toward a fresh look at teaching, teacher education, and teacher assessment. Though it does not, as I shall argue, capture the whole multifaceted endeavor of teaching, it does, as Tom intended, correct some unfortunate distortions created by the empiricist research tradition. My argument in this chapter will focus and elaborate on the notion of teaching as a moral craft. But I shall add the developmental component that Tom omitted, which I shall refer to, again metaphorically, as an "expedition." This addition, I believe, does no violence to Tom's original metaphor: indeed, it is entirely compatible with it. In fact, I shall argue that the vision of teaching as a moral craft leads directly to a number of instructional implications that are fully in line with the best insights from contemporary developmental research.

Teaching and Values

Although it is by now commonly accepted that teaching has a moral dimension (Goodlad, Soder, and Sirotnik, 1990), there is still a curious ambivalence in the profession concerning a teacher's proper stance on moral issues. I have seen this most clearly in moral education seminars that I have taught for in-service and student teachers. I often begin such seminars by asking whether it is appropriate for teachers to bring their values into the classroom at all. When phrased in this general manner, the question provokes a wide range of opinion and disagreement. It is normal for both teachers and student teachers to express great reservations about any assertion of moral or personal values in the classroom. This is commonly considered unprofessional and unfair to students who do not share the teacher's values.

When the seminar moves on to consider the proper goals of teaching itself, it quickly becomes clear that there is widespread support for the universal assertion of at least two values. In every discussion of teaching goals that I have had with teachers or student teachers, I have found strong consensus that teaching should foster, if nothing else, tolerance and critical thinking. Within our educational culture, these two goals are so widely accepted and so little questioned that I often have trouble getting teachers to see them as values at all. It always astonishes me that many teachers, for example, see a commitment to absolute tolerance in the classroom as perfectly consistent with the belief that teachers should not allow their values to affect their classroom judgments and behavior. Similarly, teachers often show a tendency to place the goal of critical thinking in a kind of natural "metacategory" outside the realm of values, as if there were no rational choice to be made in the matter. Since critical thinking is seen as an objective procedure for subjecting choices to the tests of reason and truth, it is not usually seen as itself being subject to evaluation.

The anecdote that I tell my seminars on this point is an incident that I witnessed at a conference in Toronto, Canada, about ten years ago. It is one of those rare stories that are more timely now than when they first occurred. The occasion was a presentation by a researcher from the Ontario Institute for Studies in Education (OISE) about new methods for fostering critical thinking in adolescents. Her ideas seemed noncontroversial enough to me, but they were met with indignation and even some outrage from a pair of local school board members. Didn't these new techniques, they asked, inculcate what at the time was called "divergent thinking"? And didn't Canada, that loose affiliation of diverse cultures, need to encourage more *con*vergent thinking in its young people? Who was this researcher to interject her own antinationalistic values into curriculum materials designed for public schooling?

No doubt we non-Canadians in the audience were fairly oblivious to the shifting fault lines that even then were threatening to tear that sprawling nation apart. But many of the Canadians there that day also dismissed this objection as nationalistic hyperanxiety. I suspect that, if the same incident were to take place today, many more might be persuaded. My point here, though, is not to argue for or against these particular nationalistic concerns. Rather, my point is that even the most assumed virtues can come under attack in contexts where the virtues do not function in ways that are perceived to be adaptive (and therefore valued). Who is to say that nationalism should not be an educational priority in a certain time and place? And who is to say that critical thinking may not undermine nationalistic sentiment? I am not making the case for this particular line of reasoning, but I do wish to note that the argument exists and that it is certainly a legitimate application of values to questions of instructional policy.

All educational choices—from direct moral instruction to curricular priorities—reflect values; and no matter how unassailable such values may appear at a particular time and place, they may well be questioned at a different time and place. This can be a jarring experience when one has assumed that certain choices are beyond question. I remember my own recent feeling of shock when I attended a contentious New York City community meeting and heard a parents' group complain about the school system's insistence on math and science instruction. Their children did not have a cultural background that prepared them well for numerical skills (or, they felt, that required such skills), and their children were at risk for invidious comparisons (hence low self-esteem) when their schools emphasized these skills.

Three Elemental Types of Values-Directed Choice in Teaching

The first challenge of teaching is acquiring a coherent framework of values for making educational choices. Like members of any society, teachers do not (and need not) construct their frameworks independently: there is a weighty legacy of values prescribed to them by their communities. Still, in the daily press of schooling, there is always a wide latitude of personal interpretation and choice. There are many types of values-directed choice that are critical in teaching. In this part of the chapter, I identify three of these types and discuss the intellectual and personal resources that teachers draw on to make their choices in each of these three areas.

Determining the Moral Quality of Instructional Relationships

All instruction flows from relationships. In turn, all relationships have distinguishable features that give them their moral quality. By its very nature, the teacher-student relationship has certain inevitable features that affect its moral quality. Most importantly, in any teacher-student relationship, the teacher maintains a position of authority over the student, regardless of how nondirective or egalitarian the teacher tries to be. The moral nature of the teacher-student relationship derives from the legitimacy of the teacher's authority and the manner in which it is wielded. Legitimate authority in the teaching situation has three benchmarks: fairness, specificity, and truthfulness. Let us examine each of these three in the context of teaching.

Fairness is a moral imperative of all relationships. In the teaching situation, it usually arises in issues of evenhandedness while dealing with different students and in concerns of judiciousness in doling out rewards or punishments. A common example is a teacher's response to uncompleted homework. There are many reasons why a teacher may be more patient with some students than with others, ranging from the teacher's history with particular students to the forcefulness of a student's excuses. Some of these reasons may be good and even necessary ones. But students are highly sensitive to such variations in response, and unless they perceive the variations as benignly motivated and justly administered, the teacher places his or her moral authority at risk.

Specificity is one of the benchmarks determining the legitimacy of authority in asymmetrical relationships. It means that an authority's directives to those under its command must be restricted to specific areas in which the holder of authority has a legitimate claim to leadership. A legitimate claim can derive from a number of socially recognized attributes, such as competence, experience, status, and so on. All such claims hold only for properly designated spheres of authority. They do not constitute a license for the unconstrained exercise of power. Authority figures must not overstep the boundaries of their specific area of command. It is fine for a teacher to tell a student what classroom to be in on Tuesday morning but not what church to be in on Sunday morning or whom to vote for in the next election.

Like fairness, the third benchmark—*truthfulness*—is also a general moral criterion of human relationships. Yet truthfulness raises a particular set of problems in instructional relations. These problems revolve around the most difficult and important moral challenge that teachers face: pursuing moral ends with moral means. Teachers—and other adults as well—often shade the truth when talking to children, out of the common conviction that the whole truth can lead young minds astray. No matter how well intentioned, this is a mistaken and dangerous conviction. It inevitably imparts a harmful moral message and can jeopardize students' trust in their teachers.

Truth shading can take many forms in the classroom. A science teacher working with a health curriculum may exaggerate the risks of unsafe behavior (smoking, drinking, eating high-fat foods) for the benign purpose of getting the warning across in a dramatic way. A history teacher may skip over facts that could cast revered figures in the wrong light. I have heard, for example, a teacher objecting to readings that noted Thomas Jefferson's ownership of slaves on the grounds that this would convey to students an improper attitude toward a founder of their country as well as an insufficient abhorrence of slavery. The acute sensitivity of many ethnic groups in a pluralistic society creates constant pressure on social studies teachers to tread lightly, if at all, on possibly inflammatory facts.

My primary purpose here is not simply to inveigh against the common but morally questionable practice of shading the truth. More to the point, I wish to focus on the special instructional risks that doing so—even for noble ends such as saving young people's lungs from smoke damage—can create. The teacher-student relationships, of course, is based on trust. In this regard, it is like any other relationship. But since a large part of its purpose is the communication of knowledge, it is essential to the viability of the relationship that the veracity of the knowledge be trusted. This trust can easily be undermined by an awareness that the teacher is more committed to a certain message, however noble, than to the truth.

Beyond the risks to instructional credibility, truth shading undermines a large part of the moral significance inherent in the teacher-student relationship. In many ways, the developmental effects of relationships on individuals derive directly from the interactional qualities of the relationship. The medium of exchange, in a sense, is the moral message. This is what Piaget ([1932] 1965) meant when he wrote that relationships characterized by constraint can only engender unilateral respect, moral realism, and a host of other "heteronomous" leanings, whereas relationships characterized by cooperation lead directly to mutual respect and an autonomous moral orientation. The forms of interaction within the relationship themselves have a moral meaning and in the course of development become internalized by the relationship's participants.

The great educational pitfall of a dishonest communication is that it will embody and therefore transmit a value of untruthfulness. This is a powerful form of moral education in the wrong direction. The demoralizing legacy of a dishonest communication far outweighs any verbal exhortation toward honesty that a teacher could convey. Yet, in my observations, it is the single most common miseducative experience that students encounter during their education and the single most difficult misstep for teachers to avoid in their practice. It is common and is difficult to avoid for the same reason: in human affairs, there are always compelling reasons why certain momentous ends seem to justify any means.

In human relationships generally, absolute consistency between means and ends may not always be within reach. Certainly there are times, for example, when deceit has served an essential moral purpose — as when a lie saves a refugee from the hands of an evil dictator (Oliner and Oliner, 1988). But here I wish to point to the *particular* moral risks of dishonesty between teacher and student — risks that derive from the purpose and nature of the instructional enterprise. The purpose of the enterprise, most educators agree, is to foster the student's intellectual and moral development; and the nature of the enterprise, as I have noted, is a communicational relationship in which the teacher takes on an authoritative role. Dishonest communications weaken and corrupt every aspect of the enterprise, because they impart a message that truth is not valued, they create a miseducative encounter between teacher and student, and they undermine the teacher's legitimate authority in the classroom. It is difficult for me to imagine any shading or distortion of the truth that could be justified in an instructional relationship where the teacher has assumed responsibility for the student's development. The means and ends of instruction are so intertwined that their congruence is essential — for effective teaching as much as for the usual moral considerations.

Managing Ethical Dilemmas in the Classroom

While the quality of the teacher-student relationship permeates everything that teachers do with students, ethical dilemmas often arise in the classroom in contexts that are not part of the immediate teacher-student relationship. For example, students may have conflicts with one another, or they may report on other moral problems that they have experienced, in school or out. The curricula in all humanities and social studies disciplines are studded with ethical dilemmas that quickly become apparent to students. It is common also for students to raise in class ethical issues related to current affairs. Moreover, in schools where moral education is explicitly part of the instructional agenda, ethical dilemmas may be presented directly to students for purposes of analysis and reflection.

Even after rigorous training in the methods of their profession, many teachers report being ill prepared for dealing with ethical dilemmas when they arise in the classroom. For one thing, the sheer frequency with which moral concerns arise during class time can be astonishing for a new teacher. In a recent survey, 70 percent of teachers reported that the major conflicts that they experienced while teaching were ethical in nature (Lyons, 1990). What is more, the majority of those surveyed did not see clear ways to resolve the ethical conflicts that they had faced. The main thing that they were certain about was that similar problems would recur, again without clear ground rules for resolution.

There are a number of difficult conceptual issues that teachers must work through in order to assume an effective stance toward ethical dilemmas that arise in the classroom (see Tom, 1984; Lyons, 1990). Perhaps the thorniest is the question of what to do about one's own opinions and beliefs. Does one withhold them, suggest them, advocate them, indoctrinate one's students according to them? Another is the broader question of intent: what is my goal in encouraging students to consider ethical dilemmas; what pedagogical purpose am I seeking? This raises a third, meta-issue: What is the place of ethical discussion in the overall instructional agenda? In fact, it must be asked, does a discussion of morals belong in my classroom at all?

I shall discuss these difficult conceptual issues in the context of an example of an ethical dilemma that I have witnessed virtually everywhere I have worked with teachers. I do not know whether it is the most prevalent ethical dilemma that teachers encounter these days in the United States, but I suspect that if it is not, it is very close. This is the problem of how to handle a racial or ethnic slur made by one student against another. The offense can be brought to a teacher's attention in any number of ways. A child can report a playground incident. A student can be caught scribbling an epithet on another student's belongings. Or, incredibly enough, a student can hurl a racial insult at another student right under the teacher's eyes. A beginning teacher once told me of a student in her history class who proclaimed, to the amusement of some classmates and to the horror of others, that members of a certain ethnic group had been outcasts in the United States because they were shifty and slow-witted. Not coincidentally, there was a member of this very ethnic group sitting across the room from the speaker. The insult was clearly intentional. What is a teacher to do?

The question of how (or even whether) to express one's own values in the classroom troubles many teachers (Lyons, 1990). Inclinations about this vary from never interjecting one's beliefs to ensuring that one's beliefs dominate the classroom discourse. Many teachers harbor the entire range of inclinations themselves, vacillating uncertainly from a stance of values neutrality to a stance of strong values assertion. Lyons offers an example of a black U.S. teacher torn between her desire to encourage an open discussion of South African politics and her conviction that there could be no moral justification of the apartheid system (Lyons, 1990, pp. 165–166). One moment the teacher wonders whether she should reveal her perspective to her students; the next moment she wonders whether she should let them express any pro-apartheid views at all.

Lyons argues that the teacher's first task must be to clearly know his or her own subjective beliefs and how these are related to those of his or her students. The teacher then is in a position to "manage" the dialogue that ensues, including any embedded ethical conflicts, in a way that provides both teacher and student opportunities to learn from one another. In a classroom, teachers and students are "interdependent as knowers and learners" (Lyons, 1990, p. 176). The teacher's goal must be to manage ethical conflicts with an eye toward facilitating the interaction of teacher and student perspectives, rather than to try to resolve the conflicts for once and for all. For one thing, many of the conflicts are not readily resolvable; for another, managing conflicts in an interactive manner creates communicational conditions that foster change.

I would agree with Lyons, but I believe that a further distinction is needed. It is an old and always controversial distinction, one that is frequently dismissed because of the contention that it provokes and just as frequently resuscitated because it inevitably seems required in human affairs. This is the distinction between conflicts that revolve around core moral concerns and those that do not. There are many ways of making this distinction in moral philosophy and the social sciences, and much has been written about the elusive complexities that it entails (see Weber, 1947; Spiro, 1986; Turiel, Killen, and Davidson, 1987; and Shweder, 1986). For now, I simply wish to assert that a teacher's orientation toward conflicts that raise core moral issues such as honesty, fairness, compassion, and human respect must be somewhat different from his or her orientation toward conflicts around political attitudes, conventional rules, personal customs, and other less fundamentally moral values.

It is not always easy to make this distinction, and there inevitably will be gray areas. But clear cases are not hard to recognize. In the example that I have given above, ethnic and racial slurs violate the unambiguously moral standards of fairness, compassion, and respect. In such cases, I would argue, teachers have a responsibility as well as a right to advocate the moral standard. This does not mean that teachers should restrict discussion or disallow opposing views. But it does mean that they should present their own views clearly and without equivocation. Such a response can turn a disruptive classroom conflict into an opportunity for moral education.

In a statement that I have written on guidelines for effective moral education in the classroom, I suggested an interactional principle that I have called "respectful engagement" (Damon, 1988). It is a principle that holds for adult-child communication generally and has much in common with effective relationship patterns that have been observed in parent-child dyads. Diana Baumrind, for example, has written about the developmental benefits of "authoritative" (as opposed to permissive or authoritarian) parenting (Baumrind, 1988), and in a number of ethnographic observations across several cultures, Barbara Rogoff has described a parent-child interactional mode that she calls "guided participation" (Rogoff, 1986). Both of these patterns are structured similarly to respectful engagement, although, of course, there are some unique features of classroom communications between teacher and child, especially when the discussion turns to ethical conflicts and moral values.

The elements of respectful engagement are (1) the creation of a dialogue in which the adult and the child share a common interest; (2) the structuring of that dialogue in ways that accomplish the adult's instructional agenda for the child; (3) the encouragement of the child's active participation in the dialogue, including the child's free expression of beliefs (however wrong or even repellant these beliefs may seem); and (4) the clear expression, in ways that the child can comprehend, of the adult's own perspective. All four conditions are necessary for effective moral education. I have explained respectful engagements between teachers and children in the following way:

> The teacher must foster and respect the child's own decision-making capacities if the child is to become an autonomous moral agent. But children must not be given the message that whatever they decide is automatically right. Teachers must *engage* their students with feedback, discussion, reasoning, and argumentation in order to convey the adult position strongly and clearly. In an interaction characterized by respectful engagement, neither adult nor child can be passive. The adult, in fact, must encourage the child's active participation, not only to ensure the child's attentiveness but also to bring out the very decision-making capacities that the child must further develop. At the same time, teachers owe it both to themselves and to their students to actively assert their own mature value commitments. . . . Nor do I believe that adults in our society need agonize over what these values should be. Whether or not we take a universalist stance on morality, it is evident that many of our society's most fundamental values are widely enough shared for unhesitating intergenerational transmission [Damon, 1988, p. 150].

Respectful engagements establish a climate of tolerance for divergent opinions. But tolerance in instructional dialogues need not imply, as some have wrongly deduced, that teachers should practice values neutrality while discussing ethical conflicts with their students. In fact, displays of values neutrality from teachers have an opposite effect to that intended. By failing to confront children with real values genuinely held, such displays engender in children an attitude of passive indifference — and even cynicism — toward the enterprise of moral choice. Why should a child bother working through a moral problem or risk taking a stand when the child's supposed moral mentor refrains from publicly doing so? To have a lasting effect, moral educators must confront children with basic values that are clearly stated and sincerely held.

The principle of respectful engagement assumes that the primary goal of moral discussion must be to help children to reason autonomously — and soundly — about moral issues. I believe that this goal needs little justification, for no amount of rote learning or indoctrination will prepare children for the many diverse situations that they will face in life. The child must learn to find the moral issue in an ambiguous situation, to apply basic moral values to unfamiliar problems, and to create moral solutions when there is no one around to give the child direction. The only way to master these key challenges is to develop an autonomous ability to interpret, understand, and manage moral problems.

It is in this spirit that Lyons advocates teachers taking a managerial stance toward classroom ethical conflicts rather than attempting a final resolution (Lyons, 1990). I do not wholly agree with this, since I believe that it is a teacher's responsibility to make his or her position known when basic moral issues arise. Many classroom dilemmas do indeed call for final resolutions, and avoiding these can lead to cynicism and moral apathy on the part of students (Damon, 1988). But I agree with Lyons that teachers must create in their classrooms reciprocal dialogues that acknowledge the complexity of ethical conflicts, rather than simply giving their students pat, prepackaged answers to moral problems. Only through such dialogues can teachers impart to their students a capacity to recognize and deal with the complex moral problems that arise naturally in real life.

Selecting the Ends of Instruction

Above, I stated my belief that the goal of moral instruction should be to foster children's ability to make sound autonomous moral choices. The particular goal that I asserted was a choice—one that can be questioned, my own convictions notwithstanding. All pedagogical goals for students are choices that can be questioned, because they are determined by values and subject to the test of opposing values. In fact, it is over the matter of goals that teachers' values are most frequently and most profoundly tried.

Values and Developmental Change

I began this chapter with an anecdote about a surprising (for me at least) Canadian challenge to the goal of critical thinking. I shall end the chapter by considering how one set of goals and values, deriving from a developmental perspective, would respond to this and similar teleological challenges. In this discussion, I draw both on Tom's (1984) notion of "teaching as a moral craft" and on Kohlberg's formulation of "development as the aim of education" (Kohlberg and Mayer, 1972). But I shall not adopt either position entirely, because I believe that, where the dynamics of development are concerned, both positions are insufficient.

During the winter and spring of 1989, a fascinating interchange took place on the pages of *Educational Researcher*. In a treatise on "Situated Cognition and the Culture of Learning," Brown, Collins, and Duguid (1989) cite an example from Lave (1988) that is intended to represent the notion of situated cognition as activity- and context-based: as such, situated cognition (unlike the more decontextualized kind) is supposed to be particularly "inventive" and "expedient" within the cultural framework.

The example comes from the observation of a Weight Watcher struggling with a straightforward fractions problem. The man was instructed to fix a serving of cottage cheese that was three-fourths of an original two-thirds-cup allotment. The man saw no symbolic way to solve this problem, but he did arrive at an accurate, though clumsy, solution through some concrete actions: "He filled a measuring-cup two-thirds full of cottage cheese, dumped it out on the cutting board, patted it into a circle, marked a cross on it, scooped away one quadrant, and served the rest" (Brown, Collins, and Duguid, 1989, p. 35). In applauding the inventiveness and expedience of this man's solution, the authors note that "It reflected the nature of the activity, the resources available, and the sort of resolution required in a way that problem solving that relies on abstracted knowledge cannot" (p. 35).

In a commentary that appeared two issues of *Educational Researcher* later, Anne-Marie Palincsar writes the following about this example:

> The article cites with approval the example of some poor soul at Weight Watchers confronted with the challenge of measuring three-fourths of a cup and then taking two-thirds of that to arrive at the required half-cup of cottage cheese. The authors regard the dieter's ineptitude with fractions as giving rise to an "inventive resolution" to a problem arising in a particular context. Instead, it was an act of desperation, born of ignorance. Although the authors laud this activity, I question whether it was learning at all. Where did the so-called solution lead? Nothing has been learned that could be generalized [Palincsar, 1989, p. 7].

What we have here, of course, is a conflict about the adequacy of certain cognitive acts. Implicit in both sets of comments are systems of values for assessing such acts. Brown, Collins, and Duguid value inventiveness and expedience within a practitioner's framework, and for them the reported behavior meets these criteria. Palincsar, on the other hand, is looking for something quite different. She approaches the example from a learning framework, questioning the implications of the behavior for the subject's generalized competence with fractions. Judged from this perspective, the man's actions are necessarily devalued.

Now we could leave this conflict at that, concluding simply that the value of the man's actions depends on the framework by which they are assessed. But, as Palincsar rightly suggests, questions of learning and development cannot be begged in this manner. At some point, we must determine whether a particular act of learning has contributed in a positive way to the learner's intellectual development. The only alternatives to this are to assume either that people gain nothing lasting from their experience or that all learned ideas are equally functional. Both of these assumptions are absurd on their face.

Determining what indeed is "positive" in a developmental sense requires a framework of assessment derived from the functions that intellectual activity serves in an individual's life. That is, an act of learning can be judged to have developmental significance if and only if it enhances the learner's ability to perform some specified function. The "direction" of development is always toward greater functionality: to the extent that an experience changes an individual's behavior in such a direction, it has developmental value. Of course, this still leaves room for debate concerning which intellectual functions should stand as important goals for individual development. This brings us once again to the question of values.

It is clear in the above example that Palincsar places primary value on the general function of numeracy. By this standard, the Weight Watcher's solution was almost worthless. No lasting understanding of fractions or ability to manipulate mathematical symbols was generated from the experience. Brown, Collins, and Duguid might argue that, nevertheless, the behavior was adaptive in the context of the event. But if we keep our framework of assessment firmly fixed on the acquisition of numerical competence, as does Palincsar, we cannot conclude that this was a developmental experience in any sense. The necessary directionality is simply not there.

This episode is reminiscent of recent studies of Brazilian candy vendors reported by Saxe (1988a, 1988b). Brazilian children as young as eight have been observed to perform numeric manipulations of remarkable complexity in the course of selling candy on the street. For example, they are able to accurately subdivide large units of candy, price them appropriately, and even adjust for a continually changing inflation rate. At the same time, these children have very little schooling and practically no adeptness with numeric orthography. Their behavior seems perfectly functional despite their ignorance of the standard tools of mathematical discourse. Saxe, however, refrains from claiming that these precocious candy merchants have acquired an idyllic state of mathematical competence. Rather, he points out that their conventional numeric illiteracy is indeed a real handicap, even if it does not put them at a disadvantage in the world of street candy selling. It is a handicap because these young mathematicians will need a working knowledge of formal symbol systems if they are to make further progress into algebra, geometry, calculus, and all other forms of higher math.

It is easy to romanticize the unschooled skill, particularly when charming examples of spontaneous intelligence are found among those previously suspected to be incapable. Social scientists who have observed the impressive adaptive skills of people once thought to be "primitive" (from *paisanos* to children to native groups) have done just that. But leveling the differences between spontaneous skill and formal instruction makes better romantic fiction than social science.

The developmental benefits of formal instructional experiences have long been familiar to psychologists and educators. It was, ironically enough, Vygotsky who wrote one of the most lucid accounts of such benefits (Vygotsky, [1934] 1962). (The irony is that Vygotskian theory somehow has come to represent an approach that reduces the value of knowledge to its social-contextual significance, without the implication that some forms of knowledge are developmentally superior to others, and yet Vygotsky's own writings have an unmistakable developmental thrust.) Vygotsky wrote of the gap between what he called "spontaneous" and "scientific" concepts. Spontaneous concepts arise directly from a child's own experience and are fully imbued with the vivid meaning and flavor of that experience. Scientific concepts — among which Vygotsky included social, scientific, literary, and historical ideas as well as natural science ones — are learned as part of a systematic package of formal instruction. The full range and complexity of higher-order thinking becomes available to a child only through schooling experiences that impart scientific concepts. Certain learning acts, therefore, are imbued with a developmental priority, in the sense that they enable learners to acquire advanced thinking abilities.

When the term *development* is used rigorously (that is, with explicit reference to the formation of increasingly advanced systems) rather than loosely (that is, to mean merely any sort of change during ontogenesis), it invariably makes people uncomfortable because of the values that are inevitably implied. Who is to say what is "advanced," or what represents "progress"? Yet such value choices are unavoidable if we are to look critically at any intellectual achievement, let alone participate in any planned intervention. My point here is that such choices need not reflect someone's arbitrary set of biases. Rather, they can be made on the quite objective grounds of functionality. The defining and selecting of functions, of course, is a matter of value and therefore subjective, but the determination of how well a given behavior serves an already defined function can be an objective and reliable procedure. Once, therefore, the desired functions of thought are defined, the developmental directions by which we assess change can be readily identified and calibrated. Of course, there always will be some discrepancy in how scientists define the functions, but there is also a great deal of shared consensus.

The important thing is to begin with a careful consideration of criteria for determining developmental direction so as to avoid approaching cognitive phenomena without clear standards of analysis. Most educators, for example, recognize and value the features of thought that have been called, variously, "higher-order," "complex," "abstract," "propositional," "critical," "hypothetical-deductive," "hierarchical," "formal," "systematic," and so on. This provides a common standard of analysis through which acts of learning may be consistently evaluated. In this, the question of implicit values in any statement of developmental direction can be addressed and unambiguously resolved. Of course, the nature of the resolution will vary across domains and functions of knowledge.

In some manner or other, as teachers formulate their own pedagogical priorities, they must identify the features of thinking that they wish to have their students acquire. In so doing, they implicitly have made choices about what constitutes the developmental direction toward which they hope their instruction will lead their students. Since learning in the classroom is a collaborative activity between teacher and student, the teacher somehow must convince the student to travel in the same direction. Often this requires a gradual transformation of the student's learning goals (see Griffin and Cole, 1984; Wertsch, 1987; and Damon, 1990, for discussions of student goal transformation and learning). When there is a match of goals between teacher and student, learning becomes a fairly straightforward affair. When there is not, motivational problems, literacy gaps, and alienation from schooling ensue (Damon, 1990). One of the main reasons, then, that it is so important for teachers to work out their own values concerning the goals of their instruction is that doing so is necessary if they are to persuade their students to adopt similar values. For teaching to be effective, the teacher must recruit the students to come along on the developmental journey.

References

Baumrind, D. "Rearing Competent Children." In W. Damon (ed.), *Child Development Today and Tomorrow.* San Francisco: Jossey-Bass, 1988.

Brown, J. S., Collins, A., and Duguid, P. "Situated Cognition and the Culture of Learning." *Educational Researcher,* 1989, *18* (1), 32–42.

Damon, W. *The Moral Child.* New York: Free Press, 1988.

Damon, W. "Reconciling the Literacy of Generations." *Daedalus,* 1990, *119,* 33–53.

Goodlad, J. I., Soder, R., and Sirotnik, K. A. (eds.) *The Moral Dimensions of Teaching.* San Francisco: Jossey-Bass, 1990.

Griffin, P., and Cole, M. "Current Activity for the Future: The Zoped." In B. Rogoff and J. V. Wertsch (eds.), *Children's Learning in the "Zone of Proximal Development."* New Directions for Child Development, no. 23. San Francisco: Jossey-Bass, 1984.

Kohlberg, L., and Mayer, R. "Development as the Aim of Education." *Harvard Educational Review,* 1972, *42,* 449–496.

Lave, J. *Cognition in Practice.* New York: Cambridge University Press, 1988.

Lyons, N. "Dilemmas of Knowing: Ethical and Epistemological Dimensions of Teacher's Work and Development." *Harvard Educational Review,* 1990, *60,* 159–181.

Oliner, S., and Oliner, P. *The Altruistic Personality.* New York: Free Press, 1988.

Palincsar, A. S. "Less Charted Waters." *Educational Researcher,* 1989, *18* (4), 5–7.

Piaget, J. *The Moral Judgment of the Child.* New York: Free Press, 1965. (Originally published 1932.)

Rogoff, B. "Adult Assistance of Children's Learning." In T. E. Raphael (ed.), *The Contexts of School-Based Literacy*. New York: Random House, 1986.

Saxe, G. B. "Candy Selling and Math Learning." *Educational Researcher,* 1988a, *17,* 14–21.

Saxe, G. B. "The Mathematics of Child Street Vendors." *Child Development,* 1988b, *59,* 1415–1425.

Shweder, R. "Divergent Rationalities." In D. W. Fiske and R. A. Shweder (eds.), *Metatheory in Social Science: Pluralism and Subjectives*. Chicago: University of Chicago Press, 1986.

Spiro, M. "Cultural Relativism and the Future of Anthropology." *Cultural Anthropology,* 1986, *1,* 259–286.

Tom, A. *Teaching as a Moral Craft*. White Plains, N.Y.: Longman, 1984.

Turiel, E., Killen, M., and Davidson, P. "Morality: Its Structure, Function, and Vagaries." In J. Kagan and S. Lamb (eds.), *The Emergence of Morality in Young Children*. Chicago: University of Chicago Press, 1987.

Vygotsky, L. S. *Thought and Language*. Cambridge, Mass.: MIT Press, 1962. (Originally published 1934.)

Wertsch, J. *Vygotsky and the Social Formation of Mind*. Cambridge, Mass.: Harvard University Press, 1987.

Weber, M. *The Theory of Social and Economic Organization*. Oxford, England: Oxford University Press, 1947.

Section Four

DEVELOPMENTAL PERSPECTIVES

Ronald Gallimore,
Section Editor

The "naturalization of pedagogy" is Wolfgang Edelstein's elegant description in Chapter Eleven of an educational theory and practice rooted in developmental theory and research. With this phrase, he captures the idea of developmentally based instruction as "the process of natural development intentionally applied." To understand the implications of this conception requires a brief review of some assumptions about the relationship of development to education.

Edelstein argues that a cognitive-developmental formulation of educational aims is commonly misunderstood as substituting the formal universals of stage-specific competencies for more traditional curricula. However, the stage-specific universals do not justify educational intervention under normal conditions, nor are they broad enough a program for general education. Education is concerned with more than what comes naturally with human development. It is also concerned with the content and skills needed for individual development in a normative cultural context.

Making education developmentally sound means treating development as a general aim, not as the achievement of specific tasks that indicate competence. It is not enough to say that educational goals must subserve or not contradict the developmental aims of education. It is also necessary to specify what makes "operational" educational aims serve developmental ends through a "blueprint for instruction."

A "blueprint" or theory of instruction is therefore the focus of a developmental theory of education. And such a theory, to come full circle, properly conceives education and instruction as "the process of natural development intentionally applied." An elegant formulation indeed. But there are problems with this. There always are, and Edelstein knows them well. Two that he mentioned specifically are taken up here because the three other chapters in this section address them in differing ways. The first is what is entailed by the "naturalization of pedagogy" in the artificial context of school learning. The second is the dismal history of efforts to implement developmentally based instruction in schools, given Edelstein's reminder of the organizational features that tend to thwart, impede, or subvert natural learning processes.

The chapters by Lother Krappmann (Chapter Twelve), Rolf Oerter (Chapter Thirteen), and Ronald Gallimore and Claude N. Goldenberg (Chapter Fourteen) concur in at least one fundamental way: all three feature analysis of social context as a critical and essential feature of a "natural theory of instruction." These three chapters take up Edelstein's challenge to draw a "blueprint for instruction" by attending to the issue of development in social context. All three chapters argue that taking this issue seriously can solve at least some of the problems that have prevented developmental theory and science from having an impact on education. Taking social context seriously makes educational research more difficult than it already is, but there is really no choice. For example, educational researchers not only must take the school contexts seriously; they will have to consider contexts outside of school that impinge on the child and how the school and nonschool contexts interact to affect development.

An illustration drawn from Oerter and Krappmann's chapters suggests that knowing only about the individual psychological development and the school context may lead to significant misinterpretations about development and education. Oerter offers the general principle that for a zone of proximal development (ZPD) to arise, the child's environment must include certain features. For example, developmental theory holds that for a child's normal development to take place, the social context must include self- and peer-regulated social activities as a necessary incentive to the development of social, cognitive, and personal competencies. Only in mutual social interaction and joint reasoning and problem solving can children develop understanding, judgment, and competent practice. Since such opportunities are presumed to be absent in most schools, it is assumed that most children must experience "peer regulation" in zones of development that arise in nonschool contexts.

For historical reasons, however, nonschool opportunities for self- and peer-regulated activity may be diminishing. In the Berlin community that Krappmann studied, social, economic, and demographic changes have led to increased use of adult-regulated activities and substantially eroded nonschool opportunities for self- and child-regulated social activities. "Out-of-school life is divided in several sections separated from each other like isolated islands that children can reach only with parental support." In other words, opportunities for ZPDs that include developmentally essential peer mediation are scarce in nonschool contexts.

What about school contexts? Did they reflect the teacher-dominated, impoverished peer-interaction stereotype of modern schools? Although social interaction in his Berlin classrooms is shaped by adult-regulated teaching-learning activities, Krappmann observed surprisingly frequent self- and child-regulated interactions. Peer-regulated interactions appeared between the "cracks" of adult-regulated classroom activities, in ways that served vital developmental purposes. The interactions took many forms, including abundant negotiation, quarreling, mutual helping, and joking during class time. The children seem to have created contexts in which developmentally sensitive opportunities exist in the midst of what seems the most "unnatural" of contexts. Krappmann reports that a surprisingly large proportion (40 percent) of help-giving–help-seeking interactions begin in a somewhat antisocial fashion (blunt denials of help, blaming or admonishing the help seeker, and so on).

Amazingly, Krappmann reports that these student-created interactions are put to good use as collaborative contexts for exploring different aspects of a problem, changes of perspectives, experimentation with ideas, analysis of errors, and so forth. Even when the "correct" answer was not obtained, these instances provided opportunities to develop competence of another kind. In other words, these episodes not only represent satisfying peer interactions but also provide developmentally sensitive opportunities — that is, the kinds of zones of proximal development that were once common features of nonschool settings. In other words, existing school contexts are not entirely hostile environments for natural developmental processes. In Krappmann's classrooms, natural pedagogy exists but goes largely unrecognized and unexploited.

These findings illustrate one barrier to the achievement of developmentally based education. In stronger terms, we can know everything about cognitive development and have little impact on teaching and schooling unless we know a lot more about the social contexts in which we intentionally apply the process of natural development. Unless we study contexts, we may not see existing developmental opportunities or discover ways to create them; thus, we are not doing responsible research, which, in the context of this volume, would be ironic.

Krappmann's data also suggest ways in which teachers can simultaneously increase their efficacy and assume an important developmental responsibility. For example, Krappmann reports instances in which ZPDs arise in surprising fashion, suggesting the possibility of untapped opportunities to remodel current school practices. Using student-initiated interactions, teachers can "capture" developmentally important phenomena without major alteration of classroom practices — in this case, the frequent self- and child-regulated interactions that Krappmann observed.

Indeed, Krappmann's studies suggest that such capturing is possible. In the last ten years, he and his colleagues have observed a gradual and substantial increase in the frequency with which teachers in Berlin make use of activities in which self-regulation and peer regulation are permitted. In contrast, during the 1970s, they almost never observed a teacher departing from adult-regulated activities. A similar trend toward peer-mediated and cooperative learning appears to be developing in many nations; for example, the cooperative learning movement in the United States. Does this imply the gradual evolution of schools (relatively new human inventions) toward structures that make more developmental sense? Would a gradual shift toward more peer-regulated contexts in school not only serve normative cultural aims for education but also be congruent with developmental laws and complementary to changing conditions in the larger community?

In Chapter Fourteen, Gallimore and Goldenberg examine some of the reasons why another kind of everyday, natural pedagogy is seldom observed in classrooms. Their particular example is the kind of discourse that is so common in literate households and so uncommon in contemporary classrooms. As is the case with the developmentally essential peer interactions, they note the possibility that without such discourse as part of instruction, an upper limit may be placed on development in general and a particular handicap placed on children from nonliterate households.

One reason for infrequent classroom use of the discourse patterns of literate households, Gallimore and Goldenberg suggest, is the failure to appreciate that whatever is said about developmental education for children has a parallel for teachers. Their chapter examines the social contexts that help and hinder teachers' development and concludes that some of the features that facilitate child development likewise aid teachers. To make pedagogy more natural for children, teacher work contexts must be reorganized to include naturally embedded opportunities for intellectual and professional development.

Teacher development is thus added to the responsibilities of developmental and educational researchers. Certainly, there is no argument that more attention to and research on teacher development is needed — indeed, it is the central thesis of this book. As necessary as it is to do such research, however, it is not the only major task. What also needs increased attention was put into focus at a recent meeting (August 1991) of the governors of the fifty states of the United States. Several with good credentials in the school reform movement expressed disappointment that educational research had contributed so little to school reform. Expert witnesses were challenged to cite examples of research findings that had significant impact on school improvement. A number of the experts reluctantly agreed that it was a difficult task to list unequivocal successes.

Is this gloomy assessment accurate? Researchers have to accept responsibility for this perception, if not for the substance. One reason research has had little impact is to be expected: research studies are designed to address theoretical questions deemed important to other researchers, not to answer concrete problems confronted by practitioners (Goldenberg and Gallimore, 1991). Although researchers' questions and practitioners' concerns sometimes coincide, this either happens infrequently or, if it does happen, often goes unrecognized (see, for example, the exchange between Finn, 1988a, 1988b, and Shavelson and Berliner, 1988).

Goldenberg and Gallimore argue in Chapter Fourteen that there is another, perhaps deeper reason why research alone is an inadequate basis for reform, a reason that touches on the central themes of this volume: research does not provide knowledge about local sites, the contexts in which reforms either succeed or fail. Sarason has already warned of the consequences of working in contexts with which we have no personal experience, not to mention understanding: "How well do you understand the culture of the context in which the problem arose and in which you seek to intervene? Our inadequate answers to that question explain a good deal about the failures of educational reform. And that is true for most of the educational research community as well as for those non-researchers who have, as they should, grappled with reform" (Sarason, 1990, p. 130). It is not difficult to imagine him adding "grappled with researcher effectiveness and responsibility" to his warning.

What Sarason says about research in general can be said for developmental theory and research, but even more so if the goal is truly the "naturalization of pedagogy."

References

Finn, C. "What Ails Educational Research?" *Educational Researcher,* 1988a, *17* (1), 5–8.

Finn, C. "Rejoinder to Shavelson and Berliner." *Educational Researcher,* 1988b, *17* (1), 12–14.

Goldenberg, C. N., and Gallimore, R. "Local Knowledge, Research Knowledge, and Educational Achievement: A Case Study of Early Spanish Reading Improvement." *Educational Researcher,* 1991, *20* (8), 2–14.

Sarason, S. B. *The Predictable Failure of Educational Reform: Can We Change Course Before It's Too Late?* San Francisco: Jossey-Bass, 1990.

Shavelson, R., and Berliner, D. "Erosion of the Educational Research Infrastructure." *Educational Researcher,* 1988, *17* (1), 9–12.

11

Development as the Aim of Education—Revisited

Wolfgang Edelstein

In *their 1972 article in the Harvard Educational Review, Kohlberg and Mayer (1972)*
argue that progressive education, in the theoretical formulation provided
by John Dewey, is the only viable option for an educational theory open
to educators. This is because it fits cognitive-developmental psychology
and provides a rationale that unites the aims of education with the process
leading individuals toward those aims. The cooperative structure by which
knowledge is coconstructed in the classroom under the epistemic tenets of
discovery learning matches the interactionist and pragmatist convictions in
which Dewey's progressive education has its roots. The philosophical quan-
dary of education, which justifies ends by tradition (or ideology) while operating through means that are basically divorced from the ends both in time
and in nature, appears resolved in the very unity of instructional process
and developmental product that characterizes the cognitive-developmental
brand of progressivism proposed by Kohlberg and Mayer. But the putative
unity of educational aims and instructional method provided by the imperative that the aim of the school should be to stimulate human development
indeed deserves a closer look.

It is a common misunderstanding that in a cognitive-developmental
formulation of educational aims, the formal universals of stage-specific competencies in reasoning will substitute for more traditional formal (skill) or
material (content) goals of instruction. This, for various reasons, makes no
sense: the stage-specific universals of logical reasoning represent either mile-
stones or end points of developmental sequences, whatever the developmental
(or educational) programs of the child. As Eleanor Duckworth (1987) nicely
phrased the dilemma, "either we're too early and they can't learn it, or we're
too late and they know it already." Thus, formal universals do not justify
educational intervention into the cognitive careers of normal children under normal conditions. And even if they did—under conditions of, say,

deprivation or retardation—they would represent much too narrow a program for general education. After all, education is not concerned, or at least not merely concerned, with what comes naturally with human development; rather, it is concerned with the content and skills implied in and needed for individual development in a normative culture.

The formal universals, moreover, are mere indicators of a competence that transcends the individual tasks whose successful completion represents this competence. Working toward developmental progress does not mean that educational endeavors toward competence are directed toward the achievement of specific tasks that indicate competence. The developmentalization of education, then, defines *developmental progress in general,* not specific stages or indicators of development, however broadly defined, as the aim of education. This, however, leaves the problem of the choice of educational goals (in a narrow, more operational sense) unsolved. It says only that educational goals properly defined must not contradict (weak version) or must subserve (strong version) the developmental aims of education. In other words, what a developmental formulation of educational aims calls for is the compatibility of educational goals and developmental aims. Although this may have more far-reaching implications than is obvious at first sight, it is hardly a revolutionary insight that sustains grand educational principles.

Developmental Education as a Theory of Instruction

We need to specify what it is that makes educational practice serve developmental aims. We surmise that educational aims serve developmental ends through the conduct of instruction. Any developmental imperative for education must specify a rather detailed blueprint for instruction. In any specific instructional context, the teacher must be able to knowingly apply strategies that enhance the developmental progress of the individual child while simultaneously serving the collective progress of the entire instructional group in which the individual learner is involved. At one level, this implies the diagnosis of developmental needs, or challenges, that characterize a specific individual who is grappling with the cognitive demands of a given context of instruction as defined by subject matter, instructional objectives, and general aims or goals. At another level, it implies the design of lessons and larger instructional units that provide adequate developmental challenge for the group as well as the individuals who compose it. At still another level, it calls for the design of curricula in light of the developmental knowledge and imperatives of a given age group. Thus, the teaching of a history course may require the construction of complex systems of temporal, causal, and correlational relationships and the concept of function in order to make meaning of a narratively simple sequence of events. These requirements place constraints on the what, how, and when of teacher operations. Finally, there is a level at which teachers must systematically and persistently apply general knowledge of developmental processes as microgenetic instances of construction under cognitive conflict, and toward transition, consolidation, or generalization, as the case may be.

It should now have become clear that if cognitive-developmental theory is considered as a theory of education, it must be formulated as a developmental psychology of education. This is a radical enough claim, as we shall see, but it is still quite different from the claim that Kohlberg and Mayer (1972) raised in their widely quoted paper.

The unit and the unity of developmental education, then, are incarnate in but also confined to a *theory of instruction*. Theories of instruction traditionally specify the means toward the end of education. But since this end is defined as the developmental progress of the individual, the means toward this end — the instructional process — indeed determines the nature of education. Hence, the unity of developmental education resides in the nature of instruction, and it is the theory of instruction that turns out to be the focus of a developmental theory of education. And, while constraining what are legitimate concerns and legitimate procedures of instruction developmentally defined (namely those, and only those, that are conducive to developmental progress), a developmental formulation of educational theory seems to take us back to the classical formalistic framework, the two-tiered theoretical construction, with formal procedures on the one hand and material "objects" of instruction on the other, both generating and projecting their respective goal systems.

Remember how, for example, the teaching of Latin was justified in the two-tiered system: the learner was to appropriate the content of a classical literature — the humanistic ideal — while submitting to the putatively logical discipline of a highly inflected grammar — the formational ideal. Now the formalist theory has been denounced as profoundly ideological, and the classical dualism is precisely what developmental educational theory must avoid if it is not to develop into mere ideology. It may avoid this pitfall by having the formal structure of developmental instruction maintain control over the material objects of education much in the same way that cognitive development exercises selective control over what the mind can process, assimilate, or integrate at any given stage of a child's life. While the objectives are selected from outside the very process of education so as to represent cultural goals, their educational control comes from within the structure of developmental instruction that determines their contribution to the individual's growth.

In our case, of course, exploding the formalist myth does not necessarily imply giving up Latin. But it does eliminate the particular ideological justification for Latin found in the classical argument. There are developmentally viable arguments for teaching Latin that simultaneously constrain the uses to which Latin can be put in school, as well as the developmentally adequate strategies of teaching it, just as would be the case for any other subject or skill. To take another example, neither quantification nor the theory of numbers nor computation skills are superseded by the use of electronic calculators in the classroom. But certainly the design, the choice, and the timing of developmentally adequate strategies of instruction are affected by the introduction of calculators into the classroom.

In sum, while Kohlberg and Mayer's (1972) analysis led to a position highlighting the philosophical justification of developmental *aims,* we are led to stress the system of instructional *procedures* in the service of developmental intervention. But to be functional, procedures in the service of development must represent the very process that leads to developmental progress naturally. That is, developmental instruction must harness the process of development itself, or some approximation thereof, an educational analogue to the process of development. Developmentally oriented instruction is, in effect, the process of natural development intentionally applied. Because the process of development is a process of developmental construction both of reality and of reasoning *about* reality, a developmental theory of instruction must necessarily be a constructivist theory and its practice a constructivist practice that establishes realities to think and reason about. A constructivist practice of instruction has two far-reaching implications: it aspires to be an adequate, if intentionally patterned, representation of the developmental process, and it naturalizes pedagogy. It is not clear, however, what is entailed in this naturalization of pedagogy in the artificial context of school learning.

Limitations of the Scope of Developmental Education

Constructivist instruction, while selective, can serve a wide range of goals as long as these are compatible with constructivist procedures. But it cannot serve all goals that may be worthy of recognition. Inevitably, there must be choices that go beyond the scope of constructivist instruction and imply values that transcend the merely formal claim of development as the aim of education. While the option of constructivist procedures has far-reaching consequences for the conduct of instruction, education (and instruction) may still serve cultural and social goals largely unaffected by the constructivist transformation. Development as the aim of education is neither a philosophically sufficient nor an educationally complete definition of the educational process. Indeed, the question of educational aims is left sadly underdefined when development is established as the aim of education. What we want students to learn is neither fully defined by our intention to have them progress developmentally by learning it nor indifferent to it. Conversely, if we want students to progress developmentally through learning for a given set of objectives, these objectives cannot be chosen without reference to this aim.

While this asymmetrical relationship between a procedural theory of instruction and the substantive aims of education is decidedly less elegant than the wedding between developmental psychology and educational philosophy led us to expect, it takes us closer to a more manageable relationship between means and ends. It is not entirely conventional, however, as will become clearer below, because the naturalistic pedagogy contained in a constructivist theory and practice of teaching transcends a merely instrumental or strategic means-end relationship, carrying critical potential from the domain of means (instructional and procedural) into the domain of ends. This is so because an active, discursive, inventive construction of knowledge in agreement with (or, better, inspired by and compatible with) Piaget's theory means knowledge as understanding, and this does not agree with the unquestioned establishment of any arbitrary bit of knowledge as a goal for the process of knowledge acquisition. The developmentalization of education or, in the words above, the naturalization of pedagogy therefore turns knowledge into critical knowledge and turns the means-end relationship between instructional procedures and educational aims into a critical, not merely an instrumental relationship.

Revisiting Kohlberg's analysis, we have been compelled to reverse his top-down analysis, which proceeds from the philosophical justification of development as the aim of education to the practice of instruction, and to replace it with a bottom-up, inductive construction of the process that proceeds from the psychological construction of developmentally aimed procedures to the reconstruction of education as activity and knowledge as understanding. To a degree, this forfeits the rigor and elegance of Kohlberg's deduction. But it confronts us with the problem of the developmentalization of education on the level of empirical reality.

Implications for the Organization of Learning in the Schools

What characterizes this problem on the level of the empirical reality of school systems, schools, and classrooms? It is true that constructivist principles, in order to determine the system of educational means toward developmental ends, must be applied not merely to the methods of instruction but to the entire process of teaching and learning, to curriculum design and curriculum decisions, to the organization of groups, and to the organization of schools. An interactionist, peer-oriented, collaborative orientation to the organization of learning in schools (Damon, 1984; Slavin, 1983) appears plausible. A note of caution is warranted, however: there is no one-to-one relationship between constructivist principles and the larger context of learning in the schools, and in many instances we do not even know what such principles may entail. Important facets of the educational process and significant aspects of the educational system certainly remain outside the purview of an interactionist theory of instruction. While it is true that constructivism implies development, and education represents a subset of development (or a function, an implication of what is meant by this term), conversely, constructivism or even development cannot meaningfully represent a subset of what is meant by *education*. The reciprocal implication of terms and meanings and domains thus also constrains the field by a system of mutual limitations that have great practical relevance.

If development — in a strict cognitive-structural sense — can be defined as the overarching aim of education, it follows that instruction and, a fortiori, the means and methods of instruction must serve these aims. Yet even within a design of instruction entirely dominated by constructivist principles, the methods of instruction will never represent just a single psychological principle. And while Dewey and, later, Kohlberg have argued that educational objectives are real only inasmuch as they can be defined in psychological terms, psychology is clearly not sufficient to define them. Even convinced constructivists will not extend constructivist principles beyond the descriptive terms of instructional psychology narrowly defined.

This is because educational objectives cannot be defined simply on the basis of a developmental psychology or on the basis of didactic principles, such as constructivist methods of instruction. Even constructivist educators want students to learn cherished texts of the cultural tradition by heart; to develop spelling skills, routine behaviors, conventions; to take seriously exercises, repetition, dictation, and many other activities conducive to the appropriation of contents or skills that are part and parcel of some educational objectives. And yet these contents and skills and the exercises that lead to their mastery have little to do with constructivist didactics.

Whether we are consciously planning educational contexts to fit developmental principles or are unaware of their developmental implications, instructional sequences and the pattern of educational objectives, as well as the ways in which classroom discourse is arranged and the level of questioning is set — the entire structure of the school, for better or for worse — are a function of the relationship that we assume to exist between development and learning and thus both impose and constrain the process of education. An obvious example is the way we organize progression through the years of schooling according to age. Developmental sense and nonsense are closely mixed in the ways schooling is implemented, and the failure of schools to elicit the commitment of their students may well be due to their failure to base the structure of the educational process more clearly on the developmental principles that govern natural inquiry in the growing child. In a constructivist view of schooling, the child's commitment to learning is based on and sustained by the continuing operation of cognitive construction as the foundation of organized learning activity even in the most conventional domains of the curriculum. What, if anything, then, is there in the application of cognitive structures to a learning problem in the institutional setting of schools that goes beyond the constructivist description of knowledge acquisition?

It is often claimed that a constructivist description of school learning is an idealizing mode of expression, fit, at best, for what is called *structural* learning. But what is structural learning as distinguished from other types of learning? Does it apply to the acquisition of logical or mathematical schemata, while the less noble elements of figural knowledge are acquired by the rote procedures of traditional content learning? We know that rote procedures are endemic in the schools. Is it perhaps plausible to attribute the notoriously destructive boredom of the schools, so vividly described by diverse authors from Jackson (1968) to Csikszentmihalyi and Larson (1984), to the pervasiveness of such procedures? Is it possible that only the "natural" learning processes *outside* schools are structural—that is, experiential, intentional, actional, and thus meaningful, meaning-based, and problem-oriented—while in the schools, learning is grounded in different laws? There are reasons to think that all learning is grounded in the same principles, but different contexts impose different realizations of these principles in the practice of learning. In this view, school learning is, at worst, a deformed copy of natural learning, an alienated and deprived version, that is characterized by organizational constraints on the free play of assimilation and accommodation, by interventions that upset the natural balance of figural and structural elements inherent in any situation of natural learning.

A moment's attention to natural—that is, developmental—learning, such as the acquisition of the lexicon, the taxonomies of natural objects and cultural artifacts, and the phenomenologies of the natural, the social, and the psychological worlds, will disclose that figural learning is overwhelmingly important—so much so that classical learning theories took this to be the total process and, for a time, banned everything else from the realm of a science of learning.

In sum, the situation is contradictory. On the one hand, it seems that only part of the educational process can be legitimately subsumed under the principles of constructivism. On the other hand, we remain theoretically convinced that natural learning is developmental and constructive. The concept of construction provides a useful bridge between knowledge and learning, the acquisition of knowledge and the structure of knowledge, epistemic process and product. But at least two problems remain. First, what is the role of different classes of knowledge, figural and structural, in the process of knowledge acquisition? Is a constructivist theory of structural learning valid for the construction of knowledge structures, while a different theory has to account for rote learning, for the acquisition of content, for imitative appropriation, for the entire world of labeled information? Second, is learning in schools, for some systematic or contingent reason, mainly concerned with what here has been classified as nonstructural learning?

A dual theory of learning will not solve our problem. Associationist and constructivist principles of learning do not lend themselves to easy cohabitation. Nor will an appeal to memory as a second principle in addition to construction take us far, since what we know about the functioning of memory suggests a structural rather than an associationist organization. To judge from the widespread criticism of the schools, the practice of rote learning and other memory-oriented didactic strategies has not been very successful and thus does not provide attractive arguments for a theory of "figural learning." On the contrary, the widely documented failure of learning in school settings calls for an explanatory theory of its own. In a constructivist perspective, such a theory will be a deficit theory, couched in terms of a cognitive social psychology of the school. That will take us back to a constructivist theory of successful learning.

A Constructivist Description of School Learning

What follows is an attempt to sketch very roughly the outlines of a constructivist theory of learning in the schools. For systemic reasons reported elsewhere (Edelstein, 1983), learning in the schools is organized in such a way that natural learning processes tend to be thwarted, impeded, or subverted. When successful, learning in schools contributes to equilibrated cognitive structures in spite of the power of extraneous rules imposed on the learning process and the stunting of the motivation to learn that follows from these rules. The extraneous rules tend to establish the dominance of extrinsic motivation over learning, whereas natural learning is motivationally autonomous. It is characterized by intrinsic motivation, by motivation for competence (Lepper, Greene, and Nisbet, 1973; White, 1959).

In this view, school learning fails to exhibit developmental qualities, because it is uncoupled from its natural motivational energizer. It is denaturalized learning. Thus, theories built around classroom learning deal with the ubiquitous yet specific condition of the *deformation* of learning processes in institutions, perhaps a structural analogy to socialization processes under the institutional constraints of a prison or, perhaps more to the point, to the estranged learning of the rat in the maze (Seligman, 1975). In other words, such theories are special theories for nonnatural learning. If this hypothesis is true, a constructivist renaturalization provides a key to a better economy of learning in the schools. While, as mentioned earlier, the scope for the application of constructivist principles is limited by the cultural constraints on the selection of learning objectives, those principles still define a strategic position for a transformation of the schools even beyond the somewhat limited domain where they can be applied.

If the function of the school is to enable learning to take place (which has been denied by some renowned sociologists) and to organize the acquisition of knowledge, schools must do justice to the structure of learning. If learning is situationally and contextually adequate structure building, the school must accommodate itself to this process and organize itself so as to support (or at least not to impede or subvert) the natural forms of learning. School organization concerns primarily the form and methods of instruction, which can be described in constructivist terms as disequilibrational activity serving to induce developmental processes. Elements of this activity are known; they include cognitive and social conflict, exploration, discursive teacher-pupil interaction, and conceptually activating questioning techniques (for an example of the domain of social learning, see Chapter Twenty-Five of this book; for a discussion of the domains of social studies in general, see Edelstein, 1986). Good arguments speak for such techniques, and they should be specified in detail. But beyond mere instructional strategies, what is implied by disequilibrational activity is the unity of means and ends, of method and goal, that characterizes the intentional structure of development. It is far from clear, of course, how the social organization of the school can accommodate, let alone enhance, the natural structure of the learning process. But enough is known for schools to embark on exploratory action.

We cannot here describe the unfolding of the natural process of learning and strategic means of bringing it about intentionally in the artificial context of instruction. This is the object of much Piagetian theorizing about development and learning (see Inhelder, Bovet, and Sinclair, 1974), post-Piagetian theorizing about constructivism (see Cellérier, 1987), and constructivist theorizing about instruction (see Athey and Rubadeau, 1970; Duckworth, 1987). The overarching operational principle of instruction is the principle of *exploration* (often mistakenly overstated as *discovery*), leading to various forms or implementations of the construction process. Depending on the stage or phase in microgenesis as well as on the domains of operation, what is intended is the disequilibration of a substructure; cognitive conflict; accommodation to object, scheme, preconcept, or concept; reciprocal assimilation of new and preexisting schemes; reequilibration of a (sub)structure. Exploration depends on operational context: subject matter and problem context; general developmental level of the group and specific developmental level of the individual; the individual's experiential history; and the opportunities and iniquities of class, culture, and socialization.

Understanding the operational context is the hallmark of the epistemically active and insightful teacher who is able to manage the syllabus, the curriculum, and the instructional microsituation as opportunity structures for exploration and instruction in the service of development. In order to manipulate the conditions for the establishment of opportunity structures for exploration and construction, the teacher will make use of the sociointeractional system of the classroom for the benefit of individual construction processes. Cognitive conflict is frequently, if not always, nested in interactional conflict, and social conflict generates cognitive conflict — the signal and function of collaboration. Collaboration is the socially generative mechanism of a constructivist didactic theory: it must be implemented in terms of developmental stage, subject matter, and problem at hand. There are many forms of collaboration — such as group instruction, project organization, team enterprise, learning by discussion, peer instruction, individual profile development, and differentiated group design — that can be engineered in view of a constructivist perspective as manifestations of a collaborative process serving to generate intraindividual cognitive conflict and decentering.

The essence of the epistemic process served by a constructivist organization of instruction is learning as the implementation of change or innovation, as the production of newness. This definition of learning is contrary to the criterion of conservation and memorizing that is typical of the performance valued by schools. That is why the learning process can best be described in terms that indicate change: disequilibration, stage transition, modification of a structure, emergence of a new structure, consolidation of a structure that makes the integration of new concepts possible, differentiation of structure, decentration from earlier centrations, and transcendence over functionally obsolete structures. A concept that subsumes all these terms of structural innovation is the concept of generativity. Constructivist instruction will organize learning in view of the production of generative structures through the internal construction process of individuals joined in a common effort with others who are involved in similar processes. These structures, we know, are but the structures of everyday cognition activated by exploration. They are here and there and everywhere—except perhaps in the schools, where they ought to be institutionalized but where they have been paralyzed by the elimination of motivated exploration from the process of inquiry.

The process of collaboration is less well known than the epistemic process. Its essence appears to be mutual decentration, less as a task for the teacher and as an element of construction than as a result, in the individual, of a collective process maintained across conflict, confrontation, and the crisscrossing of arguments, questions, and discordant answers. These are processes that describe the free association of individuals, united neither in preestablished harmony nor in the captivity of cognitive alignment, collectively engaged in the construction of reality; with the conflicting perspectives of individuals busily innovating on their own mental structures—participants, as it were, in a system of free cognitive exchange.

The decentration of the teacher transcends the collaborative decentration just outlined because the teacher must construct a double perspective—the perspective of the learner that he or she once was and whom he or she has to understand in his or her own actual present (How did I learn this, how did I assimilate this into which structure, when I was the child facing this task?) and the perspective of the student facing the teacher here and now (How would I learn if I were this student, if I were in his or her shoes?).

Summary and Postscript on Responsibility

All this process that we have been discussing is, of course, accommodation. A constructivist theory of teaching and learning generally tends to orient instructional action to the accommodation side of the genesis of structure. It leaves aside necessity and, with it, integration. It focuses on possibility and, with it, on differentiation. The generative process is productive of newness in the subject individually. In this limited and technical cognitive sense, creative performance is the aim of instruction. To understand this creative process is to reconstruct the conditions of the emergence of newness in the individual and the collective conditions in the classroom that foster invention (Piaget, 1976). And to engage in constructivist instruction in the service of development is to take this process into one's own hands, intentionally and understandingly.

Of course, this is not all. After accommodation, there is assimilation. After newness, there is integration. After understanding as invention, there is systematic knowledge and expertise, the discipline of functional performance. But it is the accommodative side of decentration and invention that is the salt of a constructivist practice of education in the service of development. It is limited, but it is radical and pervasive. It could change the schools.

Let me sum up the gist of the message. The limited if important function of a constructivist reconstruction of the teaching-learning process — the partial transformation of instruction imposed by the developmentalization of the aims of education — could generate major changes in the schools. The small revolution in the conditions of learning called for in this chapter aims at a naturalization of the learning process, described as a process of construction, or, as Piaget formulated it, understanding through invention. It is focused on accommodation-side didactics, on the emergence of new structures. Given the work of Dewey and other protagonists of active education, these insights can hardly be called revolutionary. Nor do they go beyond what has long been known to educators and psychologists. However, the consequences of their application are radical and pervasive, while failing to apply them leaves the schools to boredom and frustration. The consequences are no less radical and pervasive, although less visible, because they are trivially ubiquitous in today's schools.

Development as the aim of education would indeed, as Kohlberg and Mayer (1972) write, transform both educational theory and educational practice. But rather than doing so in a top-down fashion, the process would proceed upward from the local and limited transformation of instruction and the collaborative and organizational conditions necessary for and necessitated by such transformations.

In its own way, naturalizing school learning in developmentally oriented instruction serves to dissolve the contradiction between effectiveness and responsibility in teaching. To serve the development of individuals is to be responsible toward them and for them, here and now, while transcending their present. It has long been the predicament of teachers that they have had to reconcile responsibilities to the culture with responsibility for the child's welfare. This, it would seem, is eased by the transition to a conceptual structure for teaching that reconciles learning with development. Moreover, the transition will bridge the gap in teacher ethos between effective teaching — a responsibility toward society — and responsibility toward the individual taught. If the learning process is liberated from the constraints of a deformed mode of knowledge acquisition, the teacher's developmentally oriented strategies will simultaneously serve the principles of effectiveness and responsibility, freeing the latter from the sway of child-centered sentimentalism and returning it to the domain of professional expertise, where it belongs.

References

Athey, I. J., and Rubadeau, D. O. (eds.). *Educational Implications of Piaget's Theory.* Waltham, Mass.: Xerox College Publishing, 1970.

Cellérier, G. "Structures and Functions." In B. Inhelder, D. de Caprona, and A. Cornu-Wells (eds.), *Piaget Today.* Hillsdale, N.J.: Erlbaum, 1987.

Csikszentmihalyi, M., and Larson, R. *Being Adolescent: Conflict and Growth in the Teenage Years.* New York: Basic Books, 1984.

Damon, W. "Peer Education: The Untapped Potential." *Journal of Applied Developmental Psychology,* 1984, *5,* 331–343.

Duckworth, E. "Either We're Too Early and They Can't Get It, or We're Too Late and They Know It Already: The Dilemma of Applying Piaget." In E. Duckworth, *The Having of Wonderful Ideas and Other Essays on Teaching and Learning.* New York: Teachers College Press, 1987.

Edelstein, W. "Cultural Constraints on Development and the Vicissitudes of Progress." In F. S. Kessel and A. W. Siegel (eds.), *The Child and Other Cultural Inventions.* New York: Praeger, 1983.

Edelstein, W. "The Rise and Fall of the Social Science Curriculum Project in Iceland, 1974–84: Reflections on Reason and Power in Educational Progress." *Journal of Curriculum Studies,* 1986, *19,* 1–23.

Inhelder, B., Sinclair, H., and Bovet, M. *Apprentissage et Structures de la Connaissance* [Learning and structures of knowledge]. Paris: Presse Universitaire de France, 1974.

Jackson, P. W. *Life in Classrooms.* New York: Holt, Rinehart & Winston, 1968.

Kohlberg, L., and Mayer, R. "Development as the Aim of Education." *Harvard Educational Review,* 1972, *42,* 449–496.

Lepper, M. Z., Greene, D., and Nisbet, R. E. "Undermining Children's Intrinsic Interest with Extrinsic Rewards: A Test of the Overjustification Hypothesis." *Journal of Personality and Social Psychology,* 1973, *28,* 129–137.

Piaget, J. *To Understand Is to Invent.* Harmondsworth, England: Penguin, 1976.

Seligman, M.E.P. *Helplessness: On Depression, Development, and Death.* San Francisco: Freeman, 1975.

Slavin, R. E. *Cooperative Learning.* White Plains, N.Y.: Longman, 1983.

White, R. W. "Motivation Reconsidered: The Concept of Competence." *Psychological Review,* 1959, *66,* 297–333.

12

On the Social Embedding
of Learning Processes
in the Classroom

Lothar Krappmann

No *synthesis of effectiveness and responsibility in teaching is conceivable without taking* into account the social relationships in the classroom. While the teacher-student relationship has received abundant attention, above all with respect to learning and achievement (Brophy and Good, 1986), social interactions between learners, especially outside the learning processes, have been much less the focus of educational researchers. However, it is obvious and beyond doubt that teaching and learning in our schools are deeply influenced by the social life of peers in the classroom. Again and again, students talk to their classmates, giggle, yell at a classmate's mistake, and have fun together with amusing replies; they show pride in success or ashamedly hide themselves from their classmates' view when they are negligent; they look for support when they have trouble with a task and hope for comfort from a friend when they fail; they sometimes irritate each other with inappropriate suggestions and at other times stimulate each other to demonstrate the best of their competencies.

Many of these activities are considered distracting and disturbing by teachers and by achievement-oriented parents. Therefore, it is no surprise that children's social activities during periods of instruction often are listed as obstacles to effective and responsible teaching. Teachers usually try to restrict these "side activities." They often permit them only when they are directly related to the learning process. They may allow or sometimes even order mutual support or cooperation for certain periods of instruction, either to give some leeway for children's social demands or, guided by the prin-

Note: The study on the everyday life of school children on which much of this chapter is based is a joint project of the Max Planck Institute for Human Development and Education, Berlin, and the Institute for Sociology of Education, Free University of Berlin. The ongoing project receives financial support from the German Research Foundation (DFG).

ciples of "cooperative learning" (called "social learning" in Germany), to better integrate the learner as a social being in the learning process (Slavin, 1983).

The argument presented in this chapter does not contradict the educational program of "cooperative learning" introduced into the classroom, since this effort can in fact be a worthwhile step toward recognizing the social embedding of the teaching and learning processes. On the contrary, the conclusions of analyses of peer interactions in the classroom presented in this chapter support even more radical efforts to respect and value students' social interactions and relationships in the classroom. The chapter goes beyond the scope of the cooperative learning approach to maintain not only that task-oriented cooperation can contribute to effective learning but that the entire social involvement of children serves as a basis for enabling or restricting learning progress. Therefore, it argues, a teacher's responsibility has to include active attention to children's social interactions as well as operative care for the kind of social life in the classroom that elicits the fundamental competencies on which learning processes are so deeply dependent.

The aim of establishing a negotiated order in the classroom (Martin, 1976) is to create a frame in which students and teachers share the responsibility for classroom interactions, eliciting development of competencies as well as learning. Only through such sharing can children's growing autonomy be used productively, as stressed by theories elaborating on the children's own contribution to their development (for example, Oerter's zone of proximal development in Chapter Thirteen of this volume).

Theoretical Background

The theoretical perspective on which the analyses of peer interactions in the classroom are based is derived from the thinking of Mead (1934), Piaget (1926, [1932] 1965), and Sullivan (1953), who regarded children's self-regulated social activities as a necessary incentive to the development of social, sociocognitive, and cognitive competencies and of a personality structure that can produce the efforts, create the inspirations, and tolerate the ambiguities connected with the processes of solving problems. As they have pointed out, children's route to the status of a competent member of their society is characterized by two processes: on the one hand, they must be taught by mother, father, teachers, and many other loved or feared authorities about humankind's and their society's achievements; on the other hand, they must apply what has been taught to them, experiment with the acquired knowledge and skills, and thus find out what their sociocultural heritage really means. Piaget and Sullivan have emphasized that only in social interaction and mutual exchange of reasoning and argumentation with a partner of equal ranking and comparable experience will a child develop understanding, judgment, and competent practice. Therefore, the developing and learning child needs peers and friends in order to coconstruct, step by step, stage by stage, as Youniss (1980) puts it, competencies, meanings, personal autonomy, and mutual responsibility.

This thesis is too comprehensive to be tested as a whole. However, research has demonstrated that peers commonly involved in solving problems benefit from their joint efforts. In some domains, even if children working together do not initially know how to successfully deal with a problem, they can achieve a solution that promotes the development of their capacities more effectively than mere instruction by an expert. In other domains, the advice of an expert is more useful than the mutual support of two unexperienced novices in the field (see Chapters Thirteen and Fourteen). In still other domains, peer experts can often assist in the search for a solution more effectively than an adult expert. There are too many studies to be reviewed here in a few sentences, but the interested reader can find recent excellent reviews in Webb (1989) and Azmitia and Perlmutter (1989). I wish to make clear that these studies in no way suggest that adult teachers are not necessary. Rather, they highlight the finding that instruction could be more effective if students had more opportunities for mutual tutoring and collaboration. This finding should receive more recognition, and not just for fostering curriculum-related learning processes.

It is my intention in this chapter to broaden the perspective on and examine the contribution of children's natural peer activities in the classroom — originally thought of as a remote and noneducational factor — to children's developmental and learning progress. As the theories mentioned above hold that children especially profit from interactions among themselves because they must overcome dissensions, coordinate intentions, and solve problems without adult help, it seems contradictory that teachers are requested to take responsibility for a domain whose fostering impulses essentially rely on children's independence from adults' control. Some readers may even wonder whether natural peer life in the well-organized classroom exists at all. The following part of the chapter addresses these questions.

The Classroom as a Place for Peer Life

While in Western societies, school is usually considered a place of systematic teaching and learning and thereby of children's cognitive development, it is often forgotten that the classroom also presents exceptional opportunities for peer activities. More than ten years ago, when my colleague Hans Oswald and I began to study social interactions and relationships between girls and boys ages six to twelve, we were not at all sure about the quality of children's social life in the classroom. Before we analyzed our field notes on children's social activities, taken during usual school lessons, we considered our decision to investigate children's interactions and relationships in the context of school as a second choice, justified by the fact that we were unable to collect reliable data in more unstructured, natural settings, such as playgrounds or swimming pools. However, our field notes surprised us and removed all doubts: children negotiated, quarreled, helped each other abundantly, bothered each other, and joked during the lessons, which were by no means conducted in a laissez-faire style by their teachers.

Perhaps our expectations had been influenced by outdated memories of growing up in former decades when children's social life took place mainly in the streets and backyards, then as crowded with children as they are today with cars. But for the overwhelming majority of primary school–aged children today, there is no place offering more social opportunities for a child to regularly meet other children and have intense interactions with peers than the neighborhood school. This is borne out by the studies on which the discussions and conclusions of this chapter are based. The Michael Ende Primary School, host of our study of children's peer interactions and relationships (Krappmann and Oswald, 1987, 1991a, 1991b; Oswald and Krappmann, 1984, 1988), is located in an upper-lower- and lower-middle-class neighborhood of Berlin, Germany. Almost all the children from an area covering about thirty city blocks attend this school. Because of a decline in birthrates, all children of the same age within walking distance of the school are included in only two classes. There is no private alternative to the public primary school. Thus, most of the children will not, after school, meet children other than those met at school. From interviews with children from seven different classes in the first, fourth, and sixth grades, we know that children and their friends are most probably in the same class. Only a very small minority of children find their most important friends outside their class. Poor social integration of children within the relationship networks of the classroom is hardly ever compensated for by close friendships established outside the classroom (Oswald and Krappman, 1984; these results were later corroborated by studies in other classrooms).

A second study examined variations and longitudinal changes in organization, instructional methods, and the social life of twelve primary schools located in different regions of what was then West Germany (Hopf, Krappmann, and Scheerer, 1980). Although it was not possible in this study to conduct the kind of intense analyses of friendship networks conducted in the first study, the data from the second study showed the important place of school in children's social life. Considering the increasingly sparse population of children outside of schools, the classroom of the urban as well as the rural primary school offers the best opportunities for meeting other children who live within a reachable distance. In general, only the older children of the fifth and sixth grades begin to expand their social activities beyond the social borders of their classrooms. Interestingly, this expansion is often related to the establishment of first cross-gender relationships, which the preadolescents seek at a further distance outside the classrooms, perhaps because they try to conceal contacts across the gender border from their classmates' observations.

Further, peer life in the classroom has a special quality, in that children who share the classroom therefore meet again and again. Thus, the classroom context necessitates defining and differentiating relationships, reaching solutions or clarifying borders, and explaining and justifying behaviors that may be questioned by friends and nonfriends. These are developmental challenges generated by group processes that nowadays are only seldom found outside the classroom. According to our interviews with children and parents, most of the parents allow at most only two friends to be invited for play in their homes. Other studies demonstrate that children who are considered too old for the preschoolers' playgrounds have difficulty finding convenient space for meetings and games (Friedrich and others, 1989).

Socializing with other children is also often restricted by the educational aims of the parents. Parents from all social classes demand that their children do their homework carefully and often provide additional educational programs for the children's afternoons, including athletic training, playing an instrument, and other attractive, worthwhile activities, while at the same time limiting their children's opportunities for spontaneous peer activities. Referring to these extracurricular programs, Rabe-Kleberg and Zeiher (1986) have shown that children's out-of-school life is divided into several sections, separated from each other like isolated islands that children can reach only with parental support. Thus, their activities often demand planning and control of a time schedule negotiated in advance among everyone involved.

Although these observations underline the fact that the relevance of the classroom as a social meeting place has increased, one may wonder whether the classroom can offer the domain of spontaneous, self-regulated peer activities that allows for children's coconstruction of meaning, judgment, and competence as described above. Surprisingly, children are less under adults' direct or indirect control in the classroom than in many of the social situations outside school. The size of the classroom limits teachers' individual control. The philosophy of the classroom expects children to behave autonomously and to try to solve their problems independently before they ask for their teachers' help.

However, closer integration of peer-group life into the classroom has consequences for school and classroom as well as for the children's social world. It is hard to imagine that a child's peer group could remain the same once it has been taken from the neighborhood and integrated into the classroom. The range of children's social activities in classrooms is influenced by the context of school and instruction. Most probably, unstructured activities such as fantasy play, practical joking, fooling around, and teasing are less frequent than expected among children that hang around elsewhere. However, our field notes from classroom observations give ample evidence that these activities also occur in the classroom, and more frequently than many teachers seem to believe.

Children's peer-related behaviors in the classroom represent many facets of the children's world. However, interactions can be traced to the subject that engendered them. Many interactions of children in the classroom stem from the social world of childhood and take place in school simply because it is school that brought them together. Other interactions are shaped by the teaching and learning processes: children have to solve cognitive tasks and undergo training of their capacities. Although these tasks are presented by the teacher or the curriculum, the way in which children come to terms with the task is determined by the children's capacities and remains part of the social processes among children. To give an example: When we compared the number of rewarding or unfavorable outcomes of helping interactions that were related to needs emerging from school and instruction to those that referred to children's own affairs, such as sharing a Coke or support in a misfortune, we found no overall differences with regard to the rewarding or unfavorable outcomes of the interactions. Children help each other regardless of the domain in which the need has emerged (Krappmann and Oswald, 1991b). Furthermore, evidence exists that the origin of a school negotiation issue does not destroy children's coconstruction but rather stimulates children to perform at the best of their competencies. While negotiations about issues arising from the peer world vary in intensity, the school and instructional contexts place demands on children to try hard to find acceptable solutions (Krappmann and Oswald, 1991a).

These observations show that the peer world exists within the school, in part influenced by the school (and not wholly to its detriment) and in part relatively independent of school and instruction. Although historical comparison data are not available, it appears that since recent social changes have eliminated traditional resorts of peer interaction, the peer world has invaded the classroom even more than before. To examine the question of whether teaching and learning can effectively profit from these social peer world processes, sheltered by the classroom, we must take a closer look at the interactions among children in the classroom.

Social Processes Among Children in Classrooms

The following analyses of three children's peer group behaviors—helping, negotiation strategies, and self-testing—draw on data derived from observations in natural settings, mainly in classrooms during instruction and breaks but also on the school playground and on hikes. The results are based on observations of boys and girls attending fourth- and sixth-grade classrooms in an inner-city primary school located in an upper-lower- and lower-middle-class neighborhood (ages of children between nine years, one month and thirteen years, nine months; mean age of fourth-graders nine years, eleven months; mean grade of sixth-graders twelve years, five months). Two observers focused on two children sitting next to each other at one table and took notes on all interactions between these two children, as well as between these children and other classmates. Most of the children's conversations were tape-recorded.

On the basis of the field notes and the recordings, the observers elaborated detailed descriptions of the interactions independently from each other. The final protocols were compared, and dissensions were discussed. Doubtful reports were eliminated, and missing information in one observer's perspective was supplied by available data in the other protocol. For detailed analyses of children's behaviors, all interaction sequences included in the issue under examination were identified in the protocols by means of manuals defining the characteristics of the issue (for instance, "helping"). Additional codings were grounded in the interpretation of the interactions included in the data file (Glaser and Strauss, 1967; for more details about the design of the study and the methods of data collection and analysis, see Oswald and Krappmann, 1988).

Helping

Children's helping interactions were studied in four classrooms, grades 4 and 6 (Krappmann and Oswald, 1991b). Included were interactions in which help was requested or offered without request and given or denied either with a sensible explanation or without an acceptable reason. As mentioned above, children help in not only friendly ways: in more than 40 percent of all situations in which help was at issue, children bluntly denied support, blamed the petitioner, took advantage of the need, or admonished the asking child in an unfriendly manner. Even more astonishingly, there were many instances in which the child in need asked for help in a commanding tone, derogated the help given, or ridiculed the benefactor, mostly without any provocation. These behaviors were observed in situations related to children's social affairs as well as in situations related to instruction. The latter situations included times at which teachers recommended mutual help as well as times at which they did not intervene.

An interesting aspect of the problem is how children learn to deal with the asymmetrical relationship between a child asking for help and a potential helper. Children have to negotiate shared rules that determine whether a request is well established or represents unfair exploitation and whether the support given is reasonable or is designed to misuse the emergency. This refers to children's social development. Another aspect is whether children benefit from peers' support on tasks related to their learning achievements. On the one hand, we found quite a number of occasions when the helping acts were rather useless — sometimes misleading and often superficial — or when help was refused to children having difficulty with a task or with their student role. However, these antisocial behaviors (as they may be interpreted at a first glance) often aim at establishing a situation among children characterized by fair mutual demands. In cases in which such a balance already existed, which happened more frequently among friends than among nonfriends, children tended to effectively examine the core of the problem and to elaborate solutions. These collaborative efforts of peers, mostly friends, presented almost the only situations in which we found the capacities that the educational system promises to promote — exploration of different aspects of a problem, change of perspectives, experimentation with ideas, reconstruction of failed procedures, analysis of mistakes, verification of the indubitable, search for criteria of good solutions — coconstructively developed and jointly applied.

There are qualities that, according to Piaget (1926), are characteristic of group processes as well as of cognitive operations. In view of these situations, it is almost unimportant whether the children actually obtain the correct solution, because they clearly achieve competence on the fundamental level, and that is what is decisive.

Negotiations

Productive helping actions elicited intense negotiations between children. Children, however, negotiate not only helping but also rules, sanctions when rules have been broken, meanings of behaviors, and assessments of people and events. These issues are often negotiated in a very frank and rough way, frequently escalating to conflicts about problems that adults have difficulty understanding.

Our analyses of children's negotiations are based on data again collected from four classrooms in grades 4 and 6 (Krappmann and Oswald, 1987, 1991a). Briefly, we found that the procedure and the outcome of a negotiation were strongly determined by the beginning of the negotiation and again by the relationship previously established between the negotiating children. Generally, if an issue strictly regulated by norms is under negotiation and the initiating child uses a strategy that disregards the other's rights or interests, the negotiation will most probably end without an accepted solution. If the issue can be discussed freely and the initiating child acknowledges common interests, the negotiation will usually be terminated by an agreement. These predictions that forecast the outcome according to the beginning give the impression that negotiating children select a track determined by their first actions and then inevitably roll to the predetermined end. However, our analyses of negotiations among friends show that the outcome of their negotiations cannot be predicted from the beginnings. In other words, friends do not seem to move from a respectful opening of negotiations on the friendly track to an agreed-upon solution.

This result appears irritating, but it is consistent with the interpretation of productive helping actions. Friends are less influenced by initial behaviors but will try to find out what the problem really is. Thus, when interacting with a friend, children object to kindly presented proposals and insist on their dissenting opinion, and, particularly among friends, they explore why the friend initiates a negotiation in such an unfriendly manner in order to find an agreement. Through these behaviors, negotiating friends broaden the scope of phenomena under consideration, controversially debate the issue, offer and share more information and reactions, and also demand more serious efforts to reconcile different and ambiguous aspects of the problem instead of reducing the cognitive, social, and emotional agenda under the pressure of initial stimuli, as unrelated children were observed doing.

As mentioned above, the qualities of children's negotiation processes are also influenced by the origin of the controversial issue. If issues related to school and instruction are debated, the outcome of the negotiation is just as unpredictable from the beginning of the negotiation as are the outcomes of negotiations among friends. Apparently, school also stimulates negotiating children to mobilize knowledge and capacities, to consider the quality of an argument, and to overcome misunderstandings or discords caused by harsh treatment or offensive "slips of the tongue." When children intensely debate an issue, they are often able to achieve an acceptable solution even when the beginning of the negotiation was unfavorable. Thus, the close correlation between the beginning of the negotiation and the outcome found with negotiations in general also disappeared in the case of school-related issues of negotiation.

However, many observations demonstrate that capacities are elicited not only by serious topics under negotiation but also in the domain of children's jokes and pranks, because here it is urgent that the limits of tolerability and pleasure be precisely negotiated. Part of children's preferred activities is playful transgressions of the limits that separate teasing from joint fun. This is a risky domain of children's social life, as indicated by the fact that quite a number of initiatives begun with good intentions end with tears and annoyance. In contrast, some of the playful interactions recorded in our field notes show that if children manage to avoid vexation and harassment, their communicative, empathic, and cognitive capacities are seldom more intensely elicited than by these risky plays and jokes, which adults tend to call "nonsense." In contrast, the concrete problems presented by instructional tasks often do not initiate such intense negotiations, since the correct solution is undebatable. How much children like experimenting with solutions to make mundane tasks more enjoyable was evidenced by observations of children playing with words, competing with others for fun, dramatizing boring texts, and making up challenging math problems to demonstrate prowess, all of which mutually stimulate involvement and performance.

Testing of the Self

With regard to children's self-concept, the educational system is very dependent on peers' contribution to children's developing self-understanding, as teaching and learning often reveal children's difficulties in the realm of achievement. Failures that threaten the child's conception of self are easier to tolerate if children can read from the reactions of the same-aged reference group that they are socially accepted. Our own study, at the moment based on about one hundred self-threats observed in one sixth-grade classrooms, shows that children of this age group are interested in finding out who they are independently from the experience of learning in school (Krappmann, forthcoming). They even transform demands of school and instruction into issues related to the maintenance of a respected self in the peer world by changing the challenge of achievement or performance into an issue of sovereignty and equality, something that is so important in the peer world.

Interestingly, our study suggests that risky situations are actively searched out rather than simply befalling children. Successful corroboration of claimed self-concepts encourages involvement in the self-endangering learning process and thus contributes to achievement, as we know from numerous studies (Bosma and Jackson, 1990). These studies, however, do not demonstrate how closely children link the learning domain of school with social experiences with peers. According to our data, self-threats were more frequent among friends than among nonfriends. Compared to unrelated children, threats among friends were more often countered by communicative strategies, the procedures were more often appropriate, and the outcomes were more often positive. It is remarkable that communicative strategies, adequate procedures, and positive outcomes were even more frequent among children who were well integrated into the network of peer relationships; that is, among children who had established several stable friendships. Since, as demonstrated earlier, the classroom is the outstanding marketplace for friendships, these results again highlight the relevance of children's social life in the classroom for education and achievement in school.

Instruction as a Negotiated Order

Obviously, the interaction of learning processes with children's peer-related efforts to maintain a respected self are an important argument for the responsibility of school and teachers for social life in the classroom. However, it must be conceded that school cannot host children's complete peer world in its classrooms. Because peer activities are important, there should be places outside educational institutions where the peer world can manifest its developmental power. But the outdoor peer world of today in many countries is too reduced for teachers to risk banning children's negotiations from the classroom. School offers a socializing ground that is essential to the success of teaching and learning. Teachers should therefore try to integrate social processes such as the three discussed here—negotiation, helping, and affirmation of self-concepts—as overlapping aspects of children's fundamental efforts at coordinating and controlling actions.

Teachers, however, cannot tolerate the kind of social anarchy that frequently characterizes the peer world and that at times threatens to spill over into the classroom because it finds no place elsewhere. With regard to the integration of peer processes penetrating into the classroom, we discovered an interesting change of teachers' strategies in a longitudinal study of educational change in primary schools. Three researchers visited these schools, first in 1977–78, again in 1982–83, and finally in 1987–88. They collected data in every school for two to three days. More than 400 lessons of instruction were observed during the three periods of data collection. Almost all teachers were interviewed after the lesson about the models, goals, and problems that influenced the observed lesson. Teachers' behaviors toward peer interactions in the classroom were compared on the basis of about 50 lessons selected randomly from the first and the last periods of data collection. In 1977–78, teachers tended to organize their students' activities according to rules that they themselves introduced and controlled. Teacher-oriented learning was frequent and self-regulated learning in dyads or groups infrequent. These latter social forms of learning clearly increased until 1987–88, when they were observed in about 50 percent of the lessons. Also, teacher-oriented instruction was realized less rigidly, referred more to children's own experiences, and included joint searches for solutions. Often, both forms of learning were combined.

These findings indicate that the traditional distinction between teacher-oriented learning and social learning in groups appears gradually to have become less salient. It is more characteristic now for teachers to make far greater efforts to elaborate agreements with the children in their classrooms than it was in the 1970s. On the one hand, this can be regarded as a consequence of the mixed forms of instruction that demand that children recognize and apply specific regulations in the respective learning situations. On the other hand, teachers can give more leeway to children's social activities because the discussion of basic rules of classroom life ensures that children take the necessities of teaching and learning into account when interacting with peers in the classroom.

Thus, the embedding of learning in children's social life does not lead into unstructured situations. The productive integration of teaching, learning, and children's social life can be achieved within the "negotiated order" of the classroom (Martin, 1976), which allows for an integration of the seemingly unreconcilable: the curriculum-oriented and teacher-controlled learning setting and the independent and self-regulatory social processes among the students in the classroom. However, this reconciliation is possible only when negotiation is clearly based on mutual respect for the particular goals and expectations of both sides. It is in the interests of both sides that the members of the classroom come to a working agreement. With few exceptions, all children want to learn and will accept regulations if they feel accepted as social beings. Teachers can allow children's social life to penetrate into the classroom as they better understand that learning processes are rooted in basic socializing processes, to which peer interaction effectively contributes.

The Comprehensive Responsibility of Teachers

The negotiated order of instruction in the classroom apparently creates an opportunity for a tight relationship between effectiveness and responsibility for the teacher. This synthesis is more than a mere additive combination: it can be envisioned as a mutual promotion of both goals, pursued by teachers who want to educate a competent and responsible generation of women and men. There are good reasons that teachers cannot divide their activities into effective promotion of learning, on the one hand, and care for children's well-being, on the other. Our analyses confirm that teachers, at least in primary schools, are well advised to foster children's social interactions and friendships in the classroom, because competencies urgently needed for successful learning emerge in the social processes among children. Efforts undertaken to effectively help another child can stimulate taking the other's perspective; controversial negotiations can further the development of discourse capacities and comprehension of fairness and justice; and conflicts about claimed selves can nourish a stable self-understanding that helps children to cope with making mistakes in the process of learning.

The observations from classrooms and playgrounds presented in this chapter demonstrate that school does not necessarily destroy the developmental incentives inherent in the social life of children. On the contrary, because school and instruction place demands on children to find acceptable solutions, this context can contribute to a productive challenge of children's coconstructive competencies. The context of school can even compensate for a weakness of children's interactions in less demanding settings, such as their tendency to drop controversial subjects, to avoid irksome negotiations, or to agree on hollow compromises in order to have peace. In many cases, school influences interacting children in a manner similar to friendship, because both contexts underscore the necessity of trying hard to find an acceptable solution.

However, we know that in many classrooms, these desirable productive social processes are lacking because children are not friends with each other, because they envy the successes of other children or try to outdo others, because they do not share ideas or mutually exclude children, and because they form rival cliques. There are also teachers who contribute to a hostile climate by engendering a destructive atmosphere of competition. But most often, averse social relationships among students can be linked to unstable relationships with significant others in earlier childhood. Given this fact, teachers should be made aware that they can also become a developmentally important significant other for children. Although they cannot directly establish friendships and a caring climate among their students (see also Chapter Twenty-Four), teachers can offer a vital "firm base" for social experience by developing an understanding of individual children's human needs for affiliation, security, and justice (Sroufe, 1989). Again, this conception of teachers' role stresses that their responsibility stretches beyond the narrow sense of learning processes.

This chapter has tried to outline a concept of teachers' double responsibility that can link effective learning and socializing processes in peer interactions to mutually stimulate children's competence development. The concept has been illustrated rather than proved by the presentation of classroom observations. This qualitative methodological approach contains the most contextually valid information about children's social life in the classroom. It is important to keep in mind that children's worlds are richer than most of our studies can deal with. From the educationalist point of view, it is a relief to realize that children have more sources of development than those that adults organize for them.

References

Azmitia, M., and Perlmutter, M. "Social Influences on Children's Cognition: State of the Art and Future Directions." *Advances in Child Development and Behavior*, 1989, *22*, 89–144.

Bosma, H. A., and Jackson, A. E. (eds.). *Coping and Self-Concept in Adolescence*. Berlin: Springer, 1990.

Brophy, J., and Good, T. L. "Teacher Behavior and Student Achievement." In M. C. Wittrock (ed.), *Handbook of Research on Teaching*. (3rd ed.) New York: Macmillan, 1986.

Friedrich, P., and others. *Die "Lücke"-Kinder* [Children in the educational gap]. Weinheim, Germany: Deutscher Studien Verlag, 1989.

Glaser, B. G., and Strauss, A. L. *The Discovery of Grounded Theory: Strategies for Qualitative Research*. Chicago: Aldine, 1967.

Hopf, D., Krappmann, L., and Scheerer, H. "Aktuelle Probleme der Grundschule" [Present problems of primary school education]. In Max Planck Institute for Educational Research, *Bildung in der Bundesrepublik Deutschland* [Education in the Federal Republic of Germany]. Vol. 2. Stuttgart, Germany: Klett-Cotta, 1980.

Krappmann, L. "Self-Threat in the Peer World: Observations of Twelve-Year-Old Children in Natural Settings." In G. Noam and T. Wren (eds.), *Morality and the Self*. Cambridge, Mass.: MIT Press, forthcoming.

Krappmann, L., and Oswald, H. "Negotiation Strategies in Peer Conflicts: A Follow-Up Study in Natural Settings." Paper presented at the biennial meeting of the Society for Research in Child Development, Baltimore, Md., Apr. 1987.

Krappmann, L., and Oswald, H. "Aushandlungen unter zehn- und zwölfjährigen Kindern über Kinderwelt- und Schulthemen" [Negotiations among ten- and twelve-year-olds about issues from peer and school context]. Paper presented to the working group Development of Social Competence in Children and Adolescents at the tenth Conference for Developmental Psychology, Cologne, Germany, 1991a.

Krappmann, L., and Oswald, H. "Problems of Helping Among Ten-Year-Old Children: Results of a Qualitative Study in Natural Settings." In L. Montada and H. W. Bierhoff (eds.), *Altruism in Social Systems*. Toronto: Hogrefe, 1991b.

Martin, W.B.W. *The Negotiated Order of the School*. Toronto: Macmillan, 1976.

Mead, G. H. *Mind, Self, and Society*. Chicago: University of Chicago Press, 1934.

Oswald, H., and Krappmann, L. "Konstanz und Veränderung in den sozialen Beziehungen von Schulkindern" [Stability and change in the social relationships of primary school students]. *Zeitschrift für Sozialisationsforschung und Erziehungssoziologie* [Journal for research in socialization and sociology of education], 1984, *4*, 271–286.

Oswald, H., and Krappmann, L. *Soziale Beziehungen und Interaktionen unter Grundschulkindern: Methoden und ausgewählte Ergebnisse eines qualitativen Forschungs-*

projektes [Social relationships and interactions of primary school students: methods and results from a qualitative research project]. Papers in Educational Research, no. 33. Berlin: Max Planck Institute for Educational Research, 1988.

Piaget, J. *The Language and the Thought of the Child.* New York: Harcourt Brace Jovanovich, 1926.

Piaget, J. *The Moral Judgment of the Child.* New York: Free Press, 1965. (Originally published 1932.)

Rabe-Kleberg, U., and Zeiher, H. "Kindheit und Zeit: Über das Eindringen moderner Zeitorganisation in die Lebensbedingungen von Kindern" [Childhood and time: about the influence of modern organization of time on living conditions of children]. In K. Hurrelmann (ed.), *Lebenslage, Lebensalter, Lebenszeit* [Living conditions, age, and time of life]. Weinheim, Germany: Beltz, 1986.

Slavin, R. *Cooperative Learning.* White Plains, N.Y.: Longman, 1983.

Sroufe, L. A. "Relationships, Self, and Individual Adaptation." In A. J. Sammeroff and R. N. Emde (eds.), *Relationship Disturbances in Early Childhood.* New York: Basic Books, 1989.

Sullivan, H. S. *The Interpersonal Theory of Psychiatry.* (H. S. Perry and M. L. Gawel, eds.) New York: Norton, 1953.

Webb, N. M. (ed.). "Peer Interaction, Problem Solving, and Cognition: Multidisciplinary Perspectives." *International Journal of Educational Research,* 1989, *13* (entire issue 1).

Youniss, J. *Parents and Peers in Social Development: A Sullivan-Piaget Perspective.* Chicago: University of Chicago Press, 1980.

13

The Zone of Proximal Development
for Learning and Teaching

Rolf Oerter

The concept of the zone of proximal development (ZPD) first appeared in the writings of L. S. Vygotsky, who offered the now well-known definition: "The Zone of Proximal Development is the distance between the actual developmental level as determined by independent problem solving and the level of potential development under adult guidance or in collaboration with more capable peers" (Vygotsky, 1978, p. 86). The concept has been further elaborated by a number of investigators (Cazden, 1983; Greenfield, 1984; Wertsch, Minick, and Arns, 1984; Rogoff, 1986; Valsiner, 1987; Van Parreren, 1988; Tharp and Gallimore, 1988; Collins, Brown, and Newman, 1989) while still maintaining Vygotsky's fundamental notion that the assistance of competent social partners is needed to advance a child's developmental state. However, while most authors focus on the practical application of the idea of the ZPD, I would also like to attempt to provide evidence that the ZPD is more than an option—it is a necessary condition for human development. This is particularly true with regard to teaching and learning in school, where development can be understood as a process of coconstruction, mastered by both the child and the competent social partner (Valsiner, 1989). When development is viewed from this perspective, the modern concept of individuals as producers of their own development becomes just as one-sided as the assumption of instructional psychology that presenting knowledge according to a set of well-defined rules is a sufficient condition for learning.

In order to better understand the concept of the ZPD, we can distinguish three different situations that can create it. First, intentional instruction (be it the mother's help with the child's endeavor to climb a chair or the teacher's planned instruction in school) can provide the prerequisites of further development if it takes place within the child's ZPD. Second, a ZPD can be created by providing a stimulating environment (such as books, play materials, and materials for painting and sculpturing). Third, play can create a ZPD: "in play the child tries as if to accomplish a jump above the level of his ordinary behavior" (Vygotsky, 1966, p. 74). In all three of these situations, it is the child who constructs — with help — his or her learning, sometimes with unexpected results.

During my teacher training many years ago, I participated in a practicum in a small school. The teacher was excellent, but his musical capability was limited. During a music lesson, he introduced a new song in a very unmusical way. The children, obviously more patient than I, listened and then tried to sing. Amazingly enough, by the end of the lesson, they had mastered the song and could perform it well. The teacher, however, had not made any progress. What had happened? In terms of a ZPD, teacher and students had coconstructed the mastering of a song. Obviously, it was the children who made the main contribution to the learning progress, even though they would not have learned the song without the crude presentation of the teacher. They seemed to be able to apply already acquired schematas of songs to arrive at the right pitch (since deviations up and down were balanced, showing a kind of central tendency).

This example demonstrates that the concept of the ZPD is not a trivial one. On the contrary, school learning and instruction are fundamentally linked to human development. Furthermore, the effect of instruction on development during childhood and adolescence is completely different from that during adulthood. In childhood and adolescence, the most appropriate time for linking instruction to development is when new functions are beginning to emerge but have not yet unfolded. This is because school instruction canalizes the child's development toward the internalization of the sociohistorical knowledge of the culture in which the child grows up. Conversely, learning and instruction in adulthood usually lead to skills and competencies within an already established structure (actional or cognitive).

It is important to add that the ZPD also constitutes a moral challenge. Competent partners are responsible for enhancing developmental functions at the best possible time. Neglecting the benefits of ZPD means giving away chances for development. There is an interesting relationship between the notion of fostering development within the ZPD and Sandra Scarr's notion of individuals building their own environment (Scarr and McCartney, 1983). If the child's endeavor to construct and change the world according to his or her own developmental goals is supported within the ZPD, optimal development is guaranteed.

Memory Development, the Developmental Theory of Instruction, and the ZPD

Given the corpus of empirical data collected in memory research thus far, the production deficiency hypothesis is still a good model for understanding memory development. This hypothesis assumes four stages in strategy acquisition (Reese, 1976): (1) the strategy cannot be used even if it is taught (mediational deficiency); (2) the strategy is used after instruction but not generalized; (3) the strategy is used spontaneously and more or less generalized; (4) more complex or sophisticated forms (which also require more mental effort) of each type of strategy (especially rehearsal, organization, and elaboration) are produced later in development (see Schneider and Pressley, 1989, chap. 6) and often have to be taught explicitly.

Strategy development obviously occurs within the ZPD in a culturally dependent way. Our knowledge is ordered semantically, that is, according to the logic of sciences and school subjects. Furthermore, school as well as occupational life demands memory performance of lists of items in a specific way, requiring specific strategies, as described above. It would take too long for a child to acquire all those skills and competencies without social assistance. Family and, later, school create the ZPD in that they offer strategies and nonstrategic knowledge that can be used by the developing child to construct an efficient utilization of memory. Our awareness of the role of instruction and teaching in memory skills is growing (see, for example, Schneider and Pressley, 1989). Further research should focus on how parents and teachers mediate the acquisition of strategies and knowledge. If memory development in fact occurs at the ZPD — for example, through coconstruction of memory strategies — and not simply as a "natural" development, competent partners (parents and teachers) bear responsibility for a specific domain of mental skills (namely, acquisition and usage of encoding and retrieval strategies).

Since children acquire basic memory strategies, we can assume that the interaction provided for children at the ZPD is sufficient. However, this is not true for more sophisticated strategies (Kliegl, Smith, and Baltes, 1986; Pressley, 1982). Thus, "responsible teaching" should include the examination of possible domains of enhancement of development such as the domain of memory. The developmentally based theory of instruction offered by Case (1978a, 1978b, 1984) presents an approach to school learning that shows this aspect more clearly. According to Case (1978a, p. 457), this approach "advocates assessment of the learner's initial state in terms of the strategy that he applies to the criterion task spontaneously. . . . In addition, the developmental approach stresses the importance of the subject's own activity in the assembly process, with the consequent burden on working memory. Assembly of lower-order skills into higher-order skills is presumed to be possible only if the child's capacity for coordinating information is not overtaxed."

What Case describes is a particular example of an application of the ZPD. All components of the ZPD are taken into consideration: the initial developmental state, the consideration of the ZPD (in other words, what can be developed as a next step), and the organization of teaching processes that involve the individual's developmental constructing activity. Although Case does not specifically mention the concept of the ZPD, the developmental concept that he uses in analyzing specific tasks is very similar to the ZPD.

His analysis is especially fruitful when applied to individuals who are not able to master situations in the usual field of stimulation or ZPD provided; for example, handicapped children or children from a cultural minority.

Case (1978a, pp. 442–447) proposes three developmental principles and techniques for planning instruction: (1) analyze children's spontaneously generated strategies as well as the strategy to be taught; (2) design the instruction so that the limitations of the spontaneously applied strategy will be apparent and the advantage of the strategy to be taught will therefore be clear; and (3) minimize the load on working memory. The first principle contains a twofold task, the analysis of the present state of affairs and the conception of the optimal strategy. The latter is characterized as the expert's strategy. Note that contrary to Vygotsky's requirement, Case does not mention the assessment of the task level that can be reached with a teacher's assistance.

Case's approach applies to specific needs groups. While usual teacher-student interaction in school is sufficient for the development of cognitive competencies in mainstream children, a very careful planning of social interaction at the ZPD seems necessary for students who have difficulty mastering the task of memory development or concrete logical operations, such as described by Piaget (1969). Case (1978a, 1978b) was able to show that such learners can make remarkable progress if, in our terminology, an appropriate ZPD is provided at which coconstruction occurs in small steps. Teachers as well as other competent partners should feel responsible for utilizing procedures that enhance cognitive development with disadvantaged children if they are available, because knowledge and effort are necessary for fostering development.

Play as a Zone of Proximal Development

An important and excellent mediator of development, emphasized by Vygotsky and mentioned already as one of the three types of ZPD, is play. As Vygotsky (1966, p. 74) views the function of play, it "creates the zone of proximal development of the child . . . play contains in a condensed way, like in the focus of a magnifying glass, all tendencies of development; in play the child tries as if to accomplish a jump above the level of his ordinary behavior."

Play interaction requires flexibility, in contrast to Case's approach. A videotaped sequence of an eighteen-month-old child playing with her mother illustrates this point. In the sequence, the child wants to open plastic boxes and fill them with smaller items. She needs the help of the mother, because she cannot open the boxes by herself. However, the mother does not understand the intention of the child and offers a variety of other activities, such as building a tower with the boxes and fetching them from a drawer and putting them back into the drawer. Finally, the mother understands what the child wants and helps her to reach her goal. This shows reversed-

order interaction that can take place within the ZPD. The child is practicing a specific type of action that she cannot accomplish alone. She thus creates a ZPD in that she elicits assistance and suggests a zone of promoted
action (discussed in more detail below). Whether the child receives the needed
help within the ZPD and can advance to a higher developmental level depends on the social environment. (My colleagues and I have observed many
similar interactions as part of an ongoing project on child development in
play.)

The reverse of these dynamics is play situations in which a competent
partner suggests a certain play behavior and tries to promote the desired
activity in the child. For example, a nine-year-old girl plays the role of a
buyer with a five-year-old girl who plays the seller. The older girl is clearly
interested in enhancing her younger partner's ability to role play. She chooses
two strategies. First, she takes the role of a younger child who does not know
the value of money very well and who orders goods with which the seller
is well acquainted (in this case, cookies and toys). The seller responds to
this strategy by being particularly attentive to possible mistakes in role behavior. The second strategy appears when the older girl pretends to leave
without paying. When the younger girl, in the role of seller, does not respond,
she asks, "Did I forget something?" This reminds the younger child of the
money that must be paid in return for the goods. This second strategy is
a well-tuned proceeding within the ZPD.

Another opportunity for play within the ZPD is reading. Ninio and
Bruner (1978), who observed mothers reading to their infants, describe a
"scaffolding" procedure in which the child's activity is canalized toward recognizing and labeling represented objects. The process of scaffolding is a main
component of teaching activity within the ZPD (see Bruner, 1984). Wood
(1980) describes it as follows:

> Once the child could be lured into some form of task-relevant
> activity, however low level, the tutor could build around him
> a supporting structure which held in place whatever he could
> manage. That supporting activity served to connect the child's
> activity into the overall construction and to provide a frame-
> work within which the child's action could lead to and mean
> something more general than he may have foreseen. As the child
> mastered components of the task, he was freed to consider the
> wider context of what he could do, to take over more of the com-
> plementary activity. The adult could "de-scaffold" those parts
> which now stood firmly on their own [pp. 281–282].

In book-reading play, the scaffolding activity consists of drawing attention to a picture each time the page is turned, identifying the objects
depicted, and labeling them appropriately. Our observations show that adult
partners manage this task in different ways, sometimes moving out of the

ZPD. For example, in one videotaped scene, a grandmother looks at a picture book with a one-and-a-half-year-old pointing to objects and naming them. The mother, sitting nearby, occasionally interferes, using inappropriate labels. For example, she points to a car, saying, "look, this is an English one."

The three examples given above all suggest that there is a need to extend the ZPD concept. To begin with, the learner's contribution to the construction of a ZPD, as well as the role of contextual and situational conditions, needs to be more clearly understood.

Extending the ZPD Concept

Thus far, the ZPD concept has focused on the individual's present and future capacity. Individual competencies could be developed through shared interaction around a problem that could not be mastered by the developing individual alone. This view is not further elaborated by Vygotsky. However, from the perspective of action theory, which always includes the environment as basic to every action, this view is one-sided. In defining action, the relationship between person and environment is as important as the goal-directedness. By taking this "ecological" point of view, we can extend the ZPD to include the learning and developmental environment.

Three Zones of Interaction

Valsiner (1987) introduces the concept of the ZPD as a link between two other zones, the zone of free movement (ZFM) and the zone of promoted action (ZPA), which theoretically embeds the ZPD more precisely in the systemic relationship between culture and individual. The zone of free movement "characterizes the set of what is available . . . to the child at a given time. The boundaries of the ZFM are constantly being reorganized. The reorganization may be initiated by either the child or caregiver, or by all of them at the same time" (Valsiner, 1987, p. 232).

The ZFM always has constraints set up by the social environment, especially by parents and teachers, and behind them by culture and society. Valsiner describes the zone of promoted action as "a set of activities, objects, or areas in the environment, in respect of which the child's actions are promoted" (p. 100). Between these two zones is the ZPD. Only if the zone of promoted action and the zone of proximal development match each other can the instruction have its optimal effect. If there is no overlap between ZPD and ZPA, no development will occur. If, for example, a ZPA is provided that cannot be realized because of the absence of a ZFM, no ZPD can be created. Consider a child learning to read without access to books or other written materials (in an environment in which literacy activities are absent or infrequent): the learning environment needed for establishing a ZPD is missing. Figure 13.1 illustrates the interaction of the three zones. In the figure, the zone of promoted action is completely part of the zone of free movement. This means that all that is desired by education is available to the learner. In case of demands at the zone of promoted action that cannot be fulfilled by the child because those demands are not in the ZFM, the ZPA surpasses the ZFM. The ZPD, on the other hand, always possesses an area lying outside the ZFM, since only some of the person's developmental potentials can be realized, while others remain undeveloped.

If we include the ZFM into our analysis of the ZPD, a paradox mentioned by Valsiner (1987) becomes visible: the ZPD of an individual cannot be completely determined empirically. If capacity in a certain domain is tested and the ZPD assessed, only a subset of all possible realizations of the ZPD is tapped. In every social interaction where a child promotes his or her development, a canalization occurs that excludes other options of the original ZPD (illustrated by the part of the ZPD lying outside the ZFM and the ZPA in Figure 13.1). Since all interaction within the ZPD is socioculturally determined, this paradox holds for all development that occurs through the creation of the ZPD. Needless to say, this is also true for schoolteaching and education. Every curriculum canalizes potential activity into specific fields. We do not know what other things a child could learn within the ZPD if the time were not spent learning school subjects.

Figure 13.1. The Interaction of Three Zones in Human Development.

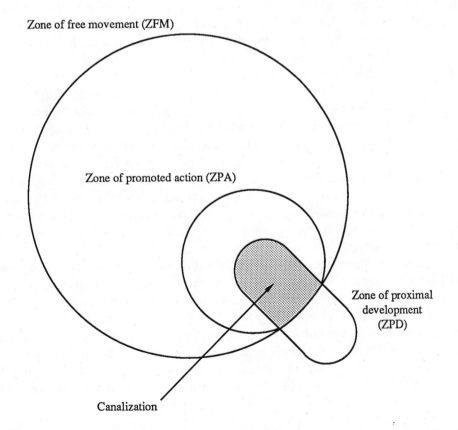

The dilemma of development by canalization, permanently deciding for one alternative against another, cannot be avoided. However, the fascinating quality of human development is its unpredictability. By extending the ZPD to offer more options and action opportunities, we can better explore human opportunity and potential development for the individual.

Moral Development and the ZPD

While we can generally claim that development and learning will occur only if and when the ZFM, the ZPA, and the ZPD all overlap, there is one domain in which the ZFM is at least partially lacking while there is a strong pressure to create a ZPA. This domain is moral development and education.

The developmental approach to moral education (Kohlberg, 1986; Oser and Schlaefli, 1986; Power and Higgins, 1981) looks like an ideal realization of the ZPD. The individual, performing at a certain stage of moral judgment, is developing with the assistance and "scaffolding" of moral education. Theoretical assumptions as well as empirical evidence have shown that enhancement in moral education is possible only in the zone proximal to the individual's current level. Furthermore, moral development occurs within a rather small area: for example, lengthy interventions have been shown to succeed in achieving only half-stage advancements in moral judgment.

The combination of development and education in moral judgment and action is certainly an excellent empirical example of what Vygotsky had in mind with the ZPD. However, research as well as theoretical work on moral education (Edelstein, 1986; Höffe, 1986) reveal that the highest stage of moral judgment, though the necessary aim of moral development, cannot be reached through education.

Here is a paradox. Every endeavor of moral development aims at the highest level (with the exception of the utilitarian position, which considers it superfluous [see Höffe, 1986], and the ethical discourse position, which sees what is conventionally considered the highest level expanding into an even higher existential level [Habermas, 1983]). Even Kohlberg, who was not able to empirically show this highest level (what he termed "stage six") claims that moral development is not completed unless it is reached. Why, then, does no one reach this level of moral development except Socrates, Jesus, and Gandhi? Scanning the literature relevant to this topic, I could not find a satisfying answer.

If we transform the problem in terms of the ZFM, the ZPA, and the ZPD, we recognize that moral action at the highest level cannot possibly be performed in our environment: society and culture do not provide a structure that allows the realization of moral thought at this level. In Figure 13.2, the dashed line marks the ZFM necessary for a ZPD at this level. Under ordinary conditions, a truly moral actor at stage six would soon become isolated from the social environment. Such an actor would violate many laws and finally would not even be able to consume food, because this is an act

Figure 13.2. The Restriction of the Zone of Free Movement in Moral Development.

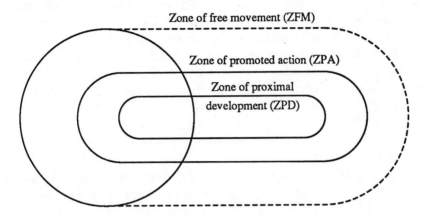

based on an economy that neglects or even increases the starvation of the
majority of the world's population.

What is true for moral action is also true for moral judgment. Arguing at stage six requires a profound and broad base of knowledge about complex relationships in society and the world as a whole. Taken as a system,
this whole is not completely analyzable and predictable. The individual looking for moral maxims gets lost in a maze of millions of conditions. If we
use the ZFM concept in a very broad sense, there is no zone of free movement for moral action at level six. The only possibility would be to change
society into a system that does realize the conditions necessary for level-six
performance.

But we need not restrict ourselves to level six in order to demonstrate
the complementary role of the environment in the ZPD. Nearly every study
within the field of moral education shows the problem of restriction through
environmental conditions. For instance, experiments with the cluster school
(Kohlberg, 1986; Power and Higgins, 1981) have shown that although an
environment for moral education and its ZPD can be created outside the
school, it is difficult to maintain moral principles that regulate interaction
within the group. Oser and Schlaefli (1986) demonstrate that the moral atmosphere originated by an intervention in a bank and the actual environment in the bank conflicted. This is no surprise given the nature of bank
business, where specific moral structures, even at stage three or four, cannot be realized.

The ZPD as an Ecological Concept

I have tried to show in the discussion above that the reintroduction of the
ZPD is meaningful only if it is considered as an ecological concept; in other
words, if the environment as "the other end of action" is systematically taken
into consideration. Environment is not merely the visible part that surrounds

the individual; it is the whole culture with its constraints and benefits. If an environment lacks some features necessary for higher development, a ZPD cannot be created. This is demonstrated by failures to transfer moral education to the social realm outside the school.

The ecological nature of the ZPD can first be demonstrated by an analysis of the object relationship of human action. Leontjew (1978) claims that there is no action without an object. Object directedness of action can be defined as

$$S \longrightarrow O$$

where S is the subject (individual) and O the object, which includes not only material objects, such as tools, animals, and people, but also every entity toward which the individual is related through overt action, thought, and emotion. Objects in this sense are culturally constructed entities. The main purpose of their construction is to perform specific actions on them that serve the individual's as well as the community's or society's well-being. The object intrinsically carries the constructor's, or tool maker's, ideas of action upon object. For instance, a hammer is a kind of materialization of the law of leverage that was put into the tool by its constructor. The child who tries to discover the functioning of the hammer is simultaneously in contact with the tool maker and his or her ideas. Thus, there is no object relationship of an individual without at least a hidden partner behind the objects defining (or teaching) its action properties.

The ZPD provides opportunities to learn appropriate ways to act upon objects. In some cases, a setting in which there is merely an object that a child manipulates in successively more appropriate ways provides a ZPD. (This would explain the effect of a stimulating environment on development.) More often, however, a second person is included in the object relationship. This shared object relationship can be symbolized as

$$S \longrightarrow O \longleftarrow S$$

Shared object relationships are an ordinary and appropriate kind of social interaction early on. They could even be considered a prototype of social interaction. Learning at the ZPD can be described and explained as the coconstruction of a shared object relationship between two or more social partners. Thus, an analysis of ZPD always includes a description of the object and the kind of actions that have to be performed on that object.

Social interaction and coconstruction have been shown at early stages of development. Bruner (1975), for example, describes how a child's attention is directed toward an object by the mother and how information processing is then regulated when the child subsequently handles the object. At later stages of development, symbolized objects become the focus of interaction. The material object no longer need be present; substitutes and, later, verbal labels for an object are the focus of shared meaning. The majority of learning processes occur this way, but if and only if the partners succeed in establishing a ZPD.

Not only the quality of objects but also the kind of interaction changes during development. While overt manipulations on a concrete object prevail at an early level, verbal interaction becomes dominant later on. A special type of verbal communication related to the ZPD is metacommunication. Metacommunication becomes the most important strategy for scaffolding the ZPD. Children first use metacommunication in free play, particularly in role playing (Fein, 1981), and profit from practice in metacommunicative language for literacy (Pellegrini and Galda, 1991). Later in school, metacommunication can be understood as a central process of learning activity scaffolding the ZPD.

From the perspective of the object-relatedness of human action and its concomitant process of communication, the ZPD, the ZFM, and the ZPA can be systematically integrated into a systems approach to personality development in culture. Culture is revealed to be the universe of possible actions available to the individual. Action opportunities are conceptualized to objects that form the substance of a culture. The zone of free movement, thus, is the segment of culturally provided opportunities or objects available to an individual. The zone of promoted action refers to the groups of objects the mastering of which is desired by competent and powerful partners (parents, teachers) as well as social groups and society as a whole. Finally, the zone of proximal development forms the segment of action opportunities (or objects) that can be acted on by common coconstructive activity.

This perspective is easily demonstrated by school subject matters. All subjects offered by society (ZFM) are limited through the curricula of a given class or school type (ZPA). Effective learning occurs at the ZPD for subjects that can be mastered by the learner through direct or indirect (for example, by structured learning material) interaction with the teacher. The notion of responsibility refers to the necessity to find the specific ZPD for each individual in order to enhance development.

The ecological approach to the person-object relationship also clarifies another characteristic of development: decontextualization (Bretherton, 1984; Piaget, 1969; McLoyd, 1983). From a cultural perspective, decontextualization refers to the segregation of a specific object (and its opportunities for action) from the immense variety of objects and their respective possibilities provided by a culture. This process of abstraction is the basic strategy for restructuring the world into logical categories, resulting in semantic rather than epistemic memory. It is obvious that only coconstruction at the ZPD guarantees this complicated process. Only competent partners can present the developing individual with objects and their opportunities for action that are important for enhancement in a given culture. No doubt, school is the central institution directed toward this task.

Is There a Theoretical Gain?

The reintroduction of the ZPD into the discussion of teaching-learning seems encouraging. First, it relates education and development in a theoretically convincing way. Second, empirical evidence in several domains (for example, memory development, play activity, and moral development) shows that much of developmental progress is indeed accomplished within the ZPD, where achievement above the spontaneously produced developmental level can be reached. The sequence deficiency of a competence, performance under instruction, and spontaneous performance is probably a general developmental law.

In a strong version of the ZPD, only developmental processes, and not learning in general, belong to the ZPD concept. From this perspective, the features of child and adolescent education that distinguish it from adult education need elaboration, something that has not been done so far. It is not even clear whether we should distinguish between learning as development and learning as merely acquisition of skills and competencies. The distinction between expert and novice seems to be somewhat between development and learning. From my own point of view, the ZPD concept should be restricted to those domains where new constructive activity occurs, be it the development of a more general structure or the development of a more specific expert structure.

Thus far, the ZPD concept has been used primarily as a paradigm that provides a promising perspective for the modeling of instruction of every kind (particularly conversation) that aims at the enhancement of development. However, a concept is useful only if it allows some sort of prediction with regard to cases that are included and those that are excluded. This necessity leads to a paradoxical problem: as was shown earlier, the ZPD cannot be fully measured empirically, since creation of the zone of proximal action and the zone of free movement restricts other possible learning chances of the individual (canalization). Therefore, prediction also means restriction of development.

Must we completely renounce prediction? Not at all. In a general way, the ZPD allows the prediction that with the help of competent partners, a child will resolve a variety of tasks that cannot be mastered alone. The selection of those tasks depends on cultural constraints and opportunities. We can also describe the if-then relation of the ZPD. We can list the following preconditions for successful development within the ZPD: (1) the student suggests an activity that is promoted by the teacher; (2) the teacher introduces an activity that is accepted by the student and improved through coconstruction; and (3) the teacher understands the student's intentions, is able to assess the student's structural level (developmental level), and is able to provide materials and interaction at the level of the ZPD. The third set of criteria can be assessed by the student's and the observer's evaluation of the teacher's competence. The fulfillment of these three conditions increases the likelihood of developmental progress.

An even more interesting theoretical advantage of the ZPD is that it can explain cases that cannot be explained otherwise. Consider our example of the music lesson, in which learning occurred in spite of bad instruction. There are many cases of instruction that is not structured as an optimal teaching-learning process in which children nevertheless make progress. One of the most amazing examples is language acquisition in a natural context. In contrast to a well-structured curriculum in which words, sentences, and domains of meaning are systematically presented, language learning in natural contexts is incidental, unstructured, and unplanned. Obviously, such a learning process demands much more spontaneous constructive activity of the involved partners than learning processes in school. Research should look at natural interactions that are successful even though they might seem to occur in a poor learning environment from the standpoint of an educational psychologist.

What can be said in summary of the above discussion? On the whole, research on the ZPD should attempt to operationalize the concepts of the ZPD, the ZFM, and the ZPA for all cases analyzed. Furthermore, a predictive capability for the ZPD needs to be developed. These predictions should apply to both events within the ZPD and those outside (or at the periphery) of it. This would allow verification or invalidation of the ZPD concept.

Outlook: The ZPD and Responsibility

As mentioned earlier, the ZPD also implies a moral challenge. If teachers feel responsible for education, they should attempt to create ZPDs and to foster development within the ZPD. The consequences of failing to create a ZPD can be illustrated by the following anecdote: A school inspector was driving his car to a little village to visit the school there. When he arrived, the car's engine died. He got out of the car, opened the hood, and stood looking helplessly at the engine. Just then, a boy approached and asked what had happened. The boy looked under the hood and made a few adjustments, and the engine ran again. The school inspector was thanking the boy admiringly until he suddenly realized that the boy should be in school. He asked, "Why aren't you in school today?" and the boy answered, "Well, our teacher told us that the school inspector was coming and that we all had to perform very well. Then he pointed to me and said, 'And you stay at home because you are the most stupid!'"

The boy in the anecdote obviously did not have much opportunity for developing in school. In fact, it is likely that in every society there are certain groups that lack appropriate ZPDs in their schools (see, for example, Ogbu, 1978). Teachers as well as the school system itself seem to be unaware that such youngsters need more specific zones of proximal development. These can be created only if there is more understanding and sensitivity to their peculiar developmental situations.

References

Bretherton, I. (ed.). *Symbolic Play: The Development of Social Understanding.* San Diego, Calif.: Academic Press, 1984.

Bruner, J. "The Ontogenesis of Speech Acts." *Journal of Child Language,* 1975, *2,* 1-19.

Bruner, J. "Vygotsky's Zone of Proximal Development: The Hidden Agenda." In B. Rogoff and J. V. Wertsch (eds.), *Children's Learning in the "Zone of Proximal Development."* New Directions for Child Development, no. 23. San Francisco: Jossey-Bass, 1984.

Case, R. "A Developmentally Based Theory and Technology of Instruction." *Review of Educational Research,* 1978a, *48,* 439-463.

Case, R. "Piaget and Beyond: Toward a Developmentally Based Theory and Technology of Instruction." In R. Glaser (ed.), *Advances in Instructional Psychology.* Hillsdale, N.J.: Erlbaum, 1978b.

Case, R. "The Process of Stage Transition: A Neo-Piagetian View." In R. J. Sternberg (ed.), *Mechanisms of Cognitive Development.* San Francisco: Freeman, 1984.

Cazden, C. "Peekaboo as an Instrumental Model: Discourse Development at Home and at School." In B. Bain (ed.), *The Sociogenesis of Language and Human Conduct.* New York: Plenum Press, 1983.

Collins, A., Brown, J. S., and Newman, S. E. "Cognitive Apprenticeship: Teaching the Crafts of Reading, Writing, and Mathematics." In L. B. Resnick (ed.), *Knowing, Learning, and Instruction: Essays in Honor of Robert Glaser.* Hillsdale, N.J.: Erlbaum, 1989.

Edelstein, W. "Moralische Intervention in der Schule: Skeptische Überlegungen" [Moral intervention in school: skeptical thoughts]. In F. Oser, R. Fatke, and O. Höffe (eds.), *Transformation und Entwicklung* [Transformation and development]. Frankfurt, Germany: Suhrkamp, 1986.

Fein, F. "Pretend Play in Childhood: An Integrative Review." *Child Development,* 1981, *52,* 1095-1118.

Greenfield, P. "A Theory of the Teacher in the Learning Activities of Everyday Life." In B. Rogoff and J. Lave (eds.), *Everyday Cognition: Its Development in Social Context.* Cambridge, Mass.: Harvard University Press, 1984.

Habermas, J. *Moralbewusstsein und kommunikatives Handeln* [Moral consciousness and communicative actions]. Frankfurt, Germany: Suhrkamp, 1983.

Höffe, O. "Autonomie und Verallgemeinerung als Moralprinzipien: Eine Auseinandersetzung mit Kohlberg, dem Utilitarismus und der Diskursethik" [Autonomy and generalization as moral principles: A discussion of Kohlberg, utilitarianism, and ethics of discourse]. In F. Oser, R. Fatke, and O. Höffe (eds.), *Transformation und Entwicklung* [Transformation and development]. Frankfurt, Germany: Suhrkamp, 1986.

Kliegl, R., Smith, J., and Baltes, P. B. "Testing-the-Limits, Expertise, and Memory in Adulthood and Old Age." In F. Klix and H. Hagendorf (eds.), *Human Memory and Cognitive Capabilities.* New York: Elsevier Science, 1986.

Kohlberg, L. "Moral Development and Identification." In H. W. Stevenson (ed.), *Child Psychology.* 62nd yearbook of the National Society for the Study of Education. Chicago: University of Chicago Press, 1963.

Kohlberg, L. "Der 'Just Community'-Ansatz der Moralerziehung in Theorie und Praxis" [The "just community" approach of moral education in theory and practice]. In F. Oser, R. Fatke, and O. Höffe (eds.), *Transformation und Entwicklung* [Transformation and development]. Frankfurt, Germany: Suhrkamp, 1986.

Leontjew, A. N. *Activity, Consciousness, and Personality.* Englewood Cliffs, N.J.: Prentice-Hall, 1978.

McLoyd, V. C. "The Effects of the Structure of Play Objects on the Pretend Play of Low-Income Preschool Children." *Child Development,* 1983, *54,* 626–635.

Ninio, A., and Bruner, J. "The Achievement and Antecedents of Labelling." *Journal of Child Language,* 1978, *5,* 1–15.

Ogbu, J. U. *Minority Education and Caste: The American System in Cross-Cultural Perspective.* San Diego, Calif.: Academic Press, 1978.

Oser, F. and Schlaefli, A. "Und sie bewegt sich doch: Zur Schwierigkeit der stufenmässigen Veränderung des moralischen Urteils: Am Beispiel von Schweizer Banklehrlingen" [And it moves after all: difficulties of changing moral judgment in stages: an investigation of Swiss bank apprentices]. In F. Oser, R. Fatke, and O. Höffe (eds.), *Transformation und Entwicklung* [Transformation and development]. Frankfurt, Germany: Suhrkamp, 1986.

Pellegrini, A. D., and Galda, L. "Spiel, Sprache und frühe Kompetenz im Lesen und Schreiben" [Play, language, and early competence in reading and writing]. *Unterrichtswissenschaft* [Science of teaching], 1991, *18,* 269–281.

Piaget, J. *Nachahmung, Spiel und Traum* [Imitation, play, and dream]. Stuttgart, Germany: Klett, 1969.

Power, C., and Higgins, A. "Moralische Atmosphäre und Lernen" [Moral atmosphere and learning]. *Unterrichtswissenschaft* [Science of teaching], 1981, *9,* 225–240.

Pressley, M. "Elaboration and Memory Development." *Child Development,* 1982, *53,* 296–309.

Reese, H. W. "The Development of Memory: Life-Span Perspectives." In H. W. Reese (ed.), *Advances in Child Development and Behavior.* San Diego, Calif.: Academic Press, 1976.

Rogoff, B. "Adult Assistance of Children's Learning." In T. E. Raphael (ed.), *The Contexts of School-Based Literacy.* New York: Random House, 1986.

Scarr, S., and McCartney, K. "How People Make Their Own Environments: A Theory of Genotype." *Child Development,* 1983, *54,* 424–435.

Schneider, W., and Pressley, M. *Memory Development Between 2 and 20.* New York: Springer, 1989.

Tharp, R. G., and Gallimore, R. *Rousing Minds to Life: Teaching, Learning, and Schooling in Social Context.* Cambridge, England: Cambridge University Press, 1988.

Valsiner, J. *Culture and the Development of Children's Action.* New York: Wiley, 1987.

Valsiner, J. *Human Development and Culture.* Lexington, Mass.: Lexington Books, 1989.

Van Parreren, C. F. *Ontwikkelend onderwijs* [Developmental instruction]. Louvain, Belgium: Acco, 1988.

Vygotsky, L. S. "Play and Its Role in the Psychological Development of the Child." *Voprosy psikhologii* [*Psychological inquiry*], 1966, *12,* 62–76.

Vygotsky, L. S. *Mind in Society: The Development of Higher Psychological Processes.* (M. Cole, V. John-Steiner, S. Scribner, and E. Souberman, eds. and trans.) Cambridge, Mass.: Harvard University Press, 1978.

Wertsch, J., Minick, N., and Arns, F. J. "The Creation of Context in Joint Problem-Solving." In B. Rogoff and J. Lave (eds.), *Everyday Cognition: Its Development in Social Context.* Cambridge, Mass.: Harvard University Press, 1984.

Wood, D. "Teaching the Young Child: Some Relationships Between Social Interaction, Language, and Thought." In D. R. Olson (ed.), *The Social Foundation of Language and Thought.* New York: Norton, 1980.

14

Tracking the Developmental Path of Teachers and Learners: A Vygotskian Perspective

Ronald Gallimore, Claude N. Goldenberg

There is a transparent kind of teaching common in the everyday life of children that the participants do not call teaching. This unnamed teaching is embedded in the social fabric in which children are "apprenticed" to more cognitively and communicatively capable others (Rogoff, 1990). For Vygotsky (1962, 1978), this unnamed teaching supports a key phase in development when a child has only partially mastered the skill but can successfully employ it with the assistance and supervision of an adult.

Performing a task with the assistance of another allows the child to internalize a skill so that in the future the task can be performed without assistance. The contrast between assisted and unassisted performance identifies the fundamental nexus of development and learning that Vygotsky called the zone of proximal development (ZPD).

In societies where literacy is a subsistence tool, "talk" and "conversation" are principal forms of assisted performance. Children are apprenticed from an early age in the uses of language and text. "Skills for the use of cultural tools such as literacy begin to be practiced even before children have contact with the technology itself. American middle-class parents involve their children in 'literate' forms of narrative in preschool discourse, as they embed their children in a way of life in which reading and writing are integral

Note: Preparation of this chapter was supported by grants from the National Institute of Child Health and Human Development, the Spencer Foundation, the University of California Linguistic Minority Research Project, and the University of California Presidential Grants for School Improvement Program. Jan Hamann provided critical and useful comments on earlier drafts and conducted some of the analyses presented. Robert Rueda also contributed to the data analysis. Our sincere thanks to the teachers in the Lennox School District, Lennox, California, who participated in the California portion of the research reported here: Betty Brandenburg, Flor Calderón, Barbara Paulsen, and Gail Williams. We are particularly grateful to Flor Calderón, who provided feedback on an earlier version of this chapter and permitted us to use extensive portions of transcripts containing her comments.

parts of communication, recreation, and livelihood. . . . Picture books made of durable materials are offered to babies, and bedtime stories become a part of their daily routine" (Rogoff, 1990, p. 115).

Despite the ubiquity of socially embedded teaching through talk and conversation in everyday life from infancy onward, schools provide learners with few opportunities for such interactions. For example, five-year-old children in Bristol, England, talk significantly less in the classroom than at home, address fewer utterances to adults, are spoken to individually less often, engage in shorter sequences of conversation, and speak with less syntactic complexity. Teachers are generally unresponsive to children's utterances and generally dominate classroom interactions (Wells, 1986; Wood, McMahon, and Cranstoun, 1980). Questions about what students have read are largely confined to known answers or convergent solutions. Similar patterns have been observed in U.S. schools for more than a century (see a review in Tharp and Gallimore, 1988, chap. 1).

It is ironic that the teachers in these U.S. schools create much richer literacy environments for their own children in their own homes. The irony is doubled for children of poverty and the many minority children who do not perform well in classrooms. Not only do teachers fail to provide the language- and literacy-learning opportunities they routinely offer their own children; they create interactional patterns that they criticize disadvantaged families for using: "The failure of many disadvantaged children in school is often explained by referring to their unfamiliarity with the middle-class ethos of school. But many schools operate in a way that is similar to the disadvantaged home in terms of using language and developing thinking skills. . . . Teachers need to recognize that many children will not have experiences through which their thinking might be extended unless these are provided in school and to recognize the critical importance of the experiences they themselves provide through their own talk with children" (Tough, 1982, pp. 14–15).

There is yet a third irony: these language- and literacy-enhancing interactions, apparently so natural and effortless at home with one's own children, are unnatural and require great effort at school. There are no doubt many reasons for this, such as the large numbers of children that teachers must deal with, which make it extraordinarily difficult to engage them in long and complex interactions. There is also tradition at work. In Western society, teaching has traditionally been equated with telling and showing. Knowledge is seen as objective, often derived from sacred or authoritative texts. The teacher's job has thus traditionally been seen as passing objective knowledge on to students (Cohen, 1988). This conception of teaching is directly antithetical to the sorts of verbal interactions that we refer to here, interactions thought to promote language and literacy development in other contexts, such as at home. Thus, the challenge for teacher educators and would-be reformers is, first, to identify and conceptualize forms of teaching to promote such interactions in the classroom and, second, to help teachers

develop the conceptual knowledge and pedagogical skills needed to instantiate such instruction (Saunders, Goldenberg, and Hamann, in press).

In our studies over the past several years, we have considered what
the processes of socialization and embedded teaching might contribute to
the conceptualization of effective teaching. In this chapter, we draw on a
line of work that began in Hawaii with native Hawaiians (Tharp and Gallimore, 1988) and that has continued in Los Angeles in a largely Latino community where many children begin school speaking only Spanish (Gallimore
and Goldenberg, 1992; Goldenberg, 1987; Goldenberg and Gallimore, 1991a,
1991b; Saunders and Goldenberg, 1992). One focus has been to draw on
developmental science.

Instruction Through Conversation

In contrast to everyday life, much of formal schooling is devoted to explicit
teaching of a more or less formal curriculum. This curriculum includes relatively well-structured domains of knowledge and skill, such as factual knowledge in science, social studies, and the humanities and skills in arithmetical
computations, reading decoding, and use of written language conventions.
In many instances, it is difficult to create "authentic" classroom contexts in
which teaching of such domains may be embedded. For these domains, a
reasonably well-defined set of teaching procedures, or functions, has been
identified that increases the likelihood of student learning (Rosenshine, 1986;
Rosenshine and Stevens, 1986). These teaching functions, which are often
grouped together and identified as "direct instruction," are especially suited
to knowledge and skill domains that are hierarchically organized and that
students can learn in a linear sequence. For these types of learning, direct
instruction has been found to be effective and efficient (Gersten and Carnine, 1986; Rosenshine, 1986; Rosenshine and Stevens, 1986).

For domains that are less clearly and hierarchically organized, however, the teaching functions of the direct instruction lesson are unlikely to
be as directly applicable (Rosenshine, 1986; Rosenshine and Stevens, 1986).
We propose that a different mode of teaching is needed for enhancing student learning in these "ill-structured" domains (Goldenberg, 1991; Goldenberg and Gallimore, 1991b). These domains include, for example, analyzing themes in history and literature, comprehending complex social, political,
or ethical ideas, and composing oral or written presentations.

While certain aspects of these less structured domains might be ame-
nable to direct instruction—and, certainly, professional teachers must have
at their disposal this cluster of skills and knowledge—we hypothesize that
other types of instruction may often be more appropriate in them. These
other types are analogous to some forms of embedded teaching described
in socialization research (for example, Rogoff, 1990). One form that we have
been exploring is the use of "conversation" in the teaching of reading comprehension:

To comprehend text — whether to read it, to write it, or to listen to it — involves the weaving of new and old information. . . . This metaphor of "weaving" is deeply connected to the basic processes of literacy. Consider the etymology of the word *text*. Deriving from the Latin verb *texere,* "to weave," text has come to mean the woven narrative, a fabric (*textile*) constructed by the relating of many elements. In the instruction of comprehension, the teacher herself is weaving a "text" composed of written and memorial materials. What we study, as researchers and students of the process, is that text created by the teacher-child interchange. That instructional conversation — the text-that-is-continually-becoming — the fabric of book, memory, talk and imagination that is being woven: that instructional conversation is the medium, the occasion, the instrument for cognitive development [Tharp and Gallimore, 1988, pp. 108–109].

The role of conversation as an instructional strategy has also been featured in many qualitative accounts of teaching students to comprehend and interpret text. For example, Rose (1989) worked with veterans of the U.S. military in a program that he described as a "crash course in the three Rs of higher education" (p. 145). The men were trying to radically change the direction of their lives, which for many of them had included either a very limited education or a school life of failure and frustration.

I knew from my own early struggles that students who have not had a privileged education often freeze up when they see readings like these, . . . the vocabulary . . . and the heady notions. . . . And they don't have the background knowledge or the conceptual grab bag of received phrases to make connections . . . [between different kinds of materials and analyses]. But give them time. Provide some context, break them into groups or work with the whole class, involving everyone. Let them see what, collectively, they do know, and students will, together, begin to generate meaning and make connections. One person once read something else [related to the first paragraph] . . . and his knowledge helps a second person understand the . . . processes in paragraph two, and that second person asks a question that remained ill-formed in the mind of a third. And the teacher darts in and out of the conversation, clarifying, questioning, repeating, looping back to line one student's observation to another's. And so it is that the students, labeled "remedial," read and talk and write their way toward understanding [Rose, 1989, pp. 145–46].

Defining Instructional Conversation

Our studies of instructional conversation (IC) began as part of the Kamehameha Early Education Project (KEEP) which was created in 1969 to research and develop a reading program for native Hawaiian students. Beginning in 1972, KEEP (Tharp and Gallimore, 1979, 1982, 1988) operated a kindergarten to third-grade research and development school in urban Honolulu. Its goal was the development of a reading program that was effective and compatible with the culture and language of the children. The KEEP team tried to implement a "good-quality" reading program that was consistent with what was then considered universally sound instructional practice. They also took account of findings from earlier ethnographic work (Gallimore, Boggs, and Jordan, 1974; Tharp and Gallimore, 1988; Weisner, Gallimore, and Jordan, 1988).

Altogether, it took five years of research and development for the KEEP team to evolve an effective reading program. It took another five years to fully evaluate its effects. Both internal and external evaluations of the program (Tharp and Gallimore, 1988) indicated that it produced grade-level or higher reading achievement both at the KEEP research school and in public school classrooms. Many of the practices implemented and evolved in KEEP are clear examples of universally sound teaching-learning practices: peer-group–cooperative learning, frequent assessment of student progress, well-run and -organized classrooms, positive classroom management strategies, teacher coaches, and an appropriate balance among word-recognition, skills, and comprehension instruction.

Reading comprehension lessons were the context in which instructional conversations occurred in the KEEP program, within an overall strategy of active, direct teaching of reading comprehension. The teaching of comprehension constituted two-thirds of a daily twenty minutes of face-to-face instruction time. The remaining third of the time was divided between sight vocabulary and analytical phonics. Thus, approximately fifteen minutes of each face-to-face lesson was devoted to instructional conversation (Tharp and Gallimore, 1988, chap. 6). However, KEEP never developed a formal and systematic definition of what constitutes an IC. Such a definition has emerged as the result of a project that we have been conducting at the University of California, Los Angeles (UCLA). Over a two-year period, one of us (Claude N. Goldenberg) met weekly with four teachers working in a school near UCLA. At each meeting, Goldenberg and the four teachers discussed and planned lessons. After the lesson had been taught and videotaped, the group reviewed the tape and discussed problems that the teachers had had in implementing ICs in their primary grade classrooms. From their discussions emerged a set of ten elements of IC that help define what we mean by the term (see Goldenberg, 1991; Goldenberg and Gallimore, 1991b):

1. Thematic focus for the discussion
2. Activating, using, or providing background knowledge and relevant schemata
3. Direct teaching, as necessary
4. Promoting more complex language and expression by students
5. Promoting bases for statements or positions
6. Minimizing "known-answer" questions in the course of the discussion
7. Teacher responsivity to student contributions
8. Connected discourse, with multiple and interactive turns on the same topic
9. A challenging but nonthreatening atmosphere
10. General participation, including self-selected turns

We must note that there is thus far little direct evidence that using IC to teach comprehension has any detectable impact on children's literacy development in particular or on their communicative and cognitive development generally. It is true that instructional conversations were a stable feature of KEEP comprehension instruction. But the KEEP evaluation data provide only indirect evidence of IC effects, and aside from exemplary lesson transcripts (see examples in Tharp and Gallimore, 1988, 1989), there are no data assessing the specific learning effects of ICs at KEEP.

We have attempted to address the question of IC effects in our more recent work in the Los Angeles area. Perhaps the most intriguing data come from a recently completed experiment (Saunders and Goldenberg, 1992) attempting to gauge the effect of an IC lesson on children's understanding of a complex concept—in this case, friendship. Children who had participated in an instructional conversation with their teacher demonstrated a more complex, sophisticated, and differentiated view of friendship than did children who had experienced a more traditional teacher-directed "reading comprehension" lesson.

Regardless of how persuasive the theoretical arguments for IC are, we are far from satisfied that the empirical case for its classroom efficacy has been made. But until we have sufficient and good examples of IC instantiated somewhere near UCLA, our opportunities to study its effects are limited. Thus, we are working to instantiate ICs in classrooms, while continuing to collect data and design studies to gauge their effects on student learning. In the remainder of this chapter, we summarize our progress to date.

When Do Instructional Conversations Occur?

As far as anyone can tell, conversation-like exchanges seldom occur in the reading lessons of most U.S. classrooms. One reason for this is that teachers see no purpose for such exchanges because they are so focused on seeking known answers to questions (Mehan, 1979; Sinclair and Coulthard, 1975).

When known-answer questions are asked, there is no need to listen to a child or to discover what the child might be trying to communicate.

Contrast to the known-answer pattern the everyday practice of literate care givers from the earliest days of a child's life: "One of the most distinctive characteristics of middle-class [European-American] caregivers is their willingness to engage in communicative exchanges [even] with the smallest of infants. . . . Long before the child has actually produced its first word, it is treated as if in fact it does have something to say. . . . When young children actually begin producing words, this set of assumptions by the caregiver continues. The caregiver, typically the mother, considers the young child to be expressing somewhat imperfectly a communicative intention" (Ochs, 1982, pp. 88–89). In most circumstances, a care giver focuses only on what the child is spontaneously trying to communicate. The conversation can meander around a topic, with digressions comfortably entertained even if they stray from a continuing focus. The purpose of the child's conversational partner is to understand what the child is trying to say. But a teacher who tries to use conversation in the classroom has an additional purpose: instruction. To open a zone of proximal development of reading comprehension, a teacher has to intentionally plan and pursue an instructional as well as a conversational purpose. To use conversation to assist performance, the teacher must also create a conversational purpose for the child to say something about a text, imperfectly or otherwise, that is aligned with an instructional purpose. In other words, students must be "drawn into" conversations that create opportunities for teachers to assist in text analysis and comprehension, including activating relevant prior knowledge.

To effectively use conversation in the classroom, teachers cannot simply be conversationally responsive—that is only a means for achieving an instructional end. Getting teachers to accept this approach is no problem in principle, even without their knowledge of Vygotskian ideas. Many are frustrated by the constraints of known-answer interactions and may have tried on their own to introduce more diverse forms. But instructing through conversation is not easy because of the paradox of planful intention and responsive spontaneity. This was quickly discovered when the KEEP project attempted to train teachers to conduct instructional conversations. Two significant barriers were encountered (Tharp and Gallimore, 1988, 1989). One barrier involved content knowledge: teachers often had a limited grasp of the texts that their primary grade pupils were reading, which made it difficult for them to recognize when a child's initial responses to a text were instructionally relevant or promising: In other words, the teachers had too little control of the content knowledge themselves to pursue an instructional purpose. The solution was a more careful reading of the text to increase their grasp of the content.

The second barrier to teachers conducting ICs, related to the first, was that they also had to learn to intentionally create and sustain a joint communicative purpose that was a means to an instructional end—assisting

students toward better text interpretation. It is not as easy to separate content knowledge and pedagogical knowledge as it may seem: not only does
it involve giving up the familiar pattern of asking known-answer questions,
it requires learning to encourage and elicit students' initial text interpretations—a hybrid of content and pedagogy. In effect, the KEEP teachers
had to learn to shift from the role of assessor of children's interpretations
to the role of assister of children interpreting texts (Tharp and Gallimore,
1988, chap. 10; 1989).

The Role of Conversation in Learning
to Conduct Instructional Conversation

The consultation sessions that KEEP used to train teachers were themselves
something like an "instructional conversation." Through conversation about
their teaching, zones of proximal development opened for the apprentice
practitioners of IC, and their performances were assisted by more experienced
staff members. The message and the medium were closely aligned.

Unpackaging the dynamics of instructional conversations among
teachers learning to conduct instructional conversations is the focus of two
studies that have been conducted since 1990 (see Goldenberg and Gallimore,
1990; Saunders and Goldenberg, 1992). In one of the studies, which began
in September 1989, Goldenberg met with four teachers once a week after
school, for a total of thirty two-hour meetings during the 1989–90 school
year. The purpose of the meetings was to discuss, identify, implement, and,
if possible, evaluate forms of instruction consistent with the new California
Language Arts Framework. In particular, we were interested in exploring
instructional conversations as an alternative to recitation or direct instruction, the most prevalent instructional approach found in schools (Gage, 1978;
Sirotnik, 1983).

In the first five meetings, Goldenberg and the teachers discussed issues and problems related to language arts instruction that the teachers faced
in their own classrooms, such as how to get beyond low-level, factually
oriented discussions, particularly with younger children. One teacher observed that while students generally can learn stories or lessons at the literal
level, questions asking for "prediction and inference" become more problematic. All agreed that discussion and oral language development were very
important, but they also agreed that making these a regular feature of their
classrooms was a formidable challenge.

The participating teachers had no difficulty talking about their classroom teaching problems. They were also eager to talk about alternative instructional strategies, and they agreed to be videotaped as they experimented
with new forms of instructional interactions with students. Reading about
and discussing instructional strategies evoked much enthusiastic talk. In fact,
during the early sessions, some of the teachers not only endorsed instructional conversation as a worthy addition but claimed to be adept practitio-

ners. One insisted that it had been her own style of teaching for a long time and that she felt ready to train others to use it.

The teachers' classroom performance, however, was another matter. What was immediately obvious was how much they talked and how seldom the children said anything. As a result, many meetings opened with teachers' excuses for the performance revealed in the tape to be viewed that day: the story was too difficult for the children; they were distracted; they had too little language or experience to respond. Gradually, the teachers began to recognize that the taped lessons were not what had been intended.

The self-consciousness that was so evident is important because it can activate self-regulatory cognition associated with behavior change. Carver and Scheier (1981) propose the following sequence: being observed by others makes people self-conscious; self-consciousness causes people to attend to the details of their own behavior; if their behavior deviates from the standards expected in the situation, they will engage in self-regulatory activity to bring their behavior into conformity. This sequence of activating conditions also appeared to be present in the accounts of KEEP teachers, who reported being highly self-conscious or reactive in the presence of an observer or video camera (Gallimore, Dalton, and Tharp, 1986). In addition, 89 percent mentioned a concern with meeting the standards of the KEEP reading program.

The four teachers with whom Goldenberg worked were also concerned about "matching to standard": they were acutely conscious that they were expected to try conducting instructional conversations. Being observed and monitored by peers seemed to have evoked self-consciousness about how well they were doing and to what extent they were conforming to expectations. As a result of this process, some substantial changes were observed that help unpackage the dynamics of conversations among teachers who are trying to conduct instructional conversations. This process is illustrated by the case of "Flor," who displayed a number of changes during the first half of the year. Case materials (classroom observations, interviews, and taped lessons) confirm that she made substantial gains not only in analyzing her own teaching but also in acquiring instructional conversation skills (Rueda, Goldenberg, and Gallimore, 1991).

To determine whether Flor had improved the ratio of teacher-to-child talk during her reading lessons with children, we compared two lessons, given approximately a month apart. In the first lesson, she tended to linguistically overwhelm the children; during the second, she decreased her own speech time by approximately 40 percent and increased the children's by a factor of approximately 3.5. The ratio of teacher-to-child talk improved from over 6:1 to somewhat over 1:1. Such a decrease in the amount of teacher talk says nothing, of course, about the quality of the interaction or the extent to which children actually learned something as a result of the discussion. But it does suggest that Flor had made considerable progress on a dimension that the group had collectively identified as a major objective of their joint activity.

Paralleling these behavioral changes were changes in Flor's talk during weekly meetings. To illustrate how her talk changed, we compared two meetings in which the group discussed two of Flor's videotaped lessons (analysis conducted by Jan Hamann): meeting 7, in October 1989, and meeting 16, in February 1990. Each of Flor's utterances was coded as a speech function according to the following categories:

1. *Explanation using cause and effect and context:* for example, "Modeling worked here in the lowest reading group because they could all hear and see how to sound out the word." This code also includes an analysis of an instructional event ("Here you were doing this constant adjusting; this isn't working, so I'll try this") as well as insights ("I realized when we read the story in more detail, then I started getting more from them").
2. *Explanation using cause and effect:* for example, "Modeling worked here because the kids could see and hear how to sound out the word."
3. *Description with pedagogical term:* for example, "She used modeling."
4. *Negative self-evaluation:* for example, "I was very general in my opening questions, not specific or concrete, and that's why I didn't get a lot of responses."
5. *Agreement:* for example, "Too abstract, yeah, that's what I thought, too."
6. *Alternative solutions:* for example, "If I would have started with the book, I would have just asked a couple of questions, instead of like I did."
7. *How I teach:* for example, "Well, I always have to start with the title and just get them thinking what they think of the story, what they'll be hearing, what the story will be about."
8. *Description without pedagogical terms:* for example, "She read a story to them."
9. *Evaluation with analysis:* for example, "I think you should concentrate on one thing that you feel is important for the kids to get out of the story."

Figure 14.1 illustrates the changes in Flor's talk.

During meeting 7, Flor's talk consisted largely of describing the lesson and explaining how she teaches. By the time she discussed her second videotaped lesson, she explained, analyzed, and suggested alternative solutions to problematic instructional events. She talked less about how she teaches and instead suggested alternative solutions. She also had a more positive response to the videotaping process and expressed support for the problem-solving approach that Goldenberg used to analyze and evaluate the taped lessons.

Transcripts of these sessions confirm a substantial shift in the level of analytical power that Flor and the others displayed. But analytical power by itself means little unless what is being analyzed has something to do with content knowledge or pedagogy. In Flor's case, the initial problem was to elicit from students sufficient response that she could begin a conversation about a text that served an instructional purpose. Flor's problem was not too many responses but too few. Getting more student response was both a goal of her joint work with Goldenberg and the others and the vehicle through which she developed greater analytical skills.

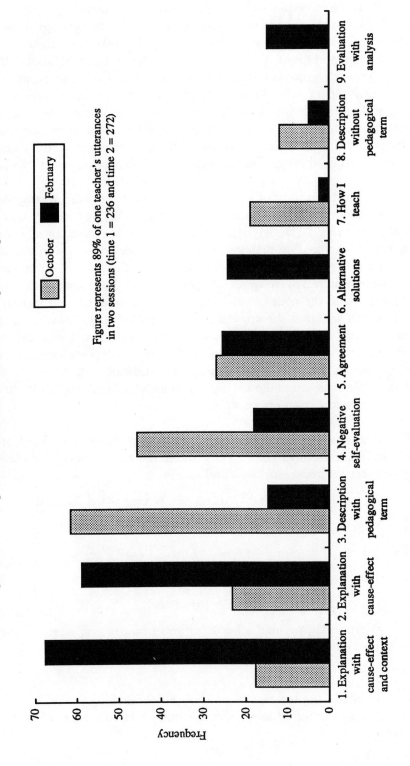

Figure 14.1. Changes in a Teacher's Talk While Viewing Videotapes of Her Lessons.

Figure represents 89% of one teacher's utterances
in two sessions (time 1 = 236 and time 2 = 272)

This effort began with a telling episode in meeting 7 (the first time one of Flor's videotaped lessons was discussed by the group). Goldenberg noted that her videotape vividly portrayed the impact of ideas on student participation and production when Flor accidently found a "hook." *Hook* was a term that the group used to describe an idea, word, or experience that activates students' prior knowledge that may help them to better comprehend and more richly appreciate the text that they are to read. Flor's lesson centered on a story about a country mouse who goes to the city to visit a city mouse; since most of the children in the class were from families who had migrated from rural Mexico, there was an obvious parallel and a potential "hook."

At the beginning of the lesson, Flor used the word *campo,* the word used in the story to refer to the countryside. This apparently was an unfamiliar term to the native Spanish speakers in her class, or at least it was not directly "hooked" to their relevant prior experiences. As long as she used *campo* (countryside) or *granja* (farm) to refer to the country mouse's experiences, the children were quiet, despite the fact Flor showed pictures and described what the countryside was like. After about five minutes, one of the children said that she knew another word for *campo: rancho.* At this moment, several of the children began to offer comments, in sharp contrast to their earlier silence. An opportunity for an instructional conversation had arisen, but in the heat of the lesson, Flor did not pick it up. (In the segments of dialogue that follow, "CG" is Claude Goldenberg; "BP," "BB," and "GW" are fellow teachers of Flor.)

CG: See now, for the previous five minutes, you've been kind of giving like a little minilecture. Here's a city and here's a *campo* and [Veronica] made the connection between *campo* and *rancho.*

Flor: Mmm. I was probably using the wrong word for that . . .

CG: Well . . .

Other teachers: No.

CG: That's right, [*rancho* is] the word that . . .

BP: They made the connection [to *campo*].

CG: [Veronica] provided a hook for you because you were talking about [the countryside] using a term that was new for them.

Flor: Right.

CG: They had the concept, they know what rural life is like, but they refer to it as *rancho* instead of *campo.* So that provided you the hook to then take off from.

(Video shown)

CG: See, and that opened up some kids who had something to say.

(Video shows several children offering comments)

Flor: (Child's speech problem—babyish) I don't know if I took too long on this part of explaining both because the whole conversation could have been just on *campo*. And forget the story.

CG: See, what struck me about that is that for a while they were just listening, when you're talking about *campo*. And then suddenly someone said *rancho* . . .

BP: Mm-hm.

CG: And this whole thing just opened up.

Flor: Yeah, that's inter . . . yeah.

CG: They had the concept, there was just a different label that was being used for it.

BP: Yeah, yeah.

Flor: Uh huh.

CG: It perhaps wasn't so much a question of teaching them stuff they didn't know, as much as getting them to realize that what they knew was related to what you were, this word that you were . . .

Flor: Right, and I think the illustrations in the book helped too.

CG: Yeah, and then when she said *rancho*, of course there was this kind of outpouring of experience on the *rancho* and so forth. (pause) Then, ok, something interesting happens.

(Video shown)

CG: You switch back here to using *granja*.

Flor: And then *campo, rancho, granja*

CG: Well . . . I don't think I heard [*rancho*] again.

Flor: (laughs)

CG: You stuck with *granja*.

BP: Well, the book probably had *granja* in it. Is it Teo? . . . and they talk about the *granja*, no *rancho*, but they're the same type of thing—ranch and farm.

CG: I don't know what your all impression was, but when you started talking about *granja*, it was like, again, they didn't know what you were talking about.

Flor: Oh yeah, that's true. I didn't realize I said *granja*.

CG: Cause we use them interchangeably. They're totally synonymous, and we just use one or the other, it really doesn't matter. But *rancho* opened up all sorts of things for them to talk about.

Flor: It was more familiar to them.

CG: Absolutely. But then when you got back into *granja,* it's like, no, I've never been on one. (laughter)

CG: "¿Han estado en una granja?" And they'd just finished telling you about *ranchos.*

Flor: Yeah.

CG: It's just so amazing how these little . . .

BP: hooks . . .

CG: these little hooks [make a difference]. And when Veronica offered *rancho,* that was it.

As the discussion continued, it was clear that Flor and the others began to appreciate the point that Goldenberg was making.

GW: (Don't drop the *rancho* hook) Until they realize it's the same word [as *campo*].

Flor: Yeah, I think, didn't I say at one point, another word for . . .

BB: Mm-hm.

Flor: No, I did say another word for *campo* is *rancho.*

BB: Yeah, you did.

Flor: But I didn't say that same thing with *granja.*

BB: Mmm.

Flor: I should have said, and another word for it, or another way to describe this environment is by saying *granja.*

Flor had accidentally found a good hook, but she had not effectively used it to increase student response. The teachers were not sure what could have been done. As the group discussion continued, the teachers debated the problem of how to get the students to make a connection among *campo, rancho,* and *granja.* They expressed frustration about time limitations that make it difficult to follow up on hooks such as *rancho;* they mentioned how hard it is sometimes to notice subtle events while teaching a lesson. But it was not yet clear to Flor and the others how to exploit opportunities such as the unanticipated *rancho* hook. This was revealed toward the end of the same meeting, when Flor made the following comments about the country mouse lesson in general:

Flor: At times . . . I was doing most of the talking.

CG: Too much?

Flor: Yeah, I felt . . . and again, when it's an experience activity I think a lot of it has to be teacher talk.

At this point in her progress, she did not appreciate that through conversation she might be able to elicit relevant prior experiences of the students, rather than providing them with relevant experiences, and in that way get more responses.

At the next meeting, Flor brought her second videotape for the group to review. She continued to be distressed by the lack of student response in the lesson. Her attempts to converse with the students about the text were frustrating: there was no conversation, and neither was she able to instruct as she would have liked. In subsequent meetings, she continued to be conscious of finding a hook through conversation, made an effort to demonstrate this, and had uneven but gradually improved success with it.

In her fourth videotaped lesson (meeting 16), Flor made three attempts to find a hook, none of which elicited much response. Her third attempt was based on an incident in her own childhood. In the meeting, she asked her peers whether that had been the right thing to do. In asking for suggestions about her teaching and considering their responses, Flor demonstrated her growing analytical powers and her increasing use of the group meetings to get specific feedback.

In the later meetings, the teachers were no longer defending their performance or explaining why things did or did not work. Rather than engaging in long accounts of "how I teach" as if they had nothing to learn, they were making use of their peers and Goldenberg to further their understanding and refine their practice. In this regard, Flor was a trend leader. She was the first to explain, during the videotapes of her lessons, what she was trying to do and to disclose what she was thinking and feeling and what insights occurred to her as she tried new techniques; she was willing to evaluate her own lessons and state what she would try in the future.

These excerpts provide only a glimpse of a complex process that unfolded over some sixty hours of meetings. Other members of Flor's group had somewhat different courses of development, although all showed increased analytical power. Some found that bending conversation to an instructional purpose required them to analyze more carefully the texts that their students read. Without that knowledge of the text, they found it difficult to decide when to allow a "conversation" to go on, rather than stopping to provide students with information. In some instances, what is intended as an instructional conversation becomes an aimless chat, which produces no greater understanding of the text and may not even engage students' prior knowledge relevant to the text. Sometimes charming conversations lead students to misinterpret stories, because the topic pursued creates the wrong "set" for approaching a text. The teachers in our study discovered that studying texts before lessons is a key to managing instructional conversations.

Did Flor develop a more conversational style of instruction as a result of instructional conversations with Goldenberg and her fellow teachers? Flor's lessons were rated according to the extent to which each lesson included the ten elements of instructional conversation listed earlier; the change was substantial, on the order of a threefold increase in IC elements over a period of a few weeks (Rueda, Goldenberg, and Gallimore, 1991). Not only did Flor become more analytical in the meetings with Goldenberg and her peers, but she was also putting into practice what she had learned to analyze. A similar analysis of the other three teachers in the study revealed that they had also made significant improvements in their ability to conduct instructional conversation.

Conclusion

In the United States, there is currently much discussion of how to improve the schools. Sooner or later, the discussion turns to ways of improving teaching. What is so discouraging is how much of today's discussion is an echo of the past (Cuban, 1990). Of all the reforms that have been tried again, again, and again, none has received more attention than changing the customary practices of teachers, including the recitation script and the reliance on known-answer questions. "The inventory of efforts aimed at changing what teachers do" is staggering (Cuban, 1988, p. 343). Yet nothing much has changed, and the recitation script still rules (Tharp and Gallimore, 1988, chap. 1).

Our research and experience suggest that one reason for these failures is the reformers' indifference to the developmental processes in which teachers themselves must engage if genuine change is to be achieved. This point was made in 1972 by Sarason as well as anyone has made it before or since:

> I have spent thousands of hours in schools and one of the first things I sensed was that the longer the person had been a teacher the less excited, or alive, or stimulated he seemed to be about his role . . . being a teacher was on the boring side. Generally speaking, these teachers were not as helpful to children as they might have been or as frequently as the teachers themselves would have liked to have been . . . *schools are not created to foster the intellectual and professional growth of teachers. The assumption that teachers can create and maintain those conditions which make school . . . stimulating for children, without those same conditions existing for teachers, has no warrant in the history of man* [emphasis added]. That the different efforts to [change teaching practices have failed] is in part a consequence of the implicit value that schools are primarily for children, a value which gives rise to ways of thinking, to

a view of technology, to ways of training, and to modes of organization which make for one grand error of misplaced emphasis [Sarason, 1972, pp. 123-124].

For their work lives to be more intellectually stimulating, for them to acquire complex new teaching skills, teachers must be collaborators as well as clients. Our research and experience suggest that teachers must be active participants in training, not passive recipients of it (Goldenberg and Gallimore, 1991b; see also Clark, 1988; Lampert and Clark, 1990). When teachers participate in this way, not only do they learn new skills, but their intellectual lives are made more stimulating as well. Unless their work lives provide ideas, academic substance, and intellectual excitement, there is no chance that teachers can rouse to life the minds of their students.

But that is not enough. Our research and experience also suggest that part of teachers' everyday work life must be devoted to developing their pedagogical skills: "We must construct settings that assist teachers to perform the new skills before they are fully competent, if they are to internalize new approaches to teaching. Teachers, like their students, have zones of proximal development; they too require assisted performance; as with students, activity settings for teachers must create opportunities for their performance to be assisted" (Tharp and Gallimore, 1988, p. 190). One way for them to develop both intellectual substance and pedagogical virtuosity is through the medium that has appeared in this chapter in several guises. It was described as a concomitant of the embedded teaching of everyday life. It is the way mothers teach their children language and literacy. It can be a third-grade reading lesson or a graduate seminar. It is a medium for teacher development. It is the instructional conversation, a medium and a message for all students, teachers, administrators, program developers, and researchers.

References

Carver, C. S., and Scheier, M. F. *Attention and Self-Regulation: A Control-Theory Approach to Human Behavior.* New York: Springer-Verlag, 1981.

Clark, C. M. "Asking the Right Questions About Teacher Preparation: Contributions of Research on Teacher Thinking." *Educational Researcher,* 1988, *17*(2), 5-12.

Cohen, D. *Teaching Practice: Plus ça Change . . .* Issue Paper 88-3. East Lansing: National Center for Research on Teacher Education, Michigan State University, 1988.

Cuban, L. "A Fundamental Puzzle of School Reform." *Phi Delta Kappan,* 1988, *69*(5), 341-344.

Cuban, L. "Reforming Again, Again, and Again." *Educational Researcher,* 1990, *19*(1), 3-13.

Gage, N. L. *The Scientific Basis of the Art of Teaching.* New York: Teachers College Press, 1978.

Gallimore, R., Boggs, J. W., and Jordan, C. *Culture, Behavior and Education: A Study of Hawaiian-Americans*. Newbury Park, Calif.: Sage, 1974.

Gallimore, R., Dalton, S., and Tharp, R. G. "Self-Regulation and Interactive Teaching: The Impact of Teaching Conditions on Teachers' Cognitive Activity." *Elementary School Journal*, 1986, *86* (5), 613-631.

Gallimore, R., and Goldenberg, C. N. "Activity Settings of Early Literacy: Home and School Factors in Children's Emergent Literacy." In E. Forman, N. Minick, and C. A. Stone (eds.), *Education and Mind: The Integration of Institutional, Social, and Developmental Processes*. Oxford, England: Oxford University Press, 1992.

Gersten, R., and Carnine, D. "Direct Instruction in Reading Comprehension." *Educational Leadership*, 1986, *43* (7), 70-78.

Goldenberg, C. "Low-Income Hispanic Parents' Contributions to Their First-Grade Children's Word-Recognition Skills." *Anthropology and Education Quarterly*, 1987, *18*, 149-179.

Goldenberg, C. "Instructional Conversations." Working paper, Center for Research on Cultural Diversity and Second Language Learning, University of California, Santa Cruz, 1991.

Goldenberg, C., and Gallimore, R. "Meeting the Language Arts Challenge for Language-Minority Children: Teaching and Learning in a New Key." Progress report for 1989-90 to Presidential Grants for School Improvement Committee, Office of the President, University of California, Sept. 21, 1990.

Goldenberg, C., and Gallimore, R. "Local Knowledge, Research Knowledge, and Educational Achievement: A Case Study of Early Spanish Reading Improvement." *Educational Researcher*, 1991a, *20*, 2-14.

Goldenberg, C. N., and Gallimore, R. "Changing Teachers Takes More Than a One-Shot Workshop," *Educational Researcher*, 1991b, *20*, 69-72.

Lampert, M., and Clark, C. M. "Expert Knowledge and Expert Thinking in Teaching: A Response to Floden and Klinzing." *Educational Researcher*, 1990, *19* (5), 21-42.

Mehan, H. "'What Time Is It, Denise?': Asking Known Information Questions in Classroom Discourse." *Theory into Practice*, 1979, *28* (4), 285-294.

Ochs, E. "Talking to Children in Western Samoa." *Language in Society*, 1982, *11*, 77-104.

Rogoff, B. *Apprenticeship in Thinking: Cognitive Development in Social Context*. New York: Oxford University Press, 1990.

Rose, M. *Lives on the Boundary*. New York: Penguin Books, 1989.

Rosenshine, B. "Synthesis of Research on Explicit Teaching." *Educational Leadership*, 1986, *43*, 60-69.

Rosenshine, B., and Stevens, R. "Teaching Functions." In M. C. Wittrock (ed.), *Handbook of Research on Teaching*. (3rd ed.) New York: Macmillan, 1986.

Rueda, R., Goldenberg, C., and Gallimore, R. "When Is an Instructional Conversation?" Paper presented at the annual meeting of the American Educational Research Association, Chicago, April 1991.

Sarason, S. B. *The Creation of Settings and the Future Societies.* San Francisco: Jossey-Bass, 1972.

Saunders, W., Goldenberg, C., and Hamann, J. "Instructional Conversations Beget Instructional Conversations." *Teaching and Teacher Education,* in press.

Saunders, W., and Goldenberg, C. "Effects of Instructional Conversations on Transition Students' Concepts of 'Friendship': An Experimental Study." Paper presented at the annual meeting of the American Educational Research Association, San Francisco, Apr. 1992.

Sinclair, J., and Coulthard, M. *Towards an Analysis of Discourse: The Language of Teachers and Pupils.* New York: Oxford University Press, 1975.

Sirotnik, K. "What You See Is What You Get: Consistency, Persistency, and Mediocrity in Classrooms." *Harvard Educational Review,* 1983, *53,* 16–31.

Tharp, R. G., and Gallimore, R. "The Ecology of Program Research and Evaluation: A Model of Evaluation Succession." In L. B. Sechrest (ed.), *Evaluation Studies Annual Review.* Newbury Park, Calif.: Sage, 1979.

Tharp, R. G., and Gallimore, R. "Inquiry Processes in Program Development." *Journal of Community Psychology,* 1982, *10,* 103–118.

Tharp, R., and Gallimore, R. *Rousing Minds to Life: Teaching, Learning, and Schooling in Social Context.* Cambridge, England: Cambridge University Press, 1988.

Tharp, R., and Gallimore, R. "Rousing Schools to Life." *American Educator,* 1989, *13* (2), 20–52.

Tough, J. "Language, Poverty, and Disadvantage in School." In L. Feagans and D. C. Faran (eds.), *The Language of Children Reared in Poverty.* San Diego, Calif.: Academic Press, 1982.

Vygotsky, L. S. *Thought and Language.* Cambridge, Mass.: MIT Press, 1962. (Originally published 1934.)

Vygotsky, L. S. *Mind in Society: The Development of Higher Psychological Processes.* (M. Cole, V. John-Steiner, S. Scribner, and E. Souberman, eds. and trans.) Cambridge, Mass.: Harvard University Press, 1978.

Weisner, T. S., Gallimore, R., and Jordan, C. "Unpackaging Cultural Effects on Classroom Learning: Hawaiian Peer Assistance and Child-Generated Activity." *Anthropology and Education Quarterly,* 1988, *19,* 327–353.

Wells, G. "The Language Experience of Five-Year-Old Children at Home and at School." In J. Cook-Gumperz (ed.), *The Social Construction of Literacy.* Cambridge, England: Cambridge University Press, 1986.

Wood, D., McMahon, L., and Cranstoun, Y. *Working with Under Fives.* London: Grant McIntytre, 1980.

Section Five

EXPERTISE IN TEACHING

David C. Berliner,
Section Editor

It is important to distinguish between "good" and "effective" teachers. Good teachers are those that meet our value systems. *Good teaching* and *bad teaching* are highly charged evaluative terms. It is a particular community's conceptions of what teaching should be that determine whether a teacher will be judged as good or bad. The parents and administrators of a fundamentalist Christian school in the United States have conceptions of good teaching that differ in important ways from those held by secular members of the community, particularly those with a more psychodynamic and child-centered view of childhood. The conception of curricula in these two groups may also differ, with the former group primarily valuing facts and the latter group thinking skills and problem solving. With such different views of what is good teaching and what is good to teach, it is no wonder that different kinds of teachers will be sought for these two different kinds of schools.

Effective teachers, on the other hand, are considered to be those that meet some criteria or standards for performance. Their students win at the science fair, or their class covers more of the curriculum than other classes, or more of their students graduate with honors, or their students pray more often, or they more often attribute their successes and failures to effort than to ability. Effectiveness always implies some objective criterion against which we can judge teachers. Such criteria can be behavioral, motivational, or affective, though most often the criterion we use is achievement test performance.

The chapters in this section discuss expert teachers and expertise in teaching, terms referring to teachers and teaching practices that are both good and effective. The teachers and teaching practices examined in these chapters may be thought of as possessing characteristics that we value and that also lead to higher performance on achievement measures. Because most of us value them, we may also think of these teachers and teaching practices

223

as inherently responsible. Three of the four chapters in this section are best described as exemplifying the complementary model of synthesis described in the introduction to this volume. All four of them consider the criteria for expertise to be evidence of productivity and morally responsible relationships with one's students—what our community of educational scholars would call both effective and good teaching.

In Chapter Fifteen, David C. Berliner offers assertions about the nature of expertise based on a series of studies that he and others have conducted. These investigators used a comparative approach; their studies provide not descriptions of exemplary teachers but descriptions of the differences between expert and novice teachers performing similar tasks. On the basis of their findings, Berliner makes a series of claims: that the knowledge of expert teachers is highly contextualized; that they rely on routines; that they are more sensitive than novices to the task demands and social situations that they face; and that they are opportunitistic in their problem solving. In addition, experts were found to have qualitatively different representations of classroom situations, fast and accurate pattern recognition, and the ability to make more sense out of what they see. Throughout the chapters we see evidence of the confluence of effective practices with consideration of the humanity of students, including concern for the affective side of teaching, and for giving responsibility to students.

In Chapter Sixteen, Franz E. Weinert, Andreas Helmke, and Friedrich-W. Schrader develop a model of expertise in teaching that is reliant on four forms of knowledge—subject matter knowledge, instructional knowledge, knowledge of classroom management, and knowledge of the students themselves, including their needs and goals, their strengths and weaknesses. The latter form of knowledge they call diagnostic ability. They cleverly find indicators for each area of knowledge and demonstrate their relative independence from one another. The expert teacher, then, is seen as developing competency in all four of these areas. The authors contrasted a group of such teachers with other, less expert teachers; their results provide a modicum of support for the model of teaching that they developed, but the data are in some conflict with the descriptions of expertise offered by the authors of other chapters in this section. Among these expert teachers, the correlations of achievement with measures of warmth and enthusiasm were negative. This suggests that the complementary synthesis model that fits the descriptions of exemplary teachers in the other chapters may not fit the data collected in this study. These discrepancies should be addressed in future research. It is important to note, however, that Weinert, Helmke, and Schrader are in agreement with the premise running through the other chapters that the socioemotional competencies, humanistic values, and moral authority of teachers are likely to be influential only in classes where instruction is effective. Responsible instruction will not often be seen in poorly managed classes. Some of their data support this assertion.

In Chapter Seventeen, by Elliot W. Eisner, we see the intertwining of effective and good teaching exemplified. When Eisner visited the third-grade classrooms of two teachers reputed to be effective, he found that their effectiveness was dependent on such factors as "comfortable" grouping practices to accomplish the goals of instruction, "affectionate" interactions, relationships in which punishment was rarely used, the communication of "seriousness of purpose," and giving students responsibility for accomplishing their own goals. This is the lived value system of a classroom that is best described by the complementary synthesis model.

Finally, in Chapter Eighteen, Brigitte A. Rollett presents a comparison of teachers in three cities—New York, London, and Vienna—who were both experienced and reputed to be excellent. Like Eisner's two exemplary teachers, the dozens of exemplary teachers in this sample made salient the overwhelming importance of the affective side of teaching. They were child-centered, not curriculum-centered, though achievement of the curriculum goals was certainly an important part of their reputations. To achieve academic goals these teachers said that they needed an intimate knowledge of each student's personality, home, culture, and community. As with Eisner's teachers, Rollett's teachers appeared to be masters of the particular—bringing general knowledge, skill, and, most of all, experience to bear on the needs of a particular child. Abstract knowledge of the type taught in universities seemed unrelated to the daily lives of these exemplary teachers. Furthermore, as with Eisner's teachers, Rollett's exemplary teachers were masters at creating a positive environment: a lived value system was in place once again. We also see in Rollett's study how notions of good teaching can differ across cultures. The New York sample emphasized self-esteem and pride for their minority students. The European teachers, however, felt that pride is not something to be valued; they emphasized instead understanding and love. As noted above, good teaching is always dependent on community values and is distinguishable from effective teaching.

There is much more to focus on in these four chapters than mentioned here: there are Berliner's notes on a five-stage theory of the development of pedagogical knowledge and the policy relevance of the findings about differences between expert and novice teachers; Weinert, Helmke, and Schrader's analysis of an empirically testable model of expertise; Eisner's musings about the limits of research on teaching; and Rollett's point about the remarkable similarities of concerns and behaviors among the exemplary teachers across three cultures. Throughout the chapters is a common thread: that expertise in teaching is both effective and good and that the label "expert" cannot really be applied to a teacher unless the teaching can also be judged responsible.

15

The Nature of Expertise
in Teaching

David C. Berliner

There are many reasons for studying expertise. For one, it is an interesting topic, and that alone is sufficient to promote a line of research. Expert mnemonists, chess players, taxi drivers, or mathematicians fascinate us, as idiot savants and geniuses do. Such individuals are rare, and their abilities seem mysterious to those of us who do not attain their levels of competence. In addition, the study of the perception and problem solving of experts sometimes provides insight into the cognitive processes and kinds of knowledge that they use, and these often differ substantially from the processes and knowledge base that are used by novices. Such information helps psychologists to understand more about the organization of memory, the way reasoning in a particular domain occurs, and the way judgments are made. This kind of knowledge can have practical benefits: it can be used to provide the scaffolding for the instruction of novices, to help them attain a greater degree of competence, though perhaps not expertise. Expertise, it should be remembered, is a characteristic that is ordinarily developed only after lengthy experience. It is descriptive of a level of performance ordinarily attained by only a small percentage of those who are competent at a task.

There are also other reasons for studying expertise in the area of teaching. With increased public criticism of teachers and schools, it has been a source of pride for teachers to learn that within the profession are individuals who resemble experts in other fields—bridge players, chess players, physicists, radiologists, and so forth (see Glaser, 1987; Chi, Glaser, and Farr, 1988). In addition, information about pedagogical expertise can help policy makers concerned about teacher testing, merit pay, career ladders, and alternative certification programs, all of which require an understanding of the kinds of performance that characterize experts and novices (Berliner, 1989).

An additional reason for pursuing the study of expertise among teachers is to make clear that there are forms of pedagogical knowledge that are quite

sophisticated and complex and take years to learn. Pedagogical knowledge—
knowledge of organization and management of classrooms, of motivation,
teaching methods, discipline, and individual differences among students—
is not generally valued by the public. Virtually anyone who has ever raised
a child or trained a dog thinks that teaching is easy. Such people have not
had to work in public school classrooms, where high levels of managerial,
organizational, and interpersonal social skills are required merely to be a
competent provider of instruction for twenty-five or thirty distinctly different individuals. What studies of expertise in the pedagogical domain seek
is a greater understanding of the sophisticated forms of pedagogical knowledge used by expert teachers to accomplish instructional goals in the complex social environment called the public school classroom.

Because studying expertise is interesting, because it enables us to learn
more about cognition, because it builds morale, and because there is a lack
of understanding of the complexity of pedagogical knowledge, a number of
studies have been undertaken to examine expert knowledge in the pedagogical domain. Of primary interest have been studies about the differences between expert and novice teachers that affect instruction and achievement.
Most of these studies have been concerned with teacher effectiveness, with
focus on how these teachers might differ with regard to responsible teaching. This chapter attempts to change that by offering a selective review of
some characteristics of expert pedagogues that highlight aspects of the literature that reflect on responsible teaching as well as effective teaching. This
review is organized around seven propositions about expert and novice
teachers for which empirical data exist.

Propositions

Proposition one: Experts excel mainly in their own domains and in particular contexts.

The obvious reasons, Chi, Glaser, and Farr (1988) state, that experts
excel primarily in single domains, is that experts have a great deal more
experience, probably reflected-on experience, in some domains than in others.
Expert radiologists surveyed in studies by Lesgold and others (1988) were
estimated to be looking at their one-hundred-thousandth x-ray. The chess
experts studied in deGroot's (1965) seminal work and in other research
(Newell and Simon, 1972; Chase and Simon, 1973) have been estimated
to have spent ten to twenty thousand hours staring at chess positions. A perspective on this is offered by Posner (1988, p. xxxi): "a student who spends
40 hours a week for 33 weeks spends 1,320 hours studying. Imagine spending more than ten years in college studying one subject, chess, and you get
some appreciation of the time commitment of master level players. . . . It
is reasonable to assume a chess master can recognize 50,000 different configurations of chess, not too far different from the number of different words
an English reader may be able to recognize."

With lengthy time commitments necessary to become expert in complex areas of human functioning, it is no wonder that individuals generally excel in only a single area. In the study of teachers, we also note that time and experience play an important role in the development of expertise. On the basis of fragmentary evidence and anecdotal reports, some scholars propose that teachers do not hit their peak until they have at least five years of on-the-job experience. The expert teacher with ten years of experience has spent a minimum of ten thousand hours in classrooms as a teacher, preceded by at least fifteen thousand hours as a student. While not all such experienced teachers are experts, there are not likely to be many expert pedagogues who achieve their status without extensive classroom experience.

It is also likely that the domain-specific knowledge that is acquired through this experience is quite contextualized. For example, in one of our research studies, experts, advanced beginners, and novices were asked to teach a thirty-minute lesson on probability to a group of high school students (Berliner and others, 1988). While they taught the lesson, they were videotaped, and after the lesson, during stimulated recall, they were asked to tell us about their thinking and to justify their actions during teaching. The interesting thing about this study was the incredible level of anger that we triggered among all the expert teachers. We had assumed that they would breeze through the teaching task and that we would use their performance to assess the lesser skills to be shown by advanced beginners and novices. While the experts did, in fact, show more skills in a number of ways (Clarridge, 1988), all of them were angry about having to participate in the task. One of them walked out on the study, while another broke down and cried in the middle of it.

The reason for the teachers' anger was that we had moved them from their classrooms to a laboratory situation, and they did not feel that they could perform well under such conditions. We had allocated thirty minutes for planning, enough for the advanced beginners and the novices to feel comfortable, but the experts claimed that they needed more time — from three hours to as much as three weeks. From our interviews, we came to understand that experts rarely enter their classrooms without having taken all the time they need to thoroughly understand the content that they will teach and planning one or more activities to teach it. In addition, they did not know the students in this study.

Our interviews revealed that expert teachers' expertise depends in part on knowing their students in three ways: (1) They know the cognitive abilities of the students they teach, and this helps them to determine the level at which to teach. (2) They know their students personally, and this allows for personal rather than bureaucratic and informal mechanisms of control to be used in teaching. (3) They have a reputation with their students. In the teachers' own schools, their students knew that they were experts and had certain expectations about what their teaching would be like. These teachers had always had students who expected to be well taught and to learn a great deal, even if they were pushed to their intellectual limits. When they faced a group of strangers, none of these three aspects of "knowing the students" was present, and the teachers felt that they suffered from that. In addition, all the experts commented on the problems created by their inability to use routines, a basic part of any expert's performance (Bloom, 1985; Leinhardt and Greeno, 1986; Berliner, 1987). By taking them out of their classrooms, we had taken away the context in which these expert pedagogues excel.

There are aspects of this study revealing concern for responsible teaching that were not made evident in the primary analyses of the data. The first of these is the experts' demand for planning time sufficient for the instructional task. This concern need not just be thought of as a way for the experts to ensure more effective instruction. Another interpretation also fits these data. Compared to novices and advanced beginners, expert teachers appear to have such high self-respect and respect for their students that they consider it markedly unprofessional to show up in class without having mastered their material completely. They seem to feel that they owe that to their students and are embarrassed when they cannot fulfill that part of their social contract with them. Participation in this study may have been perceived as requiring the breaking of a moral obligation, and that may account for some of the unexpectedly high level of anger that was expressed. A second ethical concern among the experts was seen in their need to have one or more activities planned before initiating instruction. We think that this is because most of them strive for an instructional setting that is not lecture-oriented and teacher-dominated, which does not require a lot of planning time, but prefer instead, a more indirect method of teaching. This was less true of the novices and advanced beginners, who seemed much more direct in their instruction.

A third noteworthy aspect of the experts' behavior was their concern with knowing more about their students. The interviews revealed that this was required in order to accommodate instruction to their students' needs, a form of consideration not especially noted among the novice and advanced beginning teachers in this sample. Perhaps the most interesting aspect of the experts' behavior was their perception that their lack of personal knowledge about the students that they had to teach required them to use bureaucratic rather than informal mechanisms to control student behavior. All but one of the experts seemed upset by that. The task seemed to call for them to adopt more authoritarian roles than they had become accustomed to using, roles that they had generally discarded as they acquired expertise. This too may have contributed to their anger.

Another of our studies illustrates the nature of domain-specific, classroom-bound pedagogical knowledge, which is built up over time and may not be applicable to other domains in which individuals interact (Carter and others, 1987). It also reveals a humanistic side to experts that is yet to be demonstrated as clearly among novices and advanced beginners. Experts, advanced beginners, and raw novice teachers participated in a simulation in which information about a class was given to them. They received the tests that students had taken, homework assignments that students had turned in, and a set of student information cards containing typical academic information and some personal notes about the students, their families, and their social behavior. The simulation required the subjects to imagine taking over such a class in the fifth week of school, after the regular teacher had to leave because of an emergency. The novices in this study worked very hard trying to sort student information cards into piles. Here are some quotations from the protocols obtained in the study.

> I sorted the bad kids from the good kids from some of the ones that were just good natured, if they liked to work, that type of thing. And I would do that if I started writing my own comments. If I had the class for a while, I would tend to still categorize them.

> I went through her student cards and also went through the test scores and tried to divide the students into three groups, one group which I thought might be disruptive, one group which I thought would not be disruptive and that wouldn't need intense watching. The third group I really didn't know because the back of the card was blank. So it was classified later. I realized not all the disruptive students were getting bad grades. I decided to sort of rank cards from what I thought would be the best student from the top to the obviously poorer students going down the stack just to get some sort of an idea of ranking.

This behavior was in marked contrast to that of the experts. Experts were considerably less interested in remembering specific information about students than were the novices. Moreover, experts did not trust information left to them by a previous teacher. They believed that the information was useless because they knew that children make their own deals in every classroom. Information that the child was unmotivated or highly intelligent or disruptive was not thought to be as generalizable as, say, information on a medical record reporting the child to be hypertensive or hypoglycemic. The teachers had learned that every child takes on a different character in every classroom and that educational records, unlike medical records, cannot be trusted. Because of this and because of their generic view of students — seeing them all basically as alike and teachable (Calderhead, 1983) — the experts in our study had no reason to spend time on the particulars reported in the student information cards. The experts spent their time looking at the tests and the homework assignments that students had turned in, trying to understand, at some deep level, something about what students knew. When questioned about why they did not use the student information cards, the experts responded as follows:

I just don't think names are important as far as this point in time. I haven't met the kids; there is no reason for me to make any value judgments about them at this time. And so she [the previous teacher] had a whole little packet of confidential material that I looked at, and it had trivial little things about where the parents worked and this kid was cute or something like that, and that to me is not relevant.

Especially when I start fresh, I start from a clean slate. I usually always try to . . . I like getting a little background on the students in that there are going to be severe problems or someone may need special attention on certain things, you know, learning areas, but, in general, it's a conglomeration of the students. I like to learn from them and develop my own opinions.

It was a typical classroom, some problem kids that need to be dealt with. And you have to take that into consideration when you're developing some kind of plan for them. There are the bright kids that were highly self-motivated. There were your shy kids. It was a typical class.

I didn't read the cards. I never do unless there's a comment about a physical impairment such as hearing or sight or something I get from the nurse. I never want to place a judgment on the student before they start. I find I have a higher success rate if I don't.

Among the reasons given by the experts for their distrust of the information left for them about each student was their belief that students act differently in different environments—a belief in accord with that of most personality theorists. Their unwillingness to examine the records seems to be a conscious act by these teachers to prevent expectations from forming too early and to ensure that the beliefs they form about students are derived from their own personal experience. This is behavior that is quite considerate of students; it is responsible professional behavior. The experts may ignore student information also because they possess a sense of self-efficacy and have positive expectations. With some uniformity, the experts seem to believe that every child can learn and that they personally can teach every child assigned to them. They seem to attribute the level of student performance not to ability but to effort or family—external and alterable loci. For their own behavior, the locus of control appears to be internal. They take personal responsibility for their success and failure, an example of which was seen in the anger expressed by the expert teachers but not the novice or advanced beginners in the teaching situation described above.

That expert pedagogues use less information than novices or advanced beginners was also found when experienced and novice physicians reviewed applicants for internships and residencies and when experienced and novice financial advisers reviewed financial statements of companies (Johnson, 1988). Experience in a particular domain teaches one what is worth attending to and what is not.

It is hard to speculate on what someone would do in a new situation, but this kind of specialized knowledge probably does not transfer well across domains. It is very likely that when expert teachers join a social club, attend a professional conference, or register to take courses at graduate school, they act like novices. That is, they try to categorize people, grouping them into piles, as novice teachers do with their first class of students. We have increasing understanding that knowledge is, for the most part, contextually bound. As Brown, Collins, and Duguid (1989) put it, cognitions are situated; they are not adrift in the brain, unconnected to actions and situations. The road to transfer across situations appears to be a rocky one. Transfer does not usually appear spontaneously. It usually does not occur without cognitive work, some form of mental effort (Perkins and Salomon, 1989). Thus, we can anticipate that expert pedagogues, like other experts, will excel mainly in their own domain and in particular contexts within that domain. Their expert knowledge will not transfer automatically across domains.

Proposition two: Experts often develop automaticity for the repetitive operations that are needed to accomplish their goals.

Glaser (1987) notes the efficient decoding skill of the expert comprehender in reading as an example of the way automaticity frees working memory to allow other, more complex characteristics of the situation to be dealt with. Examples of the automaticity or routinization of some teaching functions among expert teachers are abundant. For example, Leinhardt and Greeno (1986), studying elementary school mathematics lessons, compared an expert's opening homework review with that of a novice. The expert teacher was quite brief, taking about one-third less time than the novice. This expert was able to pick up information about attendance and about who did or did not do the homework and was also able to identify who was going to need help later in the lesson. She elicited mostly correct answers throughout the activity and also managed to get all the homework corrected. Moreover, she did so at a brisk pace and never lost any control of the lesson. She had routines for recording attendance, for handling choral responding during the homework checks, and for hand raising to get attention. This expert also used clear signals to start and finish the lesson segments.

In contrast, when the novice was enacting an opening homework review as part of a mathematics lesson, she was not able to get a fix on who did and did not do the homework, she had problems with taking attendance, and she asked ambiguous questions that led her to misunderstand the difficulty of the homework. At one time, she lost control of the pace. She never learned which students were going to have more difficulty later on in the lesson. Of importance is that the novice showed lack of familiarity with well-practiced routines. She seemed not to have habitual ways to act. Students, therefore, were unsure of their roles in the class.

In a small study by Krabbe and Tullgren (1989), the routines of novice and well-regarded experienced teachers, whom I will call expert teachers, were assessed. English and language arts lessons at the junior high school level were analyzed. The experts took an average of fourteen minutes to introduce a literature lesson, while the novices took two minutes to do so. The experts needed that much time to follow a routine for the set inducement or introductory phase of the daily lesson. First, they briefly stated the immediate objective of the activity (for example, "We will discuss several ways that we can learn about the qualities of people"). Then they gave clear and explicit directions about what they wanted students to do (for example, "Put everything away; here are three situations for you to think about answering"). Then they created a positive environment for the phase of the lesson that would follow. The experts found ways to increase student involvement, often arousing curiosity through use of analogies that had something to do with the central concept and theme of the lesson. The goal of the lesson was apparent throughout their introduction. This three-step routine was also accompanied by a mood shift among the expert teachers from humorous and playful at the beginning of the introduction to serious and businesslike as the presentation, discussion, or oral reading phase of the lesson drew closer (Krabbe, McAdams, and Tullgren, 1988). This regularly occurring pattern of teaching, this routine, was not evident when the videotapes of the novice teachers were analyzed. Krabbe and Tullgren (1989) also identified a routine in the way that the presentation phase of the lesson was run by the experts. The expert teachers introduced material gradually and in hierarchical order, illustrated their points by using student background and daily experiences, and provided practice opportunities as they went along. Novice teachers during this phase of the lesson tended to ask text-specific factual questions until the lesson was over. No sense of a routine was noted in the way the novices taught a literature or language arts lesson.

The well-practiced routines of expert surgeons, ice skaters, tennis players, and concert pianists (Bloom, 1986), no less than expert teachers, are what give the appearance of fluidity and effortlessness to their performance. What looks to be so easy for the expert and so clumsy for the novice is the result of thousands of hours of reflected-on experience. But once again we may speculate that the expert teachers have more than just efficiency, effectiveness, and student achievement in mind as they develop their routines. Such routinization frees the mind so that people may attend to many aspects of the situation in which they find themselves. The mind is a very limited information processor. A concert pianist with no routines would be mechanical, paying little attention to the audience, the conductor, the acous tics, the subtle and unique elements that are present in each performance. Thus, routines are so well honed that the pianist's mind is free to process much more than the position of her fingers on the keyboard. Similarly, if all the attention of a teacher were directed at simply keeping the instructional elements of a classroom moving along the proper course, the highest levels of thinking would rarely be in evidence, and the affective and moral dimensions of classrooms would be unnoticed.

Support for this thesis may be found in the classrooms of novice teachers such as the one studied by Leinhardt and Greeno (1986). With no routinization of the opening homework review, the novice could not find out which of the students had had a troubled night at home the evening before, though the expert teacher could. Routines among the experts studied by Krabbe and Tullgren (1989) may have allowed them to allocate attention to matching the content to be learned to the students' personal knowledge and common experience. That is, the quality of a teacher's pedagogical content knowledge (the teacher's explanations, metaphors, analogies, and other transformations of what is to be taught into something more easily learned) may depend in part on supportive routines. This is because pedagogical content knowledge is often developed on the run, during interactive instruction, when attention to simultaneous events is required. Thus, routinization may promote interpersonal and personal relations in classrooms as well as it promotes instructional goals.

Proposition three: Experts are more sensitive than novices to task demands and the social situation when solving problems.

Glaser (1987) notes that the mental models that experts develop to guide their behavior are constrained by the requirements of the situation in which they must work. Housner and Griffey (1985), in a study of experienced and novice physical education teachers, provide evidence of the sensitivity of experienced teachers to those issues. They found that the number of requests for information made by experienced and novice teachers during the time they were planning instruction was about the same. Each group made reasonable requests for information about the number of students they would be teaching, their gender, their age, and so forth. But in two areas, the experienced teachers made many more requests than did the novice teachers. They needed to know about the ability, experience and background of the students they were to teach, and they needed to know about the facility in which they would be teaching. In fact, five of the eight experienced teachers in this study of planning and instruction demanded to see the facility in which they would teach before they could develop their plan. Novices made no such requests. The experienced teachers were sensitive to the social and physical environment under which instruction was to take place.

When actually performing in the teaching role, the experienced teachers implemented changes in their instruction more often than did novices, using social cues to guide their interactive instructional decision making. The experienced teachers used their judgment about student performance as a cue to change instruction 24 percent more often than did novices, their judgments about student involvement 41 percent more often, student enjoyment of the activities 79 percent more often, and their interpretation of mood and student feelings 82 percent more often. The novices used student verbal statements about the activity as their primary cue for instituting a change in their instructional activity, responding to these cues 131 percent more often than did the experienced teachers. Clearly, the novice teachers changed what they were doing primarily when asked to; they seemed unable to decode the social cues emitted by students about the ways in which instruction was proceeding. The experienced teachers, however, were far more sensitive to the social cues emitted in the situation and used these social cues for adjusting their instruction. Once again, we have evidence that experts behave in ways that we would judge more considerate of their students than the ways in which novices behave. Their experience has taught them how to read the more subtle cues emitted by their students, and this makes them more sensitive to the students' needs. Their reputations for effectiveness are likely to be due in part to their heightened social sensitivity.

Proposition four: Experts are opportunistic in their problem solving.

Glaser (1987) reports that experts are opportunistic in their planning and their actions. They take advantage of new information, quickly bringing new interpretations and representations of the problem to light. Novices are less flexible. Borko and Livingston (1988) discuss these same behaviors among novice and expert teachers. The term that these researchers use to characterize the expert teacher whose lessons have an opportunistic quality is the *improvisational performer.* They see the expert teacher as having a well-thought-out general script to follow but being very flexible in following it in order to be responsive to what students do. One expert, discussing his planning, made clear the improvisational aspect of teaching: "A lot of times I just put the objective in my book, and I play off the kids." This expert also described his interactive teaching as similar to a tennis match: "I sort of do a little and then they do a little. And then I do a little and they do a little. But my reaction is just that, it's a reaction. And it depends upon their action what my reaction's going to be."

Borko and Livingston (1988, p. 20) report that "the success of the expert teachers' improvisation seemed to depend upon their ability to quickly generate or provide examples and to draw connections between students' comments or questions and the lesson's objectives." This was not the case when the novices were teaching. All three of the novices in this study ran into problems when students made comments or asked questions requiring explanations that had not been planned for in advance. Novice teachers were sometimes unable to maintain the direction of the lesson when they had to respond to student comments or questions. This was true even when the issues brought up by the students were relevant to the topic of the lesson. Experiences such as this led two of the novices to prevent students from asking questions and making comments while they presented their lesson. Although he valued student responsiveness, Jim, one of the novices, reasoned this way (p. 26): "I think . . . because I'm not that proficient yet in handling questions, it's better to cut off the questions, just go through the material, because it'll be much clearer to them if they just let me go through it. . . . I don't want to discourage questions, but there are times I'd rather get through my presentation and then get to the questions."

Opportunistic teaching is apparently much more difficult for the novice than for the expert. For novices, the pedagogical schemata necessary for improvisation or opportunism seem to be less elaborate, less interconnected, and clearly less accessible than are those of the experts. It is the flexibility arising out of self-confidence that allows the expert teacher to capitalize on the instructional opportunities that present themselves. They can personalize instruction, developing pedagogical content knowledge on the run, and this allows them to fit the lesson to the students' behavior in ways that the novice cannot. This ability must make an expert appear more sensitive and responsive to student needs than would a novice. The experience and confidence of the experts allow them to appear more considerate of students — more caring, flexible, interested in what their students know, and so forth. The display of such humanistic and effective interpersonal qualities is still beyond the reach of the typical novice.

Proposition five: Experts' representations of problems and situations are qualitatively different from the representations of novices.

Chi, Glaser, and Farr (1988) note that experts seem to understand problems at a deeper level than do novices. Experts apply concepts and principles that are more relevant to the problem to be solved. Novices' understanding seems to be at a more superficial level; they show less evidence of principled reasoning. We find some support for this general statement in studies of expertise in the pedagogical domain. In one small study of ours, Hanninen (1983) created realistic scenarios about educational problems associated with gifted children. One scenario, for example, described Mark, an eight-year-old Asian boy with severe hearing deficits who likes mathematics and science and has a strong interest in computers. Scenarios describing educational problems of this type were presented to fifteen subjects. Five of the subjects were expert, experienced teachers of gifted children; another five were equally experienced teachers but without any background in gifted education; and five more were novice teachers of the gifted, still working on their certification.

The opening sentences of some of the protocols revealed much about the thinking of experts and novices. The opening sentence from one novice reads, "Mark seems like a very talented individual with many diverse interests." Another novice comments, "Mark should be encouraged by his teacher to continue his science experiments and work on the computer." From an experienced teacher who was a novice in the area of gifted education, we have "He should be able to pursue his interests in greater depth." In contrast to these banal, unsophisticated beginnings to essays that attempted to address Mark's needs, in which superficial characteristics of the problem were noted, one expert began right off with "Mark's needs can be broken into three broad areas: academic enrichment, emotional adjustment, and training to cope with his handicap." This essay was a more organized and sophisticated representation of the problem than was obtained from the novices. The experts also concentrated more on the affective characteristics of Mark's life than did the other teachers. This is a common pattern among experts and will be discussed in more detail below.

If one views pedagogical knowledge as a complex multidimensional domain of knowledge requiring sophisticated thinking, then it could be argued that the classification of a problem as solvable by using Newton's second law — that is, considering it a conservation-of-energy problem — is no different from classifying Mark's educational needs as falling into three categories and describing action relevant to each of those categories. This was an appropriate representation for a problem in the pedagogical domain.

The scenario methodology that we used to learn about teachers' thinking was used in a better-designed study by Nelson (1988), in which expert and novice physical education teachers were the subjects. She concluded that experts "displayed a greater variety of application of sound principles of teaching" (p. 25) than did novices. The experts were also more creative and thorough in describing ways to address teaching problems and provided more solutions to each problem that they addressed. In a different study, Peterson and Comeaux (1987) used videotapes to elicit comments from experienced and novice teachers. They found that the comments of experienced teachers "reflected an underlying knowledge structure in which they relied heavily on procedural knowledge of classroom events as well as on higher-order principles of effective classroom teaching" (p. 327).

Similarities in the two studies are quite apparent. An expert in Nelson's (1988) study says of a problem with an exercise program designed for an overweight child, "I'd find something positive about his workout. . . . If I don't give him some positive reinforcement, I may lose his dedication to the task" (p. 25). And an experienced teacher in Peterson and Comeaux's (1987) study says about a teacher returning an essay test, "I guess before he handed them back, it might have been a good idea if there was an excellent paper there to have read it with no name, or excerpts from it, or at least on the board outline what a good answer would have been — that type of thing. He might have made some comments of errors that were made, again with no names, that were misconceptions, and clear those up with students right away. *You can use the test as a learning experience* rather than just hand it back, to put away, or throw away probably" (p. 328).

In the comments of both the expert and experienced teachers, we see evidence of principled thought, the former enunciating a principle about reinforcement and motivation, the latter enunciating a pedagogical principle about the usefulness of tests as learning experiences separate from their function in evaluation. Such reasoning was not typical of the responses of novices. Moreover, the comments about motivation and the use of tests for learning experiences (not just for feedback, reward, or punishment) show interest in considerate teaching. The word *genuine* characterizes a good deal of the teaching that experienced teachers do. It is teaching primarily for growth and improvement rather than for sorting children out along an ability continuum.

In another study of ours (Stein, Clarridge, and Berliner, forthcoming), we looked at the ways that expert teachers predict how students will respond to mathematics and science items used in the National Assessment of Educational Progress. From the protocols obtained while the subjects thought aloud, we learned that experts named or labeled items in a much more detailed and specific way than did novices or advanced beginners. The experts also engaged in a task analysis of the problem in a way that was quite sophisticated. They analyzed the demands of the task represented in the item to determine what sorts of problems students might experience with them. Task analysis was coded in their think-alouds when the subjects verbalized something about the reasons for an item's difficulty or when they traced out the various steps or competencies that a student would need to answer an item correctly. Eighty percent of the experts analyzed the task demands of the items; they did this for between one and four of the five items for which they had to think aloud. Among the novices and the advanced beginners, only 50 percent of each group engaged in task analysis of the items, and when they did so, it was for only one of the five items that they analyzed. The task analyses of the experts were also more elaborate or more clearly formed than those of others.

The experts also differed in their inferences about the student cognitions used in answering an item. Experts seemed to have a fund of knowledge about the way students thought and how that thinking interacted with the content of the specific mathematics or science items. In addition, the experts seemed able to think through the *mis*algorithms that students might apply. The experts had more experience dealing with student errors and therefore knew what types of errors students might make. Novices rarely discussed the issue of misalgorithms that students might apply to solve a problem. We concluded from this study that experts in mathematics and science teaching were more likely than novices and advanced beginners to represent the test items the students would address in a more sophisticated way because of their better labeling of problem types and that they gained insight into the nature of a particular problem type by more frequently doing a task analysis of it from the students' perspective. From the labeling and task analysis, the experts could more often predict the kinds of errors that students would make when attempting to answer test items. Since their predictions were more accurate, they appeared to be better explainers than novices or advanced beginners and more understanding of their students' ways of thinking.

Proposition six: Experts have fast and accurate pattern-recognition capabilities; novices cannot always make sense of what they experience.

Accurate interpretation of cues and recognition of patterns reduce a person's cognitive processing load and allow the person to instantaneously make sense of a field. For example, quick pattern recognition allows an expert chess player to spot areas of the board where difficulties might occur. Novices are not as good at recognizing such patterns, and when they do note them, they are less likely to make proper inferences about the situation.

In one of our studies, we showed subjects slides of classroom scenes and asked them to interpret what they saw. Each slide was viewed briefly three different times. After the second viewing of a slide, one expert in science said, "It's not necessarily a lab class. There just seemed to be more writing activity. There were people filling out forms. It could have been the end of a lab class after they started putting the equipment away." After the third viewing of the slide, the expert said, "Yeah — there was . . . very little equipment out and it almost appeared to be towards the end of the hour. The books appeared to be closed. Almost looked like it was a cleanup type of situation." Novices did not usually perceive the same cues in the classroom and therefore could not make the inferences that guided the expert's understanding of the classroom. The expert, by the way, was absolutely correct. It was a cleanup kind of activity.

In another study, novice, advanced beginner, and expert teachers simultaneously viewed three television screens, each depicting a different group working in the same class. We saw the same phenomena at work here as in the task using slides (Sabers, Cushing, and Berliner, 1991). During a think-aloud viewing of the videotape, one expert commented, "Left monitor again. . . . I haven't heard a bell, but the students are already at their desks and seem to be doing purposeful activity, and this is about the time that I decided they must be an accelerated group because they came into the room and started something rather than just sitting down or socializing." In fact, the students in the scene shown on the left monitor did begin working as soon as they entered the classroom and continued working throughout the entire instructional period. To us, as well as to the experts, this group of students seemed to exhibit a lot of internal motivation. Further, just as this expert noted, this was an accelerated group: it was a science classroom for students identified as gifted and talented.

We regard the reading of a classroom, like the reading of a chess board, to be, in part, a matter of pattern recognition based on hundreds of thousands of hours of experience. The ability of novices or other relatively inexperienced teachers to reliably interpret classroom information is limited precisely because of their lack of experience. The information related to pedagogical events may be so rich and complex that novices and advanced beginners simply cannot agree on what is seen. In the study where they monitored three television screens simultaneously, novices and advanced beginners seemed to experience difficulty in making sense of their classroom observations and in providing plausible explanations of what was occurring within the classroom. For example, we obtained these two comments from advanced beginners who were asked to describe the learning environment in the classroom that they were observing:

> It looked . . . I wouldn't call it terribly motivating. It was, well, not bored, but not enthusiastic.

> Very positive as well as relaxed. Very positive . . . it's good to be able to focus [student] energy into a group situation, yet at the same time, accomplishing the work that they need to do for the class and also lending to the relaxed feeling of the classroom.

Such contradictions were common. Even more discrepancy was noted when these subjects were asked to describe the students' attitudes toward this class. For example,

> It didn't look like it was a favorite class for most of them. One boy looked kind of like, "Oh no, it's not this class again." They didn't look overwhelmingly enthusiastic to be there.

> They seemed pretty excited about the class, excited to learn and a lot of times it's hard to get students excited about science, but this teacher seems to have them so that they are excited about it. They're willing to work and they want to learn.

As a group, these advanced beginners, in their first year of teaching, seemed unable to make sense of what they saw. They experienced difficulty monitoring all three video screens at once. Thus, they often reported contradictory observations and appeared confused about what they were observing and the meaning of their observations. Because novices are much less familiar with classroom events than advanced beginners, they often appeared even more overwhelmed. Many of them expressed difficulty in monitoring all three video screens at once; generally, they appeared able to focus on and make sense of only one screen. Since this limited their observations, they also made errors and contradictions when they were asked about specific events. They were unable to see the overall patterns in the information presented to them.

Another of our studies also showed this difference in interpretive competency between experts and novices (Carter and others, 1988). In that study, subjects viewed a series of slides depicting science or mathematics instruction over a class period in a high school. The subjects held a remote control and were told to go through the fifty or so slides at their own pace, stopping to comment on any slides that they found interesting. Novices and advanced beginners seemed to show no particular pattern in what they stopped to comment on and showed the same kinds of contradictions in their interpretations that we found in the study using videotapes. That is, one novice might say "Everything looks fine, they're all paying attention," and another novice might say, "It looks like they're starting to go off task, they're starting to drift." A pattern was noted among the experts that was quite different. The experts, more often than the subjects in the other groups, found the *same* slides worth commenting about and had the *same* kinds of comments to make. For example, three experts made these comments on slide 5:

> It's a good shot of both people being involved and something happening.

> Everybody seems to be interested in what they're doing at their lab stations.

> Everybody working. A positive environment.

And two experts offered these comments on slide 51:

> More students with their books closed, their purses on their desks, hands folded, ready to go.

> Must be the end of class and everybody is getting ready for the bell to ring.

This reduction in variance by the experts is particularly noteworthy. It means that they have learned to pay attention to some of the same things and to interpret visual stimuli in the same way. This similarity in what is attended to and how it is interpreted is what we hope for when we visit an expert ophthalmologist or automobile mechanic. Novices, advanced beginners — anyone in the early stages of skill acquisition — simply will not have acquired enough experience for that.

The ability to quickly make sense out of what is seen was demonstrated in a unique way by one of the experts in the study using slides. In the classroom that had been photographed, a girl had entered in a gray jacket, gone to her desk, put her purse down on the floor, and looked straight ahead throughout the lesson, neither opening a book nor engaging in any aspect of instruction or student conversation. She appeared clothed in a heavy mantle of grief. Near the end of the lesson, she silently started to cry. Tears streamed slowly down her cheeks, unnoticed by her teacher or her peers. As the bell rang, she bolted and ran from the class. From static slides, shot with a wide-angle lens, the girl's behavior could hardly be noticed. Yet one expert, as he got to a slide near the end of the tray, said, "There's something wrong with the girl in gray." And then, as he looked at the next slide, he said, "Yep, there's something really making her unhappy and it has nothing to do with this class." We think this is a remarkable example of accurate processing of subtle patterns in the visual field. We commented about this skill in social sensitivity when we discussed proposition three, above. And we will comment on a related phenomenon as we discuss proposition seven, next.

Proposition seven: Experts perceive meaningful patterns in the domain in which they are experienced.

Chi, Glaser, and Farr (1988) point out that the superior perceptual skills of experts are due not to any innate superior perceptual abilities but to the way that experience affects perception. After one hundred thousand x-rays or ten thousand hours of observing students, what is attended to and how that information is interpreted are very likely to have changed. In another experiment with slides of classroom scenes (Carter and others, 1988), we flashed slides on the screen for only a very brief time and asked experts, novices, and advanced beginners to tell us what they saw. The responses of the novices and advanced beginners to the slides were clearly descriptive and usually quite accurate.

Novice: A blond haired-boy at the table, looking at papers. Girl to his left reaching in front of him for something.

Advanced beginner: [It's] a classroom. Student with back to camera working at a table.

Advanced beginner: A room full of students sitting at tables.

In contrast to these literal descriptions, typical of novices and advanced beginners, some of our expert teachers often responded with inferences about what they saw:

It's a hands-on activity of some type. Group work with a male and female of maybe late junior high school age.

It's a group of students maybe doing small-group discussion on a project as the seats are not in rows.

For experts, the information that was often deemed important was information that had instructional significance, such as the age of the students or the teaching-learning activity in which they were engaged. They perceived more meaningful patterns than did novices. Nelson (1988) replicated these findings of ours, using expert and novice physical education teachers. When viewing a slide intended to show a common management problem, a student not dressing for the gym period, a novice teacher somehow misinterpreted the scene: "What I'm assuming is that this is an on-looker. Somebody [who's] just walked in. Maybe someone that's late to class or someone who's hesitant about doing gymnastics, a little scared so they're off in another area just watching" (p. 15). An expert viewing the same slide perceived more than the girl's lack of gym clothing. She saw the whole instructional situation in a more global way and made more meaning of it:

> Here is one girl I noticed earlier who is not dressed out [sic].
> She could have a doctor's excuse or something, but she's far away
> from the remainder of the class and she should be involved,
> maybe with spotting, or at least in a closer proximity to the rest
> of the students. She needs to learn just like everyone else in the
> class. The teacher [then wouldn't] need to be worried about what
> she is doing, either. If something is missing from the teacher's
> desk or any of the students' belongings, [that girl] may have
> to take the responsibility. [Also], the doors are so close by, if
> she wants to leave there's always a possibility, and the teacher
> is responsible for her. She's just not involved in the class in any
> way [pp. 15–16].

In any field, the information that experts extract from the phenomena with which they are confronted stems, in part, from the concepts and principles that they use to impose meaning on phenomena in their domain of expertise. That is, experts in all domains appear to be top-down processors. They impose meaning on the stimuli in their domain of expertise. In education, one such concept used to interpret phenomena is attention, or involvement. The physical education expert quoted above is interpreting the slide with this concept in mind. In our study of the interpretation of slides, a focus of the experts was on the notion of work: "students *working* at the blackboard," "students *working* independently," "teacher looking over a person *working* in lab," and so on.

This work orientation, of course, is part of what promotes high rates of achievement among the students of experts. But some characteristics of the experts that are less clearly tied to effectiveness (though contributing to it) have also been found. These have more to do with the responsibility side of teaching. For example, we have found evidence from two studies of ours (Clarridge, 1988; Rottenberg and Berliner, forthcoming) that expert teachers take student responsibility in a lesson into account, expecting students to be in some way involved in the creation of their own knowledge, perhaps through discussion, perhaps through cooperative learning, perhaps through questions or projects. Somehow, the experts seem to communicate this sense of responsibility and are sensitive to it when discussing their views of classes.

Evidence for this was found in Clarridge's (1988) study in which videotapes were rated by a specialist in non-verbal communication. The specialist found the expert teachers to be high in incorporative behavior, behavior that invites the students to work jointly with them. The specialist also found that novice and advanced beginners set up barriers to keep authority in their own hands. (The tapes, of course, were rated without knowledge of the experience level of the teachers that were viewed.) Furthermore, expert teachers seem to be unusually sensitive to the affective concerns of the students they teach (Nelson, 1988; Rottenberg and Berliner, forthcoming). The expert who recognized the unhappiness of the student from a minimum of cues in the study discussed above was displaying this kind of social sensitivity. This was also true of the physical education teachers described earlier.

A physicist may bring to bear Newtonian laws to make meaning of a problem in physics. A biologist may bring to bear concepts of homeostasis or ecological niche to make meaning of a problem in biology. A chemist, auto mechanic, and an engineer will also bring to bear on the problems that they face the most salient and useful concepts that they possess. Among the salient and useful pedagogical concepts with which teachers make meaning from the phenomena that they encounter in their work are attention, work, responsibility, and affect. While the first two of these concepts deal with effectiveness more than responsibility in teaching, the latter two concepts deal explicitly with issues of responsibility more than effectiveness. Perhaps of greater interest is that among experts, it appears that effectiveness and responsibility are fused concepts.

Conclusion

The results of the studies described in this selective review appear to be clear. First, expert teachers share characteristics with experts in other domains. Second, the domain-specific knowledge of experts is of a rather sophisticated nature. The collection of evidence supporting these two points is important for the profession. Finally, the evidence about experts suggests that their unique reputation is not based merely on their effectiveness as instructors. Certainly, the evidence supports the claim that they think and act differently from novices in ways that are likely to promote their effectiveness as instructors. But a review of the same data suggests that the experts also think and act differently in ways that promote responsible instruction. And these differences in thinking and acting do not appear to be attributable to differences in age and life experience, though such differences certainly exist; rather, they appear to result from reflected-upon classroom experience, which leads the experts, for the most part, to teach in ways consistent with the complementary synthesis model described in Chapter One of this book. The experts seem to understand better than other teachers that the two approaches are mutually interdependent. They appear to believe that effectiveness can be achieved through responsible teaching and that being responsible entails being effective. That is, a responsible teacher owes students the opportunity to obtain the knowledge and skill needed to succeed in life, and an effective teacher owes students civility and consideration. With rare exceptions, the experts that have been studied demonstrated this sense of obligation toward their students. They also had a positive motivational system at work in their classrooms, a recognition of individual differences among their students, a belief in their own efficacy and their students' ability to learn, and a concern with both the affective and the effective elements of the classroom environment in which they worked.

The research on expertise has proved to be useful in policy analysis. Understanding the contextualization of expertise helps us to understand the limits of what we can expect from teachers and the irrationality of the expectations that we sometimes have. Learning that it takes considerable time to acquire competence in the pedagogical domain, let alone expertise, changes the way we think about support systems for the beginning teacher and the limits of teacher education programs. Learning what experts attend to, what they find worth remembering, how they implement routines, and how they maintain a classroom that is considerate of their students can help in designing programs of teacher education that are more focused on the acquisition of the pedagogical knowledge needed to teach both responsibly and effectively. The research has also provided us with ways to think about the growth or development of different kinds of knowledge in the pedagogical domain. Theories about the development of pedagogical expertise have been proposed that fit the existing data quite well. An example is my own description of a five-stage theory of the development of expertise, which posits the stages of novice, advanced beginner, competent performer, proficient performer, and expert (Berliner, 1989; based on work by Dreyfus and Dreyfus, 1986). Developmental theories of knowledge growth have implications for the kinds of assessments, the content of assessments, and the timing of assessments that will be used in the evaluation of teachers.

Expertise in pedagogy is now seen as a synthesis of what we call responsible and effective instruction. It appears to be a complex and highly sophisticated kind of domain-specific knowledge and skill, developed slowly over many years by highly motivated individuals. It is not a level of development that is obtained by everyone. The small number of teachers who achieve this status should be honored. They are the people whom we should ask the public to watch when the public is criticizing education. Few among the critics could ever match the experts' pedagogical skills day after exhausting day, year after exhausting year.

References

Berliner, D. C. "In Pursuit of the Expert Pedagogue." *Educational Researcher,* 1987, *15* (7), 5–13.
Berliner, D. C. "Implications of Studies of Expertise in Pedagogy for Teacher

Education and Evaluation." In *New Directions for Teacher Assessment.* Princeton, N.J.: Educational Testing Service, 1989.

Berliner, D. C., and others. "Implications of Research on Pedagogical Expertise and Experience for Mathematics Teaching." In D. A. Grouws and T. J. Cooney (eds.), *Perspectives on Research on Effective Mathematics Teaching.* Reston, Va.: National Council of Teachers of Mathematics, 1988.

Bloom, B. S. (ed.). *Developing Talent in Young People.* New York: Ballentine, 1985.

Bloom, B. S. "Automaticity." *Educational Leadership,* Feb. 1986, 70–77.

Borko, H., and Livingston, C. "Expert and Novice Teachers' Mathematics Instruction: Planning, Teaching and Post-Lesson Reflections." Paper presented at the meeting of the American Educational Research Association, New Orleans, La., Apr. 1988.

Brown, J. S., Collins, A., and Duguid, P. "Situated Cognition and the Culture of Learning." *Educational Researcher,* 1989, *18* (1), 32–42.

Calderhead, J. "Research into Teachers' and Student Teachers' Cognitions: Exploring the Nature of Classroom Practice." Paper presented at the meeting of the American Educational Research Association, Montreal, Canada, Apr. 1983.

Carter, K., and others. "Processing and Using Information About Students: A Study of Expert, Novice and Postulant Teachers." *Teaching and Teacher Education,* 1987, *3,* 147–157.

Carter, K., and others. "Expert-Novice Differences in Perceiving and Processing Visual Information." *Journal of Teacher Education,* 1988, *39* (3), 25–31.

Chase, W. G., and Simon, H. A. "Perception in Chess." *Cognitive Psychology,* 1973, *4,* 55–81.

Chi, M.T.H., Glaser, R., and Farr, M. (eds.). *The Nature of Expertise.* Hillsdale, N.J.: Erlbaum, 1988.

Clarridge, P. B. "Alternative Perspectives for Analyzing Expert, Novice, and Postulant Teaching." Unpublished dissertation, University of Arizona, Tucson, 1988.

deGroot, A. D. *Thought and Choice in Chess.* The Hague, the Netherlands: Mouton, 1965.

Dreyfus, H. L., and Dreyfus, S. E. *Mind over Machine.* New York: Free Press, 1986.

Glaser, R. "Thoughts on Expertise." In C. Schooler and W. Schaie (eds.), *Cognitive Functioning and Social Structure over the Life Course.* Norwood, N.J.: Ablex, 1987.

Hanninen, G. "Do Experts Exist in Gifted Education?" Unpublished manuscript, College of Education, University of Arizona, Tucson, 1983.

Housner, L. D., and Griffey, D. C. "Teacher Cognition: Differences in Planning and Interactive Decision Making Between Experienced and Inexperienced Teachers." *Research Quarterly for Exercise and Sport,* 1985, *56,* 44–53.

Johnson, E. J. "Expertise and Decision Under Uncertainty: Performance and Process." In M.T.H. Chi, R. Glaser, and M. Farr (eds.), *The Nature of Expertise.* Hillsdale, N.J.: Erlbaum, 1988.

Krabbe, M. A., McAdams, A. G., and Tullgren, R. "Comparisons of Experienced and Novice Verbal and Nonverbal Expressions During Preview and Directing Instructional Activity Segments." Paper presented at the meeting of the American Educational Research Association, New Orleans, La., Apr. 1988.

Krabbe, M. A., and Tullgren, R. "A Comparison of Experienced and Novice Teachers' Routines and Procedures During Set and Discussion Instructional Activity Segments." Paper presented at the meeting of the American Educational Research Association, San Francisco, Mar. 1989.

Leinhardt, G., and Greeno, J. "The Cognitive Skill of Teaching." *Journal of Educational Psychology,* 1986, *78,* 75–95.

Lesgold, A., and others. "Expertise in a Complex Skill: Diagnosing X-Ray Pictures." In M.T.H. Chi, R. Glaser, and M. Farr (eds.), *The Nature of Expertise.* Hillsdale, N.J.: Erlbaum, 1988.

Nelson, K. R. "Thinking Processes, Management Routines and Student Perceptions of Expert and Novice Physical Education Teachers." Unpublished dissertation, Louisiana State University, Baton Rouge, 1988.

Newell, A., and Simon, H. A. *Human Problem Solving.* Englewood Cliffs, N.J.: Prentice-Hall, 1972.

Perkins, D. N., and Salomon, G. "Are Cognitive Skills Contextually-Bound?" *Educational Researcher,* 1989, *18,* 16–25.

Peterson, P. L., and Comeaux, M. A. "Teachers' Schemata for Classroom Events: The Mental Scaffolding of Teachers' Thinking During Classroom Instruction." *Teaching and Teacher Education,* 1987, *3,* 319–331.

Posner, M. I. "Introduction: What Is It to Be an Expert?" In M.T.H. Chi, R. Glaser, and M. Farr (eds.), *The Nature of Expertise.* Hillsdale, N.J.: Erlbaum, 1988.

Rottenberg, C. V., and Berliner, D. C. "Expert and Novice Conceptions of Everyday Classroom Activities," forthcoming.

Sabers, D., Cushing, K., and Berliner, D. C. "Differences Among Teachers in a Task Characterized by Simultaneity, Multidimensionality and Immediacy." *American Educational Research Journal,* 1991, *28,* 63–88.

Stein, P., Clarridge, P. B., and Berliner, D. C. "Teacher Estimation of Student Knowledge: Accuracy, Content and Process," forthcoming.

16

Research on the Model Teacher and the Teaching Model

Franz E. Weinert, Andreas Helmke, Friedrich-W. Schrader

Scientific progress is frequently stimulated by conflicts between different theoretical camps. But this does not apply when the theoretical approaches are obviously inadequate; here a theory-derived combination of seemingly contrasting lines of inquiry may provide a more comprehensive description and explanation of the phenomena concerned. We would argue that this is the case concerning the two separate tracks so far pursued in teaching research. As Stolurow (1965, p. 223) asked, "Model the master teacher or master the teaching model?"

Both these approaches are popular today and are being explored in various research programs. To "master the teaching model" is no doubt the main goal of numerous studies within the process-product research paradigm (Brophy and Good, 1986; Gage and Needels, 1989; Weinert, Schrader, and Helmke, 1989). To "model the master teacher," in contrast, is the theoretical and methodological basis of research in teacher expertise and its applications (Berliner, 1986; Leinhardt, 1986; Leinhardt and Greeno, 1986; Leinhardt and Smith, 1985; Weinert, Schrader, and Helmke, 1990; see also Chapter Fifteen in this book). At present, neither the teaching model approach nor the master teacher tradition has the theoretical power to offer an adequate explanation of the interrelationships between quality of instruction and students' learning outcomes.

This is especially true if one distinguishes two types of teaching effects: performance criteria that are taken as indicators of teacher effectiveness (for example, the average achievement growth in the class and changes in performance variance in the class) and students' personality development (for example, value orientation, self-concept, motivation to learn, anxiety reduction), interpretable as an indicator of teacher responsibility. Thus, for a comprehensive picture of teaching competence, both teacher behavior and learning outcomes must be included in a multicriterial analysis.

A Theoretical Model of Teaching Expertise

The concepts of the expert teacher and the general teaching model allow successful instruction to be analyzed from two different approaches: the teacher expertise approach and the instructional variables approach. These two approaches would provide a theoretical contradiction only if the first were interpreted within a cognitive and the second within a behaviorist frame of reference. Whereas this type of polarization may have had some validity in the past, it has no relevance in current research. The main difference between the two approaches is that the teacher expertise approach emphasizes different instructional patterns influenced by teacher attributes, whereas the instructional variables approach highlights the functional effects of single instructional variables analyzed in isolation. From this perspective, the two approaches are not incommensurable but rather are complementary approaches whose integration should result in a more comprehensive theory of instruction (see Berliner, 1989, for a similar conclusion).

The theoretical assumptions underlying a combination of the master teacher and the teaching model approaches can be summarized as follows.

Instructional Variables and Learning Outcomes

Research results, as well as everyday classroom observations, indicate that the effects on students' achievement growth and/or personality development of very few instructional variables are unconditional, that is, context-free, invariant, and stable. The efficiency of an instructional variable and to some extent even the direction of its effect depend on the occurrence of that variable within a configurative pattern of other instructional variables, or in what has been termed an "instructional gestalt" (Siegel and Siegel, 1967). This means, however, that functional relationships between isolated instructional variables and learning outcomes are often masked or invalidated. For this reason, instructional research should not continue to collect and analyze long lists of specific instructional variables but rather should focus on identifying complex instructional patterns that enable clear distinctions to be made among different teaching styles.

Patterns of Instructional Variables

Identifying and analyzing complex patterns of instructional variables is difficult because these patterns are not static; rather, they are dynamic configurations with a stable fundamental structure but high situative variance at the surface level. It is meaningful, therefore, not only to describe such patterns on the basis of classroom observation but also to consider teacher differences in pedagogic expertise and responsibility as conditions of competent teaching. We assume that with such a procedure, it should be possible to tap the stable structures of instructional patterns despite their situative oscillation, fluctuation, and variation in the classroom.

The Knowledge Principle

The expert-novice paradigm assumes that domain-specific knowledge is a necessary condition for competent action. Lack of knowledge can be compensated for only to a very limited extent by general abilities or special effort. This point is captured by the "knowledge principle": "a system exhibits intelligent understanding and action in a high level of competence primarily because of the specific knowledge that it can bring to bear: The concepts, representations, facts, heuristics, models, and methods of its domain of endeavor" (Feigenbaum, 1989, p. 179). The interrelationship among expert knowledge, competent behavior in complex situations, and high achievement postulated for experts in general has also been confirmed for teachers' classroom behaviors.

Types of Teaching Expertise

There is sufficient theoretical and empirical evidence to support the assumption that pedagogic expertise is not a uniform, homogeneous, and coherent class of knowledge. There are good reasons to assume that there are at least four subdomains of teaching expertise that are independent of each other and acquired independently of each other. Accordingly, we propose the following classification of pedagogic knowledge. (Of course, limiting teaching expertise to four classes of knowledge in no way excludes other kinds of teacher knowledge necessary for achieving the various goals of schooling.)

   Subject Matter Expertise. Subject matter expertise refers to the content of the knowledge domain to be taught. This involves a well-organized and easily accessible body of factual and conceptual knowledge, content-specific algorithms and heuristics, and metacognitive competencies to be used in decisions concerning curricular goals, optimal sequential organization of the subject matter, task difficulty, and the like. Thus, teachers' subject matter expertise includes not only content-specific knowledge but also an organization of this knowledge that facilitates optimal instruction (Berliner, 1986; Grossman, Wilson, and Shulman, 1989; Leinhardt and Smith, 1985; Shulman, 1987; Tamir, 1988).

   Classroom Management Expertise. Classroom management expertise refers to procedural knowledge about conditions supporting effective and responsible teaching and successful learning. This includes maintaining high levels of on-task behavior in the classroom, preventing and/or rapidly eliminating interruptions, and creating a positive social climate in the class (Berliner, 1986; Doyle, 1986; Evertson, 1989).

   Instructional Expertise. Instructional expertise refers to the teacher's implicit and explicit knowledge about teaching strategies and methods for achieving instructional or pedagogical goals. It is composed primarily of procedural knowledge that is organized within a complex/hierarchical system of instructional schemata (Leinhardt and Greeno, 1986; Leinhardt, Weidman, and Hammond, 1987; Peterson and Comeaux, 1987). It also includes planning, monitoring, control, evaluative, and corrective skills that allow classroom teaching to be organized in a competent way and adapted to changing situations.

Diagnostic Expertise. This subdomain refers to general and person-specific knowledge about the students in the class—their needs and goals, their abilities and achievement levels, and their particular strengths and weaknesses as learners (Clark and Peterson, 1986; Leinhardt, 1983; Schrader, 1989).

These four classes of knowledge involve declarative, procedural, and metacognitive knowledge; that is, they consist of classroom-specific facts, concepts, heuristics, and skills. In addition, such factors as a teacher's personality attributes, motives, values, and emotions no doubt also influence instruction and teaching.

Integrated Expertise

It is hypothesized that a teacher's competence, defined as the quality of teaching behavior and its outcomes, is determined by the combined use of knowledge within these four subdomains. Obviously, the term *expert teacher* should refer only to those teachers who can draw on a rich knowledge base in all four subdomains. It is presently not clear whether simultaneous activation of these four knowledge components gives rise to an additional class of integrated pedagogic expertise. This might, for example, involve instructional metacompetencies, the level of instructional awareness, the quality and verbal justification of pedagogic decisions, or the ability to undertake multiple classifications of instructional problems.

Without considering this special problem, we would emphasize again that our model is composed of three separate structural components: teacher expertise, teaching competence, and teaching outcomes (see Figure 16.1). The advantage of this model is that these three construct systems enable separate operationalization of the variables, so that data sources are not confounded: the *expertise level* is composed of the pedagogic knowledge of the teacher, the *teaching competence level* is composed of the teacher's classroom behavior resulting from pedagogic knowledge, and the *criteria level* refers to student development, such as achievement growth and changes in cognitive aptitudes, motives, and values.

Patterns of Instruction

Many though not all variables used within the process-product paradigm are components of teaching expertise. For most of the other instructional variables, it is expected that their functional relationship to teaching outcomes depends on their incorporation into a pattern of either effective or ineffective instruction. Presumably, the effects of variables such as teacher

Figure 16.1. A Model of Teacher Expertise,
Teaching Competence, and Teaching Outcomes.

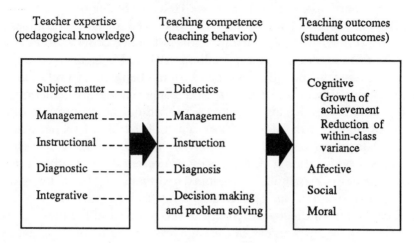

enthusiasm, use of visual aids in instruction, and amount of homework assignments are a function of the teacher's pedagogic expertise. Thus, in a theoretical model conceptualized along these lines, a complex gestaltlike pattern of teaching variables determines the quality of instruction. This global quality of instruction, in turn, is the reference system that has a considerable impact on the effectiveness of many single instructional variables.

An Empirical Illustration of Teaching Expertise

The theoretical assumptions underlying this combination of the expert teacher model and the general teaching model will be empirically tested in a preliminary way on the basis of our own research. As we have not collected data especially for this purpose, we will draw on and reanalyze data from an earlier study (Helmke, Schneider, and Weinert, 1986). Considering these data under a novel theoretical perspective can help to investigate the following questions:

- Are the four systems of pedagogical knowledge that we have postulated relatively independent of each other?
- Are there groups of teachers who differ in pedagogic expertise? Are there teachers in the sample who have a rich knowledge base in all four subdomains and who can thus be classified as expert teachers?
- Is teaching expertise related to different (for example, cognitive and affective) learning outcomes?
- Do the effects of particular instructional variables depend on the level of teacher expertise in the classroom? Do these effects differ when instrumental variables or socioemotional instructional variables are considered?

To investigate these questions, we looked at data from a study in which thirty-nine teachers from German primary schools (Hauptschule) in the Munich area participated (for details, see Helmke, Schneider, and Weinert, 1986). Nine math instruction lessons were observed; teaching variables were assessed by trained observers using a low-inference observational system (Five-Minute-Interaction System; Stallings, 1977). The items recorded were relative frequency of the following instructional behaviors in relation to the total number of all teacher behaviors and teacher-student interactions: disciplinary problems, procedural activities, individualized supportive contacts, and structuring cues. In addition, after each of the nine lessons, observers rated the following aspects of instruction on high-inference scales: effective use of rules, organizational skills, clarity of presentation of subject matter, control of homework assignments, adaptivity of teaching behavior, patience with slow learners, teacher enthusiasm, and teacher warmth.

The data from the low-inference observations and the high-inference ratings were aggregated across all the nine lessons. Some of these data were used to operationalize the four subdomains of teacher expertise listed below. However, only two of the four expertise subdomains (diagnostic expertise and subject matter expertise) could be operationalized using knowledge components; for the other two subdomains (management expertise and instructional expertise), we had to draw on observational data.

> *Management expertise.* This construct is composed of the following manifest variables: the percentage rate of disciplinary and procedural activities and the effective use of management rules and organizational skills.
>
> *Instructional expertise.* The components of this construct are the percentage rate of individual supportive contacts and clarity of subject matter presentation.
>
> *Diagnostic expertise.* This construct was operationalized as the accuracy with which teachers rated the rank order of and the variations in students' achievement outcomes in comparison to actual achievement test scores.
>
> *Subject matter expertise.* Subject matter expertise was measured by the accuracy with which teachers rated the rank order of task difficulty for two different types of test items (arithmetic problems and word problems) in comparison to the empirical level of task difficulty.

Different goals of instruction were considered and assessed separately as effect criteria:

> *Achievement growth.* The classes' mean posttest outcomes, adjusted for individual cognitive entry characteristics (level of prior knowledge and intelligence), were used as the measure of math achievement growth.

Reduction of achievement variance. Reduction of achievement variance within the class was operationalized by use of the relationship between standard deviations in the pretest (numerator) and the posttest (denominator) (Helmke, 1988). Both measures are based on achievement outcomes in a math test developed for this study (arithmetic skills and word problems) and administered at the beginning and at the end of the fifth grade.

Reduction of test anxiety. To measure changes in test anxiety in the class, we used the data from a student questionnaire administered at the beginning and at the end of the fifth grade (frequency of task-irrelevant cognitions). The data tapped at the end of the fifth grade were adjusted for the entry variables, rescaled, and aggregated for each class.

Students' motivation to learn. Students' motivation to learn was assessed through a low-inference observation system as percentage rate of various forms of on-task behavior of eight students chosen randomly in each class (Helmke, 1986).

The first empirical question was whether the four knowledge domains postulated constitute relatively independent subdomains of teacher expertise. With one exception, the four expertise domains showed no significant correlations. Only instructional expertise and management expertise were significantly correlated. This is plausible in that both are core variables of effective instruction that are closely intertwined in instructional behavior. However, as even this correlation is only moderate, the four subdomains can in fact be considered as constituting relatively independent aspects of teacher expertise.

The second question was whether it was possible to distinguish groups of teachers who differ in terms of various dimensions of expertise. A hierarchical cluster analysis was conducted with the four expertise variables, using Ward's procedure (see, for example, Aldenderfer and Blashfield, 1984). If one compares the variance that is explained by the clusters across all variables and the increase in variance as a function of the number of clusters, it is possible to select a five-cluster solution. One cluster shows an above-average mean score on all four expertise dimensions and thus represents a group of expert teachers (cluster $E+$; $n = 9$). Another cluster shows below-average scores on all four expertise variables, representing a group of teachers without expertise status (cluster $E-$; $n = 5$). The third group (cluster M_1; $n = 5$) shows below-average values for three expertise dimensions (management expertise, subject-matter expertise, and diagnostic expertise), the fourth shows below-average values for instructional expertise and management expertise (cluster M_2; $n = 12$), and the fifth shows below-average values only for subject-matter knowledge (cluster M_3; $n = 8$).

To confirm the validity of this solution, we tested whether the five expertise clusters can also be differentiated from each other in terms of some central criteria of successful teaching. The criteria that were uncorrelated were achievement growth, reduction of achievement variance, reduction of test anxiety, and students' motivation to learn. A multivariate analysis of variance revealed significant differences among the five expertise clusters across all the criteria of successful teaching. Simple analyses of variance conducted for each goal criterion showed significant group differences for achievement growth and for motivation to learn but no significant differences for reduction of achievement variance or reduction of test anxiety. It is particularly interesting to note that the means of the expert group (cluster E +) were above average for all four teaching criteria, while those for the nonexpert group (cluster $E -$) were below average for all four criteria. This may be regarded as a tentative validation of our expertise concept.

Another question that was addressed was whether the experts and the nonexperts differ in their pattern of effects for separate instructional variables. This was analyzed for selected teacher variables, comparing only the expert group (cluster $E +$) with all other (nonexpert) teachers. Figure 16.2 shows the correlations between six teaching variables and two different learning outcomes (achievement growth and students' motivation to learn) for the two groups of teachers. As seen in the figure, correlations with achievement growth are higher in the expert group than in the nonexpert group for the two cognitive teaching variables (structuring cues and control of homework), as was expected. Surprisingly, the correlation with achievement growth is negative in the expert group and positive in the nonexpert group for both affective teacher variables (teacher enthusiasm and warmth). Neither group showed a correlation between aspects of teacher adaptivity (instructional flexibility, patience with slow learners) and achievement growth. Thus, the correlational pattern only partially supported our theoretical expectations.

The correlations for the outcome variable students' motivation to learn were more straightforward. We had assumed that this variable would be influenced by both teaching effectiveness and teacher responsibility. Whereas the correlations were all positive and in some cases substantial for the expert teachers, there was no clear pattern for the nonexpert teachers. It is striking that only affective variables (enthusiasm and warmth) were correlated with students' motivation to learn for the nonexpert teachers, whereas strategic and adaptive learning variables had no or negative relationships with motivation to learn. This pattern can be interpreted as support for the claim that some instructional variables are embedded in a personal frame of reference (experts versus nonexperts). However, one should be cautious in generalizing this finding too rapidly, because the corresponding correlational patterns for the outcome variables reduction in achievement variance in the class and anxiety reduction were generally more diffuse and less straightforward.

Teacher Expertise: A Research Paradigm in the Making

In general, when a new theoretical model is elaborated but can be given only preliminary empirical support, it is likely that the results will raise

Figure 16.2. Correlations Between Teaching Variables and Learning Outcomes.

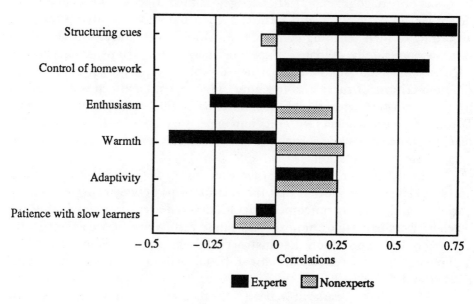

Learning Outcome I: Achievement Growth

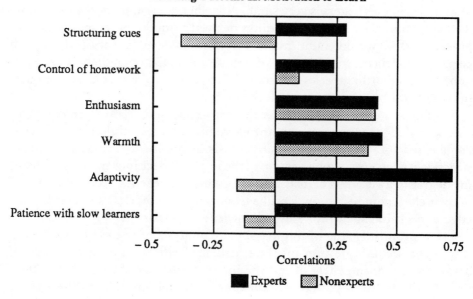

Learning Outcome II: Motivation to Learn

more questions than they answer. This holds true for the present study as well. Nonetheless, our analysis of the data does provide compelling empirical evidence supporting our central theoretical assumptions: the four subdomains of pedagogic expert knowledge, defined a priori, were largely independent of each other and formed a good basis for classifying teachers according to their teaching competence. More importantly, this classification was successfully validated. Expert teachers with a rich pedagogic knowledge base in all four subdomains achieved superior outcomes on several very different criteria of successful teaching. The opposite pattern was obtained for the group of teachers with little knowledge in the four expertise domains. For the groups of teachers with medium expertise (clusters M_1, M_2, and M_3), teaching outcomes were somewhat mixed but nevertheless could be given a plausible interpretation.

Finally, in some instances (achievement growth and students' motivation to learn), we showed that the relationships between single teaching variables and learning outcome variables differed according to whether the teachers were experts or nonexperts. These results are in accordance with the theoretical expectation that instructional effectiveness is moderated by a personal frame of reference that can be labeled an "instructional gestalt" (Siegel and Siegel, 1967).

Although our results fit well with our theoretical assumptions, we must be cautious in generalizing and interpreting them, especially because the sample size in the clusters is very small. Nonetheless, systematically expanding the expert model by means of findings derived from the process-product approach can, we would claim, make it possible to develop a fruitful research paradigm for this area. However, there are still many open theoretical questions, making further research absolutely necessary. In particular, three questions are still open.

The first question is whether there is a class of integrative (metacognitive) knowledge that operates on the elements of all the subdomains of pedagogic expertise. This is the cognitive basis for multiple classification of instructional problems, sophistication of the teacher's decisions in the classroom, the degree of awareness of instructional goals, and teachers' reflexive control of their classroom behavior. Results from general research on expert knowledge concerning such integrative knowledge components suggest that this is also a promising line of inquiry for the analysis of pedagogic expertise.

The second question involves further clarification of our theoretical assumption that the effect of specific instructional variables is tied to their incorporation into a pattern of other instructional variables. Whereas the trends in the cognitive data were in accord with our expectations, the effects for some socioemotional variables were in a direction opposite to the one hypothesized. Currently, we have no theoretical explanation for this phenomenon, which clearly must be explored in further research.

The third and final question addressed to further research concerns the overall attempt to combine the concepts of teacher effectiveness and teacher responsibility with the teaching expertise paradigm. In this context, it is important to realize that pedagogic expertise is but a part of the qualities and competencies required of teachers. Professional enthusiasm, high moral standards, humanistic values, and emotional warmth are no doubt as important for students' growth and development as is effective instruction. But these attributes should not be regarded as conflicting with teaching expertise. The level of pedagogic expertise and the level of desirable personal attributes and values of the teacher are independent of each other. Nonetheless, the assumption that expert teachers who give effective instruction will be better able to assert their moral and socioemotional competencies in the classroom than teachers whose instruction is little more than a chain of unsolved or wrongly solved instructional problems seems plausible and has been supported by some of our empirical results.

References

Aldenderfer, M. S., and Blashfield, R. K. *Cluster Analysis.* Newbury Park, Calif.: Sage, 1984.

Berliner, D. C. "In Pursuit of the Expert Pedagogue." *Educational Researcher,* 1986, *15* (7), 5–13.

Berliner, D. C. "The Place of Process-Product Research in Developing the Agenda for Research on Teacher Thinking." *Educational Psychologist,* 1989, *24,* 325–344.

Brophy, J. E., and Good, T. L. "Teacher Behavior and Student Achievement." In M. C. Wittrock (ed.), *Handbook of Research on Teaching.* (3rd ed.) New York: Macmillan, 1986.

Clark, C. M., and Peterson, P. L. "Teachers' Thought Processes." In M. C. Wittrock (ed.), *Handbook of Research on Teaching.* (3rd ed.) New York: Macmillan, 1986.

Doyle, W. "Classroom Organization and Management." In M. C. Wittrock (ed.), *Handbook of Research on Teaching.* (3rd ed.) New York: Macmillan, 1986.

Evertson, C. M. "Classroom Organization and Management." In M. C. Reynolds (ed.), *Knowledge Base for the Beginning Teacher.* Oxford, England: Pergamon Press, 1989.

Feigenbaum, C. A. "What Hath Simon Wrought?" In D. Klahr and K. Kotovsky (eds.), *Complex Information Processing: The Impact of Herbert A. Simon.* Hillsdale, N.J.: Erlbaum, 1989.

Gage, N. L., and Needels, M. C. "Process-Product Research on Teaching: A Review of Criticisms." *Elementary School Journal,* 1989, *89,* 253–300.

Grossman, P. L., Wilson, S. M., and Shulman, L. S. "Teachers of Substance: Subject Matter Knowledge for Teaching." In M. C. Reynolds (ed.), *Knowledge Base for the Beginning Teacher.* Oxford, England: Pergamon Press, 1989.

Helmke, A. "Student Attention During Instruction and Achievement." In S. E. Newstead, S. H. Irvine, and P. D. Dann (eds.), *Human Assessment: Cognition and Motivation.* Dordrecht, the Netherlands: Nijhoff, 1986.

Helmke, A. "Leistungssteigerung und Ausgleich von Leistungsunterschieden in Schulklassen: unvereinbare Ziele?" [Achievement growth and reduction of achievement variance in classrooms: incompatible goals?] *Zeitschrift für Entwicklungspsychologie und Pädagogische Psychologie* [Journal of developmental psychology and educational psychology], 1988, *20*, 45–76.

Helmke, A., Schneider, W., and Weinert, F. E. "Quality of Instruction and Classroom Learning Outcomes: The German Contribution to the IEA Classroom Environment Study." *Teaching and Teacher Education*, 1986, *2*, 1–31.

Leinhardt, G. "Novice and Expert Knowledge of Individual Students' Achievement." *Educational Psychologist*, 1983, *8*, 165–179.

Leinhardt, G. "Expertise in Mathematics Teaching." *Educational Leadership*, 1986, *43*, 28–33.

Leinhardt, G., and Greeno, J. G. "The Cognitive Skill of Teaching." *Journal of Educational Psychology*, 1986, *78*, 75–95.

Leinhardt, G., and Smith, D. A. "Expertise in Mathematics Instruction: Subject Matter Knowledge." *Journal of Educational Psychology*, 1985, *77* (3), 247–271.

Leinhardt, G., Weidman, C., and Hammond, K. R. "Introduction and Integration of Classroom Routines by Expert Teachers." *Curriculum Inquiry*, 1987, *17*, 135–176.

Peterson, P. L., and Comeaux, M. A. "Teachers' Schemata for Classroom Events: The Mental Scaffolding of Teachers' Thinking During Classroom Instruction." *Teaching and Teacher Education*, 1987, *3*, 319–331.

Schrader, F.-W. *Diagnostische Kompetenzen von Lehrern und ihre Bedeutung für die Gestaltung und Effektivität des Unterrichts.* [Diagnostic competencies of teachers and their significance for teaching and teaching effectiveness]. Frankfurt, Germany: Lang, 1989.

Shulman, L. S. "Knowledge and Teaching: Foundations of the New Reform." *Harvard Educational Review*, 1987, *57* (1), 1–22.

Siegel, L., and Siegel, L. C. "The Instructional Gestalt." In L. Siegel (ed.), *Instruction: Some Contemporary Viewpoints.* San Francisco: Chandler, 1967.

Stallings, J. *Learning to Look: A Handbook on Classroom Observation and Teaching Models.* Belmont, Calif.: Wadsworth, 1977.

Stolurow, L. M. "Model the Master Teacher or Master the Teaching Model." In J. D. Krumbholtz (ed.), *Learning and the Educational Process.* Chicago: Rand McNally, 1965.

Tamir, P. "Subject Matter and Related Pedagogical Knowledge in Teacher Education." *Teaching and Teacher Education*, 1988, *4*, 99–110.

Weinert, F. E., Schrader, F.-W., and Helmke, A. "Quality of Instruction and Achievement Outcomes." *International Journal of Educational Research*, 1989, *13*, 895–914.

Weinert, F. E., Schrader, F.-W., and Helmke, A. "Educational Expertise: Closing the Gap Between Educational Research and Classroom Practice." *School Psychology International*, 1990, *11*, 163–170.

17

What a Professor Learned in the Third Grade

Elliot W. Eisner

I*t is a truism in the social sciences that the ways in which we have been socialized* influence the ways in which we see the world. Our views of schooling and what we believe constitutes responsible and effective teaching are the result of our socialization, both professional and personal. My socialization has been fed by two major streams. The first is my experience in the arts, at first as a painter and later as a collector of arts. What I cherish and what I look for have been shaped by what I have learned how to see and what I have come to value. These values and this seeing are not limited to the fine arts; they pervade the way I lead—or try to lead—my life. Thus, for example, the kind of experience that a process or an object makes possible, whether in a museum, a concert hall, or a classroom, is important to me. In a sense, for me, the journey is the reward.

The second stream feeding my socialization has been the social sciences. I regard the concepts and theories that social scientists invent as *structures of appropriation*. They are devices through which focus is secured and certain kinds of meaning obtained. In this sense, artists and scientists share a common mission: to create structures—qualitative and theoretical forms—through which the world is viewed. Indeed, following Nelson Goodman (1978), I would say that it is through these structures of appropriation that our worlds are made.

My experience in the arts has led me to eschew abstract formalisms in so highly nuanced an enterprise as teaching. It has led me to emphasize the centrality of perception in cognition, for it is through perception that consciousness is born, and it is through consciousness of the qualities that we attend to, whether in a classroom or a concert hall, that our understanding is enlarged.

The practical consequence of these foregoing experiences has been, for me, the development of an approach to the study of schooling that, on

261

the one hand, roots itself firmly in the humanities, in the literary, and in the qualitative and, on the other, uses concepts and theories from the social sciences to try to account for what has been given an account of. My general aim has been to try to expand and to legitimate a broader, more catholic approach to educational inquiry. This approach does not aspire toward the ethnographic. I am not an anthropologist. I am an educator. Its closest relatives are to be found in the humanities, particularly in the practices of connoisseurship and criticism. My aim is to exploit the capacity of perception to see what matters in educational settings and to use whatever language, in all its forms, can deliver to make vivid what an enlightened eye has seen (Eisner, 1991). These aims are realized through what I have called *educational* connoisseurship and *educational* criticism. They require going into schools to see firsthand how schooling is played out, a practice that now, in the 1990s, is much more common than it was in the 1970s. My return to school—the third grade—was an effort to get closer to the phenomena than the comforts of a university office at Stanford make possible.

I provide this context because it is so critically important in the kind of work this orientation to research makes possible.

Two Third Grades in Stanford's Shadow

The two schools in which my observations were made are located in a well-to-do suburb near Stanford University. The parents of many, although by no means most, of the pupils are employed by the university. But virtually all the parents, as one can detect by the prevalence of the word *Stanford* emblazoned on their maroon sweatshirts, would like their children to succeed academically and to attend a prestigious university. The school district is one that is considered successful by any standard measure of academic performance. Its students rank in the ninetieth percentile or higher within the state on academic measures and have done so for decades. The parents attend school board meetings in numbers far larger than what is considered typical for a community of this size, and their expectations for school performance are very high indeed.

The two schools in which I observed are single-story structures, well supplied, orderly; an atmosphere of affluence and material comfort pervades these institutions. One school, built in the late 1960s, was originally designed for open education, an innovation at the time, but in more educationally conservative periods returned to traditional forms of school organization: the flexible folding doors that were once opened are now closed, and each teacher works in his or her own space with a group of elementary-aged children ranging in class size from about twenty-one to thirty.

What we have, therefore, are two well-appointed schools serving a student population consisting of academically motivated children coming from homes of high-aspiring parents, many of whom work for a prestigious research university. It is not a typical American school district.

I chose the two classrooms in this school district because I wanted to observe educational practice in what might be regarded as "the best of circumstances." I wanted to see teachers who were regarded by their peers and by building principals as particularly strong; indeed, among the very best. I intended to interview several teachers before making a selection, but it became clear after I had talked to the first two that interviewing others would be unnecessary. Their intelligence and commitment were hard to miss, even during a single interview session.

I describe these institutions and the characteristics of the teachers I observed in order to emphasize the "special" nature of the setting and the people. I do not know whether the teaching patterns I saw would be effective with other, less fortunate children, although I think they would. In any case, I believe that there is much to learn from excellent teachers, regardless of the context.

Just what did I learn from my three-month sojourn? Some of what I learned may appear prosaic. It is. But there is a profound difference between knowing something in the abstract and knowing it through direct experience. Consider, for example, the idea that all children are different. To professors of education, that notion is about as prosaic as can be, but seeing the ways in which a group of eight-year-olds can differ in size, temperament, maturity, interests, energy level, and personal style is quite another matter. Their presence makes plain the vacuity of the concept "the average eight-year-old." Direct experience underscores the personal idiosyncrasies of students that any elementary school teacher must deal with. It makes vivid the truth of Goethe's observation that between the universal and the particular, the particular always prevails. Teachers cannot deal with abstractions or averages when they teach. Their knowledge of individuals is crucial in enabling them to make appropriate assignments, to provide comfort and support, to impose sanctions, to define limits to behavior, to remind individual students of obligations, to encourage participation, and to foster attitudes of cooperation. It is awareness of individual children that makes it possible for teachers to encourage the development of nascent but valuable interests and the expression of well-developed talents. Spending three months in the third grade seeing these individual and irrepressible personalities in living color makes clear the pallor of textbook renditions of human development. Such renditions might well serve the interests of psychologists, but they do not portray the human realities that elementary school teachers must face.

A second thing that I learned was the ingenious ways in which teachers create a common culture, almost a special language through which the coherence of the group is maintained and the teacher's own energy level conserved. This language emerges in the kinds of signals and routines that teachers employ to get children's attention, to initiate a familiar set of activities, to bring a teaching episode to a close. The way of life that teachers share with children is complex, and modi vivendi need to be created that will make smooth transitions within the school day possible. The forms that these transitions take and the cues that teachers use are well known to students, so well known that they need not be articulated. For the visitor, however, they need to be learned. For example, one teacher used a simple but ingenious method for collecting student papers. Each of her students was assigned a number, and by counting off a set of numbers, tests or papers to be graded were turned in alphabetically. Certain mailboxes were available for students to hand in or pick up their work. Certain people in the classroom performed particular tasks, and these tasks were rotated on specific days. Certain groups—or tribes, as they were called in one class—were formed to enable students to work together, and membership in each tribe changed during the course of the year. This made it possible for students to have opportunities to learn to work with everyone in the class. A whole complex set of arrangements was designed to facilitate the achievement of the academic and social aspirations of both teachers and students. None of these routines, as far as I could tell, was hyperrationalized, overbureaucratized, or mechanical. They were a comfortable, ongoing part of a way of life that the students shared with each other and with their teacher.

Do those kinds of activities and arrangements fall under the heading of "teaching"? Does teaching include the design of these arrangements? Are people teaching when they invent the conditions through which students take responsibility for the distribution of papers and materials, when they manage and monitor cleanup, when they assume responsibility for equipment? I think that teaching encompasses these tasks as well as the conventional conception of instruction. What does the saliency of such task demands imply for research on teaching? These tasks in teaching are not simply manifestations of subject matter knowledge or pedagogical skills related to instruction. They are pedagogical all right, but pedagogical in terms of social arrangements.

A third feature that I saw was the diversity—indeed, the rhythm—among the curriculum activities that these teachers employed. The class day has some clear structured divisions. One portion of the day is devoted to whole-group activities, another to small-group instruction, and another to individual student work, defined by these eight-year-old students but pursued within general constraints defined by the teacher. These arrangements create changes in tempo. Like a ballet, the day is choreographed; indeed, one teacher analogized her work to the work of a director of a play—the entire sequence of acts needed to be planned and matters of tempo and timing considered in order to avoid tedium.

One of the ways in which tedium is avoided is by creating classrooms that have an open structure. Children are free to move about and to talk with each other, except on those occasions in which there is whole-class activity that requires the participation of everyone—the use of the overhead projector to teach spelling, for example. Indeed, conversations among children are encouraged by their seating arrangements: groups of three or four eight-year-olds sit together, face to face. One teacher encouraged students to whisper the answers that they had arrived at to their neighbors, a kind of personal sharing.

What also avoids tedium is the practice of self-regulation that the classrooms' open structure makes possible. Since children do not need permission from the teacher to move about, and since they can speak at will to other classmates, just how much moving and talking they do is something that they themselves learn to control. This structure is complemented by a procedure that both teachers employ in planning their activities.

Some classroom activities engage children in tasks in which the content or skill to be learned is highly rule-governed. The teacher's aim is to get the children to learn the material in a socially correct form. Learning to spell, learning to punctuate, and learning to do multiplication tables are examples of tasks in which innovation in outcome is not a particular virtue. Creative spellers are not sought by teachers, regardless of the innovative forms of cognition that might lead a child to spell a word in a particular way. As important as understanding is in mathematics, accuracy in computation is still a primary virtue. There are many tasks in schools, perhaps most, in which children are expected to acquire the skills of impression, that is, learning how to take something in. In a sense, the aim is to internalize social conventions.

There are other tasks, particularly in the fine arts, including creative writing, in which the child's internal life can be given leave to take flight. Here the end in view is not to internalize social conventions but to enable children to place their own stamp on their work, hopefully a stamp that has soared on the wings of imagination. These are the skills of expression. These two emphases in task features are also a part of the tempo that these two teachers orchestrate. Some tasks demand strict adherence to socially prescribed norms and outcomes, while other tasks put a premium on letting one's mind take flight. Whether eight years old or eighty, humans need such variety. We need to be able to do our accounting when we must, but we also need to walk in the forest, to move into our private worlds, and to listen to the Brandenburg Concertos.

These teachers do not rationalize their curricular choices as I have just described, but they make them nevertheless. They recognize that they are planners of a day, implementers of a program, creators of tasks that engage twenty-five children in a set of activities that will maintain their interest over the course of a day. They do this five days a week, forty weeks a year.

I would like to say a word about the teachers' temperaments. Above all, at the elementary school level, the teacher is the major shaper of the form of shared social life that students experience. How affection is provided, the particular ways in which limits are enforced, the amount of flexibility that children experience, the clarity with which tasks are assigned, the pace and mood of the day are profoundly influenced by the head of the household — the classroom teacher. At the secondary level, departmentalization mitigates such effects, since students encounter five or six teachers each day, but at the elementary level, the class teacher is clearly the major force pervading the classroom. These personal factors may be among the most difficult to influence, yet they are, in my experience, among the most important in establishing classroom tone. What children learn from their teacher as a person that does not emerge on the standardized achievement tests used to assess the outcomes of schooling may be among the most important things that they learn in school. They are clearly among the most important things that children will remember when they are asked to recall the teachers that influenced their lives.

Another factor that became clear to me during my observation was the extent to which children pick up instructional cues, not only when they are given to them directly but also as they are overheard or seen when given to other children. By the time they are eight, children are well practiced at exploiting a vast array of sources for orienting themselves to their environment. Thus, the teacher who teaches one child is often teaching the entire class. In this sense, individualized instruction is seldom individualized.

Another thing that I learned about classrooms is the extent to which these teachers think pedagogically about almost everything. What I mean is that they exploit every reasonable opportunity to get children to draw their own conclusions. Questions raised by children are seldom answered directly; instead, they are followed by another question from the teacher or by suggestions about where to look for answers. The teacher's pedagogical routines are, it seems to me, almost on automatic pilot in responding this way, just as they appear to be on automatic pilot in using positive comments to "correct" student behavior. During the three months that I spent in these classes, I heard or saw practically no significant forms of negative reinforcement used by either teacher, a feat that demands my utmost admiration. This should not be interpreted to mean that children do not know when the teacher is not pleased—they do know. What I mean is that the overt use of aversive comments or acts by the teachers is virtually nonexistent when they interact with their students.

Part of the reason for the saliency of positive reinforcement emanates from the inclination among teachers, particularly at the elementary school level in California, to be concerned about matters of self-esteem. These concerns have created a climate that has led to the practices that I have described. Whether such practices are in the child's best interests in the long run depends on what one believes to contribute to effective forms of socialization and the norms of the society in which the child lives.

The maintenance of a class as a cohesive group is a form of pedagogical achievement. These teachers employed a variety of techniques to maintain such cohesiveness. One such technique is to deal explicitly with details so that nothing is left to chance or to assumption; it cannot be assumed that children will know what adults have taken for granted. Another is to ask children themselves to review what they are supposed to do—this provides them with a kind of advance organizer and a reminder of what is to take place. Others are to review plans for the school day at the day's beginning and post the sequence of events on the blackboard and to bring the class together from time to time to review where things stand. What is clear is that these procedures are intended to keep movement and coherence present. The teacher is indeed a planner, a producer, and a director. The most apt metaphor may be that of a chef. Like a chef, the teacher has to know how to use a wide variety of ingredients, how to put them together, what level of flame is required, and when it is necessary to get back to the pots to keep them from boiling over. At times, the teacher must innovate when ingredients are unavailable. All of this must be done with a sense of orchestration to keep the whole enterprise moving forward and working well.

These features by no means exhaust what I learned from the two third-grade classrooms that I observed. I have neither the time nor the space to describe the ways in which these teachers convey the seriousness of their work to students, how they help them understand that the work they do is important. I cannot describe the physical forms of affection that they provide to their children, nor can I describe the extent to which these particular children have internalized the norms of achievement or how much the small victories — spelling a word correctly or being called on to assume a small responsibility — that to an adult seem trivial, mean to these children. I cannot describe the degree to which these teachers are psychologically fed by their students or the energy that they expend in planning and executing plans in their classrooms. I cannot comment on the degree of administrative acumen required to keep what is often a four-ring circus functioning in full gear and without a hitch. These achievements are part of what I judge to be the fine professional performance of the elementary school teachers I observed in the schools I visited. The parts of these teaching skills that pertain to subject matter knowledge are important to be sure but, I believe, minor in importance compared to the teachers' personal and organizational skills. Immersion in these elementary school classrooms relegates most university teaching demands to the minor leagues.

Expectations for Future Research on Teaching

Given the particularity, the phenomenological density, and the dynamic complexity of what these two third-grade teachers do in the course of their workday, what is it that we can reasonably expect research on teaching to provide? In what ways can research on teaching increase the effectiveness of teachers and help them become more professionally responsible? There are, I believe, five major options that we can consider. The first of these — the creation of a science of teaching — was thought to be a realistic aim for educational research by the father of educational psychology in America. I speak, of course, of E. L. Thorndike. Thorndike believed that a "complete science of psychology" was possible and that eventually we would have a tested technology of practice that would efficiently and effectively enable teachers to achieve their most lofty educational aims. Writing in the first issue of *Educational Psychology,* published in 1910, he said:

A complete science of psychology would tell every fact about everyone's intellect and character and behavior, would tell the cause of every change in human nature, would tell the result which every educational force—every act of every person that changed any other or the agent himself—would have. It would aid us to use human beings for the world's welfare with the same surety of the result that we now have when we use falling bodies or chemical elements. In proportion as we get such a science we shall become masters of our own souls as we now are master of heat and light. Progress toward such a science is being made [Thorndike, 1910, p. 6].

There are few people today who share the level of optimism that Thorndike expressed in 1910. No one whom I know believes that even in principle it will be possible to provide teachers with specific procedures for teaching specific subjects to particular children. The prospects of "getting teaching down to a science," by which I mean a procedure that can be systematically employed to yield highly predictable results, time after time, are considered extremely dim by virtually everyone.

If the aspiration for pedagogical algorithms is a wrongheaded hope for research on teaching, what expectations appear more reasonable? One is the expectation that research on teaching will provide empirically derived generalizations about variables related to teaching effectiveness and to matters associated with it. Such generalizations might be derived from correlational studies or from experiments designed to lead to generalizations about causality. I leave aside issues related to the logical status of generalizations derived from experiments whose validity depends on the existence of conditions present in the initial experimental design. Those criteria are typically too difficult to meet as a standard for justifying the use of such generalizations. It is seldom clear whether the classrooms to which the generalizations are to be applied sufficiently approximate the classrooms in which the initial studies were made: the so-called application of research conclusions to practice is made primarily on the basis of analogical reasoning, not statistical inference or deduction. But again, putting such matters aside, what can we expect reasonable and robust generalizations to provide to those who work in particular classrooms, located in particular schools, in particular parts of the country?

One thing seems reasonably clear. The farther away one is from the particular setting in which the individual teacher works, the more useful the generalization appears to be. That is, when we think about third-graders in general, we find it more congenial to invoke generalizations about third-graders. But it is equally clear that individual teachers do not work with third-graders in general. They work with little Tommy Johnson or with overweight Katy Epstein. Tommy's mother and father have just decided to divorce after several years of arguing and bickering, and Tommy is uncertain and frightened about his future. Katy, however, comes from a secure home but suffers from the pressures exerted by academically anxious parents. Katy's problem is fear of failure. She, too, is uncertain and insecure, but for different reasons and in different ways. Teachers do not deal with the abstractions that university professors and government policy makers typically address; they deal with Tommy and Katy. Effective and responsible teaching might be quite different for each of these children. Thus, generalizations are at best guidelines, rules of thumb, so to speak, that a teacher might want to consider if there is time to do so and if the generalization is thought to be relevant.

When we come to the uses of generalization, two complications are encountered. The first has been suggested by Gage (1978) in his book *The Scientific Basis of the Art of Teaching*. Gage recognizes that generalizations—that is, statements about consistent and robust relationships among variables—can be usefully employed in the context of teaching *if* the variables that are relevant for making a teaching decision are few. But when variables become numerous—more than three or four, as they always are in classrooms—artistry must take over. Gage writes:

> Scientific method can contribute relationships between variables taken two at a time and even, in the form of interactions, three or perhaps four or more at a time. Beyond say four, the usefulness of what science can give the teacher begins to weaken, because teachers cannot apply, at least not without help and not on the run, the more complex interactions. At this point, the teacher as an artist must step in and make clinical, or artistic, judgments about the best ways to teach. In short, the scientific base for the art of teaching will consist of two-variable relationships and lower-order interactions. The higher-order interactions between four and more variables must be handled by the teacher as artist [p. 20].

The artistry that Gage describes is infused in the teacher's judgment of what *this* situation at *this* time calls for. Paradoxically, as more generalizations are created through research on teaching, more rather than less artistry will be demanded from the teacher. One aspect of such artistry is great particularity in perception, what I call connoisseurship (Eisner, 1991).

One possible response to this paradox is to expect that one day something like a limited array of powerful macrogeneralizations derived from the empirical study of teaching will be created. This limited array will diminish the burden on teachers because a few generalizations will do the work of many. Aside from the improbable quality of such an expectation, the drift of research on teaching is currently toward the rediscovery of the importance of subject matter in teaching. This creates an even greater need for particularity. Although Charles Hubbard Judd (1915) wrote a book in 1915 on the psychology of school subjects, the aim of research on teaching through the 1970s was to try to understand teaching as a process that was content-free; that is, a process that could be improved and understood without reference to what was being taught. Shulman's (1987) work on teaching and Stodolsky's (1988) book *The Subject Matters* are predicated on the view that the subject does, indeed, matter.

Once the subject enters our research paradigm, we are in a position to partition generalizations about teaching. Once this partitioning is done, generalizations take on validity as they pertain to the teaching of something. In one sense, we have fewer generalizations, but in another sense, we have more. We can expect that some generalizations will hold for some subjects but not for others.

But the problem is not so simple. What one is teaching is not identical to something called a subject matter. As Schwab (1969) pointed out in 1969, there are a dozen versions of the social studies and five orientations to mathematics, and the fine arts can be taught from a wide variety of perspectives for a diverse set of ends. To paraphrase Gertrude Stein, a subject is not a subject is not a subject. Once we recognize the plurality of approaches to the teaching of any subject — and by approaches, I mean what is aimed at, what constitutes appropriate content, and how this content should or should not be related to other fields — generalizations, too, must become more numerous. Again, even greater particularity. The question of what a relevant generalization is for teaching children to memorize the multiplication tables fades into oblivion if memorization is no longer considered an important aim in mathematics education. In other words, conceptualizing teaching within a subject matter requires far more than identifying a body of content. It requires situating that content within an educational context, and this means, among other things, understanding its educational function.

The point of my analysis is not to reject the search for generalizations — we need them in all walks of life, not merely in trying to achieve effective and responsible teaching — but rather to illuminate the complexity with which we are dealing and to increase our appreciation of those fine teachers who by dint of artistry in teaching somehow manage to be both effective and responsible.

One comment with respect to the art of teaching: whether we refer to what teachers do when they effectively handle classroom complexities as intuitive, as employing the wisdom of practice, or as engaging in the craft or art of teaching, it is clear that such aspects of the teacher's performance are of critical importance. It is especially ironic, therefore, that in none of the three handbooks of research on teaching is there any index entry on the art of teaching. The latest handbook (Wittrock, 1986), for example, has 880 main index entries, and although there is indeed an entry pertaining to art, it refers to the teaching of art, not to the art of teaching. The virtual absence of attention to artistry in teaching dramatizes a critical aspect of the teacher's work that needs attention and at the same time reveals something about the assumptions with which we work.

Another area of expectations for research on teaching is its potential role in guiding the teacher's perception and interpretation of classroom events. All research on teaching or on any other aspect of educational practice is rooted in schemata of one kind or another that parse practice in particular ways. Schemata gain their power both from the windows that they provide and from the walls that they create to obstruct our vision. Put less metaphorically, schemata define what will count as relevant while at the same time they neglect other potentially important candidates for perception. These reciprocal functions — concealing and revealing — make particular classroom phenomena vivid. Wait time, for example, becomes an important candidate for attention as this aspect of the teacher's behavior is noticed and labeled. Time on task becomes important for the same reason. Researchers on teaching notice what they believe matters and assign it a name. Once named, it can be shared; once shared, it can become a part of our cognitive lexicon, a device that we use to look for the named qualities.

One virtue of schemata is that they can be used flexibly. One vice is that schemata are often used with little attention to the particular context in which the teacher functions. For example, increasing wait time is usually regarded as beneficial for students, but surely there are significant exceptions to that general expectation. How long to wait depends on the contextual conditions in which longer or shorter wait times are appropriate. These conditions are not a part of the schema, nor are they a part of the generalization about wait time or time on task. We could not deal with the vast number of subgeneralizations that specified the contingencies under which different amounts of time were appropriate. To assume that more time is better is a bit too simple.

The same caveats apply to time on task. Optimal conditions for learning might very well require *time off task*. Furthermore, whether time on task is a virtue depends, at least, on the kind of task one is on: Relief from an assigned academic task might be exactly what students need. When schemata are treated as decontextualized rules, their potential utility for improving learning is diluted.

The point of the foregoing is that even when structures as potentially flexible as schemata are used, individual pedagogical judgments must still be made. Such judgments depend on context sensitivity. Thus, the boon in using schemata in teaching — which we must inevitably employ in any case — is their contribution to focus. The bane is their potential for limiting our sight. But even when schematas are numerous and refined and our awareness of relevant classroom phenomena large, no set of schemata, regardless of how large, can encompass the particular configuration of phenomena or the competing educational values that a teacher must reconcile. The reconciliation of two competing goods that at a particular pedagogical moment may be mutually exclusive is not an uncommon pedagogical task: do I call on Harry and give him a momentary place in the sun even though I suspect that his response will lead the discussion astray, or do I neglect Harry and call on Mary, who is likely to keep the discussion on track but who at this moment does not need a place in the sun?

There is one other complication that I wish to mention regarding the use of schemata in teaching. When talking about teaching, there is a tendency to regard schemata as structures through which meditative processes called decision making occur. In fact, some educational researchers have likened this process to a kind of hypothesis testing, a form of scientific experiment. While the forms of reflection implied by an extended form of decision making might be appropriate for those domains of teaching that Jackson (1986) refers to as preactive, interactive teaching, the kind of teaching that occurs when teachers are working directly with students seldom provides time for reflective deliberation. As Clark (1990), Schön (1983), and others have pointed out, much of what teachers do in *the context of action* has an immediacy about it that differs qualitatively from the type of reflection exercised in *the context of planning.* I believe that in the context of action, the perception of qualities displayed by students is immediate. In some ways, as is the case with the highly skilled soccer player, there is no time for extended deliberation. The action must be instantaneous and on target. My observations of teachers suggest to me that not only do they possess a variety of schemata for seeing what is important, an observation that Berliner (1987) has emphasized in his work on the expert pedagogue, but they also have a broad repertoire of moves with which to quickly and gracefully act on the situation that they see. If my observations about schemata are plausible, we can ask how schemata become a part of the iconic structures that make the identification of particular classroom conditions recognizable. How does one move from linguistically portrayed schemata to their application?

I believe that this application occurs by one's acquisition of referents for the schematic structures that one learns. For example, the words *retroactive inhibition* cannot be meaningful without an image of what the words themselves point to, and one cannot secure such an image without some form of association, either through a direct empirical connection or through language sufficiently vivid to enable the reader to envision what the words mean. Extended further, this line of argument suggests that the possession of what Broudy (1987) has called a rich *allusionary base* is at the root of expert perception and that it is through this perceptual expertise that action follows. That is why, I think, someone can possess expertise without possessing a set of technical linguistic terms with which to label the conditions or qualities on which the expert acts. Following Michael Polyani (1967), we do seem to know more than we can tell.

There are two other options that we can consider for expectations pertaining to the potential contributions of research on teaching: its diagnostic potential and its usefulness in constructively undermining simplistic conceptions of causal relationships in teaching, conceptions that lead to dysfunctional prescriptions for teachers. I address each briefly.

The ways in which schemata and generalizations from research on teaching might be used to enhance practice are embedded in some of the issues that I have already addressed. To the extent to which research provides practice-relevant schemata for seeing and explaining what teachers and children do in classrooms, these schemata call to our attention what we might look for and how we might interpret what we see. As long as the caveats that I have provided are taken into account, the creation of new schemata that help us see what is occurring in classrooms is a nontrivial aspect of school improvement. Images related to terms such as *turn taking, set induction, advance organizers, null curriculum,* and *forms of representation,* as well as *time on task* and *wait time,* are tools in our perceptual arsenal. They are resources for noticing what we might not otherwise see. What they cannot do is provide prescriptions for practitioners in a form indifferent to the context in which practitioners work. In short, the conceptual devices that researchers use to study teaching can function as "perceptual maps" for seeing, but they ought not to become recipes for performance or criteria for evaluating the value of the terrain.

I emphasize this point because in the United States, there is a strong tendency, particularly in bureaucracies, to create lists of so-called research-proven teaching behaviors for use in evaluating teachers. The states of Georgia, Texas, and Florida justify their use of such lists by citing research studies. Such practices commit the *fallacy of constituency*—that is, they operate on the belief that the presence of discrete constituent elements constitutes a successful whole. What constitutes a successful whole, given a particular set of values, depends on how the constituent elements are composed, not their mere presence. The fact that Mozart used a particular number of F-sharps and B-flats in his Jupiter Symphony is no assurance whatsoever that if we used the same number, our own symphony would be as wonderful as his. In human affairs, both the configuration of elements and attention to nuance are critical. The schemata that research on teaching provides can enable us to notice those configurations and to see those nuances in the individual teaching performance of particular teachers.

The last research option that I will identify is an orthogenic one. Research on teaching can undermine simplistic conceptions of what effective teaching consists of when it does justice to the complexity of a complex act and when it provides a more replete analogue of what is involved in teaching. Research on teaching has debilitating effects when it oversimplifies and reduces the complexity of teaching and when it decontextualizes research conclusions and uses them to prescribe "what works" or "what research tells us."

My comments about using research findings to tell teachers what they should be doing should not be interpreted to mean that research findings cannot provide teachers with useful leads or ideas. Rather, my comments are aimed at prescriptions about what teachers should do in their own classrooms that are made by both researchers on teaching and bureaucrats in the field of education without considering, as they seldom can from their offices in universities and bureaucracies, what the context is. We hear, for example, from one researcher (Rosenshine, 1976) that to teach skills efficiently, teachers should follow a particular sequence of steps. We hear from other students of teaching (Hunter, 1982) that six enumerated processes are what teachers should engage in. We hear from still others that good teachers do such and such or that such and such elements are what effective teaching consists of. How many model prescriptions are there? Mastery teaching, cooperative learning, individualized instruction, the Madeline Hunter method, inductive teaching — one could go on and on. The sheer number of prescriptions is sufficient to engender more than a little skepticism among experienced teachers whose experience tells them that, as we say in the United States, there is more than one way to skin a cat.

The major focus of my remarks so far has been on the practices and forms of cognition that teachers employ when they teach, what teachers do in the course of their work as it unfolds in their classrooms. The theme of this volume, however, is effective and responsible teaching. The improvement of teaching that the terms *effective* and *responsible* suggest will require more than insightful generalizations about correlated variables, refined forms of perception, or new and more practice-sensitive schemata with which teachers might think about what they do when they teach. It will require attention to the institutional conditions in which teachers and students work and the effects of those conditions on how they function in schools. It is to this final topic that I now turn.

The Context of Teaching

To convey to prospective teachers, or even to experienced ones, the fruits of research in the expectation that such knowledge will alter what they do in their classroom is too simple. The primary feature of human behavior is its adaptive nature. We accommodate ourselves to the demands of the environment when we cannot change it. Schools are places that are difficult to change. What kinds of adaptations must secondary school teachers make to the fact that they must teach a different class every fifty minutes? What does such a structural requirement impose on students? Is there any other occupation that you can think of in which every fifty minutes a person changes jobs, moves to another location, and works under the direction of a new supervisor? This is precisely what we ask adolescent students to do, and this request has implications for what teachers do.

Consider the issue of feedback to teachers about their teaching. In most schools, teachers are afforded very little discretionary time: they are with students almost all day. This virtual absence of discretionary time makes it almost impossible under typical school conditions for teachers to observe their colleagues teaching. Since teaching is, in part, a skilled form of human performance, and since complex skills profit from coaching, where is the coaching of teaching provided for in schools? In U.S. public schools it is rare, although there is one place where it is even rarer: U.S. universities. Thus, time for planning is difficult for teachers to secure, and useful, sympathetic, and critical feedback is largely unavailable. Principals, those whom we might expect to provide it, are often preoccupied with other, less important matters.

One resource used to assist teachers is what is called in-service education. This practice consists of having teachers attend conferences or institutes to listen to experts talk about what they ought to do in their own classrooms. The problem, however, is that the experts (often university professors who have not been in schools for years) have never seen the teachers whom they advise teach. How does one know what advice to give? Do we expect voice coaches to give advice to singers whom they have never heard sing? How does one discern individual teachers' strengths and weaknesses? Is it realistic to expect that teachers will be able to apply what they have been told by visiting experts, or will their well-internalized teaching routines and the conventional norms and structural conditions that permeate their schools override the innovations that are being recommended to them?

Is it realistic to expect teachers to engage in the time-consuming features of inductive teaching when they are going to be held responsible for covering the curriculum? Is it reasonable to expect teachers to emphasize higher-order questioning when the norm-referenced tests that their students will take emphasize recall? Can teachers be expected to make intellectual connections between what they teach and what their colleagues teach when they work in a departmentalized school structure that makes it difficult to know what their colleagues teach? My point here is that the infrastructure of schools creates a powerful set of conditions to which most teachers adapt. There are some teachers, to be sure, who manage to overcome the organizational conditions imposed on them, but most teachers adapt to such conditions or leave teaching. One way to leave teaching is to find work outside the field of education. Another is to become a school administrator.

The constraints of the organizational structures that I have described include some of the aspects of schooling that affect teaching performance, but clearly not all of them. For example, there are also the conditions that Dreeben (1968) identifies in his book *On What Is Learned in School.* Dreeben's major point is that schools are agencies intended to facilitate the child's transition from dependency on adults in the context of the home to the acquisition of the social competencies needed to function as an adult in society. Schools, Dreeben argues, teach much that is not and cannot be taught pedagogically. The so-called hidden curriculum is a program that shapes learning because of the ways in which schooling is structured. Organizing children into homogeneous age groups, for example, increases the sense of competition among them. Emphasizing the norms of competition and achievement makes assistance to others a form of cheating. Learning the norm of universalism is fostered by being treated as a unit within a category. This is very much a part of what it means to be a student in school. Learning to accept, even prize, grades given by others for tasks that others assign, even though the tasks may be neither satisfying nor meaningful, is another lesson that schools teach.

Many of these lessons, once learned, are in fact conducive to socialization toward adulthood. In this sense, schools are indeed effective teachers. Whether they are responsible teachers depends on one's views of the norms that schools emphasize as well as one's views of the norms salient in the society. Successful socialization to norms that are themselves intellectually problematic is not a good way to define responsible teaching.

My point here is that the improvement of teaching is not likely to occur unless the conditions of schooling change. It is utopian to believe that large-scale improvement in teaching performance is likely in a social organization that itself teaches students lessons that are questionable and that constrains what teachers, at their best, wish to do. Making it possible for teachers to be educationally effective and morally responsible will require more than research on teaching. It will also require attention to the organizational and social structure of the school. Thus, the mission of those who wish to improve teaching must include the creation of schools that make fostering the growth of teachers almost as important as fostering the growth of students. From this perspective, the major locus of teacher education is not the university, the teacher training college, or textbooks and research journals. It is the school itself. We have yet to take this task seriously. Until we do, I have little confidence that small, piecemeal efforts will have the impact that we desire. What is called for is not only a theory of teaching but *a theory of schooling,* one that will situate the teacher and the process of teaching within a social configuration. Such a theory will not only help us understand why teachers do what they do; it will help us create the kind of schools that children will come to love.

References

Berliner, D. C. "In Pursuit of the Expert Pedagogue." *Educational Researcher,* 1987, *15* (7), 5–13.

Broudy, H. *The Role of Imagery in Learning.* Occasional Paper no. 1. Los Angeles: Getty Center for Education in the Arts, 1987.

Clark, C. "What You Can Learn from Applesauce: A Case of Qualitative Inquiry in Use." In E. W. Eisner and A. Peshkin (eds.), *Qualitative Inquiry in Education: The Continuing Debate.* New York: Teachers College Press, 1990.

Dreeben, R. *On What Is Learned in School.* Reading, Mass.: Addison-Wesley, 1968.

Eisner, E. *The Enlightened Eye: Qualitative Inquiry and the Enhancement of Educational Practice.* New York: Macmillan, 1991.

Gage, N. *The Scientific Basis of the Art of Teaching.* New York: Teachers College Press, 1978.

Goodman, N. *Ways of Worldmaking.* Indianapolis, Ind.: Hackett, 1978.

Hunter, M. *Mastery Teaching.* El Segundo, Calif.: TIP Publications, 1982.

Jackson, P. *The Practice of Teaching.* New York: Teachers College Press, 1986.

Judd, C. H. *Psychology of High School Subjects.* Boston: Ginn, 1915.

Polanyi, M. *The Tacit Dimension.* London: Routledge & Kegan Paul, 1967.

Rosenshine, B. "Classroom Instruction." In N. Gage (ed.), *The Psychology of Teaching Methods: Seventy-Fifth Yearbook of the National Society for the Study of Education.* Chicago: University of Chicago Press, 1976.

Schön, D. A. *The Reflective Practitioner: How Professionals Think in Action.* New York: Basic Books, 1983.

Schwab, J. J. "The Practical: A Language for Curriculum." *School Review,* 1969, *78* (5), 1-23.

Shulman, L. S. "Knowledge and Teaching: Foundations of the New Reform." *Harvard Educational Review,* 1987, *57* (1), 1-22.

Stodolsky, S. S. *The Subject Matters: Classroom Activity in Math and Social Studies.* Chicago: University of Chicago Press, 1988.

Thorndike, E. L. "The Contribution of Psychology to Education." *Educational Psychology,* 1910, *1,* 6, 8.

Wittrock, M. C. (ed.). *Handbook of Research and Teaching.* (3rd ed.) New York: Macmillan, 1986.

18

How Do Expert Teachers View Themselves?

Brigitte A. Rollett

What does it mean to be an expert in teaching? We know already that there are different kinds of knowledge (Shulman, 1986), and we also know that experts possess most or all of these (see Chapter Fifteen). More specifically, experts rely on a large repertoire of strategies and skills that they can call on automatically, leaving them free to deal with unique or unexpected events. They have been shown to possess a distinct and original way of approaching the task of teaching, getting right to the core of problems rather than paying attention to peripheral features. They analyze situations for a longer time and in greater depth than novices before deciding on a plan of action. The wealth of knowledge and routines that they employ, in fact, is so automatic that they often do not realize why they preferred a certain plan of action over another. However, when questioned, they are able to reconstruct the reasons for their decisions and behavior. And it seems that we in teaching research have finally begun to appreciate the fact that expert teachers also have a caring attitude toward their students. In fact, it is this caring attitude that enables them to be not just efficient but also responsible in carrying out their activities.

That is how researchers see teachers. But how do teachers see themselves? What is their self-image, and does this also have an effect on their teaching? In an international study described in this chapter, my colleagues and I tried to find answers to those questions on the basis of a belief that good teachers have positive self-images and that this optimistic, positive way of seeing themselves and their teaching plays an important role in their high capability. A positive self-image allows teachers to think positively about their work and, thus, about their students. This positive view of their students is reflected in their caring attitude toward them and also forms the basis for it.

Now, of course, one might ask, "Yes, but can't a teacher have a positive self-image and still be an uncaring teacher, more interested in his or her own professional ego than in the students?" A positive self-image, it is true, is not something easily come by or easily assessed. In fact, it is much easier to assess teachers' didactic skill or the results achieved at the end of a lesson than to assess their self-image. However, by using the "critical incident" methodology of Flanagan (1954), it is possible to approach a realistic impression of teachers' self-image.

In much of the research on expert teachers, the teachers had been prepared in one way or another before the investigation was begun. We felt that if we asked teachers in an impromptu way to explain or write about two critical incidents, a negative one and a positive one, it would be possible to carefully analyze the events for the values that entered in and to evaluate these and to thereby arrive at a more spontaneous view of teachers' thinking. We were also interested in the possibility of cross-cultural variation in how teachers valued themselves. To investigate this, a three-country research project that included researchers in New York, London, and Vienna was organized. While these countries all participate in the Western cultural tradition, there is enough of a difference that anyone moving from one culture to the other for the first time would sense a clear need to shift his or her cultural expectations in order to function smoothly and without incident in the new culture. Furthermore, when setting out to examine thought processes across very disparate cultures, one runs a risk of either comparing the wrong phenomena or asking questions inappropriate for discovering what one wants to discover (see Cole, Gay, Glick, and Sharp's 1971 classic work on this subject).

Simply put, then, our question was, if expert teachers have a positive self-image reflected in their caring attitude, is this self-image the same across three Western cultures? The answer turned out to be yes and no. Although how the teachers in the three cultures defined themselves as good teachers differed, our detailed analysis showed that the items that they viewed as contributing to their success were largely the same. This finding encouraged us to expand our hypotheses to include the consideration that it might be possible to create a sort of knowledge base for beginning teachers that is based on teachers' own perceptions of what is important and that might have international usefulness.

Intercultural Research Project

The crucial question for our study (Beckum and others, 1989; Garcia and Otheguy, 1988; Perry and Lord, 1988; Rollett, 1988, 1989) was what expert teachers see as the source of their success (knowledge base, teaching skills, belief system) and how this reflects how they view themselves as teachers. We also wanted to determine whether expert teachers interpret and handle problem situations similarly in different cultural environments. The last question becomes especially significant when we think about the growing internationalization of society caused by increasing worldwide mobility. In what follows, I outline the main thrust of our international research effort undertaken to shed light on this aspect of expert teachers.

A set of three parallel studies was organized and conducted by research groups in three different countries: Austria, the United Kingdom, and the United States. The research centers that took part in this study were the City College of the City University of New York, led by Leonard C. Beckum (who headed the research team), Ofelia Garcia, and Ricardo Otheguy; the South Bank Polytechnic in London, headed by Pauline Perry and Eric Lord; and the University of Vienna, Austria, headed by myself and my colleague Barbara Reisel. Each of these institutions is involved in training programs for teachers in urban, multiethnic, multilingual, multicultural classrooms.

Each research center selected teachers from elementary schools in its area and then asked school authorities to make the final selection of teachers. They were asked to choose teachers who met the following prerequisites: a minimum of three years' teaching experience, proven professional excellency, and continued participation in various higher-level teacher training seminars. Furthermore, we asked that the teachers have classes with a multiethnic character. The final project included 102 elementary teachers: 50 teachers in twenty schools from four community school districts in New York City; 21 teachers in four schools from two districts in London; and 31 teachers in fifteen schools from nine districts in Vienna.

The expert teachers were asked to "think back on two different kinds of situations. One should be an event or practice that you think you handled in a competent manner and that worked out well. The second situation should be an event or practice that you feel did not work out so well." Their answers could be in either written or oral form (essay or taped interview). The teachers were encouraged to analyze and describe the incidents as fully as they could, reflecting on the skills and knowledge that they thought had enabled them to cope with the positive situation successfully and had caused failure in the negative instance.

The teachers' descriptions of their successes and failures were analyzed for content through a category system developed by the New York research group (Garcia and Otheguy, 1988). On the basis of an initial reading of the essays and interview transcripts, a coding manual was developed in order to guarantee an exact application of the categories. Through this process, 105 topics were identified and coded according to the positive and negative affect expressed by the teachers. The topics were then organized into four domains that we felt were basic and essential spheres of operation for teachers: community characteristics, institutional characteristics, student characteristics, and teacher characteristics.

Community characteristics took into consideration items of social or cultural significance, mostly pertaining to the students mentioned in the description of critical incidents, such as cultural and linguistic background, household structure, school orientation of families, and so on. Institutional characteristics included more official elements of the classroom and school context that the teacher had to respond to, such as administrative support, type of curriculum, and class size and groupings. Student characteristics pertained to psychological characteristics of the students as they interacted in the classroom and included such areas as ability of students to concentrate, particular behavior problems, poor language skills, and emotional needs (the latter two could also be correlated with an item in the community characteristics group, for instance). The teacher characteristics ranged the furthest, running the full spectrum from teachers' concern for and understanding of individual children, class management, and handling of the intricate social relationships in the school community to considerations and initiatives regarding the curricula, didactic skill, and providing for their own professional development.

Obviously, there is overlap among these items, especially between those in the community and the student domains. However, if we go back to the original question, "What image do expert teachers have of themselves?" any overlap or lack of clarity becomes more a formal question than a true methodological one. Qualitative research aims at getting to the *quality* of something, not at quantification of the exact composition of elements that would be imposed by the research question. Another goal of our categories and domains was to see whether it would be possible to determine what it is that teachers themselves feel is most important to their success and whether that could be formulated into a knowledge base for beginning teachers.

The results of the analyses from all three parallel research groups were surprisingly similar. We had expected to find greater, more substantive differences in how teachers in the three different cultures viewed their teaching and to what they attributed their success. When we analyzed the data for cultural differences in their thought processes, we could identify only a few characteristics.

For example, a comparison between the New York and the Viennese data showed some interesting differences in the ranking of the categories that the teachers used to describe teacher characteristics and aims that they thought significant. New York teachers especially stressed the importance of self-esteem as a person and a teacher, of upholding high expectations, and of developing self-esteem and pride in their students, while Viennese teachers' first priority was the ability to create a general atmosphere of understanding and love in their classrooms. The London and Vienna teachers did not emphasize helping their students develop self-esteem and pride, because the European tradition holds that pride is too "self-congratulatory" (a term used by the London group) and not something to strive for. However, it is clear that having a positive self-image (self-esteem) is the foundation for having respect of others, which is again the basis for creating an atmosphere of understanding and love. Thus, while the definitions among the cultures vary, the basis seems the same.

Another area where there was apparent cultural variance was the protocols dealing with unresolved situations. Teachers across all three cultures generally showed a tendency to blame failures on extrinsic factors (community, administrative, and student domains). In Vienna, the teachers agreed that a nonschool orientation of parents was one of the main reasons for their inability to resolve a problem situation satisfactorily. In New York, on the other hand, teachers cited the disintegration of families caused by the absence of one or both parents as the predominant cause of failures. While it is statistically obvious that there are more divorces in the United States than in Austria, the two explanations come down to the same thing: parents are occupied with matters other than school and are, for economic or emotional reasons, not able to give their children or the teacher the support that the teacher feels is necessary to solve certain problems.

In the two examples just cited, where we thought we would find cultural variance, closer analysis showed that teachers, especially expert teachers, in our Western cultural tradition seem to resemble each other regardless of their specific cultural or ethnic backgrounds. Who is this culturally nonspecific expert teacher as seen through the teachers' own eyes? Our research shows that above all, it is someone who favors the positive.

A first general analysis of the teachers' narratives of critical incidents in the classroom disclosed one characteristic that all teachers had in common: they found it much easier to recall positive events than negative ones. In some cases, it was necessary to ask the teachers to go back more than two weeks in order for them to remember an event that had not worked out favorably. In addition, the teachers found it much harder to describe the negative episodes and seemed reluctant to do so. When explaining their successes, expert teachers used much more detailed information and gave more reasons for their behavior than they did in relating their failures. (A chi-square analysis of the data showed that the difference between the descriptions of successes and failures was significant in New York and Vienna, with a strong tendency in the same direction in London.) A comparison of the number of categories used by the Viennese teachers when narrating positive events and narrating negative events further elucidates this tendency. Both descriptions and explanations of positive episodes were more numerous and detailed than those of the negative ones.

That teachers across three cultures preferred to remember positive events over negative ones is a noteworthy result, since the typical outcome in studies of recall of past events is that unfavorable memories are described in greater detail. To check this, I organized a preliminary adjunct study at the University of Vienna. Sixty-eight students who were participating in an educational psychology course were asked to describe the most pleasant incident and the most unpleasant incident that they could remember happening to them during their own schooling. When we compared the lengths of the descriptions, we found that they went into much greater detail about the unpleasant events than the positive ones.

Our teachers, however, showed a strong inclination to concentrate on the brighter side of their professional experiences. In all three samples, the experts showed themselves to be a strikingly optimistic group of people: they thought of themselves positively, as teachers who enjoy teaching and who have great trust in their abilities to ensure their success. As one Viennese teacher expressed it, "Every morning I look forward to going to school, and I tremendously enjoy teaching."

Another interesting strong tendency of the teachers, along with their positive self-image and attitude toward their work, was the importance that they attribute to emotions in their descriptions of critical incidents. In all three cities, teachers most often chose categories dealing with emotions and attitudes in explaining success or failure. For instance, in explaining success in dealing with a critical incident, teachers attributed affective qualities such as patience, tolerance, empathy, and love for and acceptance of children. When describing a negative experience or an incident with a negative outcome, they again chose affective qualities, such as disappointment, anger, and frustration.

This shows that emotions play a critical role when teachers think about important incidents in the classroom. As Zajonc (1980) proposed in 1980, processing meaningful information in general seems to be mediated by "hot cognitions." He found that emotions are not postcognitive but precognitive and that conclusions based on emotions are made with much more confidence than purely rational judgments. In this way, cognitions produce the intimate meaning that a person attributes to his or her experiences. By preferring positive occurrences, expert teachers set the emotional stage for interpreting classroom situations in a favorable way, thereby producing a positive feedback loop for themselves.

Critical Incidents

The teachers in our study were chosen to participate by their school principals because they were considered good teachers who were well liked by both students and fellow staff. As noted above, an analysis of their reports of critical incidents in their classroom showed that they tended to prefer reporting on positive incidents rather than negative ones and, in fact, had difficulty remembering the negative ones and that they tended to think of these experiences in emotional terms, indicating that they made decisions and acted on these decisions in a more affective than cognitive way. What were the types of incidents that they tended to report as critical? In analyzing the issues that teachers concentrated on in the incidents that they reported, our research showed that, across all three countries, the highest percentage of episodes centered around problems generated by the teachers' interest in their students rather than curricular or managerial matters.

In all three studies, two-thirds of the incidents reported had to do with problem situations involving *individual* children, while only about one-third of the episodes dealt with situations caused by other factors. When researchers discussed these results with teachers, they mentioned that they felt at ease when handling instructional or managerial tasks but that the "emotional highlights and frustrations" of their work at school were created by their successes and failures with children who had behavioral or academic difficulties.

The content analysis also pointed out that the major concerns of beginning teachers—perfecting their knowledge of subject matter, sharpening their pedagogical skills, familiarizing themselves with the curriculum, and developing their organizational and classroom management techniques—had long ceased to be problems for these experts. What they were interested in was not the routines of the teaching profession but the extra challenges.

This finding supports what Berliner in Chapter Fifteen calls a characteristic attitude of experts: that they attend more to the atypical or unique events than the typical or ordinary events in the domain in which they have expertise. From this, I think we can also conclude that it is exactly this ability to deal efficiently with the curriculum or subject matter that allows expert teachers to go on to deal with their students in a caring, responsible way. It is hard to imagine that a novice teacher struggling to master presentation of the content could also find energy to negotiate particular issues on a more moral level with students in a responsible way. Our study also shows that it is exactly this level beyond the curriculum that expert teachers find the most challenging and interesting in their jobs.

At least half of the positive incidents recalled by the teachers dealt with their ability to integrate into the learning group a child who had been, for various reasons, an outsider. The next highest category of positive incidents was teachers' ability to successfully teach an individual child something that the child had previously found difficult to grasp. An example of this child-centered aspect of the teachers in our study is a teacher in the London project. One of the critical incidents that this teacher with fifteen years' experience found very important involved an eleven-year-old pupil who went "berserk" on the playground during a physical education period. The teacher was able to calm the child down by removing him from the situation and discussing the incident with him. She interpreted his loss of control as the result of his worries about his grandmother's health and his upcoming move to a secondary school. She attributed her success to her knowledge of his home situation, her ability to sympathize with his grief and anxiety, and her willingness to understand his emotions instead of punishing his behavior. Thus, her image of herself as an understanding, empathetic, caring teacher allowed her to act in a very responsible way, and her success in dealing with the situation reinforced her positive feelings not only about herself but about her student.

In all three cities, what teachers complained about (and saw as the extrinsic factors having a negative impact on their teaching success) was institutional and time pressures imposed on them by authorities. They saw these pressures as preventing them from being as flexible in their teaching as they thought was necessary to get the best out of every child in their class. They were especially interested in developing ways to find a compromise between these institutional limits and the needs of individual students.

This personal, child-centered way of interacting with their students seems to be one of the major reasons for these teachers' feelings of success and satisfaction. In all three samples, the detailed analysis of the teachers' descriptions revealed their conviction of the importance of being able to reach individual children and to deal with their problems in a responsible and competent way. If the teachers had generally found their successes in academic or curricular incidents, such as high overall test scores for a particular subject, we would have to have said that school efficiency was more important for them and that they saw themselves primarily as transmitters of content knowledge. Given our findings, it is clear that the large majority of them see themselves as *caring* individuals.

This is not to say, of course, that knowledge of subject matter and its competent presentation, supported by efficient classroom management techniques, is not important to them. In fact, it is these things that form the basis of successful teaching. The results of our studies indicate, however, that in teachers' views of themselves, another component plays a more important role in their conceptions of what it means to do a good job of teaching: the teachers felt that for them to be successful, it was vital to have an intimate knowledge of each student's personality and to understand how classroom, home, and community experiences affected each child. They also thought that it was important that the teacher could work with children on an individual basis as well as on a group basis in a quasi-therapeutic way so that children could make the most of their abilities and their personality growth could be enhanced. This is clearly an attitude of taking moral responsibility for their students.

One teacher felt extremely uplifted when, after four frustrating years of trying to teach a boy to read, he surprised her one day by suddenly reading aloud a whole paragraph in the book that they were discussing. She was especially pleased about the fact that the whole class started clapping and congratulated the child for his achievement, shouting excitedly, "Our Tommi can read!"

We found further support for the child-centered orientation of the teachers in our detailed analysis of the items in the category of student characteristics. In their narratives recalling problems within a critical incident, about half the teachers mentioned students' poor study habits and/or their disruptive behavior. Their perceived success or failure in dealing with the incident was based on the degree of cooperation that they felt they were able to establish with individual students in social or academic settings. This finding is closely related to one mentioned earlier in the discussion, that teachers in all three cultural settings tended to blame the child's family or home situation for failures. Now we can better see why: if the teachers view themselves as being able to establish positive rapport with their students, on both an individual and a group basis, and this effort fails with certain children, they generally choose to maintain their own positive self-image and that of their students and blame extrinsic factors such as the family instead. Of course, we could also ask why they do not blame the student directly.

We can hypothesize that doing so would require them to view at least part of the teaching relationship in a directly negative light. For example, since one of the main concerns of the Viennese teachers was forming good and loving relationships with their students and a pleasant work atmosphere in their classrooms, they probably preferred to view all their students as being capable of joining this effort (see Chapter Eight for a discussion of teachers' assumptions about students).

Since we specifically chose classrooms with a high ratio of students from ethnic backgrounds other than the target culture, we also found that the teachers in our study were highly sensitive to minority children's particular cultures in their dealings with them. Their interest in learning more about those cultures in order to understand their students better again reflects this important student-centered attitude. A striking feature of the reports was that ethnicity was never mentioned in a derogatory way but was seen as a challenge (which we know is not always the case, especially as racism becomes an increasingly more important topic in many Western industrialized nations). Quite a few of the teachers in fact blamed teacher training authorities for not providing enough information about the customs and traditions of specific nationalities, so that the teachers had to acquire the necessary knowledge by trial and error. In a critical incident reported by an Austrian teacher, a Turkish boy ordered a female classmate to pick up something that he had dropped. When the classmate refused, he then ordered the teacher herself to pick it up. The teacher, needless to say, was annoyed and baffled by this incident. Only after she had been able to reflect on it did she realize that he had acted in accordance with the customs of his culture, where males are superior to females and never bend down in the presence of females. This insight made such an impression on her that she decided to develop a cross-cultural awareness program in her classroom.

This example also shows how expert teachers are able to build the positive feedback loop mentioned earlier. This teacher felt very good about her success at understanding what was behind her Turkish student's "inappropriate" (as seen from her own culture) behavior and was further motivated to increase mutual understanding in her classroom by initiating a cultural awareness program. The success of this program, fueled by her desire to care for each one of her students, further contributed to her positive self-image and her ability to feel responsible in her teaching.

It is interesting to note at this point a study conducted at the University of Vienna by Fiedler (1987). Fiedler was interested in finding out which of the competencies acquired during teacher training at the university made young teachers more appreciated by their classes. She collected the grades received by twenty-seven prospective secondary school teachers in their final exams and compared them to their rankings on the Dortmund Scale of Teacher Behavior (Masendorf, Tücke, Kretschmann, and Bartram, 1976), a test designed to determine whether teachers use a positive (supporting), a negative (authoritarian), or an intermediate teaching style. The test was administered to 635 students in classes taught by these twenty-seven teachers.

An analysis of the data showed that the only predictor for a supportive teaching style as perceived by the students was the grade that the teacher had received on his or her psychology exam at the university.

We can suspect that the teachers who feel positive and responsible toward themselves and their students are likely to possess a certain amount of psychological tact and to be similarly perceived by their students. Thus, we can expand our hypothesis to include the assumption that an interest in and knowledge of psychology and the ability to apply it to the problems in the classroom are crucial to developing a teacher's sense of success in the classroom and thus also to developing a sort of positive feedback loop as mentioned earlier. The benefit for the students is that the teacher is able to create a climate of mutual trust and support in which they can efficiently and responsibly carry out their work. In terms of teacher training, it seems to me that this insight supports the recommendation that teacher training programs try to include psychology courses, preferably with a practical focus.

At this point, it is useful to return to our discussion of teachers' self-image. We hypothesized that expert teachers have a positive self-image that allows them to view their classrooms and their students in a positive, optimistic way. In addition to expert teachers' interest in the psychological well-being of their students, analysis of our data revealed that teaching was a very personal issue for them. This can best be illustrated by a Viennese teacher in our sample who declared, "I realized in the course of my teaching experience how much the problems of my students have to do with myself."

This attitude of taking personal responsibility for what goes on in the classroom may seem to contradict what was said earlier about teachers tending to blame extrinsic factors for their failures — why do they not also take direct responsibility for negative outcomes? — but, in fact, it does not: the teachers represented in all three research projects showed that they earnestly strove to improve themselves as persons and as professionals. They were interested in attending teacher training courses and eager to consult with other teachers at their school to share knowledge and skills, to exchange materials, and to discuss problems (items mentioned in the domain of teacher characteristics). A New York teacher expressed this connection between success and interest in personal improvement by saying, "I am successful because I am good at looking for resources." The responsibility that the teachers felt for maintaining a good relationship with their students extended to themselves: by improving themselves, they could feel more positive about themselves. This characteristic of experts is also discussed by Greeno (1990), who found that experts are especially able to draw on the resources in their environment to solve problems in their field of expertise.

Conclusion

As Clark and Peterson (1986) concluded from their review, teachers' thought processes play a crucial role in teaching. Teachers are revealed as responsible "reflective professionals," whose theories and belief systems influence, to a large degree, their perceptions of classroom occurrences and who thus monitor their thoughts and actions involved in the teaching process (see also Bromme and Brophy, 1986; Clark and Lampert, 1986; Corno and Edelstein, 1987; Floden and Klinzing, 1990; Lampert, 1984; Leinhardt and Greeno, 1986; Peterson and Comeaux, 1987; Peterson, 1988; Shavelson and Stern, 1981; Shavelson, 1983; Shulman, 1986). A strong positive self-image is part of the belief system that influences teachers' perception of classroom occurrences and their feeling of power to have a positive effect on such occurrences.

When the results of our three studies are summarized, the parallels outweigh the differences. In their accounts of critical incidents in the classroom, the expert teachers revealed themselves as optimistic, outreaching, loving personalities, interested in children and concerned about their needs, able and happy in relating with them and willing to put in any amount of time and effort necessary to make a success of this. Furthermore, the expert teachers had a firm picture of what they wanted the individual learners to achieve academically and in social and personality growth, and they were convinced that it was important to give the children the needed time to achieve these things, even when this meant departing from the prescribed curriculum.

As competent professionals, the teachers were able and eager to produce what De Corte (1990) calls a "powerful learning environment," fashioning the standardized curriculum to the requirements of their pupils. The reports of the resolved situations reflect the wealth of pedagogical and psychological knowledge that these expert teachers possess. The unresolved incidents mirror this in a way: they were experienced as doubly frustrating because the teachers were used to handling problems smoothly and successfully. As the London researchers expressed it, "It was as though in these situations what stayed in the teachers' mind was simply their bafflement. They had run through their repertoire of skills and were at a loss to know what other strategies they could try" (Perry and Lord, 1988, p. 22). The fact that they tended to avoid pondering on the negative incidents, thus possibly depriving themselves of the chance to hit on a solution, reflected their optimism and their positive self-image rather than a denial of the problem or an unwillingness to improve their skills and knowledge. Many of the positive incidents were the unresolved problem situations of the past. We can thus infer that the teachers seemed to prefer to shelve a problem for the time being when they did not have a solution rather than take a trial-and-error course of action. This kind of strategic thinking allows the teachers to further reinforce the positive feedback loop that seems to be basic to their success.

Thus, expert teachers seem to attribute an integral part of their success to their ability to understand children and their willingness to observe and listen to them, making responsible interaction the keynote of their everyday work with their students. If the driving force in the professional life of expert teachers seems to be the overwhelming conviction that, regardless of adverse factors, all children are able to learn, then it is the teachers' responsibility to enhance this growth. Their effectiveness is constantly being shaped by this force. Our study reflects the interpretative synthesis model of effectiveness and responsibility (see Chapter One), in which morality is implicitly present wherever certain humane forms of effectiveness are employed.

References

Beckum, L. C., and others. *Moving Towards Developing a Knowledge Base for Beginning Teachers of Multicultural, Multilingual Populations: An International Study Focussing on Effective Teacher Behaviors.* New York: City College of New York, 1989.

Bromme, R., and Brophy, J. "Teachers' Cognitive Activities." In B. Christiansen, G. Howsen, and M. Otte (eds.), *Perspectives on Mathematics Education.* Dordrecht, the Netherlands: Reidel, 1986.

Clark, C. M., and Lampert, M. "The Study of Teacher Thinking: Implications for Teacher Education." *Journal of Teacher Education,* 1986, *37* (5), 27-31.

Clark, C., and Peterson, P. "Teachers' Thought Processes." In M. C. Wittrock (ed.), *Handbook of Research on Teaching.* New York: Macmillan, 1986.

Cole, M., Gay, J., Glick, J., and Sharp, D. W. "The Cultural Context of Learning and Thinking." London: Methuen, 1971.

Corno, L., and Edelstein, M. "Information Processing Models." In M. J. Dunkin (ed.), *The International Encyclopedia of Teaching and Teacher Education.* New York: Pergamon Press, 1987.

De Corte, E. "Towards Powerful Learning Environments for the Acquisition of Problem-Solving Skills." *European Journal of Psychology of Education,* 1990, *5* (1), 5-19.

Fiedler, R. "Einige Aspekte der Praxisrelevanz der Universitätsausbildung von Lehrern für Allgemeinbildende Höhere Schulen." [Some practice-relevant aspects of the university's teacher training program for prospective teachers at the college-preparatory level]. Unpublished doctoral dissertation, University of Vienna, 1987.

Flanagan, J. C. "The Critical Incident Technique." *Psychological Bulletin,* 1954, *51* (4), 327-358.

Floden, R. E., and Klinzing, H. G. "What Can Research on Teacher Thinking Contribute to Teachers' Preparation? A Second Opinion." *Educational Researcher,* 1990, *19* (5), 15-20.

Garcia, O., and Otheguy, R. "The Knowledge Base of Experienced Teachers of Minority Children in New York City Public Schools." Report submitted to the Exxon Foundation Project on the Knowledge Base of Beginning Teachers, 1988.

Greeno, J. G. *Number Sense as Situated Knowledge in a Conceptual Domain.* Report NOIRL 90-0014. Palo Alto, Calif.: Institute for Research on Learning, 1990.

Lampert, M. "Teaching About Thinking and Thinking About Teaching." *Journal of Curriculum Studies,* 1984, *16,* 1-18.

Leinhardt, G., and Greeno, J. "The Cognitive Skill of Teaching." *Journal of Educational Psychology,* 1986, *78,* 75–95.

Masendorf, F., Tücke, M., Kretschmann, R., and Bartram, M. *Dortmunder Skala zum Lehrerverhalten* [Dortmund scale of teacher behavior]. Braunschweig, Germany: Westermann, 1976.

Perry, P., and Lord, E. "Knowledge-Base for Beginning Teachers in Multicultural, Multilingual, Deprived Urban Schools." Report of the London Project, 1988.

Peterson, P. L. "Teachers' and Students' Cognitional Knowledge for Classroom Teaching and Learning." *Educational Researcher,* 1988, *17* (5), 5–14.

Peterson, P. L., and Comeaux, M. A. "Teachers' Schemata for Classroom Events: The Mental Scaffolding of Teachers' Thinking During Classroom Instruction." *Teaching and Teacher Education,* 1987, *3,* 319–331.

Rollett, B. *Expert Teachers' Interpreting and Handling of Difficult Classroom Situations: Preliminary Report of a Study of 31 Primary Grade Teachers Using Flanagan's Critical Incidents Technique.* Vienna, Austria: University of Vienna, 1988.

Rollett, B. "An Examination of Knowledge Bases for Beginning Teachers in a Multicultural Environment." Report to the Vienna Project, University of Vienna, 1989.

Shavelson, R. J. "Review of Research on Teachers' Pedagogical Judgments, Plans, and Decisions." *Elementary School Journal,* 1983, *83* (4), 392–413.

Shavelson, R. J., and Stern, P. "Research on Teachers' Pedagogical Thoughts, Judgments, Decisions, and Behavior." *Review of Educational Research,* 1981, *51* (4), 455–498.

Shulman, L. S. "Paradigms and Research Programs in the Study of Teaching: A Contemporary Perspective." In M. C. Wittrock (ed.), *Handbook of Research on Teaching.* (3rd ed.) New York: Macmillan, 1986.

Zajonc, R. B. "Feeling and Thinking: Preferences Need No Inferences." *American Psychologist,* 1980, *35,* 151–175.

Section Six

CONTENT IN TEACHING

Frank Achtenhagen,
Section Editor

All teaching and learning procedures in school deal with subject matter, or content; thus, all considerations on effectiveness and responsibility in teaching must take content into account. This point is not a new one; we find from the earliest descriptions of educational processes that the main attention of pedagogy has focused on goals and content as the substance of education. And it is no wonder: from their very inception, educational organization and procedures have followed a top-down approach. Education began as a preparation for kings, pharaohs, grand viziers, and high priests to assume their leading positions; effectiveness and responsibility were the two themes that guided these teaching-learning procedures. As the division of labor and public tasks progressed, however, more people had to be brought into the formal educational process. And here — in ancient Egypt as well as in other societies — well-known problems of effective and responsible teaching immediately emerged.

In ancient Egypt, many texts were designed to convince young people of the advantages of being a "writer" or a civil servant. This motivational process is still seen today: the older generation presses the young into content-burdened programs, promising compensation later in life, in the form of salary and status, for their hard work in school. Old texts also provide us with illustrations of how the teachers of ancient Egypt viewed their students. One of them says, "The ears of the boy are his back: he hears only if he is beaten." The problem was then, as it is now, the long list of linearized content units that could not and cannot be directly related to tasks that are of actual importance to youth. Throughout its history, then, education has confronted the difficulties of the older generation as it tries to prepare the younger generation for life and the motivational problems of the youth being confronted with overburdened curricula.

The top-down process of education came to a formal end in Europe when Comenius's *Didactica Magna* (The great didactic, 1632) and *Orbis Sen-*

291

sualium Pictus (The visible world in pictures, 1653) were published. Comenius demanded that content be made broadly available and understandable to the whole population, including those at the bottom of society. To help teachers reach this goal, his approach offered a variety of content: content units appear in different form, in different representations (verbal, iconic), in different functions, and in different languages. Although he was eager to improve teaching and learning, Comenius did not solve the problem of the *amount* of content. And this problem has ruled the didactic and curricular area until now.

Numerous didactic models have been developed and used within teacher training. These models usually include the following categories: teachers' decisions on content, intentions and goals, methods, and media; students' characteristics (prior knowledge, attitudes, and so on); and sociocultural conditions. All these models conceal many problems, mainly that they are related to individual lessons, not to sequences of lessons; they do not sufficiently take into account the problems and needs of the students; and they do not sufficiently bring together the disciplinary (the content area) and the pedagogical (the student area) aspects of content and goals. Furthermore, didacticians and curriculum specialists tend not to think thoroughly enough about the empirical evaluation of their categorical models and the practical consequences of these models for teacher training. Educational psychologists, on the other hand, while specializing in teaching-learning processes, think too much in behavioral and procedural categories, to the neglect of the dimension of content and goals. This two-sided neglect has led to a curtailing of the full scope of possibilities for developing methods of effective and responsible teaching that teacher training and institutionalized teaching-learning process research could provide. This situation can be rectified — in my judgment — only if teachers can cooperate with didacticians and curriculum specialists and with teacher trainers (and maybe also with students) and succeed in bringing the disciplinary and the pedagogical structure of content together. The main advantage to this would be that it would structure teacher training around pedagogically constructed content units. This is what is meant by Shulman's (Chapter Two) term *pedagogical content knowledge* or the German term *Fachdidaktik,* which means "didactics of a special subject or content." To develop such approaches in an empirically relevant way, we need to bring together didactic, curricular, and teaching-learning research. That is exactly what the chapters in this section deal with.

Chapter Nineteen, by Magdalene Lampert, concentrates on teaching and learning in mathematics. Lampert chooses the term *authentic* to stress the special relationship between individual understanding and the public justification of mathematical knowledge. Although this subject seems to be the outstanding example of logically and very stringently organized teaching-learning processes, Lampert points out the necessity of creativity and nondirect mathematical thinking and arguing. She refers to the concept of "cross-country" mathematics, which has often been emphasized by famous mathematicians. Teaching "authentic" mathematics is considered as integrating aspects of personality and aspects of the structure of the discipline: the teaching-learning processes have to be meaningful and important for the students and, at the same time, to reflect a wider mathematical culture. To balance these goals in a responsible way urges expert didactic knowledge as well as student-sensitive teaching. By relating an example from her own math classroom, the author demonstrates a strategy that can lead to "authentic" mathematical teaching.

In Chapter Twenty, on the other hand, Frank Achtenhagen looks more at the handling of content and teacher behavior. He finds that equal chances to learn for all students can be provided only by a conscious handling of content units and by striving for an effectiveness that is not defined only by measurable outcomes. Such goals must be included in our concepts of responsible teaching and research in teaching. Achtenhagen also discusses the problem of the relationship between traditional curricular structures and the demands of real life that students are supposedly being prepared for. For youth to be effectively and responsibly prepared for the very new complex goals and tasks that they will face at work and in their private lives, new patterns of teaching and learning have to be developed. The first step is introducing complex teaching-learning arrangements into the schools. Initial investigations into these processes show that teachers are currently overstrained: they do not make use of expert didactic knowledge to effectively and responsibly handle complex content together with complex instructional methods. How this problem can be solved remains to be seen.

Anne-Nelly Perret-Clermont in Chapter Twenty-One looks at the problem of didactic expertise from a psychosocial point of view. Her central statement is that all classroom effects — the content being one angle in the triangular semantic field of instruction — are mediated by the way in which the actors, the teachers and the students, perceive and interpret them; the same objects of knowledge sometimes have quite different meaning for the teachers and the students. This psychological view helps to explain why content does not always work in the intended direction. Lampert's approach of teaching "authentic" mathematics and Achtenhagen's examples can be directly related to that phenomenon, which demonstrates that content and behavior have to be considered together in instructional planning. Perret-Clermont shows how a mathematical concept such as "set" changes within the teaching-learning processes. Effectiveness from this point of view is related to a clear and valid interpretation of instructional processes, whereas responsibility appears as a conscious awareness of possible side effects of effective action. The didactic expert must also make use of that psychologically founded knowledge.

Thus, all of the contributions in this section deal with the necessity of proper interpretation of content. Teaching will not be effective and responsible with regard to the goals of the curriculum and the needs of the students if the importance of content is neglected. The main social and political purpose of institutionalized education can be fulfilled only through the development, construction, and evaluation of pedagogically and disciplinarily proven, accepted, and legitimized content units within sequences and curricula. Only in that way will the older generation's efforts toward responsibility, carried out by publicly paid teachers, be accepted by students, allowing effectiveness in the realm of life-related content and goals to be reached with a cognitively, motivationally, and emotionally positive learning style.

19

Practices and Problems
in Teaching Authentic Mathematics

Magdalene Lampert

What is the synthesis of effective and responsible teaching of mathematics? If one were interested only in deciding whether the teaching of this subject is effective, then the question to be answered would be whether what is taught is what is learned. But if one is also interested in whether the teaching of mathematics is responsible, then the question of whether what is being taught and learned is authentic mathematics becomes pertinent. Teachers may teach and learners may do well on tests or be observed to have "target" skills without the learning having much to do with real mathematics. In order to judge whether mathematics is being taught and learned responsibly, one must look at whether the skills and knowledge being acquired contribute to students' ability to actually *do* mathematics. And one must consider not only outcomes but pedagogical methods as well, for students learn what it means to know something from the interactions that they have with the subject and the teacher.

In this chapter, I examine what can be learned about responsible pedagogical methods for teaching mathematics from looking at mathematical practice. I come at the question of how to make mathematics teaching both effective and responsible from the perspective of a fifth-grade teacher in a public school in a diverse community. My goal as a teacher is to have my students learn to do authentic mathematics. From this perspective, being effective and responsible means constructing curriculum and instruction in ways that make it possible for my students to participate in activities that are genuinely mathematical and to learn from those activities.

Investigating Effective and Responsible Teaching in a Lesson

In order to give the reader a sense of what it might be like to be a teacher who wants to do the right thing in the classroom, I want to begin by telling you about some assertions that were made by my fifth-grade students during a discussion of a problem that the class was working on. I played a role in this discussion as the teacher, but here I want to recount primarily what the students said and leave open for now the question of what an effective and responsible teacher of mathematics might do in response. Later in the chapter, after some examination of what it might mean to know and do mathematics in practice, I will return to the discussion in which these assertions were made and analyze the role that I played as the teacher.

In an introductory lesson on functions, I had asked my fifth-grade class to figure out how one might characterize the relationship between the x and y values in this chart:

x	y
8	4
4	2
2	1
0	0

Ellie, a fifth-grade student, made these observations: "Um, well, there were a whole bunch of . . . a whole bunch of rules you could use, use, um, divided by two . . . And you could do, um, minus one-half."* I followed Ellie's final assertion with a question: "And eight minus a half is?" to which she answered, "Four."

At this point, a gasp arose from the class, and several other students made a bid to enter the conversation. They either agreed or disagreed with Ellie.

Karim: Well, see, I agree with Ellie because you can have eight minus one-half and that's the same as eight divided by two or eight minus four.

Charlotte: I think eight minus one-half is seven and a half because one-half's a fraction and it's half of one whole and so when you subtract you aren't even subtracting one whole number so you can't get even a smaller number that's more than one whole [away from eight].

Suran: I think, um, I would agree with Ellie if she had said eight minus one-half of eight, because half of eight would be four because four plus four would be eight.

Sam: Um, I agree with Charlotte and, um, I don't agree with Ellie. Because, um, like one-half is not even one, so if, so when Ellie said that people would like, um, a really good mathematician would probably, like, would

---

*The student-teacher conversations in this chapter are excerpted from a transcript of a discussion that occurred in my fifth grade mathematics class. See the appendix of this chapter for the complete transcript.

probably write seven and a half, not four because they would have to know what the one half was meaning, half of a number to, um, to understand it.

Lev: I think, um, I would agree with Ellie if she had said eight minus one-half of eight because half of eight would be four because four plus four would be eight.

Tyrone: I agree with Charlotte and Sam and I disagree with Ellie and like I think Ellie meant, like, because four is half of eight, like one-half would be a half, but, and I agree with Lev when he said if she meant one-half, uh, equals, wait, eight, equals half of eight and I agree with Sam, and, uh, Charlotte because, um if, if, uh, four is not, uh, eight equals half of four is not right because it's seven and a half, because half of like, eight is the whole and um, one number away from that is seven and plus a half would be seven and half.

Suran: I would agree with Ellie if she had added something else to her explanation, if she said one half of the amount that you have to divide by two.

Ellie: Um, well, I agree with Suran and, um, when Charlotte said, um, she thought that, um, it should be one-half of eight, um, instead of just plain one-half, I don't agree with her because not all of them are eight. Not all of the problems are eight.

Consider what mathematics these students seem to know or not know and what the teacher's role might be in leading them toward a more refined understanding of mathematics. Should the relationship be called, as Lev asserts, "eight minus a half of *eight*"? Or should it be what Ellie says: "eight minus *just plain one half*"? What difference does it make? What difference does it make to judgments of whether the teaching that occurs here is effective and responsible if the teacher legitimates one expression and not the other — or neither or both? What do these students know — and what do they need to learn — about mathematics, or, more particularly, about functions or fractions or subtraction, or about the conventions of mathematical language and symbols? How should the teacher teach them what they need to learn? How should the teacher respond to Sam's assertion that "good mathematicians" would say that eight minus a half was seven and a half, while he himself asserts that "it is important to know what the 'half' is meaning"? Or to Charlotte's certainty about the idea that "one-half's a fraction and it's half of one whole"? Or to Karim's assertion that "eight minus one-half is the same as . . . eight minus four"? It is a simple matter to say that a teacher of mathematics should teach these students in a way that is true to the discipline of mathematics. But what does that mean in practice, when the practice occurs in a contemporary schoolroom? What implications does the goal of *doing mathematics* in school have for designing the kinds of ethical and intellectual interactions that should occur between teacher and students?

Two Kinds of Practices

In constructing a pedagogy that takes seriously both the nature of school-work and the nature of work in mathematics, one moves back and forth between two kinds of practices: the practice of teaching in school and the practice of doing mathematics.

Teaching involves the teacher in communicating with learners about something that the teacher knows and the students are supposed to be learning. Doing mathematics involves both teacher and learner in thinking about quantitative relationships and making and evaluating mathematical assertions. What the teacher knows could be constructed as the "findings and conclusions" of a particular domain or as a familiarity with the kinds of activities that are considered legitimate generators of findings and conclusions in that domain (or both). The most familiar way to communicate findings and conclusions in classrooms is for teachers to tell them to students or to tell students to read books in which they are written down. In order to communicate with learners about what is entailed in doing an activity in a domain, teachers can engage them in doing the activity with them, they can show learners aspects of the activity and talk about it with them, and/or they can prepare a synoptic description of what they believe people need to know to do the activity, teach it to them, and then guide their attempts to do the activity themselves (see Cohen, forthcoming). Each of these approaches to communicating teachers' knowledge to students constitutes a pedagogy or set of activities and assumptions about how the activities of teaching produce some desired learning. Which pedagogy we choose expresses our assumptions about what knowledge is, how knowledge is represented, and how usable knowledge is acquired.

Teaching practice is related to the practice of doing mathematics (or any other intellectual activity) through the question of how knowledge is justified (Tymoscko, 1986). Teachers and students make one assertion after another during lessons. The question of what makes an assertion true or understood or accepted for use is central to both pedagogy and mathematics. In conventional teaching, what makes an assertion true is the teacher's authority. But if we think about what it means to know something in mathematics, we would not accept simply repeating what an authority said or what was written in a book as "knowledge," even of facts and principles.

This way of thinking does not give the teacher clear prescriptions for practice, however. In my fifth-grade class, when one of the students asserted that "eight minus a half" could be "four," I could have resolved the disagreement in the class by telling students that $8 - \frac{1}{2} = 7\frac{1}{2}$ is correct, according to mathematical convention. And so Ellie's phrase "minus a half" could not legitimately be used to describe the relationship between the x's and the y's. But because I wanted my students to learn something about why mathematics needs linguistic conventions in the first place, to make my teaching a responsible representation of authentic mathematics, I chose not to intervene in that way. Instead, I acted as a guide while the students argued among themselves about the correct linguistic formulation for the relationship. In order for authentic mathematics to be taught and learned here, the decision about whether it should be said one way or another should have a justification that was situated in mathematical conversation, not wholly dependent on the authority of the teacher. Because I wanted my students to practice mathematics in the classroom, I wanted to make it possible for them to wander around in the territory of fractions and ratios and functions and explore the connections among these ideas. But I was torn—like Sam, I also thought that a "good mathematician" would never say "eight minus a half is four," yet I wanted the rest of the class to know that Ellie had a legitimate point: the numbers in the y column could be obtained by taking away a half from each of the numbers in the x column. And that is what functions are all about. Being effective and responsible here does not have a simple meaning. There are multiple and conflicting possibilities for how a teacher might act.

One way to understand these kinds of dilemmas is to relate them to a continuum of justification (Figure 19.1), since we are talking about both individual and social constructions of knowledge. When we talk about "teach-

Figure 19.1. Continuum of Justification.

Convincing yourself	Convincing the people you work with regularly	Convincing strangers
Making sense of what you are told	Arguing about what is true with people who share your language and assumptions	Making a formal deductive argument
Inventing conjectures	Establishing the plausibility of an argument in a community of discourse	Presenting empirical evidence according to accepted procedures
Constructing personally meaningful links between elements	Constructing links between elements that can be communicated to others	Constructing a synoptic representation of the structure of a domain that stands for the domain itself
Insight, intuition, "seeing"		Writing a proof

PRIVATE ⟵—————————————⟶ PUBLIC

ing for understanding," we are talking about only the individual, private end of the continuum. But if an individual "knows" something that does not match what others (either in or out of the classroom) believe to be true, and knowledge becomes part of the public discourse as it does in the classroom, a social confrontation occurs that must be resolved one way or another. When we talk about "effective teaching," we are usually talking about only the most public end of the continuum, in which assertions can or cannot be mapped directly onto disciplinary conventions, and controversy is resolved by the teacher's interpretations of those conventions. But in the classroom, except under unusual circumstances, students talk to one another about what they think is true. This discourse can be truncated by the assertion of the teacher's authority, or it can be a genuine intellectual argument in which the community collaborates to establish its shared assumptions—an argument in which the teacher plays a role as a clarifier and supplier of information rather than a judge.

The dilemmas that I faced as a teacher in this situation are connected to an epistemological controversy within mathematics that has been expressed in various ways throughout history and has sometimes spilled over into the realm of mathematical pedagogy. An analysis of how knowledge has been considered and communicated within mathematics thus has the potential to enlighten the way in which one might think about effective and responsible mathematics teaching. Looking at mathematical practice will not provide us with right answers to questions about what constitutes good teaching, but it will help us to better understand the nature of pedagogical practice and its problems.

Knowing in and of Mathematics

In a recent exposition on the nature of knowledge in mathematics, Philip Kitcher (1984) sought to examine the links between how knowledge valued and used in the discipline grows and changes and how practice in the discipline proceeds. He identified five characteristics of mathematical practice that provide a useful framework both for thinking about how doing and knowing are related in the discipline and for generating some hypotheses about what learning authentic mathematics might look like in school. He argues that mathematical practice is distinguished from other practices by (1) the questions that are understood as meaningful and legitimate; (2) the methods of reasoning that are accepted as supporting conclusions; (3) the goals and structures of mathematical knowledge; (4) the language that is meaningful to practitioners; and (5) statements of findings and conclusions that are accepted and established. Several researchers and reformers in mathematics education (for example, Greeno, 1991; Romberg, 1983; Bell, 1979) have complained that school mathematics seems to attend only to the last of these five characteristics. These contemporary critiques of mathematics teaching echo earlier concerns within mathematics about how findings and conclusions in mathematics are to be learned by newcomers to the field.

There is a famous project in mathematical theory building associated with the name Bourbaki. Bourbaki is not a person but the pseudonym under which a group of French mathematicians wrote about mathematics (Cartan, 1980). In 1934, this group convened and decided to write a new university textbook that would capture the substantial changes in their field around the turn of the century, now known as "modern mathematics." They were concerned that the changes in mathematical practice that had caused what they were doing to be called "modern"—changes in how one might reason about mathematical questions and what counted as evidence in a mathematical argument—were not being reflected in the material taught to university students. In the process of producing their Éléments de mathématique, the Bourbaki group came to define what was meant by "axiomatics" and reified the nature of mathematical structures by formalizing the process of establishing abstract mathematical certainty. They came to be known as "formalists" because they identified the knowledge of mathematics with knowledge of its formal structures. The structures of logic made it possible to relate mathematical entities in formulas and to transform those formulas by following deductive rules. Thus, the process whereby new truths are generated and their legitimacy secured could be described in terms of an intellectually mechanical process; this process would decrease reliance on "insight" or "genius," thereby (the Bourbaki group assumed) making practice in the discipline available to a wider range of participants.

The Bourbaki group's purpose was pedagogical. In their project, so-called modern mathematics became a body of knowledge represented in books rather than a social institution with human beings involved cooperatively in the production, organization, and changing of knowledge. In the words of a member of the group, Henri Cartan, "While the members of Bourbaki considered it their duty to elaborate all of mathematics according to a new approach, they did this with the hope and expectation of putting into the hands of future mathematicians an instrument which would ease their work and enable them to make further advancements" (quoted in Steiner, 1988, p. 9). Their fundamental intention was communication: in order to teach others about mathematics, they assumed, it was appropriate to collect everything that was known and organize it into a coherent whole, making the connections among pieces of that whole logical and coherent. And why? Because they believed that the professors who were to teach modern mathematics to future mathematicians were not as gifted as the creators of these new ideas; that is, not everyone who wanted to learn about the findings and conclusions of modern mathematics could appreciate the intuitive connections among different ideas that led to new discoveries. As Jean Alexandre Dieudonné (another Bourbaki group member) commented,

> Communication between mathematicians by means of a common language *must* be maintained . . . and the transmission of knowledge cannot be left exclusively to geniuses. In most cases it will be entrusted to professors. . . . As most of them will not

be gifted with the exceptional "intuition" of the creators, the only way they can arrive at a reasonably good understanding of mathematics and pass it on to their students will be through a careful presentation of the material, in which definitions, hypotheses, and arguments are precise enough to avoid any misunderstanding, and possible fallacies and pitfalls are pointed out whenever the need arises. . . . It is this kind of expository writing that has been, I think, the goal of those mathematicians [called] "formalists" from Dedekind and Hilbert to Bourbaki and his successors [Steiner, 1988, p. 10].

What the Bourbaki authors were worried about was something like the knowledge base for teaching and the relationship between mathematical practice and mathematical communication and its relationship to pedagogy. These writers made a distinction between mathematics as it is known by practicing mathematicians (the ones with genius and intuitions) and mathematics as it is known by mathematics teachers (the ones who could understand what had been produced by those intuitions and communicate it to others). This distinction is rooted in the difficulties of communicating about a practice to those who are not yet or never will be a part of it, and it remains a problem for all of us as we try to understand the nature of effective and responsible teaching.

Within mathematical philosophy, there is much current writing that is critical of the images of mathematical knowledge and communication that the Bourbaki group perpetrated. But the tension between the dynamics of practice and the need to codify knowledge so that it can be passed on to novices did not begin with reactions to the Bourbaki group. Arguments about whether one should engage learners in messy and creative disciplinary activities as a method of teaching them about the discipline are at least as old as the foundations of university education in the sixteenth century. At this time, instruction began to move away from having novices engage in disciplinary discourse as a method of education and toward lecturers preparing and publishing synoptic representations of knowledge in their fields and delivering them to learners (Ong, 1958). Throughout history, questions about pedagogy — that is, questions about how to communicate what is known to the uninitiated — have been deeply tied to questions about the relationship between doing mathematics and the nature of the knowledge that results from the doing. Within the discipline, there have been many variations on how this relationship was conceived and sometimes raging controversies over it (Koerner, 1960; Davis, 1988; Kline, 1985; Tymoczko, 1986).

I want to review a bit of that history here because it suggests the many ways in which we might think about teaching and learning and knowing mathematics in classrooms. Until recently, the purpose of most philosophical scholarship focusing on mathematics was to conceptualize the nature of mathematical knowledge and to examine the characteristics of the formal language in which mathematical truths are asserted. The Platonists, who include not only the ancient Greeks but such contemporary and distinguished mathematicians as G. H. Hardy and Paul Erdos, believe that there is a definite, supernatural reality of mathematical objects and that the relationships that pertain among these objects determine the truth or falsity of any mathematical proposition. The practicing mathematician recognizes these relationships in the act of "mathematical intuition." These intuitions put knowers in touch with the world of mathematical objects and suggest the axioms, or basic assumptions, on which their logical arguments are based. Descartes, among others, broke with the idea that mathematical knowledge was derived from a kind of congruence between the mathematician's mind and "the mind of God" and posited that truth was obtained by correct reasoning alone. The Cartesians see mathematical truth as objective and believe that the individual mathematician knows it through the power of his or her own logic. In this view, axioms, or basic truths, are derived from fundamental principles of logic, and they can be known by anyone who has the capacity to reason logically.

Unfortunately, attempts to set down these principles by mathematicians such as Bertrand Russell, Gottlieb Frege, and Georg Cantor turned up some basic and irresolvable inconsistencies. So another way of thinking about what it means to know mathematics developed, in which it was asserted that mathematicians arbitrarily choose which first principles they will use and follow the rules of logic from there. With this development, what it meant to know mathematics became a mix of the individual and the social: knowledge was acquired by individuals through a process of reasoning from the axioms, but the axioms themselves were a set of assumptions that were agreed on by a given discourse community. This philosophy was too arbitrary for a group of Dutch mathematicians who practiced early in the twentieth century and called themselves "intuitionists": they asserted that the axioms were constructed by mathematicians out of intuitions derived from intellectual experience. They would not assert, as the Platonists did, that mathematical reality was there to be discovered; instead, they suggested that it is created by the act of thinking mathematically. (The intuitionists are considered a "fringe" group within mathematics, but I am continually struck with the parallels between their epistemology and some of the tenets of contemporary cognitive psychology.)

All of these ways of thinking about mathematical knowing focus on the powers of the mind of the individual mathematician. They all portray mathematical knowledge as infallible and atemporal, to the extent that the mathematician is able to think correctly about the mathematical reality. They focus more on what kind of knowledge mathematics is once it is known and on the rules of the language of mathematical representations than on the processes by which that knowledge came to be acquired and that language came to have meaning in the first place. The theme of relating intuition and reasoning that runs through all of these philosophies has undoubtedly influenced the development of the popular notion that "only geniuses can do mathematics," that doing it is something of a superhuman, antisocial endeavor. And that notion certainly influences how mathematics gets taught in school and how learners think about themselves in relation to the activity of doing mathematics (see Schoenfeld, 1985). When we think about connections between the discipline and the classroom, we need to think about these sorts of potential influences as well as the ones that currently seem more appealing.

More recently, and partly in reaction to the kind of epistemology perpetrated by the Bourbaki group, philosophers of mathematics have turned away from examining the conceptual and linguistic foundations of mathematics and have begun to try to understand more about the human social activities that are involved in producing and refining mathematical knowledge. Thus, within analyses of disciplinary knowledge, there are more and more analyses of both contemporary and historical mathematical practice. Contemporary criticisms of the equation of mathematical knowledge with mathematical formalisms focus on what of mathematics is lost when the discipline is presented in terms of finished, logical structures that can be clearly, if abstractly, communicated rather than in terms of dynamic processes for discovering and arriving at mathematical assertions. They contrast the messiness of the doing of mathematics with the polished, structured character of the form in which the results of the doing are communicated and complain that those who are not directly engaged in mathematical practice cannot appreciate what is involved in arriving at the formal structures.

Those who would challenge the formalist view of mathematical truth and the Bourbaki writers' "deductivist" approach to mathematical communication assert that the practice of mathematics is ill structured; that is, that the search for truth in this discipline is as much an attempt to make fallible and tentative sense out of a tangled web as it is in other human scholarship. Steiner (1988) calls the counterpoint to the deductivist approach "analytic-genetic" and goes back to Diderot's *Encyclopédie* for a definition: "Analysis consists in returning to the origin of our ideas, developing their order, decomposing and composing them in a variety of ways, comparing them from all points of view and making apparent their mutual interrelations. . . . In searching for truth, it does not make use of general theorems, rather it operates like a kind of 'calculus' by decomposing and composing knowledge and comparing this with intended discoveries" (translation of Steiner, 1988, p. 10).

Steiner has also uncovered French mathematics textbooks from the eighteenth century that advocate the approach to mathematical knowledge embraced in the *Encyclopédie*. Alexis Clairaut, for example, rejects the classical "theorem-proof" presentation that we are all familiar with from studying plane geometry and asserts, in the preface to his text on geometry,

> If the first originators of mathematics presented their discoveries by using the 'theorem-proof' pattern, then doubtlessly they did this in order to give their work an excellent shape or to avoid

the hardship of reproducing the train of thought they followed in their own investigations. Be that as it may, to me it looked much more appropriate to keep my readers continuously involved with solving problems, i.e., with searching for means to apply some operation or discover some unknown truth by determining a relation between entities being given and those unknown and to be found. In this way, with every step they take, beginners learn to know the motive of the inventor; and thereby they can more easily acquire the essence of discovery [translation in Steiner, 1988, p. 12].

Clairaut's emphasis here is on the genesis of knowledge and the flexible and dynamic process of linking ideas that supports it. In using ideas, the mathematician does not structure them in the same formal way that they would be structured for communication. In the process of the mathematician's learning something new, process and content are inextricably linked. From a pedagogical point of view, it is notable that Clairaut recognizes the potential "hardship" involved in following another's train of thought, even as he advocates that teaching and learning should attend to that process. (The metaphor of a "train" that Clairaut [or perhaps Steiner in translating Clairaut] uses here seems somewhat inconsistent with Clairaut's purposes; that is, the inventor's thoughts might not be as linearly organized as a "train" but might be organized more like a web or a traffic jam at the Place de la Concorde.)

Along the same lines, Imre Lakatos more recently criticized the form that was assumed to communicate mathematical reasoning to students in textbooks. I quote at some length here from his diatribe because of the information he gives us about the alternative to the synoptic presentation of results:

Euclidean methodology has developed a certain obligatory style of presentation. I shall refer to this as "deductivist style." This style starts with a painstakingly stated list of *axioms, lemmas,* and/or *definitions.* The axioms and definitions frequently look artificial and mystifyingly complicated. One is never told how these complications arose. The list of axioms and definitions is followed by carefully worded *theorems.* These are loaded with heavy-going conditions; it seems impossible that anyone should ever have guessed them. The theorem is followed by the *proof.*

The student of mathematics is obliged, according to the Euclidean ritual, to attend to this conjuring act without asking questions either about the background or about how this sleight-of-hand is performed. If the student by chance discovers that some of the unseemly definitions are proof generated, if he simply wonders how these definitions, lemmas, and the theorem can possibly precede the proof, the conjurer will ostracize him for this display of mathematical immaturity.

> Deductivist style hides the struggle, hides the adventure.
> The whole story vanishes, the successive tentative formulations
> of the theorem in the course of the proof-generated definitions
> of their "proof ancestors," presents them out of the blue, in an
> artificial and authoritarian way [Lakatos, 1976, pp. 142, 144].

When Lakatos speaks of axioms and definitions being "proof generated,"
what he means is that the mathematician figures out what he or she is talking about in the process of trying to talk about it, not beforehand by some
magical intuition. Setting out to prove something, the practitioner sees that
the original terms of the argument were unclear and usually even changes
what it was that was being asserted in the first place. The activity of developing a proof is not the straightforward series of logical steps that are
portrayed to support assertions in textbooks but a "zigzag path" between con-
jectures and refutations. And the zigzag has much to do with trying to create
a plausible argument and communicate it at the same time. The distinguished
contemporary mathematician Henry Pollack talks about the importance in
his own education of being exposed to what he calls "cross-country mathematics"; in contrast to a well-marked path, the cross-country terrain is jagged
and uncertain. Pollack said of his teacher, Ed Begle:

> As a student, I had a very interesting time watching him strug-
> gle, inventing proofs and trying to think about the right way
> to do it. I learned a lot more mathematics that way than I might
> have if it had been a perfectly polished lecture and I think al-
> ready at that time I developed my feeling that I like cross-country
> mathematics. Mathematics, as we teach it, is too often like walk-
> ing on a path that is carefully laid out through the woods; it
> never comes up against any cliffs or thickets; it is all nice and
> easy [quoted in Albers and Alexanderson, 1985, p. 231].

In deductive syntheses of mathematical discoveries, what is learned
from practice is separated from learning *about* practice. The syntheses also
exclude disciplinary conversation from the epistemological picture. Recent
studies (Polya, 1954; Davis and Hersch, 1981; Wang, 1986; Hersch, 1985;
Thom, 1985) emphasize the fact that when a mathematician makes an assertion that is assumed to be plausible, he or she is trying to convince some
audience that it is plausible. What it takes to do that, in any particular instance of mathematical practice, is not the functional equivalent of a formal
deductive proof—such a proof would put a stop to the conversation and impede rather than further the process of discovery.

School Learners Doing Mathematics: What Is Effective and Responsible Teaching?

If teaching means that the teacher has some knowledge and students are
supposed to acquire some knowledge that they did not previously have, one

way to construe pedagogical practice is the way the Bourbaki writers (and many other curriculum developers) have done: as the logical presentation of well-formulated ideas. But as Lakatos complained, although such formal presentations are clearer and easier to communicate than the adventure of practice, they hide some essential aspect of what needs to be appreciated by learners: "What kind of knowledge is it that I am getting here, anyway?"

What I have taken into my fifth-grade classroom from these arguments in mathematical epistemology is the idea that the questions of where mathematical knowledge comes from and what makes it true ought to be an explicit part of the agenda. This means that we do not proceed as if whatever the teacher says, or whatever is in the book, is what is assumed to be true. It also means that lessons must be structured to pursue the mathematical questions that have meaning for students in the context of the problems that they are trying to solve. And this means that lessons are more like messy conversations than like synoptic logical presentations of conclusions.

I began the discussion of the table of relationships referred to at the beginning of this chapter with a question to the class. I said that the relationship in this table was a function and that it "did something" to the values on the left to obtain the values on the right, and I asked, "What did it do to the numbers in every case?" Ellie was one of the first to raise her hand, and she made an assertion: "Um, well, there are a whole bunch of rules you could use." After she stated one of those rules, "divided by two," I tested it out to see whether it indeed related each of the ordered pairs. I did not explicitly judge Ellie to be correct or incorrect, but I modeled a process whereby the truth of such an assertion would be assessed within mathematics. No one in the class challenged either me or Ellie at that point. Then Ellie asserted a second rule that could define the relationship among the same set of ordered pairs: "You could do minus one half." When she said that, several students gasped and began bidding for attention. Again, I did not judge Ellie's assertion to be correct or incorrect but began to test it against the ordered pairs in the exercise. Using her own language, I asked, "What would eight minus one half be?" When she answered "four," a gasp again went up from the class, and students' bids for the right to speak became even more aggressive.

In this situation, I took it as my responsibility to protect Ellie's right to practice mathematics by monitoring the discourse so that she would have the opportunity to explain her thinking and justify her assertion. Before calling on any of the students who were eager to argue with Ellie, I set the terms of the conversation: you can express an idea that is different from Ellie's, but you also need to make an attempt to take her position seriously. In mathematics, the legitimacy of an assertion cannot be judged without considering the assumptions and the reasoning that are supplied to justify the assertion. In the course of trying to prove that "eight minus one half is four" or the counterassertion that "eight minus one half is seven and one-half," the students and I together became clearer about the assumptions and definitions that underlay our assertions. My role was to participate in the conversation, raising questions when the terms were not clear and making it safe for students to raise questions about assertions made by their peers.

Ellie's assertion that the rule could be either "divide by two" or "minus one half" might be thought of as the result of a mathematical intuition. She "saw" both relationships in the set of ordered pairs that had been given in the exercise. In more formal terms, we might say that Ellie made a *conjecture* that each of two different mathematical operations would have the same effect on a given set of independent variables. Conjecturing about such relationships is at the heart of mathematical practice. Once a conjecture is made, the practitioner sets out to prove it and in doing so becomes clearer about the assumptions that led to the conjecture in the first place. The precision of mathematical language develops out of the process of seeking clearer and clearer assertions for which deductive proofs can be produced. Here the teacher's role is to legitimate the process, to accept mathematical intuitions, half-formed as they may be, as an essential part of the lesson.

Ellie and her classmates were embarking on the adventure of "cross-country mathematics" about which Pollack, Lakatos, and Polya write so eloquently. More particularly, they were doing what Polya, in his exposition on *Patterns of Plausible Inference,* calls "Examining a Possible Ground" to ascertain the plausibility of a proposition. As he begins this section of his book on the practice of generating knowledge in mathematics, Polya quotes Descartes: *"When we have intuitively understood some simple propositions . . . it is useful to go through them with a continuous, uninterrupted motion of thought, to meditate upon their mutual relations, and to conceive distinctly several of them, as many as possible, simultaneously. In this manner, our knowledge will grow more certain, and the capacity of the mind will notably increase"* (Polya, 1954, vol. 2, p. 18; italics in the original).

The process that Polya describes here is what Steiner (1988), following Jean Le Rond d'Alembert, calls "analysis": Ellie and the rest of the class were composing and decomposing ideas — about subtraction and fractions and functions — and making apparent their mutual interrelationships. For several turns in the discussion after Ellie's conjecture (and her assertion that it implied "eight minus one half is four"), the question of concern was whether "eight minus one half" should be "four" or "seven and one-half." The disposition of these assertions would determine whether Ellie's conjecture that "divide by two" and "minus one-half" are equivalent function rules should stand as true or be judged false. Judgments about the effectiveness of this kind of teaching, to use Polya's terms, need to be related to whether students have the opportunity to go through their mathematical ideas in a "continuous uninterrupted motion of thought" (Polya, 1954, p. 18). If the questions that are important to them in the discussion are questions that would also be considered mathematically important, they could be said to be engaged in mathematical practice, as defined by Kitcher (1984) and others.

Part of the problem in the discussion had to do with language; Ellie's conjecture was not stated very clearly, and so much of the talk was an attempt to say what she might have been meaning and to formulate it in more explicit terms. Lakatos (1976) gives a great deal of attention to this aspect of mathematical practice, as does Kitcher (1984). Both are concerned about the way in which mathematical terms come to have meaning in a discourse and how the resultant meaning affects the community's judgment about the verity of the proposition.

The underlying issue of concern to my students was how to interpret the meaning of "minus one-half": did "one-half" as it was being used here mean "half of one," or did it mean "half of the original number, whatever that number might be"? Several of the students who spoke said that you could look at it either way. But their acceptance of either point of view was not simple relativism, nor was it merely a social routine to avoid embarrassing a peer. They all spoke about *the conditions under which* one or the other assertion could be considered true. In my contribution to the discussion, I supported this method of reasoning. In response to Sam's challenge to Ellie, for example, I said, "You know when Charlotte was talking she said that she thought one-half meant half of a whole. And it sounds like that's the way you are interpreting it. But Ellie might be interpreting one-half to mean something else." I pointed out that the question of how we define "the unit" is important when we are talking about fractions and said, "We have to have some kind of agreement here if it's a fraction of eight or if it's a fraction of a whole"; I said that "it would be important to clarify" which of these interpretations we were using when we judged Ellie's original conjecture to be true or false. Although I did not strictly impose it on the class, I introduced the idea that it was convention to interpret the symbol $\frac{1}{2}$ as "half of one whole" in situations "when we just talk about numbers and we don't associate them with any objects or groups of objects." I also reformulated what Ellie was asserting in more precise mathematical language and tested out with her whether what I said was equivalent to the assertion that she had been trying to make. By the end of the lesson, we had collaboratively constructed a conjecture that she could live with and that other members of the class agreed was true. Ellie and the other members of the discussion came to address the importance of distinguishing between how things work in the domain of functions — where, as Ellie reminds us, "they are not all eight" — and the domain of arithmetic, where relationships and procedures determine specific ordered pairs (that is, once *eight* is assumed as the input, the operation determines whether the output will be seven and a half or four).

Problems of Doing Authentic Mathematics in School

If we are willing to think of this as "authentic mathematics," what problems does doing it in school raise for the teacher? And what kinds of pedagogical practices might be invented to support this kind of activity in school? I only briefly mention these questions here as markers for work in progress (see also Ball, 1990).

One problem is how we think about the relationship between individual understanding and the public justification of knowledge. Within mathematics and in the classroom, it probably makes sense to think in terms of a continuum and to consider every act of "knowing" as occurring somewhere on this continuum. The activities that I am calling "authentic mathematics" occur in a discourse community, but it is a community made up of individual learners who will go their separate ways with whatever knowledge they have acquired. Teaching and learning need to take account both of what is accomplished by individuals and what is understood to be "true" within the classroom discourse.

A second problem has to do with communication. Classroom discourse in "authentic mathematics" has to bounce back and forth between being authentic (that is, meaningful and important) to the immediate participants and being authentic in its reflection of a wider mathematical culture. The teacher needs to live in both worlds, in a sense belonging to neither but being an ambassador from one to the other.

A third problem has to do with establishing a culture of inquiry. This endeavor, too, is paradoxical, because school is supposed to be about learning to be a competent adult in our society. But as things now stand, not very many "competent" adults would appreciate the kind of mathematical discourse that occurs in my classroom, let alone be able to participate in it themselves. So the classroom here is a world apart, while at the same time perhaps reflecting some of the ideals that we publicly embrace.

A fourth problem has to do with the messiness of it all. Synoptic presentations of findings and conclusions based on chains of formal deductive argument would be easier and more efficient, as the Bourbaki writers believed, and would not rely so heavily on the teacher's capacity to move with the flow, supplying new tools and information as they are called for in the problem-posing and problem-solving process rather than as a series of neat packages of information. The extent to which the practice of mathematics in school lessons can mirror what is most exciting and admirable in the practice of mathematics in the discipline will depend on whether teaching practice can proceed in a way that takes these problems seriously.

References

Albers, D. J., and Alexanderson, G. L. *Mathematical People.* Boston: Birkhauser, 1985.

Ball, D. L. "With an Eye on the Mathematical Horizon: Dilemmas of Teaching Elementary School Mathematics." Paper delivered at the annual meeting of the American Educational Research Association, Boston, 1990.

Bell, A. W. "The Learning of Process Aspects of Mathematics." *Educational Studies in Mathematics,* 1979, *10,* 361–387.

Cartan, H. "Nicholas Bourbaki and Contemporary Mathematics." *Mathematical Intelligencer,* 1980, *2,* 175–180.

Cohen, D. *Teaching: Practice and Its Predicaments.* Forthcoming.

Davis, P. "Mathematics as a Social Contract." *Mathematics Magazine,* 1988, *61* (3), 139–147.

Davis, P., and Hersch, R. *The Mathematical Experience.* Boston: Houghton Mifflin, 1981.

Greeno, J. "Number Sense as Situated Knowing in a Conceptual Domain." *Journal for Research on Mathematics Education,* 1991, *22,* 170–218.

Hersch, R. "Some Proposals for Reviving the Philosophy of Mathematics." In T. Tymoscko (ed.), *New Directions in the Philosophy of Mathematics.* Boston: Birkhauser, 1985.

Kitcher, P. *The Nature of Mathematical Knowledge.* Oxford, England: Oxford University Press, 1984.

Kline, M. *Mathematics and the Search for Knowledge.* New York: Oxford University Press, 1985.

Koerner, S. *The Philosophy of Mathematics: An Introduction.* New York: HarperCollins, 1960.

Lakatos, I. *Proofs and Refutations.* Cambridge, England: Cambridge University Press, 1976.

Ong, W. *Ramus, Method, and the Decay of Dialog.* Cambridge, Mass.: Harvard University Press, 1958.

Polya, G. *Mathematics and Plausible Reasoning.* Vols. 1 and 2. Princeton, N.J.: Princeton University Press, 1954.

Romberg, T. A. "A Common Curriculum for Mathematics." In G. D. Fenstermacher and J. I. Goodlad (eds.), *Individual Differences and the Common Curriculum.* Chicago: National Society for the Study of Education, 1983.

Schoenfeld, A. H. *Mathematical Problem Solving.* San Diego, Calif.: Academic Press, 1985.

Steiner, H.-G. "Two Kinds of Elements and the Dialectic Between Synthetico-Deductive and Analytic-Genetic Approaches in Mathematics." *For the Learning of Mathematics,* 1988, *8* (3), 7–15.

Thom, R. "'Modern' Mathematics: An Educational and Philosophic Error?" In T. Tymoscko (ed.), *New Directions in the Philosophy of Mathematics.* Boston: Birkhauser, 1985.

Tymoscko, T. "Making Room for Mathematicians in the Philosophy of Mathematics." *Mathematical Intelligencer,* 1986, *8,* 44–50.

Wang, H. "Theory and Practice in Mathematics." In T. Tymoscko (ed.), *New Directions in the Philosophy of Mathematics.* Boston: Birkhauser, 1986.

Appendix 19.1
Transcript of Large Group Discussion

Lampert: But let's look at this one. This is number 6. As I was walking around and I asked people which ones they thought were hard or easy and which ones they had to revise their thinking on and so on. . . . In number 6 the function machine takes 8 and it gives out 4. If it takes in 4, it gives out 2. If it takes in 2, it gives out 1. If it takes in 0, it gives out 0. What does it do to the numbers in every case? Ellie?

Ellie: Um, well, there were a whole bunch of . . . a whole bunch of rules you could use, use, um, divided by two. . . .

Lampert: Okay, so one rule you think could be divided by two. You could try eight divided by two is four, four divided by two is two, two divided by two is one, zero divided by two is zero?

Ellie: And you could do, um, minus one half. [Several hands go up around the class and students talk privately to one another.]

Lampert: Minus one half?

Ellie: Um. . . .

Lampert: Okay. What would eight minus one half be?

Ellie: Four. [More hands go up, more talking.]

Lampert: Eight minus one half. [Pause]

Ellie: Um, four.

Lampert: You think that would be four? What does somebody else think? I started raising a question because a number of people have a different idea about that. So let's hear what your different ideas are and see if you can take Ellie's position into consideration and try to let her know what your position is. Karim?

Karim: Well, see, I agree with Ellie because you can have eight minus one half and that's the same as eight divided by two or eight minus four.

Lampert: Eight divided by two is four, eight minus four is four? Okay, so Karim thinks he can do all of those things to eight and get four. Okay? Charlotte?

Charlotte: Um, I think eight minus one half is seven and a half because . . .

Lampert: Why?

Charlotte: Um, one half's a fraction and it's half of one whole and so when you subtract you aren't even subtracting one whole number so you can't get even a smaller number that's more than one whole. But I see what Ellie's doing, she's taking half the number she started with and getting the answer.

Lampert: So, you would say one half of eight? Is that what you mean?

Charlotte: Yeah, one half of eight equals four.

Lampert: How do you know that?

Charlotte: Because, um, eight and one half is, um, eight and half of eight is four, so if you have two groups of four you would, is eight.

Lampert: Ellie, what do you think?

Ellie: Um, I still think, I mean, one half, it would be eight minus one half, they would probably say oh, eight minus one half equals four.

Lampert: Who would say that?

Ellie: I don't know. Well, well if if I saw something like that, like if we were having something and the answer was missing . . . .

312

Lampert: Um-hmm.

Ellie: Um, and it was eight minus one half I would probably say four.

Lampert: What do other people think? Sam?

Sam: Um, I agree with Charlotte and, um, I don't agree with Ellie. Because, um, like one half is not even one, so if, so when Ellie said that people, that people would like, um, a really good mathematician would probably, like, would probably write seven and a half, not four because they would have to know what the one half was meaning, half of a number to, um, to understand it.

Lampert: You know when Charlotte was talking she said that she thought one half meant half of a whole. And it sounds like that's the way you are interpreting it. But Ellie might be interpreting one half to mean something else. Lev, what do you think?

Lev: I think, um, I would agree with Ellie if she had said eight minus one half of eight, because half of eight would be four because four plus four would be eight.

Lampert: So, in your case, you're saying one half, if Ellie meant one half was half of eight wholes, then it would work. Okay, Tyrone?

Tyrone: I agree with Charlotte and Sam and I disagree with Ellie and, like I think Ellie meant, like, because four is half of eight, like one half would be a half, but, and I agree with Lev when he said if she means one half, uh, equals, wait, eight, equals half of eight and I agree with Sam and, uh, Charlotte because, um, if . . . if, uh, four is not, uh . . . eight equals half of four is not right because it's seven and a half because half of like, eight is the whole and, um, one number away from that is seven and plus a half would be seven and half.

Lampert: Uh huh. So um, that reminds me of some of the discussion that we were having yesterday, which is that if you, if you use addition, it helps you to understand what it means to take away something on the other side. Okay? Let's hear from Suran.

Suran: I would agree with Ellie if she had added something else to her explanation, if she said one half of the amount that you have to divide by two.

Lampert: Okay. You guys are on to something really important about fractions, which is that a fraction is a fraction of something. And we have to have some kind of agreement here if, if it's a fraction of eight or if it's a fraction of a whole. Let's, let's just hear from a couple more people, Ellie, and then I'll come back and hear from you, okay? Uh, Mina?

Mina: Well, I think, um, I disagree with Ellie because if she means that one half of the whole you would get seven and then if you add that half on again you would get seven and a half.

Lampert: Okay. Well, that's quite similar to what Tyrone was saying, that addition is a way of helping me think about the meaning of subtraction. But again, both you and Tyrone are assuming that one half means one of one. Okay? Alexander.

Alexander: [Inaudible] . . . if you are assuming it is one half of the original number it would be different than if it is half of a whole. So it depends on what your point of view is.

Lampert: Right. And that, that would be very important to clarity. Okay. Ellie, what do you think?

Ellie: Um, well, I agree with Suran and . . . when Charlotte said she thought that it should be one half of eight . . . um . . . instead of just plain one half, I don't agree with her because not all of them are eight. Not all of the problems are eight.

Lampert: Okay. Let's . . . one of the things that is kind of a convention in mathematics is that when we just talk about numbers and we don't associate them with any objects or groups of objects, that this symbol means half of one whole. So if, if you were gonna communicate with the rest of the world who uses mathematics, they would take this to mean eight wholes minus one half of a whole. Okay? Ellie?

Ellie: Um, well, I . . . I think that eight if, you had, all you . . . all these numbers are that are going into the, um . . .

Lampert: Function machine.

Ellie: Um, on number six, they're all, they can all be divided into halves and four minus . . . well, two is one half of four.

Lampert: Okay, so the number that comes out is one half of the number that went in. Okay. And in this case is that true?

Ellie: Um . . .

Lampert: Is one one half of two? Is zero one half of zero?

Ellie: Um, yes.

Lampert: So, what do you think about that? We could write this in words, you know, we don't have to use these equations, but it's more efficient. You, you feel that . . .

Ellie: One half is . . .

Lampert: . . . if, if you said that the number that comes out is half the number that goes in it, it would be easier for you to understand?

Ellie: That's what I meant but I just couldn't put it in there, but that's what was in my mind.

Lampert: Okay. But I think you raised a lot of interesting questions by your idea of taking away a half. Okay? Alexander?

Alexander: Um, what Charlotte meant was that a half of the original number so, the original number was eight and so half of eight is four. So, if it was a different number, you would use a different number.

20

The Relevance of Content for Teaching-Learning Processes

Frank Achtenhagen

Lee Shulman (1986b, p. 6) once used a striking formulation for schooling in the United States: "Investigators ignored one central aspect of classroom life: the subject matter." This formulation aptly applies to the type of investigators who are exclusively psychologists: they neglect — and this is my hypothesis — the dimension of subject matter or content when researching teaching-learning processes. This statement can be verified both in the United States and in Europe. We observe in both cases the fact that psychologically run research on teaching-learning processes concentrates primarily on behavior and neglects the content dimension.

In Europe, we have a tradition of thinking on teaching-learning problems that falls under the heading *didactics*. This term has its origin in the ancient Greek *didaskein*, which means "to teach." The Greek poet Hesiod in about 700 B.C. used a style called "didactic" in his poems and ballads describing agriculture, daily life, deities, and other topics central to Greek life at that time. This meaning of *didactic* remained unchanged until the seventeenth century. In 1632, the Moravian theologian Comenius wrote his *Didactica magna;* this was followed in 1653 by his *Orbis sensualium pictus*. Both, but especially the latter, were written with a strong emphasis on the dimension of content.

As it is applied today, the didactic approach is burdened by three serious problems: (1) It is more analytical than constructive, with more emphasis on criticism than on better alternatives. (2) It focuses too much on lessons given for the purpose of examinations. This leads didacticians to think in terms of intervals of forty-five or sixty minutes, not of spans of months or years or even of lifelong learning. (3) It neglects the processes of teaching and learning, since it is focused on very small products (the lesson orientation) and not on the development of knowledge and behavior over time, with its prerequisites, results, and zones of proximal development.

If we consider the psychological and the didactic orientations together, we find a very interesting phenomenon: didactics concentrates on content and neglects the behavior of teachers and students, while educational psychology focuses on behavior and neglects the content dimension. In addition, didacticians emphasize content but neglect its transformation into knowledge, while psychologists focus on knowledge as a part or requirement of behavior but neglect the weight and importance of content per se.

This gap is related to the lack of generalizable results of research on teaching-learning processes (for example, Shulman, 1986a; Brophy, 1979; Achtenhagen, 1990b). It also militates against effectiveness and responsibility in teaching and their integration. Below I outline dimensions of the relevance of content or subject matter for teaching-learning processes.

Aspects of Content

Different aspects of the content problem are easily distinguishable. There are several—in part overlapping—that are relevant to the discussion here. First, at a primary level, content is what defines the central relationship between school and life. Content is the major purpose of schooling—a fact that is emphasized by curriculum theory but often underestimated in teaching-learning research. How this connection is defined usually depends on the subject and on the type of teacher education. Second, content appears at different stages and in different modes of representation. For example, it can appear as a natural setting, as a medium, as a book, or as an oral statement by teachers. Third, there are different stages of transformation of content. Shulman (1986b, p. 9) defined three categories of content knowledge: subject matter content knowledge, pedagogical content knowledge, and curricular knowledge. This concept has been extended by other writers (Shulman, 1987; Wilson, Shulman, and Richert, 1987), as well as receiving criticism (McEwan and Bull, 1991). In any case, the distinctions are useful: knowledge is regarded as the "subjective" aspect of subject matter and content as the "objective." This allows us to make these categories more explicit:

- Content per se (represented by situations)
- Content in its diverse disciplinary structures
- Content as represented by media (including the author's goal system)
- Content as part of the knowledge of the individual teacher
- Content as part of the prior knowledge of the individual student and as the goal of the teaching-learning process
- Content as part of the examination system
- Content as part of the cognitive structure of school examiners
- Content as part of the cognitive structure of parents and the public

There is no integrative structure for these categories. They can be incompatible; sometimes content structures are hidden by teachers, examiners, or the examination system to preserve a real or an imaginary advantage in the possession of content knowledge. An example of this occurred during my own time as a teacher. A very new book came onto the market with illuminating and useful sketches and diagrams. It is clear that teachers need diagrams to structure their lessons. However, in this case, the teachers refused to introduce the new book in order to preserve their advantage over the students in the possession of new structures of content knowledge and to appear creative. The book was secretly circulated only among the children and relatives of the teachers. This situation continued for about four years until the book was finally introduced as a textbook. Why should the students not have had the same opportunity to be confronted with new content as the teachers? Why must there be a difference between teachers' and students' modes of learning?

Fourth, content should be a central medium within research processes. In Dörner's study of problem solving (Dörner, Kreuzig, Reither, Staeudel, 1983), it is clear that many problems with the interpretation of the study's results and their correlation with such variables as measures of intelligence were caused by the researchers' failure to realize that three different types of content had been embedded in the project: the content modeled by the researchers, the content in the interpretation of the experimenters, and the content in the interpretation of the problem solvers. I have seen similar problems with the interpretation of results in other studies in the field of problem solving where these three different aspects of content were not controlled by the researchers (Achtenhagen, 1990a). To avoid such problems, teaching-learning research has tended to choose physics and mathematics as its main content areas. But research on the expert-novice paradigm shows that the "content" of physics also varies: confronted with the same problems, experts observe, interpret, and handle content structures differently from the ways in which novices do. Similar statements can be made about the field of mathematics. Thus, what is understood as "content" depends on a person's degree of expertise in the specific field. "Content" is defined by highly individualized and specified understanding of that specific content and its structure and, therefore, has to be defined with regard to specific situations with all their syntactic, semantic, and pragmatic components.

A last dimension that I would like to mention here is the connection between educational goals and content (the main point of German didactic models). Is it possible for content to be discussed in a neutral way? Or does content change in relation to specific goals, questions, and perspectives? For example, a nuclear power plant may be defined by some people as a means for generating electricity and by others as a risk to the neighborhood. Here is where the interrelationship between pedagogical effectiveness and responsibility rules the structure of didactic argumentation and action. It is also here that morality, ecology, and ethics enter the didactic discourse. Failure to address these issues limits students' possibilities for learning.

Intended and Unintended Effects of
Content in Teaching-Learning Processes

In this part of the chapter, I present some research data to illustrate my issues. I start with a relatively old study to demonstrate that the content problem well known in Europe also appeared very early in the United States.

In 1966, Bellack, Kliebard, Hyman, and Smith (1966) published a study titled *The Language of the Classroom*. In this investigation of classroom discourse, the verbal actions of teachers and students in fifteen classrooms were classified into categories of pedagogical moves such as "structuring," "soliciting," "responding," and "reacting." The researchers chose to limit the content of the processes in the classrooms investigated to the first four chapters of a pamphlet on international economic problems. They furnished the teachers with copies of the pamphlet and teacher's guides to it and asked them to base their instruction during the experimental period on the content of the pamphlet.

Bellack and colleagues made two observations that are of special interest here. First, the patterns of pedagogical moves remained relatively stable over time. (It should be noted that these moves were measured without relation to a special dimension of content.) Second, "Although teachers were urged to teach in any way they chose, they were unequivocally directed and limited in the subject matter to be covered during the experimental class sessions. In view of these limitations, it is remarkable that, of all the categories of analysis, the data for the substantive meanings covered in the classroom reveal the greatest variability among teachers. While teachers structured, solicited, and reacted for about the same proportion . . . in every classroom, they showed marked differences in the substantive material covered in the class sessions" (Bellack, Kliebard, Hyman, and Smith, 1966, pp. 63, 68).

In other words, the teachers did not cover the main content aspects in the same way. Why was this so? I see five points that were not considered when the research was planned: (1) The teachers and students were given no reason to feel that the chosen pamphlet should have importance for them. (2) The content was represented by a pamphlet written in accordance with the specific goals of the author. (3) The teachers and students had different levels of knowledge and different interests. (4) The subject matter was not systematically taken into account during the research process. (5) There was no effort to achieve an adequate understanding of the underlying goals of the author. This example strengthens the argument that content is one of the most important variables in teaching-learning processes and demonstrates that there are effects of teaching content within one subject. A study by Stodolsky (1988) has shown the effects of teaching content for different subjects.

In a long-term study on teaching English to German students, my colleagues and I undertook to examine some of the effects of content in more detail (Wienold and others, 1985; Achtenhagen, 1990b). Our study included six classes in three different school grades. The classes were in two separate schools and used three different textbooks. We observed twenty-three forty-five-minute lessons (about six to eight weeks of instruction for German beginners with English). All of the lessons observed were videotaped and subsequently transcribed. (We also gathered data through questionnaires, tests, and biographical surveys.) In cooperation with some linguists, we developed a linguistic model (SYNTAKO) that allowed us to describe the syntactic rules underlying each sentence spoken in the classroom by the teacher and the students (Achtenhagen and Wienold, 1975). The SYNTAKO rules interpreted the sentences as content units and then measured their quality and quantity, showing how many content units were used by the teacher and how many content units were assigned to an individual student. After the second lesson, teachers were also asked to assign ratings to each of their students, thus giving an indication of their perception of a student's ability and effort.

The results of this study were astonishing: we found huge differences among the various classes. For example, in one class, the active use of SYNTAKO rules showed a variation of 400 percent between the student with the maximum and the student with the minimum of rules. When the teacher of this class assigned SYNTAKO rules to individual students, there was a range of about 500 percent. These differences led us to ask two questions: (1) Is there a relationship between classroom activities and learning outcomes or even grades (the problem of effectiveness)? (2) What amount of content is necessary for each student to get a fair chance to learn from the classroom activities (the problem of responsibility)? Since we had a description of the content units available for comparison, we could also correlate this variable with others, such as students' biographical data and their verbal and nonverbal classroom behavior (Wienold and others, 1985).

For this investigation, we put together sixteen variables from different data blocks, including input variables (students' gender, socioeconomic status, language proficiency, anxiety, and aversion to school); teachers' judgments of students' grammatical performance, general ability, effort, and oral performance; students' judgments of their own grammatical performance, oral performance, and classroom interaction; content units (sum of SYNTAKO rules produced by the teacher, sum of SYNTAKO rules produced by the students); teachers' classroom behavior (correction and exercise behavior, interactional standard behavior, spatial behavior); and output variables (criterion-oriented test, grade in English).

In order to investigate the effect of content on learning processes, we operationalized Brophy and Good's (1974) hypothesis about the behavior of the "overreactive teacher" — "the one most susceptible to negative expectation effects. He not only allows himself to be conditioned by individual differences in students; he exacerbates these differences by developing extreme and stereotyped expectations and by treating the students as even more different than they really are, thus increasing the differences from what they were originally" (pp. 121–122).

Twenty-five percent of the teachers in our research project showed overreactive behavior. We expected no significant correlations between these teachers' classroom processes, especially teaching and learning content units, and learning outcomes. When we counted the correlations, we found data fell into two types: process-related variables, which are dominated by the teacher's judgments of student effort and oral performance, and output variables, which are dependent on the teacher's judgments of the students' grammatical performance and general ability. It is interesting to note that we found no significant correlation between classroom activities and the effects measured by tests or grades. The results of the teaching-learning processes governed by an overreactive teacher, thus, cannot be clearly related to the teaching-learning processes themselves. The processes do not compensate for the initial differences and judgments.

The judgments on ability, however, correlated with the effects of instruction, and the judgments on effort correlated with instructional behavior. This seems to me a very good visualization of the assumptions underlying the behavior of the "overreactive teacher." In terms of responsibility and effectiveness, we can say that this type of teacher is not equally responsible toward all students. This type of teacher's effectiveness is also biased: while this teacher behavior is very effective with regard to grades (in a positive way for the students who were judged high, in a negative way for the students who were judged low), it seems to be less effective with regard to the mastering of content; the results of the criterion-oriented test are not significantly correlated with the content dimension and not highly correlated with grades. When the teachers' judgments after the second lesson were correlated with behavior, the content units within classroom processes did not show any statistically significant correlation with the achievement measured by a test and by grades. For "proactive teachers," in contrast, we found a close correlation between classroom activities and learning outcomes in their classroom management.

As did Bellack, Kliebard, Hyman, and Smith (1966), we found that the pedagogical moves of the teachers were very stable and consistent over classrooms and time. Therefore, it seems clear that the content dimension must be controlled by valid and reliable descriptions if the process-product variations of teaching-learning processes are to be adequately judged and classroom activities to be influenced as intended.

While this discussion has primarily concerned the research-oriented problem of neglecting the content dimension among educational psychologists, the pattern of overreactive teaching behavior shows that didacticians also need to focus their attention on the interaction of content and behavioral variables.

New Requirements for Complex Teaching-Learning Arrangements

In most of the industrialized countries, there are new challenges to the traditional patterns of teaching-learning processes. These challenges arise from

(1) intradisciplinary changes, (2) interdisciplinary changes, and (3) external changes, especially in large enterprises and administrative organizations. These changes are all in the same direction — toward a very new emphasis on content and higher-ranking behavior.

Intradisciplinary Changes

In the field of psychology, a new discussion of the importance of content for the development of knowledge can be observed. Examples are the expert-novice research paradigm, the field of well- versus ill-structured problem solving, the field of microworlds and simulation games, and the research on mental models. As I see it, the discussion of content is gaining permanent significance in this field. At the moment, however, this discussion is still too embedded in the debate about the development of knowledge and expertise, although there is a strong movement to take it seriously on its own terms.

Within didactics, there are also new approaches aimed at overcoming the drawbacks of short-term and linearized models by constructing more complex teaching-learning arrangements and longer and more meaningful learning sequences.

Interdisciplinary Changes

Besides the developments within each discipline, there is a strong conviction among practitioners that the new challenges — which are mainly external ones — can be met only if there is a shift to more interdisciplinary work. As a result of an investigation that it conducted in the field of vocational research, the German Research Society (1990) has called for a collaboration in this field among pedagogy, psychology, sociology, applied economics, and engineering. It seems clear that such cooperation will also be necessary in other content areas. With regard to the classic content of research in educational psychology — physics and mathematics — researchers would be well advised to cooperate with representatives of these disciplines, rather than collecting both pedagogical and psychological knowledge, on the one hand, and physical or mathematical knowledge, on the other hand, from the same person. Such cooperation might make possible research on more ambitious content areas than electrical circuits, levers, trolleys, or fractional arithmetic, although all these areas are of great importance for school learning. The discipline-oriented discussions show that there is a need for developing physical and mathematical thinking and that this will require new interdisciplinary structuring of the content.

Resnick's (1987) problem analysis of "learning in school and out" is an example of interdisciplinary work. Anthropologists and ethnologists have shown that students who fail in school and are frustrated and demotivated to learn are often able to solve relatively complicated tasks in their everyday lives. Another example of interdisciplinary work is the development of the "cognitive apprenticeship" approach (Collins, Brown, and Newman, 1989). My critique of this approach is that it deals insufficiently with modern concepts and contents of apprenticeship and too quickly shifts its focus to purely cognitive procedures (Achtenhagen, 1991). Although all these efforts must take into account the fact that the change to life-related learning models has to be controlled within the content dimension, the new interdisciplinary approaches form a first step toward considering the content-oriented relationship between everyday life and school. This relationship urges a new dimension of effectiveness and responsibility in comparison to the traditional curricula.

External Changes

Intra- and interdisciplinary approaches normally are shaped by research cycles. But the relationship between life and school learning is also challenged by new requirements in industry, administration, and the military. We find new didactic developments in progressive enterprises and in the military for teaching new content structures. These developments focus primarily on two goals: to introduce new and more complexly structured content units and to introduce new and more complex teaching-learning strategies and environments for these content units.

One reason for this change is the worldwide impact of computers and other new information and communication technologies. For Germany, as well as for other European countries, there is also the important reason of a shortage of production and clerical workers. A reduction in our population sets a limit to our economic growth. Businesses and the military, therefore, must try to combine work tasks that are usually low-level and linearized. This procedure achieves a new quality and complexity of tasks and allows information and communication systems to bridge the gap caused by reductions in personnel. These complex tasks also demand more complex teaching-learning procedures. Currently, the main problem is that these procedures are applied outside school and that schools are not at the moment prepared to change their arrangements to meet the new challenges. However, I am sure that we will see decisive changes in our school systems in the next few years.

The restrictive factor in implementing the new changes will be the teacher. Teachers will have to learn new content, content different from what they are used to teaching. The new content is not linearly structured but has the structure of networks; for the most part, it cannot be learned from books alone but requires acting processes as well. Teachers will also have to give up their reliance on stable and consistent pedagogical moves and engage in such complex teaching methods as simulation games and case studies.

In the new scientific approaches, as well as in the economic context, content must gain a new dimension of importance in teaching-learning proce-

dures. There are real problems that have to be solved if school is to be related
to real life. This does not mean that school does not also have the task of
developing students' personalities. Open-minded directors of enterprises know
that a combination of pedagogical and economic rationality is one guarantee of economic success. In fact, the demand for this combination substanti-
ates the pedagogical effort to integrate effectiveness and responsibility. I illustrate this point in the following paragraphs by considering the difference
between actual school processes and content structures and actual and future needs within industry and administration within the German vocational
system. This applies especially to the commercial and public service sec-
tors, in which about 62 percent of all German employers are found.

    1. *Content units (including goals) are not defined by situational aspects and thus
are not operationalized on all possible levels.* Various analyses using Bloom's (1956)
taxonomy of educational goals (Krumm, 1973, p. 85; Achtenhagen, 1984,
p. 179) show that goals on the lowest cognitive level are overrepresented:
97 percent of items in classroom tests, 93 percent of items in final examinations, and 85 percent of items in textbooks fit in the category "knowledge."
Only 11 percent of the textbook items were related to the category "application."

    2. *Content units are not related to usability in industry and administration.* Con-
text analyses of curricula demonstrate that only 29 percent of the curricular
content in full-time vocational schools and only 45 percent in part-time vocational schools is related to qualifications for vocational situations. The remainder is related to very general political and economic situations (Krumm,
1973, p. 43; Achtenhagen, 1984, p. 148). There is not one content unit dealing with students' needs as sellers of work. The practical needs of the work
site are neglected. It is also interesting to note that these analyses were done
even before the new technologies gained their present importance.

    3. *Content units do not take students' abilities into account.* One of the major
findings of our analyses is that students and their needs and abilities do not
really exist within the didactic literature. We analyzed teacher handbooks
in the field of economic and commercial education and found that only 8
percent of all sentences were related to students, and these were without reference to content and other instructional variables. About 44 percent of these
sentences were negatively formulated: the students were described as relatively unintelligent, unmotivated, undisciplined, and so on (Achtenhagen,
1984, pp. 25, 27). We found comparable results in the area of foreign language teaching (Achtenhagen and Wienold, 1975, vol. 1, pp. 46, 51).

    4. *Content units are linearized, chopped into pieces, distant from economic needs,
distant from personal needs and abilities, and wrongly mixed (in other words there is
an overrepresentation of traditional units, such as law).* The structure of curricula
and the construction of textbooks illustrate this problem. The following list
symbolizes the linearity of an actual content structure in a German curriculum for business administration:

Content Units	Student Goals
1. Efficiency of production processes	
1.1 Private economic goals	To know the private economic goals
1.2 Ratios of private economic efficiency	To know and distinguish ratios of private economic efficiency
• Productivity	To measure by means of the ratio of productivity the physical output caused by the input of factors
• Operational efficiency	To understand the necessity of maximizing the output and/or minimizing the input
• Profitability	To count the profitability as relationship between capital and profit
• Liquidity	To judge the solvency using the ratios of liquidity
1.3 Public economic goals	To mention examples of citizens' supplies by public economy

The actual demand of enterprises cannot be satisfied by such a linear content structure. A change is necessary. Such a change would offer a great intradisciplinary as well as interdisciplinary opportunity for educational psychology and didactics to develop new procedures of teaching and learning with regard to complex content and to higher learning and thinking processes. This does not mean that schools should be forced to completely change their approach, but they must overcome the traditional linear series of goals and content. This is possible if didactic thinking adopts networklike interpretations of curricula. A network structure can be developed through the use of scientific statements and task structures found in larger enterprises. The content structure, therefore, would contain important and rich information on real life and be of high relevance for learners.

Approaches for Future Research

I have tried to demonstrate two central points: (1) that there is a lack of systematic thinking on content problems within teaching-learning research and (2) that there is a necessity and opportunity to establish new complex teaching-learning arrangements with regard to disciplinary insights and new external challenges. The problem facing us is how to approach these tasks, which are prerequisites for effective and responsible teaching. It is my estimation that interdisciplinary approaches closely related to enterprises and schools are what is needed. Furthermore, it seems to me that designing such teaching-learning procedures in only one step will be impossible. Rather, we need cycles of analysis, development, implementation, and evaluation. The main task will be to control the content dimension throughout these very different processes.

My colleagues and I have conceptualized a model by which we are trying to develop and test such complex teaching-learning arrangements within the context of first-year commercial education in business administration (Achtenhagen and others, 1988). We have followed an interdisciplinary approach that includes experts in didactics, psychology, computer sciences, and business administration. One of our main problems has been that the individual disciplines themselves have difficulty supplying adequate information. I have already mentioned the problems of psychology and didactics; in the field of business administration, there is also a lack of consistent theory that would allow us to teach theory-oriented content in practical terms. It became clear that we need better and more systematic scientific models. At the moment, we are following a system-oriented approach developed in St. Gallen, Switzerland (Ulrich, 1984). With regard to the task of transforming the content for the students, we have considered adequacy of academic knowledge, adequacy of situational needs, significance for the students, and comprehensibility.

Figure 20.1 provides a formal demonstration of the context of our approach, which is dominated by reflection on the content domain. We start by considering the qualification problems: academic disciplines (such as business administration) and practical needs at the work site determine the goals of the teaching-learning processes. With regard to these aims, we try to formulate an idealized thematic structure—the goal and content structure that best meets the practical and academic needs. At this point, we confront problems of substantiation and legitimization—we must design constructions and evaluate and revise them. The transposition into concrete content and teaching-learning procedures requires a number of steps: considering students' needs, prior knowledge, proficiency, and motivation; relating the idealized thematic structure to single lessons and, more importantly, to sequences of lessons; constructing meaningful subnetworks through controlled procedures of content reduction; and devising a global evaluation concept that covers not only the cognitive but also the emotional and motivational domain and proves whether the curricular content and goals lead to adequate actions. The most important question is whether the teaching-learning processes in school stand the test in business enterprises and administration.

Working with this scheme over a period of more than five years, we have developed simulation games, case studies with the use of expert systems, concepts of simulated offices, working-analogue learning tasks, and so on. We have tried to combine all these approaches with the development of new complex content examples and the consistent use of computers. We are analyzing the instructional processes that apply our content material,

Figure 20.1. Content in Teaching-Learning Processes.

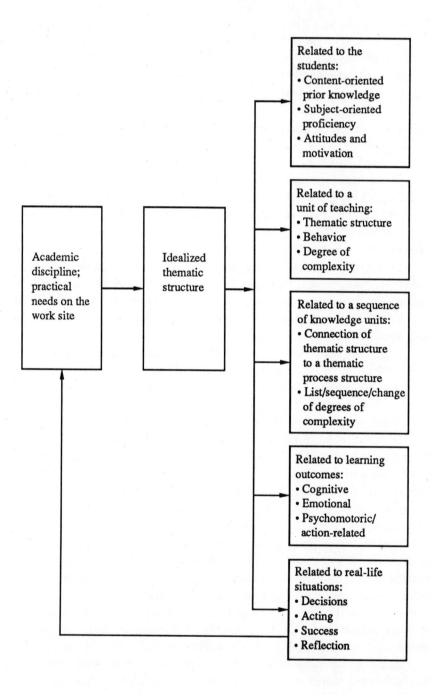

methods, and software in different classes and commercial schools by video-taping and then transcribing the teaching-learning processes that we observe. Although these steps of research and development seem to be promising, we have been confronted with some severe problems.

The main problem is that teachers are not didactic experts. They are not able to handle complex content when new complex methods are administered. An analysis of group discussion processes within simulation games demonstrates that teachers are overtaxed in being required to simultaneously manage processes with complex content and a networklike discussion structure. This is also true for students.

In sum, the role of content in teaching-learning processes is being discussed in a new light. Several disciplines are changing their approaches to consider content problems in more detail. Schools and teachers are having difficulty in adequately handling the necessary complexity of content and corresponding methods. Much research is needed to design realizable programs to meet these new needs, and much effort will be required to prepare teachers for their new jobs as "didactic experts," including the task of being effective and responsible. The fact that business enterprises also see the necessity of a combined economic and pedagogical rationality is our golden opportunity. I am optimistic that teachers can and will change their behavior. And I strongly believe that without that change, schools as we know them cannot survive.

References

Achtenhagen, F. *Didaktik des Wirtschaftslehreunterrichts* [Didactics of economics and commerce]. Opladen, Germany: Leske, 1984.

Achtenhagen, F. "Einige Überlegungen zur Bedeutung der Problemlöseforschung für die Didaktik des Wirtschaftslehreunterrichts" [Some considerations on the importance of research on problem solving for the didactics of economic and commercial education]. In H. Feger (ed.), *Wissenschaft und Verantwortung* [Science and responsibility]. Göttingen, Germany: Hogrefe, 1990a.

Achtenhagen, F. "How Can We Generate Stable, Consistent and Generalizable Results in the Field of Research on Teaching? Theoretical Considerations and Practical Tests." In H. Mandl, E. de Corte, N. Bennett, and H. F. Friedrich (eds.), *Learning and Instruction: European Research in an International Context*. Vol. 2.1. Oxford, England: Pergamon Press, 1990b.

Achtenhagen, F. "Development of Problem-Solving Skills in Natural Settings." In M. Carretero, M. Pope, R. Simons, and J. I. Pozo (eds.), *Learning and Instruction*. Oxford, England: Pergamon Press, 1991.

Achtenhagen, F., and Wienold, G. *Lehren und Lernen im Fremdsprachenunterricht* [Teaching and learning in foreign language instruction]. Vols. 1 and 2. Munich, Germany: Kösel, 1975.

Achtenhagen, F., and others. "Lernen, Denken, Handeln in komplexen ökonomischen Situationen" [Learning, thinking, acting in complex economic situations]. *Zeitschrift für Berufs- und Wirtschaftspädagogik* [Journal for vocational education], 1988, *85,* 3–17.

Bellack, A., Kliebard, H. M., Hyman, R. T., and Smith, F. L., Jr. *The Language of the Classroom.* New York: Teachers College Press, 1966.

Bloom, B. S. (ed.). *Taxonomy of Educational Objectives Handbook: Cognitive Domain.* Vol. 1. New York: Longmans, Green, 1956.

Brophy, J. E. "Teacher Behaviour and Its Effects." *Journal of Educational Psychology,* 1979, *71,* 733–750.

Brophy, J. E., and Good, T. L. *Teacher-Student Relationships: Causes and Consequences.* New York: Holt, Rinehart & Winston, 1974.

Collins, A., Brown, J. S., and Newman, S. E. "Cognitive Apprenticeship: Teaching the Crafts of Reading, Writing, and Mathematics." In L. B. Resnick (ed.), *Knowing, Learning, and Instruction: Essays in Honor of Robert Glaser.* Hillsdale, N.J.: Erlbaum, 1989.

Dörner, D., Kreuzig, H. W., Reither, F., and Staeudel, T. (eds.). *Lohhausen.* Bern, Switzerland: Huber, 1983.

German Research Society. *Berufsbildungsforschung an den Hochschulen der Bundesrepublik Deutschland* [Research on vocational education at the universities of the Federal Republic of Germany]. Weinheim, Germany: VCH, 1990.

Krumm, V. *Wirtschaftslehreunterricht* [Economics and commercial education]. Stuttgart, Germany: Klett, 1973.

McEwan, M., and Bull, B. "The Pedagogic Nature of Subject Matter Knowledge." *American Educational Research Journal,* 1991, *28,* 316–334.

Resnick, L. B. "Learning in School and Out." *Educational Researcher,* 1987, *16* (9), 13–20.

Shulman, L. S. "Paradigms and Research Programs in the Study of Teaching: A Contemporary Perspective." In M. C. Wittrock (ed.), *Handbook of Research on Teaching.* (3rd ed.) New York: Macmillan, 1986a.

Shulman, L. S. "Those Who Understand: Knowledge Growth in Teaching." *Educational Researcher,* 1986b, *15* (2), 4–14.

Shulman, L. S. "Knowledge and Teaching: Foundations of the New Form." *Harvard Educational Review,* 1987, *57,* 1–22.

Stodolsky, S. S. *The Subject Matters: Classroom Activity in Math and Social Studies.* Chicago: University of Chicago Press, 1988.

Ulrich, H. *Management.* Bern, Switzerland: Haupt, 1984.

Wienold, G., and others. *Lehrerverhalten und Lernmaterialien in institutionalisierten Lehr-Lern-Prozessen am Beispiel des Englischanfangsunterrichts"* [Teacher behavior and learning material in institutionalized teaching-learning processes]. Vols. 1–3. Göttingen, Germany: Department of Business Education, Georg August University, 1985.

Wilson, S. M., Shulman, L. S., and Richert, A. E. "'150 Different Ways' of Knowing: Representations of Knowledge in Teaching." In J. Calderhead (ed.), *Exploring Teachers' Thinking.* London: Cassell, 1987.

21

Transmitting Knowledge: Implicit Negotiations in the Student-Teacher Relationship

Anne-Nelly Perret-Clermont

My *regular involvement as a psychologist with in-service teacher training programs* has called my attention to teachers' often limited understanding of the complexity of the sociopsychological processes that mediate their actions. This is quite understandable and legitimate: the teachers' main role is not that of a psychologist interested in deciphering how people think and interact but that of an educator who has to make decisions and to act according to his or her best present understanding of pupils' needs and of his or her duty. But the drawback of this active position on the educational scene is that because of lack of time and methods to carry out observations and the need to rationalize or defend their choices, teachers run the risk of remaining anchored in oversimplified ideas about how learning functions and about their professional role. In the long run, this can have negative consequences for teachers' efficiency and responsibility when they make efforts to adjust their teaching strategies to changes in pupils, context, or knowledge.

Psychologists have an easier time taking the role of outsider. They try to mirror the educational scenes that they observe in a way that allows teachers to situate their actions more consciously within their contexts: large webs of explicit determinants and implicit expectations that affect teacher conduct and student needs and attitudes. In my search in this chapter for a general understanding of learning and teaching as a psychosocial activity, I will be referring primarily to research that has been carried out by myself and my colleagues Nancy Bell, Michèle Grossen, Michel Nicolet, and Maria Luisa Schubauer-Leoni.

To begin with, I would like to introduce a very simple model of the teaching-learning process as a *triangular semantic field*. Then, using this simple

Note: The author would like to thank the Swiss National Research Foundation, whose research grant 10-1977-86 supported this work. She also extends her gratitude to Maria Luisa Schubauer-Leoni, joint author of this research project.

triangular model as if it were a "can opener" to look into the psychology of teaching-learning situations, I will consider the *bipolar social interaction* that mediates the cognitive activity of the student. Learners do not think or acquire knowledge alone but do so in a social venture in which they to some extent monitor the activity but at the same time are strongly dependent on the dynamics of the cognitive exchanges that take place around them (thus requiring us to depart from a purely individualistic conception of learning).

In observing learning, we come to grips with the often forgotten fact that *learning is always the learning of something* and that transfer of learned competence from one skill or area of knowledge to another is always weak. Hence, we cannot assess efficiency on a general level but must consider each specific content per se: we must ask in each case why it is taught and why it is learned. These become crucial questions if learning is seldom transferred from one context to another.

The cultural context and the institutional setting in which teaching takes place largely determine both the knowledge transmitted and the type of interactive relationship established between teacher and students and among students themselves. Schools establish norms of efficiency (mostly on the student side) and definitions of teachers' duties through the rules and regulations of the institution that fix the range of behaviors expected. Curricula, examination procedures, and other, less obvious factors, such as habits and group values, determine the teachers' and students' work. And more implicit elements, such as role expectations, aims, and a general idea of what knowledge is about and learning for, structure their sense of efficiency and responsibility.

A Triangular Semantic Field

Our empirical research, done in experimental settings or directly in the classroom, draws attention to the importance of microsocial processes for successful transmission of knowledge in teacher-pupil interactions. The relationship between the teacher and the student and the interactions among students sustain cognitive development and learning. But there is a third pole to this teacher-student encounter: the object of knowledge that the teacher is supposed to transmit and the pupil is supposed to learn.

This knowledge exists independently of the present teacher-student relationship (as part of the school curriculum or cultural expectations) and partly structures the aim, the means, and the pace of the interaction (Voigt, 1989). Various institutional and cultural factors more or less explicitly define the nature, precise contents, and symbolic values of these elements of knowledge transmitted in school. Acquisition of knowledge is likely to increase competence, understanding, and mastery of the environment, but it also effects social status and self-image, according to the sociocultural context.

This brings us to an examination of the institutional setting of a didactic encounter. A classroom is a social environment that is structured according to rules. It is part of a wider context (school, educational system, culture, and society) that also has norms and rules. All these elements constitute the background of the scene on which the teacher-pupil relationship is established and develops. But these determinants are not purely "external" to the individual learners or teachers. Their effects are mediated by the way in which these actors perceive and interpret them. More or less consciously, each partner has an active role in defining what is at stake in the school interaction. In general, teacher and students usually gear their communication to establish a common intersubjectivity that allows for some kind of common understanding of their task and hence for transmission of knowledge. But this is not always the case, as can be observed in disrupted classrooms or with school failures.

A Bipolar Social Interaction

Various purely individualistic models of cognitive development consider the growth of the mind as the result of individual competencies or experiences and underestimate the role of social factors, cultural structures, and symbols and meanings. Departing from these models are different lines of research, inspired by the pioneer works of authors as different as George Herbert Mead, Lev Semenovich Vygotsky, and Jean Piaget, that converge in calling attention to the importance of *microsocial processes* in the development of cognitive competence in children.

In our own research, we have had the opportunity to observe the importance of peer interactions. We have centered our attention in particular on the role of sociocognitive conflicts that are likely to take place when two or more people who are trying to resolve the same task confront their different judgments. Even when they are both wrong, the fact of having to decenter from their own initial perspective and take into account the other's is likely to cause them to reorganize their understanding (Perret-Clermont, 1980). Many other authors have explored the role of peer interactions in fostering cognitive growth and learning (Miller and Brownell, 1975; Botvin and Murray, 1975; Rubtsov, 1981; Rogoff and Tudge, forthcoming; Glachan and Light, 1982; Doise and Mugny, 1984; Martin, 1985; Perret-Clermont and Nicolet, 1988; Azmitia, 1988). Close observations of peer interactions reveal different elements that contribute to learning efficiency and in particular the great importance of fine regulations of dialogue that make possible processes such as imitation, confrontation, joint action, and other sociocognitive operations that enlarge the child's reasoning activity. These fine regulations of communication are no less necessary in teaching than in dialogues.

Of course, such opportunities for finely geared sociocognitive interactions do not occur only among peers. They can also take place within the teacher-student relationship. The danger of this is that the asymmetrical nature of such interactions is likely to lead to behaviors such as compliance, unreflective imitation, and dependence on the teacher's expectations, thus rendering autonomous cognitive activity less likely. On the other hand, it has been observed that in many adult-child interactions, adults know how to monitor the learners' attention and to accompany them in their cognitive "ventures," helping them to accomplish tasks in which they would not have succeeded on their own (see Chapter Thirteen). Children have an active role in this monitored learning experience: asking questions, seeking help, exploring the adult's expectations, testing their responses, and looking for verbal or nonverbal confirmation (see, for example, Forman and Cazden, 1985; Nelson-Le Gall, 1985; Grossen, 1988; Wertsch, 1978, 1985; Rogoff, 1990; Brossard, 1990; Perret-Clermont, Perret, and Bell, 1991).

Another microsocial process that has received attention lately is teachers' subtle use of routines (Edwards and Mercer, 1987; Voigt, 1989; Cestari, forthcoming). Of course, these routines are likely to be oriented more toward procedural "right-answer" competence than toward principled explanation. But in fact, these routines serve at the same time as mnemonic tools allowing for quick availability of behavioral algorithms and as a means of regulating the flow of discourse between the teacher and the students (see Chapter Fourteen).

A series of implicit and explicit norms structure the encounter and make communication and consequently transmission of knowledge possible. Implicit "communicative contracts" (Rommetveit, 1974, 1979) permit the progressive establishment of a common intersubjectivity (Grossen, 1988). Specific constraints bear on these "communicative contracts" in the school situation, transforming them into "didactic contracts" (Schubauer-Leoni, 1986a, 1986b, and 1988; Brousseau, 1988). Wider socialization practices also define, often unconsciously, the "rules of the game" in the classroom during the transmission of information and skills.

The development of cognitive competence in children is also dependent on the accessibility of symbolic means in regard to cognitive endeavours (Rubtsov, 1989; Carraher, Carraher, and Schliemann, 1988; Carraher, 1989). Other interpersonal factors play a part in these transactions of individuals involved in cognitive tasks, including sympathy, identification, and the search for recognition. These cognitive processes always take place within specific social contexts with identifiable people addressing specific tasks and using specific language or symbolic means. Research on social marking (Doise and Mugny, 1984; Rijsman, 1988; Gilly, 1989) has shown the importance of norms that are activated in the interactive situation: they affect the meaning that the subjects attribute to the task and, as a consequence, the cognitive competence that they actualize. Symbolic means that are available to students (because they have been taught in school or transmitted by the social milieu) are not always perceived as relevant by the students in contexts other than those in which they have learned them (Carraher, Carraher, and Schliemann, 1988; Perret-Clermont, Schubauer-Leoni, and Grossen, 1990). This problem of the weak transfer of learned competence from one context to another leads us into the discussion of the role of specific knowledge in the development of cognitive competence.

The Third Pole: Knowledge

Knowledge is accumulated experience, structured according to cultural or scientific traditions, recorded with symbolic means in material forms. It exists prior to the encounter in which a teacher attempts to transmit it to a student. *Learning is always the learning of something:* specific information, a skill, or an object of knowledge. In conceiving of cognitive development, psychologists very often forget the *content,* reducing it to the structure (sometimes even to the logical structure) of its growth. But content is important: when it varies, so do the epistemological difficulties. Learning different contents is learning different cultural meanings.

The elements of knowledge that are transmitted in schools are determined by larger institutional, cultural, and ideological factors. Explicitly or implicitly, they fix the nature and symbolic value of curriculum contents. In schools, different objects of knowledge have different "reputations," such as being more or less "difficult," "important," or "fundamental." Different naïve systems of explanations of success and failure and various theories of learning seem to coexist (Bell, forthcoming).

The same objects of knowledge can have quite different meanings for teachers and students. This is a function of the usually very different life experiences of these two partners. First, because their past experiences such as training, social background, and professional or practical use of knowledge are so different, the universes of reference for teachers and students are not even similar. Second, their social identities are different. Hence, what is at stake during the transmission of knowledge is likely to be perceived differently by the teacher and the learner. It might, for instance, concern gender identity (particularly in regard to learning mathematics or technical skills), ethnic identity (in regard to second-language learning), or sociopolitical experience (in regard to the study of history). Third, the social roles of teacher and learner imply different attitudes toward knowledge (Schubauer-Leoni, 1986a, 1986b; Schubauer-Leoni, Perret-Clermont, and Grossen, 1992). In some cases, the transmission of knowledge as a one-way process is overemphasized in schools, which induces the identification of knowledge with social status and power and elicits defensive patterns of behavior to hide ignorance and to avoid negative evaluations of social position and role. Finally, the short-term and long-term goals of teachers and students in the school situation are different. Their investments in successful communication are based on different motivational grounds. For teachers, these may include a search for professional quality or recognition and the need to complete the curriculum by the end of the school year. For pupils, they may be a desire to get good grades, to compete with peers, or to avoid appearing overly concerned with school matters; intrinsic interest in school subjects; or fear of punishment by parents in case of school failure.

The transmission of knowledge implies the process of decontextualization and recontextualization. Taking the mathematical notion of "set" as an example, we can illustrate the process by which this object of knowledge is transformed (see Perret-Clermont, Brun, Conne, and Schubauer-Leoni, 1981). Set theory as elaborated by mathematicians becomes in the hands of curriculum experts (who are influenced by other social agents and other subject experts) the notion of "set" as an "object of the scholastic curriculum." This decontextualized object is then transformed by teacher trainers into the notion of "set" as an "object to be taught," which in turn becomes the "object of a lesson" or exercise within the classroom. Hence, when the object "set" finally reaches the child, its nature might be somewhat different from its original one within the field of mathematics. The child in turn recontextualizes this notion of "set" as an "object to be learned" within the logics of all the other learning strategies that he or she develops in school.

At the end of this process, it is not surprising when psychologists discover that there is little in common between the use that the child can make of his or her own understanding of what a "set" is and its original meaning. However, the transmission of knowledge is not only a descending process, a progressive "degradation" of "pure" knowledge to "deformed" scholastic material. It can also be an ascending process whereby teacher and student, involved in well-chosen cognitive activities, progressively appropriate the cultural tools that are available. Yet researchers have not sufficiently described how this appropriation can be made possible through relevant school activities that respect pupils' cognitive strategies (Perret, 1985; Woods, 1989).

An Encounter in an Institutional Setting

Schools are social institutions with legal foundations, roles, and norms defining the nature of the professional tasks of their agents, the time and location of activities, and the contents of lessons and examinations. These elements contribute to the definition of expectations, behaviors, values, and judgments made by teachers as well as students during their interactions. In school settings, individuals develop self-perceptions (Robinson and Tayler, 1989) and social representations of the teaching-learning process. They draw on the ideological discourse that the institution makes available to interpret their successes and failures and construct their perceptions of the school universe and of what knowledge is about (Bell and Perret-Clermont, 1985; Bell, Perret-Clermont, and Baker, 1989; Bell and Schubauer-Leoni, forthcoming). These institutional determinants are not necessarily always the same ones. Woods (1989), for instance, illustrates how changes in group relationships within a school activity can affect both teachers' and pupils' procedures for obtaining information. Carraher's (1989) considerations of in-school and out-of-school mathematical activities indicate the importance of goals in structuring meaning and scaffolding problem-solving strategies and suggest a reconsideration of the goals of daily school activities.

Within the school institution, pupils and teachers interact according to more or less tacit social "contracts" that define their respective social roles, the form of their encounters, and the content of their communication. Observations of teacher-child interactions, even during short periods of time

(Schubauer-Leoni, 1986b), reveal that these social contracts are not static. They are monitored by the teacher and evolve to include progressively new elements within the "object to be taught." I will give a simple example: In the beginning of the school year, a mathematics teacher is quite likely to teach pupils that it is impossible to subtract a larger number from a smaller one (for example, the arithmetic statement $5 - 8$ is an impermissible problem at that age). But later in the year, when the teacher introduces negative numbers, this rule will have to be replaced by one that renders possible such calculations. This example is a rather obvious one, but more subtle and more tacit unconscious changes in the didactic contract can be seen operating within the communication patterns of teachers and students. It is as if these patterns were means to establish a progressively common understanding, starting from the different universes of reference of the knower and the learner to reach gradually shared cognition (Edwards and Mercer, 1987; see also Chapter Nineteen in this volume).

Each Encounter as a New Event

The above-mentioned macro- and microdeterminants figure as the background of the sociocultural and institutional scene in which teacher-student encounters take place. They also tell us something of the grammar (communication contracts, scripts, routines, role distribution, ideological discourses, explicit and implicit rules, and so on) governing the "drama" of their encounter. But this "play" is not completely written. Each teacher-student interaction in a classroom remains a new event, in which each partner has an active role and specific goals and attributes meaning according to his or her specific past experience and present understanding of the situation (including understanding of his or her partner's actions and reactions). Each partner participates mostly unconsciously and implicitly in the definition of the task and of what is at stake in the interaction. It is a two-way process, often underestimated as such. However, it becomes easily observable when, for example, we ask children to role play teacher-pupil interactions (Schubauer-Leoni, 1986a, 1986b; Perret-Clermont, Schubauer-Leoni, and Grossen, 1990).

The teaching endeavour is a difficult one. It resembles the research process insofar as it consists in *making known the unknown*. How can this be achieved in a relationship in which, by definition, the learner does not know what the teacher is talking about? How can the learner then appropriate the teacher's knowledge? Communication skills and ability to participate in the regulation of the interaction are very important here. It is only the final mutual adjustment by interlocutors that allows for the progressive development of joint attention to the same objects, the establishment of a common use of terms, and the adequate handing over of information. Knowledge is transmitted through different kinds of negotiation in this interpersonal process between the learner and the knower. I offer here a few observations of such classroom interactions in Switzerland to illustrate these assertions.

It is a common practice in our local secondary schools for teachers to incompletely formulate their ideas and sentences, asking their pupils to complete them. They believe that in doing so, they not only attract the students' attention and make the lesson more vivid but also can check the students' understanding. Yet sometimes this discourse modality gets so distorted that lessons look like a missing-words test. They are not the hoped-for Socratic maieutic experience!

In a biology lab session, a teacher wanted her secondary school students to observe a cell under the microscope and to recognize the membrane. She had drawn a cell on the blackboard and pointed out the membrane in the drawing. Yet under the microscope, none of the students managed to recognize the membrane. They kept questioning the teacher, who finally exclaimed, "Yes, indeed, in nature, the membrane is not labeled with Chinese ink!" In this case, the discourse partners had an obvious difficulty finding the common reference of their discourse. It was only when the teacher had the idea of resorting to a special pointer that allowed her to indicate the membrane under the microscope that the students managed to enter into her discourse about the constituents of the cell.

In another biology lesson with young secondary school pupils, a teacher was trying to make the children understand the ecological notion of "cycle." After more than an hour, one child finally understood what the teacher was aiming at through the suggested discovery activity and said, "Oh, you want it to form a circle!" This pupil's remark showed that she had understood the type of graphic abstraction that the teacher wanted her to use to model the ecological process that he had in mind. However, it is not clear that the pupil understood the meaning of this model. She may simply have guessed the "trick" that satisfied the teacher.

Teachers' Responsibility, Students' "Work Sites," and Efficiency

Further understanding of the microsocial processes that render learning activity possible is likely to bring us to a reconsideration of the pupils' "work site" and what is meant by "effectiveness and responsibility" in the transmission of knowledge. A "work site" has material components; for instance, the pupils' tools for discovering information, stocking it, and checking its memorization and the symbolic tools and languages available to deal with these elements. The "work site" has social components as well: partners, such as teachers or peers with whom different kinds of help seeking or collaborative or interactive relationships can be established; norms that define within which boundaries the students can modify the flow of the interaction according to their needs; and so on.

Further research will inform us on how children understand what they are meant to do as pupils and what the meaning of pupils' activities are in the eyes of the teachers, the parents, and the pupils themselves. When children change schools or even only change teachers, these implicit expectations become more obvious: the child has to rediscover what he or she is supposed to listen to, to memorize, to write down, to illustrate, to search for, and finally to "learn." And even this last term has different meanings for different teachers, ranging from automatic retrieval to understanding or even to active, creative use of the object of knowledge that has been learned. Each teacher has his or her own representations of the prerequisites to what is being taught. How do students manage to adjust when in fact they are missing those prerequisites or working on other premises? Observing the kinds of questions asked by teachers, the type of thinking that they require from their students, the manner in which they deal with errors, the types of feedback given to students (for instance, on production, on meaning, or on learning strategies), and the effects of these practices on students' identities and metareflections will inform us of the different modes of socialization to the world of knowledge that students go through in school.

Students' main goal is not always knowledge per se, as we know from observation of classroom interactions and interviews with students outside the classroom. Nor do students regularly expect school to provide them with a sense of fulfillment (Robinson and Tayler, 1989). In fact, within this institutional context, they often experience the pain of rating low in social comparison and of failing and fear the disastrous consequences that their behavior might create for their school career. It is not obvious that through school tasks students really taste "genuine understanding" as a source of intellectual satisfaction. Often, their cognitive activity has the primary goal of succeeding at the given task (and earning a good grade) rather than responding to a serious cognitive question. Their self-perception, their school identity, and their image in their parents' eyes are at stake and are often emotionally more important to the student than cognitive mastery of the task itself. It also seems to us that the right to gain pleasure in study and inquiry, the right to master information, is not so easily recognized in the daily practice of schooling, especially for "lower-stream" students.

Emotional Costs

Even when social and emotional conditions are such that learners and teachers can concentrate their attention on problem solving, developing mastery skills, searching for information, and developing models to account for phenomena, these cognitive activities are not always painless. Indeed, if thinking extends our mastery of the environment, learning also confronts us with the limits of our actions and thoughts and with the reality of insurmountable events such as thunderstorms, earthquakes, diseases, and death. Under which psychological conditions can one be motivated to face the pain of limits? When does one take the risk to become aware of certain facts that are unpleasant for cultural, ideological, or personal reasons? When do individuals or groups accept their ignorance and wish to learn? And what do they learn, and why?

The pain of facing reality or marveling at new discoveries, the fear of repression or the search for prestige, defense of one's own identity or cultural enrichment of one's understanding — these are all partly contradictory aspects of learning. They are often simultaneously present in a given school situation but appear differently to different pupils. Teachers have to take these elements into account if they want to succeed in transmitting knowledge.

But why do teachers want to transmit knowledge? Do they know why they want children to learn? Is this really their aim, or are they engaged, more than they believe, in self-reproduction, in social role adjustment, and in defensive attitudes to protect their knowledge and status? More fundamentally, why has humanity developed symbolic tools to memorize experience and to gear relationships within social communities? The answers to these questions are multiple. They belong both to the individual and to the cultural tradition and are worth asking, not only to better understand the psychosocial processes that mediate teaching and learning but also to deepen the sense of responsibility among individuals and groups who can learn from history and culture in our joint venture on a common planet.

References

Azmitia, M. "Peer Interaction and Problem Solving: When Are Two Heads Better Than One?" *Child Development,* 1988, *59,* 87–89.

Bell, N. "La construction sociale des explications" [The social construction of explanations]. Unpublished doctoral dissertation, University of Neuchâtel (Switzerland), forthcoming.

Bell, N., and Perret-Clermont, A.-N. "The Socio-Psychological Impact of School Selection and Failure." *International Review of Applied Psychology,* 1985, *34,* 149–160.

Bell, N., Perret-Clermont, A.-N., and Baker, N. "La perception de la causalité sous-jacente à l'insertion scolaire chez les élèves en fin de scolarité obligatoire" [School leavers' perceptions of the causality of school career]. *Revue Suisse de Psychologie* [Swiss Journal of Psychology], 1989, *48* (3), 190–198.

Bell, N., and Schubauer-Leoni, M. L. Research report, University of Geneva and University of Neuchâtel (Switzerland), forthcoming.

Botvin, G. J., and Murray, F. B. "The Efficacy of Peer Modeling and Social Conflict in the Acquisition of Conservation." *Child Development,* 1975, *46,* 796–799.

Brossard, M. "Regards, interactions sociales et développement cognitif chez l'enfant de 6 à 10 ans dans des épreuves opératoires piagétiennes" [Gazes, social interactions and cognitive development in six- to ten-year-old children in Piagetian operatory tests]. *Dossiers de Psychologie* [Papers in psychology], 1990, *39* (entire issue), University of Neuchâtel (Switzerland).

Brousseau, G. "Le contrat didactique: Le milieu" [The didactic contract: The context]. *Recherches en didactique des mathématiques* [Research in mathematics teaching], 1988, *9* (3), 309–336.

Carraher, T. N. "Negotiating the Results of Mathematical Computations." *International Journal of Educational Research,* 1989, *13* (6), 637–646.

Carraher, T. N., Carraher, D. W., and Schliemann, A. D. *Na Vida Dez Na Escola Zero* [In life 100 percent, in school zero]. São Paulo, Brazil: Cortez, 1988.

Cestari, M. L. Doctoral dissertation, forthcoming.

Doise, W., and Mugny, G. *The Social Development of the Intellect.* Oxford, England: Pergamon Press, 1984.

Edwards, D., and Mercer, N. *Common Knowledge: The Development of Understanding in the Classroom.* London: Methuen, 1987.

Forman, E. A., and Cazden, C. B. "Exploring Vygotskian Perspectives in Education: The Cognitive Value of Peer Interaction." In J. V. Wertsch (ed.), *Culture, Communication and Cognition: Vygotskian Perspectives.* Cambridge, England: Cambridge University Press, 1985.

Gilly, M. "The Psychosocial Mechanisms of Cognitive Constructions: Experimental Research and Teaching Perspectives." *International Journal of Educational Research,* 1989, *13* (6), 607–621.

Glachan, M., and Light, P. "Peer Interaction and Learning: Can Two Mays Make a Right?" In G. Butterworth and P. Light (eds.), *Social Cognition: Studies of the Development of Understanding.* Brighton, England: Harvester Press, 1982.

Grossen, M. *L'intersubjectivité en situation de test* [Intersubjectivity in testing situations]. Fribourg, Switzerland: Delval, 1988.

Martin, L. "The Role of Social Interaction in Children's Problem Solving." *Quarterly Newsletter of the Laboratory for Comparative Human Cognition,* 1985, *7*, 40–45.

Miller, S. A., and Brownell, C. A. "Peers, Persuasion, and Piaget: Dyadic Interactions Between Conservers and Non Conservers." *Child Development,* 1975, *46*, 992–997.

Nelson-Le Gall, S. "Help-Seeking Behavior in Learning." In E. W. Gordon (ed.), *Review of Research in Education.* Vol. 12. Washington, D.C.: American Educational Research Association, 1985.

Perret, J.-F. *L'écriture des nombres* [The writing of numbers]. Bern, Switzerland: Collection Exploration, Editions Peter Lang, 1985.

Perret-Clermont, A.-N. *Social Interaction and Cognitive Development in Children.* London: Academic Press, 1980.

Perret-Clermont, A.-N., Brun, J., Conne, F., and Schubauer-Leoni, M. L. "Décontextualisation, recontextualisation du savoir dans l'enseignement des mathématiques à de jeunes élèves" [Decontextualization, recontextualization of knowledge in the teaching of mathematics to young pupils]. *Interactions Didactiques* [Teaching interactions], 1981, *1* (entire issue).

Perret-Clermont, A.-N., and Nicolet, M. (eds.). *Interagir et connaître* [Social interactions and knowledge]. Fribourg, Switzerland: Delval, 1988.

Perret-Clermont, A.-N., Perret, J.-F., and Bell, N. "The Social Construction of Meaning and Cognitive Activity in Elementary School Children."

In L. B. Resnick, J. M. Levine, and S. D. Teasley (eds.), *Perspectives on Socially Shared Cognition.* Washington, D.C.: American Psychological Association, 1991.

Perret-Clermont, A.-N., Schubauer-Leoni, M. L., and Grossen, M. *Le jeune enfant et l'explication* [The young child and explanation]. No. 7/8. Paris: National Center for Scientific Research, René Descartes University, 1990.

Rijsman, J. B. "Partages et norme d'équité: Recherches sur le développement social de l'intelligence" [Sharing and norms of equity: experiments on the social development of intelligence]. In A.-N. Perret-Clermont and M. Nicolet (eds.), *Interagir et connaître* [Interaction and understanding]. Fribourg, Switzerland: Delval, 1988.

Robinson, W. P., and Tayler, C. A. "Correlates of Low Academic Attainment in Three Countries." *International Journal of Educational Research,* 1989, *13* (5), 581–595.

Rogoff, B. *Apprenticeship in Thinking: Cognitive Development in Social Context.* New York: Oxford University Press, 1990.

Rogoff, B., and Tudge, J. "Peer Influences on Cognitive Development: Piagetian and Vygotskian Perspectives." In M. Bornstein and J. Bruner (eds.), *Interaction in Human Development.* Hillsdale, N.J.: Erlbaum, forthcoming.

Rommetveit, R. *On Message Structure: A Framework for the Study of Language and Communication,* New York: Wiley, 1974.

Rommetveit, R. "On Piagetian Cognitive Operations, Semantic Competence and Message Structure in Adult-Child Communication." In R. Blakar and R. Rommetveit (eds.), *Studies in Language and Thought and Verbal Communication.* London: Academic Press, 1979.

Rubtsov, V. V. "The Role of Cooperation in the Development of Intelligence." *Soviet Psychology,* 1981, *19* (4), 41–62.

Rubtsov, V. V. "Organization of Joint Actions as a Factor of Child Psychological Development." *International Journal of Educational Research,* 1989, *13* (6), 623–636.

Schubauer-Leoni, M. L. "Le contrat didactique: Un cadre interprétatif pour comprendre les savoirs manifestés par les élèves en mathématiques" [The didactic contract: an interpretative framework to understand pupils' display of competence in mathematics]. *European Journal of Psychology of Education,* 1986a, *1,* 139–153.

Schubauer-Leoni, M. L. "Maître-élèves-savoir: Analyse psychosociale du jeu et des enjeux de la relation didactique" [Teacher-pupils-knowledge: a sociopsychological approach to the endeavors of the didactic relationship]. Unpublished doctoral dissertation, University of Geneva, 1966.

Schubauer-Leoni, M. L. "Le contrat didactique dans une approche psychosociale des situations didactiques" [The didactic contract in a psychosocial approach to didactic situations]. *Interactions Didactiques* [Teaching Interactions], 1988, *8,* 63–75.

Schubauer-Leoni, M. L., Perret-Clermont, A. N., and Grossen, M. "The

Construction of Adult-Child Intersubjectivity in Psychological Research and in School." In M. von Cranach, W. Doise, and G. Mugny (eds.), *Social Representations and the Social Bases of Knowledge*. Bern, Switzerland: Hans Huber Verlag, 1992.

Voigt, J. "Social Functions of Routines and Consequences for Subject Matter Learning." *International Journal of Educational Research*, 1989, *13* (6), 647–656.

Wertsch, J. V. "Adult-Child Interaction and the Roots of Metacognition." *Quarterly Newsletter of the Institute for Comparative Human Development*, 1978, *2*, 15–18.

Wertsch, J. V. (ed.). *Culture, Communication and Cognition: Vygotskian Perspectives*. Cambridge, Mass.: Cambridge University Press, 1985.

Woods, P. "Opportunities to Learn and Teach: An Interdisciplinary Model." *International Journal of Educational Research*, 1989, *13* (6), 597–606.

Section Seven

TOWARD EFFECTIVE
AND RESPONSIBLE PRACTICE

Jean-Luc Patry,
Section Editor

Research projects that deal explicitly with both effectiveness and responsibility are rare. This section presents a few projects that have in common an attempt to increase responsibility and responsible action on the part of students, either with an explicit program, as in Chapters Twenty-Four, Twenty-Five, and Twenty-Six, or by including specific elements in an existing teacher training approach, as in Chapters Twenty-Two and Twenty-Three.

Trygve Bergem, in Chapter Twenty-Two, and Andreas Dick, in Chapter Twenty-Three, address the question of how student teachers can become more responsible in their eventual teaching. This is one of the central aims of the new synthesis to balance effectiveness with responsibility. In some chapters in this book, teachers are described as tending to focus primarily on effectiveness at the expense of responsibility. Is it possible to remedy this lack of concern with responsibility through appropriate teacher training? Are there strategies that can be employed to increase this concern? Such are the questions confronted in these two chapters.

The other three chapters — Chapter Twenty-Four, by Daniel Solomon, Marilyn Watson, Victor Battistich, Eric Schaps, and Kevin Delucchi; Chapter Twenty-Five, by Sigrún Adalbjarnardóttir, and Chapter Twenty-Six, by Heinz Schirp — focus more on issues of responsibility in school settings, particularly in terms of children becoming more responsible in different situations (dispositional responsibility). Educating toward dispositional responsibility implies the influence of responsible teaching on responsible action of the pupils. Teachers who intend to increase their pupils' responsibility need to act responsibly themselves. But can teachers influence their pupils' responsibility? And if teachers act responsibly and succeed in conveying responsibility to their pupils, does this have an impact on the teachers' effectiveness with respect to subject matter goals? In other words, is it possible for a teacher to enhance both dispositional responsibility and subject matter knowledge simultaneously?

The two emphases of the chapters in this section are closely related in several regards. Teacher training traditionally focuses on effectiveness. When talking with practicing teachers about values and other prescriptive issues, one often hears the complaint mentioned by Bergem in Chapter Twenty-Two that while the discussion of values is interesting and important, teachers have not had the opportunity to deal with them in teacher training and have no time to think about them as practicing teachers. There is no incentive to reflect on ethical questions, because daily practice requires effectiveness. Most teachers often have negative feelings, particularly in grading and selection situations, but lack training or experience in dealing with such problems and prefer not to discuss them. In fact, one of Bergem's lessons is that most teachers have not even acquired a vocabulary with which to discuss moral matters (see White's "Principle of Vocabulary" in Chapter Four). This is not to say that there are no teachers who reflect on ethical questions and act responsibly. We all know highly competent teachers who are almost perfect in this regard (and Dick presents some of these experts). But these teachers are the exception. The question is how average teachers, who have little opportunity to reflect on ethical problems because their major concern is effectiveness, can be helped to become more responsible.

One possibility, of course, would be to include responsibility issues in teacher training programs. Bergem evaluates six different teacher education programs developed in accordance with curricula guidelines in which both effectiveness and responsibility are stated as explicit aims for teacher education. In practice, however, effectiveness is the important issue, while guidelines with respect to responsibility are rather marginal. Since the teacher educators themselves show ambivalence toward the normative aspects, it is not surprising to find responsibility being dealt with on a superficial level. Clearly, issues of responsibility are underrepresented both qualitatively (the real issues are not discussed) and quantitatively (too little time is spent on these topics) in the evaluated teacher training programs. Thus, if practicing teachers act responsibly — and there is no reason to believe that they do not — it seems that this is due not to their teacher training programs but to other influences. To reduce the chanciness of responsible teaching behavior, Bergem argues for a systematization of future teacher training programs to provide student teachers with a moral language, promote their personal and moral development, and stress the personal responsibility incumbent on the teacher as a role model.

How can this be done? In Chapter Twenty-Three, Dick presents one possible answer, based on the concept of the "reflective practitioner": assigning student teachers expert teachers (who are also responsible teachers) as mentors. The student teachers have the opportunity to observe the expert teachers in action and to discuss, question, and deliberate important actions and the issues behind them. Within this exchange, different points of view quickly arise: the student teachers are dealing with a primarily preconceptual knowledge base, while the experienced teachers rely on a case knowledge base.

Such deliberate interaction provides a setting for reflecting and revising ethical points of view, thereby enhancing awareness of responsibility for both student teacher and expert teacher.

One important message of Dick's chapter is that people can evolve with respect to responsibility issues if the relevant ethical background for practical decisions is discussed freely and openly and with respect to an everyday setting (as opposed to artificial ethical dilemmas). "Telling" student teachers the "right way" probably does not enhance their dispositional responsibility; if anything, it probably would affect only the student teacher's case knowledge. The caring, open relationship of a "reflective practitioner" with students can provide a sort of "zone of proximal development" (see Chapter Fourteen) in which the students can truly develop their moral understanding.

A caring, open attitude toward enhancing children's responsibility is the focus of Chapters Twenty-Four, Twenty-Five, and Twenty-Six. In the examples presented in these chapters, rather than trying to directly influence pupils' responsibility by "directing" them to behave responsibly, teachers provide a setting or context that can foster pupils' responsibility. Such a setting is characterized by a high degree of reciprocity and mutual respect. Teachers in the program described by Solomon, Watson, Battistich, Schaps, and Delucchi (Chapter Twenty-Four) created an extraordinary caring community in which they worked to meet the psychological needs (needs for self-direction, competence, and social connectedness) of all students while providing moral guidance through examples, discussion, and exposure to morally relevant literature. The setting described by Adalbjarnardóttir (Chapter Twenty-Five) focuses more on special social problem-solving incidents characterized by the teachers' responsibility to bring children's conflicting perspectives in social relationships to light and to foster a discussion on these issues in a stress-free atmosphere. Schirp (Chapter Twenty-Six), in contrast, describes two programs in which pupils are given the opportunity to work with relevant questions dealing with both curricular and sociomoral problems. Thus, the underlying foundation of all three studies is that to enhance responsibility, at least two conditions must be satisfied: first, the teachers must act responsibly themselves; second, the pupils must be given the opportunity to take responsibility on real issues, to discuss them openly, and to find their own solutions.

Creating such a context raises several issues. One of these is the fact that when teachers teach in accordance with the principles mentioned above, they must give up control. In direct instruction and problem solving, the teacher is generally in full control of the situation and can easily anticipate possible disturbances and plan an intervention. A teacher described in Adalbjarnardóttir's chapter is a good example. Before participating in the study described, she had always been quick to intervene and advise her pupils. In the responsibility-enhancing setting, she agreed to give up control and was quite aware of the change. Giving up control means that events become less predictable, challenging the teacher to react quickly and responsibly in often critical situations. There is a certain risk involved, but the benefits can be great. Giving up control (and hence accepting a different kind of authority) can also cause anxiety and insecurity in teachers, who must delegate responsibility for certain decisions to pupils yet are still ultimately responsible for them and the situation. Interestingly, however, the teachers participating in Adalbjarnardóttir's project eventually felt an increased security in dealing with social conflicts. Obviously, teachers can learn to cope with the problems of reduced control when the program is properly implemented.

A second issue is the external conditions for programs aimed at increasing student responsibility. Schirp particularly addresses this point: his emphasis is on opening the school and creating new structures that provide an interface with the community. Implementing proposed solutions requires changes at the school level, and this can result in opposition from the outside: from concerned parents who fear that subject matter learning may fall short; from authorities who are afraid that schools may walk on paths that they regard as dangerous (for whatever reason); from society, which is suddenly confronted with pupils who want to work within the social reality and not be restricted to the classroom as a societal island; from people who may fear that children will become too critical of the prevailing social structures and will challenge them; from teachers not participating in the program who perceive it as a critique of their own approach.

The anxiety and insecurity that loss of control can cause for both teachers and external people involved can be a strong inhibitor to the implementation of such programs. This leads to the third issue: how can we encourage responsible action in teachers, and can programs to do so really be implemented as conceived? In studies to follow up on their programs, Adalbjarnardóttir and Solomon and his colleagues found that the teachers did tend to comply with the principles of the respective programs. This not only is encouraging but also tells us that there are appropriate strategies for enhancing teachers' responsibility. What are they? Solomon and his colleagues used intensive teacher training in summer institutes, monthly workshops, frequent meetings with project staff, and supporting curriculum materials. Adalbjarnardóttir trained her teachers in twenty group meetings during the school year that focused on theories of children's social development. In both studies, the teachers were given the opportunity to discuss any problems that arose in their attempts to implement the program and to commonly search for solutions. Such constant support and feedback surely play a crucial role in the implementation procedure. This type of discussion of practical teaching situations seems to be lacking in the programs that Bergem describes. Restricting discussions about responsibility to situations that the participants had not themselves experienced may have contributed to the problems that arose. In Dick's approach, on the other hand, a support and feedback system was explicitly built in by the ethnographic approach that he chose.

Did the programs reviewed in this section succeed in enhancing pupils' responsibility? The traditional criterion for judging the effectiveness of teaching is students' knowledge in subject matters. Here, however, the criterion used to evaluate teaching is evidence of pupils' responsible action. Can we assume that if someone acts responsibly in one situation, he or she will do so in other situations as well? Can we judge whether an action was responsible without knowing the rationale behind the action or the reasons given by the actor? Assessing dispositions such as responsibility or responsibleness is problematic, and it might well be that these problems contribute to the fact that little research is being done in this field, far less than in the field of subject matter knowledge, where evaluative assessment is much easier.

This leads me to my last question, one that is pertinent to all the questions mentioned above and indeed is at the core of the new synthesis attempted in this book: are students' achievements in subject matters influenced by the attempt to enhance their dispositional responsibility, or is an increase in responsibility "compensated" for by a decrease in regular school achievements? The claim here is that creating a responsible setting according to the principles of a caring community and opening the schools to interact with the community will help to enhance students' responsibility as well and that teaching according to these principles will yield not only greater responsibility but also greater subject matter knowledge than in pupils of comparable schools with traditional teaching.

What is the direct evidence for this hypothesis? Solomon and his colleagues report several studies that confirm it. In their own study, the pupils of the program did no worse on a standardized achievement test than pupils of regular schools; with a "holistic" measure of reading comprehension, the pupils of the program did even significantly better than the control group. It seems that not only was there no loss due to the implementation program, but there was a gain in higher-order thinking and development of understanding. This kind of achievement is usually even more valued than the purely knowledge-based achievement test performance.

There is other evidence, although more indirect. Bergem reports that student teachers with high professional morality indices are also rated as more effective teachers. Dick's expert teacher discusses how allowing students to gather freely and discuss their test work encourages them to talk about subject matter in a very intense way—again, responsibility enhancing effectiveness. Dick's exemplary teachers show some other relationships between responsibility and effectiveness as well. For example, they take responsibility for teaching their pupils to finish things (responsibility in the choice of the criterion for effectiveness) and for taking into account the contextual conditions in anything that they do or decide. These examples, combined with the belief that the aim of teaching is not to control the outcomes of learning but to facilitate a dialectical process between content subjects and individual subjectivities, demonstrate effectiveness of responsible action and the responsibility of effective teaching.

Schirp's contribution also fits in here nicely. He found that taking responsibility to open up schools can lead to the discovery of pupils' hidden talents, skills, and learning competencies beyond the simple knowledge of subject matters. There is also indirect evidence for the compatibility of effectiveness and responsibility at the level of the general setting. Solomon and his colleagues mention that a set of schoolwide and community activities and a parent program included in the project likely contributed to their success. Such activities are explicitly addressed by Schirp, whose program to "open the schools" was conceived both to foster responsibility and to increase the amount of meaningful learning in school. Adalbjarnardóttir also found, as a secondary effect, that the pupils of teachers who participated in the program were more open and friendly toward each other than pupils of other teachers were — and this is certainly a favorable condition for successful teaching in subject matters. A similar observation is made by Solomon and his colleagues.

These five studies indicate that the new synthesis is possible both for teachers, who indeed are able — with appropriate support — to learn to act responsibly and effectively, and for pupils, who can acquire competencies in responsibility as well as in subject matters. This success, however, is not automatic but requires much effort, know-how, and sensitivity in the implementation of programs that enhance the moral capacities of both teachers and students. The programs described here provide five examples of what can be done. We hope that these paths will be followed by future teachers and teacher educators.

22

Teaching the Art of Living: Lessons Learned from a Study of Teacher Education

Trygve Bergem

What do teacher educators actually do to develop students into effective and responsible teachers who can face the challenges of classroom teaching according to professional standards? By analyzing the content of six teacher education programs in Norway—including written documents, textbooks, and interviews with teacher educators and prospective teachers—I will attempt to draw conclusions about the formal as well as the perceived and experiential curricula with regard to both effectiveness and responsibility in teaching.

The findings of the study do not, of course, allow us to make global generalizations about the present state of teacher education. However, questioning the conceptual orientations of the teacher education programs under study does bring into focus issues that teacher educators and researchers generally have to consider when evaluating teacher education and the work of teachers in schools.

The study on which this chapter is based was started in 1986, five years after the implementation of a new nationwide curriculum for teacher education in Norway. The basic idea behind the reform was that teacher education should become more of a state-of-the-art enterprise.

In examining the content of the teacher education programs, we addressed the following main issues: What is the rationale behind the formal programs? What are the aims that the teacher educators themselves are trying to achieve? By what means are they trying to realize those aims? How do teacher educators justify the design of their own programs? In the present context, special emphasis will be placed on a discussion of how the participating colleges address questions pertaining to the development of professional morality in teachers-to-be.

The analysis of the content of teacher education programs was limited to a unit called Educational Theory and Practice (ETP). This unit, which constitutes 50 percent of the first two years of study in the three-year program, focuses on five main topics that do not logically lend themselves to the traditional classification of disciplines, such as educational psychology, educational sociology, teaching methods, and educational foundations. Yet the study shows that the majority of the teachers' colleges still cling to this tradition of classification in their design of the teaching programs.

A Theoretical Context

The Old Song Reiterated

A main assumption in the present research is that teaching is a moral endeavor. Clark (1991, p. 2) has rightly maintained that researchers whose studies have stubbornly rested on this axiom (Peters, 1974; Tom, 1984; Danner, 1985) have been singing an old song. Yet for many years, this song has been ignored. It has simply been drowned out by louder voices emphasizing the need for more effective teaching. The behavioristic research traditions that have dominated the educational field during the last forty years and the philosophy underlying them (Fenstermacher, 1986) have neglected the normative aspects of teaching.

New approaches to the study of teaching and teachers that have been developed in the wake of behaviorism (Shulman, 1986) are based on a revised understanding of the teaching concept and of the teacher's contribution in the teaching-learning process. Teachers' cognitions and the relationship between teacher thinking and professional action have come to the forefront (Day, Pope, and Denicolo, 1990). Among neither researchers nor practitioners is teaching any longer thought of as a purely technical activity. This development has necessitated a revision of the conception of the role of the teacher. Ryan (1986) maintains that the new role of the teacher is characterized by a higher degree of participation and commitment in the student-teacher relationship. Teachers are once more encouraged to express their own views on moral issues. In many countries, teachers are explicitly thought of as moral agents (Bergem, 1990a) and role models for their students. The reconceptualization of the role of the teacher has made moral responsibilities, which teachers in the Norwegian schools have always been charged with, more explicit.

Teachers as well as researchers are realizing that the ethical dilemmas of classroom management make the already difficult work of educators even more complex, for what may be considered effective teaching may be morally questionable. The ethical dilemmas of classroom life often have an existential bearing, forcing the teachers to ask themselves how they are to work and behave as educators to fulfill the needs of the individual child (Miller, 1990). By extension, the teachers of educators are charged with similar responsibilities (Clark, 1991). It is exactly this situation that prompted the critical examination of the content of teacher training reported here; I hope that we have learned some lessons.

The Conceptual Framework

The conceptual framework used in our study is derived primarily from moral philosophy and from recent research on teachers' thinking and professional action. However, since this framework has been discussed elsewhere (Bergem, 1989; Bergem and Kristiansen, 1987), I shall limit this discussion to the assumptions on which teachers' moral responsibilities are based. These assumptions are directly related to the problems addressed in this chapter.

Through the use of phenomenological analyses, the Danish philosopher K. E. Lögstrup (1905–1981) looked for the facts that constitute the true relationship between human beings. In psychological terms, he tried to reveal what elements could be said to be most fundamental to the quality of human interactions (Lögstrup, 1975). He starts his discussion by maintaining that, as human beings, we are each other's destiny. Living in a state of interdependence, we put our lives in other people's hands, showing or asking for trust. From this fact follows the demand to take care of the life of fellow beings. No matter how much or little of a person's life that person entrusts to another person in a given situation, in every encounter between humans, there is an "unexpressed ethical demand." This holds true regardless of the character of the encounter and the circumstances in which it takes place.

Lögstrup (1975) claims that trust is the basic phenomenon of every human's moral existence. That is to say, it is not an attitude that we as human beings arbitrarily choose to display toward other persons; rather, it is one of the basic elements of life. To be human implies being in a relationship of trust. Distrust is contrary to life itself.

Lögstrup (1968, pp. 92–103) further argues that existentialists such as Kierkegaard and Sartre ignore one important field of human existence: that represented by *spontaneous life manifestations,* such as forgiveness, mercy, sincerity, compassion, care, commitment, and love. According to Lögstrup, the spontaneous life manifestations correspond to the ethical demand in the existence of humans. At the same time, the ethical demand can be met only by these manifestations, which can also make it redundant. Well in advance of Noddings (1984), Lögstrup developed the idea that "To receive and to be received, to care and to be cared-for: these are the basic realities of the human being and its basic aims" (Noddings, 1984, p. 173).

Lögstrup's ontological ethic clarifies the ethical demands that teachers have to consider. It urges teachers to examine very carefully what they teach and how they treat the students whose lives they are entrusted with. Using this line of thought as a basis for our study, we first developed a number of assumptions about what can reasonably be expected from teachers (Bergem, 1990b) and then what impact these expectations should have on teacher education and training.

Assumption 1: We expect that teachers, being educators with whom we entrust our children, will teach our youth the art of living. The importance of this task is made very explicit by Lögstrup's (1975) statement that teachers always have something of their students' lives in their hands. Peters (1974) similarly argues for the view that education should imply the transmission of what is worthwhile to the parties involved and that students in school should be involved in worthwhile activities in which they willingly engage. Since teachers must themselves, after all, decide what these worthwhile activities should actually be, they do indeed need to be "reflective practitioners" (Schön, 1983, 1987). Therefore, teacher education programs, which are aimed primarily at developing prospective teachers into technicians and performers who can efficiently plan, choose, and use the proper teaching techniques and evaluate the outcomes of the teaching-learning processes, cannot enable future teachers to meet and solve some of the most difficult ethical problems that they will confront when they start teaching.

Assumption 2: We expect the teachers to whom we entrust our children to be trustworthy. Most parents trust the school system. This does not mean, however, that parents and students have *confidence* in all the teachers working in the school. It rather means that this trust has what Sockett (1990, p. 236) calls an outside and an inside. Outside trust provides parents and students with the opportunity to trust the system, but it does not guarantee the system's trustworthiness or, more precisely, the trustworthiness of each constituent element of the system.

By introducing the term *interdependence,* Lögstrup underlines the relational condition, based on mutual trust, that exists between individuals. This also implies that all parties involved in the school system have to contribute to its maintenance. When we focus on teachers, the issue of trustworthiness calls for a closer examination of the teacher's personal integrity and character. What conclusions can be drawn about the trustworthiness of teachers from their behavior during their teaching and their interaction with students? Do they respect the integrity of all the students in the classroom, even those who challenge the truth told by the teachers? Do the teachers seem to possess the virtues that constitute trust in the psychological sense of the word as well—social sensitivity, veracity, fidelity, and a caring attitude?

If teacher education programs are to promote trustworthiness in future teachers, character development should be considered an important aim for teacher preparation. Because the prospective teachers are going to work as educators, they should also be trained as such and taught how they can actively assist students in their personal development and moral growth.

Assumption 3: We expect that teachers in our schools are professionally committed to their students. As mentioned above, Lögstrup argues that we can realize ourselves as human beings only by caring for each other. The student is the weaker partner in the teacher-student relationship. Students are also the most vulnerable. They need to be taken care of by more mature individuals who know more about the demands of life than they do themselves. This implies that every teacher should continue asking questions such as "Where does the caring for my students start and where does it end?" Answers to this question will most probably vary according to the way in which teachers conceive of and interpret their professional role and moral responsibilities.

In an article discussing the ethical complexity of practical problems encountered in counseling, Tennyson and Strom (1986) distinguish between the terms *responsibility* and *responsibleness*. Referring to Frankl (1977), they maintain that *responsibility* refers to obligations relating to a given profession imposed on it by some outside authority, while *responsibleness* comes from within as a response to a moral obligation accepted by the individual. As already noted, we contend that the practice of teaching has a moral dimension that all teachers must be aware of regardless of their philosophical attitude toward teaching and the model of rationality that they adhere to, to introduce Giroux's (1981) category. As professionals, teachers must be aware of the fact that underlying professional actions there is, to quote Oser (1989, p. 108), "a value system that has to be balanced against functional standards. This implies that professional actions must not only be evaluated in terms of functionality and factual expertise but also in terms of moral expertise and reliability."

In our view, developing responsibleness in teachers entails promoting the development of *professional morality*. This should be considered an integral part of teacher education. Teachers who are entrusted to teach our youth to become reliable and productive citizens need themselves to develop a clear notion of what is implied in living and behaving as responsible human beings caring for others. It becomes clear that the burden of ethical responsibility resting on teachers is enormous. So are the challenges that teacher educators are confronted with. Because the ethical demand can be thought of as a *tacit demand* that has to be discovered by teachers, their social sensitivity (Bergem, 1986) has to be developed along with their moral reasoning abilities, their moral motivation, and the "ego strength" needed to implement moral decisions in a given situation (Rest, 1984, pp. 29–33).

Methodology

Guided by theoretical perspectives to choose both the design and the instruments for this longitudinal study, I asked six training colleges, located in different parts of the country, to participate in the study. The 284 students who participated had all started their formal training during the fall semester. In addition, there were 14 instructors who were responsible for the teaching of the ETP curricula in the twelve participating classes (two from each school). A random sample of 37 cooperating teachers (mentors) was also included in the study.

Each of the six colleges was visited twice. During the first visit, which took place shortly after the fall semester began, qualitative and quantitative data were collected from the student sample. Semistructured interviews were conducted with the two samples of teacher educators and a subsample of sixty-five students randomly drawn from the student sample. All interviews were taped for later transcription and analysis.

The second visit took place at the end of the second year. This time, data were collected from the participating students only. In addition, we asked for the final evaluation of the individual students' teaching during field practice.

Analyses of the interviews were performed according to a qualitative approach derived from hermeneutic interpretations of literary texts. The responses from the different groups were compared by computer analysis. Details about the methodology can be found in technical reports in Bergem (1989, 1992).

Lessons Learned

The first lesson that we learned from our study was that the teacher education programs that we analyzed generally seem to *lack a sound rationale* or a clear conceptual orientation. By this, we mean that the programs as a whole lack a considered set of ideas about the goals of teacher education and the means for achieving them. A program with a distinct conceptual orientation would give direction to the daily activities of teacher education and set the scene for the teaching of educational theory and practice. In her recent review of research in teacher education, Feiman-Nemser (1990, pp. 220–228) discusses characteristic features of the following five conceptual orientations presently identified in teacher education programs: academic, practical, technological, personal, and critical-social. According to Feiman-Nemser, a conceptual orientation should ideally include a view of teaching and learning and a theory about learning to teach.

In our study, we were not able to detect anything that can rightly be called a theory about learning to teach. We did, however, discover noticeable differences in the design of the ETP curricula. In the plans worked out by the individual colleges, the importance assigned to the focal topics varied markedly according to the professional views and attitudes of the faculty. Yet very few were able to defend the philosophy underlying the programs and curricula that they had designed.

During the two-year program of course work, the instructors spend an average of only 10 to 12 hours on issues pertaining to the foundations of teaching and schooling. In contrast, they spend about 150 hours teaching general and developmental psychology, 100 hours on educational psychology, and 70 hours on teaching methods. The time spent on issues related to professional ethics and professional morality varies from 5 to 0 hours.

There seems to be a relationship between the emphasis that teacher educators give to foundations and their own inability to justify the priority given to the focal topics in the formal programs and the lack of rationale for the programs. The teacher educators often seemed to be much more concerned with their own favorite disciplines than with the quality of the ETP program as such. At the same time, they also complained about the weaknesses of the present program. However, very few were able to name the weaknesses and suggest what improvements could be made. When asked about the basic ideas of the conceptual orientation of the teacher education programs for which they were responsible, the great majority of the teacher educators had difficulty responding. Most often, they answered with vague utterances on the necessity of training prospective teachers to be effective and hardworking professionals — or "craftsmen," as some educators would have it. When asked to explain what kind of strategy they used in counseling student teachers, one of the cooperating teachers typically answered as follows:

> We teach them some tricks that we know of, you see. That's a good way to start. We teach them tricks that can easily be used in the classroom. What the student teachers do wrong is easy to see. After having given a message to the whole class, they start teaching right away, unaware of the fact that more than half of the students in the class haven't yet opened their books. . . . You have to learn the name of every student in the class as soon as possible. You can't just stand there pointing at "the one in the green sweater." These are the kind of tricks we teach them.

Only rarely were the respondents concerned with the necessity of developing their students' understanding and acceptance of the complex responsibility incumbent on the teacher.

The second lesson that we learned was that *a practical-technological approach to teacher education prevails* in the participating colleges. The lack of a considered rationale as discussed above does not mean that distinct ideas about the ends and means of teacher education are not expressed by the respondents. On the contrary, we find some very articulate views on what should be given priority in teacher education and what the major aims should be. They are, however, only fragments of a clear conceptual orientation to teacher education, typically practical and technological views and opinions as to what should be considered the crux of the matter. These responses substantiate the understanding that we arrived at in the analysis of the formal programs, as can be illustrated by the following excerpts from the interviews. The first is from a teacher educator with more than twenty years' experience.

> My vision is that future teachers have acquired the kind of knowledge that enables them to explain and understand what they're going to do while teaching. My hope is that they'll be able to apply the theory they've learned to plan what they're actually going to do in the classroom. If they aren't able to

achieve that, then our transmission of knowledge has failed. According to the feedback from the students, that is what often happens, because they are always complaining about the lack of consistency between theory and practice.

One of the mentors (in the Norwegian system, a cooperating teacher responsible for counseling student teachers during internships) expresses a similar view:

> I've been in this business for eighteen or nineteen years now, and I feel that we're forced to give priority to the practical job which the future teachers are going to do. We spend most of our time commenting on the daily routines that they have to master in a proper way. By and large, they have no idea about how they are going to proceed!

While the teacher educators who express views such as these do not necessarily share the same notion of good teaching, they do share a focus on the development of techniques, practical skills, and practical knowledge. Therefore, they maintain that the primary task for teacher educators should be to teach future teachers to become skillful craftspeople. While some advocate the principle of apprenticeship, others are much more concerned with initiating the prospective students into the secrets of research on teaching and the theories and principles of effective teaching. These teacher educators conceive the development of skillful practitioners as the main goal for teacher education. We seldom met with teacher educators who were primarily concerned with developing effective and responsible teachers by promoting reflective and critical thinking. Only very rarely did we come across teacher educators who believed that good teachers are created by being shown how they can use themselves effectively and that good teaching requires individuals who are knowledgeable and possess creative and sound personalities as well.

The third lesson that we learned was that the great majority of the teacher educators *had become so by chance, not because of interest.* By this we mean that very few of the teacher educators had planned to enter the teacher education business after graduating from college. Some of the instructors had been striving toward quite different careers before they settled down to teacher education. Others had not really known what to do once they had finished their own education. This ambivalence is illustrated by the following career story told by one of the instructors:

> I became a teacher educator merely by coincidence; however, the same does not apply to my choice of a major in education. My interest in educational issues has developed gradually. It started while in training college, into which I hadn't plan to enter.

All the same, it was during my time in college that I really be-
came interested in educational issues, especially foundations.
After having got my diploma, I finally had to make a choice.
So I ended up here.

Even if few teachers were initially attracted by the challenges of teacher
education as such, the great majority of the group had enjoyed teaching
courses in education. However, after having been in teacher education for
twenty years on average, quite a few complained about burnout problems.

Only two of the fourteen instructors reported that they had quite intentionally become teacher educators. By influencing the development of
prospective teachers, they hoped to contribute to the improvement of schooling. One of the instructors said that, after some years of teaching in elementary school, he suddenly realized one day that it was not possible to change
the practice of schoolteaching from inside the classroom. So he decided to
become a teacher educator in order to work toward the improvement of the
quality of teaching in classrooms by developing a reflective and critical mind
in future teachers.

The teacher education mentors told similar stories. Most of them had
been in the business for more than twenty-three years and were very experienced, dedicated teachers. Becoming a teacher had been the first vocational preference for the great majority of the group. Two-thirds of them
maintained that they had become counselors and teacher educators by pure
chance as a result of other people's interference in their teaching career. While
some had been encouraged by colleagues to join a team of teacher educators, others had been recruited by principals. There were clearly no systematic criteria used in recruiting them. We have reason to believe, however, that most of them had the reputation of being reflective and effective
teachers, often with a special interest in one or more subjects. Although only
rarely had any of them had some kind of formal training working as counselors within the field of teacher preparation, they tended to stay with the
job for quite a long time. None had ever thought of leaving the field, since
they liked working with both children and adults.

The one-third of the mentors who maintained that they had planned
to become teacher educators gave several reasons for this. Some had been
attracted by the opportunity to share their experiences with future teachers.
Others admitted that they had considered becoming a mentor both an ad-
vancement in the school system and an honor.

We cannot tell from our research what impact teacher educator recruit-
ment may have on the quality of teacher education. Yet the stories we were
told ought to prompt further research into this issue.

The fourth lesson learned from our study was that *teacher educators show
great ambivalence toward the normative aspects of teaching*. The teacher educators'
uncertainty about the imperative nature of the role of the teacher in general
and the moral responsibilities pertaining to their own role as instructor and

mentor for prospective teachers was reflected in many parts of the interviews. I would like to address this issue by taking a closer look at the teacher educators' views on whether teachers should think of themselves as role models for their students.

The importance of model learning has been clearly demonstrated by social learning theorists and researchers such as Bandura (1971) and Mischel and Grusec (1966). In everyday language, we talk about learning by example. It should be stressed that modeling does not mean copying. Research on learning has indicated that the most important feature of modeling is that this style of learning tends to generate new structures in the knowledge of the observer more often than other forms of learning do. Modeling is of special importance in the learning of behavior governed by rules and expectations that the individual voluntarily accepts and respects.

On the basis of such considerations, we asked the teacher educators to respond to the following statement: "The teacher should be a role model for the students." Two-thirds of the teacher educators endorsed the statement, referring to the fact that the students perceive the teacher as someone with whom to identify regardless of how teachers perceive themselves. As part of the justification of her response, one of the mentors made the following comment:

> The transfer of knowledge is not the most important part of the teacher's job. Other tasks are of equal importance. Students are going to learn about life, and they're going to learn what it means to be a responsible person. It's hard to mention everything that teachers are obliged to teach their students. The best way to manage it would be for us as teachers to try to practice ourselves what we tell our students to do. The issue of smoking is a good example. We urge the kids not to start smoking, while we puff away like mad ourselves. We ought to try very hard to be good role models for our students.

The teacher educators who opposed the statement about teachers as role models for their students generally believed that it would be too much to expect of teachers that they should think of themselves as models for identification. "One cannot demand more from teachers than one can expect from people in general," they maintained. One of the instructors, who saw no reason to use the role model concept at all anymore, expressed himself in the following way:

> In today's society it's not possible to think of the teacher as more of a paragon of virtue than other people. Similarly, one cannot expect that teachers should perceive what they are doing in the classroom as a response to a calling. It's not possible to think like this any more, it's not realistic.

The responses given by this group of teacher educators indicate that they consider the shaping of students' attitudes to be an important part of schooling and an important part of teacher preparation as well. The way teachers live and behave is not, however, to be seen as a part of it. Teachers have the right to live their lives as they wish. In accordance with this view, the majority of teacher educators do not think of themselves as role models for the future teachers either.

The fifth lesson that we learned from our case study was that *prospective teachers do not acquire a moral vocabulary* during formal teacher education. On the contrary, the computer analyses of the students' responses during the interviews shows that there is a marked shift from the use of normative concepts to technical concepts pertaining to teaching and teachers' responsibilities. This fact may very well lead to the conclusion that one of the most important issues in teacher preparation is teaching prospective teachers the proper use of a technical language free of normative concepts and their moral impact. Teacher educators and future teachers as well speak fluently and with great enthusiasm about how teaching can be improved by the use of good planning and efficient teaching methods and techniques. In contrast, few are able to explain what it really means to be sensitive to the needs of the individual child, to be committed to all students in the classroom, and to behave as a figure of identification for the students.

Our data show that only a small minority of the respondents were able to reason beyond issues of dressing, personal habits, and manners when asked to explain the meaning and impact of being a role model. At this point, however, a clear difference could be seen between the vocabulary of mentors and that of instructors. While 90 percent of the first group stuck to a discussion of the teacher's manner and behavior, the latter group more often introduced aspects related to teachers' values and beliefs. According to the descriptions given by the mentors, responsible teachers who can serve as role models for their students are nondrinking, nonsmoking, well-dressed, polite, punctual, and well-adjusted citizens who treat other people decently and are universally trusted. Some of the mentors addressed this question to the classroom, as did one who expressed her conception of a model in the following way:

> It all relates to how you are going to behave as a teacher. The teacher should be well prepared and in a good mood. She should collect and hand back the assignments according to schedule. The teacher should see to it that she is herself punctual and sticks to what she has promised. The students in your class benefit tremendously from immediate feedback.

As mentioned above, the instructors tended to include personal qualities and internalized values in their discussion of teachers as role models more often than the mentors did. They strongly emphasized the fact that youth in today's society need figures of identification and that teachers serve as such whether they like it or not. Quite a few of the instructors believed that the importance of teachers as figures of identification has declined through recent years, as evidenced by the fact that people today generally do not expect as much from teachers as they did before. One of the instructors ended his reasoning about this as follows:

> Some of the most characteristic features assigned to teachers in schools have faded away. In many places, teachers have become quite anonymous citizens. Students do not look up to teachers any more. They have to look elsewhere for figures of identification. At the same time, I share the idea that there is still something special about teachers and the teaching profession. It's not like every other profession. Some still want teachers to reflect the old spectrum: middle-class values, the traditional social background, and the ideologies that teachers have had for decades.

When we look at the meaning that the future teachers assign to the role-model concept, we find a wide variety of views, which is similar to the pattern found in the group of teacher educators. The great majority of the education students responded by referring to manners and habits, as in the following example:

> If you're going to be a model for your students, you can't smoke, you can't drink, and you have to be respectable and behave properly in every way. There can't be any rumors about you painting the town, and you can't be seen out at any of the town's night spots or anything like that. You have to be an upright person who exercises self-control and doesn't let emotions show.

Some 10 percent of the teachers-to-be attach the model concept to the values, norms, and inner qualities of teachers. They think of teachers as people whom their students will naturally look up to and identify with because of their value systems. One student expressed this idea in a particularly pointed way at the beginning of her training:

> You should live a life the students learn from. It's not a question of appearance, having to be like a movie star the students are going to idealize. I'm thinking more of values. What you stand for should be compatible with what you teach kids at school. Children can learn a lot indirectly by observing the life you live as a teacher.

It is interesting to note that this student maintained her conception all the way through college training. The fact that teacher educators, as far as we can see, do little to encourage the development of prospective students' understanding of the moral dimensions of teaching may explain why nine out of ten students leave college with an understanding of the role model concept that is very similar to the one that they had when they started their formal teacher training.

Future Perspectives

The responses given by the teacher educators in our study very clearly indicate that the great majority of the group regard teacher education as a *practical-technological enterprise* whose main aim should be to develop prospective teachers into efficient professionals who can master the challenges of classroom teaching. This, they say, includes training future teachers to become good planners, effective and knowledgeable performers with highly developed communication skills, and good evaluators. Certainly, no one can object to that. It would seem, however, that these "performative" criteria rest on shallow ground, since they are not based on a solid rationale, a reflective view of the purpose of the school in today's society and of how the role of the teacher should be defined.

Most of the features that the research literature has assigned to the practical and technological conceptual orientations in teacher education were easily recognized in the responses that we analyzed in this study. However, these conceptual orientations do not address the moral dimensions of teaching. Quite a number of the prospective teachers complained that they were given few opportunities to think and reflect critically about their own role as teachers and about the work that they were actually going to do when they left college. What kinds of knowledge, skills, and values are they going to convey to their own students when they start teaching? How are they going to go about teaching the art of living — the *ars existendi* — which is the most difficult of all arts to perfect?

Some of the most reflective teachers-to-be in some way or another recognized that to be able to educate others, one must be educated oneself. If you expect to teach values and moral education, you must first clarify your own values and reflect thoroughly on how these should manifest themselves in your daily interaction with students and fellow citizens. The prospective teachers in our sample did not feel that they had been given much guidance or encouragement in their personal development during the formal teacher education program. Very few were able to point to teachers whom they would describe as a positive influence or whom they had looked up to. We met with a great number of enthusiastic teacher educators, but very few of them had serious thoughts of promoting a professional morality in prospective teachers.

We have every reason to believe that the group of prospective teachers with whom we worked are now practicing according to the best of their abilities. However, the degree to which they are teaching our youth the art of living can definitely not be attributed to formal teacher education. This does not imply that teacher educators do not encourage future teachers to do their best and to be both effective and responsible teachers. What it means is that the current attempt to reform teacher education in Norway to be a state-of-the-art enterprise has, in many instances, resulted in a noticeable neglect of the moral dimensions of teaching and the moral responsibilities that it entails. At this point, it also seems that our conclusions are quite congruent with the findings of recent research in other countries (Goodlad, 1990).

In a survey article on research on teacher education, Lanier and Little (1986) refer to teacher education as "the troubled field" (p. 527) and to the "consistent chaos in the course work" (p. 546) in teacher education colleges. We have seen some of the troubles and had glimpses into the chaos ourselves. In spite of the substantial meliorative activity and reforms that have been undertaken in teacher education, it seems that the problems remain basically the same. We wonder whether one reason for this may be that so many teacher educators enter the field without an explicit understanding of the nature of the teacher education enterprise and the task that they are going to perform. Experiencing the lack of rationale behind the program, they become more concerned with their own professional interests than with the teacher education business as such.

In spite of the new conception of teaching that has developed according to normative hermeneutic principles since the early 1970s, the teacher education field as a whole seems to still cling to old progressivist and behaviorist paradigms dating from the beginning of the twentieth century. To solve the persistent problems in teacher education, we have to develop a new and firm rationale based on a synthesis of the existing rationales. The new rationale should invite discussion as to what should be regarded as the most fundamental kinds of knowledge and the most basic values. It should provide future teachers with a moral language, promote their personal and moral development, and stress the personal responsibility incumbent on the teacher as a role model. Fenstermacher (1986) has rightly argued that "to be engaged in education as a normative enterprise one must have and exhibit the manner appropriate to this activity" (p. 47). The results from our own empirical research clearly indicate that the student teachers who score high on measures of professional morality (Bergem, 1986, 1992) are also rated as the more efficient teachers. This should suggest to us that we have a duty to develop a new and sound rationale for teacher education that forms the basis for an education capable of providing our prospective teachers with the highest possible ethical standards—indeed, capable of creating a new and firm teacher ethos.

References

Bandura, A. "Analysis of Modelling Processes." In A. Bandura (ed.), *Psychological Modelling: Conflicting Theories.* Chicago: Aldine-Atherton, 1971.

Bergem, T. *Vordende læreres tenkning og undervisnings-atferd* [The thinking and teaching behavior of student teachers]. LYH-Project Technical Report no. 3. Bergen, Norway: Norwegian Teachers College, 1986.

Bergem, T. "The Development of Professional Perspectives and Behaviour in Prospective Teachers." In H. Mandl, E. de Corte, N. Bennett, and H. F. Friedrich (eds.), *Learning and Instruction: European Research in an International Context.* Vol. 2.2: *Analysis of Complex Skills and Complex Domains.* Oxford, England: Pergamon Press, 1989.

Bergem, T. "The Teacher as Moral Agent." *Journal of Moral Education,* 1990a, *19* (2), 88–100.

Bergem, T. "Towards a Theory of Professional Morality: An Introduction to K. E. Lögstrup's Thought." Paper presented at the international symposium Values, Rights, and Responsibilities in the International Community: Moral Education for the New Millennium, Notre Dame, Ind., Nov. 1990b.

Bergem, T. *Tenkende lærere: Sluttrapport fra LYH-prosjektet* [Reflective teachers: a final report from the LYH project]. Bergen, Norway: NLA-Forlaget, 1992.

Bergem, T., and Kristiansen, A. "The Ethics of Teaching and the Teaching of Ethics: Comments on the Framework of a Study in Progress." Paper presented at the 1987 congress of the Nordic Society for Educational Research, Copenhagen, Mar. 1987.

Clark, C. "Educating the Good Teacher." Address presented to the Norwegian Conference on the Moral Dimensions of Teaching, Tjöme, Norway, May 1991.

Danner, H. *Verantwortung und Pädagogik* [Responsibility and pedagogy]. Königstein, Germany: Forum Academicum, 1985.

Day, C., Pope, M., and Denicolo, P. (eds.). *Insight into Teachers' Thinking and Practice.* London: Falmer Press, 1990.

Feiman- Nemser, S. "Teacher Preparation: Structural and Conceptual Alternatives." In W. R. Houston (ed.), *Handbook of Research on Teacher Education.* New York: Macmillan, 1990.

Fenstermacher, G. D. "Philosophy of Research on Teaching: Three Aspects." In D. C. Wittrock (ed.), *Handbook of Research on Teaching.* (3rd ed.) New York: Macmillan, 1986.

Frankl, V. E. *Man's Search for Meaning.* London: Hodder and Stoghton, 1977.

Giroux, H. *Ideology, Culture and the Process of Schooling.* Philadelphia: Temple University Press, 1981.

Goodlad, J. I. *Teachers for Our Nation's Schools.* San Francisco: Jossey-Bass, 1990.

Lanier, J. E., and Little, J. W. "Research on Teacher Education." In D. C. Wittrock (ed.), *Handbook of Research on Teaching.* (3rd ed.) New York: Macmillan, 1986.

Lögstrup, K. E. *Opgör med Kierkegaard* [The controversy with Kierkegaard]. Copenhagen: Gyldendahl, 1968.

Lögstrup, K. E. *Den etiske fordring* [The ethical demand]. Copenhagen: Gyldendahl, 1975.

Miller, A. *Banished Knowledge: Facing Childhood Injuries.* New York: Doubleday, 1990.

Mischel, W., and Grusec, J. "Determinants of the Rehearsal and Transmission of Neutral and Aversive Behaviors." *Journal of Personality and Social Psychology,* 1966, *3,* 197–205.

Noddings, N. *Caring: A Feminine Approach to Ethics and Moral Education.* Berkeley: University of California Press, 1984.

Oser, F. "Cognitive Representations of Professional Morality: A Key to Teaching Success." In T. Bergem (ed.), *I lærerens hånd* [In the teacher's hand]. Bergen, Norway: NLA-Forlaget, 1989.

Peters, R. S. *Ethics and Education.* London: Allen & Unwin, 1974.

Rest, J. R. "The Major Components of Morality." In W. M. Kurtines and J. L. Gewirtz (eds.), *Morality, Moral Behavior, and Moral Development.* New York: Wiley, 1984.

Ryan, K. "The New Moral Education." *Phi Delta Kappan,* Oct. 1986, pp. 231–233.

Schön, D. A. *The Reflective Practitioner: How Professionals Think in Action.* New York: Basic Books, 1983.

Schön, D. A. *Educating the Reflective Practitioner: Toward a New Design for Teaching and Learning in the Professions.* San Francisco: Jossey-Bass, 1987.

Shulman, L. S. "Paradigms and Research Programs in the Study of Teaching: A Contemporary Perspective." In M. C. Wittrock (ed.), *Handbook of Research on Teaching.* (3rd ed.) New York: Macmillan, 1986.

Sockett, H. "Accountability, Trust, and Ethical Codes of Practice." In J. I. Goodlad, R. Soder, and K. A. Sirotnik (eds.), *The Moral Dimensions of Teaching.* San Francisco: Jossey-Bass, 1990.

Tennyson, W. W., and Strom, S. M. "Beyond Professional Standards: Developing Responsibleness." *Journal of Counseling and Development,* 1986, *64,* 289–302.

Tom, A. R. *Teaching as a Moral Craft.* White Plains, N.Y.: Longman, 1984.

23

Putting Reflectivity Back into the Teaching Equation

Andreas Dick

The thesis of this chapter is straightforward: reliance on technical knowledge and skill in professional teacher education leaves student teachers ill prepared to think about schooling in a context-sensitive and socially constructive way and to consistently execute their practice accordingly. And yet is this not what we are demanding when we ask for responsible teaching? How can we, as teacher educators and researchers in teaching, help novice teachers cross the threshold between the theoretical-methodological-procedural side of teacher education to the complex and context-bound side of real teaching?

One of the answers lies in understanding the kind of knowledge that student teachers and experienced teachers bring to their respective tasks. In considering what beginning teachers need to know, teacher education programs have all too often failed to take experienced teachers' practical knowledge into account. At the same time, student teachers' preconceptions of teaching, learning, learners, subject matter, and other commonplaces of teaching have been neglected. Both knowledge bases offer important information for us as teacher educators. Expert-novice research, a growing field, offers teacher educators a starting point for including both prior knowledge and praxis knowledge in teacher education programs, and ethnographic techniques provide an excellent opportunity to become aware of and communicate both types of knowledge, thus offering a step across the theoretical-practical knowledge bridge.

Prior Knowledge, Professional Knowledge, Practical Knowledge

There are many different kinds of professional knowledge offered by most teacher education programs today. Feiman-Nemser (1990), for example,

Note: The author would like to thank all the teachers and students who participated in the study described in this chapter — without them it would not have been possible. He would also like to express his appreciation to David Berliner, Elliot Eisner, Gary Fenstermacher, Fritz Oser, Richard Shavelson, and Lee Shulman for their valuable influence, each in his own unique way.

differentiates five: the academic, the practical, the technological, the personal, and the critical-social, all of which often exist side by side. These various knowledge bases are grounded in research on teaching that, in the past, avoided dealing with difficult nonquantifiable knowledge (Barnes, 1989). However, while process-product research of various types (which neglected inner processes) has been supplemented or replaced by less linear or nonlinear models, the basic input-output approach has remained in teacher education. The result is the prevalence of a "what works" mentality, camouflaged as "research-based teacher competencies." These competencies are unfortunately often experienced by novice student teachers as a "deficit skills model" (Smyth, 1989) and create a large gap between the student teacher's prior knowledge of the reality of school and the professional knowledge that is supposed to be acquired.

Yinger (1987) touches on the subtlety of this matter when he draws attention to the fact that professional knowledge cannot be consistent because it combines two dissimilar types of knowledge. On the one hand, there is practical knowledge, which is often acquired in heterogeneous situations but retrieved only if it is relevant to particular instances. On the other hand, there is textbook knowledge, which can leave students ill prepared or "unintelligent" (p. 296).

When new teachers enter the profession, the conflict between these two types of knowledge often results in so-called practice shock (Müller-Fohrbrodt, Cloetta, and Dann, 1978; Veenman, 1985; Zeichner and Tabachnick, 1981). Having survived (or perhaps in order to survive), many teachers and not a few teacher educators choose to reject knowledge from conventional traditions such as teacher effectiveness research. They find that the research-based generalizations and rules cannot cope with the specificity of complex classroom phenomena and rely instead on a craft conception of professional knowledge, using professional judgment rather than positivistic generalizations (Tom and Valli, 1990).

To counter the one-sidedness of research in teacher education, increasing attention has been given to teachers' knowledge and thinking, thereby validating context-bound knowledge (for a summary, see Carter, 1990; Clark and Peterson, 1986). This research defines teacher cognition as a body of self-reflections regarding teachers' beliefs and knowledge about teaching, students, and content and as an awareness of problem-solving strategies endemic to classroom teaching. Within this framework, beliefs and knowledge are often used interchangeably. The difficult classifications within this research emanate out of the three epistemological orientations: the positivistic, the interpretive, and the critical. From these have evolved three main distinct but overlapping approaches: information processing studies, studies of pedagogical content knowledge, and research on practical personal knowledge.

The information-processing studies of research on teachers' knowledge have been the foundation for expert-novice research and partially for the research presented here. They have made it possible for us to begin to understand the depth and variety of experienced teachers' knowledge and to start formulating a definition of expertise. Berliner (1987; Chapter Fifteen in this book) has shown that experts have more complex understandings than novices and that expert teachers perceive, remember, and solve problems related to teaching differently from novice teachers. Furthermore, expert teachers appear to have rich schemata available that provide them with a framework for meaningfully interpreting information. At the same time, they know what to neglect, which means having a sense of the significant and possessing a framework that makes the search for the significant efficient. Finally, expert teachers attend more to atypical or unique events in the classroom than novices do. Interestingly, it is clear that expert teachers have the "reflective capability" to communicate knowledge about their craft to novice teachers. What is still lacking in the research, however, is the expert teacher's process of learning and the content of the kind of knowledge that such an expert teacher possesses. If these issues were pursued, the rather plausible factor of experience could be broken down into specific notions of constructed or invented forms of knowledge, acquired through repeated actions and thinking and learning from successes and failures.

Research on practical knowledge has generally come to be known as the "epistemology of practice" (Schön, 1983). Other terms used by researchers of practical knowledge are *local* or *personal* knowledge (Connelly and Clandinin, 1988; Lather, 1986; Sternberg and Caruso, 1985) and *craft* knowledge (Brown and McIntyre, 1986; Leinhardt, 1990). This current interest in theories of practical cognitions includes a number of studies of "situated," "everyday," or "practical" thinking and learning (Rogoff and Lave, 1984; Schön, 1987). All of them are related to the efforts of John Dewey ([1904] 1933), who spoke of the immediate quality of experience. This new interest in "learning the language of practice" (Yinger, 1987) seems promising both for revitalizing overly decontextualized and fragmented academic research and for providing a more realistic understanding of educational processes in teaching (Bruner, 1985).

Another type of knowledge classification, heading in the same direction, has been proposed by Shulman (1986), who distinguishes three important forms of knowledge for teachers: propositional knowledge, case knowledge, and strategic knowledge (forms that he extensively discusses in categories of content, pedagogy, and curriculum knowledge). Shulman argues that propositional knowledge, especially derived from empirical research as principles, is probably the most used form of knowledge in teacher preparation after practical experiences (maxims) and moral or ethical reasoning (norms). And while propositions are economical to use, reducing a great deal of the complexity of phenomena, they are in fact a form of "shortcut" knowledge. However, it is precisely the detail, the emotional or cognitive context, and the real situation that are often needed in order for knowledge to be remembered and responsibly used. Case knowledge is defined by Shulman as knowledge of very specific events that are well and thoroughly documented and richly described (and often cited by teachers as examples). As a synthesis, Shulman proposes the strategic knowledge that analyzes, tests, extends, and amends the other two forms of knowledge: "Strategic knowledge is developed when the lessons of single principles contradict one another, or the precedents of particular cases are incompatible" (Shulman, 1986, p. 13).

The new approaches to teacher thinking and teacher cognition accomplish several things: they validate context-bound information; they offer teachers the opportunity to communicate their perception of teaching; and they provide a more global framework for reintegrating responsibility with effectiveness in our understanding of "good" teaching. However, we must also keep in mind that, as Jackson (1986) has so clearly stated, teaching is never really "seen" but is always "read": it is interpreted in a way that is inevitably shaped by the assumptions of the observer. Since all descriptions of teaching are interpretations, the question for observers is how to lay bare the thinking that shapes the described actions. Ethnographic case studies offer the possibility to begin to do this and thus offer a research tool that can discover the relationship between effectiveness and responsibility in actual teaching practice as well as student teachers' awareness of this relationship.

Ethnography as Qualitative Inquiry

The problems in designing a truly useful teacher education program are complex. Some of the issues, as mentioned above, are the oversimplification of teaching through process-product research designs and their subsequent application to teacher education; the different types of knowledge bases that are employed in the act of teaching itself; and the traditional split between the research community and those actually working in elementary and secondary schools. Furthermore, we know little about student teachers' conceptions of the teaching profession, before or after their training. Information processing studies, particularly expert-novice research, are an attempt to address some of these issues. This chapter falls within that framework; it attempts to explore the complex interconnection between people's beliefs and actions — in this case, those of expert teachers and student teachers. Thus, a methodology that incorporates the existential experiences of the participants themselves (their language, actions, thoughts, feelings, and perceptions) was necessary for this investigation. The methods used to collect and analyze data were those associated with qualitative field studies (for example, Eisner and Peshkin, 1990; Glaser and Strauss, 1967; Goetz and LeCompte, 1984; Pelto and Pelto, 1975; Spradley, 1979; Strauss, 1987). They seemed the most appropriate because they allow a free combination of data-gathering methods. They also allow for the generation of analysis grounded in recorded data concerning the professional perspectives of teachers.

This study depends in particular on ethnographic methods of data gathering. It is based on a form of teacher-based practical inquiry, which is a characteristic feature of a kind of curriculum reform process new to teacher education. This view of education implies a shift in the concept of learning, which in turn shifts the criteria by which it is assessed: learning is viewed as the active production rather than the passive reproduction of meaning (see, for example, Chapter Fourteen). When learning is viewed as "active production," it becomes a manifestation of human powers to look at situations from different points of view and to self-monitor personal bias and prejudice (compare, for example, Chapters Ten and Twenty-Five). The development of understanding is construed as the extension of students' natural powers in relation to the things that matter in life. The manifestation of such qualities can be described and judged but not standardized and measured.

Ethnography, consisting as it does of openly recognized reflexivity, offers a tool for learning about and understanding both sides of an equation — in this case, expert teachers and student teachers. The ethnographic inquiry process, which I employed, depends on the student teacher as "coresearcher." It operates on two distinct but related levels: finding out what experienced teachers know and can communicate to novice teachers and discovering the gaps between students teachers' prior knowledge (or expectations) of classroom life and the reality of classroom life. In looking at the expert teachers' knowledge base, I concentrated on the characteristics of the teachers' theories of action in relation to their thought processes on their profession; the relationships among the teachers' philosophy of teaching, theories of action, thought processes, and classroom practice; and process aspects of the experienced teachers' thinking during the interactive phase of teaching and during narrative conversations about the profession with student teachers (evidenced in their frequent reuse of specific "themes" and examples).

In studying the student teachers, I needed to identify their current state of knowledge and to locate some kind of "minicrisis" in understanding that would cause them to recognize an insufficiency in their present knowledge and the advantages of a more advanced strategy of interpretation. I thought that by discovering crucial points of exposure to the multiple perspectives of the educational settings of teaching, I could challenge the student teachers' "familiar world of schooling" and that they would thus experience "disequilibration" and discomfort. Such a psychological state demands resolution by rethinking a situation. During this effort, however, it was sometimes necessary to gently push student teachers into analyzing what they saw and heard and linking it with their own experiences.

The major purpose of this study was to find a way to begin to fill in the large gap in our knowledge about how student teachers conceptualize their own professional perspectives. It also attempts to address questions in the literature regarding the psychosocial dynamics that take place within student teachers (for example, the way in which they process information, experience things, and learn as they develop a given perspective toward teaching).

The goal of the study was thus to probe deeply into the thinking and actions of student teachers, as well as to explore the way in which they organized their perspective into a practical philosophy of teaching by observing and dialoguing with an experienced teacher. It also set out to show the viability of an ethnographic approach as an alternative to the "deficit skills model" mentioned previously. The study of teachers' personal practical knowledge (see also Dick, 1990) is premised on the twin views that a theory of professional learning should be grounded in practice and that teachers' professional learning is a function of their ability to develop the qualities of the "reflective practitioner."

In order to achieve these goals, I designed a course for preservice teachers as part of an advanced methods course in which the students' task was to monitor the development of teachers' perspectives and to construct in-depth portraits of life in the classroom culture (in other words, an ethnographic study). This was accomplished through classroom observations and interviews with teachers (and in a few cases with pupils) over a four-month period. Each student teacher was randomly paired with one expert teacher. The study included eight teachers, each from a different secondary school in the German-speaking part of the canton of Fribourg, Switzerland. All eight schools were public secondary schools consisting of several hundred pupils. The eight teachers included five men and three women: four of them were in their forties, two were in their thirties, and two were in their fifties. Their length of experience in teaching ranged between twelve and twenty-four years. All of them were recommended by their principals as being excellent teachers in their own way. The eight student teachers involved were between twenty-three and twenty-six years of age, and all had completed a minimum of six semesters of teacher training at the University of Fribourg.

Each teacher was formally observed in the classroom at least three times. During the observations, student teachers made detailed field notes concerning various facets of teaching techniques, such as students involved, materials used, teacher talk, cognitive level, syntax of the teacher's role, types of activities used, student talk, objectives, and pacing. Following each observation, the field notes were expanded to form a comprehensive narrative of the lesson. The student teacher could also make use of videotapes of one or two class sessions, the cooperating teacher's logs, and collections of artifacts such as school documents, unit plans, and class handouts.

The ethnography that each student teacher was required to complete consisted of a beginning interview and a final interview and in some cases an intermediate interview as well. Questions were suggested by myself and then expanded by the student teachers. The type of interview questions that were developed for the students to ask required the expert teachers to reflect on the nature of teaching, the knowledge needs of new teachers, and the process of learning to teach. Furthermore, both teacher groups were encouraged to articulate their thoughts and attitudes in the form of dialogues. (As mentioned above, this work is based on the assumption that expert teachers do have the "reflective capability" to communicate knowledge about their craft in meaningful ways to novice teachers; see Berliner, 1987.) The interviews and dialogue sessions were recorded and then transcribed. It is interesting to note the student teachers' development as evidenced by just the questions they formulated. At first, the students structured their questions around various general areas of concern. However, as they analyzed their field notes and formulated their final set of interview questions, much more specific questions began emerging, which led to deeper insights and clarification of ambiguities.

In parallel to the interviews, student teachers were asked to keep journals in which they recorded classroom observations as well as their reactions to the teaching world around them. The purpose was to get them to focus on relating classroom, teacher, and school context to their own experiences in the profession. The ultimate aim was to teach the student teachers to be participant-observers in their own teaching cultures. If teaching can be viewed as a dialectical and deliberative process, the same can be said for the participant-observation field experience: it is a dialogue between the self and the environment, and the objective is to teach the student how to begin having this "situational conversation" (see Chapter Fourteen).

The final task in the ethnography was for each student teacher to create a portrait of the expert teacher based on all the materials that they had available from the interviews and classroom observations. This gave them the optimal opportunity to reflect on the thinking and actions of the experienced teachers that they had observed firsthand (with the variety of issues discussed above, including the role of teachers as curriculum developers, the nature of knowledge, definitions of learning, and the politics of teaching). Such reflection on their in-depth investigation rewarded the student teachers with insights into the types of professional perspectives that teachers develop as they become teachers, as well as helping them to explore ways in which a personal perspective can be organized into a practical philosophy of teaching.

Inquiry, Interpretation, Interaction

Besides providing insights into the practice of "real" contextualized teaching, the case approach helped student teachers to become aware of their own preconceptions and to examine them. Becoming aware of preconceptions is never an easy task. To help the student teachers to do this, it was suggested that as they drew a portrait of the experienced teacher, they try to identify the underlying beliefs that would make the actions and thoughts of that teacher plausible to someone else. Exposure to a variety of "conflicting" actions and thoughts and their underlying theories often made student teachers aware of the extent to which their own practice was theory-laden or preconceived. Thus, working on a "case" stimulated them to make their tacit beliefs and preconceptions explicit.

The eight student teacher-led ethnographic studies that form the data base for this report yielded almost a thousand pages of written text (transcripts plus portraiture). While all the student teachers started out with basically the same set of initial interview questions, they diverged widely in the depth of their final interviews. This clearly indicated to me that some expert teacher–student teacher dyads were able to profit more from the reflective experience than others. However, there were common themes — grading, differentiation, parents' role and influence, adolescence, and self-assessment — that emerged among all the student teachers' work, as evidenced by their temporal and situational recurrence. In fact, it could be exactly these common themes that indicate points of weakness in teacher education programs. Student teachers are unable to resolve the discrepancy between what they know or feel to be true, what they learn, and what they observe to be happening. The possibility for dialogue within the framework of ethnography offers teacher educators and researchers the opportunity to begin to discover the interaction between people's beliefs and actions. Exposing some of the thinking behind the actions also gives us insights into how efficiency can be carried out responsibly (see Chapter Eight).

One particular case in this study points out the impressive amount of reflection that can occur if we offer student teachers the opportunity. This case, which involved an experienced teacher with fourteen years of teaching service in a small town and a student teacher with three years of teacher training and ten weeks of supervised practice teaching and internship, showed the tremendous value of dialoguing. Through the process of questioning and responding, the student teacher experienced several "minicrises" in the course of his investigation, each of which he was eventually able to use as an opportunity for reflection. The interviews in this case also reveal the thinking and strategies of the experienced teacher. For example, following a classroom observation, the student teacher asked the experienced teacher where in that lesson the experienced teacher had perhaps shown a weakness. The experienced teacher told him — to the student teacher's great surprise — that during the main activity of the lesson, a French dictation, a child had cheated, and the teacher had noticed it and subtly let that girl know that he knew:

Experienced teacher: One of my weaknesses I felt at the start of the dictation: usually I do some relaxation exercises, so that there is a relaxed atmosphere, but today I was not able to do that. So I felt weak as I caught one pupil cheating. Did you notice it? I pity her, I feel sorry for her, since I know that she is under her parents' pressure.

Student teacher: Is that all you are going to do? I would flunk her!

The student teacher, who had also observed that something had gone on during the class, interpreted both the experienced teacher's description and his firsthand observation in a decontextualized way. Thus, the experienced teacher's response to it made little sense to him. Not so the experienced teacher, who was able to quickly judge the situation and take action on the basis of prior knowledge gained from similar context situations in the past. It is therefore not surprising that the experienced teacher immediately saw the need to point out to the novice teacher some aspects of the situation that justified his actions:

Experienced teacher: Grades and grading directly affect the further life, the path, of a child. We call it promotion and selection. And we wonder why a kid cheats. Why? Often it's actually the parents' demands and expectations that lie behind the child's behavior. But for the child, cheating is not a "cavalier's delict" at all: when they cheat, their hearts are pounding. On their own, just for fun, they'd cheat a lot less or not at all.

He then went on to compare his participation in school grading conferences with being at a math symposium, where participants exchange ciphers, forgetting their meaning.

Experienced teacher: Anybody who has thought about the problem once knows that "grading" means looking only at one side of the child. But all the teachers behave or have to behave as if the grades are an objective qualification.

When an experienced teacher employs an activity within the classroom, it is embedded within the teachers' set of premises about grades and grading. While both the student teacher and the experienced teacher probably observe the same surface qualities of the activity, it is in fact not the same activity for the two teachers, because each operationalizes a different theoretical framework, intention, and belief set. In this case, the experienced teacher communicated a strong opinion to the student teacher. He felt that there is room for so-called pedagogical grading, especially in a situation where a child is undergoing a psychological crisis, such as parental divorce. He went on to explain how teachers fear parental reactions or being accused of prejudice or are in a "state of information distress" (in other words, they do not know the contextual factors of families). This can make the task even harder and less reliable.

From this example, we can also imply that the experienced teacher in this case was convinced that good pedagogical intention, judgment, and consequently action must be supported by contextual knowledge, which subsequently must be organized into meaningful clusters that tie into a network of coherent relationships. He assumed that what learners bring with them to their learning tasks — the values, language, and cultural understandings that they have acquired from membership in particular gender, socioeconomic, religious, ethnic, or racial groups — also influences what and how they learn. By making the situation transparent to the student teacher "researcher," this teacher tried to communicate his beliefs.

This complex view of a situation, presented in such a straightforward way, caused the student teacher to reconceptualize his previous knowledge frames. This is exactly the goal of a "minicrisis." The transcript of his final interview, as well as his final portrait, shows evidence that he learned to take more of a "cultural difference" view, examining school failure in terms of the communicative misunderstanding that develops between children and teacher. Indeed, the student teacher appeared to have adopted the view, at times explicitly and at other times implicitly, that differences in school performance stem from interference between home culture and school culture: when children fail to meet a teacher's expectations, the cause is sought in the complexities of the tasks or in cultural differences in expectations rather than in deficiencies in the children themselves.

Further interview excerpts from this case illustrate the complexity of the interaction that can take place in such an ethnographic interview. The experienced teacher continued on the same theme of grading by emphasizing an aspect of testing that he thinks necessary to add at this point in the discussion lest his explanations be wrongfully categorized as a "soft-sided" conception of achievement.

Experienced teacher: But let me add one thing: in the more advanced classes I do have a lot of tests per semester, up to fifteen. [This number is rather high for Switzerland, where tests seem to be given in schools considerably less frequently than in the United States, for example.] The pupils have the need to find out how good they are in a particular subject. And there is another advantage: in a test, a pupil does not expose himself to the other classmates; it is his or her own achievement; it is silent work. This is important to keep in mind, since older pupils in puberty like privacy and tend to be more vulnerable.

This experienced teacher's use of frequent tests seems to serve more as a kind of self-monitoring technique to help pupils to be accountable for their work than as a grading measure. For example, in the case of the French dictation mentioned above, he gave pupils the possibility to freely gather and discuss their test work on their return to the regular classroom. Although this might have sounded like a contradiction to the student teacher, for the experienced teacher this kind of "opinion exchange" was much more important than the extra test that he gave. He considered it one of his strong points in teaching, since during such "free-gathering sessions," pupils usually talk very intensely about the subject matter. Methodologically, it also seems that he used this procedure as a way to occupy the pupils who finished their work quickly. This teacher was therefore dealing with the well-known problem of completion rates in a subject matter-oriented way *and* in a pupil-oriented way, a way that allows teacher and pupils to engage in learning to "see" participation, to examine learning in action, and to determine what is appropriate attention and participation in a given situation.

This is an example of the teacher individualizing his classroom teaching. In fact, as he continued to explain his position to the student teacher "researcher," he made it clear that his interest was in more than just "individualization." Throughout the interviews, he emphasized his particular interest in the weaker students, thus appearing as an "attorney of the suppressed." After a class test, he commented:

Experienced teacher: I'm very curious about the results. I've always been primarily interested in the achievements of the weaker students. . . . I think it's a shame when students get used to not finishing things — and that's something we do with our system, that the weaker students are used to not finishing things. I think it's not good for their psychic development. Students should be able to have the feeling that they can carry out every and all things to the end.

Still on the same general theme, the teacher went on to explain that giving his pupils goals that they can achieve is one of his most challenging tasks. Whenever he can, he gives them simple reinforcement possibilities. He shows a pattern of differential treatment for students in different ability-level groups by reinforcing practices of instructional tracking; this involves the coordinated use of both top-down (deductive, problem-solving) and bottom-up (inductive, rote) processes, rather than exclusively one or the other. Here is the kind of complex strategic planning that student teachers rarely meet in educational textbooks. Intrigued, the student teacher asked the experienced teacher whether his teaching in a particular class would change if one day the top five students suddenly failed to come to class. The experienced teacher answered as follows:

Experienced teacher: That's exactly what I do: I send them away myself because I've planned the lesson differently. They don't need to be present when I know that they can already do something. I send them away, and they can go read. That's something I purposely do. The reverse is also true, by the way. For example, I've already announced that I'd like to do a difficult text analysis. Whoever isn't interested can go and read. I plan this when I know that the next-door classroom is free so that they can go in there.

Student teacher: Then only the good students come to you?

Experienced teacher: Then the good students stay. I inform them, for example, that I'm going to do an analysis like they do at college. Then the potential future college students come. That's logical. [In Switzerland, secondary school children generally have to undergo an admission test in order to enter college.]

Not satisfied with this elaboration of the topic, the student teacher inquired further:

Student teacher: In teaching, do you call on the good students often?

Experienced teacher: I always try not to make any difference between the good and the bad students. I'd rather think in terms of interested and less interested students. I don't like it when fellow students know who's the best and who's the worst. That's why I try to get everybody. For example, [I'll say] "Who's interested in this text analysis?" And it's possible that a student who has only a 4 [a C] grade will be interested, so I let them [stay].

The topic of time on task interpreted in this differentiated way impressed the student teacher so much so that he specifically wrote in his portrait that he was about to understand the concept of "internal differentiation" on a practical level for the first time. In other words, a disequilibrium occurred that caused him to rethink prior (propositional) knowledge. Previously, he had been convinced of the correctness of the concept that those who fail to fit easily into the flow of social activity are to be treated as though they are deficient, rather than as though they are trying to make sense of things in their own, possibly different way. It was not exactly the view of engaging in outright favoritism, but the attention to understanding larger meaningful units of "text" was more neglected for the very children who may have needed it most (see Chapter Nine for further discussion of student motivation).

In fact, the student teacher also mentioned in several places in his ethnography that this kind of experienced knowledge meant something different from the expressions that he had learned from his teacher education program. He had learned the topic of individualized task-oriented learning as declarative knowledge only, without related procedural and conditional knowledge. Now he was beginning to grasp the explanations of the experienced teacher. At one point, the student teacher even forcefully spoke of the responsibility that he would like to take for doing everything possible to break into this cycle of reciprocity. This sensitivity stands in direct opposition to the deficit approach that he expressed at the beginning of the narrative example.

This example shows the value of recontextualization as a possible corrective, helping to place wayward actions back into the contexts to which they are thought to properly belong. It is interesting to note that the experienced teacher was somewhat sensitive to the student teacher's conflict, for he felt inspired to say the following:

Experienced teacher: One should avoid operating with abstract words like *student* and *youth*. In reality they're people, human beings, who vary from region to region, from school to school, from class, background, etc. Another way to put it is that one child can be already half-adult while another child [in the same class] is still completely a child. The discrepancy between the two extremes is even larger today. On the positive side, though, I'd like to say that children are much more independent today. Although it's true that you have to have more patience with them, in the end they know how to help themselves much better. For example, I've noticed that in school camps, nowadays the well-known phenomenon of homesickness rarely appears. Why isn't homesickness a problem for children anymore?

This quotation shows that the experienced teacher is able to differentiate among meanings of abstract psychological terms by recognizing the powerful influence of context on learning and looking beyond the surface features of classroom life to discover the social meanings constructed by the participants. And the student teacher was not unimpressed by the knowledge that he felt these remarks contained: he quoted them in his final portrait of his experienced teacher.

The portrait of the experienced teacher observed for four months was not an easy task. All the data had to be synthesized into a written portrait. Thus, the primary problem was to reduce the complexity of the rich picture that the student teachers had accumulated from the dozens of field notes, classroom materials, interview transcripts, and journal entries (altogether between 80 to 120 pages) that constituted their product-oriented assignment. The challenge of this metalevel thinking task is described in the following introduction of the student teacher's portrait (the teacher's name has been changed):

> The biggest difficulty for me is presenting Michael as Michael himself. First of all, I experience him as a person, an individual, a unique indivisible life, with light and shadows, touchable and yet finally an inexplicable phenomenon. So, as I proceed to "dissect" him into various parts for the following portrait (and I use the word "dissect" purposely) I ask the reader to always try and remember the whole person who is called Michael Zurkinden. I've rarely, and I emphasize this, rarely met a human being whose diverse sides have been so closely interwoven as with him. For these reasons I will concentrate less on his role as teacher, and pedagogical experience, recipes, and engagement as would perhaps be expected in his portrait.

The metalevel thinking required in creating his portrait of the experienced teacher led the student teacher into thinking about his own competencies as a novice teacher and the question of self-evaluation. For example:

> How to go about, what to do to assess yourself, when for example you think your teaching is good, but at the same time you want to assess yourself? I have troubles, saying whether I am a good teacher or a bad one. But I was comforted by Michael saying: *"To do the possible, and to trustfully let happen the rest! Since I do not have influence on the rest (otherwise I would do it), it shouldn't interest me. That is a very important principle that I try to train myself into. It is kind of a primeval trust and faith, a kind of religion maybe, so that you are not interested in other religions anymore."* That's amazing, I'll carry that sentence, that conviction with me all the time.

The student teacher seems to think and reflect in a way that helps him to broaden his awareness of his own beliefs and to develop his own personal justification on a difficult matter such as self-assessment. This is real empowerment. As Richardson (1990) writes, without empowerment, "teachers may become victims of their personal biographies, systematic political demands, and ecological conditions, rather than making use of them in developing and sustaining worthwhile and significant change" (p. 16). It can also be said that this is clearly a first step toward responsible action, for without reflection, action risks being only effective.

Self-Constructed Learning

As mentioned earlier, this chapter is premised on the new concept of learning in which the learner constructs his or her own learning. In the ethnographic approach presented here, the student teachers are involved as coinvestigators. Thus, the project serves as a kind of self-instruction where the student teachers assume an active role in their learning by consciously organizing and using their knowledge "to know when they do not know" (Wang and Palincsar, 1989) and to seek and find assistance with questions in future situations. This awareness of personal knowledge and the regulation of one's own cognitive processes—this metacognitive awareness—offers teachers and teacher educators the opportunity to consciously build responsibility into their effectiveness. "Erroneous" thinking or theorizing becomes an opportunity for higher-order problem solving rather than simply a wrong to be eliminated.

This strategy also requires the experienced teachers (the objects of inquiry) to be involved in a progressive approach in which they convey cultural knowledge, help the student teachers acquire higher-level thinking, and foster development beyond the usual limits. The participant observation and interview data collected revealed that experienced teachers do have coherent philosophies or ideologies and beliefs about students, knowledge, and the classroom situation that are clear and consistent and that can be communicated. The data also showed that the ideologies are consistent with the identified styles of teaching. In fact, the compatibility between style and ideology impressed all the student teachers.

The precision of the final interview questions and the portraits showed that, in the process of conceptual dialoguing, the student teachers had learned much. Their new knowledge included the fundamental realizations that theories are implicit in all practices and that theorizing consists of articulating those "tacit theories" and subjecting them to critique in free and open professional discourse—in other words, that theory derives from practice and not from a textbook—and that curriculum is not an organized selection of knowledge, concepts, and skills determined independently of the pedagogical process, solely on the basis of public structure of knowledge, but rather that the curriculum map is shaped within pedagogical practice, as the teacher selects and organizes content knowledge in response to the students' own search for meaning and then monitors their responses in the light of such criteria as relevance, interest, and challenge (Elliott, 1990). The pupils' subjective experiences constitute the data, in the light of which the teacher adjusts and modifies the emerging map. As the map unfolds and is pedagogically validated in retrospect through self-monitoring, it enables the teacher to anticipate but not predict future possibilities: "it provides the teacher with a sense of direction without prescribing a fixed agenda" (Elliott, 1990, p. 6). In Shulman's (1986) framework, this means that propositional knowledge notions (theory) must be paired with case knowledge (experiences) in order to be amended and merged into deliberate action (strategic knowledge).

This view of the theory-practice relationship is contrary to the rationalist assumption built into teacher training at this time: that good practice consists of the application of theoretical knowledge and principles that are consciously understood prior to it. One of Vygotsky's (1962) key assumptions is that concepts have their origins in social practices, rather than simply being "in one's head." And in that sense, the reflectivity of the experienced teachers in our study helped the student teachers to "reframe" (Schön, 1987) or "recontextualize" (Cazden, 1988) situations. It also meant a shift in the "game" being played: it took old moves and placed them in new domains of activity. For example, the experienced teachers responded to pupils in ways that placed them in new types of contexts, giving them meanings beyond those that the student teachers initially imagined; and in doing so, the experienced teachers pointed out additional possible meanings latent in a given situation or action, a message that was strongly received by the student teachers.

Conclusion

I hope that some of the implications of this work have become clear by now. One of them is that conceptual change can serve as an integrative concept in preservice education, representing an approach in which the teacher educator involves student teachers more actively and consciously in building knowledge and skills and in advancing their own development by means of interacting with an experienced teacher in a reflective way; for example, by doing an ethnography. Such a view of teacher education, wherein the student teachers shape their curriculum—a view analogous to Doyle's idea in Chapter Five of this book—is supported by Richardson (1990), who feels that empirical premises derived from research should be considered warranted practice and become the content of reflective teacher change. Similarly, Fenstermacher's (1986; Chapter Seven in this book) concept of practical arguments puts the value of research in the ability to change, complete, or modify premises in the minds of teachers or to introduce an altogether new premise into the practical argument of the teacher. He suggests that a way of introducing research to teachers could be encouraging them to compare their own value premises with those proposed by research.

The findings of this study illustrate the process of gathering ethnographic data and then fashioning it into a portrait of an experienced teacher, providing the preservice teachers who participated with the opportunity to examine and validate their own perspectives and legitimize their professional struggles. Within this perspective, teaching was not viewed as an activity aimed at controlling or causally determining the outcomes of learning (as it was perceived by some novice teachers); rather, it was viewed as facilitating an indeterminate dialectical process between public structures of knowledge and individual subjectivities. Furthermore, by sharing their agonies over contradictions, dilemmas, and dead ends, the experienced teachers were able to help prepare their inexperienced colleagues for the uncertainty of teaching rather than a fictitious world of teaching as a technically exact scientific enterprise.

These findings indicate that the separation between theory and practice typical of teacher education should be replaced by a view that allows each component to draw on information from the other. Student teachers need to experience many facets of classroom practice and routine if they are to be able to question and integrate the theory they learn. At the same time, we need to constantly evaluate and adjust research and theory to reflect the practical experience of teachers. Such an adjustment will also affect the recommendations for changes in practice that are based on such theory (Russell, 1988). The cumulative effect will be an intertwined theory and practice that more closely reflects reality. If reflective practice and the development of teachers' professional learning are to advance, then a much wider lens must be used, one that includes a focus on "extended professionalism" and the value of teachers' control and choice over curriculum content, planning, assessment, and evaluation (see Chapters Five and Six). This work offers, therefore, a powerful heuristic for meeting and for thinking more deeply about the needs of student teachers during their socialization into the complexities of teaching. That permits us to look at schools as enterprises where students, parents, teachers, and administrators are interlocked in a complex network of expectations and goals, more often than not diametrically opposed, whether they concern matters of effectiveness or manners of responsibility.

In reflecting on the methodology of this study, I believe that the merger of several research traditions has proved to be a powerful approach to uncovering information that would not have become visible if only one method had been used. This offered a richer picture of classroom and professional life for the teachers than would have been available from a single method of inquiry. The value of the approach can be realized only by future research that examines complex teaching and socialization processes from multiple perspectives.

References

Barnes, H. "Structuring Knowledge for Beginning Teaching." In M. C. Reynolds (ed.), *Knowledge Base for the Beginning Teacher.* Oxford, England: Pergamon Press, 1989.

Berliner, D. C. "Ways of Thinking About Students and Classrooms by More and Less Experienced Teachers." In J. Calderhead (ed.), *Exploring Teachers' Thinking*. London: Cassell Educational, 1987.

Brown, S., and McIntyre, D. "How Do Teachers Think About Their Craft?" In M. Ben-Peretz, R. Bromme, and R. Halkes (eds.), *Advances of Research on Teacher Thinking*. Lisse, the Netherlands: Swets & Zeitlinger, 1986.

Bruner, J. S. "Narrative and Paradigmatic Modes of Thought." In E. W. Eisner (ed.), *Learning and Teaching the Ways of Knowing*. Eighty-fourth yearbook of the National Society for the Study of Education, Part 2. Chicago: University of Chicago Press, 1985.

Carter, K. "Teachers' Knowledge and Learning to Teach." In W. R. Houston (ed.), *Handbook of Research on Teacher Education*. New York: Macmillan, 1990.

Cazden, C. B. *Classroom Discourse: The Language of Teaching and Learning*. Portsmouth, N.H.: Heinemann, 1988.

Clark, C. M., and Peterson, P. L. "Teachers' Thought Processes." In M. C. Wittrock (ed.), *Handbook of Research on Teaching*. (3rd ed.) New York: Macmillan, 1986.

Connelly, F. M., and Clandinin, D. J. *Teachers as Curriculum Planners: Narratives of Experience*. New York: Teachers College Press, 1988.

Dewey, J. *How We Think: A Restatement of the Relation of Reflective Thinking to the Educative Process*. Chicago: Henry Regnery, 1933. (Originally published 1904.)

Dick, A. *Researching the Familiar: Student Teachers' Long Last Look at the Teaching Profession*. Scientific Contributions on Education, no. 86. Fribourg, Switzerland: Department of Education of the University of Fribourg, 1990.

Eisner, E., and Peshkin, A. (eds.). *Qualitative Inquiry in Education: The Continuing Debate*. New York: Teachers College Press, 1990.

Elliott, J. "Teachers as Researchers: Implications for Supervision and for Teacher Education." *Teaching & Teacher Education*, 1990, *6* (1), 1–26.

Feiman-Nemser, S. "Teacher Preparation: Structural and Conceptual Alternatives." In W. R. Houston (ed.), *Handbook of Research on Teacher Education*. New York: Macmillan, 1990.

Fenstermacher, G. D. "Philosophy of Research on Teaching: Three Aspects." In M. C. Wittrock (ed.), *Handbook of Research on Teaching*. (3rd ed.) New York: Macmillan, 1986.

Glaser, B., and Strauss, A. L. *The Discovery of Grounded Theory: Strategies for Qualitative Research*. Chicago: Aldine, 1967.

Goetz, J. P., and LeCompte, M. D. *Ethnography and Qualitative Design in Educational Research*. San Diego, Calif.: Academic Press, 1984.

Jackson, P. W. *The Practice of Teaching*. New York: Teachers College Press, 1986.

Lather, P. "Research as Praxis." *Harvard Educational Review*, 1986, *56* (3), 257–277.

Leinhardt, G. "Capturing Craft Knowledge in Teaching." *Educational Researcher*, 1990, *19* (2), 18–25.

Müller-Fohrbrodt, G., Cloetta, B., and Dann, H. D. *Der Praxisschock bei jungen Lehrern*. [The praxis-shock among young teachers]. Stuttgart, Germany: Klett, 1978.

Pelto, P. J., and Pelto, G. H. "Intra-Cultural Diversity: Some Theoretical Issues." *American Ethnologist*, 1975, *2*, 1-18.

Richardson, V. "Significant and Worthwhile Change in Teaching Practice." *Educational Researcher*, 1990, *19* (7), 10-18.

Rogoff, B., and Lave, J. (eds.). *Everyday Cognition: Its Development in Social Context*. Cambridge, Mass.: Harvard University Press, 1984.

Russell, T. "From Preservice Teacher Education to First Year of Teaching: A Study of Theory and Practice." In J. Calderhead (ed.), *Teachers' Professional Knowledge*. Lewes, England: Falmer, 1988.

Schön, D. A. *The Reflective Practitioner: How Professionals Think in Action*. New York: Basic Books, 1983.

Schön, D. A. *Educating the Reflective Practitioner: Toward a New Design for Teaching and Learning in the Professions*. San Francisco: Jossey-Bass, 1987.

Shulman, L. S. "Those Who Understand: Knowledge Growth in Teaching." *Educational Researcher*, 1986, *15* (2), 4-14.

Smyth, J. "A Critical Pedagogy of Classroom Practice." *Journal of Curriculum Studies*, 1989, *21* (6), 483-502.

Spradley, J. P. *The Ethnographic Interview*. New York: Holt, Rinehart & Winston, 1979.

Sternberg, R. J., and Caruso, D. R. "Practical Modes of Knowing." In E. W. Eisner (ed.), *Learning and Teaching the Ways of Knowing*. Eighty-fourth yearbook of the National Society for the Study of Education, Part 2. Chicago: University of Chicago Press, 1985.

Strauss, A. *Qualitative Analysis for Social Scientists*. Cambridge: Cambridge University Press, 1987.

Tom, A. R., and Valli, L. "Professional Knowledge for Teachers." In W. R. Houston (ed.), *Handbook of Research on Teacher Education*. New York: Macmillan, 1990.

Veenman, S. "Perceived Problems of Beginning Teachers." *Review of Educational Research*, 1984, *54* (2), 143-178.

Vygotsky, L. S. *Thought and Language*. Cambridge, Mass.: MIT Press, 1962. (Originally published 1934.)

Wang, M. C., and Palincsar, A. S. "Teaching Students to Assume an Active Role in Their Learning." In M. C. Reynolds (ed.), *Knowledge Base for the Beginning Teacher*. Oxford, England: Pergamon Press, 1989.

Yinger, R. J. "Learning the Language of Practice." *Curriculum Inquiry*, 1987, *17* (3), 293-318.

Zeichner, K. M., and Tabachnick, B. R. "Are the Effects of Teacher Education 'Washed Out' by School Experience?" *Journal of Teacher Education*, 1981, *32* (3), 7-11.

24

Creating a Caring Community: Educational Practices That Promote Children's Prosocial Development

Daniel Solomon, Marilyn Watson,
Victor Battistich, Eric Schaps, Kevin Delucchi

Children inevitably receive much of their moral education in schools, even in societies that consider this to be an inappropriate or irrelevant role for the schools. Teachers implicitly convey moral values in their approaches to classroom governance and student motivation and in the types of goals that they emphasize, even when they feel that their concern is purely with promoting academic growth. The need for schools to attend *explicitly* to enhancing children's moral development may be greater now than ever before, as a result of social changes that have reduced the availability of other traditional sources of moral guidance. It is, therefore, appropriate to try to identify the aspects of schooling that are particularly effective for promoting moral development and to devise educational approaches that have this as a major goal.

The Child Development Project (CDP) is one such approach. The CDP was designed to enhance children's sociomoral development as well as their intellectual development during the elementary school years. Our conception of *sociomoral* (a term that we use interchangeably with *prosocial*) is a fairly broad one, including elements in each of four domains: cognitive characteristics; affective, motivational, and attitudinal characteristics; behavioral competencies; and action tendencies. To be prosocial, people must *understand* other people's motives, intentions, and needs; they must *want* to take appropriate actions to safeguard or improve the well-being of others; they must have the *abilities* needed to take the necessary actions; and they must then actually *perform* them in the appropriate situations. Moreover, prosocial people, in our view, do not develop a heightened orientation toward others at the expense of concern for their own needs, desires, and goals. They attend to their own needs and to those of others simultaneously, seeking an optimal self-other balance.

The CDP contains several elements: a comprehensive classroom program, a set of schoolwide and community activities, and a parent program.

In this chapter, we present a rationale for the approach (focusing primarily on the classroom program), describe its major elements, and present and discuss some findings from research on its effectiveness.

Creating Caring Communities in Schools

In our view, the environments or settings that are most likely to promote prosocial development are those that provide moral guidance to children while helping them to fulfill basic psychological needs for self-direction, competence, and social connectedness. Schools and classrooms in which these needs are consistently and routinely met are "caring communities." Such communities are characterized by feelings of mutual concern and respect among the members and by the knowledge that each cares about the welfare and progress of the others and is responsive and ready to give support when needed. The teacher helps this process by creating and maintaining a setting in which children can progress, with guidance, toward increasing levels of autonomy, responsibility, and interpersonal concern.

Another essential element of caring school communities is that all students feel that they are contributing members. In the classroom, this is accomplished by giving them the opportunity to have a meaningful impact on what happens there, through active (age-appropriate) participation in decision making about issues concerning classroom management, plans, and activities. What characterizes a caring classroom is not a lack of disagreement — there can be strong disagreement and disputation in decision making, and, in fact, it is each member's responsibility to state and explain his or her opinion — but a climate of respect for varying opinions and a norm of active participation by all members as the best way to reach fair and just decisions.

The teacher plays the critical role in creating a classroom that students experience as a caring community. The teacher creates a climate of mutual concern and respect by showing concern for all students and by being sincerely interested in their ideas, experiences, and products. By giving reasons and explanations for both academic and social-behavioral issues and by asking for student opinion and input, the teacher demonstrates that he or she considers students to be well intentioned and capable of useful thinking. Students are given the chance to see for themselves the importance of the things that they are asked to do and, in many cases, are allowed to decide for themselves when or in what way they will do them. They come to see themselves as doing these activities for their own intrinsic reasons rather than as a response to external coercion (that is, reasons imposed from without). It then becomes less necessary to entice students with the prospect of rewards or to threaten them with the fear of penalties or punishment in order to provide incentives for desired academic or social behavior.

Although we do not know of research on schools that has assessed the effects of participating in caring communities that include all the elements in the above description, there are a number of studies that have examined them individually. DeCharms (1976, 1984) has conducted several studies that have shown that students who are given the opportunity to exercise meaningful control over their academic lives show improvements in both their interpersonal relationships and their academic performance. Deci and Ryan (1985) found that teachers more effectively promote students' intrinsic motivation when their "control ideology" favors giving students opportunities to make their own decisions about how to solve classroom social and academic problems (as opposed to having their actions and plans imposed and controlled by the teacher). Adolescents in "just community" high schools (Higgins, Power, and Kohlberg, 1984; Kohlberg, 1985; Power, 1985), in which the students take a very active role in group norm setting and decision making, have been shown to score higher than students in traditional high schools on several measures relating to their perception of the school as a community, including their valuing of the school, their perception of shared norms among the students and of the commitment of members to uphold those norms, and the "moral adequacy" of the shared norms and values.

The Approach of the Child Development Project

In the Child Development Project, teachers foster children's prosocial development by creating classroom and school environments that meet the children's basic psychological needs and by implicitly and explicitly teaching general (or "core") prosocial values. The program plan was derived from the theoretical and research literature on prosocial development. It emphasizes the importance of children's active participation in the construction of sociomoral rules, norms, understandings, and behaviors (consistent with the positions of Piaget, 1932; and Kohlberg, 1985), as well as the crucial role of the adult as guide and transmitter of cultural values (consistent, in part, with Durkheim, 1973). It also emphasizes the importance of a meaningful and engaging curriculum focused on helping children to acquire understanding of the academic material and to develop long-term commitments to learning. The origins and initial general model of the project are presented in Brown and Solomon (1983) and Solomon and others (1985). Further elaborations of the background and rationale can be found in Watson and others (1989) and Battistich and others (1991). The program includes four major elements: cooperative learning, developmental discipline, the use of literature and other means to highlight prosocial values and promote empathy and interpersonal understanding, and helping and other prosocial activity.

Cooperative Learning

There is much evidence that cooperative learning is effective for promoting both academic and prosocial development (Johnson and others, 1981; Johnson, Johnson, and Maruyama, 1983; Sharan, 1980; Slavin, 1983). The CDP has developed a highly collaborative approach to cooperative learning, in which students work in pairs or larger groups, take different interdependent roles, are encouraged to use reason and explanation in their decision-making processes, and discuss and practice the application of specific social values in the group situation. Teachers give guidance where needed, but student work is largely self-directed. These activities, we believe, help children to develop feelings of competence, autonomy, and connectedness and to understand and adopt basic interpersonal values. Our use of cooperative learning in this project is based on a belief that two major types of experience are essential for promoting children's prosocial development.

One of these types of experience is interacting collaboratively with equal-status peers. Through such interaction, children learn the importance of attending to others, supporting them, accommodating to them, working out compromises, and the other interpersonal skills involved in working together with others. The second essential experience is provided by adult guidance and value advocacy. Peer interaction is not always or "naturally" equal-status, collaborative, and benevolent. The adult in our scheme provides direction — helps the students to think about the interpersonal and personal values relevant to their group activities (for example, helpfulness, fairness, concern and respect for others, personal responsibility) and to discuss how the values are expressed in particular behaviors. Care is taken to develop activities that truly benefit from collaboration and that are inherently interesting. (For a more detailed description of the CDP approach to cooperative learning, see Solomon and others, 1990; Watson, Hildebrandt, and Solomon, 1988).

Developmental Discipline

Developmental discipline is an overall approach to classroom management in which students are given an active role in classroom governance, in collaboration with the teacher. Students help to develop class rules at the start of the year and help to monitor and maintain classroom life through frequent class meetings. Control by direct teacher authority is minimized; students are helped and encouraged to take responsibility for their own learning and behavior. Instances of misbehavior are handled through a joint problem-solving approach (rather than through reward and punishment) whenever possible. Teachers are encouraged to be warm and sympathetic, rather than impersonal or punitive, and to develop close relationships with the students. Teachers emphasize the interest and importance of the academic activities as well as the basic value of positive interpersonal behavior and thus try to promote intrinsic rather than extrinsic incentives as motivators of academic and prosocial activities. A further description of the CDP approach to classroom management and discipline can be found in Watson and others (1989).

Use of Literature and Other Means to Highlight
Prosocial Values and Promote Interpersonal Understanding

Good literature provides children with "direct experience" of the role of values in our lives. Students are given books and stories to read that emphasize interpersonal and intercultural understanding and that express important prosocial values. Teachers then engage students in focused discussions that explore the interpersonal issues and values raised in the works. The readings and discussions give children opportunities to explore the values in supportive and unthreatening situations, to develop their abilities and inclinations to understand the thoughts, feelings, needs, and motives of others, and to build feelings of empathy and identification with people outside the immediate group and setting.

It is important for teachers to conduct these discussions in ways that involve the children as active participants and thinkers, not as passive recipients of indoctrination. Active participation in discourse around moral issues enhances children's understanding of the issues and also promotes internalization of the relevant values (see Oser, 1986). Prosocial values and interpersonal understanding are also highlighted in various other classroom settings, including class meetings and cooperative activities.

Helping and Other Prosocial Activity

Staub (1979) has summarized research showing that children benefit from engaging in prosocial activity, including helping others. In the Child Development Project, children are given frequent opportunities to help one another in their own classrooms and in the school community in general, most notably through a schoolwide "buddies" program in which older students pair with younger students and participate with them in various activities (accompanying them to school assemblies or on field trips, helping them with academics, working together on school or community service projects). This helps the older children to think about and act on specific social values and to feel competent and autonomous and helps the younger children to develop close relationships with the older students; students at all ages are helped to feel part of the general school community.

CDP and the Development of Caring
Communities in Schools and Classrooms

We believe that when this program functions effectively, students experience a sense of community both in the classroom and in the school as a whole. With the active guidance of the teacher, students develop feelings of commitment and responsibility to the class and the desire to uphold its norms. They care about one another and feel cared for in return. Each student knows that he or she has important contributions to make to the group. The same feeling is created in the school at large, so that students will feel that the school is a large "family" and that all of them are important and valued members. We believe that it is this sense of membership and identification that motivates children to want to abide by and uphold the norms and values endorsed by the teacher and the community.

We take steps to ensure that the sense of community is not achieved through a process of isolating and distancing one's own group or community from others. We discourage competition between groups within the classroom and between classes within the school. Within the class, students change membership in their cooperative groups periodically, so that by the end of the year, each student will have worked with all other students in the class. Many cross-class or schoolwide activities provide students with opportunities to feel part of the larger school community. Literature and discussions of readings are used in part to help children to understand the experiences of other settings and groups and to extend their sense of community and prosocial orientations to the world beyond their immediate community. The teacher's discussions of values and of the variety of settings and situations in which they can apply also help students learn to extend these values and the related behaviors beyond the boundaries of the classroom and school.

Plan of the Project

The CDP project was first implemented in three elementary schools in a relatively affluent suburban school district in the San Francisco Bay area, beginning in 1982. The program was provided primarily in classrooms by teachers, but it also included significant schoolwide and parental support aspects. Teachers received intensive training each year, usually consisting of a one-week summer institute, monthly workshops, frequent meetings with project staff, and supporting curriculum materials. The program moved up the grades in successive years with a cohort of children who were in kindergarten in 1982 and finished sixth grade in the spring of 1989. In addition to the schools in which the program was implemented, a set of three similar schools was selected to serve as a comparison group. In this chapter, we focus on the findings obtained with these two groups of schools.

During each year of the program, data were collected to assess the adequacy of program implementation in the classrooms and to assess student behavior and other outcomes. Program implementation was assessed primarily through classroom observations; student outcomes were assessed through class observations as well as interviews, small-group task sessions, and student questionnaires (given at third grade and above).

Assessment of Students' Sense of Community

A measure of students' sense of the classroom as a community was included in questionnaires administered to students when they were in the fourth, fifth, and sixth grades. This measure includes items representing the two major components in our conception of the sense of community: students' perceptions that they and their classmates care about and are supportive of one another and their perceptions that they have an important role in classroom decision making and direction. The mutual caring component was represented by seven items, including "Students in my class work together to solve problems," "My class is like a family," and "The children in this class really care about each other." The student participation in decision making component was represented by ten items, including "In my class the teacher and students plan together what we will do," "In my class the teacher and students decide together what the rules will be," and "The teacher in my class asks the students to help decide what the class should do." Internal consistency reliability of this scale (alpha), averaged across the three grade levels, was .74.

To see how these student perceptions related to the observers' representations of these classrooms, we correlated the sense of community scores, aggregated to the class level, with the observation indices of teacher behavior, classroom activities, and student behavior obtained at the fourth, fifth, and sixth grades, including both program and comparison classrooms (with the observation indices standardized within grade). These correlations are presented in Table 24.1. The observation indices that most closely reflect our conception of the sense of community (provision for student autonomy and input, student collaborative discussion, supportive and friendly student behavior, and spontaneous prosocial student behavior) all correlate highly with the sense of community measure (with correlations ranging from .51 to .61). This suggests a fair degree of validity for the measure. Other correlations shown in the table suggest that the way the teacher acts and organizes the classroom influences the sense of community among the students, with the encouragement and facilitation of cooperation being especially important.

Evidence of Program Implementation

All participating program and comparison classrooms were observed repeatedly during each year, and indices of each of the program components were derived from these observations. The program and comparison classrooms were found to differ strongly with respect to each of the five components, indicating that the program was much more closely approximated in the program classrooms than in the comparison classrooms. Although some teachers were better implementers than others, these findings show that, on the whole, the program was adequately conducted in the demonstration school classrooms.

Teachers' responses to questionnaires also provided evidence of program implementation. Teachers from the program schools reported less use of prizes and rewards as incentives, were more likely to say that their students had participated in the development of class rules, and scored consistently

Table 24.1. Correlations of Aggregated Sense-of-Community Scores
with Classroom Observation Indices.

	Correlations with Sense of Community	p
Teacher qualities and practices		
Provision for student autonomy and input	.51	.006
Warmth and supportiveness	.38	.044
Irritability and punitiveness	−.14	.480
Use of external control	−.09	.660
Encouragement of cooperation	.56	.002
Facilitation of cooperative activities	.55	.002
Promotion of competition	−.21	.358
Student interpersonal classroom behavior		
Cooperative group activities	.29	.136
Collaborative within-group discussion	.45	.016
Supportive and friendly behavior	.60	.001
Negative behavior	−.02	.902
Proportion of positive behavior	.35	.068
Spontaneous prosocial behavior	.61	.001
General harmoniousness	.30	.118

Note: $N = 28$ classrooms: 13 at fourth grade, 6 at fifth grade, and 9 at sixth grade.

higher on a measure of "control ideology" (Deci, Schwartz, Sheinman, and Ryan, 1981), indicating an inclination to maximize student autonomy in the classroom and minimize the use of power assertion and other forms of external control. For more details about the evidence of program implementation, see Solomon and others (1988, 1990).

Effects of the Program on Student Outcomes

Effects on Students' Sense of Community

We have said that the CDP approach to education was designed to promote students' sense of community and that we expected that the program would be most effective when it succeeded in creating this feeling. How successful were we in creating caring classroom communities?

To determine whether the CDP program as a whole influenced this feeling, we compared the individual sense of community scores between students in program and comparison schools at the fourth, fifth, and sixth grades. Students in the program schools scored significantly higher than those in the comparison schools each year (with ps of .001, .022, and .049).

Other Direct Effects on Students

In addition to its contribution to the development of a sense of community among students, the CDP program also produced a number of other consistent and significant effects on students. Although we have reported most of them elsewhere, we will briefly summarize these findings here.

The classroom observers focused on student interpersonal behavior (in addition to indices of program implementation) and found that program students engaged in more spontaneous prosocial behavior and were more harmonious in class than were comparison students (Solomon and others, 1988). From the interviews and questionnaires given to students over the life of this project, program students were found to score higher on measures of social problem-solving and conflict-resolution skills (Battistich and others, 1989), endorsement of democratic values (Solomon and others, 1990), and interpersonal understanding.

Academic achievement was assessed with a standardized achievement test (California Achievement Test) when the students were in the fourth grade. Scores on these tests were not significantly different between the students at the program and the comparison schools. The scores were generally in a very high range at both sets of schools (around the ninetieth percentile), so there was not much opportunity for further enhancement. The results do indicate, however, that the program did not *undermine* academic achievement, as measured by these tests (see Solomon and others, 1988).

We had some doubts as to the appropriateness of standardized achievement tests for assessing the aspects of achievement that are most emphasized by the program—the use of higher-order thinking and the development of understanding. We therefore adapted a "holistic" measure of reading comprehension developed by the Educational Testing Service that seemed better suited for assessing such aspects and administered it to the students in both sets of schools when they were in the sixth grade. They read two brief passages and then answered general questions about the meaning of the passages. Students from the program schools scored significantly higher on this measure ($p = <.01$), suggesting that the program was successful in helping children to more fully understand what they read.

Relationships Between Sense of Community and Other Student Measures

Sense of community was significantly correlated with a number of other student measures. At each of the three grades in which sense of community was assessed (fourth, fifth, and sixth), it was most strongly related to students' liking for school. Students apparently are most likely to enjoy a setting if they experience it as a caring community. Sense of community was also positively (and significantly) related to self-reported empathy, intrinsic prosocial and academic motivation, achievement motivation, and self-esteem.

Having shown that the CDP program experience and the sense of community were each separately related to a number of student outcome measures, we were interested in investigating the possibility that these two variables might have additional combined effects. We therefore conducted a series of regression analyses to see whether the effectiveness of the CDP program was enhanced when it succeeded in creating a sense of community among students. Each analysis investigated the effect of program status, sense of community, and their interaction on a single dependent variable.

Several of these analyses provided evidence that program status and sense of community did have combined effects on various of the assessed outcomes. The relationships showing combined effects took different forms. Some showed additive effects, such that sense of community and program status were separately and consistently related to outcomes; this occurred for the measures of democratic values, conflict resolution, and reading comprehension. In these instances, the outcome variable was significantly related to sense of community in either type of classroom but was at a generally higher level in the program classrooms, so that the program students with the highest sense of community scores showed the best outcome scores.

There were also a few instances of interactions where the effect of sense of community was positive within program classrooms and either nonsignificant or negative within comparison classrooms. These occurred for four variables in the prosocial values domain, all derived from interview questions about hypothetical situations. Some of these described potential helping situations (and were scored for both the choice as to whether to help and the reason given for that choice), while others described moral-ethical transgressions (and were scored for both the type of actions that were taken following the transgressions and the reasons given for taking those actions). In each case, higher scores represent more prosocial responses or more prosocial explanations for the responses (for example, helping because of empathy, concern for the other, or a specific value, rather than avoidance of punishment, anticipated rewards, or hoped-for reciprocation). These responses were enhanced by students' sense of their classrooms as communities in program classrooms but not in comparison classrooms.

Some of the interaction results showed comparison students with a low sense of community to have prosocial scores as high as program students with a high sense of community; we find this difficult to interpret. Within the program classrooms, however, the students' sense of community, as expected, was positively related to the prosocial measures, underlining the importance of creating a community feeling for enhancing the positive effects of this program.

The significant interactions between program status and sense of community seem largely consistent with the notion that a strong sense of community increases students' adherence to perceived classroom norms. The generally positive relationships between sense of community and the helping and transgression measures in program classrooms, for example, compared with the neutral or negative relationships in comparison classrooms, may reflect a greater salience of the relevant values in program classrooms. We know from our observations that prosocial values were more salient in program classrooms. If participating in a caring community promotes a desire to conform to the community's norms, we might expect that students in a caring classroom whose teacher stressed prosocial values and interpersonal concern (and where actions based on such concerns were the norms) would attend more to such factors as guides for their behavior (thus the positive relationship between the sense of community and the prosocial responses and reasons in the program classrooms).

These findings suggest that experiencing a caring classroom community is likely to promote students' adherence to what they see as the implicit or explicit norms and values of that community — norms and values that may take very different forms from one classroom to another.

Conclusions

We have stressed the importance of creating a caring community in the classroom and the school. The data that we have presented confirm the importance of children's feeling that their classrooms constitute such caring communities and provide evidence that the program was successful in helping to create those feelings. In spite of the differences between the program and comparison students on this variable, however, there was also substantial overlap in the distributions, indicating that some of the comparison classrooms also created this sense among their students and that some of the program classrooms did not.

There were several instances in which program status and sense of community produced a greater impact on student outcomes in combination than either did by itself. The patterns of these relationships took several shapes, but, in general, they indicated that positive results were found for program students who saw their classrooms as caring communities (and, in some cases, for comparison students who did not). Perhaps the most interesting findings suggest that classrooms that create a sense of community among their students may promote a desire among those students to abide by the norms of the classroom. This is consistent with the findings of investigations of social influence that stress the importance of "identification" and "internalization" (Kelman, 1958), "referent power" (French and Raven, 1959), and the "normative function" of reference groups (Kelley, 1952). It is also consistent with approaches to socialization that emphasize the importance of supportive and nurturant environments for the acquisition and internalization of values (see Maccoby and Martin, 1983).

If the sense of community provides students with the motivation to abide by the norms of the classroom, it does not inevitably dictate what those norms should be. We have suggested, for example, that the program and comparison classrooms differed with respect to their relative emphasis on prosocial values and that this difference may help to account for some of the joint effects of program status and sense of community. The broader implication is that developing a sense of community alone is insufficient. Attention must also be paid to the content of the norms and values enunciated by the community and to the ways in which those norms and values are upheld.

We believe that the findings described here underscore the importance of creating classroom environments that children will experience as caring communities. The findings also indicate that the actions and style of teachers are important in shaping such experiences for children and that it is important to have these communities grounded in explicit prosocial norms and values. These results support the utility of an approach to education that attends to children's developmental needs; that tries to create school and classroom environments that are cohesive, supportive, and involving; and that engages students' intrinsic interest in academic activities and in promoting prosocial interpersonal relations. While we do not claim that such ideal circumstances were approached in more than a few classrooms in this project, we do believe that the evidence presented here indicates that they are possible—that classrooms and schools that simultaneously promote students' academic development and interpersonal concern through the creation of caring and prosocial communities can be achieved. The Child Development Project represents one approach to helping schools and teachers to realize these goals.

References

Battistich, V., and others. "Effects of an Elementary School Program to Enhance Prosocial Behavior on Children's Cognitive Social Problem-Solving Skills and Strategies." *Journal of Applied Developmental Psychology*, 1989, *10*, 147-169.

Battistich, V., and others. "The Child Development Project: A Comprehensive Program for the Development of Prosocial Character." In W. M. Kurtines and J. L. Gewirtz (eds.), *Handbook of Moral Behavior and Development*. Vol. 3: *Application*. Hillsdale, N.J.: Erlbaum, 1991.

Brown, D., and Solomon, D. "A Model for Prosocial Learning: An In-Progress Field Study." In D. L. Bridgman (ed.), *The Nature of Prosocial Development: Interdisciplinary Theories and Strategies*. San Diego, Calif.: Academic Press, 1983.

deCharms, R. *Enhancing Motivation: Change in the Classroom*. New York: Irvington, 1976.

deCharms, R. "Motivation Enhancement in Educational Settings." In R. E. Ames and C. Ames (eds.), *Motivation in Education*. Vol. 1. San Diego, Calif.: Academic Press, 1984.

Deci, E. L., and Ryan, R. M. *Intrinsic Motivation and Self-Determination in Human Behavior*. New York: Plenum Press, 1985.

Deci, E. L., Schwartz, A. J., Sheinman, L., and Ryan, R. M. "An Instrument to Assess Adults' Orientation Toward Control Versus Autonomy with Children: Reflections on Intrinsic Motivation and Perceived Competence." *Journal of Educational Psychology*, 1981, *73*, 642–650.

Durkheim, E. *Moral Education*. New York: Free Press, 1973.

French, J.R.P., Jr., and Raven, B. "The Bases of Social Power." In D. Cartwright (ed.), *Studies in Social Power*. Ann Arbor: University of Michigan, 1959.

Higgins, A., Power, C., and Kohlberg, L. "The Relationship of Moral Atmosphere to Judgments of Responsibility." In W. M. Kurtines and J. L. Gewirtz (eds.), *Morality, Moral Behavior, and Moral Development*. New York: Wiley, 1984.

Johnson, D. W., Johnson, R. T., and Maruyama, G. "Interdependence and Interpersonal Attraction Among Heterogeneous and Homogeneous Individuals: A Theoretical Formulation and a Meta-Analysis of the Research." *Review of Educational Research*, 1983, *53*, 5–54.

Johnson, D. W., and others. "Effects of Cooperative, Competitive, and Individualistic Goal Structures on Achievement: A Meta-Analysis." *Psychological Bulletin*, 1981, *89*, 47–62.

Kelley, H. H. "Two Functions of Reference Groups." In G. E. Swanson, T. M. Newcomb, and E. L. Hartley (eds.), *Readings in Social Psychology*. New York: Holt, Rinehart & Winston, 1952.

Kelman, H. C. "Compliance, Identification, and Internalization: Three Processes of Attitude Change." *Journal of Conflict Resolution*, 1958, *2*, 51–60.

Kohlberg, L. "The Just Community Approach to Moral Education in Theory and Practice." In M. W. Berkowitz and F. Oser (eds.), *Moral Education: Theory and Application*. Hillsdale, N.J.: Erlbaum, 1985.

Maccoby, E. E., and Martin, J. A. "Socialization in the Context of the Family: Parent-Child Interaction." In E. M. Hetherington (ed.), *Handbook of Child Psychology*. Vol. 4: *Socialization, Personality and Social Development*. New York: Wiley, 1983.

Oser, F. "Moral Education and Values Education: The Discourse Perspective." In M. C. Wittrock (ed.), *Handbook of Research on Teaching*. (3rd ed.) New York: Macmillan, 1986.

Piaget, J. *The Moral Judgment of the Child*. New York: Free Press, 1965.

Power, C. "Democratic Moral Education in the Large Public High School." In M. W. Berkowitz and F. Oser (eds.), *Moral Education: Theory and Application*. Hillsdale, N.J.: Erlbaum, 1985.

Sharan, S. "Cooperative Learning in Small Groups: Recent Methods and Effects on Achievement, Attitudes and Ethnic Relations." *Review of Educational Research*, 1980, *50*, 241–271.

Slavin, R. *Cooperative Learning*. White Plains, N.Y.: Longman, 1983.

Solomon, D., and others. "A Program to Promote Interpersonal Consideration and Cooperation in Children." In R. Slavin and others (eds.), *Learning to Cooperate: Cooperating to Learn*. New York: Plenum Press, 1985.

Solomon, D., and others. "Enhancing Children's Prosocial Behavior in the Classroom." *American Educational Research Journal*, 1988, *25*, 527–554.

Solomon, D., and others. "Cooperative Learning as Part of a Comprehensive Classroom Program Designed to Promote Prosocial Development." In S. Sharan (ed.), *Cooperative Learning: Theory and Research*. New York: Praeger, 1990.

Staub, E. *Positive Social Behavior and Morality.* Vol. 2: *Socialization and Development.* San Diego, Calif.: Academic Press, 1979.

Watson, M., Hildebrandt, C., and Solomon, D. "Cooperative Learning as a Means of Promoting Prosocial Development Among Kindergarten and Early Primary Grade Children." *International Journal of Social Education,* 1988, *3,* 34–47.

Watson, M., and others. "The Child Development Project: Combining Traditional and Developmental Approaches to Values Education." In L. Nucci (ed.), *Moral Development and Character Education: A Dialogue.* Berkeley, Calif.: McCutchan, 1989.

25

Fostering Children's Social Conflict Resolutions in the Classroom: A Developmental Approach

Sigrún Adalbjarnardóttir

A student has been attacked by several of his classmates, accused of being a tattle-tale. All the students are very upset. How do teachers react to common conflicts among students such as this one? Some teachers might not deal with the conflict at all. They might avoid confronting both themselves and the students with the problem, thinking that it is not their main role and responsibility as a teacher to deal with children's social conflicts. Other teachers might feel that as an authority figure, they have to solve the conflict for the sake of the children's well-being. In a unilateral manner, they might talk to the students, blame them for their behavior, and tell them that they should never attack their classmates. Still other teachers might feel that as professionals, they have the responsibility to solve the problem *with* the students. They might provide a setting for discussing the problem from each participant's point of view and working out a solution. These teachers would be concerned about both fostering individual well-being in the classroom and promoting children's social-cognitive competence and skills.

In the Western world, educators today seem to be facing increasing problems in social interactions among students, as well as problems in student-teacher relationships, including discipline problems. In many cases, there is lack of respect, lack of empathy, and even increased violence among young people. It is a societal problem that we need to react to, searching for effective ways to work against the trend. School is no exception in this regard;

Note: The research reported in this chapter was supported by grants from the Icelandic Council of Science, the Research Foundation of the University of Iceland, and the Ministry of Culture and Education of Iceland. I gratefully thank the teachers and their students who participated in the intervention program and the intervention study for their contributions. I would also like to sincerely thank Kristjana Blöndal, Elísabet V. Gudmundsdóttir, and Elín Thorarensen for their assistance in conducting the intervention study and Wolfgang Edelstein for his helpful comments on the chapter.

indeed, the school and the classroom environment may provide special opportunities for activating children to consider and solve social problems successfully, given the various daily social problems that arise in school and the relatively equal status of the students involved in these problems.

The work presented in this chapter aims at relating our responsibility in fostering children's sociomoral growth to effective school practice. The chapter describes an intervention program that the author organized with this aim in mind. More precisely, in working toward the aim of fostering children's social competence and skills in dealing with social conflicts, the program emphasized teacher training, focusing on the competence and teaching strategies of the responsible professional teacher. As part of the program, a curriculum was developed around children's social interactions for the use of teachers, and an intervention study was conducted to explore whether children who receive special training in resolving social conflicts in the classroom improve their social competence and skills more than children who do not receive structured training.

Intervening in Social Conflicts

The attempt to promote children's interpersonal understanding and successful social conflict resolution in the schools depends essentially on the teacher's competence and motivation to deal with social issues in the classroom (Oser, 1989), as well as on the teaching approach (DeVries, Morgan, and Learned, 1990). In this regard, teacher education plays an important role. However, teacher training programs have tended to neglect the preparation of teachers for working on sociomoral issues with children. Not surprisingly, teachers are often insecure about dealing with these various issues, both those in the curriculum and those that arise among classmates. Teachers need knowledge, support, and encouragement in working with students on sociomoral topics (Edelstein, 1977).

In this light, I organized a special intervention program for Icelandic elementary school teachers. Well-integrated theoretical and practical knowledge was considered one of the prerequisites to being able to promote children's social competence and skills. To achieve this, I adopted a two-sided approach. On the one hand, an emphasis was placed on working with theories of children's sociocognitive development (for example, Piaget [1932], 1965; Kohlberg, 1969; Selman, 1980; Youniss, 1980; Damon, 1983; Turiel, 1983; Adalbjarnardóttir, 1988; Keller and Wood, 1989). According to this tradition, individuals in interaction with others constantly construct and reconstruct their social world, gradually improving their ability to face and solve social conflicts. The teachers were introduced to these theories to improve their understanding of how children gradually develop their sociomoral competence. They were stimulated to consider what to expect of children's competence in dealing with social issues and to evaluate their sociomoral growth.

On the other hand, the program focused on teaching strategies that have been found effective in promoting children's social competence and skills in conflict resolution (Oser, 1981; Brion-Meisels and Selman, 1984; Berkowitz and Gibbs, 1985; Power, Higgins, and Kohlberg, 1989). These teaching strategies focus on setting up a cognitive conflict in children's minds by using either real-life or hypothetical social dilemmas, followed by Socratic questioning. In the Piagetian tradition, theories of socio-cognitive development claim that thinking about the various sides of the conflict induces disequilibrium in the child's sociomoral thought structures. Children must assimilate new information into their thought structures and accommodate to new reasoning. Gradually, this struggle of coordinating conflicting perspectives, which the teacher provides in the classroom, makes the child's reasoning structures more complex and flexible. In other words, the struggle promotes children's sociomoral growth.

Fifteen Icelandic elementary school teachers working with children aged seven through twelve participated in the intervention program. The teachers were trained in twenty group meetings held once every week or two during the academic year. In those meetings, they had to participate in discussions about theoretical and practical issues that concerned the promotion of children's sociomoral growth and then decide which tasks should be dealt with and how. Classroom experiences were shared, and the teachers reflected on what had worked well, what had worked less well, and how they could improve their teaching. In addition, the teachers allowed me to observe them in the classroom while they worked on social issues with the children. Afterward, I gave them feedback on their teaching.

The teachers were responsible for bringing to the classroom issues of conflicting perspectives in social relationships among children and to work on these issues with the children. Previous experience suggested that the most appropriate way to sustain children's motivation to deal with social issues over a long period of time is to work on a theme for some time and then switch to another topic. The teachers accordingly ran an organized program with the children for four weeks during the fall and for ten weeks during the spring. In the fall, the program started with tasks about friendship (for example, conflicts in friendship, what makes a good friend, how to make a friend, how to keep a friend, and trust in friendship). During the spring, the program focused first on events in recess periods, with time devoted to dealing with conflicts between classmates (teasing, calling names, fighting, telling on, leaving out), and later on classroom interactions. Topics included the interaction between the children (for example, in cooperative work) and differences between students' and teachers' points of view about such issues as classroom rules.

The three themes of the program — "Let us be friends," "Let us play together: recess periods," and "Let us work together: in the classroom" — served as frames for subject matters. The teachers did not all necessarily deal with exactly the same issues, nor did they deal with them in the same way. They used their various types of "pedagogical content knowledge," to use Shulman's term (Chapter Two), as they prepared and worked with their students on sociomoral issues. In addition to the three themes, the teachers used opportunities for discussion and problem solving provided throughout the entire academic year by the many real-life social conflicts between the children.

The teachers further were responsible for creating a comfortable atmosphere in the classroom, where students not only felt free to express their ideas, felt that they were heard, and felt the need to listen to each other but also were motivated to argue, debate, and reach agreement. In this regard, the teachers were encouraged to emphasize with the students a mode of discussion that focused on the different perspectives in social relationships. The aim of such discussion around conflicting opinions was to stimulate children to face and define different perspectives in the process of solving interpersonal conflicts. In this process, children are encouraged to understand the conflict and to consider various types of conflict resolution and their consequences for the participants before they take action that is simultaneously responsible and effective.

In line with the Piagetian tradition, stressing the importance of activating children's reasoning processes for the promotion of their social development, teachers were warned not to do the thinking for the children and to actually listen to children's voices (Adalbjarnardóttir and Edelstein, 1989; Chapter Fourteen in this volume). Here is one teacher's report that sheds light on her awareness of her responsibility to encourage her students to solve their social conflicts themselves, instead of thinking for them, and to encourage them to think before they act:

> My participation in this project has brought about many changes in my work. Earlier, when problems came up, I think I was very quick to intervene. Certainly, I asked the kids involved to express themselves "very briefly" about what had happened. But I was quick to judge, to comment, to advise, and to try to reconcile them, such as by saying "Well, now you must be friends." Thus, the students themselves were not active in the problem solution. Rather, it was I who found the solutions and I who controlled. Now I am no longer as quick to intervene. I ask the children to stop and think, to express themselves about what has happened, and I withdraw more and listen to the children. Certainly, it is more effective if they themselves face and solve the problems. Then the solution and the whole experience are more likely to stay with them. I feel I have changed a lot in this manner.

This teacher is aware of how her way of exerting her authority when she works on social problems with her students has changed. She is aware that she is giving up some control in the classroom. She believes that if she encourages her students to take responsibility for working out their problems themselves, they will be more likely to act on their solutions. In addition, she is clearly aware of the developmental implications of her teaching with regard to the interplay between her students' progress and her own change in dealing with social conflicts.

Discussion was an important element of the program. The teachers were encouraged to conduct discussions with the whole class, as well as within groups or pairs of students. Peer discussion was emphasized in light of findings that it promotes growth because of the relatively equal status of the participants (Damon, 1984; Slavin, 1988). The teachers were encouraged to use other types of instruction as well: the students wrote stories and poems about social interaction and problem solving, and they expressed themselves through drawing and painting and by role playing social conflicts.

Teachers' responsibility was also reflected in the way they organized and conducted the classroom discussion. In line with Dewey's ([1904] 1933) findings on how people solve problems step by step, the teachers were encouraged to systematically lead the discussion through the use of specific "open questions." These questions require the students first to define the problem and to express their feelings about it (step 1), then to generate alternative ways of solving the problem (step 2), next to choose the best way (step 3), and finally to evaluate the outcome (step 4). The following example shows how one teacher dealt with the problem mentioned at the beginning of this chapter by using these steps (the name of the student involved has been changed):

> In the beginning of the school day, the students were very upset. One of the students, Tryggvi, had not shown up, and I found out that he had been attacked by a number of his classmates and that he was too scared to come to class. As the students were very upset, I started with asking them to explain their point of view (What happened? Why did this happen?). But soon I asked one of the three students who seemed to be on Tryggvi's side to see whether he could find him. He came back with Tryggvi, and we sat down in our discussion corner. Then he explained his point of view. The facts of the situation seemed clear. The students had been going to a gym lesson. As their lesson had not started yet, most of the class had sat in the balcony to watch another gym class. Tryggvi thought this was not permitted and said to his classmates that the teacher had forbidden it, but they didn't listen to him. Then he went to the teacher and told on his classmates. The teacher did not make any comments about the matter to the class, since the students came down from the balcony before the lesson started. After the gym lesson, Tryggvi was attacked, hit, spanked, kicked, and

abused. His classmates said that he was always a tattle-tale. Only three kids were on Tryggvi's side and said he had just been trying to ask the kids not to do forbidden things. I worked through the steps by having them define the problem and think about the feelings of those involved. Then I asked them to come up with alternative ways to solve the problem and to find the best way to solve it. The solution they suggested was that the class would agree to stop teasing Tryggvi if he would stop telling on the others. Tryggvi agreed to be less meddlesome but thought he should tell if it was obvious that his classmates were violating rules. The class agreed to this.

The teacher reported that this discussion had been very effective. Tryggvi's classmates had considered him to be a tattle-tale and had demonstrated their disapproval in various ways before this event. After this discussion, however, the children held to their agreement for months. She reported how lively the discussion had been and how concerned and eager to solve the problem the students were. She emphasized how helpful it had been to use the standard questions, the steps, in leading the discussion. This approach had provided her with increased security and assurance of working through the social conflict with her students in an organized and constructive way.

This example demonstrates how a teacher can face conflicts among her students in a way that is both effective and responsible. This teacher acted responsibly toward the students by providing them with an opportunity to work through a conflict that, if left unresolved, would have cemented an outsider position for a member of the class and deprived the class of an opportunity for social, emotional, and cognitive progress. As she applied her professional knowledge and skills, her approach was highly effective.

Researching Social Competence

We empirically validated the effectiveness of the intervention program by exploring whether children who participated in the program improved their social competence and skills more than did children who had not received training. The focus of the study was on children's ability to differentiate and coordinate conflicting perspectives in social interactions when solving social conflicts. Perspective-taking competence is taken to be a grounding element of the development of reasoning about social conflicts, required for interpersonal understanding and consensus (Selman, 1976; Kohlberg, 1976; Habermas, 1984; Keller and Reuss, 1984).

Previous Research

It is well known among researchers how difficult it is to design studies that show the influence of educational intervention on children's and adolescents' sociomoral competence and skills. Researchers have, however, detected rather positive effects of educational interventions emphasizing active classroom discussion around sociomoral conflicts on either judgments or actions of participants. In a meta-analysis of moral intervention studies, it was found that educational programs focusing on group discussion of moral dilemmas and programs emphasizing personality development improve adolescents' and adults' moral judgment (Schlaefli, Rest, and Thoma, 1985). Academic courses in the humanities and social studies have not shown this influence on moral judgment development.

In a review of sociocognitive problem-solving interventions, Urbain and Kendall (1980) report that studies designed to assess improvement of children's perspective-taking competence have generally been successful. The intervention programs that they review focused mainly on role playing and discussion (see, for example, Chandler, 1973). In their pioneering work, Spivack and Shure (1983) postulated a model that assesses children's interpersonal cognitive problem-solving (ICPS) skills. Shure (1982) reports that most studies using this model have shown evidence of the improvement of ICPS skills of elementary school children following intervention. These intervention programs focus on skills in solving social problems, such as the generation of alternative strategies, anticipation of consequences, and selection of a strategy. In addition, Solomon and his colleagues (Chapter Twenty-Four) have found positive effects of their Child Development Project on several aspects of sociomoral development, such as prosocial behavior, interpersonal understanding, feelings of loneliness, and social anxiety. In their project, they emphasize warm and supportive relationships in the classroom, students' autonomy and influence, and effective guidance regarding social values.

Few studies have explored the relationship between what children *say* they will do to solve a problem and what they actually *do* in real-life conflict situations (see, however, Shure, 1982). This is the classic problem of the relationship between thought and action (Blasi, 1980). Focusing merely on either thought or behavior provides limited effects of educational intervention (Urbain and Kendall, 1980). Exploring only reasoning and not real-life actions is a limited approach, because it lacks the pressure to act that is present in a specific setting. In real-life situations, components of inner dispositions, personal history, and context interact in complex ways to influence an individual's actions. Also, exploring only actions limits the understanding of an individual's competence and motivation to solve social problems (Oser, 1989; Selman and Schultz, 1988).

Selman and his colleagues (Adalbjarnardóttir and Selman, 1989; Schultz and Selman, 1989; Yeates and Selman, 1989) have attempted to address this issue in a theory of interpersonal negotiation strategies (INS). The theory focuses on development in thought and action that children and adolescents use in resolving conflicting opinions in social interactions. The theory of interpersonal negotiation strategies was used in the intervention study described here as a framework to explore whether children who receive

constructive training in resolving social conflicts in the classroom improve
their social competence and skills more than children who do not receive
such training.

The INS Model

There are several reasons for using the model of interpersonal negotiation
strategies in this study. The theoretical background of the intervention program and of the study is the Piaget-Dewey approach mentioned earlier.
Within the structural-developmental tradition (Piaget [1932] 1965; Kohlberg, 1969), Selman (1980) postulates that the ability to take another person's perspective is developmental: it requires a person to pass through a
series of ordered *levels*. These levels are impulsive (level 0), with no consideration of perspective expressed; unilateral (level 1), with a consideration of only one participant's perspective expressed; reciprocal (level 2), with
each participant's perspective expressed cooperatively but separately; and
collaborative (level 3), with mutuality expressed in the coordination of both
participants' perspectives. In our intervention program, teachers attempted
to promote this natural development by providing the children with opportunities to resolve interpersonal problems.

    Within the social information processing approach (Rubin and Kras-
nor, 1986; Spivack and Shure, 1983) rooted in Dewey's ([1904] 1933) for-
mulations, *steps* are identified in the INS model that individuals use to resolve
conflicts in interpersonal negotiation. As noted earlier, these steps are defining
the problem (step 1), generating alternative strategies (step 2), selecting and
implementing a strategy (step 3), and evaluating the outcome (step 4). In
a structured interview, children are presented with hypothetical dilemmas
involving social conflicts. Responding to questions that illustrate the four
steps, children report on the conflict and its solutions. This interview technique is easily applied to the questioning strategies used in the intervention
program where sociomoral conflicts are discussed.

    The structural-developmental approach and the information process-
ing approach are integrated in the INS model by postulating that the four
levels of perspective coordination underly each of the four steps. For example, individuals may *generate* alternative strategies or *act* in real-life situations
in either an impulsive, a unilateral, a reciprocal, or a mutually collaborative way. Below, these levels are distinguished and illustrated with interpersonal negotiation strategies at each of the four levels:

> *Level 0: Impulsive-egocentric strategies.* Strategies classified as impulsive
> are primarily physical in nature, either withdrawing (flight) or ag-
> gressive (fight). These strategies reflect an egocentric point of view
> that fails to differentiate subjective perspectives.
> *Level 1: Unilateral–one-way strategies.* Strategies classified as unilateral
> are primarily one-way directed, taking only one person's perspec-

tive into account. Strategies are either submissively obedient (give in, apologize, be helpless) or assertively commanding (give orders, bully).

Level 2: Reciprocal-reflective strategies. Strategies classified as reciprocal reflect a coordination of both participants' perspectives but with a priority on the perspective of either the self or the other. These strategies are oriented toward exchange, either in a deferential style (ask for reasons, barter, accommodate, go second) or in a persuasive style (give reasons, influence, go first).

Level 3: Collaborative-mutual strategies. Strategies classified as collaborative involve the integration of the needs and wishes of self and other in dialogue. A mutual third-person perspective is reflected in the contribution of both participants to the resolution of social conflicts, with considerations of psychological effects for a long-term relationship.

In this light, the INS model allows for the exploration of social development in both thought (using hypothetical interactions) and action (using observations in the classroom). Also, the model allows for the examination of the relationship between thought and action; that is, the relationship between what children say and what they do in real-life situations. In addition, the model allows for the exploration of social context differences; that is, whether children are involved in interaction with a classmate or a teacher.

Studying Social Conflict Intervention

Method

Four teachers from the pool of the fifteen Icelandic elementary school teachers participating in the intervention program assisted in the study by giving permission to have their students interviewed and observed in the classroom. These four teachers worked with children aged eight (two classes) and eleven (two classes). Twelve children (six girls and six boys) were selected randomly from each class to participate in the study, for a total of forty-eight children. Children from four other classes were assigned to a control group and received no structured training. The control group also comprised forty-eight students, twelve (six girls and six boys) from each class, aged eight and eleven.

All ninety-six children were similarly interviewed and observed in the beginning of and again at the end of an academic year (fall and spring). Children were interviewed to assess their developmental level of *INS thought* (INS reasoning). Each child in the study had to respond to four brief school dilemmas focusing on strategies in negotiating with either a teacher or a classmate concerning different perspectives about classroom activities. For example, "Anna (Árni) thinks she (he) is working hard on a project in social studies that she (he) and her (his) classmate Thora (Thor) are doing together.

One day, however, while they are working, Thora (Thor) accuses Anna (Árni) of not working hard enough." The interviewer asked the child a series of eight standard questions followed by probes. The questions asked the child to define the problem as the child saw it (step 1a), express the feelings of the participants (step 1b), suggest several good ways for the protagonist to negotiate with the teacher or the classmate (step 2), choose the best way to negotiate (step 3a), evaluate how the participants would feel if the proposed action were taken (step 4a), think of an obstacle that might hinder that action from working (step 3b), find a good way to handle such a situation (step 3c), and, finally, explain how he or she knew that the problem was being solved (step 4b). Children's responses to these questions were classified according to their ability to differentiate and coordinate the conflicting perspectives involved (levels 0–3).

To assess children's developmental level of *INS action,* we observed them in their social interactions with their classmates and their teacher. The observers stayed in each class for one week both in the fall and in the spring. They observed each of the participating children for at least two hours, writing down every social act of the child in negotiating with either classmates or teacher (minimum of five and maximum of fifteen interaction scenes for each role situation). As with the children's responses to the hypothetical dilemmas, each of the actions observed with either a teacher or a classmate was classified according to an underlying developmental level of social perspective coordination (0–3).

Results

The effectiveness of the program is indicated by the fact that children in the intervention group increased their INS reasoning level scores more than children in the control group ($F[1,88] = 5.48, p = .021$). Moreover, a three-way interaction was obtained between participation in the program, gender, and role ($F[1,88] = 4.02, p = .048$). As expected, girls in the intervention program improved more in their thinking about a conflict with a classmate than in their reasoning about a conflict relating to the teacher. Contrary to what was expected, however, boys in the intervention program increased their level scores more in teacher-oriented problems than in thinking about a problem with a classmate. It had been expected that the change in level of INS reasoning for both genders would be more pronounced in situations with classmates than with teachers, given the constraints in student-teacher relationships as compared to peer relationships (Adalbjarnardóttir and Selman, 1989). This unexpected finding with regard to boys may further illustrate the effectiveness of the program. Instead of using unilateral ways of blaming boys for their known misbehavior in the classroom (Dweck, Davidson, Nelson, and Enna, 1978), teachers in the program used more reciprocal ways by encouraging the boys to consider both their own point of view and the teacher's perspective when solving student-teacher social problems. This change in teaching approach may have influenced the relatively high progress in the boys' level of INS reasoning in dealing with student-teacher conflicts.

An interaction between program and role emerged in the *observed INS action level* (F [1,88] = 4.22, p = .043). Children in the intervention group improved their level scores in negotiating with a classmate more than children in the control group, while practically no difference was obtained between the groups in the increase in level of INS negotiation with a teacher. This failure to detect difference between the groups in level of action in negotiating with teachers may illustrate the constraint in adult-child relationships compared to peer relationships (Piaget, [1932] 1965; Youniss, 1980; Damon, 1983). Student-teacher relationships tend to be unilateral, given the teacher's authority (Adalbjarnardóttir and Selman, 1989). With this constraint, it may be difficult to detect progress in children's level of action in negotiating with teachers in real-life situations as affected by only a one-year intervention program.

A significant correlation between INS reasoning level scores and INS action level scores (r = .49, p < .0001) was found. Further exploration of this relationship indicated that once the effects of age and gender were removed, INS reasoning level predicted INS action level (F [3,92] = 16.84, p < .0001). These results suggest that children scoring high in INS reasoning level are also likely to do so in INS action level. This correspondence between reasoning and action indicates that there must be a relationship and validity between the concepts underlying INS reasoning and the behavioral reality of everyday life.

Fostering Social Reasoning and Conflict Resolutions

The Piaget-Dewey approach of the theory of interpersonal negotiation strategies can be used as a model to link the sociopsychological theory of social cognition to educational implications as a way to foster children's social competence and conflict resolutions. The same theoretical model underlies both the promotion of children's social-cognitive understanding and effective conflict resolutions in the classroom by using discussion and role playing and the exploration of children's progress as affected by their participation in such an intervention program.

The intervention program appeared to be effective both with regard to teachers' competence and motivation in handling sociomoral issues in the classroom (a qualitative observation) and with regard to children's social competence and skills (a quantitative study). The teachers in the intervention program reported that they felt that participation in the project had increased their security in dealing with social conflicts because of their richer understanding of children's interpersonal competence and actions and their improved teaching skills in working with children on social conflicts. Observations in the classrooms and discussion meetings about the teachers' work with the children indicated this increased security among them and reflected their professional responsibility.

Second, girls and boys who participated in the intervention program showed more improvement in their ability to solve hypothetical classroom conflicts (INS level of reasoning) than girls and boys who did not receive training in dealing with such conflicts. Children in the intervention program thus considered both participants' perspectives in a social conflict more often than did the children in the regular program.

Finally, when negotiating with classmates in real-life situations, children in the intervention program showed more improvement in their INS action level than did children in the regular program. They negotiated with their classmates on a more reciprocal level, taking both people's perspectives into account more often than did children who received no structured training in social conflict resolution. These children might argue more often instead of fighting, ask questions instead of commanding, engage in discussion instead of quarreling.

These results may support the intuitions of the teachers that the atmosphere in their classrooms had become more relaxed and positive because of their classes' participation in the program. They reported that the students had become more open and friendly toward each other, had begun to express more empathy, tolerance, and altruism, and were less judgmental. In addition, children tried more frequently to solve their conflicts in a peaceful way than they had done before. One nice example of the increased responsibility among the children in dealing with sociomoral issues is this teacher's report:

> The day before the last day of school, Ása came to me and asked me whether I would believe that Sigga had been stealing. I said no, except if I had seen it or if she would admit to having taken the thing. The rumor went on, and at the end of the school day, more children came to me and said that three girls in the class were suspected of having together taken some candy from a store. Clearly, the children were under considerable pressure because of their concern about working things out as a group before school vacation. They felt a lack of trust toward the girls and did not want to leave without discussing the matter. Even that night, three kids called me at home emphasizing how important it was that the issue should be discussed in class. As time was running out, I decided to call the three girls and ask them to meet me an hour before school started the very next day, which they did. We discussed the problem. They were sincere about what they had done and expressed their own feelings, as well as how they thought their classmates felt about the matter. Then I asked them to discuss the problem among themselves and come to an agreement about how to solve it with their classmates. And I left. When they had come up with a solution, they presented it to their classmates for discussion. They

told their classmates that they regretted having taken the candy and that all three of them were equally guilty. They said that they felt very sorry about this and that they would never do such a thing again. They also suggested that the problem should not be discussed further in class. After some deliberation, the class agreed to this solution. I could feel the relief among the children that the issue had been dealt with. For example, afterward, two of the boys came to me and expressed how pleased they were.

This teacher felt convinced that the children would not have demonstrated such care and concern as a group and such competence in solving the problem had they not taken part in a program where they were encouraged to solve social conflicts by studying a variety of solutions and their consequences before acting according to the best solution chosen. This example, however, not only reflects children's awareness of their responsibility as members of a group that has to solve problems in order to keep a strong, trusting relationship alive in the classroom; it also shows how the teacher had created a supportive community in the classroom by encouraging students to deal with sociomoral conflicts responsibly. To use Oser's terms (Chapter Eight), the teacher's professional morality is reflected in how he or she works with the children toward coordinating the three moral dimensions of *justice* (in this example, it is not right to steal), *care* (the concern of classmates and teachers, as a group, with the importance of maintaining trust), and *truthfulness* (ascertaining sincerity in the discussion) when searching for the adequate solution of a sociomoral problem (see also Habermas, 1984).

In addition, the study indicated that children's developmental level of reasoning was positively related to their developmental level of action (Yeates, Schultz, and Selman, 1991), a finding of interest for both educators and theorists. For example, children who scored high in reasoning were also likely to score high in action. This suggests that reasoning about conflict resolutions may extend to real-life settings (Shure, 1982). Yet there is not a one-way street between level of INS thought and level of INS action. For example, Schultz and Selman (1989) have shown that psychodynamic processes such as defense mechanisms and object representation predict INS action level, even when the effects of INS thought level (which also predicts action level) are controlled for. As Rest (1983) claims, reasoning is only one component among others, such as character and motivation, that predict sociomoral behavior.

In sum, the results of this attempt to bridge the gap between sociopsychological theory and educational practice appear promising. In fact, the findings indicate greater effectiveness of the intervention program than I had expected, given the time it takes for teachers to assimilate new teaching styles and to accommodate to them and the relatively slow natural progression of children's social development (Adalbjarnardóttir and Selman, 1989; Edelstein, Keller, and Schröder, 1990). These findings should encourage educators to engage in constructive endeavors in the schools, fostering the social competence of the students and their ability to resolve conflicts. To pursue this goal, teachers should not only focus on classroom management but also attempt to promote students' sociocognitive development by dealing with sociomoral issues.

Many questions remain concerning the promotion of children's social development. Here I would like to emphasize two. First, there is the theoretical problem of evaluating the relationship between children's progress in social reasoning and their progress in successful conflict resolution in real-life settings. We have just begun to explore the complex psychological processes of judgment, motivation, character, and personal history that influence conflict resolutions in social settings. Second, there is the practical problem of providing teachers with enough support to face and deal with sociomoral conflicts with their students. Sociomoral conflicts are sensitive issues that are often difficult for teachers to handle, given the demands of the many children in class and the time-consuming and complicated nature of adequate solutions to the problems. Further research and educational interventions are needed to strengthen the bridge between sociopsychological theory and educational practice so that it can be traversed smoothly to the advantage of the next generation.

References

Adalbjarnardóttir, S. "Children's Communicative Actions in Conflict Situations with Teachers and Classmates: A Developmental Study." Unpublished doctoral dissertation, Department of Human Development and Psychology, Harvard University, 1988.

Adalbjarnardóttir, S., and Edelstein, W. "Listening to Children's Voices: Psychological Theory and Educational Implications." *Scandinavian Journal of Educational Research,* 1989, *33* (1), 79–97.

Adalbjarnardóttir, S., and Selman, R. L. "How Children Propose to Deal with the Criticism of their Teachers and Classmates: Developmental and Stylistic Variations." *Child Development,* 1989, *60,* 539–550.

Berkowitz, M. W., and Gibbs, J. C. "The Process of Moral Conflict Resolution and Moral Development." In M. W. Berkowitz (ed.), *Peer Conflict and Psychological Growth.* New Directions for Child Development, no. 29. San Francisco: Jossey-Bass, 1985.

Blasi, A. "Bridging Moral Cognition and Moral Action: A Critical Review of the Literature." *Psychological Bulletin,* 1980, *88,* 593–637.

Brion-Meisels, S., and Selman, R. L. "Early Adolescents' Development of New Interpersonal Strategies: Understanding and Intervention." *School Psychology Review,* 1984, *13,* 278–291.

Chandler, M. "Egocentrism and Antisocial Behavior: The Assessment and Training of Social Perspective-Taking Skills." *Developmental Psychology,* 1973, *9,* 326–332.

Damon, W. *Social and Personality Development: Infancy Through Adolescence*. New York: Norton, 1983.

Damon, W. "Peer Education: The Untapped Potential." *Journal of Applied Developmental Psychology*, 1984, *5*, 331–343.

DeVries, R., Morgan, P., and Learned, H. "Interpersonal Understanding in Children from Distar, Constructivist, and Eclectic Kindergarten Programs." Paper presented at the annual meeting of the American Educational Research Association, Boston, Apr. 1990.

Dewey, J. *How We Think: A Restatement of the Relation of Reflective Thinking to the Educative Process*. Chicago: Henry Regnery, 1933. (Originally published 1904.)

Dweck, C. S., Davidson, W., Nelson, S., and Enna, B. "Sex Differences in Learned Helplessness." *Developmental Psychology*, 1978, *14*, 268–276.

Edelstein, W. "Educational Application of Theories of Social Cognitive Development." In C.F.M. Van Lieshout and D. J. Ingram (eds.), *Simulation of Social Development in School*. Amsterdam: Swets & Zeitlinger, 1977.

Edelstein, W., Keller, M., and Schröder, E. "Child Development and Social Structure: A Longitudinal Study of Individual Differences." In P. B. Baltes, D. L. Featherman, and R. M. Lerner (eds.), *Life-Span Development and Behavior*. Vol. 10. Hillsdale, N.J.: Erlbaum, 1990.

Habermas, J. *The Theory of Communicative Action*. Boston: Beacon Press, 1984.

Keller, M., and Reuss, S. "An Action-Theoretical Reconstruction of the Development of Social-Cognitive Competence." *Human Development*, 1984, *27*, 211–220.

Keller, M., and Wood, P. "Development of Friendship Reasoning: A Study of Interindividual Differences in Intraindividual Change." *Developmental Psychology*, 1989, *25*, 820–826.

Kohlberg, L. "Stage and Sequence: The Cognitive-Developmental Approach to Socialization." In D. A. Goslin (ed.), *Handbook of Socialization on Theory and Research*. Skokie, Ill.: Rand McNally, 1969.

Kohlberg, L. "Moral Stages and Moralization: The Cognitive-Developmental Approach." In T. Lickona (ed.), *Moral Development and Behavior*. New York: Holt, Rinehart & Winston, 1976.

Oser, F. K. *Moralisches Urteil in Gruppen* [Moral judgment in groups]. Frankfurt am Main: Suhrkamp, 1981.

Oser, F. K. "Cognitive Representations of Professional Morality: A Key to Teaching Success." Address presented at the annual meeting of the American Educational Research Association, San Francisco, Mar. 1989.

Piaget, J. *The Moral Judgment of the Child*. New York: Free Press, 1965. (Originally published 1932.)

Power, F. C., Higgins, A., and Kohlberg, L. *Lawrence Kohlberg's Approach to Moral Education*. New York: Columbia University Press, 1989.

Rest, J. R. "Morality." In J. Flavell and E. Markmann (eds.), *Cognitive Development*. Vol. 4 of *Manual of Child Psychology*, edited by P. Musses. New York: Wiley, 1983.

Rubin, K., and Krasnor, L. "Social-Cognitive and Social Behavioral Perspectives on Problem Solving." In M. Perlmutter (ed.), *Minnesota Symposia on Child Psychology*. Vol. 18. Hillsdale, N.J.: Erlbaum, 1986.

Schlaefli, A., Rest, J. R., and Thoma, S. "Does Moral Education Improve Moral Judgment? A Meta-Analysis of Intervention Studies Using the Defining Issues Test." *Review of Educational Research*, 1985, *55*, 319–352.

Schultz, L. H., and Selman, R. L. "Bridging the Gap Between Interpersonal Thought and Action in Early Adolescence: The Role of Psychodynamic Processes." *Development and Psychopathology*, 1989, *1*, 133–152.

Selman, R. L. "Social-Cognitive Understanding." In T. Lickona (ed.), *Moral Development and Behavior*. New York: Holt, Rinehart & Winston, 1976.

Selman, R. L. *The Growth of Interpersonal Understanding*. San Diego, Calif.: Academic Press, 1980.

Selman, R. L., and Schultz, L. H. "Interpersonal Thought and Action in the Case of a Troubled Early Adolescent: Toward a Developmental Model of the Gap." In S. Shirk (ed.), *Cognitive Development and Child Psychotherapy*. New York: Plenum Press, 1988.

Shure, M. B. "Interpersonal Problem Solving: A Cog in the Wheel of Social Cognition." In F. C. Serafica (ed.), *Social-Cognitive Development in Context*. New York: Guilford, 1982.

Slavin, R. E. "Cooperative Learning: A Best-Evidence Synthesis." In R. E. Slavin (ed.), *School and Classroom Organization*. Hillsdale, N.J.: Erlbaum, 1988.

Spivack, G., and Shure, M. "The Cognition of Social Adjustment: Interpersonal Cognitive Problem-Solving Thinking." In B. Lahey and A. Kazdin (eds.), *Advances in Clinical Child Psychology*. Vol. 5. New York: Plenum Press, 1983.

Turiel, E. "Domains and Categories in Social-Cognitive Development." In W. F. Overton (ed.), *The Relationships Between Social and Cognitive Development*. Hillsdale, N.J.: Erlbaum, 1983.

Urbain, E. S., and Kendall, P. C. "Review of Social-Cognitive Problem-Solving Interventions with Children." *Psychological Bulletin*, 1980, *88*, 109–143.

Yeates, K. O., Schultz, L. H., and Selman, R. L. "The Development of Interpersonal Negotiation Strategies in Thought and Action: A Social-Cognitive Link to Behavioral Adjustment and Social Status." *Merrill-Palmer Quarterly*, 1991, *37*, 369–406.

Yeates, K. O., and Selman, R. L. "Social Competence in the Schools: Toward an Integrative Model for Intervention." *Developmental Review*, 1989, *9*, 64–100.

Youniss, J. *Parents and Peers in Social Development: A Sullivan-Piaget Perspective*. Chicago: University of Chicago Press, 1980.

26

Where is the Sense in Learning? Opening the Schools to Promote Moral-Cognitive Development

Heinz Schirp

Let me set the scene for this chapter by presenting two current approaches. First is that of Sloterdijk (1983, p. 12): "Incorporation into society through schooling, as it occurs in this country, is a calculated stultification after which no learning gives the prospect of things ever being better. The destruction of the relationship between life and learning, the end of faith in education, the end of European scholarship is imminent. And conservatives and pragmatists, cynical or well-meaning, equally find it disturbing. Basically, nobody believes any more that today's 'learning' will solve tomorrow's problems; it is far more likely to cause them." Then there is that of Greffrath (1989, p. 40): "Ethics are fashionable at the moment: business ethics, ethics of the environment, ethics of technology. Morality can apply the brakes to the momentum of progress, shortly before it crashes into the wall. . . . Morality is good. Politics is better. Best of all, however, are the people who care." With these lines as introduction, Greffrath takes up the questions "Where does the urge to care spring from? How does it come about that we feel responsibility?" To tackle this question, he cites a fairy tale with the contrasting characters of Goldmarie and Pechmarie.

In the fairy tale, Goldmarie wakes in a beautiful meadow. On her way, the maiden passes an oven full of bread. The bread calls out, "Oh, pull me out or I'll burn, I'm already overdone." The girl empties the oven. She goes further along the meadow and comes to an apple tree, which calls to her, "Shake me, shake me, my apples are all ripe!" The girl shakes the tree and puts the apples in one large pile. At the end of all her social involvement, Goldmarie is showered with gold. Seeing this splendid reward, Pechmarie jealously follows the track of her sister. But although she passes through the same scene somewhat later and also sees the overflowing oven and the overripe apples, she ignores both and goes on her way unconcerned. As a "reward" for her unsocial behavior, she is showered with pitch.

It is the right of a fairy tale to have protagonists that represent good and evil. The good are rewarded for their observation and involvement; the evil are punished for looking away, for their insensibility in the face of need. Of course, fairy tales have a moral message. In this story, the message could be put as "Be observant, do something, help—and you will be rewarded." Alas, reality seldom operates in this way. Social behavior rarely brings a direct reward. School and classroom learning therefore cannot be based on motives of gratification and reward, nor can teachers refer to such motives when they want to get their pupils to care or to be involved.

Is it in fact possible for school and instruction to make a meaningful contribution to the development of personal involvement? In the final analysis, are such aims as "values education" not just hazy aspirations ritually mentioned in our educational schemes? Is the hope of being able to solve problems by learning, or at least of making a modest contribution, absurd? Can education make a practical contribution to the development of an "ethic of self-responsibility" that would be an important step on the way to a sturdy and humane moral system? Is it possible for the aims of school learning to be transposed from the abstract into the everyday experience of our pupils? "A humane moral system and, even more, a feeling of responsibility toward all those living, these are still abstractions. Whether they come to exist, whether they exist in sufficient strength, is a problem of quantity. An infinitive number of decisions—from Goldmaries and Pechmaries—will decide the issue: decisions of human beings who appreciate the condition in which the world is; who, through their sympathy with the world, forge a conscience and acquire knowledge; who interfere; and also from those who turn away or who make themselves deaf—through stupidity, through ineptitude, through vulnerability. Why?" (Greffrath, 1989, p. 40).

What are the real achievements of school and schooling in a process at the end of which cognitive and positive social attitudes and abilities should be evident? These qualities should be the basis for solidarity, for participation in the community, for the ability to make decisions and take action—in short, for taking on full social responsibility. How can such aims as "judgment and behavioral competence" be accommodated in the framework of school teaching and learning? How can the concepts "schooling for instruction" and "schooling for life" be reconciled? The concept "the organization of school life and the opening of schools," in our experience, offers the chance to incorporate sense- and values-oriented issues while providing opportunities to make decisions. Put another way, the promotion of moral-cognitive abilities is an important activity that enables people to arrive at reasoned decisions when faced with the possibility or necessity of choice. In our view, the two concepts complement one another. On the one hand, if learning is not open to the realities of everyday life, moral-cognitive promotion runs the danger of being reduced to an intellectual system, the subject of ritual discussions of no practical utility. On the other hand, without being embedded in moral-cognitive work, activity aimed at giving greater accessibility may become action for its own sake, undertaken without reflection. Therefore, the question is, how can teaching and learning be structured so that pupils can connect school learning and their everyday experience, can experience the practical utility of what they have learned, can recognize the value of their own efforts, and can understand the necessity for their own involvement?

An Approach to Opening the Schools: Sense and Motivation in Learning

There is no shortage of critical analyses on the contribution of "schooling for instruction" and on what is sometimes seen as meaningless and irrelevant learning. It might be more to the point to go to pupils themselves and ask them whether they feel that enough is being done to demonstrate the point of learning during schooling. A large proportion of pupils say that they learn "just" for the next vocabulary test, the next class test, the next qualifying examination, and that learning has a point only insofar as one can (or must) get good grades. They feel that the content and processes of learning are chosen and stipulated by "the school" without consideration of their own interests, problems, and experience, so that they do not see them as valuable to themselves or as personally affecting them. They feel that even when lessons treat topics and content apparently springing from the wishes of the pupils, this is often no more than an introductory and motivating phase, after which instruction quickly returns to the everyday routine, with the teacher and subject matter dominant once again. And they feel that instruction (astonishingly, when one considers the various subjects and the constantly changing content) goes on in a similar, monotonous form (see Schirp, 1987). Where, therefore, is the sense in learning?

Pupils' subjective reactions coincide with a strain of current criticism of schools. It does indeed appear to be the case that the vast majority of lessons are conducted in such a way that the point of learning and making an effort to learn cannot be communicated at all or can be put across only by referring to grades, by appealing to future gratification in the form of a greater range of career possibilities, and/or through associated social pressure from parents.

These subjective theories put forward by pupils in more or less explicit form are analytically confirmed in many publications on the quality of schooling. Oerter, for instance says that learning, its content and materials, have what he calls an "abstract valence" (Oerter, 1985, p. 210). He goes so far as to suggest that the educational value of something is directly related to its abstraction and remoteness from the everyday world and experience of the pupils. Pupils learn in our schools to distinguish between learning materials and their real content; in other words, to see them independently of their usual context. What is learned is an object with abstract valence; it is valuable irrespective of its use in a particular context. Memory as a psychic phenomenon "is valuable independent of the content stored in it.

This changes with the different curriculum. Learning and knowledge are seen as valuable without particular intellectual skills being intended for a specific purpose. On the contrary, competence appears the more valuable the wider it can be applied. The real value of formal education is seen in its independence from specific tasks and in its universal applicability" (p. 210). Put bluntly, one could say that "abstract valence" leads to alienated learning. One learns content in which one is not interested, with the help of learning processes that one cannot influence, in order to come to conclusions that one cannot use. How can motivation toward involvement, toward "caring," arise out of this?

Such criticism of the low level of pupil involvement particularly affects those staff members who, day by day, are at pains to bridge the discrepancy between the demands of the syllabus, the requirements of the subject area, the content of the textbook, and the rhythm of a forty-five-minute lesson, on the one hand, and the interests, questions, and problems of the pupils, on the other. What teacher would not wish for pupils who show an interest, realize why they are making an effort, enjoy their work, are proud of the end product, and retain what they have learned and use it as the basis for further work? Seen from the perspective of current educational research, the dilemma of our school system can be sketched in the following way.

The quality of learning and of the schools themselves depends on finding a balance between the requirements of curricular subjects and meaningful learning. The school systems of Western nations have concentrated primarily on the first part. On the one hand, the high standard of teacher training, the mandatory syllabi and teaching plans, the subject-oriented instruction methods, and so on ensure a high level of education compared to that in other countries. On the other hand, many of these elements stand in opposition to the real daily interests and experience of young people and bring with them the risk of destroying any sense of purpose in learning. At its worst, school can lead to the loss of enjoyment in learning. When pupils say, more out of resignation than rebelliousness, "Literature classes took away my interest in literature, art instruction showed me how clumsy I was at drawing and painting, and music lessons showed me that I was too untalented to learn to play a musical instrument," then something is wrong with the theory behind this teaching or the practice that it represents. One could conclude that some kind of system was conspiring to make those things that really interested pupils generally boring.

An extreme alternative would be a school that was a "life school" in content and organization. Such a school would draw its aims, content, and process of learning from the current needs of the young, and it would be based on an implicit "system" from which could be learned what was currently engaging their interest and feelings, rather than the explicit methodology of individual subjects. Perhaps the problem of individual motivation would be solved in this way, but only at the cost of the positive results that have characterized our educational system up to now. Among other things, a reduction of learning standards would inevitably follow the adoption of such a vision, along with the loss of comparability of qualifications and problems with the requirements for professional qualifications. Such a vision could simply not be reconciled with the needs of a specialized industrial society based on achievement and efficiency, nor with individual awareness and the promotion of educational opportunities in a democratically constituted society.

The Ministry of Education of North Rhine–Westphalia, Germany, has initiated a program on the organization of school life and the opening of the schools. This school- and research-based project is supported by the State Institute for School and Adult Education in Soest. The program sketches out ideas, suggestions, and examples showing how schools can cooperate with partners in their community, trying to steer a course through the extremes of the dilemma outlined above. Essentially, it aims to bring school learning much closer to real life where it can be attuned to the obligatory aims and tasks of schools. The guiding philosophy of this approach is that the starting point for learning should be relevant to the real world and interests of pupils. Learning should be organic and close to life and should strive for an individualization of learning opportunities. Furthermore, it should foster social competence, self-reliance in thought and action, and an awareness of appropriate modes of conduct. In this way, an important contribution can be made to the future development of schools and classroom learning and to the promotion of a moral-cognitive capacity — both explicitly and implicitly.

Classroom Learning

The best chances for change are when classroom learning uses the "educational resources" of the school environment and when real-life situations are sought "on the spot" to make individual subjects and cross-curricular areas more accessible and transparent. Using pupils' life experience in this way offers the best opportunity to bring together in a meaningful and motivating context subject learning and real-life experience, subject knowledge skills and life skills, pupil-oriented experience and its cognitive assimilation, and social learning and the framework of knowledge specific to the individual subjects.

This kind of approach is based on such sound didactic principles as correlation (the bonding of "message" and pupils' experience) and conduct, product, and future orientations, which belong to the didactic norm of almost all subject areas. These guiding principles can be put into effect in different areas of activity. However, classroom learning is the most significant of these, offering as it does the framework that can most easily be opened up to school and outside activities.

School Life

School life is the second area of activity where the relationship between effectiveness and responsibility can be brought into play. This means not just special occasions such as festivals, celebrations, theater performances, and parents' days but also the forms of coexistence that characterize everyday life in the school. The manner in which the relationship among teachers, pupils, and school authorities is conducted is ultimately more influential than all the lessons on tolerance, values, and social "virtues." In fact, pupils' awareness of a discrepancy between the morality taught to them and that which governs school life is likely to be deeply counterproductive. Pupils can see from their own immediate experience that values such as tolerance, fairness, justice, consideration, politeness, and partnership cannot really be so important if those involved abandon them so lightly. Thus, they experience a classic case of "double morality."

School and Community

The third field of activity is the neighborhood of the school itself—the community, with its many opportunities for experience in cultural, technical, economic, social, political, and religious areas; its people, groups, clubs, institutions, movements; its specialists and experts of all kinds in the topics treated and learned in the school. Taking advantage of these educational resources can bring together work on specific subjects and everyday experience. This has a double effect: many things can be better appreciated and understood when they are seen, experienced, inquired into, examined, and documented. The awareness gained on the spot can help in the assimilation of subject knowledge. On the other hand, systematic learning methods help pupils to judge the reality that they encounter more rationally and deeply. In this way, school and classroom learning fulfill their original function of helping pupils rely on themselves to confront and appreciate circumstances and events in society, to explain them, and to learn to understand them better. Thus, the community setting is a genuine area of activity and experience, the educational aspects of which should be integrated into school life. Of course, it is not just the community that is of significance to the school; school can also increase its relevance for community life.

The School as Meeting Place

A fourth area of activity demonstrates that the school itself can be a meeting place. Much of what happens in the neighborhood of the school is of such interest and of such potential use to the teacher that it should be brought into the school. Art exhibitions, historical documentations, theatrical performances, and technological products and processes, along with the people associated with them, demonstrate that there are many interesting things in the immediate environment. These things in turn are impulses and starting points for various kinds of learning: linguistic, historical, political, technical, and artistic. There is also a very practical reason for the community to cooperate apart from school interests: rooms, media, scientific laboratories, language laboratories, technical facilities, and so forth, that are available in schools can be used communally. In consequence, this kind of cooperation has value for the community.

The following examples show the necessity of combining external and general school activities with classroom learning. However, the motivation and triggering impulse can originate in any of the fields of activity and proceed through them in any order. This sketch should not be interpreted to mean that all areas of activity can always be integrated; it merely shows how typical "opening" activities undertaken by a school can be recognized and indicates the structure of this "learning and opening."

Example 1: "A Project Week and Its Results." The theme of a project week was "Our town looked different—scenes from the past." First, the pupils began to collect old pictures, photos, maps, and historical documents. Then they tried to find out how buildings, streets, and the whole structure of their town had changed over the centuries. The further they went back into history, the more difficulties they had to overcome in exploring the development of their town. They soon realized that specialists, experts, and institutions could help them to gather more and more details. Exhibitions of ancient tools in a museum, interviews with old people, and books about regional history in the public library were used to get more and more detailed information. In the course of their inquiry, the students dug out an old school chronicle that no one could read at first because it was written in ancient characters. A real historic find was discovered in a farmstead: a contract of inheritance from 1808, written in both French and German, brought new information about the partition of fields and woodland at the time when the town was governed by civil servants of Napoleon. At the end of their research on the spot, the results of the project week were presented for the public at school. A lot of these materials could be used intensively by teachers and students in their subject-specific work during the following weeks. So elements such as "opening," subject-specific learning, school as meeting place, and school and community could be combined in a student-oriented way.

Example 2: "First You Need the Correct Tools!" In a project-oriented unit, the question came up as to whether and to what extent ecological systems in the neighborhood of the school had been damaged by environmental influences. The first step in answering this question was to reflect on what kinds of instruments and methods could help to achieve valid results. At the same time, the students had to discuss what environmental problems they wanted to tackle: various types of pollution (air, water, soil, noise), the destruction of nature by growing traffic, and industrialization. Very soon, they realized the interdependence between specific environmental problems and appropriate "tools" and the difficulty of exploring them in a suitable way. In different subject-specific courses, they learned to use chemical, physical, and technical methods and procedures. In the following research phase, they could practically apply their fresh instrumental knowledge on the spot. The results of these studies were exhibited in the foyer of the school building and later on in the rooms of a bank on the occasion of a local environmental campaign. The success of this project-oriented work stimulated two other classes to investigate environmental problems in the local community. These classes did not only simply repeat the inquiry; they succeeded in improving methods, tools, and results of the study. Today, environmental studies are among the most interesting activities of the school and play an important role in school life. The different steps of this unit show how "opening" and classroom learning overlap and help to develop a sense of responsibility.

Example 3: "A Theater Performance Gets Something Going!" A performance of Sophocles's *Antigone* led to a variety of reactions on the part of the students: complete mystification, indifference, curiosity. In various classes, the classical text was read and explained so that the moral dilemma of Antigone in deciding whether to obey her conscience or the laws became evident. The students remained quite unmoved and indifferent throughout these routine interpretive activities. The situation changed quite distinctly when someone suggested that they write their own stories on the pattern of the same dilemma: conscience versus legal rules. A lot of stories deriving from the social experiences of the students were written and discussed. Moral debate led to an even better understanding of the classical text. At the end, they staged a theater production: *Four Times Antigone*. The steps show how the whole learning and teaching process was structured by the idea of opening the school and how a classical value problem could be linked with the everyday experience of students and society.

Example 4: "Our Market Is a Microcosm." At the very beginning of a unit, the students went on an excursion to familiarize themselves with their town. They explored the marketplace to find interesting aspects for subject-oriented themes. At the end of this excursion, the most interesting examples were pinpointed on a map: a memorial for the "heroes" of the German-French war of 1870–71; modern iron sculptures of a local artist; an old fountain in a park that served as a meeting place for people from various age groups and cultures; market stalls where farmers offered their products; a recently established Turkish cafe; political posters from an election campaign; the booth of a local group opposing the community's plan to build a new highway through an old neighborhood. Numerous classroom activities were inspired by these findings. At a very practical level, historical, economic, cultural, social, political, ecological, and technical issues emerged. To suitably analyze these issues, students had to get into contact with many experts in the field. The outcome of all these activities was a small booklet entitled *Our Marketplace: A Microcosm* and an exhibition that attracted the attention of local authorities. It became evident how the social awareness of the students could be fostered and how open chances for practical cooperation between school and community were focused and processed by the learners. At the same time, the quality of subject-oriented teaching was improved.

It should be clear from these examples that simply carrying out these external events is not sufficient. A broader rationale, oriented toward pupil, experience, and conduct, is essential to classroom learning. This rationale bases classroom learning on a sound foundation that includes what we might call the head (abstract, schematic, teacher-centered) and the feet (concrete, representing a totality, pupil centered). The activities that schools have mounted in response to our project show that this effort is indeed practical and can be applied in many ways. The reactions and comments that we have received from schools have also made clear that although time pressures on teachers and pupils alike restrict the number of opening activities that can take place in any one school year, even a few limited activities can have an impact. They can inspire motivation and increase interest in particular subjects, release hidden talents and skills (technical, organizational, social, practical, artistic) that can be fruitfully employed in the classroom, improve pupils' ability to work independently, help to develop self-confidence and the stamina to tackle long-term tasks, provide insights into complex problems, and improve the cooperative faculty in many pupils. In this way, the concept of "the organization of school life and the opening of schools" ensures a better balance between systematic work in subject areas and real-life motivational elements and between effectiveness and responsibility.

The Moral Cognitive Approach and the Opening of Schools

The areas of activity introduced in the discussion of the organization and opening of schools can also be applied to the approach of another school- and research-based innovation project of the State Institute in Soest: "Democracy and Education in the School: Fostering a Capacity for Judgment." The approach of this project is based on the analytical and sociomoral work of the American psychologist and pedagogue Lawrence Kohlberg (see Kohlberg, 1978). Its major aim is to promote pupils' capacity for judgment and responsibility through the discussion of dilemma stories and subsequent action and the involvement of pupils in solutions to school problems.

Applying the Kohlbergian approach to the structural, organizational, and curricular areas of our schools has met with reservations and required some modifications (see Edelstein, 1985). For instance, it was quickly appreciated that, in the long run, purely fictional dilemma stories were suited only to sustaining interest in "moral problems" and made no contribution to a realistic, informed grappling with "conflicts of values." We felt that the concept "organization of school life and the opening of schools" indicated how we could adapt the Kohlbergian approach. It should be clear from the four areas of activity sketched above just how and why the moral-cognitive approach can be used together with the main principles of the opening of schools. This combination, deployed in a practical pedagogical manner, can contribute to the improvement in the quality of schooling.

Classroom Lessons: Community-Based Dilemmas

The function of fictional dilemmas lies in the area of analysis. With their use, pupils' moral-cognitive level can be ascertained by abstracting from their "problem awareness," their state of knowledge, and how that knowledge is structured. In the classroom, however, subject- and community-based dilemmas are of greater curricular importance. Our schools are centered on subject learning. Thus, a clear connection between dilemma stories and the topics, content, and problems of individual subjects makes the dilemma stories more acceptable to teachers, who regularly complain about not having enough time to complete even their required material. Value conflicts that rely heavily on the content of a particular subject are more likely to be taken up than the fictional ones, which teachers often see as a distraction from the set syllabus. Individual teachers do not feel that they are the ones responsible for dealing with fictional values conflicts.

The situation looks quite different, however, for dilemma discussions that are directly related to particular subject problems. It is also evident that much subject content could be made more interesting to pupils and, to the advantage of the subject, be presented in a more refined and structured way. Take, for example, a moral-cognitive discussion that might arise when pupils examine the behavior of Antigone: it could motivate a search for a personal position in regard to the conflict between the power of the state and personal conscience and simultaneously challenge pupils to give reasons for "correct" and "incorrect" behavior. A discussion of such value conflicts can lead to questions of the moral-historical context of a drama, possibly change or verify moral principles, and stimulate a search for the validity of such moral criteria in one's own decision making. Another example could be dilemma discussions as part of a geography unit on "economic and ecological interests in the Alps" that focus on the topic "A ski lift for our village?" Such discussions could deal directly with subject aims and knowledge, lead to a discussion of the very different economic and ecological interests involved in such a community issue, and demand a personal judgment of those interests by the pupils.

The statement of aims for this project is "the ability and readiness to, on the one hand, assert one's own personal rights and interests — when possible, in a manner showing solidarity and the readiness to compromise — and, on the other, to recognize the interests of society and the disadvantaged, and on occasion to give them precedence" (North Rhine–Westphalia Ministry of Education, 1987). This statement points directly to the bond between a dilemma approach (When and why are my interests more important than those of the society?) and the pedagogical demands of the subject. Lessons in politics and government offer a rich field of topics that are particularly closely related to the concept of moral-cognitive promotion through the use of dilemma discussions. In all subjects whose content allows the dilemma approach to be applied, it proves its usefulness both in didactic preparation and in investing the lessons with an inner rhythm (see Dobbelstein-Osthoff, 1987).

The concept "organization of school life and the opening of schools" also indicates that the chosen dilemma stories should be related to and have an affinity with the real-life experiences of the pupils and should provide opportunities for research, examination, collection of information, and the independent consideration of reality. Thus, a realistic interest in the problem can be created and then discussed. Dilemmas that do not spring from the direct experience of pupils should be considered to see whether they have parallels with familiar situations. Such analogies are important for the quality and intensity of moral-cognitive fostering: they help to establish a connection between experiences, knowledge, attitudes, and patterns of judgment from very different "close" or "distant" areas. By approaching the strange and unfamiliar through what is already known, pupils can more readily recognize similarities and peculiarities and compare systems of values with one another.

The different levels on which analogies are to be found could be arranged as follows:

- Individual experience
- Experience and relationships in the family environment
- Experience, relationships, and interests in small groups (peer group, learning group, recreation group)
- Experience, relationships, interests, and structures in community, society, state institutions, and organizations
- Experience, relationships, interests, and structures in and "bridges" to other cultures and societies

It is impossible to overlook the parallels to the first five stages of Kohlberg's model. In fact, "analogous" dilemmas from the different areas help to question the extent and validity of solutions and whether they can be generalized; this ensures that the question of generalization is kept in the foreground. Sequences could be developed on sex discrimination, for example, that have the pupils' subjective experience ("boys" and "girls") as their starting-point and go on through dilemmas based on small groups ("Boys/girls don't do that!"), role expectations for the sexes and discrimination in the context of society (women's rates of pay), and finally role expectations for women in other societies and cultures ("In Islamic societies, women aren't allowed to . . . "). Thus, the connection between individually desired rules and rights (human rights) can be created (see Schirp, 1989).

The Organization of School Life and
the Promotion of a Moral-Cognitive Sense

The school itself is a genuine area for opening and organization activities. The extent to which subject and cross-curricular learning is organized in a communicative, cooperative manner in which pupils play their part and pupils, teachers, and people from the surrounding area are drawn into school activities—festivities, exchanges of experience, common learning—determines whether and to what extent one can identify with the school and feel "at home" there. The learning climate and the school atmosphere are thus crucial variables in the quality of a school, and school life is a genuine area of activity and conduct for the development and promotion of a capacity for judgment. This is consistent with Kohlberg's (1978) idea of the "just community" and the fostering of a moral-cognitive sense through the "dilemma approach"— an attempt to involve pupils in the discussion and solution of conflicts within the school. Recognizing that the promotion of moral-cognitive development must be complemented by interventions appropriate for the level of understanding necessary to influence behavior, Kohlberg and his colleagues attempted to establish "just communities" in the form of cluster schools. These schools gave children the opportunity to resolve conflict in a collective, discursive, and responsible manner.

The application of the "just community" approach to schools in Germany has met with organizational and legal obstacles preventing the implementation of voluntary cluster schools. If this approach is to be implemented, it will most likely be because it is taken up as a pedagogical challenge by individual schools. Moral-democratic education could become an internal project of schools that do not wish to leave the aims of social learning, insight into democratic rules and regulations, the ability to engage in rational discussion, the culture of conflict, participation, and collective conduct and democratic behavior to the hidden curriculum.

From the approach that we take here, the organization of school life is not merely a matter of making joint decisions on regulations and agreements. It also includes determining what practical things can be done to make the school more friendly, more interesting, more lively, more pleasant. This approach to the school as a building, as an institution, and as a place of learning requires, among other things, a capacity for judgment, empathy, just solutions, the pursuit of individual and collective interests, and organizational ability. It requires the taking of responsibility by all concerned for mutual benefit. For example, a class deciding to transform its sterile and ugly classroom into a friendly and congenial learning space will have to address questions such as the following:

> Must everybody help because everybody will benefit?
> Is this not taking work away from local craftspeople?
> What changes to the classroom are allowed?
> Who decides on this?
> How can we ask the community for support (materials, paint, appliances)?
> Should, must, can the parents be involved?

What should be done when other learning groups join the class that
    has decorated the room?
Should or must a new set of class rules be set up?

These types of practical problems are based on a real situation rather than
a fictional or hypothetical one. The pupils are not merely participants in
the discussion; each of them will be potentially affected by the decisions of
the majority. Must one go along with the majority decision even when one
has the better arguments or "right" on one's side?

Many real-life situations can be used to illustrate how the organization of schools, the promotion of a moral-cognitive capacity, and the opening of schools intertwine with and support one another. For example, a class
decides that the children and their parents will offer a "whole-food break-
fast" during the main morning break: homemade whole-grain rolls, muesli
and fruit, and so on. This brings up a string of questions to be discussed,
such as "Is such a thing allowed?" and "What will be the reaction of the health
and licensing authorities, the shopkeepers and snack-bar operators in the
area, the school principal, the school governors, the other classes?" One can
find many more examples of practical efforts that can serve as opportunities
for discussion or moral responsibility: a school sets up a bicycle repair shop
together with the community; the pupils' representatives decide to set up
a school cafe, a group of female Turkish pupils plan and set up a tea shop;
a group of advanced older pupils plan and set up an exhibition in the school
on the history of Nazism in the town; the biology teachers in a school plan
a school garden with the pupils. What all these examples have in common
is that they require planning, deciding, negotiating, discussing, and per-
suading to be done along with practical work, and the results must be evaluated to determine whether what was intended was indeed achieved or whether
there was a discrepancy between intention and outcome. Practical "caring"
of this kind about an area of life and work also draws on specific subject
learning. This is true not just of social studies; it applies equally to languages,
technical, artistic, and scientific areas. These, too, benefit from a pragmatic
opening to include a more concrete content and learning procedure.

Community-Oriented Learning and the
Promotion of a Moral-Cognitive Capacity

How school learning is related to what it takes to be successful in the various areas of social reality encountered outside school has always been a moot
point. It is accepted that school learning differs from "other learning." What
the differences are and what is necessary to bridge the gulf between them
has been the subject of increased research in schools for some years. Resnick (1987) summarizes four characteristics of mental activity outside school
and contrasts them with typical in-school activities: (1) individual, cognitive

learning in the school versus group activities and work procedures in everyday life; (2) abstract-logical "pure mentation" versus instrumental, practical "tool manipulation"; (3) symbolic procedures in the school versus reasoned, practical procedures in other contexts; and (4) generalized learning versus competence specific to a particular situation.

It is exactly those realistic, everyday areas of competence referred to as "group," "practical," or "specific to situation and context" that can be developed when school learning admits the "community" as an area of activity. At the same time, it is clear from the terms used that such community-oriented learning is closely allied to the promotion of a moral-cognitive sense and a sense of responsibility to the school and community. This affiliation has for some years been part of the practice of U.S. schools that have applied Kohlberg's moral-cognitive approach. The "social action model" described by Hersh, Miller, and Fielding (1980), with its guiding principles of "caring, judging and acting," demonstrates this particularly clearly.

The environment outside the school is full of unanswered questions, controversial decisions, and concrete problems, some of which have a direct effect on the everyday lives and the long-term perspectives of pupils. As the controversial springs from different sets of values, options, and interests, the promotion of a moral-cognitive sense, as in the "democracy and education in the school" approach, represents a particularly important area of learning. Values education can and must therefore be concerned with real social conditions. This points to the increased inclusion of subject areas and the consequent treatment of particular dilemmas arising from specific school subjects. At the same time, it should be noted that almost all values problems can be solved only in an interdisciplinary, cross-curricular manner (see Schirp, 1988). For example:

- A chemical analysis of water samples in class shows significant traces of toxic substances. An approach to the local authorities leads to a jointly developed plan to oversee and purify the water. (A cross-curricular project links issues of biology, chemistry, literature, and social science.)
- A church parish deliberates how a considerable sum of money that has been donated should be spent: for the renovation of the parish hall, for charitable purposes, to support partner parishes, to assist people in Third World countries. Pupils involve themselves both during and outside classes by offering reasoned suggestions. A new awareness of problems emerges. (Discussion links religious education, social science, and geography.)
- A unit in literature studies requires pupils to analyze the local supplement to the town newspaper. They find the reporting astonishingly biased. The pupils draw attention to this state of affairs with their own research and articles in the school newspaper and in the town paper. Their own reports are offered as an alternative and published. A new discussion ensues. (A project links literature and politics.)
- A reconstruction plan for a town includes the building of a new bypass,

which will shift traffic problems to another district. The controversy that arises among the different groups affected is the starting point for a project in which a number of classes will work on devising technological and social solutions. The problem of "just" decisions becomes central. (A project links geography, arts, politics, and technology.)

All these community-oriented questions and problems raise concepts of values and their justification. What, then, is new about these possibilities for moral-cognitive development? First, they involve *the generation of moral dilemmas from real life*. When the community is used as the context, a dilemma does not have to be artificially created—it arises from a particular situation and from the concerns of those involved. Second, they provide for the expression of *reasoning based on a sense of values*. Citizens involved in the conflicts and problems express the values on which their decisions are based in many different ways. Thus, the various structures of argumentation—rather like Kohlberg's moral-cognitive levels—can be recognized. Third, they involve the use of *intervention materials* that can stimulate argument about the practicality of the values decisions made. Fourth, they illustrate the essential *seriousness of values decisions* and their effect on everyday life—the fact that decisions in a social context have a significant impact on people's lives and are not simply abstract and theoretical options. Fifth, they make clear the connection between *moral-cognitive reasoning and personal involvement*. Deciding and rationalizing are one thing; it is quite another to see whether and how far each person is prepared to engage him- or herself in advocating solutions the justice and correctness of which he or she is convinced of. Finally, the serious nature of values decisions and the real effects that they can have show the *difference between holding opinions and taking responsibility for those opinions*. If the aim of school and lessons is to imbue pupils with social responsibility, to render them capable of functioning in and changing a democratically constituted community, then school learning must be made more sensitive to questions of values, especially in community-oriented teaching, and to the links established between these questions and moral-cognitive development through the opening of schools.

Can Sloterdijk's (1983, p. 12) prediction of the "end of faith in education" be justified? The answer depends on whether and to what extent schools can succeed in establishing a better balance between systematic subject-based instruction and a form of learning that helps pupils to reflect on and work with the real, everyday world. Learning to care, to be observant of what is going on around one, and to involve oneself constructively in it requires classroom learning and school to help pupils build up the appropriate subject knowledge, positive social abilities, and capacity for judgment.

References

Dobbelstein-Osthoff, P. "Das Kohlbergkonzept der moralischen Kompetenzentwicklung" [The Kohlberg approach to moral development]. In P. Dobbelstein-Osthoff and H. Schirp (eds.), *Werteerziehung in the Schule — aber wie?* [Values education in school — but how?]. Soest, Germany: Landesinstitut, 1987.

Edelstein, W. "Moral Intervention: A Skeptical Note." In M. W. Berkowitz and F. Oser (eds.), *Moral Education: Theory and Application.* Hillsdale, N.J.: Erlbaum, 1985.

Greffrath, M. "Das Prinzip Goldmarie" [The Goldmarie principle]. *Die Zeit,* No. 6, Feb. 9, 1989, p. 40.

Hersh, R. H., Miller, J. P., and Fielding, G. D. *Models of Moral Education.* White Plains, N.Y.: Longman, 1980.

Kohlberg, L. "The Cognitive-Developmental Approach to Moral Education." In P. Scharf (ed.), *Readings in Moral Education.* Minneapolis, Minn.: Winston Press, 1978.

North Rhine–Westphalia Ministry of Education. *Curriculum Politik* [Curriculum politics]. Düsseldorf: North Rhine–Westphalia Ministry of Education, 1987.

Oerter, R. "Die Formung der Kognition und Motivation durch Schule" [The formation of cognition and motivation through school]. *Unterrichtswissenschaft* [Science of teaching], 1985, *3,* 203–219.

Resnick, L. B. "Learning in School and Out." *Educational Researcher,* 1987, *16* (9), 13–20.

Schirp, H. "Jugendliche zwischen Schule und Beruf" [Adolescents between school and professional work]. Soest, Germany: Landesinstitut, 1987.

Schirp, H. "Öffnung von Schule und projektorientiertes Arbeiten" [The opening of school and project-based learning]. In W. Gagel and D. Menne (eds.), *Politikunterricht* [Didactics for political science]. Opladen, Germany: Leske & Budrich, 1988.

Schirp, H. "Human Rights and Moral-Cognitive Development." Soest, Germany: Landesinstitut, 1989.

Sloterdijk, P. *Kritik der zynischen Vernunft* [Critique of cynical reason]. Frankfurt am Main, Germany: Suhrkamp, 1983.

Section Eight

THE NEW SYNTHESIS

27

Toward Relational Responsibility

Christopher M. Clark, Karen I. Jensen

Several years ago, educational researchers were challenged to ask self-critical questions about the relevance of their work to the pressing needs of teachers and children (Clark, 1986). In the intervening years, those needs have multiplied in number and increased in intensity. Poor urban schools have become desperately poor battlegrounds where lives are literally at risk. In the United States today, more young black men live in prisons than are enrolled in colleges. Teachers try to cope with ever-lengthening lists of social responsibilities and expectations while budget cuts and heavy-handed evaluation and accountability schemes drive the most dedicated to the edge of exhaustion and the most mobile to less enervating careers or into early retirement. As in Edgar Allan Poe's famous story "The Pit and the Pendulum," the walls are closing in, and something sharp and sinister hangs over our heads.

Problems noted in ethnocentrism, nationalism, racism, elitism, and economic exploitation have become epidemic in North America and Europe and show themselves in many ugly forms in our schools, some conspicuous and many subtle. Tactics of control, punishment, denial, and exclusion that seemed superficially to bring order to the classrooms of thirty and fifty years ago are now seen to be immoral, illegal, and ineffective in any case. And now the epistemologists tell us that the one domain that we thought we could count on to hold still, consisting of scientific theories, historical facts, scholarly knowledge about literature, mathematics, and the arts — the content of instruction — is itself shifting, changing, subject to reinterpretation, becoming obsolete before our eyes. We are living in the first days of a shift from the age of technology and anxiety to the age of uncertainty, and there are few states more uncomfortable than pervasive uncertainty.

In light of these claims that the needs of teachers and schoolchildren are greater than ever and that pervasive uncertainty marks the tenor of the times, how can we, as researchers on teacher thinking, respond in some constructive way? Our answer is to turn our attention, our skills at analysis and synthesis, our technical tools, our minds' and hearts' energies toward research in the moral domain of teaching—toward studying the ways of care.

The argument that follows examines the cognitive bias in our research traditions and the unfortunate legacy of the "knowledge base" metaphor in the social sciences, suggests prospects for a transformed research agenda, outlines two perspectives on morality and care, and concludes with a set of questions that we offer as points of departure for a program of thoughtful research in the moral domain.

Cognitive Bias and Control

Contemporary research on the profession reflects a preoccupation with cognitive processes and subject matter knowledge (Shulman, 1987). Even chronic anxiety and depression among teachers have been interpreted as symptoms of dysfunctional beliefs about self-efficacy or as the consequences of boundedly rational decisions to preserve autonomy through isolation. The high-status image of the fully functioning teacher to emerge from this work is that of the reflective professional acting dispassionately to solve instructional design problems and manage recurring dilemmas (Schön, 1983; Lampert, 1985). The migration away from prescriptive models of technical rationality to descriptive representations of reflection in action remains firmly within the cognitive domain, as to teacher evaluation schemes.

In contrast, when teachers and practicing members of other caring professions (for example, nurses, physical therapists, counselors, physicians) speak out about their needs and strengths, we hear a very different, non-cognitive priority. They report that the quality of human relationships is vital to good teaching and professional satisfaction (Clark, 1989; Fullan and Hargreaves, 1991). Many thousands of prospective teachers, doctors, and nurses chose their vocation out of love of children and of learning and healing, rather than other, more instrumental motives. A lived ethic of care and a felt sense of community are the hallmarks of healthy helping professionals everywhere. The moral dimension seems, from the insiders' perspective, to be closest to the heart of the matter.

In sum, we see a dialectic tension between the priority of individual cognition and efficient information transfer, on the one hand, and of relationship and care, on the other hand, in teaching and in other helping professions. Or, as Michel Foucault (1988) has put it, we see a tension between the ancient imperatives *to know* (oneself) and to *take care* (of oneself). How might attending to this dialectic tension serve to reframe questions, methods, and roles in research, professional preparation, and practice in the caring professions? This is the question around which this chapter is composed.

If we take Foucault's distinction to heart, we see that social scientists, especially researchers on teacher thinking, have been pushing "know thyself" as the first imperative of understanding and improving the professions.

The bulk of this work has been in the cognitive domain, with researchers serving as brokers and technologists of the self, inventing and using techniques to help teachers make the implicit and secret details of their plans, beliefs, attributions, and theories visible and public. The privacy of teachers' thoughts, motives, doubts, and struggles is being stripped away. The justification for this research program is that those who would control and improve teaching, its processes and its consequences, must get below the superficial level of obvious behavior to describe, understand, and eventually diagnose and prescribe remedies for faulty thinking, for inadequate knowledge, for theoretically incorrect beliefs (Shulman and Elstein, 1975). The explorer becomes a missionary; the guest becomes informer; the therapist becomes social engineer. And practitioners who cooperate in this drama become collaborators in a more sinister sense than we are used to seeing celebrated in the literature. All this in the name of compiling a "knowledge base" about efficient and effective teaching from which teacher trainers, evaluators, and administrators might draw. The research community is organized to accumulate information about a small number of others as a basis for shaping and constraining, directing and defining, the work of a large number of others whom the researchers will never meet.

Prospects for a Transformed Agenda

How might the character of research on the professions be different if the ways of care were given priority over the ways of knowing? One likely consequence would be that practitioners would begin to see and hear answers to their own authentic questions in the writings of researchers. The so-called gap between research and practice, we believe, is not merely an artifact of language differences and inadequate dissemination. Rather, it is a reflection of the irrelevance of what researchers are so fascinated by to the everyday certainties and doubts of a teacher's world (Clark, 1984). In addition, cultivation of a caring community might become a candidate for a prized outcome of good teaching and good schooling, reframing the singular quest for increases in scores on individual achievement tests of cognitive performance as one of a broader range of desired outcomes of education. The mental health of children and teachers and the conditions in schools that support or threaten mental health would be up for examination (for example, Wagner, 1983; Clark, 1991). Practices of humiliation, manipulation, and punishment, long justified as necessary to enforce respect for authority and to goad children on to higher levels of academic performance, would be seen in a new light (Miller, 1983). Long-term field experiments such as the inspiring work of Fritz Oser on "just community" schools (Oser, 1991) would become a research design of choice. The moral dimensions of teaching, long neglected but deeply felt to be important, could move to the foreground (Tom, 1984; Goodlad, Soder, and Sirotnik, 1990). Caring tactfulness and respect for teachers and children, as reflected in the writings of Max van Manen (1990,

1991), could replace the legalistic conventions of "informed consent" and the voicelessness of anonymity (Shulman, 1990). And researchers, we think, would be changed as a consequence of thoughtfully attending to the ways of care in context. We might even become better teachers ourselves.

Two Perspectives on Morality and Care

Calling attention to the importance of morality and care in teaching and other helping professions brings problems of its own. In particular, Jensen (1991) has shown that, paradoxically, the direct pursuit of goodness and morality may in effect undermine them. Depending on the perspective taken on morality and care, we may tilt the balance toward alienation or toward suppression of individual identity. Consider two contrasting perspectives on morality and care: the perspective of eternity and the relational perspective.

The Perspective of Eternity

In this view, morality is conceived of as in essence selfless, impartial, and impersonal. To act morally is to subordinate the self and to put aside all particularistic commitments for a set of principles or imperatives that appeal to us as rational beings. To illustrate this view, we can point to the closing sentences of John Rawls's (1971) book *A Theory of Justice.* Here he discusses the "perspective of eternity" that is impartial across all individuals and times and writes that it is a "form of thought and feeling that rational persons can adopt in the world" (p. 587). He goes on to say that "purity of heart would be to see clearly and act with grace and self-command from this point of view" (p. 587).

The problem with holding teachers to the perspective of eternity in their moral and caring behavior is that this view of morality promotes alienation. Alienation can be roughly characterized as a kind of estrangement, distancing, or separateness (Schacht, 1971). Distance is not always a bad thing and may be necessary at times. For example, the surgeon's steadiness of hand might be compromised by strong physical and emotional identification with a patient. But alienation always implies loss; in the case of teachers, loss of the very forms of intimacy with students that they claim are essential for establishing trust foundational to a learning community (Clark, 1989). The eternal view of morality assumes that taking care of oneself is an automatic thing, while taking care of others is counterintuitive and must be learned. According to this view, learning to become moral (as a teacher, for example) implies suppression of the self and distancing from and objectification of others.

A Relational View of Morality

In contrast, views of morality have been forwarded that take into account the fact that individuals are situated in society and have identities, commitments, and relations to others (Heidegger, 1981). In this view, it becomes artificial to impose a dichotomy between what is done for the self and what is done for the other. Relationships cannot be validly decomposed into separate realms of self and other, because the other is seen as, if not a part of self, a reference point for the self. This can best be seen in relationships of deep commitment, but it applies to all types of relationships. Consider two examples that clarify and give credibility to this view.

The first example is perhaps the closest of all relationships: that between parent and child. This relationship is so intertwined that it becomes a basic part of our identity, so fundamental that it actually outlives the people involved. In parent-child relationships, it is more difficult to hold the entities apart than to hold them together. After the birth of a child, one is not only oneself but a "parent" as well. The welfare of our children reflects and confirms our identity as a parent. I feel an insult to my mother as an insult to myself. My child's joy is my own as well.

The second example comes from the reflections of a survivor of a Nazi death camp: "In our group we shared everything; and at the moment one of the group ate something without sharing it, we knew it was the beginning of the end for him" (Des Pres, 1976, p. 96). When collective survival becomes the urgent purpose of a relationship, then solidarity to the point of organic identification with the group and loss of individual identity define moral behavior. The common good becomes the individual good.

A relational perspective on morality requires that we transcend the notion held by theorists such as Rawls and Kohlberg that morality can best be secured by individuals exercising autonomous, disembodied, and decontextualized judgment. It even contests our current notion of reason as something universal that goes beyond the idiosyncrasies of partial and individual perspectives. In opposition to these notions, which expel particularity and define feelings as the greatest enemy of rationality, a relational perspective requires a model that urges us to contextualize and to seek understanding through difference, through contrast. Likewise, it requires that we understand how emotions, sympathy, compassion, and concern not only provide motivation for moral action but underlie all that we do and think (Scheffler, 1991).

Perhaps Habermas's (1983) idea of a *communicative ethics* can provide a promising starting point for an alternative model of morality and reason. In his theory of communicative action, Habermas seeks to develop a conception of rationality with a pragmatic starting point in the experience of discussion that aims to reach understanding. Reason and morality in such a model do not require impartiality and universality; rather, they require that through dialogue we learn to give reasons in the commonsense meaning of the word and that we cultivate the practical stance of *being reasonable.* This model of reason supplants the transcendental ego sitting at a height from which it can see and judge all by reducing it to a synthetic unity. It therefore eliminates the authoritarian monologism implicit in traditional theories of moral reasoning. (By claiming to be impartial, one also claims authority to decide an issue in place of those whose interests and desires are manifest. From an impartial point of view, one need not consult others, because the impartial view has already taken into account all possible perspectives.)

A dialogic conception of rationality acknowledges that there is no impartial point of view in which a subject can stand detached and dispassionately assess all perspectives. It invites all to participate in discussion, believing that good answers are gained through plurality of perspectives. As long as the dialogue allows all voices to speak freely and to be heard and taken into account, the expression of needs, motives, and feelings will not have merely private significance and will not bias or distort the conclusions because they will interact with other needs. Within this model, therefore, there is no need to exclude feelings, needs, and desires from either discourse or moral rationality.

One problem with holding teachers to the standard of a relational view of morality is that it requires an intensity of community that is rare in typical schools and cannot be commanded or manipulated into existence. Other features of formal schooling militate against intense community, including the large size of many schools and classes; fragmentation of the school day and year; specialization of educators by subject matter and function (for example, counselors, reading specialists, behavioral therapists, social workers); ethnic, cultural, and linguistic differences between teacher and students; and the inherent conflict between a teacher's roles as nurturer and as evaluator of student learning. The cultivation and celebration of individuality so fundamental to Western cultures is directly at odds with the most radical implications of a relational morality.

In spite of these obstacles, current research on village schools in rural Alaska (Noordhoff and Kleinfeld, 1991) suggests that a relational morality is active here. Indeed, the Alaskan researchers claim that understanding and tuning in to the relational morality of the village is essential for success or even survival as a village teacher. In contrast, a recent study of democratic participation in small-town schools in Oregon (Schmuck and Schmuck, 1990) found "only superficial forms of democracy in our small town schools. Whether they are aware of it or not, small town educators and parents seem to be mimicking a mass-production model of academic life that many of their urban counterparts are striving to give up" (p. 18). In other words, small scale and close community are not sufficient conditions for activating a relational morality.

Toward a Research Agenda on Morality and Care

By laying out two perspectives on morality and care and the problems and dilemmas attendant thereto, we are not suggesting that a simple choice can or ought to be made, nor that these two perspectives exhaust the reasonable possibilities. Rather, we mean to demonstrate the importance and complexity of the thought patterns, belief systems, and ideologies of care that operate just below the surface of every school and classroom. Further, we mean to make the case that matters of morality and care are susceptible to philosophical and empirical analysis. They are not merely matters of natural virtue, religious doctrine, or personal taste.

One further point worth making explicit is that taking morality and care seriously in research and in practical situations does not mean adopting an ethos of being nice, or lenient, or perpetually agreeable. In fact, in a morally mature and caring organization, there will be many times when adherence to previously agreed on principles or processes of deliberation is difficult, uncomfortable, effortful, and confrontational. The key feature of a consciously moral and caring social system is universal commitment to principles and processes that *all* members of the system agree are just. Each member has a voice, and no member has authority that puts him or her above the law and outside the negotiating process. Such a just community will at times seem inefficient in its deliberations when compared to the workings of a hierarchical, top-down model of decision making and decision enforcement. And, especially during the early phases of becoming a just community, there will arise predictably strong objections that the lowest ranks of a formerly hierarchical system (for example, teachers, schoolchildren) are incapable of taking a meaningful part in important decisions or will always be governed in their decisions by motives of self-interest, laziness, and so on.

The antidote to these concerns is that the social systems of which we speak will remain mission-oriented. The raison d'être of a school will be some locally and collectively explicated forms of learning; the mission of a group home for the mentally retarded will be some locally and collectively specified forms of care and integration of clients into the larger society. Morality and care are qualities of the ways and processes by which these missions will be pursued. If a possible decision path leads away from learning for all students in a school, that decision should be argued against by any voice in the system on fundamental grounds. Seymour Sarason (1990) also grounds his call for teacher and student participation in school decision making as "political-moral in that it rests on the value that those who are vitally affected by decisions [indeed, who are responsible for bringing decisions to action] should stand in some meaningful relation to the decision-making process" (p. 63).

A second feature of the morally conscious process worth highlighting here is that it is meant to be a dynamic ongoing process throughout the life of the institution. The highest goal is not to make no bad decisions but to pay attention to the consequences of all decisions and to be always open to reconsidering our ways in the light of experience and principle. In this way, a morally conscious organization becomes a self-correcting social system, unfettered by obsolescent routines and less vulnerable to the pride or denial of a single strong executive or to the mindlessness of a bureaucracy without responsibility. (Classic tragedies from *Hamlet* and *Julius Caesar* to Vietnam and the Gulf War depend on stubborn adherence to morally dysfunctional patterns of organization, paternalistic decision making, narrow privileged voice, projection of blame for failure away from the executive center, and powerful resistance to reconsideration of any decision and its consequences.)

In the language of organizational development, the school becomes a "learning organization" (Argyris, 1991). In the language of research on teaching, it becomes a locus of perpetual formative research on its own process and outcomes. In the latter case, a new twist in the character of "researching oneself" as advocated by Clark (1976), Florio (1978), Erickson (1986), and others is that the authority to act as a researcher is not limited to a few specially designated adults in the organization. Paying attention, collecting evidence, and arguing persuasively from that evidence become everyone's privilege and duty. Indeed, learning how to do this may become a most important and valued outcome of living in such organizations.

Conclusion

In this short chapter, we have merely opened a topic and offered it as a line of conversation in deliberations about the future of research on teaching. Must we limit our questions to the cognitive domain and our models and theories to bloodless information processing and knowledge representation? Or is it time to turn the considerable creativity, practical insight, and wisdom of this research community toward the *social* side of the social sciences — specifically, toward questions of morality and care? Clearly, we believe that it is time to turn, and the voices of philosophers (Goodlad, Soder, and Sirotnik, 1990; Noddings, 1984; Sarason, 1990), practicing teachers (Clark, 1989; Oser, 1991) and other helping professionals (Jensen, 1991) support our call.

References

Argyris, C. "Teaching Smart People How to Learn." *Harvard Business Review,* May–June 1991, pp. 99–109.

Clark, C. M. "The Effects of Teacher Practice on Student Learning and Attitudes in Small Group Instruction." Unpublished doctoral dissertation, Stanford University, 1976.

Clark, C. M. "Research in the Service of Teaching." Paper presented to the conference the Contexts of School Literacy, Snowbird, Utah, June 1984.

Clark, C. M. "Ten Years of Conceptual Development in Research on Teacher Thinking." In R. Halkes, M. Ben-Peretz, and R. Bromme (eds.), *Advances in Research on Teacher Thinking.* Lisse, the Netherlands: Swets and Zeitlinger, 1986.

Clark, C. M. "The Good Teacher." Paper presented to the conference Education from Cradle to Doctorate, Trondheim, Norway, Oct. 1989.

Clark, C. M. "Educating the Good Teacher." Address to the Norwegian Conference on the Moral Dimensions of Teaching, Tjöme, Norway, May 1991.

Des Pres, T. *The Survivor: An Anatomy of Life in the Death Camps.* New York: Oxford University Press, 1976.

Erickson, F. "Qualitative Methods in Research on Teaching." In M. C. Wittrock (ed.), *Handbook of Research on Teaching.* (3rd ed.) New York: Macmillan, 1986.

Florio, S. "Learning How to Go to School: An Ethnography of Interaction in a Kindergarten/First Grade Classroom." Unpublished doctoral dissertation, Harvard University, 1978.

Foucault, M. "Technologies of the Self." In L. H. Martin, H. Gutman, and P. Hutton (eds.), *Technologies of the Self.* Amherst: University of Massachusetts Press, 1988.

Fullan, M., and Hargreaves, A. *What's Worth Fighting for? Working Together for Your School.* Toronto: Ontario Public School Teachers' Federation, 1991.

Goodlad, J. I., Soder, R., and Sirotnik, K. A. (eds.). *The Moral Dimensions of Teaching.* San Francisco: Jossey-Bass, 1990.

Habermas, J. *The Theory of Communicative Action.* Vol. 1: *Reason and the Rationalization of Society.* Boston: Beacon Press, 1983.

Heidegger, M. *Varat och tiden* [The being and the time] Vols. 1 and 2. Lund, Sweden: Doxa Press, 1981.

Jensen, K. "Beyond Virtue and Command: A Study of Care." Paper presented to the American Educational Research Association, Chicago, Apr. 1991.

Lampert, M. "How Do Teachers Manage to Teach? Perspectives on Problems in Practice." *Harvard Educational Review,* 1985, *55* (2), 178–194.

Miller, A. *For Your Own Good: Hidden Cruelty in Child-Rearing and the Roots of Violence.* New York: Farrar, Straus & Giroux, 1983.

Noddings, N. *Caring: A Feminine Approach to Ethics and Moral Education.* Berkeley: University of California Press, 1984.

Noordhoff, K., and Kleinfeld, J. "Preparing Teachers for Multicultural Classrooms: A Case Study in Rural Alaska." Paper presented to the American Educational Research Association, Chicago, Apr. 1991.

Oser, F. "Combining Effective and Responsible Teaching: The Nature of the New Synthesis." Paper presented to the conference Teacher Professionalization and Professional Morality, Bergen, Norway, May 1991.

Rawls, J. *A Theory of Justice.* Cambridge, Mass.: Harvard University Press, 1971.

Sarason, S. B. *The Predictable Failure of Educational Reform: Can We Change Course Before It's Too Late?* San Francisco: Jossey-Bass, 1990.

Schacht, R. *Alienation.* New York: Doubleday, 1971.

Scheffler, I. *In Praise of the Cognitive Emotions.* New York: Routledge & Kegan Paul, 1991.

Schmuck, P., and Schmuck, R. "Democratic Participation in Small-Town Schools." *Educational Researcher,* 1990, *19* (8), 14–19.

Schön, D. *The Reflective Practitioner: How Professionals Think in Action.* New York: Basic Books, 1983.

Shulman, J. H. "Now You See Them, Now You Don't: Anonymity Versus

Visibility in Case Studies of Teachers." *Educational Researcher,* 1990, *19* (6), 11–15.

Shulman, L. S. "Knowledge and Teaching: Foundations of the New Reform." *Harvard Educational Review,* 1987, *57* (1), 1–22.

Shulman, L. S., and Elstein, A. S. "Studies of Problem Solving, Judgment, and Decision Making: Implications for Educational Research." *Review of Research in Education,* 1975, *3,* 5–42.

Tom, A. *Teaching as a Moral Craft.* White Plains, N.Y.: Longman, 1984.

van Manen, M. *Researching Lived Experience: Human Science for an Action Sensitive Pedagogy.* Albany: State University of New York Press, 1990.

van Manen, M. *The Tact of Teaching: The Meaning of Pedagogical Thoughtfulness.* London, Ontario: Althouse Press, 1991.

Wagner, A. "Contradictory Imperatives Produce 'Knots' in Teachers' Thinking." Paper presented to the International Study Association on Teacher Thinking, Tilburg, the Netherlands, 1983.

Afterword

Responsible Action as the Hallmark of Effective Teaching

Fritz K. Oser, Andreas Dick, Jean-Luc Patry

This book has offered a journey of thought toward some ideal place where teachers, researchers, school administrators, parents, and students are able to find a synthesis of responsibility and effectiveness in their everyday lives and actions. We do not consider responsibility as a set of "should's" but rather as a broad term for a particular way of making decisions that then form the basis of an action that can be judged as morally right. It should be included in both the effectiveness and the moral dimensions of schools. We hope that this integration that we strongly feel is needed will one day lead to that ideal place, which all of us in education feel a need for, where effectiveness and responsibility are synthesized into a meaningful life-respecting form of daily action.

The authors of this book have shown different ways of thinking about responsibility and its synthesis with effectiveness in schools, education, and teaching practice. We see this synthesis in the teacher who interrupts a lesson for a roundtable discussion, who takes the time to discuss problems with students, who appreciates students' need for peer-group interaction in the classroom, who shows students how to think about a subject rather than just telling them what to answer, and who is aware of a child's ethnic background and the role that it plays in the child's ability to perform lesson tasks. We see it in teacher educators who take the time to find ways to help future teachers discover the need for thinking about their students, not just their lesson plan. We see it in researchers in education who take the opportunity to go out and discover what is happening in a real classroom, not just a theoretical classroom. We see it in those who take the time to reflect on how each individual child can be creatively supported to reach his or her full potential.

One of the strengths of the chapters presented in this volume is that they present the state of research in important fields of action from different points of view at the same time that they consider, implicitly or explicitly, the relationship between effectiveness and responsibility. When effectiveness and responsibility are looked at simultaneously, one of the first questions that arise is For what effects of teaching is it necessary to take responsibility, and how? Or put another way, How is responsibility seen in professional actions—how does it appear in the actions of teachers in the process of communication, in caring for each individual student?

The four models of mediation that we presented at the beginning of Chapter One (the interpretive synthesis model, the additive synthesis model, the complementary synthesis model, and the regulative synthesis model) are heuristics for a cognitive process in the minds of teachers or researchers. The mind of an acting person must combine what cannot be combined simply by external regulations. As it turns out, effectiveness and responsibility are highly correlated: most authors have shown that teachers who are indeed effective are also responsible.

We are advocating a professional responsibility, one that lies at the core of all professional decision making and action. If responsibility is the ability to balance different role demands, and if it consists of a high self-commitment (in the sociological sense of the term used by Kaufmann, 1989), then it must be acquired through an education toward this professionalism. This is a point that we feel strongly about and that helps explain why we chose a procedural approach to the mediation of effectiveness and responsibility.

As we began this enterprise, our problem was that the only philosophical analysis that has so far captured this mediation was that found in *The Principle of Responsibility* by Hans Jonas (1986). Jonas proposes that the scope and depth of our knowledge should be equal to the long-term causal effects of our actions. However, he sees a continuous ethical problem in the fact that predicting knowledge does not equal technical knowledge. With our actions, we create ethical dubiousness that has to be resolved with new actions (Lyons, 1990). An inner uneasiness must restrict teachers' actions as it restricts the actions of natural scientists, economists, or technicians. Thus, responsibility restricts the range of feasible alternatives; morality means abandoning the belief that anything goes (Baethge, Denkinger, and Kadritzke, 1991).

A number of approaches to investigating the relationship between effectiveness and responsibility are possible. For instance, researchers could isolate variables that sustain affective, behavioral, and cognitive learning and order them according to their effectiveness, as has been done in meta-analyses of research on teaching, and then examine the degree of responsibility correlated with each of them. But such hierarchies of variables do not represent the complexities of classroom situations. To take Eisner's beautiful metaphor in Chapter Seventeen, knowing how many F-sharps Mozart used in a symphony does not help us to understand why this music is so wonderful.

It is the harmony between responsibility and effectiveness that is one of its most important assets — and also, of course, one of the sources of difficulty in research in this domain. Furthermore, information about such variables would not provide evidence for the development of responsibility within the process of action, since they do not allow us to identify changes in how decisions are being made and the extent to which the consequences are being integrated into the process.

Theoretically, it would also be possible to investigate the relationship between effectiveness and responsibility by taking the approach developed by Rutter, Maughan, Mortimer, and Ouston (1979) in their sociological study of "ethos" in secondary schools. Such a method would allow us to compare empirical variables for effectiveness with variables rating participants' subjective perception of responsibility. However, it would not reveal the inner processes of how effectiveness and responsibility are simultaneously constructed, which is what is needed if we are to really understand the synthesis between the two.

Mediating Between Effectiveness and Responsibility

We would like to summarize the discussion presented in these pages by focusing on the central aspects of our procedural approach to mediating effectiveness and responsibility in teaching: the direction of responsibility, the act of taking responsibility, and mutual understanding.

The Direction of Responsibility

Rather than teachers being responsible for one single facet, such as content, methods, structures, or children, we are aiming at a more complex responsibility that involves both students' learning of content matter and their personality development. Such a direction requires that teaching be viewed as a process in which students help shape what the curriculum eventually means. When applying this conception in research and in practice, one cannot interpret the curriculum as something that is objectively given but must see it as a function of interactive learning processes. Similarly, in regard to methods, teachers must feel responsible not just for the method but for the entire "processes and outcomes of learning, despite the power shift that experiential learning entails; and giving serious consideration to the desirable and less desirable long-term effects of the constantly improvised learning environment" (Chapter Three). Even being completely directed toward the child can lead to a "child-centered romanticism" (Chapter Eleven), missing the holistic meaning of responsibility. We are responsible for the acts of the children in a concrete situation, where we are dealing with the subject matter and being a part of a caring community. It is this intertwined direction that counts, and it is not possible to deal with overly simple concepts.

The Act of Taking Responsibility

Responsibility can be expressed only in specific actions, in contrast to moral judgment (for example, according to Kohlberg, 1981), which can be seen as detached from specific actions, as judgment as to what one should do in a generalizable and thus simplified situation (see Blasi, 1983; Kohlberg and Candee, 1984; Oser and Althof, 1992). It is not enough to verbally claim responsibility for a child. One can determine whether someone is responsible only by considering that person's actions — in our case, professional action (Dreyfus and Dreyfus, 1990). This means that, while we are oriented toward effectiveness, the degree and quality of responsibility must be experienced only in the action itself. The action thus becomes the fulcrum of the new synthesis. The action is sign and meaning.

What about the quality of the action? Here we add to the research on expertise the concept that quality is consequence-bound: one is always responsible for the future of a particular child in a specific *action* situation, and the consequences are always complex and multifaceted, since the teacher must actively "read" the social aspects of the situation where responsibility is involved.

Mutual Understanding

The third element of the process is mutual understanding and consent among all parties working toward a mutual agreement about a particular question. This means, for instance, that conflicts will not always be resolved in a clear-cut, definite way. It means finding interpersonal negotiation strategies, wherein effectiveness and responsibility converge for teachers, students, colleagues, school principals, and educational administrators alike. Fenstermacher's "manner" (Chapter Seven) is the prototype model of the quality, moral orientation, and practical rationality that are among the characteristics of any professional.

Never Lose a Child . . .

In the course of education, there are children who become lost. Many of us know of such examples: they leave school, are tracked into an inappropriate school or level, or learn to hate school with such passion that they "commit mental suicide" by their inner dismissal. It is the task of the new synthesis to minimize the risk of such "getting lost."

Unfortunately, we observe a two-sided erosion in the teaching profession. On the one hand, many people doubt the effectiveness of pedagogy and regard subject knowledge transmission and selection as the only justified criteria for education. Such an attitude can be found among teachers and politicians as much as among educational researchers, many of whom have been strongly influenced by inadequate theoretical models. On the other hand, teachers are often given jester's license as long as they uphold the curriculum: provided that they do not beat or obviously abuse a child, they can do whatever they want. Teachers who see learning as an interactive process for which readiness is more important than knowledge and the journey more authentic than the result can get into deep troubles of conscience within a school system that maintains a fossilized knowledge-transmission machinery and recall rituals. In such cases, responsibility can require that which cannot be done.

Here we are at a crossroad. If the results of research that have been collected in this volume are taken seriously, one can say that professionals, politicians, and researchers do not or cannot always do what they should do. They are still restrained by the positivistic, technological viewpoint they espouse. Such a viewpoint basically relies on good methods and strategies and nothing more. Responsibility remains a concept foreign to the school context. However, schools, researchers, and teachers are indeed changing, as the models, intervention studies, and research data presented in this book show. There are teachers who show a particularly high ethos. And there are students who demonstrate great responsibility toward their peers and their school. However, we wish that the overwhelming majority of the people involved with schooling would be touched by such concerns.

Is this a pessimistic stand? No, it is not, but the issue of losing students in school is one in which the questions of responsibility and effectiveness are particularly difficult. In the great majority of classrooms, there will always be differences among children: differences in their talent, their cultural, social, and ethnic backgrounds, their characters and characteristics, and their home situations. Whenever teachers adapt their teaching to a specific child or group of children, other children may be disadvantaged. Any particular method or approach applied systematically without regard to children's individual differences cannot be called responsible. The new synthesis asks that everyone involved in education think about the consequences of their acts so that all students can be engaged in and profit from education and so that we never lose a child.

References

Baethge, M., Denkinger, J., and Kadritzke, U. "Homo Faber in Bedrängnis" [Homo faber in distress]. Paper presented at the Symposium on Professional Morality, Berlin, Oct. 18–19, 1991.

Blasi, A. "Moral Cognition and Moral Action: A Theoretical Perspective." *Developmental Review*, 1983, *3*, 178–210.

Dreyfus, H. I., and Dreyfus, S. E. "What Is Morality? A Phenomenological Account of the Development of Ethical Expertise." In D. Rasmussen (ed.), *Universalism vs. Communitarianism: Contemporary Debates in Ethics.* Cambridge, Mass.: MIT Press, 1990.

Jonas, H. *Das Prinzip der Verantwortung: Versuch einer Ethik für die technische*

Zivilisation [The principle of responsibility: essay on an ethic for the technical civilization]. Frankfurt am Main, Germany: Insel, 1986.

Kaufmann, F.-X. "Über die soziale Funktion der Verantwortung und Verantwortlichkeit" [On the social function of responsibility and responsibleness]. In E.-J. Lampe (ed.), *Verantwortlichkeit und Recht* [Responsibleness and law]. Opladen, Germany: Westdeutscher Verlag, 1989.

Kohlberg, L. *Essays on Moral Development.* Vol. 1: *The Philosophy of Moral Development. Moral Stages and the Idea of Justice.* New York: HarperCollins, 1981.

Kohlberg, L., and Candee, D. "The Relationship of Moral Judgment to Moral Action." In L. Kohlberg, *Essays on Moral Development.* Vol. 2: *The Psychology of Moral Development. The Nature and Validity of Moral Stages.* New York: HarperCollins, 1984.

Lyons, N. "Dilemmas of Knowing: Ethical and Epistemological Dimensions of Teachers' Work and Development." *Harvard Educational Review,* 1990, *60* (2), 159–180.

Oser, F., and Althof, W. *Moralische Selbstbestimmung: Modelle der Entwicklung und Erziehung im Wertebereich. Ein Lehrbuch* [Moral self-determination: models of development and education in the domain of values. A textbook.] Stuttgart, Germany: Klett-Cotta, 1992.

Rutter, M., Maughan, B., Mortimer, P., and Ouston, J. *Fifteen Thousand Hours: Secondary Schools and Their Effects on Children.* London: Open Books, 1979.

Name Index

Subject Index